Chaos and Complexity in Psychology

Although many books have discussed methodological advances in nonlinear dynamical systems (NDS) theory, this volume is unique in its focus on NDS's role in the development of psychological theory. After an introductory chapter covering the fundamentals of chaos, complexity, and other nonlinear dynamics, subsequent chapters provide in-depth coverage of each of the specific topic areas in psychology. A concluding chapter takes stock of the field as a whole, evaluating important challenges for the immediate future. The chapters are by experts in the use of NDS in each of their respective areas, including biological, cognitive, developmental, social, organizational, and clinical psychology. Each chapter provides an in-depth examination of theoretical foundations and specific applications and a review of relevant methods. This edited collection represents the state of the art in NDS science across the disciplines of psychology.

Dr. Stephen J. Guastello is a professor of psychology at Marquette University, Milwaukee, Wisconsin, where his teaching and research specialize in industrial-organizational psychology, human factors engineering and ergonomics, psychological testing topics, advanced statistics, and applications of nonlinear dynamics in psychology and economics. He is the author of three books and more than 100 journal articles and book chapters. He is the founding Editor in Chief of the journal *Nonlinear Dynamics, Psychology, and Life Sciences* and served as president of the Society for Chaos Theory in Psychology & Life Sciences.

Dr. Matthijs Koopmans is Senior Education Research and Evaluation Officer at the Center for School and Community Services at the Academy for Educational Development in New York. His expertise is in the use of advanced statistical modeling to analyze educational data and in the applicability of nonlinear dynamical systems to educational and developmental phenomena. He has published in numerous scholarly journals, including *Nonlinear Dynamics, Psychology and Life Sciences, Journal for the Education of Students Placed at Risk*, and *Evaluation and Program Planning*.

Dr. David Pincus is an assistant professor in the Psychology Department at Chapman University in Orange, California. Dr. Pincus's teaching, clinical, and research interests focus on applications of NDS theory to understanding interpersonal processes underlying healthy exchanges of information. He has published journal articles, book chapters, workbooks, and videos applying nonlinear dynamics to diverse subjects such as relationship development, psychotherapy, family systems, pain management, and child weight management. Dr. Pincus is a licensed psychologist and a member of the American Psychological Association and the Association for Psychological Science.

Chaos and Complexity in Psychology

THE THEORY OF NONLINEAR DYNAMICAL SYSTEMS

Edited by

Stephen J. Guastello
Marquette University

Matthijs Koopmans
Academy for Educational Development

David Pincus
Chapman University

CAMBRIDGE
UNIVERSITY PRESS

CAMBRIDGE UNIVERSITY PRESS
Cambridge, New York, Melbourne, Madrid, Cape Town,
Singapore, São Paulo, Delhi, Tokyo, Mexico City

Cambridge University Press
32 Avenue of the Americas, New York, NY 10013-2473, USA

www.cambridge.org
Information on this title: www.cambridge.org/9781107680265

© Cambridge University Press 2009

First published 2009
First paperback edition 2011

Printed in the United States of America

A catalog record for this publication is available from the British Library.

Library of Congress Cataloging in Publication Data

Guastello, Stephen J.
Chaos and complexity in psychology : the theory of nonlinear
dynamical systems / Stephen J. Guastello, Matthijs Koopmans, David Pincus.
  p.   cm.
Includes bibliographical references and index.
ISBN 978-0-521-88726-7 (hardback)
1. Psychology – Philosophy. 2. Chaotic behavior in systems. 3. System theory.
I. Koopmans, Matthijs. II. Pincus, David, 1969– III. Title.

BF38.G79 2009
150.11857–dc22   2008014866

ISBN 978-0-521-88726-7 Hardback
ISBN 978-1-107-68026-5 Paperback

Contents

Contributors

Deborah J. Aks, Ph.D.
Center for Cognitive Science (RuCCS)
Rutgers University – New Brunswick
Piscataway, New Jersey

Guillaume Albert, Ph.D.
Department of Educational Psychology
    and Psychology
University of Quebec at Outaouais
Gatineau, Quebec, Canada

Peter Allen, Ph.D.
Complex Systems Management
    Center
Cranfield University
School of Management
Bedford, England,
United Kingdom

Kathleen M. Carley, Ph.D.
School of Computer Science
Carnegie Mellon University
Pittsburgh, Pennsylvania

Sylvain Chartier, Ph.D.
School of Psychology
University of Ottawa
Ottawa, Ontario, Canada

Thomas J. Dishion, Ph.D.
Child and Family Center
University of Oregon
Eugene, Oregon

Kevin J. Dooley, Ph.D.
Department of Supply Chain
    Management
Arizona State University
Tempe, Arizona

Terrill L. Frantz, Ed.D.
School of Computer Science
Carnegie Mellon University
Pittsburgh, Pennsylvania

Robert A. M. Gregson, Ph.D., D.Sc.
School of Psychology
Australian National University
Canberra, ACT, Australia

Stephen J. Guastello, Ph.D.
Department of Psychology
Marquette University
Milwaukee, Wisconsin

Geoff Hollis, B.Sc.
Department of Psychology
University of Cincinnati
Cincinnati, Ohio

Uli Junghan, M.D.
University Hospital of Psychiatry
University of Bern
Bern, Switzerland

Heidi Kloos, Ph.D.
Department of Psychology
University of Cincinnati
Cincinnati, Ohio

Matthijs Koopmans, Ed.D.
Academy for Educational
  Development
New York, New York

Larry S. Liebovitch, Ph.D.
Center for Complex Systems
Florida Atlantic University
Boca Raton, Florida

Erika S. Lunkenheimer, Ph.D.
Child and Family Center
University of Oregon
Eugene, Oregon

Tullio A. Minelli, Ph.D.
University of Padova
Galileo Galilei Department of
  Physics
Padova, Italy

Andrzej Nowak, Ph.D.
Department of Psychology
University of Warsaw
Warszawa, Poland

David Pincus, Ph.D.
Department of Psychology
Chapman University
Orange, California

Patrice Renaud, Ph.D.
Department of Educational Psychology
  and Psychology
University of Quebec at Outaouais
Montreal, Quebec, Canada

William Sulis, M.D., Ph.D.
Department of Psychiatry and Behavioral
  Neuroscience
McMaster University
Hamilton, Ontario, Canada

Wolfgang Tschacher, Ph.D.
University Hospital of Psychiatry
University of Bern
Bern, Switzerland

Robin R. Vallacher, Ph.D.
Department of Psychology
Florida Atlantic University
Boca Raton, Florida

Paul van Geert, Ph.D.
University of Groningen
The Heymans Institute
Groningen, the Netherlands

Guy C. Van Orden, Ph.D.
Department of Psychology
University of Cincinnati
Cincinnati, Ohio

Preface

Nonlinear dynamical systems (NDS) theory is the study of how complex processes unfold over time and is sometimes known as chaos theory or complexity theory. Perhaps it was one of those experiences in which "You had to be there," but the early days of NDS in psychology were rife with excitement. There was so much potential for solving old and new problems and transforming the way psychology was studied that everyone present knew it could occupy entire careers. The days of saying, "Here's what chaos and complexity can do!" were gone years ago, however. NDS scholars have embarked on the less glamorous but ultimately more important task of systematic model building and developing an empirical research agenda. We estimate that about 50 books are published each year that are relevant to some aspect of NDS, psychology, and the life sciences, as well as numerous articles in peer-reviewed journals, such as *Nonlinear Dynamics, Psychology, and Life Sciences*, signifying that the field is moving forward at a rapid pace.

The waterfall of progress creates two dilemmas that we attempt to resolve by composing this book. The first is to answer a simple question: "What should I read first?" The second is how to reconcile the escalating gap between the state of the science in NDS and the average level of awareness of its accomplishments by professionals in psychology. At the same time, the number of university courses in NDS for advanced undergraduates and graduate students has started to grow, and thus the number of psychologists devoting concerted attention to the topic is also growing. Yet with all the widely dispersed knowledge and dense mathematical content in much of the literature, the question of what to read first is difficult to answer with the resources that are currently available.

We wanted to be able to say, "Try this book! It's a compendium of the landmark developments and the state of the art in NDS science in psychological theory and research." To do so, we assembled a team of researchers who have already expanded the frontiers of NDS in a wide range of topics that are of central importance to psychology and who are actively engaged in empirical research. Each chapter delineates where conventional thinking leaves off and

NDS has been necessary to answer difficult questions. The chapters then move on to capture the state of the art in each topic area.

The opening chapter explains the basic concepts and principles of NDS – attractors, bifurcations, chaos, fractals, self-organization, catastrophes, and agent-based and other simulation models – and how they interrelate. We also encounter turbulence, sensitivity to initial conditions, the Lyapunov exponent, entropy, information, and a few types of dimension. We made a point not to become sidetracked into extensive expositions of NDS methods, although they are sometimes fascinating in their own right. The most important points about methods are covered in the last section of Chapter 1, and the authors of subsequent chapters expand on the methods that have been particularly relevant to the problems addressed in their topic areas. Although all the chapters in the book review existing work in given areas of knowledge, Chapters 5 and 6 also present some original data that illustrate the methodological issues inherent in sensation and perception.

Subsequent chapters provide in-depth coverage of substantive areas, including neuroscience, psychophysics, sensation, perception, cognition, and developmental, social, organizational, and clinical psychology. Taken together, these chapters indicate that NDS can be meaningfully applied in all of those areas and that it offers quite a few original perspectives on new questions as well as old questions to which we thought we already knew the answers. Chapter 2 presents the principal theme of collective intelligence as studied in social insect populations. The chapter could be just as readily positioned with the material about human groups, but we thought the nonhuman social dynamics would be a great way to start the psychological material, especially given that foraging behavior pops up in human sensation and perception dynamics.

Chapter 3 reviews and consolidates what is now known about neural activity and synchronization of neural circuits in the brain. Although the "binding problem" (*binding* is the translation of neural activity to actual thoughts) has not yet been solved, it is noteworthy that NDS has catalyzed progress in this area, and there is no real competing linear theory at the present time.

Chapters 4 through 7 close in on the binding problem from the other direction. The divisions among psychophysics, sensation, perception, cognition, and psychomotor response may have been historically convenient, but real-world behavior involves synchronizations among these psychological processes. Thus there is a preoccupation with perception-action sequence among neuroscientists, cognitive scientists, and information-processing professionals, just for starters. Given the nature of synchronization itself, it would be difficult for mainstream psychological research to continue the way it has been going without cheating a little bit and using NDS constructs and methods.

Chapters 8 through 11 address topics that have been traditional concerns of clinical and counseling psychologists. Children and adults develop socially and intellectually across the life span. Many of the influential theories in psychology are stage theories in which discontinuous changes in schemata occur. Chapter 8 examines the nature of developmental stages along with the literature that supports the notion of catastrophe models for those discontinuous changes. Although nature-versus-nurture remains an important principle of development, Chapter 9 on adolescent psychopathology makes the case that adaptive and maladaptive responses by children and parents in microsocial interactions play at least as great a role in shaping the functional autonomous processes that we observe among adolescents. Chapter 10 concerns the major psychopathologies. Here we encounter theories of dynamical disease and evidence that shifts to normal perceptual gestalt processes underlie the various stages of psychosis.

Chapter 11 on psychotherapy starts by considering the true differences among the prominent therapeutic models currently in use. In the early 1990s, the Dodo Hypothesis, "Everybody has won, and all must have prizes," was used to characterize the status of empirical evaluations of various types of psychotherapy;[1] it was probably as accurate as it might have been offensive to the true believers in specific psychotherapy models. The potent moments in psychotherapy, however, are evident to the dynamically aware therapist who engages the processes of self-organization that can reconstruct the self and the interpersonal relationships with which the self engages.

Chapter 12 covers some well-developed NDS themes in social attraction and social influence. Other important themes include interpersonal and behavioral synchronization, which carry over into the next chapters.

Chapters 13 through 15 address group dynamics and organizational behavior. Chapter 13 notes that the current interest among organizational theorists in adaptive behavior and emergence is laudable, but NDS developed the ideas much further a decade earlier in the form of complex adaptive systems (CAS). Important questions concerning coordination in work groups and the 50-year-old enigma of how leaders emerge from leaderless groups were not unraveled until the perspective changed to include NDS constructs. Similar issues are all the more apparent in Chapter 14, in which the goal is to understand what an organization *is*. Chapter 15 expands on CAS issues by considering evolutionary behavior, the role of learning, and the impact of those dynamics on organizational behavior.

Chapter 16 describes the contributions of agent-based modeling and similar techniques to the understanding of social influence networks and the behaviors of groups and organizations. It could make us wonder whether the notion of social building blocks that expand from dyads to groups to organizations was a naïve idea, and whether network dynamics are more fundamental after all. The concluding chapter takes stock of the field as a whole and its growing points for new developments.

We are honored that Sir Michael Berry gave us permission to use one of his graphics for the cover of this book. He describes "Chaotic Quantum Falling" to us as follows:

> Neutrons, all initially traveling at the same speed, are thrown upwards in random directions and then fall under gravity. The wave shown here represents these quantum particles, and its strength gives the probability of finding one. Red indicates the brightest places in the wave, and the black snakes are the zero lines where the particle will never be found. In classical physics, the particles would never get above a certain height (here about two-thirds up the picture); in quantum physics, the waves occasionally penetrate this "classical boundary" and reach greater heights. The study of patterns like this is part of an international research effort in "quantum chaology."

What we learn from this experience, among other things undoubtedly, is that it takes a paradigm shift to break through a boundary. With that thought in mind, we delay no further.

Stephen J. Gaustello
Matthijs Koopmans
David Pincus

Note

1. In Lewis Carroll's *Alice in Wonderland*, the characters ran a "caucus race," which involved a racecourse that was approximately circular. The participants did not start from the same place or at the same time. They stopped running when they felt like doing so. The Dodo presided over the race, determined when it was over, and uttered the pointed phrase about who won. The fairy-tale race was used as an analogy to summarize the results of psychotherapy research, given that the various therapies were used for different purposes and that the amounts and methods of study afforded to any particular types were very irregular.

1 Introduction to Nonlinear Dynamics and Complexity

STEPHEN J. GUASTELLO AND LARRY S. LIEBOVITCH

Elephants and Horses

Things change. Sometimes they change gradually, sometimes dramatically. The prevailing concept of change in psychology consists of only one form of change, linear change, which is simply undifferentiated, and with the assumption that outcomes are proportional to inputs in a straightforward manner. The overreliance among psychologists and others on the general linear model as a statistical tool for depicting change has only served to reinforce this monochrome conceptualization of change. Perhaps the most significant deviations from the concept of linear change are the concepts of *equilibrium* and *randomness*. For most intents and purposes, the concept of equilibrium has been used to describe places or times when change stops occurring. Randomness suggests that the changes are unpredictable and not explicable by any known concepts or predictors.

Nonlinear dynamical systems (NDS) theory significantly enriches our capability to conceptualize change, and it provides a rich array of constructs that describe many types of change. The concept of equilibrium is no longer specific enough to describe either the change or the events that surround the point where change stops. The new constructs are the attractors, bifurcations, chaos, fractals, self-organization, and catastrophes. As this chapter explains, each of these constructs contains several more, including those associated with the "complexity" of a system. Importantly, change is not proportional to inputs. Large inputs sometimes produce small results, and a small input at the right time can produce a dramatic result.

Psychology is not the first science to break out of the linear rut. According to Stewart (1989), the physical sciences made the transition more than a half-century ago:

> So ingrained became the linear habit, that by the 1940s and 1950s many scientist[s] and engineers knew little else.... [W]e live in a world which for centuries acted as if the only animal in existence was the elephant, which assumed that holes in the skirting-board must be made by tiny elephants, which saw the soaring eagle as a

wing-eared Dumbo, [and] the tiger as an elephant with a rather short trunk and stripes (1989, p. 83–84).

Some nonlinear phenomena, particularly chaos, force us to reconsider what it means for an event to be random. According to Mandelbrot (1983), the word *random* came into English by way of a medieval French idiom meaning "the movements of a horse that the rider cannot predict" (p. 201). Later-day statistics and experimental design have placed a great deal of emphasis on what the rider does not control, resulting in the notion that variability in observations is either "due to the model" or "due to error." NDS places more emphasis, however, on the horse's point of view: There are reasons for the horse's motions, and its rider can get used to them or not. Less metaphorically, simple deterministic equations can produce processes that appear random, but closer scrutiny may indicate that they are not. It follows that a lot of so-called error variance can be accounted for if we can identify the processes that generated the observations; those processes are most likely to be overwhelmingly nonlinear.

In contemporary colloquial English, people speak of "random events" when referring to events that occur without any apparent connection to prior events or to any clues about which the speaker is aware. In NDS, these events are called *emergent phenomena*. Their important features are their disconnection with recent past events and that they occur without the deliberate action of any person or agent. In other words, those phenomena are novel, and they can sometimes be clear examples of nonlinear events and deterministic processes, as will become apparent throughout this book.

General Systems Theories and Paradigms

One of the conceptual foundations of NDS is the general systems theory (GST), an interdisciplinary theory that contains rules, propositions, and constructs that extend beyond the confines of a single academic discipline. Within the realm of GSTs, there is a strong representation of mathematically centered theories; this approach is usually attributed to von Bertalanffy (1968) and Wymore (1967). NDS is also an example of GST that is centered on principles of mathematical origin.

A GST can be regarded as a metatheory and as an overarching methodological approach in some cases. A metatheory is a theory that organizes concepts, objects, or relationships inherent in several local (or specific) theories and places those into an overarching conceptual framework. The development of such theories facilitates interdisciplinary cross-fertilization because at the metatheoretical level, scholars from different disciplines will share a conceptual framework. For instance, a theory that successfully solves a problem in macroeconomics with principles of evolutionary biology would qualify as an example of such cross-fertilization. Thus specific objects can be interchanged from one application to another, but the relationships among those objects could remain approximately the same. Another approach might show interchangeability of objects and relationships, but the "blueprint" that defines the metatheory would tell the scientist where to look for objects and relationships that could be useful. GST and NDS can both be seen as examples of metatheories. In fact, the same concepts that are encountered in this book can also be found in texts that are concerned with the subject matter of other academic disciplines, such as economics and biology.

When viewed as a methodology, a general systems analyst would typically begin with a description of the phenomenon of interest and assess the relevance of particular tenets of the GST to that phenomenon. For example, if one were to observe a nonnormal frequency distribution with a sharp peak near the left and a long tail to the right, one might hypothesize that a power law distribution and the dynamics that usually go with it (see later in this chapter) were involved. The next step would be to create a model to represent the system using the tools and constructs of the GST plus any adaptations that are specific to the application. The model-making process typically draws on the past successes and failures encountered with applications of the general theory. If the GST is truly meritorious, the knowledge gained from a successful application would increase the knowledge about the core principles of the theory and thus facilitate the hunt for further applications. Hence one good application serves as a metaphor for another (Guastello, 1995, pp. 4–6), and NDS applications have indeed found their way into many applications within physics, chemistry, biology, psychology, economics, sociology, and political science. With repeated successes, one can develop one's intuition as to where dynamical events of different types might be found.

Scholars have pondered whether NDS can be considered a paradigm of science itself (Allen & Varga, 2007; Dore & Rosser, 2007; Fleener & Merritt, 2007; Goerner, 1994; Guastello, 1997, 2007; Ibanez, 2007). A new scientific paradigm would represent a new approach to a wide range of problems and ask entirely different classes of questions. It would pursue its answers with its own set of standards and challenges. Thus a new paradigm unearths and explains phenomena that could not have been approached through pre-paradigmatic means. Additionally, the new paradigm could be shown to provide better, more compact, and more accurate explanations for existing questions.

NDS shows other symptoms of paradigmatic behavior beyond its new perspective on randomness, nonlinear structures, and system change. For one thing, the concept of a *dimension* is not what it used to be. Although society at large has assimilated the four basic dimensions of Euclidean space and time, mathematicians have rendered 5 through N dimensions as comfortable abstractions, and social scientists have extensively analyzed complex multidimensional data spaces using factor analysis and multidimensional scaling. NDS offers a new development: fractional dimensions. There are entities between lines and planes, planes and volumes, and so on. Fractional dimensions, or fractals, are described later in this chapter. It is worthwhile to point out early that the fractals serve as good indicators of the complexity of a system.

Our notions about the nature of a system have shifted as well. In Newton's view of a mechanical system, the function of the whole can be understood by understanding the function of each of the parts. A correction of a flaw in a system can be accomplished by removing and replacing one of its parts. In a *complex adaptive system* (CAS), however, the whole is greater than the sum of its parts. This description should surely ring familiar to psychologists because of the Gestalt laws of perception. The parts of the system, perceptual or otherwise, interact with each other, shape each other, and pass information around, and they are not replaceable or removable without fundamentally altering the dynamics of the system as a whole. Furthermore, attempts to correct "flaws," or to change otherwise a part in a CAS, often do not succeed because the parts adapt in such a way as to protect the system from the intrusions of the outside tinkerer. By the same token, a CAS can survive intrusions or assaults by the same means; the tendency for brain tissue to pick up a function that was lost by a nearby tissue area is an example. These self-organizing tendencies are a primary area of interest in the study of NDS, and they are expanded further in this chapter and throughout the remainder of this book.

Has NDS produced better explanations of phenomena? The answer in each chapter that follows is "yes." It has described phenomena that could not be described in any other way, especially when temporal dynamics are concerned. In some cases, they provide an organizing center where several partially relevant theories were needed to describe a phenomenon; work-group coordination is one such example. Although the explanations may appear more complex in one respect, they become more efficient to the extent that the general principles transcend many problems in psychology and also expand beyond the usual confines of psychology.

Does it account for more of the data than conventional linear models? In most cases reported in this book, there was no linear alternative available, so the answer is a simple "yes." In the cases in which it was possible to compare R^2 coefficients for linear and nonlinear models, the cumulative advantage is 2:1 in favor of the nonlinear models (Guastello, 1995, 2002). That is to say that about 50% of the explanation for a phenomenon comes from knowing what dynamics are involved.

Elements of NDS Functions

It is no secret that the central concepts of NDS have mathematical origins, some of which might qualify as exotic even among mathematicians. Fortunately, the majority of the concepts can be represented in pictorial or graphic form, which helps interpretations greatly. In psychological applications, we only need to use the products of the mathematics; we do not need to reperform derivations, solve differential equations, or anything of that nature. The principles are analytic when applied to psychology, nonetheless. Some equations have a great deal of meaning, and they serve to codify the dynamical principles concisely. There are some novel computations that are often used in NDS research, and some of them can be rendered statistically, which is perhaps more compatible with the analytic habits of social scientists.

The equations that we do encounter are all *functional* and sometimes structural as well. Some functions that we encounter state that a dependent measure Y is a nonlinear function of another variable X. Some functions are *iterative*, in which Y at Time 2 (Y_2) is a function of Y_1 and other variables in the system.

In an iterative function, a time series of Y is produced by running Y_1 through the equation to produce Y_2; Y_2 is then run through the equation to produce Y_3, and so on, thereby producing a forecast of future behavioral patterns. Many psychological phenomena that occur over time are iterative in nature, such as the flow of a conversation or series of conversations between two people; see Chapters 9 and 11 through 13 in this volume. If we do not know what equation is the best representation for the phenomenon, it helps to recognize when an iterative function could be implied.

Structural equations are similar to functional equations, but they have the added feature of allowing, if not encouraging, the user to plug complex functions into a position that might have been signified by a single variable. For instance, we might have a function containing a bifurcation effect called c, but c might consist of several psychologically defined variables. Sometimes an element that looks as simple as c could turn out to be a constant, a variable, or an entire complex function.

Control parameters are essentially independent variables, with the important difference that they can act in ways that are often more interesting than the simple additive relationships that are found in conventional research designs. Several distinct types of control parameters are described in a later section of this chapter and in subsequent chapters. *Order parameters* are essentially dependent measures in the social scientist's worldview. There may be more than one order parameter in some complex dynamical systems, however. Order parameters within a system might be completely independent of each other, or they might interact with each other as they evolve over time.

The basic principles of nonlinear dynamics are presented next. In addition to the references that are interspersed in the text, we recommend Abraham and Shaw (1992), Bassingthwaighte, Liebovitch, and West (1994), Kaplan and Glass (1995), Korsch and Jodl (1999), Liebovitch (1998), Nicolis and Prigogine (1989), Puu (2000), Scott (2005), Sprott (2003), and Thompson and Stewart (1986) as broad technical references to the mathematical literature.

The chapter concludes with an overview of the analytic techniques that one might apply to real data to determine which types of dynamics are present. The authors of the subsequent chapters elaborate on their uses of particular techniques.

Attractors and Chaos

An *attractor* can be seen as a box of space in which movement could take place or not. When an object, represented by a point, enters the space, the point does not leave, unless a strong enough force is applied to pull it out. An attractor, like a magnet, has an effective range in which it can draw in objects, known as its *basin*. Some attractors are stronger than others, and stronger attractors have a wider basin.

An attractor is regarded as a stable structure because all the points within it follow the same rules of motion. There are four principal types of attractors: the fixed point, the limit cycle, toroidal attractors, and chaotic attractors. Each type reflects a distinctly different type of movement that occurs within it. Repellors and saddles are closely related structures that are not structurally stable.

Fixed-Point Attractors

As its name suggests, a *fixed-point attractor* is one where the trajectories of points that are pulled within it gravitate toward a fixed point. Figure 1.1A illustrates points that are being pulled in from all directions toward the epicenter. A point might start its path by shooting by the attractor, and might even have a chance of breaking free, but is pulled into the attractor, where it rests. Figure 1.1B is a *spiral* attractor, also known as a *sink*; the point spirals into the epicenter rather than moving in directly.

Attractor behavior that is viewed in a time series would look similar to the trends shown in Figure 1.1D, which would correspond most closely to the case where points are being pulled in from all directions. The structural equation that generates that type of motion is:

$$Z_2 = \theta_1 \exp(\theta_2 Z_1). \tag{1.1}$$

Equation 1.1 shows the function in iterative form, where the order parameter Z_2 is a function of itself at a previous point in time (Z_1). θ_i are empirical weights that can be determined through nonlinear regression. θ_1 is a proportionality constant (this is likely to become important when two or more attractors are involved in the dynamical field); θ_2 is the more important of the two weights because it reflects how quickly the points are converging onto the fixed point. Notice that the trajectories of the points in the figure all started with different initial values but ended up on the same attractor. If θ_2 is a negative number,

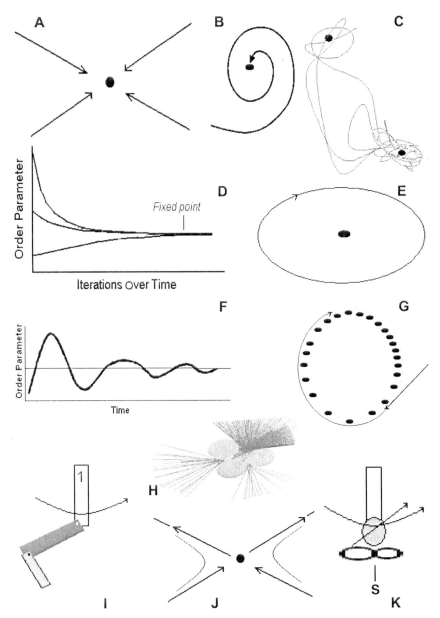

Figure 1.1. Gallery of basic dynamics: A, fixed point attractor (Eqs. 1.1 and 1.2); B, spiral attractor (Eqs. 1.3); C, trajectory of a control point in a field containing two fixed points; D, time series of points gravitating to a fixed point; E, limit cycle (Eqs. 1.4 and 1.5); F, time series for a dampened oscillator (Eq. 1.6); G, limit cycle created by organizing fixed points into a circle; H, system of three repellors; I, three coupled oscillators; J, saddle point; K, saddle created by a perturbed pendulum.

the points are indeed converging; otherwise the points' trajectories would be expanding exponentially.

Another equation for a fixed-point attractor that is used often is:

$$Z_2 = K/[1 + \theta_1 \exp(\theta_2 Z_1)]. \qquad (1.2)$$

A particular value of Z in Eq. 1.2 is recognized as the asymptotic point, which is designated as K. The regression weights would indicate how quickly the points were reaching K. A close variation on Eq. 1.2 is one in which the researcher wants to determine whether an exogenous independent variable X is responsible for the movement of Z to K. In that case, one would substitute X_1 for Z_1.

A spiral attractor is a more complicated phenomenon to analyze, but we can describe it nonetheless. Imagine that the trajectory of points on the spiral has the usual X and Y coordinates, and both X and Y are changing over time, t. We would need to write equations for both the X and Y functions (Puu, p. 21):

$$X = \theta_1 \exp[\theta_2 t \, \cos(\theta_3 t + \theta_4)] \qquad (1.3)$$
$$Y = \theta_5 \exp[\theta_2 t \, \cos(\theta_6 t + \theta_7)].$$

Equations 1.3 allow for the full range of possibilities that the spiral can be perfectly circular or stretched (elliptical) by some amount in the vertical or horizontal direction by changing $\theta_1, \theta_3, \theta_5,$ or θ_6. θ_4 and θ_7 denote the lower boundaries of the cosine functions in real numbers. Notice that the forcing function, θ_2, is common to both axes. If θ_2 were negative, the system would be converging to the fixed point and thus stable. If θ_2 were positive, however, the points would be floating away from the epicenter, and the spiral would be unstable. The spiral attractor functions become more interesting when we consider repellors and saddles a bit later.

Figure 1.1C illustrates what can happen in a dynamic field containing two fixed-point attractors. A point that might have been entered into the dynamic field in the neighborhood of the upper attractor makes a few irregular turns around the attractor and then travels to the other attractor. Nothing prevents the point from revisiting the first attractor before landing on the second one, where it appears to be spending most of its time. The convoluted pathways take different forms, depending on the relative strength of the two attractors, their proximity to each other, and the exact location where the traveling point is entered.

Figure 1.1C is, in essence, the three-body problem that got the entire study of nonlinear dynamics going. Henri Poincaré made a profound contribution in the 1890s by identifying the problem that we did not have the mathematics available to characterize the path of a "speck of dust" in the neighborhood of two celestial bodies, that is, two strong attractors (Stewart, 1989). Those trajectories were eventually characterized as chaotic several decades later.

Limit Cycles

A *limit cycle attractor* is also known as a periodic attractor. Its behavior is cyclic, in the same way that the earth orbits the sun or the moon orbits the earth. The motion of the point is thus depicted in Figure 1.1E. Once again, if a traveling point enters the basin of attraction, it does not leave. Points entering from the outside of the limit cycle are drawn into the attractor. Points that happen to be inside it are pulled outward into the orbit but do not move toward the epicenter in the way that fixed-point or spiral attractors do. Instead, there is an ongoing oscillation around the epicenter value. Oscillating functions are common in biology (May, 2001) and economic business cycles (Puu, 2000), although both types of oscillators tend to become more complex by the presence of other oscillators in the niche or economy.

A classic limit cycle can be generated by a simple function:

$$Z = \sin(X). \tag{1.4}$$

Again, one might substitute time, t, for the exogenous variable, X. One might characterize the function in both an iterative and statistically tractable form as:

$$Z_2 = \theta_1 \sin(Z_1 - \theta_2) - \theta_3 \cos(Z_1 - \theta_4). \tag{1.5}$$

Fourier analysis or spectral analysis is often employed to separate compound oscillators. This is a common practice in auditory signal processing where the sinusoidal components are additive. The generic structure of a compound oscillator is defined as a sine function, a subtracted cosine function, plus another sine function, and so on. θ_1 and θ_3 are forcing constants that adjust the amplitude of the sinusoidal functions. θ_2 and θ_4 are lower limits of the oscillating variable Z and depend on the scale used to measure Z. Note that if θ_2 or θ_4 becomes a variable, then f(Z) becomes aperiodic.

Another way to obtain a limit cycle is to place a number of point attractors in a circular configuration. If a point is injected into the neighborhood of this configuration, it will exhibit the behavior of a limit cycle (Fig. 1.1G).

We can also have *dampened oscillators*, which exhibit periodic behavior, but the amplitude of the fluctuations gradually becomes smaller until the order parameter gravitates to a fixed point. The temporal signature of a dampened oscillator would look like the time series that is shown in Figure 1.1F. A dampened oscillator might not be easily discerned from a spiral fixed point. One would be looking for a control variable that induced the dampening effect. Equation 1.6 would be a likely place to start:

$$Z_2 = \theta_1 \exp[\theta_2 X \cos(\theta_3 Z_1 + \theta_4)], \tag{1.6}$$

where $\theta_2 X$ is the variable that induces the dampening with its regression coefficient. Note that Eq. 1.6 is structurally the same as Eq. 1.3, with a substitution of X and Z_1 for t.

In light of the potential similarity of spiral points and dampened oscillators, psychologists who might encounter these dynamics should sample a long enough time series to view the full dynamics of the system. The concept of "restriction of range" is probably familiar to most psychologists from linear statistical analysis. A comparable concept here is *restriction of topological range*, meaning that the full range of topological events or movements needs to be captured in the data set to draw reliable conclusions about the dynamics of the model under study (Guastello, 1995). This principle will recur later in conjunction with other dynamics.

We can also couple oscillators so that two or more are linked to each other. Again using Eq. 1.6 as a starting point, X would be a second order parameter, and it would also have an equation that is structured like Eq. 1.6. We can also imagine a third oscillator Y in the system that is responsible for the sinusoidal forcing of X. To close this system of three variables, let Z be the forcing parameter of Y:

$$
\begin{aligned}
Z_2 &= \theta_1 \exp[\theta_2 X \cos(\theta_3 Z_1 + \theta_4)], \\
X_2 &= \theta_5 \exp[\theta_6 Y \cos(\theta_3 X_1 + \theta_4)], \\
Y_2 &= \theta_1 \exp[\theta_2 Z \cos(\theta_3 Z_1 + \theta_4)].
\end{aligned} \tag{1.7}
$$

According to a theorem by Newhouse, Ruelle, and Takens (1978), three coupled oscillators are minimally sufficient to produce chaos. Chaos, for present purposes, is a highly unpredictable time series of numbers or events that appears random but that is actually the result of a deterministic process. Chaos in the form of coupled oscillators can be readily demonstrated by joining one pendulum to another (Fig. 1.1I), so that they all swing freely. Swing the pendulum marked "1," and watch the highly volatile motion of the others.

Not all combinations of three oscillators will produce chaos, however. Puu (1993) examined different combinations that could occur in intertwined economic cycles and concluded that although some combinations produce chaos, some serve to dampen the volatility of the others in the system. It is also possible to take two or more oscillators that are oscillating at different speeds, couple them, and synchronize the whole set (Strogatz, 2003).

Repellors

A *repellor* is also a box of space, but it has the opposite effect on traveling points. Any point that gets too close to it is deflected away from the epicenter. It does not matter where the traveling point goes, so long as it goes away. Thus repellors characterize an unstable pattern of behavior. We already encountered a type of repellor when we considered the spiral with a positive coefficient.

Another type of repellor is more akin to the fixed point. A system containing three such repellors is shown in Figure 1.1H. A beam of points coming in from the left hits the edge of an attractor basin and is deflected outward, as indicated by the thin lines around the repellor regions. In some cases, the repellors deflect the point into another repellor's basin, whereupon it is deflected again until it gets free of the repellor region.

Saddles

Saddle points have properties of both attractors and repellors. On one hand, they attract traveling points. On the other, the points do not stay on the saddle point very long before they are deflected in another direction. The saddle phenomenon is similar to the flow of people to and from an information booth in an airport or other major facility. The information booth attracts people, but the booth is not their destination. The visitors remain there only long enough to find out what they need to know to get to where they are going. Again, because the points are following different rules of flow, the system is not stable.

Figure 1.1J shows one type of saddle node where the vectors cross at an intersection. The intersection is the saddle. Other trajectories, shown to the sides, are more pathways where the traveling points approach the intersection and then turn. This is the classic busy urban intersection that facilitates the placement of all sorts of businesses. The businesses, if they are interesting enough, form an attractor in their own right, but that is another matter.

Figure 1.1K shows a saddle that is obtained by perturbing a pendulum. The arc indicates that the pendulum is swinging in the normal fashion on one axis, but the oblique vector indicates that a force has been placed on the pendulum so that it also swings closer to and further from the page. The result is a figure-eight pattern; the saddle point is marked "S."

Toroidal Attractors

A *toroidal attractor* is the result of a limit cycle that is cycling along two axes rather than one. The result is a bagel-shaped set of pathways. Figure 1.2 shows two snapshots of the evolution of a toroidal attractor early and late in its regime. The movement of the traveling point is not systematically "eating" the bagel. Rather, it is following its travel rule (equations) that takes it along unpredictable local pathways. It is not until the process has evolved far enough that one is able to see the full structure of the attractor take shape.

Because of the unpredictable motion of the traveling point, a toroidal attractor might be mistaken for chaos. It is not quite as complex as chaos, however. Rather, it is known as an aperiodic attractor, which is an important transition from limit cycles to chaotic attractors, which are considered next.

Chaos and Chaotic Attractors

As with other attractors, *chaotic attractors* can be described as points that are pulled into and stay within the space, even though they are allowed to move

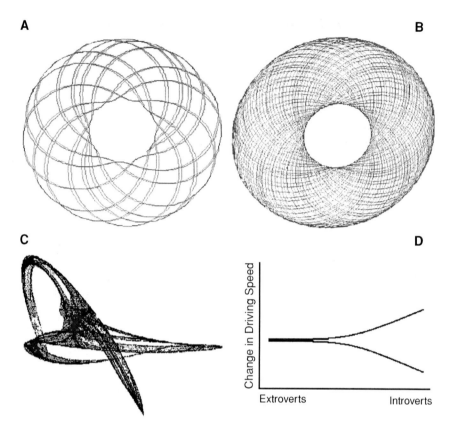

Figure 1.2. Gallery of basic dynamics: A, toroidal attractor in its early iterations; B, toroidal attractor in its later iterations; C, one of many possible strange attractors; D, simple bifurcation, pitchfork or cusp type.

within the space. The internal motion within the attractor space is more complex than is the case with the other attractors discussed here. Chaos has three primary features: unpredictability, boundedness, and sensitivity to initial conditions (Kaplan & Glass, 1995). *Unpredictability* means that a sequence of numbers that is generated from a chaotic function does not repeat. This principle is perhaps a matter of degree, because some of the numbers could look as though they are recurring only because they are rounded to a convenient number of decimal points. Rounding of this nature is going to happen in psychological applications because most psychological measurements simply do not have much meaning beyond a couple of decimal places; very small differences in most measurements are drowned in measurement error. *Boundedness* means that, for all the unpredictability of motion, all points remain within certain boundaries.

The principle of *sensitivity to initial conditions* means that two points that start off as arbitrarily close together become exponentially farther away from each other as the iteration process proceeds. This is a clear case of small differences producing a huge effect.

Chaotic motion itself is characterized by both expansion and contraction. When a point veers too close to the edge of the attractor, it is pulled inside. If it gets too close to the center, it steers outward. A school of fish behaves in the same manner (Semovski, 2001).

Figure 1.2C is one of many known chaotic attractors. It was chosen for display simply because it looks good, as well as to provide some comparison with other attractors. The typical chaotic attractor is operating in more than two dimensions. Most often, it is generated by two or more equations joined together, although there is a famous exception, which is considered next. Each equation reflects the behavior of an order parameter; each order parameter is affected in part by the behavior of other order parameters; this is not unlike the structure of Eqs. 1.7. Control parameters are usually present.

The different types of chaotic functions generate time series that may vary in complexity. The meaning of the complexity depends on the nature of the system and the theory behind it. For instance, a higher-level complexity could denote greater adaptability of a living system, whereas lower complexity could denote rigidity in the system. Two indicators of complexity in a dynamical time series that is potentially chaotic are the Lyapunov exponent and the fractal dimension.

Lyapunov Exponents and Turbulence

The *Lyapunov exponent* is based on the concept of turbulence or entropy, such as might be found in the motion of water or air (Ruelle, 1991). In signal processing, entropy is the amount of change in a system over space or time that cannot be predicted by available information (Shannon, 1948). In dynamical systems, however, a turbulent system is *generating* information (Nicolis & Prigogine, 1989; Prigogine & Stengers, 1984); information generated at one point in time might then be used to predict the state of the system at the next point in time. From either perspective, the exponent reflects the rate at which information that allows a forecast of a variable y is lost. The faster the information is lost, the greater the entropy. It is calculated (Kaplan & Glass, 1995, pp. 334–335; Puu, 2000, p. 157) by taking pairs of initial conditions y_1 and y_2 and their iterations one step ahead in time, which would be y_2 and y_3. If the ratio of absolute values of differences,

$$L \approx |y_3 - y_2|/|y_2 - y_1|, \qquad (1.8)$$

is less than 1.0, the series is contracting. If the value of L is greater than 1.0, the function is expanding, and sensitive dependence is present. The Lyapunov exponent, λ, is thus

$$\lambda \approx \ln[L]. \qquad (1.9)$$

For an ensemble of trajectories in a dynamical field, exponents are computed for all values of y. If the largest value of λ is positive, and the sum of λ_i is negative, then the series is chaotic in the sense that the trajectories are unpredictable, bounded, and sensitive to initial conditions.

The calculation of Eq. 1.9 is made on the entire time series and averaged over N values, where N is the last entry in the time series:

$$\lambda = (1/N) \sum_{N=1}^{N} |\ln(L)|. \tag{1.10}$$

As N increases to infinity, Eq. 1.10 generalizes as:

$$y = e^{\lambda t}, \tag{1.11}$$

which is actually insensitive to initial conditions. A positive value of λ indicates an expanding function, which is to say, chaos. A negative λ indicates a contracting process, which could be a fixed point or limit cycle attractor.

Bifurcations and Chaos

A bifurcation is a pattern of instability in which a system attains greater complexity by accessing new types of dynamical states (Nicolis & Prigogine, 1989). It could take the form of a split in a dynamical field in which different dynamics are occurring in each part. It can also denote a change in an attractor itself, such as the *Hopf bifurcation*, in which a fixed point attractor becomes a limit cycle. A bifurcation structure could be as simple as a critical point, or it could be a more complex structure such as the bifurcation diagram that appears in Figure 1.2D. Bifurcation mechanisms are usually observed when a control parameter is changing value beyond a given threshold value. A bifurcation effect is probably present if a modulus by^n appears in an equation for an f(y), such as Eq. 1.12 that follows; in those cases, b is the control parameter, and y is the order parameter.

Pitchfork or Cusp Bifurcations

The bifurcation shown in Figure 1.2D is known either as a *pitchfork* or a *cusp*, depending somewhat on the context. The example was first introduced by Zeeman (1977) as an explanation for some curious results of the impact of alcohol consumption on driving speed. Participants in the study drove an automobile simulator before and after the consumption of sufficient quantities of alcoholic beverage. They completed a measurement of extroversion–introversion before the driving tasks. After alcohol consumption, extraverted drivers were able to maintain the same speed, but introverts were divided into two groups, those who increased their speed and those who drove more slowly. The change in speed for the introverts was verified as two attractor states (Cobb, 1981). The

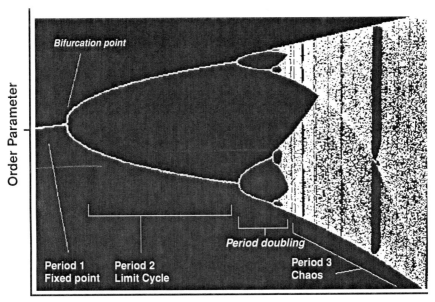

Figure 1.3. Logistic map showing its various dynamics as the control parameter increases in value (Eq. 1.12).

configuration of two attractor states and the bifurcation variable (introversion–extraversion) forms a cusp catastrophe model, which is considered later in the chapter.

Logistic Map

The *logistic map* (Fig. 1.3) is one of the more famous bifurcations in NDS and was studied extensively by May (1976). It represents the transition from a fixed point attractor to a limit cycle, and from a limit cycle into chaos all through one equation:

$$Y_2 = BY_1(1 - Y_1), \quad 0 < Y_1 < 1, \tag{1.12}$$

where Y is the order parameter, and B is the control parameter. In the region of Figure 1.2 labeled as Period 1, the system is globally stable, with dynamics that are characteristic of a fixed point attractor. The bifurcation point marks the transition from Period 1 to Period 2 where the attractor becomes a limit cycle (Hopf bifurcation) as B increases in value.

Toward the end of Period 2, where B has increased further in value, the bifurcation pattern bifurcates again, dividing the system into four smaller regions. Here one observes cycles within cycles. This is the phenomenon of *period doubling*, which later became also known as a *Feigenbaum bifurcation*. When B

becomes larger still, the system bifurcates again, so that there are oscillations within oscillations within oscillations again.

The system enters Period 3, which is full-scale chaos, after one more set of bifurcations. The behavior of Y bears little resemblance to the relative order of Periods 1 or 2. Of further interest are the windows of relative order that striate the chaotic region. The windows contain ordered trajectories that create a path, with additional bifurcations, from one chaotic period to another.

The logistic map can be expanded to reflect a dynamic that has the option of going into period doubling or not, such as the cubic variant in Eq. 1.13:

$$Y_2 = BY(1 - Y_1)(1 - Y_1). \tag{1.13}$$

The logistic map function generalizes to an exponential function:

$$Y_2 = BY_1 \exp(Ay_1 t), \tag{1.14}$$

which has seen a good deal of application in population dynamics (May & Oster, 1976), where B is the birth rate of the organisms and A is a crowding parameter of ecological importance.

Other Bifurcations

The bifurcations that have been discussed to this point, including all those associated with catastrophe theory, are known as *subtle* bifurcations. There are two other classes of bifurcations known as *catastrophic* and *annihilation* bifurcations (Abraham & Shaw, 1992). In catastrophic bifurcations, new attractor regimes pop in and out of the dynamical field as a control parameter changes. In *annihilation bifurcations*, a control parameter induces two or more dynamical structures to collide, producing a dynamical field that did not exist previously. Neither of these types of bifurcations has surfaced in psychological applications, and to our knowledge, an annihilation bifurcation only surfaced once in sociology in an application to urban growth and renewal (Guastello, 1995).

Fractals and Power Laws

Fractals are geometric structures with noninteger dimensions. They have some important properties that characterize nonlinear events: their scale–scale property, scaling relationships, and a characteristic probability density function (PDF).

Look outside your window. Out there are trees in the grass, clouds in the sky, roads on the land, and people in cities. A normal (or Gaussian) distribution has a few small things, a lot of things of about an average size, and a few big things. Trees, clouds, roads, and people are not at all like this, however. The tree has an ever larger number of ever smaller branches. There is an ever larger number of ever smaller clouds in the sky. There is an ever larger number of narrower roads (from Interstate 95, to State Road 808, to 20th Street, to the path to the Behavioral Sciences Building outside our window). There is an ever larger number of tiny villages than large cities. Objects in space, or processes in time, or sets of numbers, with this kind of statistical relationship that we so often see in nature, are called *fractals*.

Self-Similarity

A property that all fractals have in common is that they are *self-similar*, which means that the small pieces are like their larger pieces. For a purely mathematical fractal, the small pieces can be exact smaller copies of the larger pieces, which is called *geometric self-similarity*. However, the small tree branches, clouds, roads, and villages are not exact smaller copies, but are only kind of like their larger branches, clouds, roads, and cities. This is called *statistical self-similarity*. It means that the statistics describing the small pieces are similar to the statistics that describe the larger pieces.

Scale-Free

If I hide the rest of the tree, it is quite hard for you to tell whether you are looking at a small branch or a large branch. If I hide the rest of the sky, it is quite hard for you to know whether you are looking at a small cloud or a large cloud. Thus these images are independent of the scale at which they are seen. They seem to be the same at all scales; they are *scale-free*. There is no one scale that best characterizes the size of the tree branches or clouds or the roads or the number of people in a city. The PDF for the normal distribution is

$$\text{PDF}(x) = \frac{1}{\sqrt{2\pi s^2}} e^{\frac{(x-m)^2}{2s^2}}. \tag{1.15}$$

The values of the variate x are characterized by two parameters: the mean, m, and the standard deviation, s.

For a fractal, however,

$$\text{PDF}(x) = Ax^{-b}, \tag{1.16}$$

the values are characterized by the shape parameter, b, rather than m or s. The values extend over many scales, and so no one scale is a good way to characterize the data. The property of statistical self-similarity described earlier – namely, that the statistics of the small pieces at size x are similar to the statistics of the larger pieces size Ax – is formally that PDF(x) has the same shape as PDF(Ax). Equation 1.16 is a power law distribution. Two examples are shown in Figure 1.4A, each with a different (negative) shape parameter. The shape parameter is not affected by s for the variate x ($z = x/s$ in Fig. 1.4A).

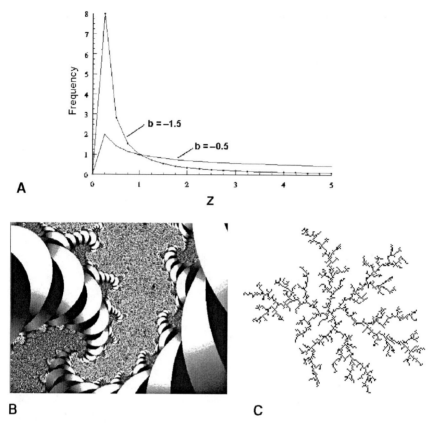

Figure 1.4. Gallery of fractal functions: A, two power law distributions with different shape parameters (Eq. 1.16); B, example of a fractal image (Eq. 1.18) showing Julia and Fatou sets (Sprott, 2000, reprinted by permission from J. C. Sprott); C, diffusion limited aggregation.

For a normal distribution, as we collect more and more data, the averages of those samples, called the *sample means*, get closer and closer to a single value called the population mean, which we identify as the "true" mean of the data. For a fractal distribution, however, as we collect more and more data, those sample means either keep getting smaller and smaller (or larger and larger), and so there is no population mean. Exactly how those sample means depend on the amount of data, or its resolution, tells us a lot about the fractal.

Scaling Relationship

The coastline of Britain has an ever larger number of ever smaller bays and peninsulas. It is self-similar and therefore fractal. As we measure the coastline at finer scales, we catch more of these bays and peninsulas, and so the length of the coastline looks longer. There is no single value that best describes the length of the coastline. Instead, what is meaningful is how the property that we measure depends on the resolution at which we measure it. This relationship is called the *scaling relationship*, which typically has the power law of the form

$$L(x) = Ax^{-f(D)},\tag{1.17}$$

where L is the measurement, x is the scale at which it is measured, $f(D)$ is a simple function that depends on each type of measurement, and D is an important quantity called the *fractal dimension*. Richardson (1961) found that for the west coastline of Britain, $L(x) = Ax^{-0.25}$. For the coastline, $f(D) = 1 - D$, and so the length $L(x) = Ax^{1-D}$, and thus $D = 1.25$.

Fractal Dimension

Why is D called a dimension? We are used to dimensions such as 1, 2, and 3 (and maybe 0 if we include single points and 4 if we include time). How can 1.25, a number that is definitely not an integer, be a dimension? First, intuitively, there is something really odd about the coastline of Britain. If it were a regular one-dimensional line, then its length should always be the same no matter how we measure it. So, somehow, it must be more than just a simple one-dimensional line. It is so wiggly that it fills up more space than just a one-dimensional line. But it is clearly not so wiggly that it covers a two-dimensional area. So, intuitively, it should have a dimension greater than 1 and yet less than 2.

   More formally, if we break up a length, area, or volume each of size 1 into tiny pieces each of size x, the number of pieces $N(x)$ is proportional to x^{-D}, where D is the dimension. $D = 1$ for lengths, $D = 2$ for areas, and $D = 3$ for volumes. For example, when we cut a line into thirds, we get $(1/3)^{-1} =$ three pieces; when we cut a square into thirds on each side, we get $(1/3)^{-2} = 9$ pieces; and when we cut a cube into thirds on each side, we get $(1/3)^{-3} = 27$ pieces. If we approximate the total length of a coastline by $N(x)$ pieces each of length x, then $L(x) = x N(x) = Ax^{1-D}$. Richardson (1961) found that for the west coastline of Britain, $L(x) = Ax^{-0.25}$, which means that $1 - D = -0.25$ and $D = 1.25$, so that it is reasonable to say the dimension of this coastline is 1.25-dimensional.

   This dimension D (hereafter D_F) is called the *fractal dimension*. It tells us how an object fills up space. It tells us that the 1.25-dimension coastline fills up more space than a one-dimensional line, but not so much space as a two-dimensional area. Details of the mathematical formulation of the fractal dimension can be found in Edgar (1990), Bassingthwaighte et al. (1994), and Liebovitch (1998). The fractal dimension thus gives us a quantitative measure of the properties of self-similarity and scaling. Even though there is no single value that characterizes the length of the coastline, how the measured length of the coastline depends on the scale at which we measure it becomes the meaningful way to describe the coastline. This is a pretty dramatic shift in our statistical thinking, compared with the statistics courses that are commonly taught at the college level.

Topological Dimension

The scaling relationship of the coastline of Britain tells us that its fractal dimension is 1.25. It is so wiggly that its dimension is greater than 1. But even though it is that wiggly, each point is connected just to the two points on either side of it on the coastline. How the points of an object are connected is called the *topological dimension*; for amplifications see Edgar (1990), Bassingthwaighte et al. (1994), and Liebovitch (1998). The topological dimension of the coastline is 1. What is really interesting about the coastline is that its fractal dimension of 1.25 (how it fills space) is larger than its topological dimension of 1 (how it is connected). This is the reason why so many new *fragmented* pieces appear as we enlarge it at finer resolution and why its fractal dimension has a *fraction* in it. Mandelbrot (1983) tells us that he coined the word *fractal* to represent just these fragmented and fractional properties. He defined a fractal as "a set in a metric space [where distances can be measured] for which the Hausdorff Besicovitch [fractal] dimension exceeds the topological dimension" (p. 361).

Embedding Dimension

The dimension that a fractal set lives in is called the *embedding dimension*. The coastline of Britain is embedded in the two-dimensional surface of our globe.

Fractal Networks

Fractal patterns are present not only in physical structures but also in the more abstract structures of physical, biological, and social networks. Networks consist of nodes and connections between them (or vertices and edges if you're a mathematician). These nodes and connections can be genes connected by transcription factor proteins that are expressed by one gene and bind to and regulate the expression of another gene, proteins connected by biochemical reaction pathways, neurons connected by synapses, computer IP addresses connected by the Internet, Web pages connected by URLs, authors of scientific articles connected by trails of coauthorship, actors connected by joint appearances in movies, sick people connected by their routes of infection, or the ideas that people have formed through their social interactions (Alon, 2007; Barabasi, 2002). These networks are characterized by their degree distribution, the number of nodes $g(k)$ that have k connections. If the nodes were connected at random, the degree distribution would be a Poisson distribution $g(k) = m^k e^{-m}/k!$ with $m =$ mean of k. Instead, the degree distribution of all these networks, and many more, has the power law form $g(k) = Ak^{-b}$, typical of a "scale-free" fractal scaling relationship (Newman, Barabasi, & Watts, 2006).

Fractals in Time

So far, we have concentrated on fractal objects in space. They are self-similar (small pieces resemble larger pieces), have a scaling relationship (the value of a property measured depends on the scale used to measure it), have the fractal statistics that there is no population mean, and their self-similarity and scaling relationship is quantified by the fractal dimension. We can now generalize these fractal concepts to include time series also, which are of so much importance in social psychology. Similar to a fractal object, a fractal time series has ever larger variations at ever longer time scales. No single value best describes these variations. The longer you look, the larger the variations. The power spectra (the energy in each frequency of the sine waves that can be added together to reconstruct the data, as illustrated by Eq. 1.5) of these time series has a power $P(f) = f^{-b}$. This means that there is ever larger power $P(f)$ in the fluctuations over ever smaller frequencies f that correspond to ever longer times. In physics, this behavior is called "one-over-f noise," even when the exponent b is not equal to 1.0. This type of fractal time series behavior is found in many physical, biological, and psychological systems, including the noise in electronic circuits, the kinetics of ion channels in the cell membrane switching between shapes that allow or prevent ions from crossing the cell membrane, and the dynamics of self-reported emotional states (Liebovitch, 1998; Nowak & Vallacher, 1998).

Fractals in Data

The same statistical properties that characterize fractals in space and time can also be found in the distribution of numbers measured in an experiment. Unlike normal distributions with many values near the mean and few values in the tails of the distribution, fractal distributions of data have a few large values, many medium-sized values, and a huge number of small values. Just like the distribution of the sizes of the pieces of fractal objects, the distribution of the values of a fractal data set has the power law form that the $PDF(x) = Ax^{-b}$. As mentioned earlier, fractal or power law distributions do not have population means. Rather, it is the ratio of the number of large values to the number of small that determines whether the sample means increase or decrease. In fact, it is exactly this ratio that is quantitatively described by the fractal dimension (Liebovitch, 1998). Because all of these fractal distributions have a much higher probability than a normal distribution of having extreme values, they are also called *heavy-tailed* or *fat-tailed* distributions.

Mechanisms That Make Fractals

Different types of mechanisms produce fractals. The geometric self-similarity of mathematical fractals can be generated by several types of mathematical transformations. Similitudes (which preserve angles) and affine transformations (linear transformations, rotations, and translations) can reproduce a whole object on smaller and smaller scales. Sets of affine transformations, called *iterated function systems*, generate realistic images of fractal and even nonfractal scenes (Barnsley, 1988). Fractals can also be generated as the attractors, the final stable end products of dynamical systems. The images generated by iterated function systems are the attractors of the set of transformations used. Adding some random noise to these methods can produce realistic models of the fractals in the natural world.

Equation 1.18 is a generic affine transformation for a fractal function:

$$Z_2 \leftarrow Z_1^2 + C, \qquad\qquad (1.18)$$

where Z is a variable and C is a constant. The *Julia set* refers to the points in space that are the values of the repeated iterations of this equation. The elaborate example in Figure 1.4B is one of many examples of a Julia set; the Mandelbrot set that appears in many books is another example. The fractal images become more elaborate as the degree of the polynomial exceeds 2.0 if we substitute a f(X, Y) for Z, or if C becomes complex; for example, $Z = X + iY$, and $C = A + iB$ (Sprott, 2004). In other words, if we tweak the parameters by a little or a lot, the image changes.

The resulting fractal patterns may be open or closed; Julia sets are closed. The interior space of a closed region is a *Fatou set* (Kuvshinov & Kuzmin, 2005; Weisstein, 2003, p. 1598). Fatou sets are shown in Figure 1.4B as black-and-white patches. In a two-dimensional image, they are usually shown simply as black patches.

The flashy graphics that made fractals famous have not, for the most part, crossed into nonlinear psychological research, except for a few studies in aesthetics (Sprott, 2004; Taylor et al., 2005). The properties of Julia and Fatou sets and the role of complex numbers do appear in Chapter 4 on psychophysics, however. The properties of fractals that affect the analysis of time-series data are used much more frequently.

Some simple mechanisms can also generate fractal patterns, which may be the reason so many natural objects in space, processes in time, or data from nature are fractal. The very simple rule that an existing structure grows fastest at its sharper tips produces fractal patterns in electrical discharges, a light fluid pushed into a denser liquid, and perhaps the growth of blood vessels. These patterns are called *diffusion-limited aggregations* (DLAs); an example appears in Figure 1.4C. DLAs have been implicated in numerous applications in which transportation or spatial spreading phenomena are involved (Bunde & Havlin,

1996). In each case, the physical mechanism is different, but the equations that represent them are the same, and so the same type of fractal pattern is formed (Liebovitch & Shehadeh, 2007).

Another very simple rule is that when the stress at one location exceeds a threshold, it is spread to its nearest neighbors. This mechanism is called *self-organized criticality* (SOC). It can produce fractal patterns in the sizes, masses, and timing of avalanches of sand in a sandpile and may be the underlying cause for the fractal properties of earthquakes, forest fires, and the spread of measles (Bak, 1996).

Fractals and Chaos

A chaotic time series can be analyzed for fractal structure and D_F (Mandelbrot, 1983, 1997). Not all fractals denote chaos, however; thus a test for chaos should be based on the Lyapunov exponent, as mentioned earlier. Fortunately, D_F can be approximated by a dimension that is based on the Lyapunov exponent, D_L. D_L becomes a function of the largest value of λ in the series (Frederickson, Kaplan, Yorke, & Yorke, 1983; Wiggins, 1988):

$$D_L = e^{\lambda}. \tag{1.19}$$

Self-Organization

Self-organization is a process that occurs when a system is in a state of high entropy, or far-from-equilibrium conditions, and takes on a structure that allows the system to operate in a more energy-efficient manner (Prigogine & Stengers, 1984). The structuring does not require the intervention of outside agents; rather it is often characterized as *order for free* (Kauffman, 1993). The primary mechanisms of self-organization are discussed later as synergetics, the rugged landscape, multiple basin dynamics, and the sandpile. The four mechanisms vary in their emphasis on feedback loops between subsystems and bilateral interactions among agents (subsystems) within a system. The reader will probably notice that the distinction between these two principles is subtle at best, and writers from different perspectives on self-organization have noted that all forms of self-organization rely on information flows in one manner or another (Haken, 1988; Kauffman, 1995). Indeed the concepts of self-organization, together with agent-based models and cellular automata, are all consistent with von Neumann's postulate that all life can be expressed as the flow of information (Levy, 1992).

Emergence

The concept of order for free provides an important advancement for social scientists who were deliberating about principles of emergence in the early 20th century. The original question for sociology was whether groups or societies have any properties that cannot be reduced to the action of individuals. A related question for psychologists at the time was whether there was any principle of cognition that could not be reduced to the action of neurons within the brain (Sawyer, 2005). The eventual development of group dynamics in psychology and sociology answered the first question affirmatively. Psychologists would probably also answer the second question affirmatively, although noting that neuronal and brain mechanisms are currently explaining a good deal of social behavior that had not been explained that way before.

Explanations for emergence processes, all of which predated NDS, considered several points: (a) actions of many individuals, (b) interactions among individuals, (c) the history of their interactions, (d) the complexity of those interactions, (e) whether a superordinate structure occurs as the result of any of the foregoing types of actions or interactions, and (f) whether any downward causality occurs once a superordinate structure has occurred. The development of a superordinate structure was known as *supervenience*. Theorists varied with regard to their emphasis on individualistic explanations or those who leaned toward the conclusion that "the whole is greater than the sum of its parts." Durkheim (1895/1964) developed the first theory about group dynamics and sociology around this point, which, according to Sawyer (2005), he had borrowed from philosophers of the late 19th century; Gestalt psychology, which made the remark famous, did not arrive until a couple decades later. Some phenomena might be understood insofar as a superordinate structure is created, but it is probably true that some systems will vary in their ability to exert strong downward influences on the lower levels of the system.

Synergetics

There is no reason to assume that the output of any subsystem is specifically steady, oscillating, or chaotic. In any event, though, the dynamics of one output do become the input for another subsystem. The output of the secondary subsystem will reflect, in part, the dynamics of its input. The general set of relationships, known as *coupled dynamics*, are central to Haken's (1984) *synergetics*, which is the study of nonlinear dynamics in interacting subsystems. Supervenience occurs in the form of a *driver–slave* relationship. A driver is usually observed as a relatively slow dynamic that modulates the behavior of a faster-moving slave. When a system reaches a sufficient level of entropy, hierarchical structures emerge that act as drivers. Drivers in the "upper" level of the hierarchy control the dynamics of the "lower" level. For instance, we could have a periodic oscillator driving a chaotic slave. The result would be a periodic function that, when it reaches a certain point, triggers the fast-moving chaotic behavior (Guastello, 1998).

The emergence of a hierarchical structure follows the same mathematical and physical dynamics as a phase transition, such as the transition of a solid to a

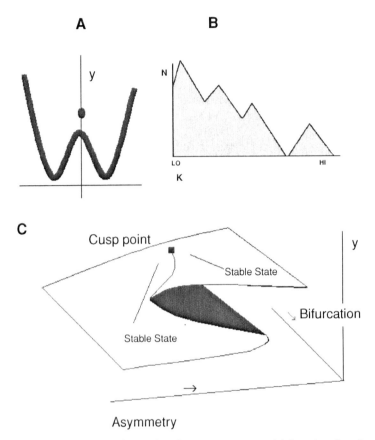

A

B

C

Cusp point

Stable State

y

Bifurcation

Stable State

Asymmetry

Figure 1.5. Gallery of complex dynamics: A, potential function for phase transitions (Eq. 1.20); B: the $N|K$ distribution for a rugged landscape; C: the cusp catastrophe response surface (Eqs. 1.20 and 1.23).

liquid. The Ginzberg–Landau model for chemical phase transitions (Gilmore, 1981; Haken, 1988; Thompson, 1982) exemplifies this process; it describes conditions of high and low potential energy within a system as a function of two control parameters, b and a:

$$f(y) = y^4/4 - by^2/2 - ay. \tag{1.20}$$

Figure 1.5A shows such a system with two equipotential states ($b > 0$, $a = 0$). The control point could fall into either one depending on whether the asymmetry (a) parameter is allowed to deflect in one direction or the other. The valleys to the left and right of the central axis reflect points of local stability, high-probability density, and low potential energy for further system change.

Synchronization, or phase-locking phenomena (Strogatz, 2003) are a special case of synergetic dynamics. The process begins with two entities that are oscillating independently, such as the flashing patterns of fireflies. After a period of time, the two oscillation patterns become synchronized, flashing at the same rate and at the same time. The synchronization results from two additional ingredients – a feedback loop between the two entities, and a control parameter that speeds up the oscillation pattern. When the oscillations speed up sufficiently, the two entities oscillate simultaneously. The principle has been demonstrated in numerous living and nonliving systems, such as the synchronization of clocks on a wooden shelf, the synchronization of a forest full of fireflies of a particular Southeast Asian variety (Strogatz, 2003), and a human tapping two fingers in response to a metronome (Pressing, 1999).

The principles of synergetics and synchronization are thought to explain a variety of human motor movements and gross body coordination (Jirsa & Kelso, 2004; Pressing, 1999; Turvey, 1990). In the simpler cases such as the fireflies or finger tapping, pronounced phase locking between the two oscillators is observed. In instances that involve more complex arrays of subsystems such as autonomic arousal levels for two people in a conversation, distinct transfer effects are observed between the two people; they influence each other's autonomic arousal levels, but the phase locking is not so clear-cut (Guastello, Pincus, & Gunderson, 2006). The phase-locking result could go either way for two people dancing, and it matters whether the two people actually know how to dance (Boker, 2006). The variety of possible results from synchronization experiments with human systems also appear to depend in part on whether the subsystems are tightly or loosely coupled (Nowak & Vallacher, 1998).

The Rugged Landscape

The *rugged landscape* model of self-organization describes changes in the adaptive behavior of species. The theoretical scenario (Kauffman, 1993, 1995) begins with a species that is well adapted to its ecological niche. It is normally distributed along many variables that are *not yet* relevant to its survival. Eventually a cataclysm of some sort hits, and the species must find a new source of food and a new place to live. The species disperses itself around the rugged landscape, trying out new niches. Some niches work well so long as the species members that are trying to occupy it share some traits that facilitate their survival in that niche.

Different niches, or locally stable ecosystems, require different adaptations. Kauffman refers to the locally stable ecosystems as *fitness peaks* in reference to the concentrated probabilities of organisms surviving in those locations. The fitness peaks are, for all intents and purposes, the low-entropy valleys of the Ginzberg–Landau phase transition. Figure 1.5B depicts the distribution of survivors as a function of the number of traits shared. This is the $N|K$ distribution. There is a large portion (N) of the original species that survives by sharing only one (K) trait. Progressively smaller numbers of organisms are found that share progressively more traits as might be required of an ecological niche. The distribution is lumpy, showing subgroups of organisms living on *fitness peaks*, or particularly favorable $N|K$ ratio values.

The distributions of clusters of K was determined with a spin glass algorithm. The idea behind the algorithm is that a complex molecule contains several atoms, the electrons for which spin in different directions. If we subject the chemical to a spinning procedure, molecules with similar spins will cluster together. If the molecule is indeed complex, there are many possible combinations of electron spins that will produce the clusters. This principle has led to other applications of the algorithm to explain, for example, how a population of people might cluster into meaningful groupings (Trofimova & Mitin, 2002).

The distribution of organisms can thus be restated in terms of the landscape's properties. If the landscape is "rugged," selection forces must be strong to hold a species in a specific area. Under those conditions, the surviving species members will need to exhibit a relatively greater number of special characteristics that distinguish them from the general population. If the landscape is "smooth," selection forces are relatively weak. Under those conditions, the surviving species members are much less differentiated from the general population (Kauffman, 1995; McKelvey, 1999).

The landscape scenario also requires another parameter, C, to denote the ruggedness, or complexity, of an organism's interaction with other species in the environment. Some of the interactions may be competitive. In either case, there is a coevolutionary process taking place in which the species that occupy a location adapt to each other (Kauffman, 1995; McKelvey, 1999). An important dynamic, therefore, is the potential movement of a species from one local niche to another. Two adaptive strategies are the *adaptive walk* and *niche-hopping*. The adaptive walk requires that some members of a niche venture out to see what other niches have to offer. New niches might be more adaptive to their circumstances than the present niche, other new niches less so. Niche-hopping is less sequential than the adaptive walk, because it involves random (or pseudo-random) visitation of niches that are not immediately adjacent to the present one.

Multiple Basin Model

The *multiple basin dynamic* (Crutchfield, 2003) builds on the rugged landscape concept to describe how small changes in genetic structure can self-organize into new and different species. The basins represent subgroups of species members, which are in turn connected to each other through narrow portals. The relationship between a genotype and a phenotype is subject to many sources of imperfection. There are similar imperfections in the relationship between the phenotype and actual fitness. Furthermore, transitions between one dominant phenotype expressed by a species and a new phenotype later in time are not always gradual. Rather, they often occur in sudden dramatic shifts, or *punctuated equilibria*.

According to the multiple basin scenario of self-organization, an organism expresses variability on numerous and potentially adaptation-relevant traits. Trait combinations within certain ranges of values predispose the organism toward fitness in a particular attractor basin. Some combinations of traits, however, predispose the organism toward low fitness in one basin, but at the same time position the organism toward the edge of a portal that connects to a new basin where the organism's fitness will be much greater. The sudden shift through a portal explains the sudden discontinuities in fitness inherent in punctuated equilibrium models for evolutionary processes.

Sandpiles and Avalanches

The sandpile model of self-organization addresses a fundamental question: Can a global structure emerge from local interaction among agents or subsystems? According to Bak (1996), who literally studied sandpiles with his coworkers, the mechanism begins with a sandpile onto which we allow more sand to trickle. At first the pile just gets a little taller. Then sand runs down the sides to increase the size of the pile overall. Eventually, however, enough sand has trickled onto the pile that the shape of the pile shifts dramatically. Here we observe an avalanche from the initial pile into several piles of different sizes. The frequency of small piles is greater than the frequency of large piles, according to the inverse power law, as described in Eq. 1.16.

It is convenient, if not fascinating, that parameter b in Eq. 1.16 is also a fractal dimension, and thus makes a bridge among statistical distributions, fractals, and numerous examples of self-organizing phenomena (West & Deering, 1995). Chaotic attractors have fractal-shaped basins. Systems in a state of chaos tend to self-organize but often continue to display fractal properties. The values of D_F that are usually associated with self-organizing systems range between 1 and 2. One should bear in mind, nonetheless, that not all self-organizing systems exhibit $1/f^b$ distributions; some exhibit catastrophe distributions instead (Guastello, 2005).

Catastrophe Theory

A mathematical catastrophe involves a sudden change in a system's state. The sudden change is propelled by one or more (most often two) control parameters. Bifurcation functions are always involved, and they range from a single critical point to a complex manifold. The system's states also involve attractors, repellors, unstable points, and saddles.

The central proposition of catastrophe theory is the classification theorem (Thom, 1975), which states (with qualifications) that, given a maximum of four control parameters, all discontinuous changes of events can be modeled by one of seven elementary topological forms. The forms are hierarchical in the sense that the topologies of the more complex models subsume the simpler models as subsets. The seven forms vary in the complexity of the behavior spectrum they encompass. The models describe change between (or among) qualitatively distinct forms for behavior, such as remaining on a job versus quitting; they do not necessarily infer any notion of desirable or undesirable outcome. Steady states and changes in behavior are governed by one to four *control parameters*, depending on the complexity of the behavior spectrum under consideration.

The elementary catastrophe models are classified into two groups: the cuspoids and the umbilics. The elementary *cuspoid* models involve one dependent measure, have potential functions in three to six dimensions, and response surfaces in two to five dimensions. They are the fold, cusp, swallowtail, and butterfly. The names reflect fanciful interpretations of what parts of their geometry resemble. The elementary *umbilic* models involve two dependent outcome measures, three or four control parameters, and response surfaces with dimensionality totaling five or six dimensions. The umbilics are the wave crest (or hyperbolic umbilic), hair (or elliptic umbilic), and mushroom (or parabolic umbilic) models. There are also catastrophe models that are more complex than the elementary seven. Only the simplest three are encountered in this book, however, but psychological applications of the butterfly and mushroom models can be found elsewhere (Guastello, 1995, 2002). The first two, the fold and the cusp, are discussed next; the third, the swallowtail model, is described and used in Chapter 13.

An overarching point for modeling, nonetheless, is that Thom's (1975) taxonomy of models allows us to reduce the plethora of possible discontinuous change functions to a paltry few. Because topological models are rubberized rather than rigid, catastrophe models can withstand perturbations without changing their fundamental structure, so long as a tear in the response surface is not introduced. This principle is known as *diffeomorphism up to transversality* and means, more simply, that the bifurcation structure of a model changes when a tear is introduced.

Fold Catastrophe Model

All catastrophe models have a *potential function*, a *response surface*, and a *bifurcation set*. The response surface describes the change in behavioral state over time, and it is the most interesting aspect of the catastrophe models in the social science applications. The potential function is the integral of the response surface function. The bifurcation set is the pattern of instabilities underlying the catastrophe response surface; it is the derivative of the response surface, or the second derivative of the potential function.

The potential function for the fold catastrophe is:

$$f(y) = y^3/3 - ay \qquad (1.21)$$

and its response surface is defined as the set of points where

$$\delta f(y)/\delta y = y^2 - a, \qquad (1.22)$$

where y is the dependent measure and a is the control parameter. The fold model is the basic geometric building block of the seven elementary models and beyond. It describes a change in behavior from a stable steady state or attractor to an unstable state as a function of a. The relationship between a and y is a common threshold model. The behavior is observed to remain steady, even though a is changing. Once a reaches a critical value, however, behavior changes abruptly. Change occurs toward instability; the point leaves the basin of the attractor and flies outward, never to return.

Cusp Catastrophe Model

The cusp surface is three-dimensional and features a two-dimensional manifold (unfolding). It describes two stable states of behavior (Fig. 1.5C). Change between the two states is a function of two control parameters, *asymmetry* (*a*) and *bifurcation* (*b*). At low values of *b*, change is smooth, and at high values of *b*, it is potentially discontinuous, depending on the values of *a*. At low values of *a* when *b* is high, changes occur around the lower mode and are relatively small in size. At middle values of *a*, changes occur between modes and are relatively large, assuming *b* is also large. At high values of *a*, changes occur around the upper mode and are again small.

The cusp response surface is the set of points where

$$\delta f(y)/\delta y = y^3 - by - a. \qquad (1.23)$$

Change in behavior is denoted by the path of a control point over time. The point begins on the upper sheet denoting behavior of one type and is observed in that behavioral modality for a period of time. During that time its coordinates on *a* and *b* are changing when suddenly it reaches a fold line and drops to the lower value of the behavior, which is qualitatively different where it remains. Reversing direction, the point is observed in the lower mode until coordinates change to a critical pair of values, at which moment the point jumps back to the upper mode. There are two thresholds for behavior change, one ascending and one descending. The phenomenon of *hysteresis* simultaneously refers to relatively frequent changes between the two behavioral states and the two different thresholds for change.

The shaded area of the surface is the region of inaccessibility in which very few points fall. Statistically, one would observe an antimode between the two stable states that would correspond to the shaded region of the surface.

The cusp and higher-order models also have a control surface on which the bifurcation set is sometimes drawn, mapping the unfolding of the surface in (for the cusp) two dimensions. When highlighted on the response surface itself, the cusp bifurcation set induces two diverging response gradients, which are joined at a *cusp point*. The diverging gradients are labeled A and B on the cusp surface in Figure 1.5C. Behavior at the cusp point is ambiguous. The cusp point is known as the *point of degenerate singularity* and is the most unstable point on the surface. Analogous points exist in other catastrophe models as well.

The cusp model has a potential function also, which just happens to be the same as Eq. 1.20 for phase transitions. Thus there is a close relationship between self-organizing systems, phase shifts, and cusps. Self-organizing events aside, catastrophe models were among the first NDS principles to be introduced to psychology (Zeeman, 1977), and the number of applications that have been studied in the past 30 years frankly has been enormous.

Computational Methods for NDS

There are several approaches to the formation and testing of hypotheses in NDS. It is only possible to capture the most distinctive groups of techniques here. We consider convenient relationships, analytic strategies, and computationally intensive simulations, along with references for further exploration.

Convenient Relationships

There are some convenient relationships among the nonlinear principles discussed in this chapter so far. First, the data sources are usually time series of one type or another. According to an important theorem, all the information that is needed to determine the dynamics of a system is encoded in the time series (Packard, Crutchfield, Farmer, & Shaw, 1980). The principle is similar to the groove of a phonograph record: All the needed information is in the groove.

Second, there are a few closely related forms of the fractal dimensions (D_F), but in principle they are meant to capture the same property of the data. D_F is asymptotically equal to e^λ, where λ is the largest Lyapunov exponent, which is a measure of turbulence in the data (Ott, Sauer, & Yorke, 1994). A negative shape parameter (exponent) of a power law distribution is a D_F for a distribution of data points, which could signify a self-organizing process if $1 < D_F < 2$.

Third, Shannon's measure of entropy and information, topological entropy, and the Lyapunov exponent are closely related also (Gregson, 2006; Guastello, Hyde, & Odak, 1998; Lathrop & Kostelich, 1989). Not surprisingly, Shannon's information function converts to an *information dimension*, which is reasonably equivalent to D_F (Sprott, 2003). Alternative constructs of entropy, such as *Komolgorov–Sinai* (K-S) and *Approximate Entropy* (*ApEn*; Heath, 2000; Sprott, 2003), also have useful converging relationships with other forms of entropy and D_F. K-S, however, indicates how fast information is *lost* over time, for example, in a chaotic system. *ApEn* is an indicator of how unpredictable a sequence of states will be over time. They were derived from different perspectives to frame the "chaos question" a bit differently. The indicators of dimension and entropy denote the complexity of the events occurring within a time series. They can also provide some indication as to whether the dynamics emanate from a fixed point, chaos, or self-organizing processes.

Fourth, the elementary catastrophe models involve combinations of attractors, bifurcations of varying complexity. Within elementary catastrophe theory, there is a clear relationship between the dimension of the order parameters and the number of control parameters in a system. The relationship between the number of control parameters and the system's dimensionality is not so clear in more generalized NDS, however. Following from catastrophe theory, it would be a useful heuristic nonetheless to start with a fractal dimension, round down to the nearest integer, and subtract 1.0 (for the order parameter) to obtain an estimate of the number of control parameters in the system. This heuristic assumes that the control parameters themselves are one-dimensional, although they could have interesting nonlinear behaviors over time themselves.

Fifth, catastrophe models also encompass phase shifts such as those that are observed in many self-organizing processes. The connection is literal, as Eq. 1.20 indicates.

Analytic Strategies

As with any mundane statistical analysis, the more one knows about the process beforehand, the stronger the hypotheses and the stronger the potential conclusions about the process. The currently available analytic strategies range from blunt instruments that detect simply whether nonlinearity is present in the data to those that allow explicit tests of specific functional relationships among variables. The variety of techniques reflects the different types of research questions that might be posed by mathematicians, physicists, biologists, and psychologists.

For mathematical questions, the functions are intrinsically interesting. For instance, one might be interested in the effect of control parameters on order parameters and critical points where qualitative shifts in the dynamics occur. One would then generate numbers from the known functions and make calculations on those number series. Note that noise and error are not yet involved to any meaningful extent.

Biology and physics encounter noise to varying extents. There have been times when a series of observations appeared chaotic in the numeric analysis but were eventually found to display simpler oscillations coupled with noise that was generated by the lab equipment (Parker, 1996). Technical questions inevitably arose as to whether filters would knock out unwanted noise without losing too much real information (Gregson, 2006; Theiler & Eubank, 1993). Gregson (2006) observed that *any* data-analytic system is going to filter information in or out, so judgment calls will be necessary.

Many of the indicators of information and dimension are not statistical in origin; thus the technique of surrogate data was introduced (Theiler, Eubank, Longtin, Galdrikian, & Farmer, 1992) to evaluate whether a given result truly characterizes a deterministic process or is the product of chance events. The idea is to generate a data set that has the peripheral properties of the real data, but none of the serial relationships between points that would be inherent in a deterministic process. Surrogate data sets are generated by randomly shuffling the points so that they appear in a pseudo-series that one can analyze. The surrogate data set would display dynamical indicators that are higher or lower than that of the real set; statistical tests can be applied here (McSharry, 2005).

The robustness of the nonstatistical algorithms for dynamics is limited by noise, missing data (Heathcote & Elliott, 2005; Kreindler & Lumsden, 2006), and whether they are sampled too closely or too far apart in time (Theiler & Eubank, 1993). One advisement is to use a time lag that is representative of the true time interval over which the system generates its data points. The relevant time frame may be 40 to 50 seconds for electroencephalographic data (McSharry, 2005), but 3 months for some types of economic data (Guastello, 2002). Topologically, any nonlinear system will appear locally linear if the points are taken too closely together in time so that the system has not had sufficient time to change its state. It is not until the system has had sufficient time, or is viewed over a broader range of topological space, that the nonlinearities become apparent (Wiggins, 1988).

Most of the studies of the effectiveness of algorithms in the presence of noise employ independent, Gaussian error, which is also known as *independently and identically distributed error* (IID). IID error is added in specified amounts to the output from an error-free equation system. The algorithms are then deployed to recover the function after removing the error by one means or another. Nonlinear functions, however, contain *dependent* or non-IID error. For this reason, the Brock-Dechert-Scheinkman (BDS) statistic was actually developed to determine whether non-IID error exists in significant quantities, and if so, the inference from the test is that a nonlinear system is present (Brock, Hseih, & LeBaron, 1991). The BDS statistic does not state what type of nonlinear system is present, however. For that, one would need to conduct some more specific tests. The presence of dependent error, however, is actually a signature that a nonlinear function exists (Brock et al., 1991; Guastello, 1995; Wei, 1998).

Psychologists' habits of data analysis typically do not involve filtering. Rather the deterministic function, IID, and non-IID error are all assumed to intertwine. One would then test a deterministic function by defining it as a polynomial regression equation or a nonlinear regression equation. Only a limited range of nonlinear dynamical functions, for example, the catastrophes, lend themselves to polynomial regression. Nonlinear regression is more flexible in that it allows regression weights in exponents, numerators, and divisors, and thus the broadest possible range of mathematical models. The price of flexibility is that one must specify the entire equation and where the regression weights should go; there is no automatic modeling feature. One would then compare the R^2 for the nonlinear model against that obtained for a linear model and inspect all the regression weights for statistical significance. One could then draw conclusions about the efficacy of the nonlinear model and the theory that it represents versus a model that was defined from the vantage point of conventional linear thinking (Guastello, 1995, 2002).

Choices of particular techniques involve, in part, whether the order parameter is measured as a continuous (e.g., interval or ratio scale) variable or as a series of discrete states. The latter lend themselves to *symbolic dynamics* analysis (Gregson, 2005; Guastello, Hyde, & Odak, 1998; Lathrop & Kostelich, 1989), which can isolate meaningful patterns from series of discrete observations. The structure of the patterns is tied in turn to entropy and information functions, and they have some important relationships to Markov chains as well.

The search for optimal methods for testing nonlinear hypotheses with psychological data is still active. Transient dynamics are a source of annoyance that has not been addressed particularly well. A transient is a dynamical process that interrupts one that is already ongoing. The transient can be brief or long, but when it ends, the initial dynamic resumes. A nonlinear regression approach could, nonetheless, find the initial dynamic if it were stronger than the transient; one might then analyze the residual to find the nature of the transient. The success of this approach depends on the investigator having a good idea of what to look for. Symbolic dynamics and related matrix-based techniques are now being explored to maneuver transient dynamics (Gregson, 2006).

Gregson and Guastello (2005) also challenged what they called the "myth of the million data points," which is the often-heard lament, "Huge quantities of data are required to test for chaos and other nonlinearities" (p. 372). The long history of nonlinear regression indicates otherwise. The myth breaks down further if we consider the differences of expressed opinion (catalogued in Liebovitch, 1998, p. 211) as to how many points are required to evaluate a six-dimensional attractor range from 10 to 5 billion. Thus the ordinary time series lengths encountered in psychology, which could run between 50 and a couple hundred points, should be sufficient if they indeed sample the full range of the phenomena that they were meant to represent.

Experiments can be designed to compare indicators of dimension and entropy across conditions to determine what variables control the observed process (Delignières, Torre, & Lemoine, 2005). Although the various indicators of dimension and entropy should be close numerically if they are taken from the same process of generating data, some indicators could capitalize on the structural aspects of some data sets more than other techniques might do. In an experimental study with suitable quantities of participants, the frailties of any particular type of computation are equally active across experimental conditions. Although the results of such experiments may be somewhat relative to the combinations of metrics and types of data that are used, differences that are observed across experimental conditions can still lead to useful conclusions about what variables produced an impact on the dynamics of a situation.

Simulation Strategies

Those whose tastes run toward mega-computation should not be disappointed. There are three classes of simulation strategy that have made substantial contributions to applied nonlinear dynamics, in addition to the spin glass system mentioned earlier: *cellular automata*, *agent-based models*, and *genetic algorithms*. These are all deployed for problems where there are many people (agents) in a system that could be interacting in a very complex manner, and it is not possible to specify in advance all the ways they could interact. Yet it is expected that after the myriad interactions, the system would self-organize, and emergent structures would be observed.

Briefly, cellular automata begin with a two-dimensional spatial grid, not unlike a checkerboard. Indeed one of the earliest applications in the social sciences literally involved the use of a checkerboard rather than a slick computer program (Schelling, 1971). Each cell interacts with adjacent cells according to rules specified by the investigator. There are no limits to the quantity or complexity of rules that could be deployed, except that they should be meaningful to the problem that one intends to simulate. Eventually something interesting emerges, and often what emerges is sensitive to the initial conditions of the system. The literature on cellular automata rules and techniques is extensive (Wolfram, 2002).

An agent is a piece of programming that perceives, cognates, and acts according to rules supplied by the investigator. An *agent-based model* takes thousands of agents and puts them into a system in which they can interact but are not necessarily confined to a checkerboard. Frantz and Carley discuss agent-based models in Chapter 16 of this volume.

Genetic algorithms have an agent-based character to them, with the major exception that the rules of interaction are confined to rules of genetic recombination. They were initially developed to simulate biological evolutionary processes and to avoid having to wait for thousands of generations of an organism's life span to see the outcome. Genetic algorithms permitted many new hypotheses about systems that were not tied to the literal rules of genetic recombination, resulting in *evolutionary computations*. Numerous applications appeared in organizational behavior and urban planning (Allen & Varga, 2007; Allen, Chapter 15, this volume).

Summary

NDS theory offers some markedly different perspectives on chance and determinism in scientific explanations of phenomena, mechanical systems versus

CAS, the concepts of dimensions and complexity, and basic notions of change and equilibria. Its inventory of new concepts for understanding change includes attractors, bifurcations, chaos, fractals, self-organization, and catastrophes, all of which can be formalized as nonlinear functions as opposed to the linear functions that permeate the mainstay of psychological theory and research at the present time. When combined with domain-specific knowledge about psychological phenomena, NDS constructs can contribute to new and improved theories and reveal commonalities in dynamical structure among phenomena that might not have been compared or connected otherwise.

NDS also offers new methodologies to accompany and test its theories using both real and simulated data. Improvements in theory can, in principle, be observed as more efficient theories, explanations for phenomena that could not be explained otherwise, and a more accurate accounting of actual observations in data compared with what could be afforded by conventional linear thinking and techniques. The following chapters of this book explain what has been delivered on these promises so far.

References

Abraham, R. H., & Shaw, C. D. (1992). *Dynamics, the geometry of behavior* (2nd ed.). Reading, MA: Addison-Wesley.

Allen, P. M., & Varga, L. (2007). Complexity: The co-evolution of epistemology, axiology, and ontology. *Nonlinear Dynamics, Psychology, and Life Sciences, 11,* 19–50.

Alon, U. (2007). *An introduction to systems biology: Design principles of biological circuits.* Boca Raton, FL: Chapman & Hall/CRC.

Bak, P. (1996). *How nature works: The science of self-organized criticality.* New York: Springer-Verlag/Copernicus.

Barabasi, A.-L. (2002). *Linked: The new science of networks.* Cambridge, MA: Perseus Books.

Barnsley, M. (1988). *Fractals everywhere.* New York: Academic Press.

Bassingwaite, J. B., Liebovitch, L. S., & West, B. J. (1994). *Fractal physiology.* New York: Oxford.

Boker, S. M. (2006, August). *Information flow and symmetry breaking in interpersonal coordination.* Invited address to the Society for Chaos Theory in Psychology & Life Sciences, Baltimore.

Brock, W. A., Hseih, D. A., & LeBaron, B. (1991). *Nonlinear dynamics, chaos, and instability: Statistical theory and economic evidence.* Cambridge, MA: MIT Press.

Bunde, A., & Havlin, S. (Eds.). (1996). *Fractals and disordered systems.* New York: Springer.

Cobb, L. (1981). Parameter estimation for the cusp catastrophe model. *Behavioral Science, 26,* 75–78.

Crutchfield, J. P. (2003). The evolutionary unfolding of complexity. In J. P. Crutchfield & P. Schuster (Eds.), *Evolutionary dynamics* (pp. 101–133). New York: Oxford.

Delignières, D., Torre, K., & Lemoine, L. (2005). Methodological issues in the application of monofractal analysis in psychological and behavioral research. *Nonlinear Dynamics, Psychology, and Life Sciences, 9,* 435–461.

Dore, M. H. I., & Rosser, J. B. Jr. (2007). Do nonlinear dynamics in economics amount to a Kuhnian paradigm? *Nonlinear Dynamics, Psychology, and Life Sciences, 11*, 119–147.

Durkheim, E. (1895/1964). *The rules of sociological method.* New York: The Free Press.

Edgar, G. A. (1990). *Measure, topology, and fractal geometry.* New York: Springer-Verlag.

Fleener, M. J., & Merritt, M. L. (2007). Paradigms lost? *Nonlinear Dynamics, Psychology, and Life Sciences, 11*, 1–18.

Fredrickson, P., Kaplan, J. L., Yorke, E. D., & Yorke, J. A. (1983). The Lyapunov dimension of strange attractors. *Journal of Differential Equations, 49*, 185–207.

Gilmore, R. (1981). *Catastrophe theory for scientists and engineers.* New York: Wiley.

Goerner, S. J. (1994). *Chaos and the evolving ecological universe.* Langhorne, PA: Gordon & Breach.

Gregson, R. A. M. (2005). Identifying ill-behaved nonlinear processes without metrics: Use of symbolic dynamics. *Nonlinear Dynamics, Psychology, and Life Sciences, 9*, 479–503.

Gregson, R. A. M. (2006). *Informative psychometric filters.* Canberra: Australian National University Press.

Gregson, R. A. M., & Guastello, S. J. (2005). Introduction to nonlinear methodology, part 1: Challenges we face and those that we offer. *Nonlinear Dynamics, Psychology, and Life Sciences, 9*, 371–373.

Guastello, S. J. (1995). *Chaos, catastrophe, and human affairs: Nonlinear dynamics in work, organizations, and social evolution.* Mahwah, NJ: Lawrence Erlbaum Associates.

Guastello, S. J. (1997). Science evolves: An introduction to nonlinear dynamics, psychology, and life sciences. *Nonlinear Dynamics, Psychology, and Life Sciences, 1*, 1–6.

Guastello, S. J. (1998). Creative problem solving groups at the edge of chaos. *Journal of Creative Behavior, 32*, 38–57.

Guastello, S. J. (2002). *Managing emergent phenomena: Nonlinear dynamics in work organizations.* Mahwah, NJ: Lawrence Erlbaum Associates.

Guastello, S. J. (2005). Statistical distributions and self-organizing phenomena: What conclusions should be drawn? *Nonlinear Dynamics, Psychology, and Life Sciences, 9*, 463–478.

Guastello, S. J. (2007). Commentary on paradigms and key word index for NDPLS articles 1997–2006. *Nonlinear Dynamics, Psychology, and Life Sciences, 11*, 167–182.

Guastello, S. J., Hyde, T., & Odak, M. (1998). Symbolic dynamics patterns of verbal exchange in a creative problem solving group. *Nonlinear Dynamics, Psychology, and Life Sciences, 2*, 35–58.

Guastello, S. J., Pincus, D., & Gunderson, P. R. (2006). Electrodermal arousal between participants in a conversation: Nonlinear dynamics and linkage effects. *Nonlinear Dynamics, Psychology, and Life Sciences, 10*, 365–399.

Haken, H. (1984). *The science of structure: Synergetics.* New York: Van Nostrand Reinhold.

Haken, H. (1988). *Information and self-organization: A macroscopic approach to self-organization.* New York: Springer-Verlag.

Heath, R. A. (2000). *Nonlinear dynamics: Techniques and applications in psychology.* Mahwah, NJ: Erlbaum.

Heathcote, A., & Elliott, D. (2005). Nonlinear dynamical analysis of noisy time series. *Nonlinear Dynamics, Psychology, and Life Sciences, 9*, 399–433.

Ibanez, A. (2007). Complexity and cognition: A meta-theoretical analysis of the mind as a topological dynamical system. *Nonlinear Dynamics, Psychology, and Life Sciences, 11*, 51–90.

Kaplan, D., & Glass, L. (1995). *Understanding nonlinear dynamics.* New York: Springer-Verlag.

Kauffman, S. A. (1993). *Origins of order: Self-organization and selection in evolution.* New York: Oxford.

Kauffman, S. A. (1995). *At home in the universe: The search for laws of self-organization and complexity.* New York: Oxford.

Kreindler, D. M., & Lumsden, C. J. (2006). The effects of the irregular sample and missing data in time series analysis. *Nonlinear Dynamics, Psychology, and Life Sciences, 10*, 187–214.

Korsch, H. J., & Jodl, H.-J. (1999). *Chaos: A program collection for the PC* (2nd ed.). New York: Springer Publishing Company.

Kuvshinov, V., & Kuzmin, A. (2005). Fractals. In A. Scott (Ed.), *Encyclopedia of nonlinear dynamics* (pp. 325–329). New York: Routledge.

Jirsa, V. K., & Kelso, J. A. S. (Eds.). (2004). *Coordination dynamics: Issues and trends.* New York: Springer Publishing Company.

Lathrop, D. P., & Kostelich, E. J. (1989). Characterization of an experimental strange attractor by periodic orbits. *Physical Review A, 40*, 4028–4031.

Levy, S. (1992). *Artificial life: A report from the frontier where computers meet biology.* New York: Random House.

Liebovitch, L. S. (1998). *Fractals and chaos, simplified for the life sciences.* New York: Oxford.

Liebovitch, L. S., & Shehadeh, L. A. (2007). *The mathematics and science of fractals* [CD-ROM]. Boynton Beach, FL: DecoBytesEducation.

Mandelbrot, B. B. (1983). *The fractal geometry of nature.* New York: Freeman.

Mandelbrot, B. B. (1997). *Fractals and scaling in finance: Discontinuity, concentration, disk.* New York: Springer-Verlag.

May, R. M. (1976). Simple mathematical models with very complex dynamics. *Nature, 261*, 459–467.

May, R. M. (2001). *Stability and complexity in model ecosystems* (2nd ed.). Princeton, NJ: Princeton University Press.

May, R. M., & Oster, G. F. (1976). Bifurcations and dynamics complexity in simple ecological models. *American Naturalist, 110*, 573–599.

McKelvey, B. (1999). Avoiding complexity catastrophe in coevolutionary pockets: Strategies for rugged landscapes. *Organization Science, 10*, 294–322.

McSharry, P. E. (2005). The danger of wishing for chaos. *Nonlinear Dynamics, Psychology, and Life Sciences, 9*, 375–397.

Newhouse, R., Ruelle, D., & Takens, F. (1978). Occurrence of strange attractors: An axiom near quasi-periodic flows on T^m, m $\geq$ 3. *Communications in Mathematical Physics, 64*, 35–41.

Newman, N., Barabasi, A.-L., & Watts, D. J. (2006). *The structure and dynamics of networks.* Princeton, NJ: Princeton University Press.

Nicolis, G., & Prigogine, I. (1989). *Exploring complexity.* New York: Freeman.

Nowak, A., & Vallacher, R. R. (1998). *Dynamical social psychology.* New York: Guilford Press.

Ott, E., Sauer, T., & Yorke, J. A. (Eds.). (1994). *Coping with chaos.* New York: Wiley.

Packard, N. H., Crutchfield, J. P., Farmer, J. D., & Shaw, R. S. (1980). Geometry from a time series. *Physics Review Letters, 45,* 712–716.

Parker, B. (1996). *Chaos in the cosmos.* New York: Plenum.

Pressing, J. (1999). The reference dynamics of cognition and action. *Psychological Review, 106,* 714–747.

Prigogine, I., & Stengers, I. (1984). *Order out of chaos: Man's new dialog with nature.* New York: Bantam.

Puu, T. (1993). *Nonlinear economic dynamics* (3rd ed.). New York: Springer-Verlag.

Puu, T. (2000). *Attractors, bifurcations, and chaos: Nonlinear phenomena in economics.* New York: Springer-Verlag.

Richardson, L. F. (1961). The problem of contiguity: An appendix to statistics of deadly quarrels. *General Systems Yearbook, 6,* 139–187.

Ruelle, D. (1991). *Chance and chaos.* Princeton, NJ: Princeton University Press.

Sawyer, R. K. (2005). *Social emergence: Societies as complex systems.* New York: Cambridge.

Schelling, T. C. (1971). Dynamic models of segregation. *Journal of Mathematical Sociology, 1,* 143–186.

Scott, A. (Ed.). (2005). *Encyclopedia of nonlinear dynamics.* New York: Routledge.

Semovski, S. V. (2001). Self-organization in fish school. In W. Sulis & I. Trofimova (Eds.), *Nonlinear dynamics in the life and social sciences* (pp. 398–406). Amsterdam: IOS Press.

Shannon, C. E. (1948). A mathematical theory of communication. *Bell System Technical Journal, 27,* 379–423.

Sprott, J. C. (2000). *Sprott's fractal gallery.* Retrieved November 18, 2007, from http://sprott.physics.wisc.edu/fractals/old/2000/fd000104.gif.

Sprott, J. C. (2003). *Chaos and time series analysis.* New York: Oxford.

Sprott, J. C. (2004). Can a monkey with a computer generate art? *Nonlinear Dynamics, Psychology, and Life Sciences, 8,* 103–114.

Stewart, I. (1989). *Does God play dice? The mathematics of chaos.* Cambridge, MA: Basil Blackwell.

Strogatz, S. (2003). *Sync: The emerging science of spontaneous order.* New York: Hyperion.

Taylor, R. P., Spehar, B., Wise, J. A., Clifford, C. W. G., Newell, B. R., et al. (2005). *Nonlinear Dynamics, Psychology, and Life Sciences, 9,* 89–114.

Theiler, J., & Eubank, S. (1993). Don't bleach chaotic data. *Chaos, 3,* 771–782.

Theiler, J., Eubank, S., Longtin, A., Galdrikian, B., & Farmer, J. D. (1992). Testing for nonlinearity in time series: The method of surrogate data. *Physica D, 58,* 77–94.

Thom, R. (1975). *Structural stability and morphegenesis.* New York: Benjamin-Addison-Wesley.

Thompson, J. M. T. (1982). *Instabilities and catastrophes in science and engineering.* New York: Wiley.

Thompson, J. M. T., & Stewart, H. B. (1986). *Nonlinear dynamics and chaos.* New York: Wiley.

Trofimova, I., & Mitin, N. (2002). Self-organization and resource exchange in EVS modeling. *Nonlinear Dynamics, Psychology, and Life Sciences, 6,* 351–362.

Turvey, M. T. (1990). Coordination. *American Psychologist, 45,* 938–953.

von Bertalanffy, L. (1968). *General systems theory.* New York: Wiley.

Wei, B.-C. (1998). *Exponential family nonlinear models.* Singapore: Springer Publishing Company.

Weisstein, E. W. (2003). *CRC concise encyclopedia of mathematics.* Boca Raton, FL: CRC Press.

West, B. J., & Deering, B. (1995). *The lure of modern science: Fractal thinking.* Singapore: World Scientific.

Wiggins, S. (1988). *Global bifurcations and chaos.* New York: Springer-Verlag.

Wolfram, S. (2002). *A new kind of science.* Champaign, IL: Wolfram Media.

Wymore, A. W. (1967). *A mathematical theory of systems engineering.* New York: Wiley.

Zeeman, E. C. (1977). *Catastrophe theory: Selected papers 1972–1977.* Reading, MA: Addison-Wesley.

2 Collective Intelligence: Observations and Models

WILLIAM SULIS

An organism is a complex, definitely coordinated and therefore individualized system of activities, which are primarily directed to obtaining and assimilating substances from an environment, to producing other similar systems, known as offspring, and to protecting the system itself and usually also its offspring from disturbances emanating from the environment.

(Wheeler, 1911, p. 308)

Introduction

Collective intelligence refers to collective behavior that is stably correlated with ecologically meaningful features of the environment, salient for the survival of the collective, adaptive to changes in the environment, and that transcends the capability of any single member of the collective. Social insect colonies provide an ideal subject for study because they comprise a large number of individuals that can be easily maintained in laboratory environments and are readily reproduced, thus providing an opportunity for the replication of statistically robust experiments. The American myrmecologist W. M. Wheeler was the first to propose the idea of the social insect colony as an organism in its own right, having the ability to regulate both its behavior and its environment to fulfill particular salient needs. The colony is able to do all of this in the absence of a central authority through the interactions among and activities of its individual members, none of whom possesses the cognitive and physical abilities to carry out these tasks on its own. The social insect colony provides the prototypical example of a collective intelligence.

The behavioral repertoire of the social insects is astonishing (Wilson, 1971). For example, when workers of the species *Eciton burchelli* are placed on a small surface, they are capable of carrying out radially distributed statory raids and constructing nests of their own bodies, both of which can be regulated within tight limits, given the presence of an entire colony of more than 200,000 workers. On the other hand, when only small numbers are present, they will walk endlessly in never-decreasing circles until they die of exhaustion (Franks, 1989). A wide range of methods of nest construction exists among different species of social insects. Nests range from large underground mazes (*Atta sexdens*), to mounds on the forest floor (*Formica exsectoides*), to complexes formed from mud (*Macrotermes bellicosus*), to hanging baskets of paper (*Polistes fuscatus*), to combs of wax (*Apis mellifera*), to nests formed from the bodies of the individual workers themselves (*E. burchelli*). The environments so formed can be regulated within quite tight constraints (*Eciton hamatum*). The colony may remain fixed in a given nest until it is time for a new colony to separate off (*Monomorium pharaonis*) or may migrate from season to season (*Iridomyrmex humilis*) or several times within a season (*E. burcelli*). Colonies are able to find suitable nest sites despite changing conditions (*Leptothorax albipennis*). Each species specializes to particular food sources, some vegetarian (*Pogonomyrmex barbatus*), some carnivorous (*E. burchelli*). Some harvest leaves with which they cultivate the opportunistic fungus that they eat (*A. sexdens*). Usually only one particular species of fungus is harvested. The maintenance of a colony generally involves many tasks, including brood care, foraging, patrolling, defense, and midden work. The distribution of workers carrying out these tasks can be regulated according to the local demands being placed on the colony (Gordon, 1999).

The association between local environs and task – nest building, midden work, brood care, foraging, patrolling, and so on – is robust across a wide range of environmental conditions despite significant variability in the specific manner in which these tasks are performed. For example, every instance of foraging will differ in terms of the number and identities of the workers involved, the particular paths traversed, the regions explored, and the food sources discovered and harvested. Nevertheless, at the end of the day, food is brought to the nest. The notion of task is defined at the colony level, and the relation between environment and task is robust and stable at that level. These properties illustrate the inherent adaptive and systemic character of the behavior of these colonies.

This ability of a system of interacting agents to respond stably to global features of the environment is typical of many complex systems models. When the global features are global dynamical transients, then a stable coupling between these environmental transients and the transient responses of these systems (Sulis, 1993a, 1993b, 1994, 1995a, 1995b, 1996) can occur. This phenomenon, known as TIGoRS (transient induced global response synchronization or stabilization) appears in a wide variety of complex systems models, including cellular automata, tempered neural networks, and cocktail party automata, and serves as a basis for information processing in a class of automata called Sulis machines (Lumsden, Brandts, & Trainor, 1997). Thus these systems may extract their own salient classification of environmental contexts to which their responses become dynamically bound. A mechanism such as evolution could arrange for this correspondence to serve ecologically valid goals.

Relatively stable patterns of behavior at the colony level are associated with much variability at the individual level. There is little apparent correlation among the actions of the individual workers participating in these colony-level activities, so that they appear to be random. Nevertheless there are systematic features when engaged in particular tasks even though there is no central coordination over the actions of individual workers. Moreover, any particular environmental context frequently observed allows for many different outcomes for the colony, yet more often than not, the actual behaviors performed by the colony appear to be optimal relative to some criterion that is ecologically salient for the colony. For example, a colony of *Lasius niger*, if presented with two distinct paths to a food source, will have the majority of workers tending to follow the shortest path.

Models of Collective Intelligence

Intelligence as applied to individual humans, when broadly considered, involves three main characteristics: (a) the capacity to learn from experience, (b) the ability to adapt to the surrounding environment, and (c) the use of metacognition, that is, the entity's ability to understand and control its own thinking processes to enhance learning (Sternberg, 1999). The first two criteria can be observed directly, whereas the third is inferential and biased in favor of the presumption of introspection, self-awareness, internalized representations, symbolic processes, and their expression through language. Different criteria are therefore necessary when applying the notion of intelligence to nonhuman entities. Fundamentally, intelligence should describe how well an entity meets the challenges of procuring sustenance, providing defense, achieving reproduction, and caring for offspring in dynamic, nonstationary environments. McFarland and Bosser (1993) argued for a notion of intelligence that avoids a human bias by emphasizing the role of intelligent behavior. They have three requirements for intelligent behavior: (a) behavior requires a body, (b) it is only the consequences of behavior that can be called intelligent, and (c) intelligent behavior requires judgment.

A social insect colony clearly meets the criteria of McFarland and Bosser, and so the application of the term *intelligence* to the behavior of a social insect colony has legitimacy. Moreover, a social insect colony lacks a leader, so that the processes that generate the intelligent behaviors exhibited by a colony must arise through the collective actions and interactions of its workers. For this reason we describe the intelligence of a social insect colony as a *collective intelligence*.

A collective intelligence provides an ideal experimental setting in which to study intelligent behavior that does not, in general, involve symbolic processes. Indeed, most collective intelligence takes the form of situated cognition (Johnson, 2001; Kelly, 1994; Thelen, 1995, Varela, Thompson, & Rosch, 1993) that involves knowledge without representation (Brooks, 1991), although there are competing paradigms (Langton, 1995; Maes, 1990; Minsky, 1986). A collective intelligence is a quintessential dynamical entity involving interactions among thousands of individual agents. It carries out its intelligent behaviors by capital-izing on regularities inherent in these dynamical processes, and so such systems demand an approach that includes nonlinear dynamical systems methods for their analysis and understanding.

Bonabeau and Theraulaz (1994) further developed these themes. They pointed out that collective intelligence systems possess several advantages over traditional systems. In particular such systems are more reliable, flexible and robust than traditional architectures. They emphasize the need to focus on the constraints imposed on the agents and their interactions that permit intelligent behavior to emerge at the collective level. They argued that there exists a dynam-ical coupling between the perceptions and actions of the agents that make up a collective intelligence that results in a kind of circular causality of a type first elaborated by J. Gibson (1979) in which perceptions to some degree become linked to those actions that they in turn support.

Usually there is a range of behaviors available to any given organism in the face of any environmental transient, and some mechanism needs to be invoked to explain why one particular behavior is manifested as opposed to some other. Generally this is termed decision making. Some mechanism reduces the range of possible behaviors to those that may actually be implemented. Usually such decision making has been associated with language (Pylyshyn, 1989), mental models (Johnson-Laird, 1983), and their manipulation through deductive rea-soning (Sternberg, 1999). Classical decision theories, which emphasized ratio-nal decision making, assumed that individuals (a) were fully informed about all possible options and all possible outcomes, (b) were infinitely sensitive to the distinctions among the options, and (c) were rational, meaning that they would make their choices so as to maximize something of value to themselves, often conceived of as utility (Newell & Simon, 1972). Simon (1957) introduced a weaker constraint with the idea of *bounded rationality*, exemplified in the strategy of *satisficing*. In this strategy, options are examined until one is found that is "good enough" or satisfactory to meet some minimum level of expecta-tion. Tversky (1972) and Tversky and Kahneman (1973) extended the notion of bounded rationality to include such methods as elimination by aspects, and heuristics such as representativeness and availability. Thus began work into nonrational decision making. Later it was realized that human decision making was often influenced by unrecognized biases that lead to a host of so-called irrational decision-making processes (Sutherland, 1992). Irrational decision-making methods are particularly poor because they are most likely to lead to nonoptimal outcomes. Nonrational decision making more frequently splits the difference between rational and irrational approaches.

A collective intelligence such as a social insect colony lacks the use of language and symbolic reasoning, although it does have the use of various signs such as pheromones (chemical signals secreted by specialized glands of workers) and stigmergic relics (physical modifications to the local environment by the direct actions of workers) that can serve as triggers to particular classes of behaviors. Thus the processes by means of which its decision-making strategies are implemented must reside in the dynamical interactions that arise between the members of the colony following exposure to the environmental context. It is therefore expected that a detailed understanding of the nature of the dynamics of interactions within the collective intelligence through such approaches as complex systems theory and nonlinear dynamical systems theory will help to inform us about the types of decision making that can be carried out by a collective intelligence and the mechanisms by means of which these decisions are implemented by the collective. An important question is whether the decision making carried out by a collective intelligence can be nonrational or irrational, or worse, merely random.

Computer scientists have looked to collective intelligence in their search for effective algorithms for parallel processing (Dorigo, Bonabeau, & Theraulaz, 2000), especially to help with the difficult synchronization problem. Computer scientists often speak of collective computation or emergent computation. Forrest (1991) defined emergent computation as follows:

> This is the essence of the following constituents of emergent computation: i) A collection of agents, each following explicit instructions; ii) Interactions among the agents (according to the instructions), which form implicit global patterns at the macroscopic level i.e. epiphenomena; iii) A natural interpretation of the epiphenomena as computations.

> The term *explicit instructions* refers to a primitive level of computation, also called *micro-structure, low-level instructions, local programs, concrete structure*, and *component subsystems.* . . . The important point is that the explicit instructions are at a different (and lower) level than the phenomena of interest (p. 2).

Hirsh and Gordon (2001) reviewed various models of collective intelligence viewed as distributed and parallel processing systems. They focused on models that deal with an individual ant's judgment of its own success, usually based on its level of activity and on its wait time for either delivering or receiving information from its nestmates. Both of these can induce the ant to carry out particular tasks. They also highlighted work by Lachmann and Sella (1995), showing that the stochastic model of an ant colony,

$$\mathrm{d}p_i/\mathrm{d}t = \sum_{j=1}^{M}(A_{ji}p_j - A_{ij}p_i) + \alpha(N)\left(\sum_{j,k=1}^{M}(B_{jki}C_{jk}P_jP_k - B_{ijk}C_{ij}P_iP_j)\right),$$

was computationally complete, meaning that the colony could carry any computation that a computer could. Here, p_i represents the probability that an ant performs task i; A_{ij} is the probability per unit time for an ant in task i to switch to task j; B_{ijk} is the probability per unit time for an ant in task i; meeting an ant in task j; to switch to task k; c_{ij} is the probability for an ant in task i to meet an ant in task j; and α is a scaling factor.

Engelbrecht (2005) provided a comprehensive survey of techniques for the solution of problems in optimization using algorithms derived both empirically and analogically from the behavior of swarms and ant colonies. The goal of this work is to provide methods for the solution of optimization problems, attempting to find the minima or maxima of some function of several variables subject to some set of constraints on the possible values of those variables. The emphasis is on the applications of these collective intelligence–derived algorithms rather than on understanding the behavior of naturally occurring collective intelligence systems. More than 60 algorithms are considered, illustrating the utility of collective intelligence concepts in real-world applications. Additional applications of social insect behavior to the study of optimization problems can be found in Bonabeau, Dorigo, and Theraulaz (2000).

Bock (1993) described an approach to adaptive artificial intelligence based on a collective learning systems theory. This approach involves the play of a particular form of combinatorial game that involves two or more players, each of whose strategy involves either association or dissociation, and that interact either competitively or cooperatively. Bock studies collective learning in the context of a particular game called the Little Universe Game. These principles are illustrated through a discussion of ALISA (Adaptive Learning Image and Signal Analysis), a sophisticated pattern analysis program developed by the author.

Szuba (2001) has developed a computational model of collective intelligence that is implemented in a Random Prolog Processor, a particular version of Prolog developed by Szuba. Prolog is a high-level programming language developed in the 1970s for use in artificial intelligence research. It was a procedural interpretation of logical inference based on first-order Horn clause logic. This system implements the following features: (a) mathematical logic is used at the highest level of the model, (b) agents ("information molecules") are used as symbolic carriers of logic formulas and structures, (c) rendezvous and a unification-based model of single inferences are assumed, (d) inference has the form of a quasi-chaotic noncontinuous process performed in a structured computational space, and (e) inference evolves with no supervision of any nature (including no operating system).

Szuba derived an approach to the formalization, modeling, and measurement of collective intelligence using a nondeterministic architecture. In part this is based on earlier work of Siegelmann and Fishman (1998) dealing with the computational properties of analogue computation of the type carried out by naturally occurring dynamical systems. In particular Siegelmann has suggested that many such systems are capable of carrying out computations that exceed the so-called Turing limit. These are termed Supra–Turing computations. Szuba conceived of collective intelligence computations as representing the actions of a chaotic dynamical system, thus fulfilling Siegelmann's conditions and therefore potentially capable of Supra–Turing computation.

A more general approach is that of Sulis (1999, 2002). This approach, termed *archetypal dynamics*, views collective intelligence as an example of an *emergent situation*. Thus it can be expected that approaches to the study of emergence and emergent situations may help in the understanding of collective intelligence. Archetypal dynamics is one such general approach to emergence based on a study of meaning-laden information flows within complex systems. It postulates that emergents are distinguished by their entities and their states, actions, reactions, and interactions; by the spatial and temporal scales at which these play out; by the rules governing these; and by the overall goals that such dynamics help to fulfill. Archetypal dynamics asserts that these are distinguished by means of semantic frames and that an emergent situation is one that admits description (and dynamics) by multiple independent semantic frames.

A collective intelligence is an example of an emergent situation. The low level of the individuals and the high level of the collective have distinct descriptions and dynamics. Archetypal dynamics represents the history of meaningful information in the system by means of a labeled directed multigraph that evolves through the play of a combinatorial game. The dynamic is given by means of a game to provide the theory with a nondeterministic character, necessary if the evolution of the history of such a system is to be determined by decisions rather than by random chance or predestination. Archetypal dynamics has been used to understand some aspects of emergent computation in the cellular automaton game of Life, in particular the role of pattern isolation and reconfiguration (Sulis, 2002).

Several important features of the dynamics of collective intelligence have been identified (Sulis, 1997).

1. *Self-organization* (Bonabeau, Theraulaz, Deneubourg, Aron, & Camazine, 1997; Camazine et al., 2001) is the idea that the stable behavior of a complex system arises from positive and negative feedback and the amplification of fluctuations in the absence of leaders, blueprints, templates, or recipes.

2. *Stochastic determinism,* the determination of a property through stochastic processes, underlies mass action. Wilson (1971) described this in *Eciton burchelli*: "As workers stream outward carrying eggs, larvae, and pupae in their mandibles, other workers are busy carrying them back again. Still other workers run back and forth carrying nothing. Individuals are guided by the odor trail, if one exists, and each inspects the nest site on its own. There is no sign of decision making at a higher level. On the contrary, the choice of nest site is decided by a sort of plebiscite, in which the will of the majority of workers finally comes to prevail by virtue of their superior combined effort."

3. *Interactive determinism* is the determination of a property of a system as a result of interactions occurring among the constituent components of the system (Sulis, 1995c) such as occurs in task allocation in *P. barbatus*.

4. *Nonrepresentational contextual* dependence refers to the fact that knowledge within a collective intelligence is nonrepresentational. The environment carries the information that a collective intelligence requires, and this information is most often expressed either as pheromones or as stigmergic artifacts. Pheromone responses are often highly tuned. The same pheromone, for example, results in the rapid assembly of workers of *Acanthomyops claviger*, whereas in *Lasius alienus*, workers scatter widely. (Wilson, 1971).

5. *Nondispersive temporal evolution* refers to the fact that the probability measures that describe the possible behaviors arising from exposure to environmental contexts do not disperse over time. Colonies, for example, tend to generate similar task distributions in similar environments despite intervening experience.

6. *Phase transitions, critical parameters*, and *control parameters* describe situations in which a system is able to exhibit a range of patterns of behavior that correlate with the values of some variable parameter, a control parameter, and that are stable over some range of this parameter. This is in analogy to the phases of matter – solid, liquid, gas – that are stable over a range of the control parameter – temperature. The critical parameter describes the phase itself. For example, in an *E. burchelli* colony, the number of workers serves as a control parameter for the distinct phases of collective motor behavior, from endless milling to ecologically salient foraging.

7. *Broken ergodicity*, a term coined by Palmer (1982), is a typical feature of complex systems in which the dynamics of the system is frustrated and certain regions of the phase space are avoided. This feature is also expected because of coupling to environmental contexts. One consequence is that averages lose meaning, and the classical statistical approaches to modeling, such as through statistical mechanics, break down and lose applicability.

8. *Broken symmetry* is closely related to broken ergodicity and refers to situations in which the dynamical symmetries observed in the behavior of individual agents of the collective are not preserved in the collective, complicating theoretical analysis. This symmetry breaking often occurs through the amplification of fluctuations. For example, given a choice of two equal paths from colony to food source, the majority of workers will, over time, tend to utilize just one of the paths, and this occurs through amplification of fluctuations of pheromone levels on the paths.

9. *Pattern isolation and reconfiguration* refers to the appearance of dynamical regularities among the dynamical transients exhibited by a system such that these transients can be identified as entities or as states of entities in their own right, having their own temporal evolution and patterns of action and interaction. The original description of the system goes over to a new description in terms of these new entities and their dynamics. Such pattern isolation and reconfiguration is in general nongeneric and dependent on initial conditions and context. Different descriptions and criteria are required for colony-level behavior compared with

that of individual workers, and these are derived through pattern isolation and reconfiguration (Sulis, 2002).

10. *Salience* refers to the identification of dynamical stimuli that are capable of influencing the dynamical behavior of a system in a meaningful and consistent manner (Sulis, 2002) such as occurs in TIGoRS. Salient stimuli produce dynamically robust and stable effects. Conversely, *irrelevance* (Laughlin, 2005) refers to the situation in which specific features of the dynamical behavior of a system at one level, say, for example, the functional form of a phase transition curve, do not depend in any meaningful manner on knowledge of the dynamical behavior at lower levels, such as the specific nature of microscopic interactions. Salience and irrelevance play opposite roles in understanding the relationships between the dynamics of individuals and the dynamics of the collective. Salience can be observed in the differential responses of different species to the same pheromone. For example, both *A. claviger* and *L. alienus* utilize undecane as an alarm trigger, but in response to its release, *A. claviger* workers aggregate in a truculent manner, whereas workers of *L. alienus* disperse (Wilson, 1971, p. 237). On the other hand, irrelevance underlies the ability of researchers to examine behaviors such as nest selection in laboratory as opposed to naturalistic settings (Mallon, Pratt, & Franks, 2001).

11. *Compatibility and the mutual agreement principle* refers to the notion that interactions between the individuals of a collective are not always random but frequently involve a choice to interact or not that depends on extrinsic factors salient to the individuals, and an interaction does not occur unless both parties agree (Trofimova, 2002). This may play a role in task selection. By contrast, interactions during foraging appear to be random.

Observations of Social Insect Behavior

The next sections present empirical observations and formal models of social insect behavior that highlight many of the ideas mentioned earlier, particularly the role of stochastic processes, nonrepresentational contextual dependency, phase transitions and control parameters, and the amplification of fluctuations. In these discussions, I focus on the following behaviors: the formation of clusters (aggregation), nest-site selection, foraging, task allocation, and the incitement of work through its products (stigmergy).

Aggregation

E. burchelli raids provide a striking example of aggregation. At the height of its development, the head of the raid will be of approximately rectangular shape, 15 meters by 2 meters in size. Proceeding from the nest in a random direction initially, the raid will eventually coalesce along one direction and move radially outward from the nest with less than a 15-degree deviation to either side.

Generally about 16 raids will occur over the course of 20 days, and each raid will proceed in a direction that forms an angle of about 123 degrees relative to the preceding raid (Schneirla, 1956). These raids show remarkable organization despite the apparent chaos manifesting within the raid itself.

Aggregation, the formation of clusters, is a fundamental behavior underlying many tasks such as foraging, nest selection, nest construction, and brood care. Depickere, Fresneau, and Deneubourg (2004) studied aggregation in the Palaearctic ant *L. niger*. The ants were allowed to interact in an empty field, and the numbers remaining within a cluster (defined as being within 1 cm of each other) were determined at fixed time intervals. The results showed a high level of aggregation resulting in the rapid formation (within 10 minutes) of a large cluster. This appeared to occur through a process of amplification – the greater the number of ants in a cluster, the longer the duration an ant remained in the cluster. This may be related to subtle contextual factors involving the geometry of packing, as ants within the cluster have great difficulty getting past the surrounding ants so as to exit the cluster. Population density had only a weak influence on the aggregation process. The fraction of ants moving at a given time followed an exponential law, whereas the probability of leaving a cluster followed a power law, $P = aA^{-b}$, where A is the number of ants in a cluster and a and b are generic constants to be fitted through comparison with data. The results were confirmed using a simple agent-based stochastic model. In another study, Depickere et al. (2004) showed that *L. niger* also utilizes ground marking via deposition of pheromone to enhance the fidelity and rate of aggregation to a particular site, although the numbers aggregated to the site are not affected. They noted that a choice between two identical options was made randomly with equal probability, showing that the decision arises through random spontaneous symmetry breaking. The presence of the ground marking serves to bias the symmetry breaking in favor of the marker option, allowing for an additional level of control over the choice.

A different aggregation process is chain formation in the arboreal ant *Oecophylla smaragdina*, in which these ants form chains from the bodies of workers to bridge gaps. Lioni and Deneubourg (2004) allowed ants from a single nest to explore a space containing two identical gaps forming a 60-degree angle to the nest. Ants formed chains across these gaps with equal probability, consistent with a random, spontaneous symmetry breaking. They showed empirically that the probability of an ant to enter a chain was of the form $Pe = C + DX/(E + X)$, where X is the size of the chain and C, D, and E are the rates of attachment to no chain, chain 1, or chain 2, respectively; and the probability to leave had the form $Pl = G/(H + X)$, where G and H are rates of leaving chain 1 or 2, respectively, so that there is a bias favoring entering a large chain. Thus amplification of fluctuations in chain size drives the colony toward completing just one chain. They also noted that a critical nest size was needed, below which chains did not form. As the nest size increased above this critical size, symmetry breaking occurred, resulting in one large chain, but the time to breaking increased directly as well. Nest size thus serves as a control parameter governing the phase transition related to chain formation. These empirical results were confirmed with a simple model consistent with the local activation – the long-range inhibition idea of Gierer and Meinhardt (1972).

Contact rate plays a role in enabling workers to determine the density of nest mates, important in both aggregation and task selection. The rates of antennal contact were studied in three ant species, *Solenopsis invicta*, *Myrmica rubra*, and *L. fulginosus* (Gordon, Paul, & Thorpe, 1993). Rather than following the pattern of Brownian motion, which would predict that contacts would increase quadratically with colony density, the contact rate increased linearly for small densities and then saturated at higher densities, showing that the ants regulated their contact rates. The ants tended to aggregate at low densities and avoided contact when the density was high. The contact rate did increase when the colony was disturbed, for example, by the introduction of foreign workers into the nearby environment. This shows that some colonies can self-regulate control parameters.

Millonas (1993) examined a related form of spontaneous symmetry breaking in the selection of one of two identical paths from nest to food source. Millonas used a detailed balance model derived from a mean field approximation based on nonequilibrium statistical field theory in which there were nonlinear couplings between the movement of the ants and the pheromone field. Millonas was able to demonstrate how slaving of the agent density to the morphogenetic field allows an explicitly coupled global dynamics to emerge from the strictly local interactions of the agents. This dynamic undergoes a phase transition reflected in the spontaneous symmetry breaking that marks a choice in the case of two identical paths. Moreover a similar mechanism ensured that when two unequal paths were presented, it was the shorter path that was chosen.

Nicolis and Deneubourg (1999) presented a mean field model of collective decision making involving a choice of trails between nest and food source. Pheromone concentration was the main parameter governing a trail. The model, built around a set of coupled birth–death process-type differential equations, accounted for positive nonlinear feedback related to new deposition of pheromone on a trail, negative linear feedback from evaporative loss, and negative nonlinear feedback resulting from competition with other trails. A qualitative analysis of the model generated a phase diagram corresponding to different foraging patterns.

A follow-up study (Nicolis, Detrain, Demolin, & Deneubourg, 2003) carried out using a Monte Carlo simulation of the model utilized parameters estimated from studies of *L. niger*. This provided a more direct study of fluctuation behavior and the validity of the model. The simulated ants were able to optimize their foraging, selecting the most rewarding source by modulating pheromone concentrations according to food quality. There appeared to be an optimal quantity of laid pheromone for which the selection of source is at a maximum. Large colonies appeared to focus their activities on one source more easily. Moreover the selection of the source was more efficient if a large number of individuals laid small amounts of pheromone rather than a few individuals laying large amounts.

Stochastic differential equations have been used to model raid formation in *E. burchelli* and can generate many of the salient geometrical features of actual raids (Franks, 1989). They have also been used in models of collective sorting (Deneubourg et al., 1991) and of foraging (Fletcher, Cannings, & Blackwell, 1995; Lachmann & Sella, 1995). Resnick (1994) has developed an extensive collection of simulations of collective intelligence using stochastic agents, as have Collins and Jefferson (1992) for ant colonies in particular. Some of these ideas have been applied to problems of hoarding in collective robotics (Beckers, Holland, & Deneubourg, 1994).

Overall, simulations have supported the contention that the organization observed in these collective behaviors can arise through the amplification of local interactions in the absence of any central control or decision maker. These interactions are stochastic in nature and do not rely on the presence of knowledge about the situation on the part of the individual workers. Rather these collective behaviors arise in a self-organizing manner from interactions among the workers and between the workers and the local environment. Thus the simulations provide support for the importance of the role of collective processes in the expression of collective intelligence.

Nest Site Selection

Nest site selection is a complex task. Potential nest sites vary in the degree of light, heat, humidity, exposure to threat, spatial expanse, elevation, and so on. A colony may be forced to choose between a wide range of options. *L. albipennis* (also known as *Temnothorax albipennis*, see Figures 2.1, 2.2, and 2.3) has been extensively studied because colonies are small (less than 500 monomorphic workers and a single queen), can survive in nests of remarkably simple construction, and appear to tolerate frequent emigrations. When emigration begins, scouts leave to seek out new sites, assessing each by several criteria and integrating these into a quality measure expressed as a wait time before recruitment that varies inversely with quality. Recruitment initially occurs through tandem running, but if a site already contains a number of workers exceeding its quorum threshold, the scout will initiate social carrying. Low thresholds mean that a scout initiates social carrying earlier, implying a more individualistic decision making, whereas higher thresholds require more recruitment to the site, allowing more scouts to make their own decisions (Mallon et al., 2001; Moglich, 1978; Moglich, Maschwitz, & Holldobler, 1974; Sendova-Franks & Franks, 1995). This scenario was modeled using a stochastic model

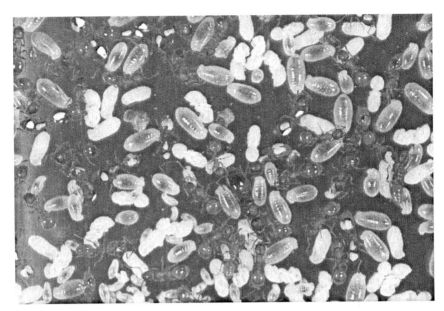

Figure 2.1. Close-up of nest of *Temnothorax albipennis* showing workers and eggs. Several individuals have been marked for movement studies. Photograph copyright 2007 by Nigel R. Franks, used by permission.

Figure 2.2. Close-up of two workers of *Temnothorax albipennis*. Photograph copyright 2007 by Nigel R. Franks, used by permission.

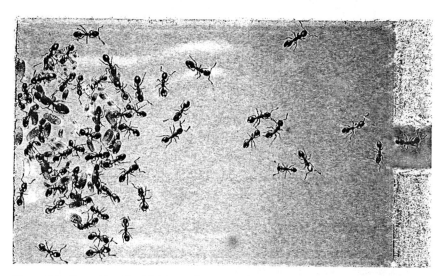

Figure 2.3. Overview of artificial nest for *Temnothorax albipennis* illustrating the enclosure formed between two glass slides and the entrance. The area of the enclosure and the height and the width of the entrance were tunable parameters. Photograph copyright 2007 by Nigel R. Franks, used by permission.

of the distribution of emigration tasks that reproduced many of the observed features (Pratt, Mallon, Sumpter, & Franks, 2002).

Mallon et al. (2001) exposed a colony of *L. albipennis* to a choice of two nest sites, mediocre and superior. A superior site matched naturalistic observations, having a floor area of 825 mm^2, a height of 1.6 mm, and an entrance width of 2 mm. A mediocre site was a site that was structurally acceptable but usually rejected if a better alternative was available, in this either half the height of a superior nest or half the superior nest in both height and floor area. Both the colony and individual ants preferentially chose the superior site. An ant's ability to recruit additional ants to a site depended on the quality of the site, so ants that were exposed only to the mediocre site had a lesser ability to initiate recruitment. Thus individual ants improved the overall response of the colony to the discovery of a superior site. Performance in such a small colony was likely due to a mixture of stochastic decision making at the colony level augmented by individual decision making by well-informed individuals, illustrating the complexity of the underlying processes.

Franks, Mallon, Bray, Hamilton, and Mischler (2003) explored decision making in *L. albipennis* in detail. These ants appear to select nest sites on the basis of three main features: darkness of the nest, internal height of the cavity, and width of the entrance. A colony was given a choice of two nest sites and allowed to emigrate, its final site being considered its "decision." From an archetypal dynamics perspective, this served as the basis for a colony-level "decision" frame in addition to the usual individual behavior frame. The properties of the two sites were varied over all possible combinations of the three attributes, light–dark, high–low, and narrow–wide. In a later study, the colony could choose from five sites simultaneously. By presenting the colony with several alternatives, they were able to explore whether the colony chose a site on a consistent basis, which would suggest the presence of a decision strategy. Using the decision frame, they compared several decision-making strategies (Payne, Bettman, & Johnson, 1993; Simon, 1957): (a) *satisficing*, (b) *elimination by aspects* (the attributes are ranked, then the alternatives are examined for the first-ranked attribute, and all that fail to suffice for that attribute are eliminated; then the next-ranked attribute is tested for, and so on until only one selection remains), (c) *the lexicographic heuristic* (the attributes are ranked, and each alternative is ranked for each attribute, then the highest ranked for the highest attributes are selected; if there are ties, then the procedure is repeated for the next-ranked attribute, and so on), (d) *the equal-weight heuristic* (there is no ranking of attributes; instead, each attribute of each alternative is scored and multiplied by the same coefficient followed by a pooling of such subscores for each alternative to give a grand total for each alternative), and (e) *the weighted additive strategy* (in this procedure, every attribute of every alternative is given a score according to its importance, and individual choices are ranked according to their total score). This is the most computationally expensive strategy but also the most thorough.

The authors determined the following: (a) The ants were fairly consistent, preferring dark over bright, thick over thin, and narrow or medium over wide, (b) The ants appeared to rank different attributes, with light level ranking higher than cavity height and cavity height ranking higher than entrance size. However, they did appear to show some ambivalence when distinguishing nest sites solely on the basis of differences in the least-ranked attribute, showing that there may be some context dependency in preferences, (c) The preferences appeared to exhibit transitivity, and (d) The ants appeared to weight the different attributes; for example, they seemed to prefer bright, thick, narrow to dark, thin, wide, showing that first-ranked preferences can be defeated by a combination of stronger, although lesser-ranked, preferences. A satisficing strategy was unlikely because the individual ants were exploring all sites simultaneously. Elimination by aspects and the lexicographic heuristic also appeared to be unavailable because the individual ant's primary response to exposure to a potential site is to vary its wait time before initiating recruitment, with virtually zero wait time for the best sites and longer times for the poorer sites. Although the equal-weight heuristic could not be entirely ruled out, the authors concluded that on the whole, decision making for nest selection appeared to follow the most computationally expensive and time-consuming strategy, the weighted additive strategy. They hypothesized that the colonies are able to implement such a strategy in an effective manner because they use a distributed process arising through the involvement of hundreds of searchers exploring widespread regions simultaneously.

Pratt, Sumpter, Mallon, and Franks (2005) developed a detailed stochastic agent–based simulation of the emigration behavior of *T. albipennis*. The simulation modeled each stage in the decision-making process of each individual ant when evaluating a site. The parameters involved in this simulation were estimated from the observations of 12 actual emigrations. The model was then validated by comparing the results of simulations against the actual behavior observed in 6 different emigrations. The model reproduced many of the features of the observed emigrations and predicted the emergence of variation in individual behavior despite the use of identical parameters for all of the ants.

Small and large colonies of *L. albipennis* appeared equally adept at nest selection, although the large colonies were faster, probably because of greater scout employment (Franks, Dornhaus, Best, & Jones, 2006). Larger colonies appeared to use higher quorum thresholds to make collective decisions so as to reduce splitting and also used more reverse tandem runs, which would help reunite split colonies. Interestingly, both small and large colonies preferred nest sites that could accommodate a fully grown colony, apparently anticipating future needs.

Franks et al. (2003) demonstrated that under harsh conditions (the presence of wind or predators), colonies of *L. albipennis* chose a nest site more quickly and with less discrimination. These were errors of judgment because the colonies discovered all of the potential sites. Under harsh conditions, individual ants appeared to lower their quorum thresholds, shifting the balance of decision making by the colony toward the individual, resulting in a form of satisficing decision making. This speed-accuracy trade-off was examined in more detail using an agent-based model called the ant house-hunting algorithm (Pratt & Sumpter, 2006). This was a stochastic model of the behavior of each individual ant in the colony, with assessment of quality being reflected in the wait time for recruitment, and the choice of recruitment (tandem running vs. social carrying) being related to a context-dependent quorum threshold, which selects social carrying if the number (quorum) of scouts at the site exceeds the quorum threshold. The threshold decreases under harsh conditions. The model reproduced most empirical observations. Marshall, Dornhaus, Franks, and Kovacs (2006) showed that this decision process was Pareto optimal in the sense that the willingness of individuals to change their decisions cannot improve collective accuracy without impairing speed.

In a fascinating study, Langridge, Franks, and Sendova-Franks (2004) showed that colonies could improve their collective performance when they were made to repeat the same process. Colonies of *L. albipennis* decreased their total emigration time with successive emigrations. If the trials were separated by 24 hours, then the subsequent trials showed a trend toward decreasing emigration times. Moreover, the number of workers engaged in transporting nest mates tended to decrease, showing that the decrease in time was not simply due to the recruitment of more workers. If the interval between trials was increased beyond 6 days, then there was no noticeable trend, suggesting that no modification in performance took place. The authors attributed this to either a lack of reinforcement or a form of forgetting of previous experience. This loss of effect makes the presence of a developmental process underlying the effect unlikely. Priming, recruitment, and facilitation did not appear to account for the observations, leaving the conclusion that some form of collective learning took place, possibly because of a change in the efficiency of interactions between the ants rather than in the performance of individual ants.

Foraging

Foraging is a major activity for most social insects that varies profoundly from species to species. Most species forage on an individual basis, but army ants forage collectively in either column (*E. hamatum*) or swarm raids (*E. burchelli*; Wilson, 1971). Leaf-cutter ants (*A. sexdens*) forage for food for the fungi that it grows. The regulation of foraging appears to be dynamic in nature, although there may be genetic factors as well (Ingram, Oefner, & Gordon, 2005). Contextual factors are significant in the regulation of foraging.

Colonies of the seed-harvesting ant *Messor andrei* show a preference to forage at sites close to the nest, presumably to reduce travel time (Brown & Gordon, 2000). However, if they encounter another species while harvesting, there is an increased probability that they will return to the same locale in which the encounter took place, possibly because the presence of another species in the same area suggests the presence of resources. There appeared, however, to be little overlap between the foraging areas of neighboring colonies, possibly because the encounters tend to involve fighting.

Patrollers of the seed-harvesting ant *P. barbatus* begin the day's activities searching the nest mound and later exploring the foraging trails (Gordon, 2002). Foraging is stimulated by the return of the patrollers. Once initiated, the rate at which foragers egress is sensitive to changes in the rate of return of patrollers and, less so, to changes in the rate of return for foragers. The inducement of foraging depends on the rate at which the patrollers return, maximal at about one patroller every 10 seconds (Greene & Gordon, 2007).

In *L. albipennis*, the lipid stores of workers are negatively correlated with their propensity to forage and with measures of spatial occupation in the nest and of activity (Blanchard, Orledge, Reynolds, & Franks, 2000). It appears that the propensity to forage depends on a balance between forging income and energetic consumption. Metabolic factors also appear to play a role in *L. niger* (Portha, Deneubourg, & Detrain, 2000). Given a choice between proteinaceous and sugar droplets, scouts prefer the sugar regardless of the presence of brood. A scout needs to drink a critical volume before returning to the nest, and this critical volume was independent of food type or brood. However, food type and brood do affect the proportion of ants laying trails (more so for sugar and brood), although not their intensity. The intensity of trails appears to arise through self-organization rather than individual decision.

Redefining the concept of team as a set of individuals performing a team task that itself requires the concurrent performance of different subtasks, Anderson and Franks (2001) studied retrieval teams in the army ants *E. burchelli* and *Dorylus wilverthi*. Such teams consist of an unusually large front-runner, who initiates prey retrieval, followed by an unusually small worker, then possibly by additional members. These teams are superefficient, the combined weight of the prey retrieved exceeding the sum of the maximal weights that the individual members could carry. Moreover it appears that ants engaged in teamwork have both upper and lower workload thresholds. Cooperation among individuals thus increased foraging efficiency.

Halley and Burd (2004) studied the feeding patterns of the Argentine ant *Linepithema humile*. These ants gather at a food source but are easily disturbed, resulting in a number of the feeding ants leaving the group to wander around in an agitated state. The authors found that the size of these disturbances measured by the number of ants leaving the group followed a power law pattern similar to that seen in states of self-organized criticality, the system here being sub-critical because the perturbations did not extend to the entirety of the feeding group. This appeared to allow the system to balance the benefits of rapid alarm communication with the costs of interrupted foraging.

Social insect colonies have provided a source of models for more than 40 years. Some of the earliest modeling efforts applied notions from "cybernetics" (Meyer, 1966). Modern approaches derive from the theory of complex adaptive systems. Couzin and Franks (2003) used a multiagent model to simulate the behavior of *E. burchelli*. The internal angle of the perceptual zone, which influenced the distance at which approaching nest mates could be detected, and the avoidance turning rate, which determined the extent to which ants turned away from each other in an encounter, provided the main critical parameters governing whether unidirectional locomotor patterns emerged. The model exhibited regions in the parameter space corresponding to bidirectional and unidirectional flows. When fitted to empirical parameters, the model reproduced the natural traffic patterns of *E. burchelii*, which tends to form trilane flows with incoming ants occupying the center lane and outgoing ants occupying the two outside lanes.

Information offers a fruitful avenue for study. Dornhaus et al. (2006) studied a model of foraging between two food sources, one constant, one intermittent. The constant source was modeled using an economically inspired constant food patch model, and the intermittent source was modeled schematically in terms of time spent at the source and rewards received. Three models were considered: constant unlimited, reflecting a continuous food source; diminishing returns, in which the resource strictly decreases over time; and capacity limited, in which the resource decreases slowly to a time corresponding to a maximal load and then decreases sharply. The model did not require cooperation among the workers.

Following both qualitative and numerical analysis, they found that central place foragers may profit from returning earlier with partial loads from food sources if there is the possibility of gaining information about the presence of new superior food sources. This strategy failed for honeybees and leaf-cutting ants. Instead, the efficient dissemination of information by successful foragers appeared to be more important than the collection of information by unsuccessful foragers in these species.

Dechaume-Moncharmont et al. (2005) developed a detailed coupled differential equation model fitted from honeybee data, describing the distribution of workers among six categories – inactive; proactive searching; unsuccessful proactive; reactive searching; unsuccessful reactive; and successful. Proactive foragers search independently, whereas reactive foragers rely on information to carry out their searches. Focusing on energy balance, they found quite robustly the rather counterintuitive result that under certain conditions the optimum strategy for the colony is completely independent, proactive foraging, apparently because the information that reactive foragers might gain from successful foragers is not worth waiting for. This seems to come about because food sources do not last forever, highlighting a problem with steady-state equilibrium models.

Spatial factors also need to be taken into account. Boi, Couzin, Del Buono, Franks, and Britton (1999) developed a coupled differential equation model of transitions between three groups in the nests of *L. acervorum*. They compared their model to observations of activity cycles in actual colonies, with and without foragers, and concluded that the relationship between nest entrance and brood workers could be treated as a coupled oscillator with intermediate degrees of coupling. Other approaches to these problems include the differential-equation–based model (Hemerik, Britton, & Franks, 1990), mobile cellular automata (Cole & Cheshire, 1996; Miramontes, Sole, & Goodwin, 1993), and neural networks (Sole, Miramontes, & Goodwin, 1993).

Adler and Gordon (2003) developed a coupled differential equation model of foraging activity in *P. barbatus* that explicitly included the spatial distribution of the foraging by examining foraging at each site on a spatial grid and examining the flow of resources and the costs associated with different foraging patterns. The interactions of multiple colonies could be simulated simultaneously. Models were chosen that optimized at the colony or individual level. The best fit was to strategies that optimized at the individual level, with or without inclusion of conflict, and at the colony level if conflict was included. Thus a balance between exploitation and conflict on the part of individuals appears to be responsible for determining the foraging range of these colonies.

Task Allocation

A major issue in the study of collective intelligence is to understand how social insect colonies allocate workers to different tasks in a manner that is responsive to the needs of the colony and robust to changes in the environmental context. Tasks have generally been defined in behavioral terms, but there have been attempts to classify tasks according to some presumed complexity hierarchy (Anderson, Franks, & McShea, 2001). Early work suggested a link between task and caste, termed *physical polyethism* (Holldobler & Wilson, 1990). Oster and Wilson (1978) were the first to attempt a game theoretic model for caste selection, assuming that the workers of these castes were specialized according to task, and so interaction with the environment created the feedback necessary to drive natural selection in the birthrates of workers assigned to these castes. This was termed an *ecological release model*. Holldobler and Wilson (1990) suggested that as ant workers became older, there was a trend for them to move from inside to outside work, known as *temporal polyethism*. Later studies of task allocation have shown it to be far more dynamic than was originally thought (Gordon, Chu, Lillie, Tissot, & Pinter, 2005; Traniello & Beshers, 1991).

Gordon (1989, 1995) studied task allocation in the harvester ant *P. barbatus*. Workers engage in one of four main activities – patrolling, foraging, nest maintenance, and midden work. Individual ants were identified by task and marked for the task being carried out at the time of collection. In response to perturbations, workers did change tasks. All workers appeared capable of switching to foraging, and nest-maintenance workers were the most flexible and could switch to patrolling or foraging. Foragers rarely appeared to switch tasks, yet their numbers often decreased in response to perturbations that increased the demand for other worker groups, suggesting that some kind of interaction was causing them to remain in the nest.

The regulation of contact rates may provide an important signal for modifying the performance of tasks (Gordon et al., 1993). Gordon and Mehdiabadi (1999) showed that in *P. barbatus*, the time an ant spent performing midden work was positively correlated with the number of midden workers encountered while it was away from the midden, and the probability of beginning to carry out midden work was higher when their rate of encounter with midden workers was high.

All of the workers in a colony of *L. unifasciatus* were individually marked and their behavior tracked over a 27-hour period (Sendova-Franks & Franks, 1993). Older workers tended to occupy one of four distinct spatial locations within the nest, and each location appeared related to a specific task. Workers were able to move from location to location and, in doing so, change the task performed. Only a weak temporal polyethism was seen. The authors suggested that task allocation arose through a mechanism of foraging for work, whereby ants would physically search the nest and switch tasks when a location was found within which they could be employed (Franks & Tofts, 1994).

This idea was studied using a process algebra system called the weighted calculus of communicating systems, which permitted the simultaneous calculation of probabilistic, priority, and temporal effects within a discrete interacting system

(Tofts, 1993). Tofts assumed that tasks were arranged in the form of a sequential production line, with each ant working at a site performing some transformation on the "product," which was then passed to the next stop on the line. If an ant was unable to continue to work at a given task, it moved to the next site either up or down the line for which there remained an excess of work, sometimes choosing randomly when there was no clear choice. This algorithm, together with additional modifications allowing for type of work, amount of work, and so on, was able to distribute workers in an optimal manner across the tasks. Moreover, when an aging process was also added, the model correctly generated the weak temporal polyethism previously observed in vivo as an emergent phenomenon in the absence of any specific encoding of this into the generation algorithm. Robson and Beshers (1997) criticized the model for many unsupported assumptions.

Sendova-Franks, Franks, and Britton (2002) developed a mathematical model of colony emigration in *L. albipennis*. They first carried out an empirical study of emigration in eight colonies of the species and determined that there are three main tasks that need to be carried out in a sequential manner, even though the stimuli to carry out these three tasks all increase simultaneously. The tasks are transport of nest mates, sorting of the brood, and building of the nest. They then constructed a mathematical model based on a set of coupled ordinary differential equations describing the amount of each task to be done and the number of workers involved in each task. The model possessed 34 tunable parameters that were estimated directly from the empirical data. The model was able to reproduce the temporal structure of the empirical data. Colony-level task switching was manifested, even though the sequence of tasks carried out by any individual worker did not need to follow the colony sequence, typical of a colony-level emergent phenomenon.

Pacala, Gordon, and Godfray (1996) developed several stochastic models of task allocation and explored the effects of group size. They showed (a) simple interactions among individuals with limited ability to process information can lead to group behavior that closely approximates the predictions of evolutionary optimality models, (b) large groups may be more efficient than small groups at tracking a changing environment, and (c) group behavior is determined by both each individuals' interaction with environmental stimuli and social exchange of information. To be effective, an individual regulates the rate of social interaction.

Expanding on earlier work (Gordon, Goodwin, & Trainor, 1992), Pereira and Gordon (2001) approached similar issues using a mathematical model based on a set of coupled nonlinear ordinary differential equations similar to those of Lachmann and Sella (1995). In particular they studied how the sensitivity of task allocation to the environment and the rate of response to environmental changes were influenced by colony size and by the behavioral rules used by individual workers. They showed that if workers used social cues in their choice of task, then the response time decreased with increasing colony size. They also showed that the sensitivity of task allocation to the environment could increase or decrease with colony size depending on the rules used by individuals. This produced a trade-off in task allocation – short response times could be achieved by increasing colony size but at the cost of a decreased sensitivity to the environment. When a worker's response to social interaction depended on the local environment, then the sensitivity of task allocation to the environment was not affected by colony size, and the trade-off was avoided.

Brandts and Longtin (2001) employed an iterated function system or birth–death jump process model to simulate ants that could switch between two "category" states according to rules involving category-dependent coupling coefficients. These categories could be fixed points, stochastic attractors, and so on. Perturbations gave rise to noisy trajectories such as random walks with state-dependent biases in the "category population" phase space.

Stigmergy

The physical construction of nests is another fascinating aspect of social insect behavior (Hansell, 2005). Members of the wasp genus *Polybia* can construct nests up to 1 m in height, whereas members of the termite subfamily Macrotermitinae can construct nests up to 7 m in height. The range in size and shape and internal complexity is truly astonishing. For example, the termite *Apicotermes* creates an underground oval nest of stacked chambers connected by helical spiral staircases.

Several mechanisms have been suggested for how a colony is capable of constructing such elaborate structures under such varied conditions. There is little evidence for internally represented blueprints (Theraulaz, Bonabeau, & Deneubourg, 1998), particularly given the collective nature of much nest construction. Inherited building programs become convoluted in the face of increasing complexity in nest architecture. Hierarchical levels of nest evaluation, subroutines, and higher cognitive and learning capacities than previously recognized could occur, but there is little evidence for these (Karsai, 1999). Recipes are rigid behavioral programs that unfold sequentially in time, possibly working for solitary wasp species but unlikely to work for social species because of the coordination problem. Templates are preexisting forms that guide construction. Although not able to account for all aspects of construction, it is clear that some usage of templates does occur at some stages of construction. For example, in some termite species, the queen emits a pheromone field, and as she grows, workers remodel the brood chamber according to this field (Theraulaz, Gautrais, Camazine, & Deneubourg, 2003). Templates do not require communication between nest mates but do not provide for efficient coordination of activities. Some behaviors appear to arise in the absence of any form of explicit coding (Deneubourg & Franks, 1995).

Stigmergy is a term coined by Grasse (1959) and refers to the idea of the inciting of work by the products of work. This means that the physical artifacts produced during the construction process incite behaviors that either facilitate in modifying those products or in creating new ones. The process has been extensively reviewed (Karsai, 1999; Theraulaz & Bonabeau, 1999). The overarching idea is that of self-organization with positive and negative feedback mechanisms influencing the expression of inherited behavioral repertoires, and the amplification of fluctuations through the appearance of construction artifacts that serve as stigmergic stimuli or as templates for further activities. Spatiotemporal structures arise spontaneously, and there will many stable states for these construction processes resulting in many variants of the nest form. For example, in *L. niger*, changes in humidity affect the moisture of the nest-building material, resulting in chimney-like growth after rainfall and disclike growth during dry periods (Theraulaz et al., 2003). Some species use various forms of marking to provide stigmergic feedback (Depickere, Fresneau, Detrain, & Deneubourg, 1994).

Polistes wasp species have received a great deal of attention. *Polistes* colonies usually consist of 100 wasps, and nests consist of a comb of around 150 hexagonal cells connected to some substrate via a petiole. Nest construction typically falls into two phases. The first involves a linear sequence of actions similar to those performed by solitary wasps. The substrate is cleaned, the petiole is attached, and a flat paper sheet is extended from the end and holds the first two cells. Then the second phase begins, during which time the full nest is constructed by adding and lengthening cells (Karsai & Penzes, 1993). More than 60 types of nest architectures have been identified.

Downing and Jeanne (1986, 1987) studied nest construction in 12 *Polistes* species. Nests varied from horizontal, oval, or round, with a central petiole to tear shaped with eccentric or lateral petioles. The angle between substrate and petiole was close to 90 degrees for all species. The nests varied more significantly with regard to the width of the postemergence nest, cell diameter, shape of the comb, and angle of the comb. Cell diameter seemed to vary with head diameter, whereas the other factors seemed to reflect behavioral differences. A subsequent study compared nest construction between *Polistes fuscatus variatus* and *Polistes instabilis*. The nests constructed differed between the species, although the individual behavioral acts carried out during construction were quite similar for the most part. The transition frequencies between these acts differed, however, and the species differed in the angle of cell lengthening, the application of pulp, and the location of nests. Thus there is some evidence for species differences being due to their having different behavioral patterns. Downing (1994) suggested *Polistes* wasps gathered information about the construction process using a hierarchical search strategy with an equal weighting of cues and that the effect of cues was additive and synergistic. The evidence, however, was weak and was criticized by Karsai (1999) as being insufficient to rule out an emergent hierarchical search process and requiring more cognitive ability to carry out the additive procedure than the wasps seemed to possess.

Downing and Jeanne (1988) showed that *P. fuscatus* used a variety of cues to initiate activity, and these cues were in fact related to features of the construction to that point in time. In addition, they showed that these wasps did not appear to follow some embedded construction algorithm or blueprint.

Penzes and Karsai (1993) and Karsai (1999), using a two-dimensional model, compared four different construction rules to see whether wasps could construct nests using local information only and without using a sophisticated decision strategy that required cognitive resources that they might not possess. The rules were (a) ideal – a new cell was initiated next to the youngest cell, (b) random – any site meeting the constraint (at least two ready walls to support the new cell) could be built on, (c) if a site has three ready walls, then a cell is initiated, and all sites having the same value are selected at random, and (d) differential – sites are picked at random but cells are initiated with a probability that varies directly with the number of ready walls. Of the four strategies, only the differential strategy produced nests that closely matched all of the features observed in vivo. A three-dimensional algorithm was devised, supplementing the differential rule by assigning a height to each cell, and a wasp added to the height of a cell with a probability that increased proportionately to the difference in height between the largest and smallest walls at a site. Both models showed that only local information was required. Downing (1994) later noted that some of the behavioral patterns observed in the simulation were later observed in vivo in nest construction.

Karsai and Penzes (1993) also devised a detailed model of comb building in *Polistes* based on a lattice swarm model in which individual wasps were simulated using 19 parameters (which were generally fitted with data derived from direct observations of trends expected from the literature) to direct control of this probabilistic algorithm. It is interesting to note that although this model was quite detailed, it seemed to do no better than the differential model, which had virtually no fitted parameters and used a simple local rule algorithm.

Noting that many *Polistes* species appear to prefer to complete a row rather than simply initiate cells, Karsai and Penzes (1998) introduced a new algorithm in which the probability of adding a buildable row was related to the number of cells needing to be added to complete such a row. They were able to produce a wide variety of nest shapes. Growth was emergent and tended to be isotropic. Eccentricity in the nests resulted from differences in the initiation preference toward particular sides of the previously built structure, which in turn depended on the local vagaries of prior construction.

Theraulaz and Bonabeau (1995a, 1995b) presented a formal model of distributed building using a lattice swarm paradigm. They characterized a set of distributed stigmergic algorithms that allowed a swarm of simple agents to build coherent nestlike structures. The agents that constituted the swarm of builders moved randomly on a two-dimensional lattice and deposited elementary bricks without communication and without a global representation of the architecture being built and perceiving only the local configuration. A few of these configurations served as stimuli for building actions.

They showed that such behavioral algorithms could produce coherent biological-like architectures, that the algorithms required specific coordination properties, and that such algorithms produced only very specific coherent architectures. These "coordinated algorithms" rely on a partition into modular subshapes of the shape to be built. If a swarm of agents is to build a given coherent architecture, the shape has to be decomposed into a finite number of building steps with the necessary condition that the local stimulating configurations that are created at a given stage differ from those created at a previous or a forthcoming building stage so as to avoid disorganization of the whole building activity. Shapes generated with noncoordinated algorithms were unstable and did not correspond to known biological structures. These coordinated algorithms exploit nonrepresentational contextual dependence to the full.

They also noted that deterministic rule schemes resulted in combs that were rendered unnaturally with abnormal features such as lobes and indentations. Probabilistic algorithms rendered natural-looking, round, tightly packed combs similar to Karsai and Penzes (1993).

Conclusion

It is quite fair to say that the fields of complex adaptive systems (CAS), and to a lesser extent nonlinear dynamical systems (NDS) and the field of collective intelligence have coevolved in a mutually beneficial manner. Indeed, models of collective intelligence, especially that exhibited by social insects, have provided a wealth of examples for study under the evolving paradigms of both CAS and NDS. Collective intelligence provides one of the prototypical examples of emergence in a complex system. Without the notion of emergence, it is not clear that the notion of intelligence as applied to a collective of entities would even have gained legitimacy. Conversely, without the striking, and easily perceived, intelligent behaviors exhibited by social insect colonies, the idea of emergence might not have captured so much public attention. An ant colony provides a far more accessible and striking example of emergence than does a block of ice.

NDS theory has also played an important role in fostering our understanding of collective intelligence. Without an understanding of the significance that nonlinearity plays in feedback control systems, the crucial role that the amplification of fluctuations plays in collective intelligence decision processes might have been missed.

The study of collective intelligence has fostered the development of new theoretical understandings of its underlying processes and given rise to new models and to applications in many areas outside its origin within the social insects – for example, in collective robotics and algorithm design. Someday our understanding of collective intelligence may help increase our understanding of collective behaviors in humans, such as crowds, mobs and fads. On the other hand, ideas from the study of CAS and NDS have allowed researchers to develop more effective experiments for studying naturally occurring collective intelligence systems. There is every reason to believe that this fruitful interchange will continue to years to come.

Acknowledgment

Thanks are due to Michael Sanderson for his assistance with the section on stigmergy.

References

Adler, F. R., & Gordon, D. (2003). Optimization, conflict, and nonoverlapping foraging ranges in ants. *The American Naturalist, 162*, 529–543.

Anderson, C., & Franks, N. R. (2001). Teams in animal societies. *Behavioral Ecology, 12*, 534–540.

Anderson, C., Franks, N. R., & McShea, D. W. (2001). The complexity and hierarchical structure of tasks in insect societies. *Animal Behaviour, 62*, 643–651.

Beckers, R., Holland, O. E., & Deneubourg, J. L. (1994). From local actions to global tasks: Stigmergy and collective robotics. In R. A. Brooks & P. Maes (Eds.), *Artificial life IV* (pp. 181–189). Cambridge, MA: MIT Press.

Blanchard, G. B., Orledge, G. M., Reynolds, S. E., & Franks, N. R. (2000). Division of labour and seasonality in the ant *Leptothorax albipennis*: worker corpulence and its influence on behaviour. *Animal Behaviour, 59*, 723–738.

Bock, P. (1993). *The emergence of artificial cognition: An introduction to collective learning.* World Scientific: Singapore.

Boi, S., Couzin, I. D., Del Buono, N., Franks, N. R., & Britton, N. F. (1999). Coupled oscillators and activity waves in ant colonies. *Proceedings of the Royal Society B, 266*, 371–378.

Bonabeau, E., & Theraulaz, G. (1994). *Intelligence collective.* Paris: Hermes.

Bonabeau, E., Dorigo, M., & Theraulaz, G. (2000). Inspiration for optimization from social insect behaviour. *Nature, 406*, 39–42.

Bonabeau, E., Theraulaz, G., Deneubourg, J.-L., Aron, S., & Camazine, S. (1997). Self-organization in social insects. *Trends in Ecology and Evolution, 12*, 188–193.

Brandts, W., & Longtin, A. (2001). Two-category model of task allocation with application to ant societies. *Bulletin of Mathematical Biology, 63*, 1125–1161.

Brooks, R. (1991). Intelligence without representation. *Artificial Intelligence, 47*, 139–159.

Brown, M. J. F., & Gordon, D. (2000). How resources and encounters affect the distribution of foraging activity in a seed-harvesting ant. *Behavioral Ecology and Sociobiology, 47*, 195–203.

Camazine, S., Deneubourg, J.-L., Franks, N., Sneyd, J., Theraulaz, G., & Bonabeau, E. (2001). *Self organization in biological systems.* Princeton, NJ: Princeton University Press.

Cole, B. J., & Cheshire, D. (1996). Mobile cellular automata models of ant activity: Movement activity of *Leptothorax allardycei. American Naturalist, 148*, 1–15.

Collins, R. J., & Jefferson, D. R. (1992). Ant farm: Towards simulated evolution. In C. G. Langton, C. Taylor, J. Doyne Farmer, & S. Rasmussen (Eds.), *Artificial life II* (pp. 579–601). Menlo Park, CA: Addison-Wesley.

Couzin, I. D., & Franks, N. R. (2003). Self-organized lane formation and optimized traffic flow in army ants. *Proceedings of the Royal Society B, 270,* 139–146.

Dechaume-Moncharmont, F. X., Dornhaus, A., Houston, A. I., McNamarra, J. M., Collins, E. J., & Franks, N. R. (2005). The hidden cost of information in collective foraging. *Proceedings of the Royal Society B, 272,* 1689–1695.

Deneubourg, J. L., Goss, S., Franks, N., Sendova-Franks, A., Detrain, C., & Chretien, L. (1991). The dynamics of collective sorting: Robot-like ants and ant-like robots. In J.-A. Meyer & S. W. Wilson (Eds.), *From animals to animats: Proceedings of the First International Conference on the Simulation of Adaptive Behaviour* (pp. 356–365). Cambridge, MA: MIT Press.

Deneubourg J.-L., & Franks, N. R. (1995). Collective control without explicit coding: the case of communal nest excavation. *Journal of Insect Behavior, 8,* 417–432.

Depickere, S., Fresneau, D., & Deneubourg, J.-L. (2004). A basis for spatial and social patterns in ant species: dynamics and mechanism of aggregation. *Journal of Insect Behavior, 17,* 81–97.

Depickere, S., Fresneau, D., Detrain, C., & Deneubourg, J.-L. (1994). Marking as a decision factor in the choice of a new nesting site in Lasius niger. *Insectes sociaux, 51,* 243–246.

Dorigo, M., Bonabeau, E., & Theraulaz, G. (2000). Ant algorithms and stigmergy. *Future Generation Computer Systems, 16,* 851–871.

Dornhaus, A., Collins, E. J., Dechaume-Moncharmont, F. X., Houston, A. I., Franks, N. R., & McNamarra, J. M. (2006). Paying for information: partial loads in central place foragers. *Behavioral Ecology and Sociobiology, 61,* 151–161.

Downing, H. (1994). Information analysis by the paper wasp, *Polistes fuscatus,* during nest construction (*Hymenoptera, Vespidae*). *Insects Sociaux, 33,* 361–377.

Downing, H., & Jeanne, R. L. (1986). Intra- and interspecific variation in nest architecture in paper wasp *Polistes* (*Hymenoptera, Vespidae*). *Insects Sociaux, 33,* 422–443.

Downing, H., & Jeanne, R. L. (1987). A comparison of nest construction behavior in two species of *Polistes* paper wasps (*Insecta, Hymenoptera: Vespidae*). *Journal of Ethology, 5,* 63–66.

Downing, H. A., & Jeanne, R. L. (1988). Nest construction by the paper wasp *Polistes:* A test of stigmergy theory. *Animal Behavior, 36,* 1729–1739.

Engelbrecht, A. (2005). *Fundamentals of Computational Swarm Intelligence.* West Sussex, UK: Wiley.

Fletcher, R. P., Cannings, C., & Blackwell, P. G. (1995). Modeling foraging behavior of ant colonies. In F. Moran, A. Moreno, J. J. Merelo, & P. Chacon (Eds.), *Advances in artificial life* (pp. 772–783). Berlin: Springer-Verlag.

Forrest, S. (1991). *Emergent computation.* Cambridge, MA: MIT Press.

Franks, N. R. (1989). Army ants: A collective intelligence. *American Scientist, 77,* 139–145.

Franks, N. R., Dornhaus, A., Best, C. S., & Jones, E. L. (2006). Decision making by small and large house-hunting ant colonies: One size fits all. *Animal Behavior, 72,* 611–616.

Franks, N. R., Dornhaus, A., Fitzsimmons, J. P., & Stevens, M. (2003). Speed versus accuracy in collective decision making. *Proceedings of the Royal Society of London B, 270,* 2457–2463.

Franks, N. R., Mallon, E. B., Bray, H. E., Hamilton, M. J., & Mischler, T. C. (2003). Strategies for choosing between alternatives with different attributes: Exemplified by house-hunting ants. *Animal Behavior, 65*, 215–223.

Franks, N. R., & Tofts, C. (1994). Foraging for work: How tasks allocate workers. *Animal Behavior, 48*, 470–472.

Gibson, J. J. (1979). *The ecological approach to visual perception.* Boston: Houghton-Mifflin.

Gierer A., & Meinhardt, H. (1972). A theory of biological pattern formation. *Kybernetik, 12*, 30–39.

Gordon, D. (1989). Dynamics of task switching in harvester ants. *Animal Behavior, 38*, 194–204.

Gordon, D. M. (1995). The development of organization in an ant colony. *American Scientist, 83*, 50–57.

Gordon, D. (1999). *Ants at work: How an insect society is organized.* New York: Norton.

Gordon, D. (2002). The regulation of foraging activity in red harvester ant colonies. *The American Naturalist, 159*, 506–518.

Gordon, D., Chu, J., Lillie, A., Tissot, M., & Pinter, N. (2005). Variation in the transition from inside to outside work in the red harvester ant *Pogonomyrmex barbatus. Insectes Sociaux, 52*, 212–217.

Gordon, D. M., Goodwin, B., & Trainor, L. E. H. (1992). A parallel distributed model of ant colony behavior. *Journal of Theoretical Biology, 156*, 293–307.

Gordon, D., & Mehdiabadi, N. J. (1999). Encounter rate and task allocation in harvester ants. *Behavioral Ecology and Sociobiology, 45*, 370–377.

Gordon, D., Paul, R. E., & Thorpe, K. (1993). What is the function of encounter patterns in ant colonies? *Animal Behavior, 45*, 1083–1100.

Grasse, P. P. (1959). La reconstruction du nid et les coordinations interindividuelles chez *Bellicositermes natalensis* et *Cubitermes* sp. la theorie de la stigmergie: Essai d'interpretation du comportement des termites constructeurs [Nest construction and interindividual coordination among the *Bellicositermes natalensis* and *Cubitermes* species, and the theory of stigmergy: Essay on the interpretation of the behavior of construction termites]. *Insectes Sociaux, 6*, 41–83.

Greene, M. J., & Gordon, D. (2007). Interaction rate informs harvester ant task decisions. *Behavioral Ecology, 18*, 451–455.

Halley, J. D., & Burd, M. (2004). Nonequilibium dynamics of social groups: Insights from foraging Argentine ants. *Insectes Sociaux, 51*, 226–231.

Hemerik, L., Britton, N. F., & Franks, N. R. (1990). Synchronisation of the behaviour within nest of the ant *Leptothorax acervorum* (Fabricius). II. Modelling the phenomenon and predictions from the model. *Bulletin of Mathematical Biology, 52*, 613–628.

Hansell, M. H. (2005). *Animal architecture.* New York: Oxford University Press.

Hirsh, A. E., & Gordon, D. (2001). Distributed problem solving in social insects. *Annals of Mathematics and Artificial Intelligence, 31*, 199–221.

Holldobler, B., & Wilson, E. O. (1990). *The ants.* Cambridge, MA: The Belknap Press.

Ingram, K. K., Oefner, P., & Gordon, D. (2005). Task specific expression of the foraging gene in harvester ants. *Molecular Ecology, 14*, 813–818.

Johnson, S. (2001). *Emergence: The connected lives of ants, brains, cities, and software.* New York: Scribner.

Johnson-Laird, P. (1983). *Mental models.* Cambridge, MA: Harvard University Press.

Karsai, I. (1999). Decentralized control of construction behavior in paper wasps: An overview of the stigmergy approach. *Artificial Life, V,* 117–136.

Karsai, I., & Penzes, Z. (1993). Comb building in social wasps: Self-organization and stigmergic script. *Journal of Theoretical Biology, 161,* 505–525.

Karsai, I., & Penzes, Z. (1998). Nest shapes in paper wasps: Can variability of forms be deduced from the same construction algorithm? *Proceedings of Royal Society London, Series B, 265,* 1261–1268.

Kelly, K. (1994). *Out of control.* New York: Addison-Wesley.

Lachmann, M., & Sella, G. (1995). The computationally complete ant colony: Global coordination in a system with no hierarchy. In F. Moran, A. Moreno, J. J. Merelo, & P. Chacon (Eds.), *Advances in artificial life* (pp. 784–800). Berlin: Springer-Verlag.

Langridge, E. A., Franks, N. R., Sendova-Franks, A. (2004). Improvement in collective performance with experience in ants. *Behavioral Ecology and Sociobiology, 56,* 523–529.

Langton, C. G. (Ed.). (1995). *Artificial life: An overview.* Cambridge, MA: MIT Press.

Laughlin, R. (2005). *A different world.* New York: Basic Books.

Lioni, A., & Deneubourg, J.-L. (2004). Collective decision making through self-assembling. *Naturwissenschaften, 91,* 237–241.

Lumsden, C. J., Brandts, W. A., & Trainor, L. E. H. (1997). *Physical theory in biology: Foundations and explorations.* Singapore: World Scientific.

Maes, P. (Ed.). (1990). *Designing autonomous agents.* Cambridge, MA: MIT Press.

Mallon, E. B., Pratt, S. C., & Franks, N. R. (2001). Individual and collective decision-making during nest site selection by the ant *Leptothorax albipennis. Behavioral Ecology and Sociobiology, 50,* 352–359.

Marshall, J. A. R., Dornhaus, A., Franks, N. R., & Kovacs, T. (2006). Noise, cost and speed-accuracy tradeoffs: Decision-making in a decentralized system. *Journal of the Royal Society Interface, 3,* 243–254.

McFarland, D., & Bosser, T. (1993). *Intelligent behavior in animals and robots.* Cambridge, MA: MIT Press.

Meyer, J. (1966). Essai d'application de certains modeles cybernetiques a la coordination chez les insectes sociaux. *Insectes Sociaux, 13,* 127–138.

Millonas, M. (1993). Swarms, phase transitions, and collective intelligence. Santa Fe Institute Preprint, 93-06-039.

Minsky, M. (1986). *The society of mind.* New York: Simon and Schuster.

Miramontes, O., Sole., R. V., & Goodwin, B. C. (1993). Collective behaviour of random-activated mobile cellular automata. *Physica D, 63,* 145–160.

Moglich, M. (1978). Social organization of nest emigration in *Leptothorax* (Hym., Form.). *Insectes Sociaux, 25,* 205–225.

Moglich, M., Maschwitz, U., & Holldobler, B. (1974). Tandem calling: A new kind of signal in ant communication. *Science, 186,* 1046–1047.

Newell, A., & Simon, H. (1972). *Human problem solving.* Newark, NJ: Prentice-Hall.

Nicolis, S. C., & Deneubourg, J. L. (1999). Emerging patterns and food recruitments in ants: An analytical study. *Journal of Theoretical Biology, 198,* 575–592.

Nicolis, S. C., Detrain, C., Demolin, D., & Deneubourg, J.-L. (2003). Optimality of collective choices: A stochastic approach. *Bulletin of Mathematical Biology, 65,* 795–808.

Oster, G., & Wilson, E. O. (1978). *Caste and ecology in the social insects.* Princeton, NJ: Princeton University Press.

Pacala, S. W., Gordon, D., & Godfray, H. C. J. (1996). Effects of social group size on information transfer and task allocation. *Evolutionary Ecology, 10,* 127–165.

Palmer, R. (1982). Broken ergodicity. *Advances in Physics, 31,* 669–736

Payne, J. W., Bettman, J. R., & Johnson, E. J. (1993) *The adaptive decision maker.* Cambridge: Cambridge University Press.

Penzes, Z., & Karsai, I. (1993). Round shape combs produced by stigmergic scripts in social wasp. In J. L. Denebourg & S. Goss (Eds.), *Proceeding manuscript of the European Conference of Artificial Life (Brussels)* (pp. 896–905). Bruxelles: Université Libre de Bruxelles.

Pereira, H. M., & Gordon, D. (2001). A trade-off in task allocation between sensitivity to the environment and response time. *Journal of Theoretical Biology, 208,* 165–184.

Portha, S., Deneubourg, J.-L., & Detrain, C. (2000). How food type and brood influence foraging decisions of *Lasius niger* scouts. *Animal Behaviour, 68,* 115–122.

Pratt, S. C., Mallon, E. B., Sumpter, D. J. T., & Franks, N. R. (2002). Quorum sensing, recruitment, and collective decision-making during colony emigration by the ant *Leptothorax albipennis. Behavioral Ecology and Sociobiology, 52,* 117–127.

Pratt, S. C., & Sumpter, D. J. T. (2006). A tunable algorithm for collective decision-making. *Proceedings of the National Academy of Sciences of the United States of America, 103,* 15906–15910.

Pratt, S. C., Sumpter, D. J. T., Mallon, E. B., & Franks, N. R. (2005). An agent based model of collective nest choice by the ant *Temnothorax albipennis. Animal Behavior, 70,* 1023–1036.

Pylyshyn, Z. W. (1989). Computing in cognitive science. In M. I. Posner (Ed.), *Foundations of cognitive science* (pp. 51–91). Cambridge, MA: MIT Press.

Resnick, M. (1994). *Turtles, termites, and traffic jams.* Cambridge, MA: MIT Press.

Robson, S. K., & Beshers, S. N. (1997). Division of labour and "foraging for work": Simulating reality versus the reality of simulations. *Animal Behaviour, 53,* 214–218.

Schneirla, T. (1956). The army ants. In *Report of the Smithsonian Institution for 1955.* Washington, DC: Smithsonian Institute.

Sendova-Franks, A., & Franks, N. R. (1993). Task allocation in ant colonies within variable environments (a study of temporal polyethism: Experimental). *Bulletin of Mathematical Biology, 55,* 75–96.

Sendova-Franks A. B., & Franks, N. R. (1995). Division of labour in a crisis: Task allocation during colony emigration in the ant *Leptothorax unifasciatus* (Latr.). *Behavioral Ecology and Sociobiology, 36,* 269–282.

Sendova-Franks, A., Franks, N. R., & Britton, N. F. (2002). The role of competition in task switching during colony emigration in the ant *Leptothorax albipennis. Animal Behaviour, 63,* 715–725.

Siegelmann, H., & Fishman, S. (1998). Analog computation with dynamical systems. *Physica D, 120,* 214–235.

Simon, H. (1957). *Adminstrative behavior.* Newark, NJ: Littlefield Adams.

Sole, R. V., Miramontes, O., & Goodwin, B. C. (1993). Oscillations and chaos in ant societies. *Journal of Theoretical Biology, 161,* 343–357.

Sternberg, R. J. (1999). *Cognitive psychology.* Orlando, FL: Harcourt-Brace.

Sulis, W. (1993a). Emergent computation in tempered neural networks 1: Dynamical automata. *Proceedings of the World Congress on Neural Networks 1993* (pp. 448–451). Hillsdale, NJ: Elrbaum.

Sulis, W. (1993b). Emergent computation in tempered neural networks 2: Computation theory. *Proceedings of the World Congress on Neural Networks 1993* (pp. 452–455). Hillsdale, NJ: Erlbaum.

Sulis, W. (1994). Naturally occurring computational systems. *World Futures, 39,* 225–241.

Sulis, W. (1995a). Driven cellular automata, adaptation, and the binding problem. In F. Moran, A. Moreno, J. J. Merelo, & P. Chacon (Eds.), *Advances in artificial life* (pp. 824–840). Berlin: Springer-Verlag.

Sulis, W. (1995b). Driven cellular automata. In *1993 Lectures on Complex Systems. Lecture Volume VI in the Santa Fe Institute Studies in the Sciences of Complexity* (pp. 565–578). New York: Addison-Wesley.

Sulis, W. (1995c). Causality in naturally occurring computational systems. *World Futures, 44,* 129–148.

Sulis, W. (1996). TIGoRS and neural codes. In W. Sulis & A. Combs (Eds.), *Nonlinear dynamics in human behaviour* (pp. 1–24). Singapore: World Scientific.

Sulis, W. (1997). Fundamentals of collective intelligence. *Nonlinear Dynamics, Psychology, and Life Science, 1,* 30–65.

Sulis W. (1999). A formal theory of collective intelligence. In W. T. Schacher & J. P. Dauwalder (Eds.), *Dynamics, synergetics, autonomous agents* (pp. 224–237). Singapore: World Scientific.

Sulis, W. (2002). Archetypal dynamics: An approach to the study of emergence. In J. Nation, I. Trofimova, J. Rand, & W. Sulis (Eds.), *Formal descriptions of developing systems* (pp. 185–228). Dordrecht: Kluwer Academic.

Sutherland, S. (1992). *Irrationality: The enemy within.* London: Constable.

Szuba, T. (2001). *Computational collective intelligence.* New York: Wiley.

Thelen, E. (1995). Time scale dynamics and the development of an embodied cognition. In R. F. Port & T. van Gelder (Eds.), *Mind as motion* (pp. 69–100). Cambridge, MA: MIT Press.

Theraulaz, G., & Bonabeau, E. (1995a). Coordination in distributed building. *Science, 269,* 686–688.

Theraulaz, G., & Bonabeau, E. (1995b). Modeling the collective building of complex architectures in social insects with lattice swarms. *Journal of Theoretical Biology, 177,* 381–400.

Theraulaz, G., Bonabeau, E., & Deneubourg, J.-L. (1998). The origin of nest complexity in social insects. *Complexity, 3,* 15–25.

Theraulaz, G., & Bonabeau, E. (1999). A brief history of stigmergy. *Artificial Life, 5,* 97–116.

Theraulaz, G., Gautrais, J., Camazine, S., & Deneubourg, J. L. (2003). The formation of spatial patterns in social insects: From simple behaviours to complex structures. *Philosophical transactions Series A: Mathematical, physical, and engineering sciences, 361,* 1263–1282.

Tofts, C. (1993). Algorithms for task allocation in ants (a study of temporal polyethism: Theory). *Bulletin of Mathematical Biology, 55*, 891–918.

Traniello, J. F. A., & Beshers, S. N. (1991). Polymorphism and size-pairing in the harvester ant *Pogonomyrmex badius:* A test of the ecological release hypothesis. *Insectes Sociaux, 38*, 121–127.

Trofimova, I. (2002). Sociability, diversity and compatibility in developing systems: EVS approach. In J. Nation, I. Trofimova, J. Rand, & W. Sulis (Eds.), *Formal descriptions of developing systems* (pp. 231–248). Dordrecht: Kluwer Academic.

Tversky, A. (1972). Elimination by aspects. *Psychological Review, 79*, 281–299.

Tversky, A., & Kahneman, D. (1973). Availability: A heuristic for judging frequency and probability. *Cognitive Psychology, 5*, 207–232.

Varela, F. J., Thompson, E., & Rosch, E. (1993). *The embodied mind: Cognitive science and human experience.* Cambridge, MA: MIT Press.

Wheeler, W. M. (1911). The ant colony as an organism. *Journal of Morphology, 22*, 307–325.

Wilson, E. O. (1971). *The insect societies.* Cambridge, MA: Belknap Press.

3 Neurodynamics and Electrocortical Activity

TULLIO A. MINELLI

Introduction

In the past two decades, a great deal of attention has been devoted to possible descriptions of electroencephalogram (EEG) activity in the context of chaos – that is, in terms of hypothetical underlying low-dimensional nonlinear dynamics, where trajectories that are initially close together diverge exponentially in time. This assumption is justified by neuron-synchronous firing and by the instability of EEG even to weak attentive stimuli. Moreover, Hebbian synaptic reinforcement implies that parallel synchronization should increase as a basic mechanism for perception and memory. The observed low dimension provides justification for the use of moderately populated artificial neural networks of low computational cost. Artificial neural networks are suitable to determine, or to reproduce, EEG rhythms on a macroscopic scale but are unable to simulate neurophysiological functions. In contrast, clusters of very few neurons, described by nonlinear differential systems that are highly expensive computationally, can realistically reproduce action potential generation and propagation mechanisms. The resulting electric signal traffic, crossing the brain, is sensitive to the electromagnetic (EM) perturbation, which can even alter functional correlates. This property legitimates transcranial magnetic stimulation (TMS) as a research tool to study aspects of human brain physiology with regard to motor function, vision, language, and brain disorders. TMS is also used in diagnostics and therapy.

Basics of Cortical Activity and EEG

The EEG essentially reflects the underlying electrical activity of the brain cortex. This six-layered structure represents the most complex constituent of the central nervous system (CNS), an organ that includes approximately 10^{10} connected neurons in mammalians. The neuron cell body, or soma, comprises a semipermeable lipidic bilayer membrane (75Å thick) surrounding the cytosol plasma, which, in turn, contains the nucleus. The neuron receives input from approximately 10^4 similar units from the dendrites, which are wire-shaped membrane extensions that form a sort of tree in pyramidal excitatory cells, or a star-like shape in stellate cells. Nonetheless, a neuron produces a single output, action potential (AP). The AP travels as a depolarization pulse through the axon, a long and tight membrane, branching out in proximity to target neurons; it is followed by repolarization and then by transient hyperpolarization. At the synapses (the junctions between incoming axons and target neurons), the AP induces a release of chemical neurotransmitters, selectively activating the opening of membrane receptor protein gates to ions, which are termed ion channels. Voltage gating can also occur. In addition to chemical transmission, direct electrical connections between cells are also possible. This type of gap junction creates specific channels that match pre- and postsynaptic membranes.

The cell membrane can be viewed as a capacitor. The equilibrium potential difference across the membrane (approximately -60 mV) is determined by the ion concentration on both sides, the temperature, the energy required to separate a given charge, and the relative permeabilities to each ion species (according to an extension of the Nernst equation, attributable to Goldman) (Junge 1981). Unlike passive transport, which follows the electrochemical gradient, active transport requires energy expenditure. The membrane potential is increased by the activity of excitatory synapses and decreased by inhibitory synapses. In excitation, the passively transported sodium (Na^+) ions flow inward, and potassium (K^+) ions flow outward. Chloride (Cl^-) and other minor species are also involved. Depolarization of the membrane potential increases the probability of Na^+ channels being in the activated, but not yet inactivated, state. At a critical membrane potential, the resulting inflow of Na^+ ions tips the balance of the net ionic current. At this membrane potential $V_{threshold}$, of about -50 mV, known as the AP threshold, the Na^+ ion flow into the cell depolarizes the membrane and further opens Na^+ channels, causing additional depolarization. Repetition of this process produces a rapid feedback loop, bringing the potential close to the reverse value for Na^+. This moment coincides with the triggering of an AP at approximately 100 mV in the initial segment of the axon, termed hillock.

After discharge, the membrane charge restarts, and no further AP firing is possible until the potential again reaches the critical value. This refractory period, a consequence of the voltage inactivation of Na^+ channels, is followed by a transient threshold enhancement due to the stochastic nature of reactivation. Thus, for the required level of synaptic input, a train of AP is produced, characterized by bursts of a few Hertz, the regularity of which depends on equilibrium membrane polarization level. Excitation during basal activity can stimulate the generation of AP of dozens of Hertz.

In a more precise description, the balance between the opposing sodium and potassium currents explains the AP time structure. The explicit main ion channel activity inspired the Hodgkin–Huxley (H-H) circuit (Hodgkin & Huxley, 1939,

1952): a capacitor in parallel to two nonlinear impedances ruling the Na^+ and K^+ currents and a third leak impedance. Impedances, in series with batteries representing the ionic-specific Nernst potentials, synthesize probabilistic channel opening–closure kinetics (White, Rubinstein, & Kay, 2000). This random behavior, together with the probabilistic nature of quantized synaptic release, provides evidence for noise in transmembrane currents and the fractal behavior observed in both ion channel gating and neuronal spiking patterns (Lowen, Liebovitch, & White, 1999).

The cortical column, 200 to 300 microns in diameter, emerges at the intermediate scale. The physiological significance of an assembly of approximately 10^5 synchronous neurons inspired the concept of neural mass used in Freeman's (1975) model of the olfactory cortex and justifies the use of low-dimensional descriptions of EEG activity and low-dimensional artificial neural networks. In a real CNS, interconnections between columns greatly outnumber those between the cortex and the thalamus, which are excitatory, as the main long-distance connections. The inhibitory activity, however, is generated by local circuit neurons, termed interneurons. The nature of the synapses is a characteristic of the cell. Excitatory neurons mainly use glutamate as a neurotransmitter; inhibitory neurons mainly use gamma-aminobutyric acid (GABA). The combination of glutamate gating with voltage gating produced by input from other neurons induces a large Ca^{2+} ions release in N-methyl-D-aspartate (NMDA) synapses. This is the origin of a chain of chemical reactions that ultimately alter the strength of the synapse, a mechanism described by Hebb (1949) to explain the memorization process.

Digital EEG, Records, and Measure

EEG electrodes detect the potential difference between two points at which the electrodes are placed. Because of the short duration and microscopic scale, the direct contribution of a single AP to the EEG is negligible. The measured voltage reflects fluctuations of excitatory postsynaptic potentials and inhibitory in the pyramidal cells of the upper layers of the cortex. Postsynaptic potentials are graded changes in the membrane potential of the postsynaptic terminal of chemical synapses, added together algebraically in space and time to result in an extracellular depolarization, or polarization, lasting dozens of milliseconds. The measured values are roughly proportional to the associated extracellular current flow. However, low extracellular tissue conductivity reduces the signal from the original scale of dozens of millivolts to dozens of microvolts.

Concerning filtering between the cortex and scalp, according to Pfurtscheller and Cooper (1975), high amplitude activity can often be observed on the subdural electrodes, together with rhythms of low amplitude and lower frequencies with maximum power in the beta band (discussed later). Only a small part of this high-frequency activity is seen on the scalp, and the lower frequencies

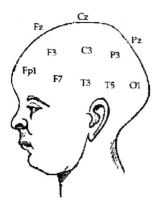

Figure 3.1. Electrode placement in the 10-20 International System. On the left hemisphere the electroencephalogram channel labeling consists of a letter followed by an even number. On the right hemisphere the numbers are odd.

dominate. Moreover, the fast muscle activity obscures complete comprehension of the small-amplitude – high-frequency activity observed in EEG.

An EEG analyzer consists of electrodes, an amplifier (with filters), and a recording apparatus. Commonly used electrodes consist of Ag-AgCl disks with long, flexible leads (or optical fibers) that can be plugged into the amplifier. The contact impedance must be adjusted to match the electrode–skin interface, of the order of 10 kΩ. In the 10-20 International System, the electrodes are placed as in Figure 3.1.

In digital records, the EEG signal is sampled at a fixed sampling rate. The high sampling rate and digital resolution of current EEG records allow (a) more accurate resolution in spectral analysis and (b) practice of proper methods of nonlinear dynamics and fractal geometry, requiring large data sets. The price of this performance improvement is the encumbrance of data memory requirements. In the frequency domain, according to the Nyquist theorem (Bendat & Piersol, 1986), if the spectral contents overcome the Nyquist frequency, which amounts to one-half of the sampling frequency, the signal appears contaminated by a sort of quantized noise. This loss of signal information due to undersampling is called *aliasing*.

The spectrum of EEG activity is usually divided in the following bands: delta, 0 to 4 Hz; theta, 4 to 8 Hz; alpha, 8 to 12 Hz; beta, 12 to 30 Hz; and gamma, 30 to 80 Hz. The spectral extension suggests a minimum sampling rate of 128 Hz. In the time domain, the undersampling produces overestimates for the correlation dimension of healthy subjects (Jing & Takigawa, 2000). This phenomenon can be attributed to the smallness of data sets for a fixed epoch, according to Mayer-Kress (1987); see also Kantz and Schreiber (1995). Their estimation requires a 4,096-Hz sampling in the EEG dimension, if one assumes the EEG signal to be stable for nearly 2 seconds. However, according to Abraham et al. (1986) and Havstad and Ehlers (1989), the previous criterion is pessimistic. Thus 2-second epochs can be considered a reasonable compromise among epoch stability, algorithm convergence, and practicality for the sampling rates in current use.

The dependence of a measure on the choice of sampling rate is not surprising. It amounts to fixing the marker of a decomposition of the EEG tracing in a low-dimensional and high-complexity component. Whereas the former (which is assumed to be a signal) is analyzed in terms of chaos, the latter is rejected as noise.

According to Steriade (2006), different brain rhythms, with both low and high frequency, must be grouped within complex wave sequences; it is conceptually rewarding to analyze their coalescence in terms of neuronal interactions in corticothalamic systems. Recent studies in humans reported by Steriade have provided congruent results in grouping different types of slow and fast oscillatory activities. Spontaneous brain rhythms have an important role in synaptic plasticity. The role of slow-wave sleep oscillation in consolidating memory traces acquired during wakefulness is being explored in both experimental animals and human subjects. Highly synchronized sleep oscillations may develop into seizures that are generated intracortically and lead to inhibition of thalamo-cortical neurons through activation of thalamic reticular neurons, which may explain the obliteration of signals from the external world and unconsciousness during some paroxysmal states.

Clinical and Cognitive Mathematical Phenomenology of EEG

EEG rhythms undergo changes during the life span, because of anatomical and morphological development, as the growth of specialized synchronous circuits do, because of synaptic plasticity and myelination – the coating of nerve fibers with a sheath that increases AP speed. Various research shows that, in addition to gradual changes, discrete growth spurts in EEG spectra may be found and may be linked to stage transitions in cognitive development (Nunez, 1995).

A posterior rhythm of approximately 4 Hz develops in the first 3 months. As a child ages, delta activity gradually disappears, and the frequency gradually increases until it attains the value of approximately 10 Hz at the age of approximately 10 years. This dominant basal activity, called alpha rhythm, consists of oscillations at approximately 10 Hz, subjected to a spindlelike modulation. This normal EEG pattern persists into senescence, when episodic theta and delta activity may be observed.

In recent years, significant attention has been devoted to a possible description of EEG activity in terms of deterministic chaos, as reviewed by Stam (2005). Such an approach is justified by neuron synchronization, the basic mechanism leading neurological phenomena such as low EEG rhythm dimension or the high spectral coherence (see Appendix) and by the instability of the EEG even to weak stimulation. After the pioneering work, which was state of the art in the early 1990s, on a possible description of EEG using chaos theory, warnings about the inaccuracy of dimension evaluations have been suggested by additional research on, for example, singular value decomposition, false nearest neighbors, and surrogate data tests (Theiler, Eubank, Longtin, Galakandrian, & Farmer, 1992), all of which are intended to confirm whether the apparent irregularity of the data is due to chaotic unpredictability or to randomness. According to Stam, Pijn, Suffczynski and Lopes da Silva (1999), only a small fraction of a time series of alpha rhythms could be employed for an analysis in terms of nonlinear dynamics. In the remainder, alpha activity could not be distinguished from linearly filtered noise. By employing a model of alpha rhythm, Lopes da Silva, Hoeks, Smits, and Zetterberg (1974) showed that linear Type I alpha epochs could be explained by a point attractor and the nonlinear Type II alpha epochs by a noisy limit cycle. It was also suggested that a normal EEG might reflect critical dynamics that are close to a bifurcation between these two types of attractor (Stam et al., 1999).

Stam (2005) noted that many pathological conditions have been examined in terms of functional sources and functional networks. Examples range from toxic states, to seizures, and neurodegenerative conditions such as Alzheimer's, Parkinson's, and Creutzfeldt–Jacob's diseases. Such analysis allows identification of three neurodynamic patterns: (a) normal, ongoing dynamics during a no-task, resting state in healthy subjects (this state is characterized by high dimension and a relatively low and fluctuating level of synchronization of the neural networks), (b) hypersynchronous, higher-dimensional nonlinear dynamics of epileptic seizures, and (c) lower-dimensional dynamics of degenerative encephalopathies with loss of cholinergic neurons and an abnormally low level of area synchronization. In a classification of functional sources, an Alzheimer's EEG is more noisy and less nonlinear than the healthy EEG (Stam, 2005). The decomposition of the tracing of patients affected by neurodegeneration into a low-dimensional signal and noise has been performed in a measure of the correlation dimension by Minelli et al. (2004) and Nofrate et al. (2007). This index significantly reaches and overtakes that of control subjects (young and elderly) with an increase of sampling rate. At low sampling, such a result raises the possibility of a cortical-connectivity lowering related to cholinergic neuron loss, and at high sampling, that of a worse signal-to-fast-activity noise ratio (SNR) in patients compared with control subjects. The increase of the correlation dimension with aging, mainly in frontal regions, is a general phenomenon, reported by Stam (2005) and studied by Anokhin, Birbaumer, Lutzenberg, Nikolaev, and Vogel (1996), in terms of independent synchronous networks in the brain.

Later, Anokhin, Lutzenberg, and Birbaumer (1999) focused on the increase of brain complexity related to the development of intelligence. The effects of cognitive and memory activity on EEG rhythms were described by Klimesch (1999). Specific nonlinear measures of mental activity using the correlation dimension were performed by Stam, van Woerkom, and Pritchard (1996) and Lamberts, van der Broek, Bener, van Egmond, and Dirksen (2000). In both sets of data, an increase in the correlation dimension during calculation tasks was measured. Lamberts et al. (2000) also observed an increase during time estimation tasks. Stam et al. (1996) observed an increase in mutual dimension between brain areas during arithmetic operations.

Petsche (1997) applied spectral coherence to the study of mental activity while listening to music and spoken language. He found that coherence changes while listening to language are greater than changes while listening to music. The former seems to require more cooperation between the two temporal regions, and foreign languages generally produced more significant coherence changes. Moreover, a greater number of coherence decreases in the right hemisphere in the beta band indicated greater involvement of smaller processing areas when listening to language. Petsche also studied memorization and mental drafts of pictures by artists and common subjects. He found that in memorization, artists produced more connections between left occipitoparietal and frontotemporal areas in the delta band than did nonartists. Most conspicuous were the differences measured while creating a picture. This finding indicates that artists require less effort to complete this task.

Artificial Learning and Neural Networks

Artificial neural networks (ANNs) are composed of interconnected units simulating local collections of neurons. As a real neuron, each unit processes the complex of incoming information, producing a single output toward the other units. This conversion is performed in two stages: (a) each incoming activity, multiplied by synapticlike weight, is added to all other weighted inputs to produce the total input and (b) an activation function f converts the total input $x_j = \sum_i w_{ji} S_i$ at discrete time t into the outgoing activity at time $t + 1$, according to the short-term memory (STM) equation:

$$S_j(t + 1) = f(x_j(t)) = f\left(\sum_i w_{ij} S_i(t) + \theta_j\right), \qquad (3.1)$$

where S_j is the output from the node j at time t and w_{ij} synaptic weights, positive or negative, as they represent excitatory or inhibitory inputs to the jth neuron. Real neurons with the characteristic dendritic arbor are compared with artificial ones in Figure 3.2. In the original version (McCulloch & Pitts, 1943), the activation function f was a binary Heaviside step with the threshold controlled by the polarization term θ_j. An extension of this hard threshold function replacing the step with a sigmoid simulating saturation effect was used by Freeman (1979a), as discussed in the next section. The two kinds of activation function are illustrated in Figure 3.3. The additive model (Grossberg, 1988) is an extension of Eq. 3.1 in the continuous limit

$$\frac{dS_j}{dt} = -\gamma(S_j) + \left(\sum_i g_i(S_i) w_{ij}^{(+)}\right) - \left(\sum_i g_i(S_i) w_{ij}^{(-)}\right) + I_j, \qquad (3.2)$$

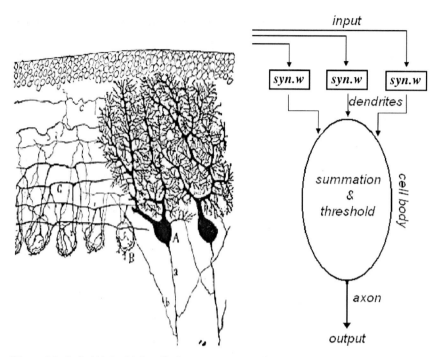

Figure 3.2. Left: (**A**) Purkinje cells, larges neurons with an intricately elaborate dendritic arbor. Illustrated by Roman y Cajal. The letters refer to the original caption. Right: The artificial-neuron–producing addition of weighted input and output activation with threshold.

where the first term after the equal sign expresses saturation and loss; the second and third, positive and negative feedback, respectively, are due to excitatory and inhibitory synapses; and the g_i are activation functions. The fourth term expresses a direct input.

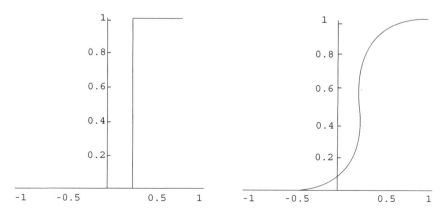

Figure 3.3. Examples of activation functions: threshold step function (left) and sigmoid function (right).

ANNs are typically multilayer structures consisting of an input layer connected to hidden ones, which are in turn connected to an output layer. Classical
ANNs are apt to learn but do not fire APs along ideal axons. Learning is the consequence of changes in synaptic strengths so that the influence of one neuron on
another varies. Hebbian learning, physiologically explained in the section of this
chapter devoted to cortex physiology in terms of plasticity of NMDA synapses,
can be formalized by a long-term memory equation as follows:

$$\frac{dw_{ij}}{dt} = \alpha\, S_i x_j - \text{decay terms} \geq 0, \tag{3.3}$$

where the decay terms express loss of old information.

ANNs are intended to perform definite tasks. In supervised learning, the
network is trained to respond correctly to selected stimuli. To this end, the
weights must be adjusted, step by step, to minimize the error between desired
and actual outputs. In practice, it must evaluate how the error changes as each
weight undergoes infinitesimal increases or decreases. The back-propagation
algorithm, based on the control of an error derivative of the weights, is the most
common method to train an ANN. Unsupervised ANNs can be regarded as
self-training pattern detectors.

Freeman Cortical Networks and Other Sigmoidal Models

In a collection of seminal papers, Freeman (1979a, 1979b, 1979c) developed
a model of perception in the olfactory bulb, suitable to reproduce the chaotic
dynamics of basal EEG, but also degenerative activities such as a seizure of
the olfactory system. In a 1975 paper, the olfactory EEG was described as a
broadband spectrum resembling $1/f$ noise. The model was extended further
to brain cortical dynamics and was capable of simulating the spatiotemporal
patterns of an actual cortex (Freeman, 1991).

The basic module of the cortex model is termed *KO* and represents the dynamics of a local collection of noninteractive neurons in parallel, being either all
excitatory or all inhibitory. The basic model blocks are termed *KII* and represent
lumped approximations of interactive aggregates of *KO* subunits. Interactions
between *KII* sets in the cortex are provided by long-range transverse couplings –
the excitatory axonal fields of pyramidal cells. Freeman (1991) predicted that
the cortex would show properties similar to those found for neuronal aggregates
in the olfactory cortex.

The neurons in each collection simultaneously perform four serial operations: (a) nonlinear conversion of afferent axon impulses to dendritic currents,
(b) linear spatiotemporal integration, (c) nonlinear conversion of summed dendritic current to a pulse density, (d) linear axonal delay, temporal dispersion,
translation, and spatial divergence. The operation of the basic *KO* integrator
consists of a linear time-dependent differential equation and of a nonlinear

relation expressing the output variable in terms of the voltage V and of parameter Q_m: the asymptotic value of Freeman's sigmoid. This curve plays a central role in model dynamics because of the bilateral saturation mechanism, giving stability to a bulbar mechanism. Freeman's sigmoid relates normalized pulse probability, for a single unit, to the amplitude and time of a concurrent EEG signal. Its shape was derived to reproduce, on phenomenological grounds, the axonal firing rate related to dendritic current. Thus parameter Q_m can be interpreted as the maximum pulse density that can be sustained by a group of neurons.

A characteristic of the model is the lag time response of dendrites to synaptic input. In conditions of sufficient excitation of all the neurons in the local cortical network, the delay, estimated to be 4.5 msec, evokes oscillations. This phenomenon, centered around 40 Hz, can be explained in terms of interaction between excitatory cells with the surrounding oscillatory cells. According to Freeman, although both the sigmoid curve and the refractory time guarantee overall stability, the sharp nonlinearity of the neuronal threshold confers a sensitive dependence on initial conditions and on stimuli such that above a critical level of excitation, the firing rate and field potential of pyramidal cells become chaotic. A fruitful concept introduced by Freeman is that of neural mass, which uses only a few state variables to describe the mean activity of neuron populations, such as macrocolumns or even cortical areas.

Many other theoretical models have been developed to study group interaction between the cortex and EEG. Relevant constituents are delays, sigmoidal pulse wave transformations, and cortical anatomy. The nonlinear dynamics underlying EEG are expected to be explained in terms of competition between coherent electric oscillations resulting from synchronized neuron clusters and desynchronizing sensor stimuli. According to this assumption, the phenomenology of rhythm production can be expressed in terms of the architecture of the network of synaptic connections between oscillators and in terms of external driving (Liljenström, 1991; Wu & Liljenström, 1994). An inclusive model would require that neuronal interactions differ in their dynamics as a function of the scale, so that locally nonlinear interactions could give rise to linear superposition of waves when averaged over a large number of cells. Wave linearity, in turn, implies the possible occurrence of linear resonant modes at a global scale.

According to Nunez et al. (1994), EEG is viewed as a linear wave process for which the underlying dynamics are treated as a problem of mass action of coupled units. The characteristics of the model are as follows: Significant delays are due to axonal conduction. The quantitative predominance of long-range interactions is mediated by the corticocortical fibers. There are boundary conditions that imply the possibility of global resonance and standing waves. There is also the assumption that EEG waves are essentially subjected to linear superposition and are based on the proportionality between synaptic action density and cortical depolarization. Nunez's model reproduces the alpha-wave phenomenology and other EEG findings. To bridge the microscopic and global scales, Nunez et al. used techniques, also used in quantum field theory, that are designed to renormalize groups.

An approach inspired by quantum field theory was also suggested by Penrose (1994) and studied by Freeman and Vitiello (2007). Here the macroscopic activity of the cortex appears to consist of the dynamical formation of spatially extended domains in which widespread cooperation supports brief epochs of pattern oscillations modulating carrier oscillations in the beta and gamma bands and recurrence rates in the theta and alpha domain. In this scheme, the formation of coherent domains of synchronized oscillations of increasing complexity and scale is described as a phase transition from one brain state to another.

A neural mass approach was also pursued by Wright, Liley, and coworkers (Wright & Liley, 1994, 1996; Wright, Sergejev, & Liley, 1994). In this case, the basic units are minicolumns, which are syntheses of excitatory and inhibitory neurons that are capable of oscillation. Each unit is symmetrically and reciprocally coupled to multiple neighbors by couplings that are predominantly excitatory. The system is described by stochastic second-order differential equations with variable control parameters, and each unit oscillator defines a local field variable. The time variation of such parameters describes deviations from the basal case, resulting from the nonlinearities of underlying neurons and noisy input from the activating system. Despite the nonlinearity of elementary constituents, it follows that the macroscopic oscillations tend to approximate a linear superposition of coupled oscillators at low frequencies. The simulations performed with this model reproduce spectral, autoregression, and frequency-wavenumber properties of real electrocortical waves, including the major rhythms. Procedures based on neural masses and mean field approximations are still largely used to reproduce EEG rhythms (Babajani & Soltanian-Zadeh, 2006; David & Friston, 2003; Sotero et al., 2007).

Hopfield's Integrate and Fire Neurons: Networks of Spiking Neurons

The classical ANN, which is capable of learning, can be composed of a large number of unrealistic units that are unable to simulate the neuron firing but are endowed with a low computational cost. Hopfield (1982, 1984) initially proposed a model for a large network of neurons with a graded sigmoid input–output relation that was in close correspondence with earlier stochastic simulations based on the McCulloch–Pitts neurons described by Eq. 3.1. He proposed an interpretation of the sigmoid as a continuous and monotonic increase of the mean soma potential of its excitatory and inhibitory inputs and claimed the existence of more realistic firing neurons. Therefore, Hopfield (1995) later proposed a pattern recognition network using AP timing. In this network, the comparison of patterns of APs over sets of analogue variables was performed using different delays for different information paths. The use of transient synchrony of a group of neurons as recognition units in this scheme was more pertinent to basic functions than to elementary sigmoids. A more advanced version, termed MAE (many-are-equal), in which a large set of neurons synchronize their spiking when the inputs are approximately equal, reproduces the olfactory bulb phenomenology (Brody & Hopfield, 2003).

In Hopfield's networks, memory and learning are related to global modifications in connectivity. Similar approaches focus on monitoring the response of network activity to sessions of stimulation, looking for induced alterations in the patterns of neuron firing (Izhikevich, Gallay, & Edelman, 2004). Similar phenomena have been confirmed by observations in cultured neural networks in which, at stimulated locations, neurons initiate synchronized bursting collective modes, each with a specific space–time firing pattern (Maeda, Robinson, & Kawana, 1995; Segev, Baruchi, Hulata, & Ben-Jacob, 2004). Further, in vitro neuronal networks provide the appropriate tool for studying the relationship between network structures and their functions (Blinder et al., 2005).

Firing-rate information in large neuronal networks is currently under study. The comparison of the interspike duration, on the order of 200 msec, with the AP, lasting near 2 msec, legitimates the AP's impulsive approximation by a spike and suggested to Hopfield the so-called integrate-and-fire (I&F) model (Hopfield, 1994; Hopfield & Tank, 1986). However, I&F neurons neglect ion channel details, which require a moderate computational cost of nearly 10 floating-point operations (FLOP) per millisecond. The leaky version of the I&F model can be expressed by the differential system suitable to a reset integrator simulation with a structure similar to that of the additive STM Grossberg model (Eq. 3.2):

$$C\frac{dV_i}{dt} = -\frac{V_i}{R} + \sum_j w_{ij}\delta(t - t_{jk}) + I_{\text{out}}, \quad V_i\left(t_{ik}^-\right) = V_{\text{threshold}}, \quad V_i\left(t_{ik}^+\right) = V_{\text{reset}},$$

$$(3.4)$$

in which $V_i(t)$ represents the voltage of the ith cell and the threshold $V_{\text{threshold}}$; reset V_{reset} voltages represent values limiting the membrane voltage excursions; C and R measure membrane capacitance and leak resistance, respectively; and t_{ik} the time of the kth spike of the jth neuron. Quantities w_{ij}, weighting the information coming from the jth to the ith cell, can excite or inhibit the firing according to their sign. Finally, I_{out} expresses the level of background synaptic current. The model dynamics start producing increasing membrane depolarization, accompanied by further opening of voltage-gated channels, interrupted when the membrane potential reaches the critical level $V_{\text{threshold}}$ of approximately −50 mV. This instant coincides with the onset of an ion-active reflux, accompanied by a potential fall to the reset value V_{reset} of approximately −70 mV and by the triggering of an AP. This version of the model (Eq. 3.4) has been used by Ferro Milone, Minelli, and Turicchia (1998) to reproduce synchronization

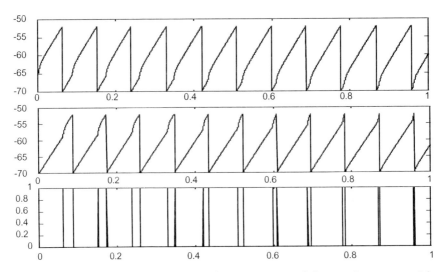

Figure 3.4. Synchronization and firing of two integrate-and-fire membrane potentials with excitatory coupling.

phenomena (see Fig. 3.4) and in numerical experiments in which a phenomenological black-box filter was employed to simulate scalp transduction and rhythm generation (see also Balduzzo, Minelli, & Turicchia, 1999).

Studies on neural hardware focusing on spiking properties fall into two groups: those using less realistic neurons suitable to learning, and those aiming at reproduction of physiological functions. An example of the second group is offered by the reproduction of the kinetics of NDMA synaptic dynamics using both short- and long-term memory equations (Giugliano, Bove, & Grattarola,1999; Izhikevich et al., 2004; Volman, Baruchi, Persi, & Ben-Jacob, 2004). A synthesis of the two lines is expected by the next-generation basic circuits of neural processors by virtue of very large-scale integrated circuits (VLSIs). This is the case studied by Kanazawa, Asai, and Amemiya (2002) on the feasibility of competitive and pattern recognition networks on a single semiconductor chip.

The Hodgkin–Huxley Circuit and Other Neurodynamic Models

The I&F model neglects ion-flow details. In the treatment of cell membrane electrical activity, only the commonest diffusible ions species, Na^+, K^+, and Cl^-, are considered. Cell membranes are endowed with Na^+– K^+ exchange pumps, which actively pump three Na^+ ions outward for every two K^+ pumped inward. The diffusion occurs through specialized proteins: the passive channels. In the steady state, the active flux of an ion must be balanced by an equal passive flux (driven by the gradients of potential and concentration) of that ion; this way, a resting potential is achieved (-100 to -50 mV). The electrical activity of a cell membrane consists of perturbations of the resting potential as a consequence of excitatory or inhibitory stimulation. In excitable cells such as the neuron, when the threshold potential $V_{threshold}$ is reached, the voltage-dependent channels open out, and an action potential is generated.

The current models of the cell membrane are based on the idea that the related electrical–physiological properties can be modelled by an equivalent simple electrical circuit with ionic voltage-dependent conductances, which represent specific ionic channels that are functionally assembled in series with batteries, representing the ionic-specific Nernst potentials that account for the concentration jumps, across the membrane, of the various ion species. Hodgkin and Huxley (H-H, 1952) proposed the proto-model of cell-membrane electrical activity. Using space-clamp and voltage-clamp techniques, these authors (1939) also measured the membrane potential and the ionic currents in the squid giant axon. The patch clamp is a refinement of this kind of measure that allows the study of ion channels in cells at the microscopic level (Sakmann & Neher, 1995). Hodgkin and Huxley (1952) were able to demonstrate that current flowing through a membrane capacitor has only two major components, I_{Na} and I_K, which in turn proved to be strongly influenced by membrane potential V. They built a consequent model based on the idea that the electrical properties of a segment of nerve membrane could be modelled by an equivalent electrical circuit in which the conductances G_{Na} and G_K changed as a function of membrane voltage; their macroscopic value could be thought of as the combined effect of a very large number of channels. An individual voltage-dependent channel had some "gates" that could be open or closed. The essence of the H-H model is that (a) the voltage depends on channel-opening probability and (b) the macroscopic conductance G is proportional to the resultant of individual probabilities. More precisely, the sodium conductance involves an activation and an inactivation voltage-dependent gate, whereas the potassium conductance has a single activation gate, representing the ionic conductances in the form

$$G_{Na} = g_{Na}m^3 h, \ G_K = g_K n^4, \tag{3.5}$$

where g_{Na} and g_K represent maximal conductances, m and n activation, and h inactivation gating variables. The exponents in Eq. 3.5 are chosen to fit measures. A third constant conductance, g_L, accounts for a leak in the membrane. The H-H differential system can be written as follows:

$$C\frac{dV}{dt} = -g_{Na}m^3 h(V - V_{Na}) - g_K n^4(V - V_K) - g_L(V - V_L) + I \tag{3.6}$$

$$\frac{dm}{dt} + \frac{(m - m_\infty)}{\tau_m} = 0, \ \frac{dn}{dt} + \frac{(n - n_\infty)}{\tau_n} = 0, \ \frac{dh}{dt} + \frac{(h - h_\infty)}{\tau_h} = 0,$$

$$\tag{3.7}$$

where m_∞, n_∞, and h_∞ are equilibrium open probabilities; τ_n and τ_m are activation times; τ_h are inactivation times; V_{Na}, V_K, and V_L are Nernst equilibrium reversal potentials; and I is the background synaptic current. Hodgkin and Huxley (1952) empirically derived for the voltage dependence of equilibrium open probability and time behaviors qualitatively similar to those later deduced by channel opening–closure kinetics. The computational cost of the H-H differential system is very high (near 1,200 FLOP per millisecond).

An oversimplification, characterized by lower computational cost (72 FLOP per millisecond) but capturing the key features of the H-H system, is offered by the FitzHug-Nagumo (F-N) (FitzHug, 1961; Nagumo, Aximoto, & Yoshizawa, 1962) nonlinear differential system:

$$\frac{dV}{dt} = a + bV + cV^2 + dV^3 - w + I, \quad \frac{dw}{dt} = \varepsilon\,(eV - w), \quad (3.8)$$

coupling the membrane voltage V with the gating variable w, proportional to the membrane current.

The H-H and F-N nonlinear coefficients are derived on phenomenological grounds, and the role of Ca^{2+} was ignored. Calcium, however, plays a dual role as a carrier of electrical current and as a second messenger. Morris and Lecar (or M-L; 1981) proposed a simple but realistic model to describe voltage-gated fast K^+ and slow free cytosol Ca^{2+} currents in which nonlinear conductances are founded on channel opening–closure kinetics (Fall, Marland, Wagner, & Tyson, 2002). Its computational cost amounts to approximately 600 FLOP per millisecond.

In the M-L model, the calcium ion level simply acts as a voltage-dependent variable. It consists of coupled differential equations:

$$C\,dV/dt = -g_{Ca}m_\infty(V)(V - V_{Ca}) - g_K w(V - V_K) - g_L(V - V_L) + I,$$
$$dw/dt = \phi[w_\infty(V) - w]/\tau(V),$$
$$m_\infty(V) = 0.5\,\{1 + \tanh[(V - V_1)/V_2]\},$$
$$w_\infty(V) = 0.5\,\{1 + \tanh[(V - V_3)/V_4]\}, \quad (3.9)$$
$$\tau(V) = 1/\cosh[(V - V_3)/(2\,V_4)],$$

where variables V and w, respectively, represent the membrane voltage and the gating variable for the potassium channel; m_∞ and w_∞ the equilibrium open fractions of voltage-dependent Ca^{2+} and K^+ channels; τ the transition rate; g_{Ca}, g_K, and g_L, the maximal conductances of calcium, potassium, and of a passive model leak, respectively; and V_{Ca}, and V_K, and V_L the corresponding reversal potentials; C represents the membrane capacitance; and I the synaptic background current. For application to periodic stimulation, see Han, Yim, Postnov, and Sosnovtseva (1999); Izhikevich (2001); Verechtchaguina, Schimansky-Geier, and Sokolov (2004); and Xie, Xu, Kang, Hu, and Duan (2005).

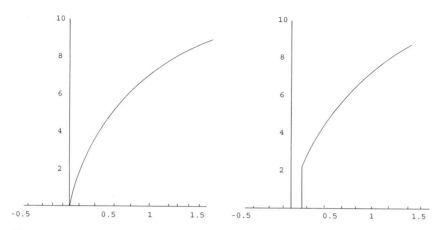

Figure 3.5. Frequency-stimulus curve for Type 1 (left) and Type 2 models (right).

Bifurcation, Chaos, and Stochastic Resonance in Neurodynamics

The F-N model is characterized by a sudden transition from rest to finite frequency firing, when the control parameter I, ruling the synaptic current background and so the polarization level, reaches a threshold value. The H-H system does not have so clear-cut a firing threshold value. Similar transition to neuron firing, usually involving a subcritical Hopf bifurcation, characterizes Type 2 models. In Type 1 models, the frequency–stimulus curve is continuous, so that low-frequency firing can be achieved for stimuli just over bifurcation (Gerstner & Kistler, 2002). The behavior of the two types of models in terms of the control parameter is illustrated in Figure 3.5.

Neurons endowed with coexistence of resting and spiking states are termed bistable, and excitability is related to the contiguity of equilibrium and bifurcation. Neurons that are excitable via Hopf bifurcation are termed resonators, as opposed to integrators, which are excitable via a saddle-node bifurcation (Izhikevich, 2001). Resonators can exhibit damped subthreshold oscillations in opposition to integrators. Moreover, according to Xie et al. (2005), resonators are more sensitive to endogenous frequency stimulation than integrators, both accounting for the activation of alpha-band oscillations and for the low intensity required by subjective sensitivity. The M-L dynamical system can act as a Type 1 or 2 model and as an integrator or resonator neuron, depending on the value of parameters (Gerstner & Kistler, 2002; Xie et al., 2005).

Shilnikov and Cymbalyuk (2005) introduced an example of an integrator model to describe the transition of a heart interneuron from a normal to a pharmacological stimulation. In simulation, a continuous and reversible transition between periodic tonic spiking and bursting activities is produced by varying a control parameter. As this quantity passes the critical value, the saddle-node periodic orbit is replaced by a stable periodic orbit.

Models of membrane bursting essentially can be based on the cycling between a silent phase and a periodic spiking, mimed by the transition from the rest point to the limit cycle of a Hopf bifurcation. This cycling can be mediated by the calcium slow dynamics as a slow varying control parameter. Chay and Keizer (1983) proposed an integrated model, extending the M-L to include calcium dynamics and thus the cycling between bursting and silent phases (as a repetitive alternation between two states of a Hopf bifurcation). Chay (1997) later extended it to account for the free-stored calcium oscillations. For an overview, see Fall et al. (2002). However, the simplest model to include the calcium dynamics was developed by Hindmarsh and Rose (1984; H-R model). The H-R model acts as a Type 1 resonator, bumping between a stable equilibrium point to a stable limit cycle. For applications under periodic stimulation or synaptic coupling, see Wu, Wei, He, and Huang (2001); Dhamala, Jirsa, and Ding (2004); Falcke et al. (2000). The H-R model consists of a system of three coupled nonlinear, first-order differential equations (Dhamala et al., 2004) describing the bursting behavior of a firing neuron:

$$\begin{cases} \dfrac{dx}{dt} = y - ax^3 + bx^2 - z + I \\[2mm] \dfrac{dy}{dt} = c - fx^2 - y \\[2mm] \dfrac{dz}{dt} = r\,[s\,(x - x_0) - z]\,, \end{cases} \qquad (3.10)$$

where variable x represents the membrane potential; y and z are, respectively, the fast (Na^+ or K^+) and the slow (Ca^{2+}) current; the control parameter I is associated with the synaptic input; and the other coefficients, here chosen according to $a = 1$, $b = 3$, $c = 1$, $f = 5$, $r = 6^* \ 10^{-3}$, $x_0 = -1.6$ (reversal potential) and $s = 4$ (ratio of fast/slow time scales), are phenomenological parameters. The computational cost is 120 FLOP per millisecond.

The system (Eq. 3.10) possesses a unique stable equilibrium point and undergoes a transition from the fixed point to a limit cycle (oscillatory regime) via Hopf bifurcation. The quantity I-I_c, where $I_c = 1.26$ is the bifurcation point, can be assumed as the membrane depolarization level. For values above I_c, the regime is characterized by regular trains of spike-burst firing. For $2.9 < I < 3.4$, the system exhibits a spike-burst chaotic behavior (Dhamala et al., 2004). Above the chaotic region, the firing becomes uninterrupted. Figure 3.6 (left and right, respectively) illustrates the interspike interval versus control parameter I and the bursting dependence of an H-R neuron in regular (top) and chaotic (bottom) regimes.

Hypersensitivity to stimulation has been observed when control parameter I, just over the boundary between chaotic and regular regime, is underpushed. Such a mechanism, producing alpha-rhythm enhancement, was offered by Minelli, Balduzzo, Ferro Milone, and Nofrate (2007) to explain sensitivity to

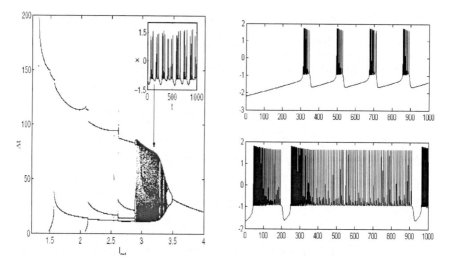

Figure 3.6. Bifurcation diagram for a Hindmarsh and Rose (H-R) model neuron: inter-spike interval versus control parameter (left; from Dhamala et al., 2004). Copyright 2004 by the American Physical Society. Reprinted by permission. Illustration of H-R bursting for different values of control parameter I (right).

light or mobile-phone-pulsed stimulation. Wu et al. (2001) obtained rhythm regularization in the presence of noise.

Resonators can exhibit, in general, stochastic resonance (SR) – namely, noise-induced enhancement in the SNR near the stimulus frequency, a phenomenon first observed by Benzi, Stutera, and Vulpiani (1981). The classical model of SR is a bistable system in which an alternate weak stimulus, perturbed by noise, pushes a damped particle from one minimum to the other of the potential well, as in Figure 3.7 (left). The oscillations, even under the escaping threshold, can be occasionally reinforced to escaping by the contribution of noise, so that the output appears in approximate synchronization with the stimulus, for a certain range of noise intensity. The signature of SR is the existence of an optimal SNR for some intermediate value of noise strength for which the resonant output to stimulation reaches its maximum, as in Figure 3.7 (right). The optimal value of noise strength occurs when the noise-induced escape time is near one-half the modulation period. In the case of the double potential well of Figure 3.7 (left), this can be estimated as mean first passage time τ of a randomly forced damped particle, according to Langevin's equation and Kramer's formula:

$$\partial_t x = -\partial_x U + \sigma \xi(t) \tag{3.11}$$

$$\tau \approx \frac{\sqrt{2}\pi}{a} e^{2U_0/\sigma^2}, \tag{3.12}$$

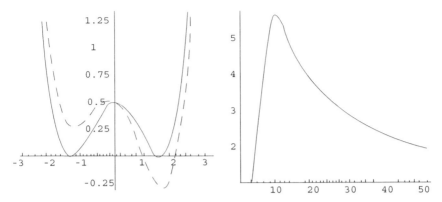

Figure 3.7 The double-well potential unperturbed (continuous line) and modulated by a weak alternant force favoring the particle escape (dashed line) ruled by the equation $U = -(a/2)x^2 + (b/4)x^4 - e\,x\cos(w_s\,t)$. Left: The picture fixes an instant in which nearly one-half the height of left well is raised. Right: The signal-to-noise ratio (in dB) versus noise power density of formula (3.13).

where ∂ stands for partial derivative with respect to the subfix variable; $\xi(t)$ represents Gaussian noise, characterized by the standard deviation σ; and $U_0 = a^2/4b$ is the barrier height. The SNR is approximated by the formula

$$SNR \approx \frac{\varepsilon^2 U_0}{\sigma^4} e^{-2U_0/\sigma^2}. \qquad (3.13)$$

The SNR tends to zero both for small and large values of σ, as in Figure 3.7 (right), and the maximal value is expected at an intermediate value, for an intensity, measured by variance $D = \sigma^2$, of the order of the barrier height U_0.

SR from voltage-gated ion channel noise has been studied by White et al. (2000). Noise sources contributing to polarizing and depolarizing current are numerous: fluctuations in the number and duration of channel opening, fluctuations in the transmitted quanta release, the number of activated receptors, ion concentrations, and membrane conductance. The underlying idea is that, near the firing threshold, the time structure of a subthreshold stimulus can be transmitted as a perturbation of the polarization level (see Gerstner & Kistler, 2002, section 5.8). In impaired neurons, the distance between the membrane potential and the threshold can be lowered by a membrane leakage. In clusters of impaired neurons, there is noise due to asynchronous firing, and the threshold can resemble that of recruitment. SR-like phenomena have been observed in studies on EEG spectrum under light stimulation, at 10 Hz, on control subjects, elderly and Age associated memory impairment (AAMI) subjects, and Alzheimer's patients (Ferro Milone et al., 2003). Also, the observed presence of harmonics of stimulus for only pulsations under the proper frequency (alpha peak) is a characteristic of some kinds of SR (Gomes, Mirasso, Toral, & Calvo, 2003). I&F leaky neurons, exploiting a mechanism different from the bistable system modulation, have been employed by Bulsara, Elston, Doering, Lowen, and Lindenberg (1996) to study neuronal dynamics, and SR in calcium oscillations has been theoretically previewed by Perc and Marhl (2004) and Sandblom and Galvanovskis (2000).

Seminal experiments on SR in life sciences were performed by Moss and coworkers (Douglass, Wilkens, Pantazelou, & Moss, 1993). They designed experiments to study the neural response to oscillatory stimulation of mechano-receptor cells of crayfish and demonstrated that the firing of stimulated neurons actually exhibits stochastic resonance. For a review of applications of SR to neuroscience, see Traynelis and Jaramillo (1998) and Moss, Ward, and Sannita (2004); for a general survey, see Gammaitoni, Hänggi, and Marchesoni (1998).

AP Propagation and TMS

In the continuous limit, a dispersive axon-cable system for the membrane potential V,

$$rc\partial_t V = \partial_{xx}^2 V - rg\left[V - H\left(V - a\right)\right] - w - E_x, \partial_t w = \varepsilon\left(V - bw\right),$$

$$(3.14)$$

is obtained by adding a diffusion term to nonlinearity, accounting for the sodium-regenerative mechanism characteristic of nerve fibers (see, for instance, the FitzHug-Nagumo differential system 3.8). Equation 3.14 exhibits a traveling solitary wave solution, simulating the AP (Fall et al., 2000, p. 192; Scott & Luzard, 1979), for suitable values of parameter a controlling (the) fiber polarization. Other variables and parameters of the model are the gating variable w, proportional to the membrane current; the longitudinal resistance r of the fiber core; the transverse capacitance c of the membrane; and the membrane conductance g per unit length in the x direction. b and ε are phenomenological parameters, whereas H represents the Heaviside step function. The action potential can be generated by proper initial conditions, simulating an ingoing AP generated at the hillock. It can also be produced by the source term E_x, accounting for the ion charge density inhomogeneities due to the EM field. Also, subthreshold phenomena, as AP distortion and velocity propagation perturbation and up-threshold action potential generation, can be induced by EM stimulation (Myers, 1999).

There are some important differences between electrical and magnetic stimulation in extremely low-frequency (ELF) electromagnetic fields. Concerning the mechanisms, in contrast to the neuron body membrane, which percepts only transverse field components, the axon is sensitive to the field-gradient components parallel to the membrane (Myers, 1999; Ruohonen, Ravazzani, & Grandori, 1998; Warman, Grill, & Durand, 1992). Moreover, magnetic fields easily penetrate the body, because the permeability of living tissue and of the

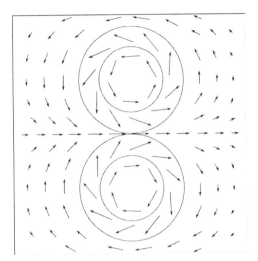

Figure 3.8. Electric field gradient lines generated by an figure-eight-shaped coil, simulating the section of a toroidal solenoid around the fiber by an inclusive plane. The coil outlines are shown as circles. The coil current grows in clockwise direction in the upper wing. In the lower wing, the current direction is opposite. Notice the field gradient along the fiber.

air is nearly the same. Conversely, effective conductivity of the air and metals are respectively strongly lower and higher than that of tissue. For this reason, electric-field stimulation is effectively practicable only by electrode application. Notice that magnetic stimulation avoids the painful sensations experienced by subjects from Electrode 1, caused by the concomitant activation of pain fibers of cutaneous nerves (Cracco, Cracco, Maccabee, & Amassian 1999; Ruohonen et al., 1998), as required in long-standing stimulation or to unperturb the cognitive tests.

In magnetic stimulation, a current pulse $I(t)$, achieved by discharging a capacitor charged up to some kilovolts through a coil, produces a strong magnetic field pulse, which induces a local electric field gradient $E_x = \partial_x E$ parallel to the membrane, as in Figure 3.8. The pulse is usually a decaying sine wave, lasting near 300 μs, the duration of the ionic current pulse accompanying the AP (Deutsch & Deutsch, 1993, p. 61). The threshold for its activation has been estimated of the order of -10 mV/mm^2 (Cracco et al., 1998; Ruohonen et al., 1998). The corresponding magnetic field can be evaluated, being the activation function proportional to $dI(t)/dt$, and results on the order of one Tesla.

When a nerve is bent, the threshold of excitation is reduced and depends on the bend angle, producing field-gradient equivalent effects (Abden & Stuchly, 1994; Suihko, 1998). However, there is a fundamental difference between magnetic stimulation of the central and peripheral nervous systems in that, whereas stimulation of the straight peripheral nerves requires a high gradient of electric field **E**, bent and short cortical neurons are dominantly activated at the site of the maximum **E**, because the strongest depolarization is achieved where the activation function is most negative. Thus the present TMS has been designed exclusively for brain stimulation and will not operate optimally in functional neuromuscular stimulation because the dominant activating mechanisms are different (Ruohonen et al., 1998). For literature on the activation function, see Warman et al. (1992), Ruohonen et al. (1998), Myers (1999), Nagarajan (1996), Rattay (1998), Grill (1999), Schnabel and Struijk (2001), and Zierhofer (2001). For an introduction to the axon excitability, see Sabah (2000); for a review, see Burke, Kiernan, and Bostock (2001).

A realistic extension of AP propagation accounting for the structure of the myelinated axon is discussed in Balduzzo, Ferro Milone, Minelli, Pittaro Cadore, and Turicchia (2003). A myelinated fiber has very short segments of unmyelinated regenerative membrane (Ranvier nodes) separated by much longer myelinated nonregenerative membrane segments (internodes). The usual realization of this repetitive structure is a compartment model based on its representation by an electrical equivalent repetitive circuit. This circuit consists of two subcompartments relative to the myelinated and unmyelinated zones. Whereas the compartment circuit of myelinated zone is rather simple, containing only discrete linear components, the unmyelinated zone is puzzlingly entangled by the presence of nonlinear voltage-dependent circuit components. These components are the circuit equivalent to G_{Na} and G_K of the H-H original model. A myelinated segment is assimilated to an "RC cable" and serves to propagate the AP with high speed and low distortion. However, the distortion and the resistive attenuation of the signal along the myelinated segment is compensated at the regenerative nodes. The myelin sheath closes the ionic channels; if its thickness diminishes because of a pathological disease such as multiple sclerosis in the CNS, or Guillaine–Barrè syndrome in the peripheral nervous system, distortion and attenuation increase because the time constant increases. The signal slows down, and its amplitude can fall to a subthreshold value, hindering the regeneration and blocking the conduction of the AP. The regular and pathological AP propagation is shown in Balduzzo et al. (2003).

In contrast to AP generation, an electrical stimulation producing suppression of synchronous neuron firing, in the band of tremor, is the deep brain stimulation (DBS) for Parkinson's disease therapy (Kuncel & Grill, 2004). DBS administrates permanent pulse trains, at a sampling rate greater than 100 Hz, via electrodes implanted in the thalamus and controlled by a pacemaker. The pulses are biphasic to reset, first by regulating sodium channel inactivation, and then properly desynchronizing the neuron cluster. The AP propagating along nerve axons can also be disrupted by outer fields. The threshold for the disruption by an electromagnetic field at 60 Hz has been evaluated by King (1999) as a 16% change in internal ion sodium concentration. This value corresponds to a current density on the order of 0.5 A/m², only two orders of magnitude over the limiting exposure stated by a guideline of the International Commission on Non-Ionizing Radiation Protection (Stuchly & Dawson, 2000).

Cortex Stimulation: Associative Memory and Binding

An essential overview of mechanisms and applications of TMS can be found in Hallet (2000). At present, the trains of transcranial magnetic stimuli can reach the pulsation rate of near 60 Hz. Repetitive TMS (rTMS) of specific cortical areas can either inhibit or facilitate the excitability of brain structures (Pascual-Leone et al., 1994). More precisely, TMS can modulate the excitability of the cortex and exert transsynaptic phenomena on corticocortical or corticosubcortical structures remotely from stimulation foci. The effects of this modulation appear related to long-term facilitation and long-term inhibition, depending on stimulation parameters. Thus transient artificial functional lesions can be created, allowing functional mapping of cortical regions (Schurmann et al., 2001; Walsh & Rushworth, 1999).

TMS is currently used as a research tool to study aspects of human brain physiology, such as motor function, vision, language, and brain disorders. It is also used in diagnostics and therapy, particularly in psychiatry and sleep control (Massimini et al., 2007). For a review of therapeutic applications, see Wasserman and Lisanby (2001).

The best-documented functional correlates are the gating function, the matching function, and the binding function (Lopes da Silva & Pfurtscheller, 1999). The gating function is the activation and deactivation of brain states and oscillatory modes as a consequence of the gating to the signal transfer, due to changes of a control parameter such as the membrane cell polarization level (alpha rhythm/desynchronization of alpha). The matching function is the optimal coupling between two brain areas displaying frequency activity. The matching effect of rTMS and the gating performed by periodic stimuli, such as light pulses, have been illustrated in this chapter. In addition to activation of brain states (Pastor, Artieda, Arbizu, Valencia, & Masdeu, 2003), light flicker in the alpha band can enhance human memory, mainly in older people (Williams, Ramswaamy, & Oulhaj, 2006). The molecular basis of the increased synaptic activity underlying long-term potentiation has been studied by Berardi, Pizzorusso, Ratto, and Maffei (2003).

The binding function is the achievement of a precise degree of synchronicity among a population of neurons that, in this way, would form a functional assembly underlying perception, memory, and motor commands. According to the feature binding model, synchronization is a typical mechanism underlying cognitive processes, as it is with associative learning. For instance, it has been proposed (Singer, 1994) that neurons, encoding features suitable for grouping operations in a visual scene, are selectively coupled with each other through reciprocal excitatory connections and engage in rhythmic responses to their preferred stimuli.

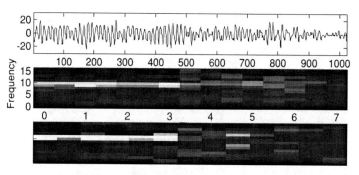

Figure 3.9. The figure exhibits enhancement of the alpha activity in the time domain, during the first 5 seconds of light pulsation, at 10 Hz in the channel Cz, sampled at 128 Hz (top), and enhanced activity in the frequency domain in a tight band centered at 10 Hz, both for the windowed spectrogram of channel Cz (middle) and for the windowed spectral coherence in the region around electrode Cz (bottom) during the photostimulation. The spectral power and coherence are measured with levels of gray, and tones increasing from black to white and the scansion scale has been chosen to mark the window progression (from Balduzzo et al., 2003).

These rhythmic responses can become synchronized after repeated stimulation, and the cellular firing rate may suffice to encode image properties, permitting the binding of a single visual object. Such time-dependent functional aggregates might be qualified as transiently activated neuronal units (Sannita, 2000). During binding, the peak of spectral coherence between involved EEG channels is near 40 Hz; because of this, phase locking with coherence increase may be expected in the ELF fields. Possible mechanisms underlying the binding are outlined in Munk, Roelfsema, Koenig, Engel, and Singer (1996), and recent experiments have provided evidence for the synchronization of cortex-area at frequencies on the gamma band (20–80 Hz) as postulated by the feature binding model (Miltner, Braun, Witte, & Taub, 1999; Rodriguez et al., 1999).

Spectral coherence and alpha-activity enhancements observed for EEG under periodically pulsed photostimulation, as shown in Figure 3.9, are reasonably expected for binding under EM oscillatory stimulation. This phenomenon supports the mode coupling of the EM field with feature binding rhythms as the attainable mechanism, leading the possible behavioral effects of the EM stimulation (Balduzzo et al., 2003). In this case, however, the reliability of EEG recording during the stimulation is doubtful because of the heavy interference of the magnetic field generated by the recording device; however, it is possible that oscillatory changes, if there are any, may last longer than the period of stimulation as the persistence of the effects of rTMS (Jing & Takigawa, 2000; Siebner et al., 1998) so that they can be observed. The existence of this transient cortical status, related to differing return in the domains of EM induction and pulsed microwaves, has been used by Ferreri et al. (2006). They demonstrated symmetry breaking of intracortical TMS excitability curves performed by the radiation emitted from a mobile phone placed near the ear. As observed in the previous section, rTMS operates in the domain of EM induction, where the field undergoes a strong attenuation in tissue. In contrast, microwaves emitted by mobile phones strongly penetrate tissue. Whereas the carrying microwaves are filtered by thermal agitation, the ELF envelopes are demodulated by nonlinearities of membrane channels, where the ELF field can perturb ion gating (Minelli et al., 2007; Panagopoulos, Messini, Karabarbounis, Phlippetis, & Margaritis, 2000).

Perturbations of neuron cell membrane gating and calcium release, ascribed to a periodic forcing of intracellular calcium oscillators at endogenous frequencies, have been suggested as a possible mechanism underlying activation of brain states and EEG modes (Balikci, Ozcan, Turgut-Balik, & Balik, 2004; Blackman, 2000; Croft et al., 2002; Freude, Ullsperger, Eggert, & Ruppe, 2000; Hamblin, Wood, Croft, & Stough, 2004; Hermann & Hossman, 1997; Hyland, 2000; Kramarenko & Tan, 2003). This particularly concerns the pulse repetition of the GSM (Global System for Mobile communications) signal. At the single neuron scale, low-intensity and ELF fields, or low-intensity pulse-modulated microwave radiation from mobile phones, dramatically modify the membrane bioelectric activity recorded from single neurons and produce neuron pool recruiting and synchronization (Azanza, Calvo, & del Moral, 2001; Azanza & del Moral, 1998; Calvo & Azanza, 1999; Pérez Bruzon, Azanza, Calvo, & del Moral, 2004; Salford, Brun, Eberhardt, Malmgren, & Persson, 2003). At the scale of the CNS, low-intensity pulse-modulated microwave radiation from mobile phones could modify the brain's functional state by increasing EEG alpha power during awake and rapid eye movement (REM) sleep stages, with concomitant REM suppressive effects (Achermann et al., 2000; Edelstyn & Oldershaw, 2002; Hyland, 2000; Lebedeva, Sulimov, Sulimova, Kotrovskaya, & Gailus, 2000; Lin, 2004; Mann & Röschke, 2004; Marino, Nilsen, & Frilot, 2003). Effects of pulse-modulated microwave radiation on test performance, memory tasks, and neurological disturbances have also been observed (Edelstyn & Oldershaw, 2002; Freude et al., 2000; Hermann & Hossman, 1997; Krause et al., 2000; Santini, Santini, Danze, Le Ruz, & Seigne, 2003; Wagner et al., 2000). Also, the effects on cognitive function of exposure to EM fields at 50 to 60 Hz is still open to debate (Cook, Graham, Cohen, & Gerkovich, 1992; Graham, Cook, Cohen, & Gerkovich, 1992; Persinger, Richards, & Koren, 1997; Preece, Wesnes, & Iwi, 1998; Trimmel & Schweiger, 1998).

Concluding Remarks and Perspectives

Chaos and fractals have turned out to be more successful as paradigms of the mechanisms underlying neurosynchronization and membrane noise than as tools for the current clinical diagnostics. Nonlinear dynamical models of neurons, in contrast, have been proven to simulate neuron functions in detail or improve the performance of the designs for neural networks that are suitable both to Hebbian learning or the simulation of EEG activity. A synthesis of the two lines is expected by next-generation basic circuits and neural processors, by virtue of VLSI circuits on a single semiconductor chip. An update of the present status of research is offered in the plan of the conference "Neuroscience Today" (Florence, March 2007):

> Non-temporal information can be carried by time patterns in neuronal spiking and neural assemblies can be identified by collective (synchronous) firing rather than only by transient change in the firing rate. According to models and experiments, this arrangement would allow fast dynamics, robustness, flexibility, and coexistence of several assemblies in the same cortical region. Synchronization, spiking accuracy, modulation of spiking rate, and spatiotemporal coherent patterning may therefore represent distinct but interacting computational codes for functionally diverse neurons.

Simulation of neuroelectrical activity with nonlinear circuits provides a theoretical framework to study EM effects on AP propagation and thus EM stimulation of the CNS. Among these applications, deep brain stimulation is making progress in the understanding of CNS disorders, and the use of TMS to study brain functional mapping and for diagnostics and therapy is increasing widely.

Appendix: Spectral Coherence

Although the correlation dimension remains the principal method to measure EEG single-channel cooperation, spectral coherence is a widely used instrument to index areas of connectivity and channel cooperation. Coherence function $C_{xy}^2(\omega)$ associated with two stationary sampled signals, $x(t)$ and $y(t)$, can be defined as

$$C_{xy}^2(\omega) = \frac{\left[G_{xy}(\omega)\right]^2}{G_{xx}(\omega)\,G_{yy}(\omega)} \ , \tag{3.A1}$$

$$G_{xy}(\omega) = 2 \lim_{T\to\infty} \frac{E\left[X_k^*(\omega,\,t)Y_k(\omega,\,t)\right]}{T} \ , \tag{3.A2}$$

in terms of the expected values of finite Fourier transforms $X_k(\omega,\,t)$ and $Y_k(\omega,\,t)$, of sample records $x_k(t)$, $y_k(t)$. Formula (3.A1, and 2) is suitable for numerical applications in time series from sampling of stationary random signals. For the equivalent current definition of the spectral coherence, see Bendat and Piersol (1986).

Being $0 \le C_{xy}^2(\omega) \le 1$, the coherence function can be used as an index, ranging from 0 to 1 and measuring the deductibility of one signal from the other as a linear response, at the frequency ω. For $C_{xy}^2(\omega) = 0$, unpredictability is absolute, whereas for $C_{xy}^2(\omega) = 1$, there is total deductibility. An average of the channels related to a reference point provides a zonal estimation. After time and frequency discretization, as detailed in Minelli and Turicchia (1999), formula

(3.A2) can be replaced by a two-dimensional array called a windowed coherence matrix, which is analogous to the windowed spectrogram.

Acknowledgments

The author is indebted to Dr. M. Balduzzo for the critical reading of the chapter.

References

Abden, M. A., & Stuchly, M. A. (1994). Modeling of magnetic field stimulation of bent neurons. *IEEE Transactions on Biomedical Engineering, 41*, 1092–1095.

Abraham, N. B., Albano, A. M., Das, B., De Guzman, G., Yong, S., et al. (1986). Calculating the dimension of the attractors from small data sets. *Physics Letters A, 114*, 217–221.

Achermann, P., Huber, R., Graf, T., Cote, K. A., Wittmann, L., et al. (2000). Exposure to pulsed high-frequency electromagnetic field during waking affects human sleep EEG. *Neuroreport, 11*, 3321–3325.

Anokhin, A. P., Birbaumer, N., Lutzenberg, W., Nikolaev, A., & Vogel, F. (1996). Age increases brain complexity. *Encephalography and Clinical Neurophysiology, 99*, 63–68.

Anokhin, A. P., Lutzenberg, W., & Birbaumer, N. (1999). Spatiotemporal organization of brain dynamics and intelligence: An EEG study in adolescents. *International Journal of Psychophysiology, 33*, 259–273.

Azanza, M. J., Calvo, A. C., & del Moral, A. (2001). 50 Hz-Sinusoidal magnetic field induced effects on bioelectric activity of single unit neurone cells. *Journal of Magnetism and Magnetic Materials, 226–230*, 2101–2103.

Azanza M. J., & del Moral, A. (1998). ELF-magnetic field induced effects on the bioelectric activity of single neurone cells. *Journal of Magnetism and Magnetic Materials, 177–181*, 1451–1452.

Babajani, A., & Soltanian-Zadeh, H. (2006). Integrated MEG/EEG and fMRI model based on neural masses. *IEEE Transactions on Biomedical Engineering, 53*, 1794–1800.

Balduzzo, M., Ferro Milone, F., Minelli, T. A., Pittaro Cadore, I., & Turicchia, L. (2003). Mathematical phenomenology of neural synchronization by periodic fields. *Nonlinear Dynamics, Psychology, and Life Sciences, 7*, 115–137.

Balduzzo, M., Minelli, T. A., & Turicchia, L. (1999). Signal analysis and simulation of the EEG activity. *Chaos Theory and Applications, 4*, 7–14.

Balikci, K., Ozcan, I. C., Turgut-Balik, D., & Balik, H. H. (2004). A survey on some neurological symptoms and sensations experienced by long term users of mobile phones. *Pathologie Biology, 53*, 30–34.

Bendat, J. J., & Piersol, A. G. (1986). *Random data*. New York: Wiley.

Benzi, R., Sutera, A., & Vulpiani, A. (1981). The mechanism of stochastic resonance. *Journal of Physics, A 14*, L457–L453.

Berardi, N., Pizzorusso, T., Ratto, G. M., & Maffei, L. (2003). Molecular basis of plasticity in the visual cortex. *Trends in Neurosciences, 26*, 369–377.

Blackman, C. F. (2000). Alterations in calcium ion activity caused by ELF and RF electromagnetic fields. In G. Oberfeld (Ed.), *Proceedings of the international conference on cell tower siting* (pp. 75–80). Salzburg: G. Oberfeld.

Blinder, P., Baruchi, I., Volman, V., Levine, H., Baranes, D., & Ben-Jacob, E. (2005). Functional topology classification of biological computing. *Neural Computing, 4,* 339–361.

Brody, C. D., & Hopfield, J. J. (2003). Simple networks for spike-timing-based computation with application to olfactory processing. *Neuron, 37,* 843–852.

Bulsara, A. R., Elston, T. C., Doering, C. R., Lowen, S. B., & Lindenberg, K. (1996). Cooperative behavior in periodically driven noisy integrate and fire models of neuronal dynamics. *Review of Modern Physics, 70,* 3958–3969.

Burke, D., Kiernan, M. C., & Bostock, H. (2001). Excitability of human axons. *Clinical Neurophysiology, 112,* 1575–1585.

Calvo A. C., & Azanza, M. J. (1999). Synaptic neuron activity under applied 50 Hz alternating magnetic fields. *Comparative Biochemistry and Physiology Part C, 124,* 99–107.

Chay, T. (1997). Effects of intracellular calcium on electrical bursting and intracellular and luminal calcium oscillations. *Biophysics Journal, 73,* 1732–1743.

Chay, T., & Keizer, J. (1983). Minimal model of membrane oscillations in the pancreatic beta-cells. *Biophysics Journal, 42,* 181–190.

Cook, M. R., Graham, C., Cohen, H. D., & Gerkovich, M. M. (1992). A replication study of human exposure to 60 Hz fields: Effects of neurobehavioral measures. *Bioelectromagnetics, 13,* 261–285.

Cracco, R. Q., Cracco, G. B., Maccabee, P. J., & Amassian, V. E. (1999). Cerebral function revealed by transcranial magnetic stimulation. *Journal of Neuroscience Methods, 86,* 209–219.

Croft, R. J., Chandler, J. S., Burgess, A. P., Barry, R. J., Williams, J. D., & Clarke, A. R. (2002). Acute mobile phone operation affects neural function in humans. *Clinical Neurophysiology, 113,* 1623–1632.

David, O., & Friston, K. J. (2003). A neural mass model for MEG/EEG coupling and neuronal dynamics. *NeuroImage, 20,* 1743–1755.

Deutsch, S., & Deutsch, A. (1993). *Understanding the nervous system.* New York: Institute of Electrical and Electronic Engineers.

Dhamala, M., Jirsa, V. K., & Ding, M. (2004). Transition to synchrony in coupled bursting neurons. *Physical Review Letters, 92,* 0281011–0281014.

Douglass, J. K., Wilkens, L., Pantazelou, E., & Moss, F. (1993). Noise enhancement of information transfer in crayfish mechanoreceptors by stochastic resonance. *Nature, 365,* 337–339.

Edelstyn, N., & Oldershaw, A. (2002). The acute effects of exposure to the electromagnetic field emitted by mobile phones on human attention. *Cognitive Neuroscience and Neuropsychology, 13,* 119–121.

Falcke, M., Huerta, R., Rabinovich, M. I., Abarbanel, H. D. I., Elson, R. C., & Severston, A. I. (2000). Modeling observed chaotic oscillations in bursting neurons. *Biological Cybernetics, 82,* 517–527.

Fall, C. P., Marland, E. S., Wagner, J. M., & Tyson, J. J. (2002). *Computational cell biology.* Berlin: Springer.

Ferreri, F., Curcio, G., Pasqualetti, P., De Gennaro, L., Fini, R., & Rossini, P. M. (2006). Mobile phone emissions and human brain excitability. *Annals of Neurology, 60,* 188–196.

Ferro Milone, F., Aporti, F., Minelli, T. A., Nofrate, V., Porro, A., & Leon Cananzi, A. (2003). EEG patterns in Alzheimer's disease: Intermittent photic stimulation and sampling rate. *European Journal of Neurology 10* (Suppl. 1), 92–93.

Ferro Milone, F., Minelli, T. A., & Turicchia, L. (1998). Neuron synchronization and human EEG phenomenology simulation. *Nonlinear Dynamics, Psychology, and Life Sciences, 2*, 21–33.

FitzHug, R. (1961). Impulses and physiological states in theoretical models of nerve membrane. *Biophysics Journal, 1*, 445–466.

Freeman, W. J. (1975). *Mass action in nervous system.* New York: Wiley.

Freeman, W. J. (1979a). EEG analysis gives model of neuronal template-matching mechanism for sensory search with olfactory bulb. *Biological Cybernetics, 35*, 221–234.

Freeman, W. J. (1979b). Nonlinear dynamics of paleocortex manifested in the olfactory EEG. *Biological Cybernetics, 35*, 21–77.

Freeman, W. J. (1979c). Nonlinear gain mediation of cortical stimulus response relations. *Biological Cybernetics, 33*, 237–247.

Freeman, W. J. (1991). Predictions on neocortical dynamics derived from studies in paleocortex. In E. Basar & T. H. Bullock (Eds.), *Induced rhythms of the brain* (pp. 183–199). Boston: Birkhaeuser.

Freeman, W. J., & Vitiello, G. (2007, July). *Brain dynamics, dissipation and spontaneous breakdown of symmetry.* Paper presented to 2007 Brain Network Dynamics: Conference in occasion of the 80th birthday of Walter Freeman, Berkeley, California.

Freude, G., Ullsperger, P., Eggert, S., & Ruppe, I. (2000). Microwaves emitted by cellular telephones affect human slow brain potentials. *European Journal of Applied Physiology, 81*, 18–27.

Gammaitoni, L., Hänggi, P., & Marchesoni, F. (1998). Stochastic resonance. *Reviews of Modern Physics, 70*, 223–287.

Gerstner, W., & Kistler, W. (2002). *Spiking neuron models.* New York: Cambridge University Press.

Giugliano, M., Bove, M., & Grattarola, M. (1999). Activity-driven strategies of dynamically regulated integrate and fire model neurons. *Journal of Computational Neuroscience, 7*, 247–254.

Gomes, I., Mirasso, C. R., Toral, R., & Calvo, O. (2003). Experimental study of high frequency stochastic resonance in Chua circuits. *Physica, 327*, 115–119.

Graham, C., Cook, M. R., Cohen, H. D., & Gerkovich, M. M. (1994). Dose response study of human exposure to 60 Hz magnetic and electric fields. *Bioelectromagnetics, 15*, 447–463.

Grill, W. M. (1999). Modeling the effects of electric fields on nerve fibers. *IEEE Transactions on Biomedical Engineering, 46*, 918–928.

Grossberg, S. (1988). Nonlinear neural networks: Principles, mechaniams and architecture. *Neural Networks, 1*, 17–62.

Hallet, M. (2000). Transcranial magnetic stimulation and human brain. *Nature, 406*, 147–150.

Hamblin, D. L., Wood, A. W., Croft, R. J., & Stough, C. (2004). Examining the effects of electromagnetic fields emitted by GSM mobile phones on human event-related potentials and performance during an auditory task. *Clinical Neurophysiology, 115*, 171–178.

Han, S. K., Yim, T. G., Postnov, D. E., & Sosnovtseva, O. V. (1999). Interacting coherence resonance oscillators. *Physical Review Letters, 83*, 1771–1774.

Havstad, J. W., & Ehlers, C. L. (1989). Attractor dimension of nonstationary dynamical systems from small data sets. *Physical Review A, 39*, 845–853.

Hebb, D. O. (1949). *The organization of behaviour: A neuropsychological theory.* New York: Wiley.

Hermann, D. M., & Hossman, K. A. (1997). Neurological effects of microwave exposure related to mobile communication. *Journal of Neurological Sciences, 152*, 1–14.

Hindmarsh, J. L., & Rose, R. M. (1984). A model of neuronal bursting using three coupled first order differential equations. *Proceedings of the Royal Society of London B, 221*, 87–102.

Hodgkin, A., & Huxley, A. (1939). Action potentials recorded from inside a nerve fiber. *Nature, 144*, 710–711.

Hodgkin, A., & Huxley, A. (1952). Currents carried by sodium and potassium ions through the membrane of the giant axon of Loligo. *Journal of Physiology, 116*, 449–472.

Hopfield, J. J. (1982). Neural networks and physical systems with emergent collective computational abilities. *Proceedings of the National Academy of Science USA, 79*, 2554–2558.

Hopfield, J. J. (1984). Neurons with graded response have collective computational properties like those of two-state neurons. *Proceedings of the National Academy of Science USA, 81*, 579–583.

Hopfield, J. J. (1994). Neurons, dynamics and computation. *Physics Today, 47*, 40–46.

Hopfield, J. J. (1995). Pattern recognition computation using action potential timing for stimulus representation. *Nature, 376*, 33–36.

Hopfield, J. J., & Tank, D. W. (1986). Computing with neuronal circuits: A model. *Science, 233*, 625–633.

Hyland, G. J. (2000). Physics and biology of mobile telephony. *Lancet, 356*, 1833–1836.

Izhikevich, E. M. (2001). Resonate-and-fire neurons. *Neural Networks, 14*, 883–894.

Izhikevich, E. M., Gallay, J. A., & Edelman, G. M. (2004). Spike-timing dynamics of neuronal groups. *Cerebral Cortex, 24*, 933–944.

Jing, H., & Takigawa, M. (2000). Low sampling rate induces high correlation dimension on encephalograms from healthy subjects. *Psychiatry and Clinical Neurosciences, 54*, 407–412.

Junge, D. (1981). *Nerve and muscle excitation.* Sunderland, MA: Sinauer Associates.

Kanazawa, Y., Asai, T., & Amemiya, Y. (2003). Basic circuit design of neural processor: Analog CMOS implementation of spiking neurons and dynamic synapses. *Journal of Robotics and Mechatronics, 15*, 208–218.

Kantz H., & Schreiber T. (1995). Dimension estimates and physiological data. *Chaos, 5*, 143–154.

King, R. W. P. (1999). Nerves in a human body exposed to low frequency electromagnetic field. *IEEE Transactions on Biomedical Engineering, 46*, 1426–1431.

Klimesch, W. (1999). EEG alpha and theta oscillations reflect cognitive and memory performance: a review and analysis. *Brain Research Review, 29*, 169–195.

Kramarenko, A. V., & Tan, U. (2003). Effects of high-frequency electromagnetic fields on human EEG: A brain mapping study. *International Journal of Neuroscience, 113,* 1007–1019.

Krause, C. M., Sillanmäki, L., Koivisto, M., Häggqvist, A., Saarela, C., Revonsuo, A., et al. (2000). Effects of electromagnetic field emitted by cellular phones on the EEG during a memory task. *Cognitive Neuroscience, 11,* 761–764.

Kuncel, A. M., & Grill, W. M. (2004). Selection of stimulus parameters for deep brain stimulation. *Clinical Neurophysiology, 115,* 2431–2441.

Lamberts, J., van der Broek, P. L. C., Bener, L., van Egmond, J., & Dirksen, R. (2000). Correlation dimension of human electroencephalogram corresponds with cognitive load. *Neuropsychobiology, 41,* 149–153.

Lebedeva, N. N., Sulimov, A.V., Sulimova, O. P., Kotrovskaya, T. I., & Gailus, T. (2000). Cellular phone electromagnetic field effects on bioelectric activity of human brain. *Critical Review of Biomedical Engineering, 28,* 323–337.

Liljenstrom, H. (1991). Modeling the dynamics of olfactory cortex. *International Journal of Neural Systems, 2,* 1–15.

Lin, J. C. (2004). Human EEG and microwave radiation from cell phones. *IEEE Microwave Magazine, June,* 34–36.

Lopes da Silva, F. H., Hoeks, A., Smits, H., & Zetterberg, L. H. (1974). Model of brain rhythmic activity. *Kybernetic, 15,* 27–37.

Lopes da Silva, F. H., & Pfurtscheller, G. (1999). Basic concepts on EEG synchronization and desynchronozation. In G. Pfurtscheller & F. H. Lopes da Silva (Eds.), *Handbook of elecroencephalography and clinical neurophysiology VI* (pp. 3–11). Amsterdam: Elsevier.

Lowen, S. B., Liebovitch, L. S., & White, J. A. (1999). Fractal ion-channel behavior generates fractal firing patterns in neuronal models. *Physical Review E, 59,* 570–580.

Maeda, E., Robinson, H. P. C., & Kawana, A. (1995). The mechanisms of generation and propagation of synchronized bursting in developing networks of cortical neurons. *Journal of Neuroscience, 15,* 6834–6845.

Mann, K., & Röschke, J. (2004). Sleep under exposure to high-frequency electromagnetic fields. *Sleep Medicine Reviews, 8,* 95–107.

Marino, A. A., Nilsen, E., & Frilot, C. (2003). Nonlinear changes in brain electrical activity due to cell phone radiation. *Bioelectromagnetics, 24,* 339–346.

Massimini, M., Ferrarelli, F., Huber, R., Esser, S. K., Singh, H., & Tononi G. (2007). Breakdown of cortical effective connectivity during sleep. *Science, 309,* 2228–2232.

Mayer-Kress, G. (1987). *Directions in chaos.* Singapore: World Scientific.

McCulloch, W., & Pitts, W. (1943). A logical calculus of the ideas imminent in nervous activity. *Bulletin of Mathematical Biophysics, 5,* 115–113.

Miltner, W. H. R., Braun, C., Witte, H., & Taub, E. (1999). Coherence of the gamma band activity as a basis for associative learning. *Nature, 397,* 434–436.

Minelli, T. A., & Turicchia, L. (1999). Progressive coherence patterns. *Nonlinear Dynamics, Psychology, and Life Sciences, 3,* 129–142.

Minelli, T. A., Aporti, F., Ferro-Milone, F., Cananzi, A., Nofrate, V., et al. (2004). On the EEG complexity in the frequency domain. In A. Gatta (Ed.), *Proceedings of the Conference Alterazioni neuropsichiche in medicina interna* (pp. 123–128). Padova: Villaggio Grafica.

Minelli, T. A., Balduzzo, M., Ferro Milone, F., & Nofrate, V. (2007). Modeling cell dynamics under mobile phone radiation. *Nonlinear Dynamics, Psychology, and Life Sciences, 11*, 197–218.

Moss, F., Ward, L. M., & Sannita, W. G. (2004). Stochastic resonance and sensory information processing: A tutorial review of application. *Clinical Neurophysiology, 115*, 267–281.

Morris, C., & Lecar, H. (1981). Voltage oscillations in the barnacle giant muscle fiber. *Biophysics Journal, 35*, 193–213.

Munk, M. H. J., Roelfsema, P. R., Koenig, P., Engel, A. K., & Singer, W. (1996). Role of reticular activation in the modulation of intracortical synchronization. *Science, 272*, 271–274.

Myers, J. M. (1999). Modelling the effect of an external electric field on the velocity of spike propagation in a nerve fiber. *Physical Review E, 60*, 5918–5925.

Nagarajan, S. S. (1996). A generalized cable equation for magnetic stimulation of axons. *IEEE Transactions on Biomedical Engineering, 43*, 304–312.

Nagumo, J., Aximoto, S., & Yoshizawa, S. (1962). An active pulse transmission simulating nerve axon. *Proceedings of the Institute of Radio Engineering, 50*, 2061–2071.

Nofrate, V., Minelli, T. A., Ferro Milone, F., Aporti, F., Aricò, V., et al. (2007). *Sampling dependence of EEG nonlinear and fractal structure in healthy and Alzheimer subjects.* Manuscript submitted for publication.

Nunez, P. L. (1995). *Neocortical dynamics and human EEG rhythms.* New York: Oxford University Press.

Nunez, P. L., Silberstein, R. B., Cadusch, P. J., Wijesinghe, R. S., Westdorp, A. F., & Srinivasan, R. (1994). A theoretical and experimental study of high resolution EEG. *Electroencephalography and Clinical Neurophysiology, 90*, 40–57.

Panagopoulos, D. J., Messini, N., Karabarbounis, A., Phlippetis, A. L., & Margaritis, L. H. (2000). A mechanism for action of oscillating electric fields on cells. *Biochemical and Biophysical Communications, 272*, 634–640.

Pascual-Leone, A., Valls-Sole, J., Wassermann, E. M., Brasil Neto, J. P., & Hallett, M. (1994). Response to rapid rate transcranial magnetic stimulation of the human motor cortex. *Brain, 117*, 847–858.

Pastor, M. A., Artieda, J., Arbizu, J., Valencia, M., & Masdeu, J. (2003). Human cerebral activation during steady-state visual-evoked responses. *Journal of Neuroscience, 23*, 11621–11627.

Penrose, R. (1994). *Shadows of the mind.* Oxford: Oxford University Press.

Perc, M., & Marhl, M. (2004). Frequency dependent stochastic resonance in a model for intracellular Ca^{2+} oscillations can be explained by local resonance. *Physica A, 332*, 123–140.

Pérez Bruzon, R. N., Azanza, M. J., Calvo, A. C., & del Moral, A. C. (2004). Neurone bioelectric activity under magnetic fields of variable frequency in the range of 0.1–80 Hz. *Journal of Magnetism and Magnetic Materials, 272–276*, 2424–2425.

Persinger, M. A., Richards, P. M., & Koren, S. A. (1997). Differential entrainment of electroencephalographic activity by weak complex electromagnetic fields. *Perceptual & Motor Skills, 84*, 527–536.

Petsce, H. (1997). EEG coherence and mental activity in analysis of the electrical activity of the brain. In F. Angeleri, S. Butler, S. Gianquinto, & J. Majkowski, (Eds.), *Proceedings of the International Conference Clinical Applications of Advanced EEG Data Processing-Rome-May 1995.* New York: Wiley.

Pfurtscheller, G., & Cooper R. (1975). Frequency dependence of the transmission of the EEG from cortex to scalp. *Electroencephy and Clinical Neurophysiology, 38,* 93–96.

Preece, A. W., Wesnes, K. A., & Iwi, G. R. (1998). The effect of a 50 Hz magnetic field on cognitive functions in humans. *International Journal of Radiation Biology, 74,* 463–467.

Rattay, F. (1998). Analysis of the electrical excitation of CNS neurons. *IEEE Transactions on Biomedical Engineering, 45,* 766–772.

Rodriguez, E., George, N., Lachaux, J. P., Martinerie, J., Renault, B., & Varela, F. J. (1999). Perception shadow: Long-distance synchronization of human brain activity. *Nature, 397,* 430–433.

Ruohonen, J., Ravazzani, P., & Grandori, F. (1998). Functional magnetic stimulation: theory and coil optimization. *Bioelectrochemistry and Bioenergetics, 47,* 213–219.

Sabah, N. H. (2000, November/December). Aspects of nerve conduction. *IEEE Engineering in Medicine and Biology, 19,* 111–117.

Sakmann, B., & Neher, E. (1995). *Single channel recording.* New York: Plenum Press.

Salford, L. G., Brun, A. E., Eberhardt, J. L., Malmgren, L., & Persson, B. R. R. (2003). Nerve cell damage in mammalian brain after exposure to microwaves from GSM mobile phones. *Environmental Health Perspectives, 111,* 881–883.

Sandblom, J., & Galvanovskis, J. (2000). Electromagnetic field absorption in stochastic cellular systems: Enhanced signal detection in ion channels and calcium oscillators. *Chaos, Solitons and Fractals, 11,* 1905–1911.

Sannita, W. G. (2000). Stimulus-specific oscillatory responses of the brain. *Clinical Neurophysiology, 111,* 565–583.

Santini, R., Santini, P., Danze, J. M., Le Ruz, P., & Seigne, M. (2003). Symptoms experienced by people in vicinity of base stations: II/ Incidences of age, duration of exposure, location of subjects in relation to the antennas and other electromagnetic factors. *Pathologie Biologie, 51,* 412–415.

Schnabel, V., & Struijk, J. J. (2001). Calculation of electric field in a multiple cylindrical volume conductor induced by magnetic coils. *IEEE Transactions on Biomedical Engineering, 48,* 78–86.

Schurmann, K., Nikouline, V. V., Soljanlahti, S., Ollikainen, M., Basar, E., Ilmoniemi, R. J. (2001). EEG responses to combined somatosensory and transcranial magnetic stimulation. *Clinical Neurophysiology, 112,* 19–24.

Scott, A., & Luzader, S. D. (1979). Coupled solitary waves in neurophysics. *Physica Scripta, 20,* 395–401.

Segev, R., Baruchi, I., Hulata, E., & Ben-Jacob, E. (2004). Hidden neuronal correlations in cultured networks. *Physical Review Letters, 92, 118102* (1–4).

Shilnikov, A., & Cymbalyuk, G. (2005). Transition between tonic spiking and bursting in a neuron model via the blue-sky catastrophe. *Physical Review Letters, 94, 048101* (1–4).

Siebner, H. R., Willoch, F., Peller, M., Auer, C., Boecker, H., et al. (1998). Imaging brain activation induced by long trains of repetitive transcranial magnetic stimulation. *NeuroReport, 9,* 943–948.

Singer, W. (1994). The role of synchrony in neocortical networks. In E. Domany, J. L. van Hemmen, & K. Shulten (Eds.), *Models of neural networks II* (pp. 141–167). New York: Springer-Verlag.

Sotero, R. C., Trujillo-Barreto, N. J., Iturria-Medina, Y., Carbonell, F., & Jimenez, J. C. (2007). Realistically coupled neural mass models can generate EEG rhythms. *Neural Computation, 19*, 478–512.

Stam, C. J. (2005). Nonlinear dynamical analysis of EEG and MEG: Review of an emergent field. *Clinical Neurophysiology, 116*, 2266–2301.

Stam, C. J., Pijn, J. P. M., Suffczynski P., & Lopes da Silva, F. H. (1999). Dynamics of the human alpha rhythm: evidence for nonlinearity? *Clinical Neurophysiology, 110*, 1801–1813.

Stam C., van Woerkom, T. C. A. M., & Pritchard, W. S. (1996). Use of non-linear EEG measures to characterize EEG changes during mental activity. *Electroencephy and Clinical Neurophysiology, 99*, 214–224.

Steriade, M. (2006). Grouping of brain rhythms in corticothalamic systems. *Neuroscience, 137*, 1087–1106.

Stuchly, M., & Dawson, T. W. (2000). Interaction of low-frequency electric and magnetic field with human body. *IEEE Proceedings, 88*, 643–664.

Suihko, V. (1998). Modeling direct activation of corticospinal axon using transcranial electrical stimulation. *Electroencephalography and Clinical Neuriphysiology, 109*, 238–244.

Theiler, J., Eubank, S., Longtin, A., Galakandrian, B., & Farmer, J. D. (1992). Testing for nonlinearity in time series: The method of surrogate data. *Physica D, 58*, 77–94.

Traynelis, S. E., & Jaramillo, F. (1998). Getting the most of noise in the central nervous system. *Trends in Neurosciences, 21*, 137–144.

Trimmel, M., & Schweiger, E. (1998). Effects of an ELF (50 Hz, 1 mT) electromagnetic field (EMF) on concentration in visual attention, perception and memory including effects on EMF sensitivity. *Toxicology Letters, 96–97*, 377–382.

Verechtchaguina, T., Schimansky-Geier, L., & Sokolov, I. M. (2004). Spectra and waiting-time densities in firing resonant and non resonant neurons. *Physical Review Letters E, 70, 031916* (1–7).

Volman, V., Baruchi, I., Persi, E., & Ben-Jacob, E. (2004). Generative modelling of regulated dynamical behavior in cultured neural networks. *Physica A, 335*, 249–278.

Wagner, P., Röschke, J., Mann, K., Fell, J., Hiller, W., et al. (2000). Human sleep EEG under the influence of pulsed radio frequency electromagnetic fields. *Neuropsychobiology, 42*, 207–212.

Walsh, V., & Rushworth, M. (1999). A primer of magnetic stimulation as a tool for neurophysiology. *Neuropsychologia, 37*, 125–135.

Warman, E. N., Grill, W. M., & Durand, D. (1992). Modeling the effects of electric fields on nerve fibers: Determination of excitation thresholds. *IEEE Transactions on Biomedical Engineering, 39*, 1244–1254.

Wasserman, E. M., & Lisanby, S. H. (2001). Therapeutic application of TMS: A review. *Clinical Neurophysiology, 112*, 1367–1377.

White, J. A., Rubinstein, J. T., & Kay, A. R. (2000). Channel noise in neurons. *Trends in Neurosciences, 23*, 131–137.

Williams, J., Ramaswamy, D., & Oulhaj, A. (2006). 10 Hz flicker improves recognition memory in older people. *BioMed Central Neuroscience, 7*, 1–7.

Wright, J. J., & Liley, D. T. J. (1994). A millimetric-scale simulation of electrocortical wave dynamics. *Network, 5*, 191–202.

Wright, J. J., & Liley, D. T. J. (1996). Dynamics of the brain at global and microscopic scales: Neural networks and the EEG. *Behavioral and Brain Sciences, 19*, 285–320.

Wright, J. J., Sergejev, A. A., & Liley, D. T. J. (1994). Computer simulation of the electrocortical activity at millimetric scale. *Electroencephalography and Clinical Neurophysiology, 90*, 365–375.

Wu, X., & Liljenstrom, H. (1994). Regulating the nonlinear dynamics of olfactory cortex. *Network, 5*, 47–60.

Wu, S., Wei, R., He, K., & Huang, Z. (2001). Burst and coherence resonance in Rose–Hindmarsh model induced be additive noise. *Physics Letters A, 279*, 347–354.

Xie, Y., Xu, J. X., Kang, Y. M., Hu, S. J., & Duan, Y. B. (2005). Critical amplitude curves for different periodic stimuli and different dynamical mechanisms of excitability. *Communications in Nonlinear Science and Numerical Simulation, 10*, 823–832.

Zierhofer, C. M. (2001). Analysis of a linear model for electrical stimulation of axons. *IEEE Transactions on Biomedical Engineering, 48*, 173–184.

4 Psychophysics

ROBERT A. M. GREGSON

Psychophysics: the investigation of the relations between physical stimuli and the psychic action in the production of sensations (1879)

Introduction

It is interesting to find this old definition in one of the world's most prestigious dictionaries of the English language, the *Oxford Shorter Dictionary* in two volumes "based on historical principles." Who today writes of "psychic action," and who would gather that the word emerged in Fechner's 1860 book *Elemente der Psychophysik* (translated by Adler in 1966)?

To know what actually was intended and what has become the activity of psychophysics, we must both go back in time and then return to the present. Although it is common to write of stimulus–response relations in summarizing the results of quantifying experimental psychology data, it is wiser to write of externally observable events for *stimuli* and to write specifically of reports of personal sensory experiences or choice actions, leaving *responses* to include a wide diversity of behaviors, including physiological processes that have no necessary conscious correlates.

Psychophysics usually leads to some mathematical representation of mapping from inputs to outputs, in which the environment is given and the behavior is dependent and the mapping is written outside time, being static and not dynamic. This does not exclude the use of psychophysical methods in studies of topics such as fatigue or vigilance, when behavior is variable and even transiently erratic. Despite arguments between physicists and psychologists about the measurability of sensation per se and about the additivity or nonadditivity of levels of reported sensation, which culminated in a sterile and unresolved committee report of the British Association for the Advancement of Science in 1940, what is actually done in psychophysics is to match judgments, of magnitude or probability, made in various forms of choice or discrimination against increments of stimulus activity levels, usually of intensity or duration.

A weak ordering of such operations (Gregson, 1992, p. 9) for which both linear and nonlinear psychophysical models can be developed, comprises, from the simplest upward, (a) detection, (b) discrimination (what Fechner basically used), (c) inequality assessment, (d) recognition, (e) identification, (f) bisection, (g) relative magnitude assessment, (h) direct magnitude assessment, (i) similarity assessment, and (j) matching.

Specific psychophysical methods were developed for some of these operations and remain in laboratory use. Each can be given an operational definition. Fechner used difference judgments to quantify just-noticeable differences as well as just-not-noticeable differences expressed in physical units. A probability cut-off of 0.5 was selected, drawing both on Weber's work and on Gaussian assumptions about error probability distributions. What is interesting is that when time vanishes from the equations, responses are treated as single-valued (although smudged by error) and so are in effect instantaneous. With the resolution of measurement available to Fechner in the 1850s, and the phenomenology of observers, as described in meticulous detail in Fechner's 1850 papers in the Proceedings of the Royal Academy of Sciences of the Kingdom of Saxony, dynamics had to take a backseat except in what evolved as separate nineteenth-century studies of reaction times.

Although this was a backward step to achieve some tractability in an emerging experimental science, theoretical psychology had already shown the first signs of dynamical modeling by Herbart in 1812 (translated by Gregson, 1998); Herbart's mathematics stemmed from Euler and did not involve probability distributions, but rather differential equations of processes running through time to stability or convergence. Herbart had his disciples, but their work had no lasting impression on psychophysics by the time Wundt's laboratory in Leipzig built up a body of results by the 1890s.

To Gauss we can attribute the partitioning of a regression into a linear form and added residual least-squares error, which derived from his work as both codirector of an astronomical observatory and a surveyor for the rebuilding of Hannover after the Napoleonic Wars. To Weber, who worked with Gauss, we have the law

$$L_{50} = f(\delta S.S^{-1}), \ S_{min} < S < S_{max}, \tag{4.1}$$

in which the term inside $f(.)$ becomes an approximate constant. In Eq. 4.1, the L_{50} refers to the 50% limen, an old word for threshold; the equation is not strictly valid to integrate if another percentage limen is substituted. This is a dimensionless mapping from an increment of physical input to the first moment of a probability distribution, so fundamentally it says nothing about psychophysical relations expressed as units in both domains. As a generalization, it is locally false (Nizami 2006) over some restricted stimulus ranges where it might be expected to hold; the reasons for this involve nonlinearities specific to a stimulus modality. Fechner used a pseudo-integration on $f(.)$ to cumulate increments that he called just-noticeable differences, ending up with a log law.

This law, which was endlessly disputed, is quite useful in applied contexts. What is important to note is that Fechner believed he was doing something in physiology and distinguished between sensory (experienced) psychophysics above, and below (in German, von unten) a psychophysics being hypothetically rooted in neurophysiology. Fechner would have known of the anatomy of the sensory cranial nerves but not about the microstructure of the frontal lobes or of the hippocampus, which play an important role in judgmental processes.

The development, or rather resurgence, of psychophysics in the later twentieth century is usually attributed to Stevens at Harvard. However, all Stevens did was revive a model that Plateau, a Belgian psychophysicist in the 1890s, had already postulated – namely, that if we write S for stimulus and R for response, then

$$R = aS^b + N(\mu, \sigma). \tag{4.2}$$

In words, "the response in psychological units is a power law of the stimulus levels in physical units, raised to some power b." Stevens made two contributions that have been disputed mathematically. He used relative magnitude assessment tasks and direct magnitude assessment tasks and advanced a theory of scale types: nominal, ordinal, interval, and ratio. The scale types were shown by Coombs (1964) to be incomplete, and their foundation was properly questioned by Pfanzagl (1968).

It should be emphasized that the classical psychophysical equations are steady-state input–output maps. They cannot, without augmentation, tell us anything about internal dynamics, complexity or the presence of chaos, and fractal relationships; for this reason, the relation between overt psychophysics and psychophysiological substrate processes is not meaningfully explored without further consideration of how complex channels and networks might function.

Hundreds of experimental studies have been conducted in the past 150 years on psychophysical modeling, and any generalizations will be associated with exceptions due to the peculiarities of the various sensory dimensions. The N term added in Eq. 4.2 represents additive superimposed Gaussian noise with the two moments mean, μ, and standard deviation, σ. These parameters will have to be in physical stimulus units, such as brightness or sound pressure.

The constants a and b are real scalars. a makes numerical values tractable, but b was thought to be very important by Stevens (1951), who tried to associate various values of b with different sensory continua. The matrix of continua and individual observer differences appears to be of indeterminate rank, so there are no necessary unique b values for a one-sensory modality.

Equation 4.2 has been popularly used in applied work, not just in the United States but also in Europe. It has defects, however; first, as applied mathematics, it is poor. Any equation needs boundary conditions on its applicability as a model, here S_{min} and S_{max}. All biological processes function within a narrow window. For example, human color vision lies between infrared and ultraviolet wavelengths. Equation 4.2 does not contain dynamics, and because it represents a process that takes place in real time, limits on its temporal evolution are necessary.

We also know that processes not mapping into Eq. 4.2 arise at the lower limits (the lower detection threshold of sensitivity) and at the upper or saturation threshold to a lesser extent. An example is negative masking (Gregson, 2001; Laming, 1973), where subthreshold stimuli can elicit greater perceived intensities than threshold stimuli. We may also dispute that the threshold exists as a point process, because signal detection theory (which is a special case of statistical decision theory) does away with the threshold as a single-valued entity.

Responses can be modified if they are elicited rapidly, under time pressure, and in contrasting environments such as when field or context effects are exhibited. Successive responses can be autocorrelated (Gregson, 1983, 2006), even when the stimulus sequence is not. Specific models of the effects or presenting reference stimuli, called anchors, in a sequence of judgments were studied by Helson (1964), whose adaptation-level theory should be seen as an elementary form of dynamic modeling. Some of the more modern treatments employ a non-linear dynamical system that is capable of performing Bayesian inferences, can make explicit use of local sequential dependencies, and can be used to model a variety of problems including the integration of cues from various sensory dimensions (Beck & Pouget, 2007).

This so far does not address the question "How long does it take to map from S to R, and is this duration itself (the response latency) related to the magnitude of the mapped difference, in some sense, from S and R?" Early on, it was realized that time to respond had components, some due to the basic physiology of neural impulse transmission and some related to cognitive load. For example, detecting very weak stimuli can take a long time and can have an error rate that is not simply related to perceived task difficulty. So, as expressed in Eq. 4.1, there is no mention of sensory dynamics and no contribution to dynamical theory. Contemporary developments in applications of dynamics to response latency data are presented later in this chapter.

The S term is expressed in physical units (except when it is a dimensionless probability), which means it has two defining properties, dimensionality and admissible operations. The simplest psychophysics was concerned with things such as line length, which has dimensions L(length), or weight, which has M (mass). Many measurement scales in physics are functions of L, M, and T(time); temperature (θ); or E (electric charge). In addition, there are operations we can perform, such as L^2 to represent area, but we do not multiply temperatures together or create products such as L^4.

We can use L^3 to represent volume, but we do not do such things as take square roots of temperature in physics, although we might find that warmth or pain behaves over some restricted range like the square root of θ. The physical side of the equation can be internally consistent in terms of dimensionality but not correspond to the left-hand side, so it is expedient to distinguish and write about physical dimensions, φ, and psychological dimensions, ψ, if they exist.

For example, if we ask a subject to judge ratios of lengths, which is dimensionless $\varphi(L/L)$, then she may respond by putting a mark on a line, which has dimensionality ψL^1. Worse, the physical variable φL satisfies additivity axioms. One can meaningfully add lengths, but psychological lengths, ψL, may not be strictly additive, because they break down at thresholds and exhibit such quirky things as being different in the vertical and horizontal directions.

Because analyses in dynamics involve metrics and rates of change over time, if one is to use the results collated in Chapter 1 of this book, then it is necessary to ask how much carries over, with or without modification in measures and admissible operations, in psychophysics. Falmagne (1985) gave a valuable treatment of the problem of meaningfulness in psychophysics that parallels in some details the issues raised here.

Let us consider an imaginary experiment that is easy to do on a computer screen. We have rectangles, and they are made to start very small and increase in size over time while keeping their shapes. In time, we now have something like the sequence

and so on up to the limit of the screen. We can then ask a question that is really about dynamics and not only about the static perception of shapes such as: "Did this sequence you have just seen grow slower or faster than the previous sequence?" Sequences can grow linearly, each increment a fixed unit of linear size, or nonlinearly, by a multiple, which from Weber's Law should be seen as more uniform. More interestingly, we can have the rate of growth accelerate, and this acceleration (d^2L/dT^2) itself can vary. Can the observer at least put various degrees of acceleration into a weak order? To our knowledge, this experiment has not been conducted.

The Ubiquitous Ogive

It is reasonably obvious today that any neural pathway from a sensory receptor input to experienced sensation passes through a network and not along a single isolated pathway. Networks leak information, transform information, and can hold memories. The ogival, or sigmoid, form, plotting response levels against stimulus levels, can be derived mathematically in various ways (Fig. 4.1), its empirical existence not confirming any one model.

The earliest treatment,[1] in more detail than in some later texts, is found in Külpe's *Grundriss der Psychologie* (1893) and is on page 70 in Titchener's translation of 1895. There, two threshold ogives are given, falling and rising, as

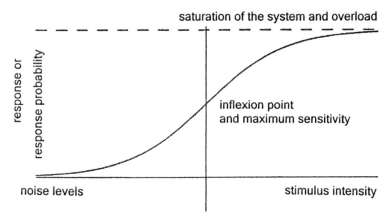

Figure 4.1. The ogival form, and its interpretation in psychophysics.

derivatives from a Gaussian error curve. This was, of course, a few years before
the existence of and interest in nonlinear dynamics that Poincaré pioneered.

The ogival relationship between detection probability (or magnitude) and
physical stimulus intensity (or difference) is ubiquitous because it appears
in nearly every well-known text on psychophysics, such as the long-lasting
Woodworth's *Experimental Psychology* (1938, p. 407), Guilford's classic *Psychometric Methods* (1936, p. 32), or specifically as the impulse response function
or the threshold curve (McBurney & Collings, 1984, p. 13). The ogival relationship also appears in physiology and in artificial neural network texts (an der
Heiden, 1980, p. 6), where its necessary nonlinearity may be commented on.
Walsh (2006) has employed it in a model of economic decision making that
interestingly involves both period-doubling and period-halving in the emergent
nonlinear dynamics. The reasons the curve flattens out at top and bottom are
not the same; in psychophysics, the bottom end is the region where gradually
increasing signal input eventually overcomes the environmental noise in the
system if we think of the process as signal detection, whereas the top of the
curve is a region of system saturation and overload that can run into oscillatory
behavior, as in motor tremor.

All these early depictions of ogival forms are either empirical or created from
stochastic arguments about probability distributions of inequality judgments.
However, ogival forms, with a diversity of second-order irregularities, can just
as well be derived from nonlinear dynamics. A collection of examples, which
does not include the Γ process to be considered later but rather employs more
familiar examples from physics, was shown by Bontempi and Casciati (1994),
including the Chirikov, Henon, and Arnold maps, as well as the Lorenz, Rossler,
and Duffing oscillators. The important point here is that these oscillators, used
in physical models, have different algebraic definitions and differences in the
number of their free parameters. The Duffing oscillator (Schuster, 1984, p. 133)

represents the action of a sinusoidal perturbing stimulus on a nonlinear system, a situation that can arise in some biological contexts and is therefore potentially of more interest to us.

Exponential, cubic polynomial, and network assumptions all generate similar forms and can be tuned in their shape with the addition of secondary parameters. The simple integration of the familiar bell-shaped Gaussian function, used, for example, in modeling responses to intelligence tests with an associated IQ distribution, is one solution. More interestingly, it can be derived from a model of networks with many sparse or null entries, where the proportion of such null entries varies (Migler, Morrison, & Ogle, 2006). Phase synchronization within networks is yet another source of ogival functions, these synchronization processes being a complex function of the degrees of connectivity in a network and the distribution of weights on connections (Motter, Zhou, & Kurths, 2005).

There is yet another way to conceptualize the ogive as a system that is almost linear around the set point of the stimulus–response mapping but nonlinear away from there, with complete failure to map at the ends of the narrow window that constitutes a sensory transmission channel. It is important to reiterate that Eqs. 4.1 and 4.2 are outside time. They tell us what would be the relation between S and R, suitably encoded numerically, after the process of judgment has come to a stop.[2] However, these equations say nothing about what pathway the system takes to achieve its stable mapping, with some attendant variation symbolized by the N, that is, the noise term in Eq. 4.2. They do not predict the ogival (or sigmoid) form but only what can be a part thereof, leaving out the extreme end ranges.

There have been many equations (of some function F) used to describe dynamics evolving through time in biological systems. Many of these equations exhibit chaos and bifurcating trajectories under appropriate conditions. One property that could be important in psychophysics, where the observer comes back repeatedly to some sort of relative stability after responding to a transient stimulus, is that of a snap-back repeller (Marotto, 1978). It can be shown that the existence of a trajectory that begins arbitrarily close to an unstable fixed point of the function F is repelled from this point as the gain increases (resulting, say, from an increase in stimulus intensity) but then suddenly snaps back precisely to this unstable fixed point. This property of the dynamics is sufficient to imply chaos. More recently it has been shown that some neural networks can embody snap-back trajectories (Zhou, Wang, Jing, & Wang, 2006). Bringing together these modeling features in one context is worth serious consideration in seeking dynamic representations of psychophysical processes.

The basic equation in nonlinear psychophysical dynamics (NPD; Gregson, 1988, 1992, 1995, 2006) is

$$\Gamma : Y_{j+1} = -a(Y_j - 1)(Y_j - ie)(Y_j + ie), i = \sqrt{-1} \qquad (4.3)$$

for given starting values Y_0 and fixed values of a and e. Y is the internal variable of the system that is never coupled directly to input levels of the stimulus S. S only acts directly on the gain parameter, a, to modify the dynamics of the Γ trajectory. It should be noted that Eq. 4.3 is a complex number recursion in Y_j. The variable Y is complex. The real part of Y, Re[Y] corresponds to R, and hence is externally observable. The imaginary part of Y, Im[Y], fluctuates differently and takes on a special role when we move to coupled multidimensional systems.

There are two linear mappings between which Γ is sandwiched: $S \rightarrow a$ and Re[Y_j] $\rightarrow R$. The series of Re[Y_j] and Im[Y_j] are called the *trajectory* of the process, $0 < x$Re[Y_j] < 1. To avoid degeneracy, chaotic dynamics or explosions, $2 < a < 5.5$, is a practical choice in exploratory modeling of real data. a serves the same role as S in Eqs. 4.1 and 4.2, and because e allows the form of the ogive to vary a little, we have called it a *sensitivity parameter*. Γ is a complex cubic polynomial, which is why it generates an ogival form, and its trajectories in time (the j variable) can be chaotic, as defined by a positive sign of the largest Lyapunov exponent.

There is no stochastic term in Γ. Instead of writing psychophysics as stochastic within a deterministic environment, the relationship is reversed, and we write the stochastic variation on a as linked to the environment and restrict such a process to a deterministic evolution within a sensory channel. The process stops with the value Re[Y_η], which can happen when the process is overwritten by a new value of a and hence of the current Y_0.

The Γ function can be represented by a map of terms of its Julia set, in the way that Mandelbrot pioneered for the logistic function, but with a variety of different shapes. The maps in the complex plane vary considerably as a function of the two parameters a and e (see Fig. 4.2). The response surface Re[Y] for various values of a and e is shown in Gregson (1998) under various conditions.[3]

The response surface has an escarpment, a feature that corresponds to a series of psychophysical functions of the sort that are sometimes modeled as a cumulative normal ogive. Any one psychophysical experiment yields a section plane through the surface's escarpment with a suitable choice of stimulus levels. This idea of experimental data being the realization of a section plane with *a priori* internal activity levels symbolized by Y is inherent in this representation.

The response surface or escarpment (Fig. 4.3) can be differentiated, each point having an altitude that can be replaced at that point by the steepest local gradient located there. This then constitutes a sensitivity surface (Fig. 4.4). The ridge is the locus of maximal sensitivity to small changes in stimulus input.

If we have a series of trials on each of which a stimulus from some related family is presented, then the Y_0 values will float, each depending on where the previous trial left off. The range and spacing in time of trials is crucial. Helson (1964) showed that if some stimuli are designated as reference or anchor values, then on any trial k, R_k is a function of three terms: anchors, context, and

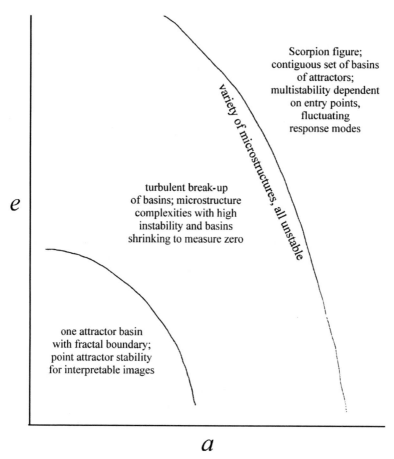

Figure 4.2. Plot of the complex plane: Fatou and Julia set shapes as a function of the two Γ parameters a and e.

the stimulus presented. Helson derived formulae for some special cases. These sequential effects are sometimes called assimilation or contrast.

Here they are partially modeled by putting $Y_{0,k} = f(Y_{\eta,k-1})$, that is, the starting value of Y on a trial is the terminal value of Y on the previous trial, not the original Y_0. Some alternative cases in the time series of psychophysics are diagrammed by Gregson (2006).

Transients

We use the term *transient* to refer to a brief episode within the evolution of a trajectory, recorded as a time series, in which there are two discontinuities, entering and leaving the transient. Within such a transient the dynamics are different in character. The simplest sort of transient, which has been studied in

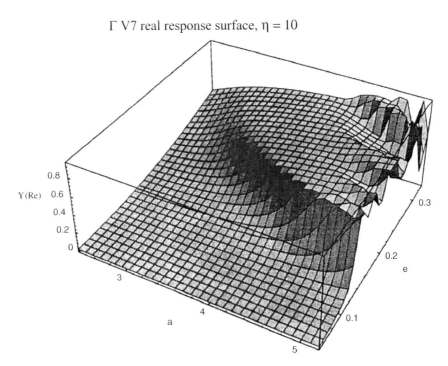

Figure 4.3. A perspective figure of the Γ escarpment over a range of *a* and *e* values.

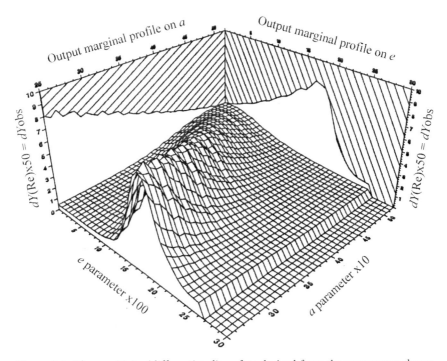

Figure 4.4. The sensitivity (differentiated) surface derived from the escarpment shown in Figure 4.3.

linear time series analysis, is a local shift in the mean. This can be caused by external interference or be intrinsic to the dynamics of the underlying process.

If the latter holds, then searching for external causes is a sterile exercise, but still a check that needs to be made. In psychophysical tasks executed over a long time, there can be short failures of attention or shifts in scale usage, as has been known, for example, in studies of sustained vigilance in radar operators.

Trajectories of attractors in nonlinear dynamics can exhibit not only bifurcations but also short embedded episodes that can resemble what in music are called arpeggios. A phrase with a recurrent form can be interpolated in the dynamics and may recur, but the lengths of intervals between the appearance of the phrase may themselves be randomly distributed, and hence stochastic.

If we allow for the presence of transients, then it is necessary to use as the generating equation of the psychophysics some nonlinear function that at least captures the qualitative appearance of the data. The Pomeau–Manneville scenario of transition to chaos is potentially relevant here (Manneville & Pomeau, 1980) when we consider also the phenomena of turbulence, a special sort of chaotic dynamics that was first characteristically found in hydraulics.

Hysteresis

Hysteresis is formally defined as the lagging of changes in an effect behind changes in its cause over time. It gives rise to what is called a hysteresis loop. The shape of that loop can be a valuable diagnostic tool in exploring the internal dynamics of a time series based on knowing both S and R terms in a psychophysical process.

Although it is carefully arranged in many psychological experiments (particularly in classical psychophysics) that a stimulus series is random; that is, one without autocorrelations, response sequences are frequently autocorrelated, at least over a short time span. Such autocorrelation gives rise to the contrast and assimilation phenomena already noted.

A hysteresis loop may be clockwise, the climbing branch being above, as shown by directional arrows in Figure 4.5, or counterclockwise, the climbing branch being below, the latter being the more usual. If the area within the loop can be entered by branches, the area of the loop can vary, and the rotation direction can be reversed. If the area in the loop cannot be entered, then a cusp catastrophe might be present in the dynamics. A empirical way to explore hysteresis is to present an autocorrelated time series of stimuli that has a slow sawtooth waveform (Gregson, 1983). This conveniently shows what happens at points where the input reverses direction and the hysteresis creates lags in the outputs that are not locally depicted as straight lines.

In nonlinear psychophysics, the hysteresis can be generated by serially coupling the Jth terminal Y_{Jn} to the next reset $(J + 1)^{th} Y_{(J+1)0}$ terms, so hysteresis can be taken as exploratory evidence of such coupling. Varying the rate of stimulus presentation can show whether the serial coupling is time dependent (the interstimulus interval is crucial) or time independent, and possibly only a

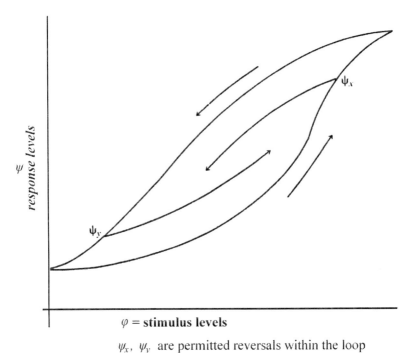

φ = **stimulus levels**

ψ_x, ψ_y are permitted reversals within the loop

Figure 4.5. A hysteresis loop showing possible reentry with truncation on the stimulus range. From Gregson (1983), *Time Series in Psychology*, with permission of Taylor and Francis.

function of the stimulus levels themselves. There are huge differences in serial effects if we compare sensory modalities. For example, vision can have after-images, whereas the chemical senses can have long-lasting masking effects.

The instability of hysteresis, in terms of the direction of travel around the loop and the area within the loop, is well displayed in tasks that induce a conflict between motion and nonmotion perception (Hock & Ploeger 2006). The two systems may be set in conflict, and each has its own psychophysical parameters.

None of these hysteresis phenomena can be derived from the static modeling of the ogive, even though each part of the hysteresis loop is itself a somewhat distorted ogive. This situation arises because sequential effects between stimulus inputs are not represented in the error function approach to deriving the ogive. However, one example of hysteresis that is derived from the predictions of an adaptive accumulator model is given by Vickers and Lee (1998, Fig. 3, p. 187).

Dimensions in Parallel

The traditional psychophysical models are created for single sensory dimensions. Extension to multidimensional mixed inputs requires some fundamental augmentation of the algebra. In NPD theory, the treatment of two-dimensional

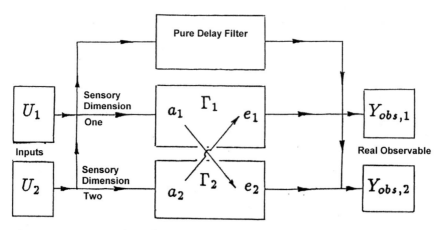

Figure 4.6. Cross-coupling of two dimensions in the 2Γ model.

sensory systems follows from a relatively simple cross-coupling of two replications of the basic equation, which we will call 2Γ.

A 2Γ process is by definition the evolution of two complex cubic polynomials in parallel (Fig. 4.6). In the Case 2 dynamics, they are cross-coupled. At any step j in their evolution in time, the state of the total trajectory can be summarized by a 22 matrix of the form

$$Y_{(2\Gamma, j)} = \begin{bmatrix} \mathrm{Re}[Y_{1,j}] & \mathrm{Im}[Y_{1,j}] \\ \mathrm{Re}[Y_{2,j}] & \mathrm{Im}[Y_{2,j}] \end{bmatrix}. \tag{4.4}$$

A multichannel situation requires $n\Gamma$ theory that has, in Case 2, interaction between channels (Gregson, 1992). Case 1 is the name reserved for situations in which parallel channels do not interact, this being a special and relatively rare restricted case. The local occurrence of phenomena such as a cusp is not predictable from two uncoupled Γ processes, neither of which independently exhibits bifurcations within the parameter range used to model the normal range of psychophysical data. So consideration of the cross-coupled form is immediately pertinent. I now define that 2Γ process.

Let the two dimensions be labeled h, w. The notation may be read as a mnemonic for h(eight) and w(idth) when viewing rectangles, but the algebra is quite general.[4]

The total within-loop $\mathrm{Im}[Y]$ level at any recursion step $1 < j < \eta$ is taken to be the union of the component parts, so in each cycle j, the two $\mathrm{Im}[Y]$ terms are replaced by the term

$$\mathrm{Im}[Y_{hw,j}] = \max\{\mathrm{Im}[Y_{h,j}], \mathrm{Im}[Y_{w,j}]\}. \tag{4.5}$$

Because the imaginary components of Y go into limit cycling more readily (that is, at lower system parameter values) than their real counterparts, the effect of Eq. 4.5 will depend crucially on the set of values (a_h, a_w, e_h, e_w) (Campbell & Gregson, 1990). Then define

$$Y^*_{w,j} = (\text{Re}[Y_{w,j}], \text{Im}[Y_{hw,j}]) \qquad (4.6)$$

and an analogous expression for $Y^*_{h,j}$.

The e terms in Eq. 4.3 are made to be functions of the a terms in the opposing dimension. This may be seen as a process of mutual inhibition (or excitation, depending on the relative levels of the components). Each dimension is desensitized to differences, δa, in its own input as the input to the other dimension is increased, namely:

$$e_h = \lambda_h \bullet a_w^{-1} \qquad (4.7)$$

$$e_w = \lambda_w \bullet a_h^{-1}, \qquad (4.8)$$

where $\lambda_h > 0$, $\lambda_w > 0$, and $2.6 < a_{min} < 4.4$ is a working range for $0.05 < e < 0.40$. Approximately setting $0.20 < \lambda < 1.2$ will avoid the explosive condition of $ae > 1.7$ (Gregson, 1988, chapter 2).

An advantage of writing Eqs. 4.7 and 4.8 is that in some cases, the number of parameters in the model can be reduced by one, e_h and e_w are removed, and λ is introduced with $\lambda_h = \lambda_w = \lambda$. Expanding Eq. 4.3 for each dimension now yields for h

$$Y_{h,j+1} = -a_h \left(Y^*_{h,j} - 1\right)\left(Y^*_{h,j} - i\lambda_h a_w^{-1}\right)\left(Y^*_{h,j} + i\lambda_h a_w^{-1}\right) \qquad (4.9)$$

and correspondingly for w

$$Y_{w,j+1} = -a_w \left(Y^*_{w,j} - 1\right)\left(Y^*_{w,j} - i\lambda_w a_h^{-1}\right)\left(Y^*_{w,j} + i\lambda_w a_h^{-1}\right) \qquad (4.10)$$

if the two λ terms are allowed to be unequal. Otherwise Eqs. 4.9 and 4.10 simplify. The Case 2 Γ model with unequal λ has been used to fit an apparently paradoxical finding in line bisection during visuospatial neglect (Gregson, 2000).

The evolution of these two coupled trajectories through time (over j) depends for their numerical values on the initial parameters $Y_{h,0}$ and $Y_{w,0}$ and the Γ parameters a_h, a_w, λ_h, and λ_w. Whether the trajectories are in the Fatou set or the Julia set of the system determines the extent of the sensitivity to initial conditions. Whereas the Julia set contains the set of points that diverge from their original positions under repeated application of the recursion, the Fatou set contains the complementary set of points that remain invariant under such an iterated perturbation.

Higher-order mixtures, those with more than two components, are commonly found in everyday life, but no single model could wisely be advanced to cover all sensory modalities. Musical chords, perfumes, and color mosaics all produce sensory psychophysics that are in some way peculiar to, even becoming defining characteristics of, a modality. Nonlinear interactions between components, masking and enhancement, can occur (Gregson, 1968). After-images in vision have their analogues in other senses. In taste, for example, we have at least four ways in which mixtures may behave: (a) interactions of two or more suprathreshold tastes in terms of the relative intensity of other components (Kamen, Pilgram, Gutman, & Kroll, 1961), (b) changes in absolute thresholds due to the presence of other subthreshold tastes, (c) changes in the absolute threshold of one primary taste (sweet, acid, bitter, salty) in the presence of another suprathreshold primary, or (d) simulation of natural tastes, such as raspberry, by mixtures of synthetic primaries.

Extensions to Networks

An example of how interaction between adjacent pixels occurs in a network where each pixel holds the evolution of a Γ recursion can be illustrated by a familiar visual illusion. If we close up the spacing vertically and horizontally of the four black squares shown below, a gray patch will appear at the central intersection of the two white channels between the patches. This pattern also induces a complex contour plot at the intersection in a $(n \times n)\Gamma$ network (Gregson, 1995), of which one version is shown below the black squares (Fig. 4.7). The creation of nets with each element having a Γ recursion within it, and coupling to its immediate neighbors, has been named $(n \times n)\Gamma$ (Gregson, 1995). It produces patterns that are more commonly thought to be perceptual, but this intermediate stage between sensation and perception is called *apperception* by some theorists. The squares depicted here may need to be brought closer together to get the full phenomenological effect.

The interaction between one pixel and its nearest dominant neighbor from the eight that surround it resembles what is called a Moore neighborhood in spatial game theory (Nowak, 2006, p. 147). Spatial game theory, as its name suggests, is a blending of game theory and cellular automata. As Nowak shows, it leads to some beautiful and complex patterns, resembling Persian carpet designs, and can handle a two-dimensional version of the familiar Prisoners' Dilemma game. This $(n \times n)\Gamma$ extension leads into complex and sometimes chaotic pattern generation when any given pixel can be categorized as cooperating with or defecting from its neighbors. There are also parallels with evolution theory and population competition dynamics that have been explored mathematically (May, 1973).

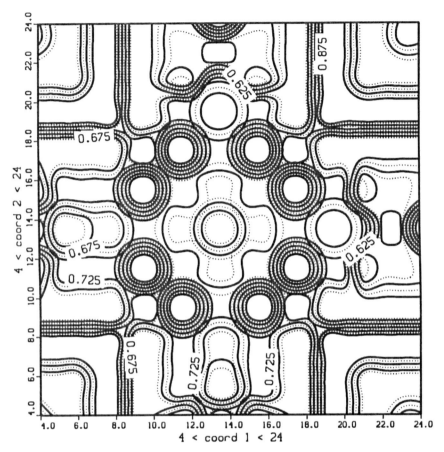

Figure 4.7. Induced $(n \times n)\Gamma$ contours in a 5×5 region at the intersection of four squares, from the methods of Gregson (1995).

Fast and Slow Dynamics

Some biological processes exhibit a mixture of both fast and slow dynamic evolution of trajectories, and the two may interact. This principle is not represented in classical psychophysics, unless implicitly the residual error term in Eq. 4.2 is taken to map any fast but second-order low-amplitude dynamics. In simulations of Eq. 4.3, however, the imaginary component of Y may be seen to oscillate rapidly, whereas the real component has a relatively smooth evolution as the input level, a, is increased. The problem in identifying internal psychophysical dynamics is that externally input noise itself may be evolving at a relatively higher frequency than a series of deterministic stimulus inputs that it partly obscures and cannot readily be separated from a fast component of the internal dynamics that is already present, autonomous, and not itself noise.

The Existence of Inverses

A psychophysical function gives us the elicited response, as a probability or a deterministic value, from a given stimulus that has been encoded symbolically. The inverse would be the expected stimulus that could, with maximum likelihood, elicit the observed response. In the most commonly used representations of the psychophysical function, the Gaussian, Weibull, or Logistic models (Gilchrist, Jerwood & Ismaiel, 2005), the mapping is single-valued in the reals, and the inverse is readily defined.

In NPD, we have a complex function as the kernel, and the inverse may be not a function but a functional; that is, a class of inverses may nearly always exist. That is, there is not one (perhaps noisy) inverse solution, but a set of mathematically acceptable alternatives and insufficient data in a real experiment of finite length to choose between them. The inverse problem has been discussed by Gregson (1992, p. 255 et seq.), but the general problem of when inverses exist and when they do not is one that requires consideration of more advanced mathematics. The issue plays a central role in nonlinear iterative dynamics and is reviewed in detail by Barnsley (2006).

If Eq. 4.2 is accepted, then a possible inverse would be, where the noise distribution may be different from the original in some details,

$$aS^b = R + N'(\mu, \sigma). \tag{4.11}$$

This could be essayed as a model of such phenomena as pitch identification, moving from hearing to writing down musical notation. The problem with inverses of NPD is that there will be a family of inverses, not one.

The existence of local singularities in psychophysical data is readily postulated to arise in nonlinear dynamics. However, actually confirming that the forms of real data do involve any singularities, which look like abrupt sharp jumps, as opposed to local high values of the derivatives, raises problems. Contextual effects arising from properties of frames of reference can create local discontinuities in the psychophysics of discrimination tasks (Simmering, Spencer, & Schöner, 2006, p. 1031) and induce local second-order irregularities in the ogival function.

As Thompson and Stewart (1986, p. 261) observed, "the behavior at a single mathematically precise value of a control is unlikely to be observed in any real dynamical system. From this point of view, it is preferable to exclude removable discontinuities from consideration, so that the transcritical bifurcation becomes a continuous one." From this standpoint, it is wiser to postulate canards than to postulate cusps when psychophysical data are involved. Amari, Park, and Ozeki (2006) reviewed the serious problems that the presence of singularities creates for modeling perceptual processes.

Under some conditions in discrete time, a sinusoidal mapping with both stable and unstable points can be derived (Magnitskii & Sidorov, 2006, p. 196) and shown in what is called a Lamerey diagram. Such a dynamical system is invertible because it is one-dimensional and strictly monotonic, so there are some nonlinear systems that have bifurcations, as well as limit cycles that can be born or vanish and still in theory be invertible. Psychophysical functions, and some ogives from dynamics as listed earlier, are not strictly monotonic at or beyond an upper limit, so inversion only obtains within a restricted range corresponding to near-average stimulus inputs.

Variations in Response-Time Durations

The interest in the time taken to make a response goes back to the nineteenth century; in earlier work, all that was available was an eternally observable sensory stimulus and a motor response of some sort. Attempts to separate the physiological component of response times (RT), variously also called response latencies or reaction times, from a decision component were not convincing. A resurgence of interest in RTs in the 1950s prompted examination of sequential, or trial-to-trial, correlational effects, which now can lead naturally into models of nonlinear dynamics.

There are other important reasons to use RTs as indices of cognitive function, because they provide measures of individual differences in personality, fatigue, stress, brain damage, and psychopathologies (Welford, 1980). Potential links between the use of psychophysical methods and clinical psychology are valuable in part because they help demonstrate the underlying dynamics of normal and abnormal behavior.

With modern developments in cognitive neuroscience, it is now possible, using electroencephalograms, functional magnectic resonance imaging, and other recordings of brain activity, to record the onset and duration of brain events that mediate the overt Stimulus-Response (S-R) relationships and their elapsing durations. Operations in the brain that affect RTs can, for example, in some cases be localized to the intraparietal sulcus (Göbel, Johansen-berg, Behrens, & Rushworth, 2004). That additional information can provide checks on the plausibility of mathematical assumptions about how the RTs are generated. Developments in neural network theory have added more mathematical approaches to the description of information flow between perception and action (Klyubin, Polani, & Nehaniv, 2007). Without that additional information, the modeling is what in systems theory is called a black-box model.

The methods for estimating RTs vary, and three paradigms need to be described.

1. A sequence of four events, on any one of a series of trials, is a warning signal (W); then, after a variable time duration (VT) under the experimenter's control, a stimulus (S) of variable duration; then, after the RT, a response (R); then a terminating signal (E) to show that the trial

is finished. If no response is made, or response is delayed too long, E precedes R. The use of W with VT is to make it possible to detect false anticipatory responses to S. In earlier work, blank trials were interposed and called trick-stimuli (in German, *Vexierversuchen*) for this purpose.

2. Sequence 1, but with two different S_1 and S_2 in immediate succession. The task is for R to select in which successive part of the sequence a nominated S is present. The task is called 2AFC (a two-alternative forced choice) paradigm and is preferred in some studies of signal detection (Estes & Taylor, 1964). It clearly involves an additional layer of decision processing.

3. A psychophysical method of production to check on time estimation processes. A time interval, $S_1 S_2$, is presented, and then the subject replicates this as S_1 R. The task is to match the duration of the two intervals. This process convolutes the estimation of time and the RT delays.

In all three paradigms, we have (a) speed of response R observed at a point in time, (b) correctness, or accuracy in precision, for detection in Sequence 1, identification in Sequence 2, or estimation in Sequence 3, and (c) subjective confidence of accuracy of response. The relationships between (a), (b), and (c) are variable; speed of response is not necesssarily simply associated with the accuracy in tasks based on Sequences 2 and 3. Ratcliff (1978, p. 96) suggested that confidence may be assumed to be an inverse function of the time required to reach a decision, but Vickers and Packer (1982) showed this to be empirically false. A ubiquitous finding is the time-conditioned RT-difference effect, which states that errors are quicker than correct responses in speeded tasks, whereas errors take longer than correct responses when either accurate responding is required or the perceptual discrimination is difficult (Luce, 1986).

In the case in which the duration of stimulus exposure is variable and under the control of the observer, not the experimenter, and the discriminability is held constant, both the probability of a correct response and the confidence are inversely related to the time taken. A review of these complicated results with regard to the relationships between confidence and performance is given by Vickers and Lee (1998). For simple judgments, as in Sequence 1, the important development of accumulator models (La Berge, 1962; Vickers, 1970; Vickers & Lee, 1998) evolved because of the demonstrated inadequacy of models that are elaborations of a random walk.

Heath (2000, p. 302) provided an example of a two-dimensional coupled cubic recursion given by

$$x(t+1) = x(t)[a_1(t) - b_1(t)y^2(t) - d_1(t)x^2(t)] \qquad (4.12)$$

$$y(t+1) = y(t)[a_2(t) - b_2(t)x^2(t) - d_2(t)y^2(t)]. \qquad (4.13)$$

This pair of equations is a nonlinear, cubic, one-step recursion and is in two dimensions, so it resembles the complex form of the Γ model in that sense. As t

increases, the vector $z(t) = (x[t], y[t])$ approaches either the origin $(0,0)$ or an ellipse, the major axes of which depend on the stimulus parameters. It is possible to show that such a model predicts shorter error RTs when the critical distance between successive $z(t)$ values is large and longer error RTs when compared with correct RTs when the critical distance between successive $z(t)$ values is small. This result is consistent qualitatively with the literature on two-choice responding (Ratcliff & Rouder, 1998).

Consistent with the idea of using a deterministic nonlinear process for information acquisition (Brown & Heathcote, 2005), an interesting nonlinear model that can predict RT data as well as relative response frequencies proposes a nonlinear recursion, such as that represented by Eq. 4.3 for a single decision, or some coupled nonlinear recursion such as Eqs. 4.9 and 4.10. The only requirement of such a model is that its dynamics converge on an attractor region as the process evolves. The response elicited is that associated with the attractor region to which the nonlinear process converges after sufficient iterations. There may be several attractor regions, and their associated response choices depend on both the nature of the nonlinear system and its internal parameters.

It was interesting to note that some of the phase plots from Experiment 1 of Kelly, Heathcote, Heath, and Longstaff (2001) had the appearance of the chaotic Lorenz attractor with its two clear lobes with a crossover point in between. Heathcote and Elliott (2005) showed that nonlinearity in noisy attractors of the Lorenz type can be detected using prediction analysis, as was shown to be useful in detecting nonlinearity in the RT series presented in Kelly et al. (2001). Such detection of nonlinearity can occur even when there is no filtering of the original RT series and even when up to 80% Gaussian noise is added to the Lorenz time series.

It is not uniformly easy to demonstrate the presence of nonlinear dynamics in RT tasks. The induced cognitive set of a speed–accuracy trade-off can induce a local simple linearity, and the use of task Sequence 3 (production matching of time intervals) mixes up two sorts of time processing. The important findings of Eisler and Eisler (1992) on breaks in the perception of time intervals indicate that short and long intervals are processed differently, and so data analysis should separate them out when looking for evidence of nonlinear dynamics in the judgment process elicited. The parallels between 2Γ and Eqs. 4.12 and 4.13 are interesting because both are cubic and embody some cross-linkage but have not been explored in terms of their relative fit to data.

Conclusion

The biologist Richard Dawkins insightfully observed that our brains had evolved to navigate and survive through an environment that is about the same scale as ourselves. We do not perceive events at the molecular level. We cannot, unlike some butterflies, detect the presence of the odor of another of our species from more than a kilometer away. Through language, we share details of experiences.

From later-developed technologies and mathematics, we have become symbiotes with our augmentations that extend the range of our senses. This capacity for symbiosis is what in part makes us uniquely human. First there were telescopes and now there are electron microscopes, and we can now receive radio by converting it to sound at levels we can tolerate. We can only safely respond to environments that have strong autocorrelation through time. A perfectly stable environment induces ganzfeld phenomena followed by sensory deprivation. A completely random environment is incomprehensible and so accident-prone as eventually to be lethal. The brain models the outside world, after learning through the senses, with sufficient fidelity for us in turn to manipulate it. We are in almost continuous feedback with the world at our scale. The dynamics of feedback and self-correction are what underlie psychophysics, not merely simple copying of some of the selected properties of our immediate environment. Nonlinear psychophysics aims to model what is a flexible but approximate system and capture both its transitory features and its endless capacity for resetting its internal parameters. It can only do this by drawing on the mathematics of complexity.

Notes

1. The ogival curve was of interest well before its role in Gaussian error functions. The English artist Hogarth, in his own portrait, engraved as a frontispiece to his works in 1745, drew a serpentine line on his palette and denominated it *the line of beauty*. In 1753 he published a treatise titled *The Analysis of Beauty* to show that the line of beauty is serpentine.
2. Guastello (2006, p. 95) used an ogival form as a representation of a speed–accuracy trade-off. This is legitimate but does not derive from classical psychophysics. According to Ratcliff's diffusion model, variability in the stimulus representation from trial to trial produces a speed–accuracy trade-off function that asymptotes at a fixed accuracy level as time increases.
3. The map in the complex plane of the Γ recursion, showing its Julia set, is illustrated on the cover of Gregson (2006). It is not the familiar Mandelbrot set, which is rather based on the logistic equation. All maps of Julia sets in the complex plane have a family resemblance, but the cubic recursions are more intricate. The maps provide additional evidence of fractal dynamics.
4. The 2Γ model has found application and conformity to some data properties in the perception of rectangles (Eisler, Eisler, & Gregson, 1995), for which the existence of a local singularity has been predicted and found, and in tactile perception (Mahar, 2005), in which its improved fit compared with a linear model was found. Similarity judgments may also be modeled (Gregson, 1994) using NPD. Its original development was for the psychophysics of odor mixtures (Gregson, 1992).

References

Amari, S., Park, H., & Ozeki, T. (2006). Singularities affect dynamics of learning in neuromanifolds. *Neural Computation, 18*, 1007–1065.

An der Heiden, U. (1980). *Analysis of neural networks* (Lecture Notes in Biomathematics, Vol. 35). Berlin: Springer-Verlag.

Barnsley, M. F. (2006). *Superfractals: Patterns of nature*. Cambridge: Cambridge University Press.

Beck, J. M., & Pouget, A. (2007). Exact inferences in a neural implementation of a hidden Markov model. *Neural Computation, 19*, 1344–1361.

Bontempi, F., & Casciati, F. (1994). Chaotic motion and stochastic excitation. *Nonlinear Dynamics, 6*, 179–191.

Brown, S., & Heathcote, A. (2005). A ballistic model of choice response time. *Psychological Review, 112*, 117–128.

Campbell, E. A., & Gregson, R. A. M. (1990). Julia sets for the Gamma recursion in nonlinear psychophysics. *Acta Applicandae Mathematicae, 20*, 177–188.

Carleson, L., & Gamelin, T. W. (2007). *Complex dynamics*. New York: Springer.

Coombs, C. H. (1964). *A theory of data*. New York: Wiley.

Eisler, H., & Eisler, A. D. (1992). Time perception: Effects of sex and sound intensity on scales of subjective duration. *Scandinavian Journal of Psychology, 33*, 339–358.

Eisler, H., Eisler, A. D., & Gregson, R. A. M. (1995). A cusp in the subjective width of rectangles. In G. Neely (Ed.), *Perception and psychophysics in theory and application* (pp. 147–153). Stockholm: Stockholm University.

Estes, W. K., & Taylor, H. A. (1964). A detection method and probabilistic models for assessing information processing from brief visual displays. *Proceedings of the National Academy of Sciences, 52*, 446–454.

Falmagne, J.-C. (1985). *Elements of psychophysical theory*. Oxford: Oxford University Press.

Fechner, G. T. (1860). *Elemente der psychophysik*. Leipzig: Breitkopf & Härtel. (First part only translated by H. E. Adler, 1965.)

Gilchrist, J. M., Jerwood, D., & Ismaiel, H. S. (2005). Comparing and unifying slope estimates across psychometric function models. *Perception and Psychophysics, 67*, 1289–1303.

Göbel, S. M., Johansen-berg, H., Behrens, T., & Rushworth, M. F. S. (2004). Response–selection-related parietal activation during number comparison. *Journal of Cognitive Neuroscience, 16*, 136–155.

Gregson, R. A. M. (1968). Simulating perceived similarities between taste mixtures with mutually interacting components. *British Journal of Mathematical and Statistical Psychology, 21*, 31–44.

Gregson, R. A. M. (1983). *Time series in psychology*. Hillsdale, NJ: Erlbaum.

Gregson, R. A. M. (1988). *Nonlinear psychophysical dynamics*. Hillsdale, NJ: Erlbaum.

Gregson, R. A. M. (1992). *n-Dimensional nonlinear psychophysics*. Hillsdale, NJ: Erlbaum.

Gregson, R. A. M. (1994). Similarities derived from 3-d nonlinear psychophysics: Variance distributions. *Psychometrika, 59*, 97–110.

Gregson, R. A. M. (1995). *Cascades and fields in perceptual psychophysics*. Singapore: World Scientific.

Gregson, R. A. M. (1998). Effects of random noise and internal delay in nonlinear psychophysics. *Nonlinear Dynamics, Psychology, and Life Sciences, 2*, 73–93.

Gregson, R. A. M. (2000). Magnitude estimations for line bisection under lateral visuospatial neglect. *Nonlinear Dynamics, Psychology, and Life Sciences, 42*, 219–223.

Gregson, R. A. M. (2001). Responses to constrained stimulus sequences in nonlinear psychophysics. *Nonlinear Dynamics, Psychology, and Life Sciences, 5*, 205–222.

Gregson, R. A. M. (2006). *Informative psychometric filters.* Canberra: Australian National University Press.

Guastello, S. J. (2006). *Human factors engineering and ergonomics.* Mahwah, NJ: Erlbaum.

Guilford, J. P. (1954). *Psychometric methods.* New York: McGraw Hill.

Heath, R. A. (2000). *Nonlinear dynamics: Techniques and applications in psychology.* Mahwah, NJ: Erlbaum.

Heathcote, A., & Elliott, D. (2005). Nonlinear dynamical analysis of noisy time series. *Nonlinear Dynamics in Psychology and Life Sciences, 9*, 399–434.

Helson, H. (1964). *Adaptation-level theory.* New York: Harper and Rowe.

Hock, H. S., & Ploeger, A. (2006). Linking dynamical perceptual decisions at different levels of description in motion pattern formation: Psychophysics. *Perception and Psychophysics, 68*, 503–514.

Kamen, J. M., Pilgrim, F. J., Gutman, N. J., & Kroll, B. J. (1961). Interaction of suprathreshold taste stimuli. *Journal of Experimental Psychology, 62*, 348–456.

Kelly, A., Heathcote, A., Heath, R., & Longstaff, M. (2001). Response-time dynamics: Evidence for linear and low-dimensional nonlinear structure in human choice sequences. *Quarterly Journal of Experimental Psychology, 54*, 805–840.

Klyubin, A. S., Polani, D., & Nehaniv, C. L. (2007). Repesentations of space and time in the maximization of information flow in the perception-action loop. *Neural Computation, 19*, 2387–2432.

La Berge, D. (1962). A recruitment theory of simple behaviour. *Psychometrika, 27*, 376–396.

Laming, D. (1986). *Sensory analysis.* London: Academic Press.

Luce, R. D. (1986). *Response times: Their role in inferring elementary mental organization.* New York: Oxford University Press.

Magnitskii, N. A., & Sidorov, S. V. (2006). *New methods for chaotic dynamics* (World Scientific Series in Nonlinear Science, Vol. A 58). River Edge. NJ: World Scientific.

Mahar, D. (2005). The psychophysics of tactile amplitude summation. A test of the $n\Gamma$ nonlinear model. *Nonlinear Dynamics, Psychology, and Life Sciences, 9*, 281–296.

Manneville, P., & Pomeau, Y. (1980). Different ways to turbulence in dissipative dynamical systems. *Physica D, 1*, 219–225.

Marotto, F. R. (1978). Snapback repellers imply chaos in R^n. *Journal of Mathematical Analysis and Applications, 63*, 199–223.

May, R. M. (1973). *Stability and complexity in model ecosystems.* Princeton, NJ: Princeton University Press.

McBurney, D. H., & Collings, V. B. (1984). *Introduction to sensation/perception* (2nd ed.). Englewood Cliffs, NJ: Prentice Hall.

Migler, T. A., Morrison, K. E., & Ogle, M. (2006). How much does a matrix of rank k weigh? *Mathematics Magazine, 79*, 262–271.

Mira, C. (2006). Fractal sets from noninvertible maps. In M. M. Novak (Ed.), *Complexus mundi: Emergent patterns of nature* (pp. 83–102). New Jersey: World Scientific.

Motter, A. E., Zhou, C., & Kurths, J. (2005). Weighted networks are more synchronizable: How and why. In J. F. F. Mendes, S. N. Dorogovtsev, A. Povolotsky, F. V. Abreu, & J. G. Oliveira (Eds.), *Science of complex networks: From biology to the Internet and WWW* (pp. 201–214). New York: American Institute of Physics.

Nizami, L. (2006). The intensity-difference limen for 6.5 kHz: An even more severe departure from Weber's law. *Perception and Psychophysics, 68*, 1107–1112.

Nowak, M. A. (2006). *Evolutionary dynamics: Exploring the equations of life.* Cambridge, MA: Harvard University Press.

Pfanzagl, J. (1968). *Theory of measurement.* Würzburg: Physica-Verlag.

Ratcliff, R. (1978). A theory of memory retrieval. *Psychological Review, 85*, 59–108.

Ratcliff, R., & Rouder, J. N. (1998). Modeling response times for two choice decisions. *Psychological Science, 9*, 347–356.

Schuster, H. G. (1984). *Deterministic chaos.* Weinheim: Physik-Verlag.

The Shorter Oxford English Dictionary (3rd ed., with corrections). (1985). Oxford: Clarendon Press.

Simmering, V. R., Spencer, J. P., & Schöner, G. (2006). Reference-related inhibition produces enhanced position discrimination and faster repulsion near axes of symmetry. *Perception and Psychophysics, 68*, 1027–1046.

Stevens, S. S. (1951). Mathematics, measurement and psychophysics. In S. S. Stevens (Ed.), *Handbook of experimental psychology* (pp. 1–51). New York: Wiley.

Thompson, J. M. T., & Stewart, H. B. (1986). *Nonlinear dynamics and chaos.* Chichester: Wiley.

Titchener, E. B. (1895). *Outlines of psychology by Oswald Külpe.* New York: Macmillan.

Vickers, D. (1970). Evidence for an accumulator model of psychophysical discrimination. *Ergonomics, 13*, 37–58.

Vickers, D., & Lee, M. D. (1998). Dynamic models of simple judgments: I. Properties of a self-regulating accumulator module. *Nonlinear Dynamics, Psychology, and Life Sciences, 2*, 169–194.

Vickers, D., & Packer, J. S. (1982). Efects of alternating set for speed or accuracy on response time, accuracy, and self-confidence in a unidimensional discrimination task. *Acta Psychologica, 50*, 179–197.

Walsh, J. A. (2006). Surprising dynamics from a simple model. *Mathematics Magazine, 79*, 327–339.

Welford, A. T. (Ed.). (1980). *Reaction times.* London: Academic Press.

Woodworth, R. S. (1938). *Experimental psychology.* New York: Henry Holt & Co.

Zhou, Z., Wang, J., Jing, Z., & Wang, R. (2006). Complex dynamical behaviors in discrete-time recurrent neural networks with asymmetric connection matrix. *International Journal of Bifurcation and Chaos, 16*, 2221–2233.

5 Temporal and Spatial Patterns in Perceptual Behavior: Implications for Dynamical Structure

DEBORAH J. AKS

Introduction

Perception and action are continuously changing processes unfolding in space and time. Their seamless coordination with the surrounding environment gives the impression that they are part of a unitary system efficiently integrating incoming sensory information with prior experience. Critical to understanding such fluid systems is the need to learn how behavioral patterns evolve over time, are time-dependent, and how they scale (assume a particular proportionality or nonproportional relation) with their surrounding context. Moreover, we need to learn how internal states and external conditions modify these patterns so that even dramatic shifts in behavior can be explained by a common mechanism. Nonlinear dynamical systems (NDS) theory and its tools offer the means to study such ever-changing systems. The aim here is to illustrate the relevance of NDS to perceptual and related cognitive–motor problems using visual search as a working example. I also hope to show how the use of NDS tools can escape some of the impasses of traditional cognitive approaches. Although perceptual behavior is the focus here, the logic and theory extend to all forms of behavior, with the presumption that sensation, perception, and cognition lie on a continuum of a common mental system, one that is emergent from the complex short- and long-range interactions across neural ensembles of the human brain.

Varela (1999) provided a vivid account of the flowlike nature of perception, its dynamical emergence and reciprocal interaction with brain, body, and environment (Varela, Thompson, & Rosch, 1991). This view matches closely the theoretical framework outlined here: a dynamic perceptual–motor system *embedded* and strongly influenced by environmental forces. Like Tononi and Edelman's (1998) extended dynamic core stressing dynamical fluctuations, I emphasize both the ebb and flow of perceptual behavior however, to mark the importance of the system's natural variability over time, as opposed to assigning prominence to the continuity of perceptual processing (cf. Spivey, 2007). The *behavioral pattern* defines what is fundamental to perception, and these are both continuous and relatively discrete in form. Together these constitute the *patterns of information* driving human perception and cognitive behavior. Exactly what these are remains an open question, as is knowing what may be the most effective way to find answers. After careful consideration and questioning of various methods, including common general linear models (GLM), a compelling case can be made for a dynamical systems approach to understanding the forces that shape our mind and drive our behavior.

Shifts to the NDS Paradigm

Many researchers have called into question the information obtained from conventional experiments and GLM analyses in cognitive research (e.g., for reviews, see Gilden, 2001; Sornette, 2004; Van Orden, Holden, & Turvey, 2005), with some reminding us of the consequences of the *framing problem* in experimentation (e.g., Carello & Moreno, 2005). To solve any problem, it is necessary to work within some coherent framework to provide a context from which to study. However, an inevitable cost is bias. Thus when driven by our assumptions, and framing drives our analyses, we may miss out on subtle patterns of behavior that may be signatures of fundamental processes. Many of these patterns we now understand from NDS theory and research (e.g., Beer, 2000; Buzsáki, 2006; Freeman, 1991, 2001; Gilden, 2001; Gilden, Thornton, & Mallon, 1995; Kelso, 1995; Skarda & Freeman, 1987; Ward, 2002). The field appears to be at a tipping point (Shelhamer, 2006), with increasingly dire calls for change (e.g., Spivey, 2007; Werner, 2006, 2007). Thanks to increasingly legitimate research and efforts to distill some of the more complicated mathematics, NDS is finally penetrating mainstream areas of cognitive science (Spivey, 2007).

Many studies now focus on time as a critical variable in the investigation of human perceptual behavior (e.g., Ögmen & Breitmeyer, 2006). Perhaps most telling are shifts in mainstream experimental jargon; for example, reference to behavioral "dynamics" is now commonplace in the literature. The term "homeodynamics" has replaced "homeostasis" in some biologically oriented circles to capture the constantly changing intersystem and symbiotic interactions fundamental to complex life, as well as the emergence of mental phenomena (Yates, 1994). Also, "epochs" have usurped experimental "blocks" in most experimental psychology circles, denoting a series of trials grouped together in time during which a percept is being formed. These changes in terminology represent implicit acknowledgment of the central role of dynamics and dynamical "recurrence" in mental processing (e.g., Edelman & Tononi, 2000).

A sampling of recent empirical studies illustrates how NDS can provide a parsimonious account of how unique behaviors, with a common mechanism, emerge under a wide range of conditions. As in standard experimentation, manipulation of conditions (or control parameters) remains critical. However, the goal has shifted from understanding simple cause-and-effect relations to learning about system dynamics. Such an approach has the potential to lead to a general theory of perceptual–cognitive behavior encapsulating context-specific behaviors into a broader framework.

One may begin with the common assumption that behavioral variability across experimental trials is independent and identically distributed (IID). Although such IID properties of the central limit theorem are well proven and robust under a wide variety of circumstances (i.e., when a system's components are truly independent), there are many demonstrations to the contrary (e.g., Carello & Moreno, 2005; Gilden et al., 1995; Shelhamer, 2005a, 2005b, 2006; Ward, 2002). Given the accumulation of illustrations of trial-to-trial dependencies, perhaps researchers should be asking some new questions such as the following: Under what conditions do IID properties emerge? What is their source? Are the shapes of our distributed data due to intrinsic psychological factors or to constraints induced by our experiments? If we restructure experimental constraints, do our probability distribution functions (PDFs) change from Gaussian to power laws (or other long-tailed) distributions, or vice versa? What models are best at describing these changes? And what are the implications?

Similar questions arise when we consider the connection between the human tendency to categorize the world and behavioral theory's attempts to explain various phenomena: Are discrete processes an accurate description of natural behavior, or a consequence of our experimental tests? In our enthusiasm to learn about the influence of independent variables on our perceptual–cognitive system, are we losing important information about the intrinsic properties of this system? Thus the rigorous controls used in "proper" experimental design may play a significant role in producing data with GLM properties. Randomization of conditions, for example, abolishes order effects, along with intrinsic dependencies. Thus to uncover intrinsic dynamics, it is necessary to minimize artificial constraints likely to interrupt temporal dependencies and their resulting scaling and skewing effects.

There are numerous other examples of how rigorous laboratory manipulation can distort intrinsic dynamics or produce discrete behaviors. We see this in studies of *perceptual masking*, in which one percept may interfere with another because information is systematically blocked at different time courses of the stimulus-response sequence: just before (forward masking), during, and after (backward masking). Various interesting (ordinal and figural) illusions are produced, along with much theorizing that perceptual changes are manifestations of separate perceptual mechanisms (e.g., Ögmen & Breitmeyer, 2006). Although these provide helpful clues as to the time course and phenomenology of perceptual processing, (typical) judgments in these studies are inferred from manual responses only after the sequence of manipulations has occurred. Thus we may ask ourselves: Are observed changes in perceptual behavior driven by *discrete-sequential* (information processing) *stages*, or discrete-sequential *manipulations* (e.g., of masking)? Perhaps we ought to heed warnings about the limits to static glimpses of behavior and how relying on these may induce discretization in our theories (Posner, 1986). Clearly, there are consequences for cognitive theory reflected in the perpetuation of stage-based models (Posner, 2005). Such reflection might help us understand why we are still far from understanding how humans perceive, think, and behave, especially in novel and dynamic situations, and why general-purpose models of human behavior are still far off on the horizon (Pfeifer & Bongard, 2007).

Response Time and Eye Tracking

The large body of research using response time (RT) offers an excellent base for further exploration of empirically oriented dynamical research. A critical point about the most common use of RTs in cognitive research is this: These reflect distributions of manually recorded "finishing times," and thus miss the time course leading up to the final response. Because they are a cumulative measure (a net combination of multiple implicit processes), RTs are by definition "confounded." RT researchers, rightfully, counter that finer resolution of response sampling, or stimulus presentation, helps resolve this problem (see Chapter 4, this volume). However, most also appreciate that no advantage is to be gained from finer RT resolution beyond millisecond samples because these are already well within the range pertinent to the time scale of perceptual–cognitive processing. We need instead to supplement RTs with real-time measures that can track mental processes leading up to courser manual RTs such as those commonly used in neuroscience research (e.g., magnetoencephalography, encephalography, functional magnetic resonance imaging, and eye tracking; Bassett, Meyer-Lindenberg, Achard, Duke, & Bullmore, 2006; Vincent et al., 2007).

Several characteristics of eye movements make them ideally suited for supplemental analyses based on NDS: (a) They provide a real-time behavioral record, (b) they are highly coordinated with attention, manual RTs, and various physiological measures, and (c) they operate at the interface of sensory-motor processes (i.e., see frontal-parietal-thalamic and the Frontal Eye Fields (FEF), Lateral–Intra-Parietal (LIP), and Superior Colliculus (SC) network described in Kastner & Pinsk, 2004; or Glimcher, 2003). Such a system at the border of internal and external forces displays many of the "critical" properties found in complex systems, including flexibility, coordination, and efficiency.

The general organizing theme here relates to "dynamic patterns" and how these can be revealed through studying the range and pattern of correlation across behavioral time series: Do RT, search, and other behaviors display long- or short-range dependencies and patterns of scaling? Do unique temporal patterns reveal information about system function? Answers to these questions, which essentially are about a statistical form of memory, require a systematic investigation of scaling behavior and of the behavioral noise that experimentalists usually try to contain or dismiss as irrelevant in GLM research (i.e., Gilden, 2001; Gilden et al., 1995; Ward, 2002).

RT, Search, and Data Skew

One potential violation of GLM can be found in the pervasiveness of positively skewed PDFs in RT and eye-tracking data. To address skewed RT PDFs, Hohle (1965) proposed a three-parameter solution, which includes one parameter for an exponential part, due to response choice, and two representing the Gaussian part, capturing the sum of all other processes involved in RT. Subsequent research has debated which types of processes give rise to the constituent components of "long-tail" PDFs. In contrast to Hohle, McGill (1963) believed the Gaussian part was due to response choice and the exponential part to residual processes. These models, like many contemporary ones, are based on the belief that task manipulation can influence, and therefore probe, independent (i.e., exponential and Gaussian) components.

Sternberg (1969) went on to be indifferent to RT PDFs because he recognized, importantly, that long-tail distributions can result from a combination of several distributions. This is a major theme and source of debate in contemporary work (e.g., Clauset, Shalizi, & Newman, 2007; Delignières, Torre, & Lemoine, 2005; Thornton & Gilden, 2005; Wagenmakers, Farrell, & Ratcliff, 2004, 2005). Instead of maintaining a focus on explaining away long-tail PDFs, Sternberg turned to studying linear interactions of component systems, which presume that independent mechanisms generate additive behavior, whereas a common mechanism (or interacting ones) will have an interacting impact on performance; see Sternberg (1969) for a description of additive factors logic and see studies using it (e.g., Aks & Enns, 1992, 1996; Posner, 2005). Unfortunately, these sorts of linear interactions are oversimplifications and provide limited descriptions of most perceptual–cognitive phenomena. Despite tremendous effort, there seems to be no solid evidence of separable linear-processing components. Rather, these seem at best an oversimplified approximation of what are naturally integrated and nonlinear mechanisms underlying perceptual–cognitive systems.

Visual Search Methodology

One behavior studied extensively with both RT and eye-tracking methodology and in need of dynamical investigation is visual search – particularly, challenging forms of search. Such forms of search are a major research priority because of their ubiquity and applied relevance. For example, in radiology, the significance of finding tumors in medical images is self-evident. Yet even with extensive research, we are still far from understanding what makes for effective search.

What have we learned so far? We do know that challenging search tasks produce complex behavior (as can be seen, for example, in the task shown in Fig. 5.1) and that long-range temporal dynamics may play an important role in effective search (Aks, Zelinky, & Sprott, 2002), as well as in perceptual behaviors in general (e.g., Aks & Sprott, 2003; Gao et al., 2006). In the vast literature on

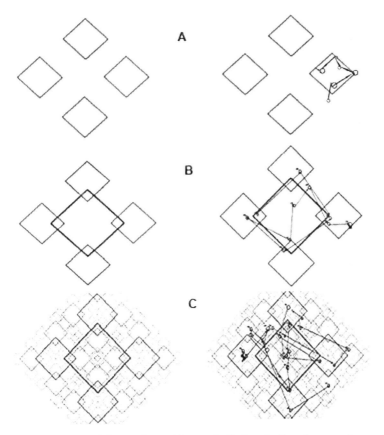

Figure 5.1. Fractal diamonds used in search displays (left) and scan path samples (right) showing representation of fixation durations (circles) and saccades (connecting lines). The search image contained an obscured gray dot, which was visible only when subjects' gaze was directed at its correct location. (**A**) Simplest 4-diamond figure from search and baseline edge-scanning conditions. (**B**) Intermediate complexity 10-diamond fractal figure. (**C**) Most complex ~341-diamond fractal figure.

feature saliency, we know that the bulk of what guides search can be boiled down to stimulus-driven and goal-driven processes (e.g., Duncan & Humphrey, 1989; Wolfe, 1998a). This point is confirmed by neuroscience and behavioral modeling (e.g., Itti & Koch, 2001) and reflected in the dominant theory of visual search (Wolfe, 1994). There are also strong top-down influences on search processes triggered by instruction, prior experience, expectations, effort, attention, and individual goals, along with other endogenous sources (e.g., Wolfe, Butcher, Lee, & Hyle, 2003).

Visual search theory assumes two fundamental processes: There are early, preattentive, and late-attentive processes that are purported to underlie parallel and serial patterns of search behavior (Bergen & Julesz, 1983; Treisman &

Gelade, 1980). Since then, thousands of studies have investigated and challenged this popular view. Wolfe (1998a, 1998b) has been most influential in putting to rest the false dichotomy between early and late stages of visual search and a strict parallel–serial distinction. This theoretical shift exemplifies growing recognition of the continuous nature of perception. In one contribution, Wolfe describes repeated instances of skewed PDFs in RT data (even with outliers removed), leaving the impression that these are typical of search performance. Skew also is pervasive in RT slope data, which measure RTs across item number (i.e., set size) and have been a standard way to distinguish parallel and serial behaviors. In many studies, skew appears greater under certain conditions (e.g., when there are many search items and a target is present in the display). Wolfe argued that this is an artifact due to individual differences and can be removed with proper normalization procedures. Importantly, skewed performance was not the focus of this study, nor is it predicted by Wolfe's (1994) guided search theory. Rather, these long-tail PDFs presented a challenge to assessments of the parallel–serial dichotomy. These require combining data across subjects and making comparisons across conditions. Palmer, Wolfe, and Horowitz (2004) devised clever ways to normalize PDFs, rendering them suitable for inferential analyses. In their initial attempt to normalize their data, they found Z scores problematic because of their extreme sensitivity to outliers. So they turned to an alternative procedure, X normalization, which involves alignment of the 25th and 75th percentile points of each distribution and matching bin numbers across RT histograms. Because these are much less vulnerable to outliers, Palmer et al. were able to average across subjects and compare PDF shapes across conditions. In their conclusion stating that their data falsify models predicting that different set sizes should produce differently shaped PDFs (for target present trials), we see an excellent example of the "GLM reflex": "Successful models should be *constrained* to produce RT PDFs of the same shape for feature and conjunction search" (p. 674). The reflex to constrain (e.g., normalize) our data when we encounter deviations from "normality" is commonplace in the GLM world.

Linearity and Nonlinearity in Eye Movements

Many parallels exist between RT and eye-tracking work. Numerous search studies have shown that short-duration fixations are common, as are the resulting long-tail PDFs (Findlay, Brown, & Gilchrist 2001; Mazer & Gallant, 2003; McPeek, Skavenski, & Nakayama, 2000; Sommer, 1994). Findlay and Gilchrist (2003) detailed the nuance of eye movements in visual search. Their characterization of "active" search as a form of "visual sampling" is critical here, as is the role of the "gaze–shift–gaze" rhythm formed by the most obvious type of eye movements – the rapid saccades interspersed with fixations. These make up "active vision" used in visual search. Additional noteworthy properties of these rhythmic movements include the ballistic nature of saccadic "shifts" ordinarily occurring at about 3 to 4 per second, with each lasting about 20 to 200 milliseconds. The duration of a saccade depends on its amplitude: Larger saccades tend to be faster than smaller saccades. The relation between speed and amplitude appears linear up to some maximum – around 60 degrees of visual angle, with a peak velocity of larger saccades leveling off at approximately 100 degrees per sec. Thus the duration of these very large, fast saccades is no longer linearly dependent on amplitude, and we see here our first instance of a nonlinearity in eye movements. Another important property is intermittency, in which long-range saccades are sporadically emitted every so often amid the much more frequent small saccades. As we shall see in the concluding section of this chapter, intermittency is associated with optimal and highly adaptive behavior (Kwok & Smith, 2005).

There are a number of exceptions to so-called typical eye movements and assertions that they follow a "regular" pattern. The first pertains to the wide range of variability in saccades and fixations (Duchowski, 2005) and how they depend on context. In open and unconstrained environments, saccade amplitude tends to be larger than in small and restricted environments. As the need to explore detail increases, however, saccades decrease in their range and fixations increase in duration. Supporting research shows saccade amplitude increases with spatial extent (Over, Hooge, Vlaskamp, & Erkelens, 2007) and decreases with greater display density (i.e., increasing number of items in a search display; Beintema, van Loon, & van den Berg, 2005). Thus size, detail, and other contextual information can cause substantial deviations from average eye movements.

A second caveat to the notion of typical eye movements relates back to the pervasive influence of GLM thinking in cognitive science and how it dominates eye-movement theory. Carpenter's (1981) theory, linear approach to threshold with ergodic rate (LATER), is a classic case, as are the many proposals for multiple (separable) mechanisms to explain perceptual–cognitive behaviors. In the LATER model, *ergodic rate* refers to random (short-range) deviations across a linear rise to threshold. This is one way to account for positive skew – as the (cumulative) sum of saccade latency distributions. Another suggested explanation uses a "two-process competitive model": a start-and-stop mechanism operating independently and believed to generate relatively independent eye movement sequences, allowing for short-range influences (van Loon, Hooge, & van den Berg, 2002). Like the LATER model, any additional variation is assumed to be negligible and simply due to random influences.

Importantly, the bulk of the earlier studies on which many of these models are based focus only on first and second saccade behavior. Arguably, a reasonable approach given a primary research agenda has been to determine what information is most salient in "pulling" our eyes. Studying initial eye movements is informative for this purpose but does not necessarily inform a more general, and perhaps more fundamental, theory of eye movements, say, when individuals engage in more challenging, and realistic, tasks requiring multiple eye movements.

Recognizing these limitations, van Loon et al. (2002) included an assessment of subsequent eye movements in their study and showed additional lingering effects. PDFs of later saccades (i.e., reciprocal latencies, standard units representing eye-movement rate), unlike those of the first saccade, were highly asymmetrical and, importantly, were found to grow even more asymmetrical over subsequent saccadic eye movements – even more than the cumulative PDFs of initial saccades (vis-à-vis Carpenter, 1981). Beintema et al. (2005) similarly showed that in extended sequences of saccades, rates for subsequent saccades were skewed. Moreover, PDF tails grow (i.e., scale) as saccade rate grows. These findings are consistent with the recurring finding of long-tail PDFs in visual search data (Findlay & Gilchrist, 2003) and of how skew for second and later saccades scales with spatial context, as do fixations and saccade amplitude (Beintema et al., 2005; Over et al., 2007).

One possible source for these skewed distributions may be the presence of temporal dependencies across eye movements. This possibility is supported by a number of findings: (a) effects from prior trials on subsequent saccades (e.g., Kapoula & Robinson, 1986; Kowler, Martins, & Pavel, 1984), (b) dependency of the first saccade latency on sequence length (Zingale & Kowler, 1987), and (c) influences from accumulated history of preceding fixations on subsequent fixation duration (Hooge & Erkelens, 1998; Vaughan & Graefe, 1977). However, such temporal dependencies and a prevalence of long tails is not sufficient evidence for long-range dependencies, nor does it discount the GLM approach. After all, many models (linear and nonlinear) can generate hyperbolic PDFs such as catastrophe and exponential PDFs (Guastello, 2005), lognormal processes, or the summing of a variety of other types of distributions (Newman, 2005).

Other possible sources of PDF skew found in alternative models include those that use gamma, beta, diffusion, and power law PDFs. Many perception studies, for example, have used two-parameter beta and gamma PDFs. Brascamp, van Ee, Pestman, and van den Berg (2005) used two shape parameters, α and β, to describe a bistable beta distribution. When the distribution is bound between 0 and 1, and when $\alpha = \beta = 1$, the beta distribution is uniform, but when these values diverge, skewing emerges. Brascamp et al. (2005) also described a popular two-parameter model, which produces gamma PDFs (e.g., Kovacs, Papathomas, Yang, & Feher, 1996). In a model of eye movements, Beintema et al. (2005) used rate and scale in their gamma fit to positively skewed PDFs. Similarly, Van Loon et al. (2002) used a shape parameter, k (symmetry increases with higher k), and scale parameter to describe the shift in PDFs from first to subsequent saccades. Shape (k) is high for first saccades and drops off with later saccades (i.e., PDF becomes asymmetric), and scale increases fourfold over many saccades (i.e., fourfold decrement in threshold). If a decision mechanism controls a latency distribution by a changing threshold, then the ratio of the mean and the SD of the reciprocal latency, the *coefficient of variation*, should be constant as predicted by Carpenter's (1981) linear model: $v = $ mean/SD $=$ K. However, the results demonstrated that v changed over time. Interestingly, this v measure is similar to *relative dispersion,* an NDS tool (i.e., SD/M).

Finally, many *diffusion (random-walk)* processes are used to incorporate stochastic influences into models describing behavioral changes over time. Smith and Ratcliff (2004), for example, described a *sequential-sampling diffusion model* of (two-alternative force choice) RT with subject's response choice sampled from a sequence of noisy observations. To make a decision, successive observations of the stimulus process are sampled and summed until a threshold is met. The accumulated information on any trial is represented by a continuous, but highly irregular, sample path, whose mean and variance are both linear functions of time. Two parameters, the drift, ξ, and the diffusion coefficient, s, describe this path. ξ represents the average rate of change in the sample path and the quality of the encoded stimulus information; s represents observer noise. For given values of ξ and rate (and when not constrained by boundaries), sample paths are represented as a function of time, t, with mean ξt and variance $s^2 t$. This description is just one of many models that could account for long-tail PDFs and variable eye-movement or RT behavior that emerge in simple decision-making tasks.

Scaling: Proportional Versus Power Law Relationships

The most general, and the simplest, description of a long-tail PDF is the *power law* (a.k.a. *Pareto* or *Zipf* PDFs) with the unique property of having slow decay over its entire range. The entire distribution is scale-free and can be described as $\Pr[X > x] \sim x^{-\alpha}$ as $x \to \alpha, 0 < \alpha < 2$. Unlike beta and gamma distributions, a distinguishing feature of the power law distribution is its infinite tail. Identifying this can be difficult, however (Clauset et al., 2007). This is especially true in psychological research in which human subjects are prone to fatigue, and it is difficult to obtain sufficiently long data sets to distinguish between power law and alternative PDFs. Therefore, to seek out more definitive answers, it is critical to use tests beyond a single assessment of PDFs.

The scale-free property of power laws is worth distinguishing from other forms and terms for scaling. Often, *scale-invariance* refers to a *stable* or *stationary* behavior, but one that can change linearly over time: The value of a function $f(x)$ is proportional to x or some constant k of x, $f(x) = kx$. Conventional descriptive statistics represent these systems with means and variance converging to relatively stable values. Variability is uncorrelated and relatively uniform over time. As we shall see, the time series of *saccade directions* in visual search is scale invariant.

Conversely, scale-free systems have means and variance that change with time in a nonproportional way. Systems described by power laws are scale-free. Variability changes over time, often in subtle (but occasionally dramatic) ways because successive behaviors influence one another. In addition to temporal dependencies, scale-free systems are likely to show spatial dependencies in which

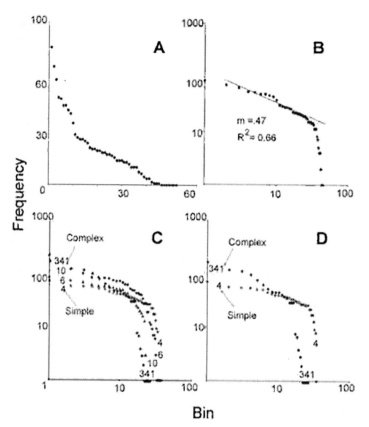

Figure 5.2. Sample plots of search probability distribution fuction (PDFs) across various complexity conditions for one subject. (**A**) PDF of rescaled-x fixations from the complex search condition with suggestion of a long tail. (**B**) a log–log plot of the same PDF with a power scaling region in the high-frequency range and a regression slope m = −0.5 (R^2 = 0.66, $p < .05$), up to exponential cutoff resulting from restricted viewing range. (**C**) log–log PDFs of simple, intermediate, and complex search conditions. (**D**) A within-subject comparison across the simplest and most complex search conditions.

behaviors change with spatial context, say, when surrounding space changes in size. This type of spatial scaling occurs in the visual search task tested in the present study: Scan paths tend to be more variable and cover a wider range when searching the larger search regions of complex displays. Hints of scaling can be seen in Figure 5.1 and the corresponding PDF analysis in Figure 5.2. The steeper regression slope in the log–log PDF plots of complex search paths confirms that greater scaling occurs in these unstructured displays relative to simple and more structured displays. Additional measures of scale-free power law behaviors include analyses of dispersion and rescaled range capturing how first and second "moments" (i.e., means and variances) change over space and time.

In the power law scaling relation, the value of $f(x)$ equals some power α of x, $f(x) = x^{\alpha}$. The source of this hyperbolic long-tail PDF shape is of great theoretical interest in the perceptual-cognitive field (e.g., Brascamp et al., 2005). Assuming we have correctly identified that our long-tail PDF is best described by a power law, there are a number of possible sources to consider. Among the more intriguing are those based on simple interactions (i.e., self-organized criticality rules; Bak, 1996) and on sources with short- and especially long-range influences that propogate across the system. As Van Orden, Holden, and Turvey (2003, 2005) described, spreading effects occur when local and global correlations coexist across different parts of the same system. Scale-free properties permit an individual to maintain a consistent set of states (e.g., ideas) over time and yet be sensitive and responsive to external information. Such adaptability is clearly helpful in our continuously changing world and attains useful predictive value in currently evolving techniques, enabling us to quantify various characteristics of behavioral patterns: their type (PSD), their persistence (tau), and whether they scale (R/S), recur (as illustrated by recurrence plots, recurrence quantification analysis [RQA]; Webber & Ziblut, 1994), or show fractal properties across behavioral time series. After reviewing some of these techniques, I will discuss a crucial step in learning about system dynamics – the need to examine the system over time under varying conditions – and illustrate with a working example from an ongoing visual search study.

Measuring Temporal Dependencies, Scaling, and Rates of Decay

Power law mechanisms, common to complex systems, produce a general form of scaling reflected in a number of NDS measures including long-tail PDFs, power spectra, and autocorrelations (tau). PDF shape can reveal important information about the rate of "memory" decay within a system: Earlier I described a statistical form of memory that captures the degree to which sequential behaviors depend on past behaviors: How far back in a behavioral sequence does any particular behavior exert an influence on future behaviors? Whereas a Gaussian distribution has rapid (exponential) decay along with a stable mean, power law PDFs have slow decay, with means and variance changing slowly over time. This slow decay produces an infinitely long tail in an ideal power law, but it is near impossible to produce this with human data. This accounts for some of the difficulty in identifying that a power law process underlies a PDF. A common strategy for attempting to identify a power law relation is to assess whether a PDF shape falls along a straight line when plotted on log–log coordinates. Newman (2005) and Clauset et al. (2007) cautioned against use of linear (regression) estimates of the scaling exponent α because they are prone to bias, and suggested instead using maximum likelihood ratios to estimate α. Once an accurate estimate of α $\iota\sigma$ is obtained, it is useful to evaluate how it is influenced under changing conditions. This is one way to learn about the dynamics of a system.

Another way to assess PDF shape and the impact of different conditions on rate of decay is through descriptive measures of kurtosis (K) and skew (Sk) or various ratios of variance (e.g., R/S or S/M). A key strategy here is to evaluate whether any of these change over different windows of time. Signs of change may suggest power law behaviors, but again careful assessments are needed to characterize these changes properly. Sampling various windows of data is critical, as is consideration of the role of stochastic influences and quantifying if and how variance changes over time across these windows of data. Performing separate analyses of descriptive statistics over different windows of time can be a tedious process. Fortunately, an expanding set of methods, commonly used in *fractal analyses*, help consolidate some of these procedures into a single measure. Various windowing procedures quantify the degree to which a behavior scales or changes over time. These include *scaled windowed variance (SWV)*, *detrend fluctuation analysis (DFA)*, *dispersion analyses (S/M or S^2/M)*, and *Hurst rescaled range analysis ($R/S = H$)*. Their windowing strategy captures time-dependent statistical changes and is what distinguishes them from traditional GLM approaches that rely on a summary of behavior presumed to be stationary. Excellent summaries of the fractal analyses can be found in Liebovitch (1998), Shelhamer (2006), Delignières et al. (2006), and Stam and de Bruin (2004).

Here we focus on *rescaled range analysis (R/S)* while taking heed to cautionary notes of Delignières et al. (2005, 2006). A number of variations of R/S analysis are available, but they all capture how variance changes with the size of the measuring window. I apply three versions to the visual search data: the first is a simplified example of R/S to illustrate how variance scales with the measuring instrument, or how disperse eye movements become over time. The second, S^2/M, is a simplified version of a common measure of dispersion described in Delignières et al. (2005). Here R/S and S^2/M are calculated for each of four different bin sizes: 256, 512, 768, and 1,024 fixations.

The other rescaled range measure is the *Hurst R/S* described by Feder (1988). Briefly, a time series containing n points is subdivided into n/p segments, each of length p. For each, the maximum range (R) and the standard deviation (S) are calculated, and then R/S is averaged for all segments. The fraction R/S is related to the Hurst exponent (H) by the formula: $R/S = (p/2)^H$. Usually, H is calculated by estimating the value of R/S for all values of p, the pairs obtained are log transformed, and a linear regression is performed with H estimated from its slope.

One important scaling property captured by H includes quantification of correlation in temporal variance to help classify the "color" of noise: brown ($H \sim 0.5$), white ($H \sim 0$), and pink ($\sim 0 > H > 0.5$). The other property captures *persistent* versus *antipersistent* patterns. Persistent trends ($H > 0.5$) occur when successive points in a data series tend to change in a similar way: Either small behaviors follow small behaviors or large follow large. Antipersistent trends ($H < 0.5$) occur when small and large behaviors tend to alternate over time and across different time scales. As we shall see, the fixation series produced by visual search consistently produces antipersistent patterns falling within the pink $1/f$ range. In the modeling section, I also discuss how antipersistent patterns may facilitate search and provide important insights into a controversial search pattern known as *inhibition of return* (IOR; Klein & MacInnes, 1999).

A much more widely known test of correlation and scaling across a data series is the *spectral analyses* (see Peak & Frame, 1994; Shelhamer, 2006; Sprott, 2003 and references within). Although based on linear and frequency-based algorithms, spectral analysis can effectively be used to study a wide range of behavior regardless of whether it emerged from a linear or nonlinear process. Fast Fourier transform (FFT; Press, Flannery, Teukolsky, & Vetterling, 1986) is an efficient spectral analysis and is commonly used to evaluate whether data scale across spectra of frequencies and are correlated in a unique way. It does so by exploiting the fact that any data series can be described as a complex waveform, which can be estimated with a composite of simple regular (sine and cosine) waves that span a range of frequencies. After decomposing the series, we plot the power (mean square amplitude) against frequency to determine what combination of waves best describes our complex waveform. The resulting plot of the power against frequency reveals dominant frequencies and correlated patterns in the series. Presence of power law scaling is indicated if a straight regression line approximates and can serve as a reasonable estimate of a trend across frequencies. As with PDF assessments of power law, this can be challenging because both tend to be susceptible to noise. Assuming a linear regression is a reasonable description of our log–log spectral plot, its slope can be used as an estimate of the power exponent or unit of scaling. Once again, there are many cautionary notes described by various authors (e.g., Delignières et al., 2005). Appropriate use of a combination of methods provides the most reliable description of these behaviors.

Assuming a trend emerges in spectral analysis and our regression slope estimate is $\alpha = -1.0$, the behavior may be classified as one form of power law that scales as the inverse of the frequency (f) or as $1/f$ noise. In this particular form of scaling, a large amount of fine structure is readily visible, as can be seen in fixation series of Figure 5.3 (top) and Figure 5.4. Less obvious are the similar patterns of fluctuations that recur across all scales of the data. These are the subtle undulating high- and low-frequency patterns that repeat across the length of the fixation series. The scaling exponent estimated from the power spectra quantifies the strength and duration of the memory across the system. Pink $1/f^1$ noise has a shallow slope, indicating long-range correlation, and is intermediate to *brown* and *white* spectra (those that are easily predicted by conventional GLM models): Brown $1/f^2$ noise, although usually defined by its short-range random increments, has a steep slope, reflecting the highly predictable long-range patterns that emerge from consecutive points always being near one another.

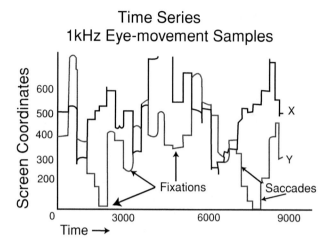

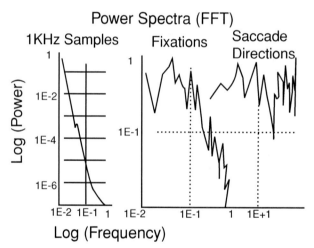

Figure 5.3. Sample of 1 KHz time series (top) showing x- (dark-gray series) and y-coordinate (light gray) for each msec eye sample over ~9 sec period of complex search. Trial starts with subject fixating center of screen (0.5 sec), after which the time series appears unsystematic. Corresponding scan paths and diamond image are shown in Figure 5.1C. Bottom figure from left to right shows three power spectra based on the following time series: 1 KHz *sampled eye positions* ($1/f^2$ brown noise), consecutive (*x*-coordinate) *fixations* ($1/f$ pink noise), and saccade *directions* ($1/f^0$ white noise). FFT = Fast Fourier transform.

White $1/f0$ noise has a flat spectrum, indicating no correlation across data points and no predictable pattern either in the short or long term. Examples of each of these can be seen in Figure 5.3. Implications for these trends are discussed subsequently and in various sources (e.g., Aks, 2005; Gilden, 2001).

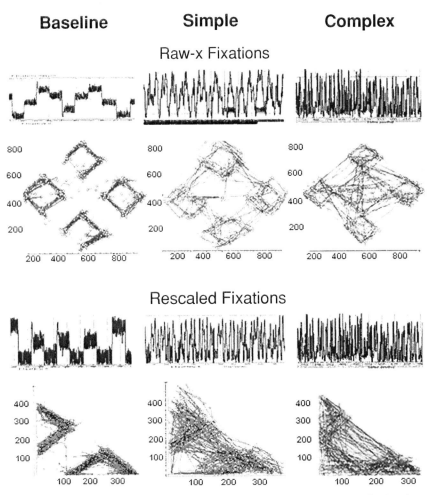

Figure 5.4. Sample fixation series and cumulative record of scan paths for baseline, simple, and complex display conditions for one subject. Raw-x fixations are shown in top two rows, and rescaled fixations are shown in the bottom two rows. First row shows ~9-sec samples of fixation series, with time represented along horizontal axis and *x*-coordinate for each eye position on the vertical axis. In the baseline condition, subjects scan diamond edge, alternating their fixation between two vertices of the diamond edge until instructed to proceed clockwise to the next diamond. Alternating eye movements produce clear periodic patterns in the fixation series. Corresponding scan paths (in second row) follow a rough path along edges of each diamond. Although diamond edges clearly guide eye movements, there remains a large amount of variability in these baseline trials. During search, magnitude of variability is much greater, and this variability increases with complexity. Scan-path images show more widely distributed eye movements and increased traversing of central regions of the display. Rescaled fixations (last two rows) emphasize all of these patterns: the periodic patterns of baseline

(*continued on page 148*)

The power spectra can be transformed to its temporal counterpart: the *auto-correlation function (tau; τ)*:

$$\hat{P}_k = \frac{\dfrac{1}{n}\displaystyle\sum_{f=k}^{N-(k+1)} (y_t - \bar{y})(y_{f+k} - \bar{y})}{\dfrac{1}{n}\displaystyle\sum_{f=0}^{N-1} (y_t - \bar{y})^2}.$$

Using a time-lagged version of itself, τ reveals whether correlations exist across a time series and quantifies the period over which these patterns decay. In short-range processes, the correlation (i.e., coupling) between values at different times decreases rapidly over time. Its distinguishing feature in a plot of the autocorrelation is its rapid fall near the zero point. An immediate drop-off is a sign of exponential decay, and the variability in the behavior is a form of white uncorrelated noise. The rapid or exponential decay is also readily seen in the symmetrical tails of the corresponding Gaussian distribution. Contrasting slow (power law) rate of decay emerges in the autocorrelation of systems with long-ranging memory, such as in $1/f$ noise. Slow decay emerges due to behavioral dependencies (i.e., coupling), which extend over long stretches of the time series, and τ represents the decay as a power of the correlation lag appearing hyperbolic in shape. The corresponding PDF is typically long tailed, and the time series contains many slowly changing sequences: There are many low-frequency sequences nesting rapidly changing or high-frequency sequences (see search time series in Fig. 5.4). One final distinguishing feature of short- versus long-range patterns is the finite area under short-range autocorrelations as opposed to the infinite area found under the plot of a long-range process.

Changing Behavioral Patterns Across Conditions: Previous Findings

Perhaps the most important tool in the NDS arsenal can be found in traditional experimentation: manipulating independent variables and observing

---

Figure 5.4 (*continued from page 147*) conditions and the variability for all conditions. In rescaled images, dimensions of scan paths are collapsed to outer and inner diamond boundaries for *x*- and *y*-coordinates. These appear as rotated and inverted V patterns in the last row and reaffirm that scan paths adhere to the diamond edge structure most strongly in the baseline trials where they are most visible. Search also adheres more closely to the diamond figures in simple trials than in complex conditions. Finally, the large amount of fine structure in the eye movements is one of the defining features of $1/f$ behaviors. Less obvious are the similar pattern of fluctuations, which recur across all scales of the data. These are most visible in the more complex fixation series and appear as subtle undulating high- and low-frequency patterns that repeat across the length of the series.

their impact on dynamic behavior. Many recent studies looking at the time course of perceptual–cognitive behavior are also informative. Yet to learn about intrinsic dynamics and how they are mediated by external influences, we need to examine how behavior unfolds within different conditions and to make use of NDS tools to capture scaling properties not revealed through standard GLM statistics. A sample of conventional and NDS studies are noted here as illustration. Shifts in temporal dependencies across conditions may reveal changes in the type of information being used, such as a switch from external to internal information. Or the shift may be in the amount of effort required to perform a task. Such effects form predictions for the visual search study presented later.

Many conventional RT studies that use challenging tasks produce positively skewed distributions. Whether these may be accurately described by power laws remains an open question, but a good starting point is in the pervasiveness of long-tail distributions even under highly constrained conditions in which we would expect a "normalizing" effect on PDFs. In a pertinent example, Wolfe's (1998b) meta-analysis of visual search studies shows that the detection of spatial conjunctions (i.e., a target defined by a unique combination of visual features such as color *and* orientation) produces more skewed PDFs than detection of features (i.e., a target defined by a simple piece of information such as color *or* orientation). In further evaluation of these effects, Palmer et al. (2004) showed that distributions "normalize" as set size increases in feature search. In their (GLM-type) analysis of temporal dynamics, they found that as RT bin size increases (from 50 to 100 msec), additional shifts emerge in the distributions, whereby the tails lengthen with complexity. This finding is consistent with that which occurs in behavior that scales as a power law: Increasing sample time includes more of the "rare" (slow search) events – perhaps providing the visual system with a "wider reach" of visual search over time. NDS tests are needed to assess the possibility that search RTs are scale-free and best described by power laws.

There are a variety of tests of perceptual–cognitive load, including those assessing behavioral dynamics. Van Orden et al. (2003) and Ward (2002) presented useful summaries of seminal NDS work (e.g., Beltz & Kello, 2004; Clayton & Frey, 1997; Ding, Chen, & Kelso, 2002; Gilden, 1997, 2001; Thornton & Gilden, 2005). These suggest that increases in *cognitive load* diminish behavioral correlations (i.e., slopes of power spectra are reduced). However, there is at least one exception to this pattern. In tests of motor coordination, Chen, Ding, and Kelso (2001) found the opposite pattern: spectra slopes *steepen* during the more difficult syncopated (i.e., unsynchronized) task than in synchronized tapping tasks. Interestingly, syncopation not only increased correlated behavior but was also better characterized as $1/f$.

What might account for these differences? A usual culprit can be found in confounds, because tasks varied widely and other factors were operating. In Clayton and Frey (1997), memory load was assessed by discriminating stimuli across one (low-load) versus two (high-load) trials; Gilden (2001) compared *blocked* (low-load) versus mixed (high-load) conditions in a classification task. In both, extraneous noise and predictability were among the inadvertent confounds. Any of these factors could decorrelate performance. Other RT studies have refocused on the role of stimulus predictability. Beltz and Kello (2004), for example, found that unpredictable cues produce weaker long-range dependencies on RTs. In studies of eye-movement behavior, Shelhamer (2005a, 2005b; Shelhamer & Joiner, 2003) found similar effects in tests of periodically paced targets: *Reactive* saccades responded to alternating stimuli of low-pacing rate and produced no correlation across trials. *Predictive* saccades, on the other hand, occur during fast pacing in which a (negative latency) saccade begins (50–70 msec) before the target jumps. Predictive saccades, in a sense, anticipate the appearance of the target and, interestingly, produce $1/f$ long-term correlation across trials. Additional dynamical properties emerged, such as the clear transition from reactive to predictive saccades at around .5 Hz, resembling a form of *hysteresis* because it showed an asymmetry depending on the direction of alternating stimuli. Most pertinent here is the correlated performance in predictive saccades with $1/f$ power law scaling in power spectra, autocorrelation, and Hurst exponent measures.

All of these studies may be best understood if viewed in terms of how intrinsic dynamics are modified by external forces. Broadly framing questions around intrinsic dynamics may be helpful in guiding us to a universal perceptual–cognitive theory. Van Orden et al. (2003, 2005) described a similar approach, as did Beltz and Kello (2004), when speculating that their nonpredictive cues might serve as an external source of variability and thus mask intrinsic behavioral dynamics. Similarly, in Shelhamer's work, predictive saccades were driven by an intrinsic dynamic tied to anticipation, whereas the reactive saccades were driven by the changing external information.

Intrinsic Versus Extrinsic Dynamics in Neural Activity

One neural account for changing behavioral dynamics points to activity across brain structures that vary in their degrees of coordination across multiple time scales (e.g., Ding et al., 2002; Van Orden et al., 2003). Such coordination, sometimes triggered by external events, can give rise to "long-range" behavioral responses. With the benefit of direct testing and marked advances in technology, much work in neuroscience is supportive of these ideas (e.g., Vincent et al., 2007) and indicates that perceptual–cognitive behavior emerges from a complex, yet coordinated, pattern of synchronization and desynchronization across brain regions (Rodriguez et al., 1999). Determining and decoding these patterns are among the remaining challenges to learning their link with emergent behavior. Recent clues suggest that to proceed from one perceptual state to another, desynchronization is crucial. Such decoupling across neural populations has been neglected to the extent that most theoretical focus has been on synchronous activity across neural oscillations. Singer (e.g., 1993, 1999) has shown many compelling illustrations of brain synchrony producing spikes in power spectra with a characteristic scale in the gamma (γ; 30- to 70-Hz range, which is purported to account for the binding of information (Singer & Gray, 1995) and even consciousness. The influence of Singer's theory of temporal synchrony is easily seen across the cognitive neuroscience literature, including application to eye movements. Brecht, Singer, and Engel (1999), for example, showed saccades initiated by cross-correlation patterns across various layers of the (thalamic) superior colliculus (SC).

Although intuitively appealing, temporal synchrony accounts for perceptual integration (i.e., binding) find support in limited situations (for a review and reinterpretation of a wide series of related work, see Shadlen & Movshon, 1999). Even in work claiming support, asynchrony can be seen to play an important role as well. First, any code based on synchronous signals by definition includes asynchronous information. Simply by intervening, their start and stop points define synchronous events. Second, the wide range of oscillation events classified as synchronous is problematic (i.e., synchrony thought to be unique to 40 Hz has been extended to the 20- to 80-Hz range). Not only does the range continue to widen, but studies such as Brecht et al. (1999) show a surprisingly large amount of variability across trials. Perhaps *relative* degrees of synchrony may be a far more important signature of changing perceptual events.

That coding may be based on a continuum, or a pattern of synchrony and asynchrony, rather than discrete (synchronous) events, ties in well with the distinction between systems described in terms of a characteristic time scale versus those described as scale-free. The 40-Hz designation for synchrony and information binding is a case in point. Perhaps the revised, broader, 20- to 80-Hz classification is a sign of scaling in mental events. Studies already reflecting this shift show evidence that brain events display scale-free and self-similar dynamics (Gong, Nikolaev, & Leeuwen, 2003; Stam & de Bruin, 2004). Most pertinent here may be the recent work showing asynchronous signals triggering saccade activity (Engel & Singer, 2001), demonstrating that a 5-msec offset in SC stimulation results in summing and activation of saccades). As Shadlen and Movshon (1999) suggested, there is indeed a compelling case for looking beyond synchrony.

Recent studies are focusing directly on baseline brain activity in the absence of any external stimulation. Vincent et al. (2007) showed coherent and active patterns across neural ensembles and how this "idling" activity disappears in the presence of external stimulation. In contrast to Singer's findings, when subjects engage in meaningful tasks, neural desynchronization dominates. What distinguishes these findings pertains to the approach taken in studying brain activity – a parallel to the GLM-NDS distinction and also to how "framing" a problem influences the outcome. The traditional Singerian approach sets out to uncover (synchronized) activity to account for more stable cognitive states, whereas Vincent's approach focuses on changing states and their deviations from intrinsic dynamics. With this new empirical focus comes a straightforward method of assessment: Compare internal versus external influences on behavior and evaluate corresponding changes in spontaneous baseline dynamics.

Are intrinsic dynamics likely to be $1/f$? Are these most likely to emerge in unconstrained conditions? Demonstrations of intrinsic long-range temporal correlations and scaling of brain oscillations suggest this may be so, especially when coupled with demonstrations of stimulus-induced changes in these brain activity patterns. For example, Linkenkaer-Hansen, Nikouline, Palva, Kaila, and Ilmoniemi (2004) showed that β oscillations (10- to 20-Hz range) modulated by somatosensory stimuli continue to exhibit long-range temporal correlations and power law scaling. The magnitude of the temporal correlations is simply attenuated as reflected in decreases in power law exponents. Other studies also demonstrate that stimuli can indeed degrade the network's memory of its past: Varela, Lachaux, Rodriguez, and Martinerie (2001) showed asynchronous electroencephalogram (EEG) responses (in the γ, 30- to 70-Hz range; 360–720 msec) after an image was presented to awake monkeys during their "perception condition" versus the more synchronous activity found in their "no-perception" conditions. Stam and de Bruin (2004) examined EEG during a no-task, resting condition and found episodic spontaneous patterns resembling those present during thought. Farid and Adelson (2001) showed externally induced temporal structure interfering with intrinsically induced synchrony, and Engel and Singer (2001) showed a similar finding in an eye-movement study in which externally induced asynchrony leads to summed neural activity and a subsequent saccadic response.

If we presume $1/f$ behavior as a baseline intrinsic dynamic, a reasonable assumption, given the accumulating evidence from behavioral and neuroscience research (e.g., Linkenkaer-Hansen et al., 2004), then empirical questions may be better framed thus: *How do external constraints modulate internal dynamics?* This view should prompt behavioral researchers to confirm that $1/f$ patterns do characterize intrinsically driven behavior (predicted to be evident in least constrained conditions) and then focus on what causes deviations from this baseline $1/f$ state. At least two benefits may emerge with this approach: (a) reconciliation of what appear to be inconsistent results and (b) rather than postulating particular, and highly idiosyncratic, theories of mental or motor influence on behavioral dynamics, each laiden with confounds and unnecessary discretization of underlying process, a theory of $1/f$ behavior can be assessed across a wide range of studies and conditions. A full description of the theory requires considering the source of the $1/f$ behavior, and as we shall see in the discussion, there are many possible sources. However, more crucial to our understanding of human and many other natural behaviors may be their common set of properties. They all are *complex systems* with *many constituent components interacting locally* (likely with variations in the exact rules), yet all give rise to similar global

$1/f$ behaviors. Thus it is the universal properties that form the basis of the theory of $1/f$ intrinsic behavior and the basis of the proposed NDS approach to understanding behavior.

Assessing Image Complexity and Visual Search Dynamics

In a series of ongoing studies, beginning with Aks et al. (2002), we have been assessing the challenging search of a *volitional* form known to require attention. In these experiments, subjects *actively* searched a complicated scene for a subtle target. Here we found evidence for long-range ($\sim 1/f$) search across the sequence of fixations. Recall the description of *fixations* as the steady-gaze component in the gaze–shift–gaze rhythm of typical eye movements. Being interspersed with saccades makes the fixation sequence comparable to a series of saccade amplitudes, and together they make up "active vision." This active property reinforces that $1/f$ patterns are pertinent to a top-down, goal-driven form of visual search.

In the present search study, we test another active search task, but here we also vary the complexity of the search context. Although the task is simply to find a gray dot, the target is not obvious because the dot is hidden until the subject's gaze (and the gaze-contingent [GC] window) is directed at the target. With increasing complexity of the surrounding display, location uncertainty also increases, so that we expect the role of endogenous search to increase with complexity (and its less informative structure). Similar to the prediction alluded to earlier, and consistent with the findings from the "cognitive load" studies, we expect dynamics to change with a shift in the use of external to internal information or vice versa. When Beltz and Kello (2004) found that unpredictable cues produce weaker long-range dependencies on RTs, they interpreted this dissociation in terms of external sources of variability acting to mask long-range intrinsically driven behavior. Whether masking, or some related cognitive phenomenon, critical is the inherent pattern of (long-range) dependencies in human behavior. Also, the extent to which a long-range pattern is observed depends on a balance of internal (memory-based) versus external (stimulus-based) sources of information. In the present visual search study, we expect that more complex displays (with their less informative guide to target location) will produce search behavior dominated by intrinsic dynamics. Based on our earlier work, we also expect scaling properties to emerge in the eye-position series. Scale-free behavior is expected in changes in search behavior over time and space so that search over progressively longer periods of time, or larger regions of space, is expected to change (i.e., stretch) accordingly. Key signatures of scaling include (a) long-tail data distributions with means or variances that change over time and (b) power law scaling in PDFs, power spectra, and various measures of behavioral scaling. In essence, manipulations of stimulus structure provide a means to assess how internal and external influences mediate behavioral dynamics.

Participants and Procedure

Four undergraduate students and one research faculty member from Rutgers University participated in the visual search experiment. Students received $15 compensation for participating. All subjects had normal or corrected-to-normal vision. Upon arriving, participants completed a consent form and received a set of instructions describing the visual search task. The entire experiment lasted less than 45 minutes, and each condition consisted of two sets of 20 trials with an approximately 5-min rest between sets.

While sitting in a comfortable chair, participants viewed the screen from about 80 cm with their chins resting on a padded chin rest. Immediately before the search tasks, a 5-min calibration of each subject's eye movements was performed. Participants fixated a sequence of nine (0.5°) calibration dots presented in an unpredictable order on a 3 × 3 (24° × 18°) invisible grid on the computer display. To ensure correct calibration was maintained throughout the experiment, a "drift correction" procedure was performed at the beginning of each trial while participants were fixating on a dot at the center of the screen. Immediately afterward, subjects pressed a key to commence searching for the target. Throughout the experiment, x and y screen coordinates of gaze position were sampled every millisecond and recorded with SR-Research Osgoode ON Canada http://www.eyelinkinfo.com/contact.php Eye Track software running off of the host PC computer.

Search Task and Stimuli

Immediately following calibration, experiments began with five practice search trials followed by 40 recorded experimental trials. The EL-1000 eye tracker (described later) recorded participant's eye movements while they searched for a 4-pixel (diameter) gray dot presented randomly within (1,024 × 768 pixel) figures on the computer display. In all conditions except the baseline task, subjects were instructed that a gray dot would appear within one of the diamonds shown on the display (see Fig. 5.1 for samples). Subjects were instructed to search for the dot using a GC window (described later) and press a button on a response pad indicating whether and when they found the target. Each trial lasted a maximum of 15 sec, and the gray dot was present in all trials. Correct responses were confirmed by eye-movement recordings and eliminated the need for the target-absent conditions standard to most visual search studies. Using only target-present trials has the key benefit of maintaining a constant set of conditions over time. This is an important experimental design feature to effectively evaluate a system's temporal dynamics.

Search Displays and Gaze-Contingent Masks

Each display contained one of four figures varying in complexity, as illustrated in Figure 5.1. An additional baseline figure was identical to the simplest four-diamond figure (Fig. 5.1A). The four diamonds were simply a subset of the remaining two-fractal figures designed with Stone Work's (2006) StarMores fractal-generating software. Four-point diamonds were used as the base figure, and the fractals were generated using a recursive algorithm stepping up from a single iteration case (Fig. 5.1B) to the complex five-iteration case (Fig. 5.1C). All diamond figures were violet colored and were within two-thirds of the full display ($\sim25°$ of visual angle).

Search for the gray-dot target was deliberately made challenging by use of a gaze-contingent (GC) mask superimposed on top of each search display so that information about the location of the gray dot was minimal. The GC mask contained a 100-pixel window, the location of which was under each subject's (eye movement) control: that is, the GC window moved in tandem with the subject's eye movements. Thus the gray-dot location, unbeknownst to the subject prior to finding it, was only revealed when the subject's eye gaze was directed at the dot location; otherwise, the gray dot was not visible, but the diamond figures were. Subjects received a complete explanation of the GC property of the mask, as well as five practice trials to ensure that they understood and were able to control the GC window with their eyes.

Complexity of the display was also manipulated to evaluate the influence of stimulus structure on search. Search is expected to be easiest in the simplest four-diamond case (Fig. 5.1A) compared to the more complex cases (Figs. 5.1B and 5.1C). Information about target location decreases with complexity in two important ways. First, with regard to *extent of search region*, the progression of complexity across all figures increases the size of the potential search regions where the dot may appear. Thus in the most complex condition, the dot may appear anywhere within the large (25°) diamond shape, whereas potential search regions are progressively more restricted with simpler shapes. Smaller search regions are likely to facilitate and help guide search. The second effect from the complexity manipulation relates to changes in *degree of figural embedding*. Unless subjects adopt a strategy to ignore the hierarchical embedding, this additional level of complexity is likely to further hinder search by increasing the number of possible search locations to include these overlapping diamond regions, with the likely effect of increasing repeat visits to the same locations.

To assess further the effect of informative structure, two additional, more extreme tasks were tested. A minimal structure condition used a homogeneous white GC mask so that virtually no information was available to guide the eyes to the target. One subject simply searched a blank field until the eyes were centered on the location of the gray dot. The gray dot no longer was restricted to appear within the diamond regions; it could appear anywhere on the computer display. A final *baseline-scanning* task was included to provide a highly structured contrast (in both stimulus structure and task) to the complex and very noisy scan paths likely to be produced in the other search conditions. Using the simplest (four) diamond figure, subjects simply scanned a single edge (top right) of each diamond for 2 to 5 seconds until the experimenter told them to move to the

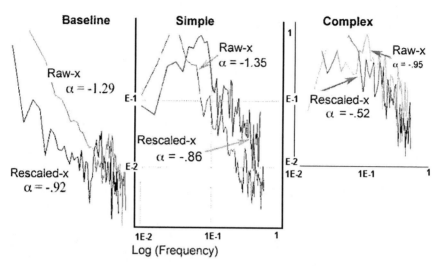

Figure 5.5. Fast Fourier transform spectra for baseline, simple, and complex search. Regression slopes of power spectra of fixation series decrease with complexity ($\alpha_\Delta = -.37$), suggestive of a "whitening" effect. However, power spectra are closest to $1/f$ in conditions in which intrinsic dynamics are expected to dominate: rescaled fixations of simple search ($\alpha_{ave} = -.92$) and raw fixations of complex search ($\alpha_{ave} = -.92$). Rescaling is appropriate to isolating the extrinsic diamond structure and its influence on simple search, whereas rescaling is less relevant to complex conditions, and thus to producing spectral whitening.

next (clockwise) diamond. Because subjects did not know exactly when they would shift to the next diamond edge, this added some uncertainty to the task. Figure 5.4 shows the cumulative record of sample scan paths of one subject moving his eyes back and forth from one vertex to another of each diamond. Results of the scaling tests are shown in Figures 5.5 and 5.6. Including this highly structured task is useful in interpreting and understanding a variety of the analyses reported in the results.

Eye-Tracking and Computer Equipment

Eye movements were measured with a video-based eye-tracking system (SR-Research Eyelink1000) with temporal resolution of 1,000 Hz and spatial resolution of 0.5 degrees. A Dell Precision 380 served as the host computer to control the eye-tracking software. This PC was connected to a 19-inch LCD monitor that showed, in real-time, participants' eye movements as they performed the search task. This display permitted the experimenter to monitor participant eye movements throughout the experiment. The host PC was connected to both the eye tracker and a Dell Dimension XPS 600 that served as the Display PC to run the visual search tasks. Search stimuli were presented on View Sonic G225fb 21-inch CRT monitor at a refresh rate of 120 Hz.

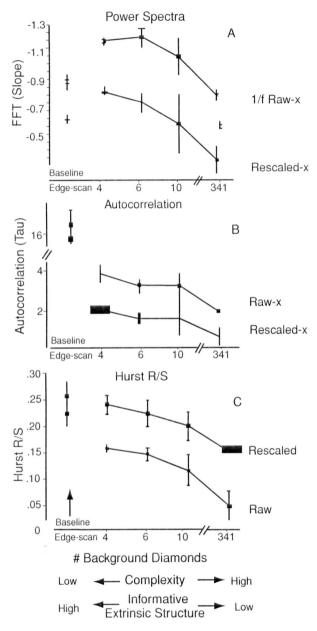

Figure 5.6. Summary of the effect of figural complexity on raw-x and rescaled-x fixation series for power spectra, autocorrelation, and Hurst R/S. Overall, as complexity increases, power spectra become shallower, and τ (T) and H decrease. In the most complex search task, there is a significant decrease in α, autocorrelation, and Hurst rescaling (raw to rescaled differences, respectively: α-diff $= 0.6$, τ-diff $= 0.9$, and H-diff $= 0.1$). These values reflect whitening, with rescaled values closer to white noise.

Eye Movement Parameters and Time Series Analyses

The search task was designed to be sufficiently challenging to require effort and the use of attention. The aim was to learn about the mechanism guiding eye movements, as revealed through patterns that may emerge in the sequence of eye movements. We evaluated the influence of figure complexity on the search dynamic and attempted to tease apart external from internal influences by rescaling eye movements to the display center, and through the use of the baseline "edge-scanning task."

To evaluate temporal patterns across the sequence of eye movements, x and y eye positions were sampled every millisecond as subjects scanned the computer display. Eye-movement parameters derived from these samples were used to map the trajectory of the eyes as they moved from fixation to fixation. Data series included consecutive eye samples and fixation series (equivalent to saccade amplitude, but analysis reported here is based on separate x and y series). Dependent measures included consecutive (x, y) eye positions, differentiation of consecutive eye positions (e.g., $x_n - x_{n+1}$), eye movement distance $(x^2 + y^2)^{1/2}$, and eye-movement direction ($arc\ tan\ [y/x]$). Each measure was treated as a vector of data points with temporal properties analyzed over the course of search.

To evaluate temporal pattern, a variety of NDS and descriptive tests were performed. Those reported here include power spectral analysis (FFT), autocorrelation (τ), Hurst rescaled range analysis (R/S), and two simplified measures of dispersion: R/S and S^2/M. Detailed descriptions of these tests can be found in Shelhamer (2006) and Sprott (2003). One visual search application of FFT and other NDS tests are also described in Aks (2005).

For each analysis, we used a complete search sequence consisting of 40 trials (except in the most difficult [homogeneous] search condition with 20 trials), and we removed eye movements that extended beyond the display screen boundaries (<0.1% of data series). An additional adjustment made to the data series compensated for any potential influence from initial (1 or 2) central fixations marking the start of each trial. Subjects fixated the center of the screen to ensure correct eye calibration by performing any needed drift correction and to ensure subjects were ready to begin the search task. To assess whether central fixations produce an artifact (i.e., a separate source for temporal correlations), we tested two versions of the time series: one with and one without the initial central fixations. Even though there was virtually no difference in our findings across the two series, the results reported here are based on time series, which exclude initial central fixations.

One final adjustment of the fixation series helped isolate (amplitude vs. direction) eye parameters and extrinsic versus intrinsic influences on eye movements. The first, *raw (x-coordinate) fixations*, measure saccade amplitude (i.e., distance between fixations), location, and direction of the eyes as the display is scanned.

These range from 0 to 1,024 pixels and represent the sequence of horizontal eye movements used in the search and scanning tasks. Raw scores were rescaled to the center of the display to tease apart factors that may influence search. Rescaling was performed by subtracting each fixation point from the average fixation position corresponding roughly to the center of the display ($x = 512$). Results on these ($x_n - x_{ave}$) time series were virtually the same as the raw (x_n) series. Thus effects found for raw scores reflect an impact on amplitude and direction; absolute (screen-based) location information plays little role in search performance. Finally, we calculated the absolute value of $x_n - x_{ave}$, thus removing direction information but maintaining information about relative saccade amplitude. Thus our second time series measure, *rescaled fixations*, may be described as:

$$X_{RSC} = |x_n - x_{ave}|.$$

Results for Image Complexity and Visual Search Dynamics

Visual search was most systematic in the simplest diamond conditions, as can be seen in a sample of the scan paths shown in Figure 5.1. The range (R) of eye movements increased with complexity (low $= 422$, medium $= 431$, and high $= 539$ pixels, on the basis of the first 512 data points using the rescaled measure of fixations; $F(2, 10) = 4.5$; $p < .05$). Overall, mean deviation from the display center was $M = 177$ and $SD = 131$. The average number of fixations to locate the gray dot increased with display complexity. Total number across 40 trials of the simple (794 fixations), intermediate (832 fixations), and complex ($\sim$2,326 fixations) figures. *Baseline scanning* produced an average of 923 fixations, largely determined by the experimenter who instructed how long subjects were to scan each of the diamond edges. Stimulus structure had the greatest influence in guiding eye movements in this edge-scanning task. Dominating the scan patterns were the periodic alternations between two diamond vertices (Fig. 5.4). Yet even with the obvious structure, there was large variability superimposed on scan path (baseline $M = 163$, $SD = 412$). This is true of all conditions, thus accounting for no significant difference in SD across complexity, $F(2, 10) = 2.1$; *ns.*

PDF Analyses

Figure 5.2 shows PDFs of the rescaled fixation series and their log–log plots across different complexity conditions. Nontransformed PDFs had a consistent positive skew ($M = 0.39$; $SD = 0.37$), which increased marginally with display complexity, $F(2, 10) = 3.6$; $p = .06$. The log–log plots appear to have a power-scaling region extending over two orders of magnitude in the high-frequency region. Just beyond is an exponential cut-off likely due to the outer boundary of the diamond figures, which restricts the range of eye movements and triggers an abrupt reversal of the eyes.

Linear regression estimates performed on the high-frequency region of the log-log PDF (i.e., those closer to the ordinate with a downward sloping linear trend) produce reliable scaling exponents (estimated by the slope of the linear regression line). A significant amount of the variance is accounted for in these analyses (i.e., $0.52 > R^2 > 0.83$). Additional assessments of the scaling range would be useful to confirm this pattern, as would performing maximum likelihood analyses to minimize bias in estimates of the scaling exponents (Newman, 2005). A noteworthy trend in the log–log PDFs (not subject to the linear regression bias) is the change in relative scaling across complexity conditions: Simpler-structured search produces shallower slopes in the (high-frequency) scaling region of the PDFs (Fig. 5.2C). This suggests that stimulus structure may attenuate the magnitude of (spatial) scaling. This difference is most obvious when making a within-subject comparison across the simplest and most complex cases, as is shown in Figure 5.2D.

Time Series Analysis of Temporal Patterns

Among the most consistent trends are temporal scaling effects and temporal dependencies found in power spectra, autocorrelation, and Hurst analyses: $1/f^2$ (brown noise) pattern across the 1-msec samples of raw eye positions, $1/f^0$ (white noise) across the sequence of fixation *directions* and *durations*, and $1/f$ (pink noise) patterns across the *sequence of fixation positions*. A sample time series is shown in Figure 5.3, along with representative spectral results for the different parameters of the eye movements. These patterns were remarkably consistent across conditions. The remaining analyses focus on the *fixation sequences* in which $\sim 1/f$ trends dominate. The various scaling effects are similar across x- and y-coordinate fixation sequences. Time series of x-coordinate positions are reported here. These capture the dominant horizontal movement of the eyes.

Simplified dispersion measures, R/S and S^2/M, provide an intuitive illustration of how eye movements scale with time and display complexity. There was a significant increase in R/S across four bin sizes: 256, 512, 768, and 1,024, $F(3, 36) = 5.0, p < .01$, indicating that eye-movement dispersion increases with longer windows of search time. Separate analyses of range and SDs show that the bulk of this effect is due to an increase in range with window size, $F(3, 36) = 2.8$; $p < .05$. Another measure of dispersion: S^2/M shows a further interaction with complexity ($F(6, 36) = 3.0$; $p < .02$), indicating that the dispersion increases with complexity. Similar scaling effects emerge in descriptive statistics. Skew, for example, increases with window size $F(2, 26) = 3.4$; $p < .05$, confirming the scale-free properties of eye movements. The most informative scaling statistics tested here include the power spectra, Hurst R/S exponent, and autocorrelation. Because these measures sample a much broader range of windows, they provide a much more comprehensive assessment of the pattern and magnitude of scaling. As noted, these show consistent $1/f$ patterns across the sequence of fixations over a wide range of conditions: *power spectra* regression slopes α (M = -1.12;

Table 5.1. Power spectra Fast Fourier transform (FFT), autocorrelation (τ), and Hurst (R/S) analyses for raw-x and rescaled-x fixation series

Fixation series		Power spectra (FFT) slope (α) (Bin window size)				Ave α	Tau (τ)	Hurst (R/S)
		16	32	64	128			
Raw-x	Ave	−1.5	−1.4	−1.2	−1.2	−1.31	6.02	0.22
	SD	0.20	0.25	0.23	0.17	0.20	7.94	0.05
Rescaled-x	Ave	−1.1	−1.0	−0.9	−0.8	−0.93	3.29	0.14
	SD	0.29	0.27	0.26	0.19	0.23	3.99	0.06

SD $= -0.20$), *Hurst* (H)R/S (M $= 0.17$; SD $= 0.05$), and autocorrelation τ (M $= 2.42$; SD $= 1.12$).

Display Complexity and Raw Versus Rescaled Fixations
Table 5.1 shows the results of FFT (α; calculated for five [bin] frequency windows: 16, 32, 64, 128), autocorrelation (τ), and Hurst (H) analyses for raw- and rescaled-fixation series. The first noteworthy finding is that α ranges from −0.8 to −1.5 – values all within the "1/f zone." Similarly, average $\tau = 4.7$, indicating slower memory decay across the fixation series than we find in the shuffled, uncorrelated time series ($\tau = 0$). Finally, H is consistently in a range (0.14 −0.22) indicating a clear pattern of antipersistence, in which short and long saccades tend to alternate between successive fixations. These values are significantly higher than the shuffled, uncorrelated series ($H = 0$) and typical of 1/f patterns.

Figures 5.5 and 5.6 show the effect of figural complexity on raw and rescaled fixation series. As complexity increases, power spectra get shallower, and τ and H decrease. In the most complex search tasks, there is a substantial decrease in all three (raw to rescaled differences, respectively: α-diff $= 0.6$, τ-diff $= 0.9$, and H-diff $= 0.1$). These values reflect "whitening" of the rescaled values. With greater complexity and less informative structure to guide search, long-range correlations diminish.

Recall that rescaling the fixation series helps tease apart the influence of different eye-movement parameters on visual search. Whereas the raw-x series combines *amplitude and direction* information, rescaled scores isolate *amplitude* information. If both series are affected equally by changes in complexity, than we can infer that amplitude is critical to search performance and that direction may be superfluous. However, this did not occur: Compared with the raw fixation series, the rescaled series had significantly shallower spectra [ave $\alpha = -1.3$ vs. −0.9; $F(1, 28) = 48.6$, $p < .05$], and higher Hurst exponents [$F(1, 28) = 26.5$, $p < .01$], but a nonsignificant difference in τ [$F(1, 28) = 48.6$, ns], although alternative grouping of complexity levels do produce significant effects for all three measures. The differences suggest that eye-movement *direction* (i.e., what distinguishes raw from rescaled measures) seems to have a significant impact across raw fixations. However, when considered along with our independent (angular) measure of direction, showing no correlation over search series (Fig. 5.3), a different interpretation emerges: Rather than direction, raw versus rescaled differences may reflect unique influences from extrinsic and intrinsic information and may interact with stimulus complexity in a subtle way.

Extrinsic Versus Intrinsic Influences

How raw and rescaled measures capture influences from extrinsic structure versus intrinsic dynamics is not obvious. The structure in *simpler displays* guides the eyes more strongly than that in complex displays. Figure 5.4 shows this for the raw fixation series: Search adheres more closely to the diamond figures in baseline and simple compared with complex trials. Search scans are much more distributed across the display in this complex case, with only 5 of the approximately 341 diamond structures showing a clear impact on search. In the rescaled figures, the influence of stimulus structure is far more subtle. Here we see two clusters for the simple case, which is what we would expect from having removed the direction information. But in the complex condition, there are three clusters, with the unique cluster now closest to the origin $(0,0)$. These correspond to the large number of fixations nearer to the central region of the screen. This pattern likely reflects a diminished influence from extrinsic structure in these complex cases, coupled with increased influence of intrinsic dynamics.

Whitening in the spectral analyses when fixations are rescaled, and as displays increase in complexity, is consistent with a loss of (useful) extrinsic information for guiding eye movements. This is especially true of the most complex homogeneous case, which occludes all but the 100-pixel GC region of the diamond figures. Based on these results, loss of information would seem to be due to extrinsic structure (from the complexity manipulation) and direction information (from the rescaling measure). However, the contribution from direction information on search is questionable given the separate analysis showing an absence of temporal correlation. This leaves open the possibility that relative intrinsic–extrinsic contributions may be the primary source for spectral whitening of rescaled measures, and these vary with display complexity.

Deviation From $1/f$ Baseline

Notice in Figure 5.6 spectral analysis, when fixations are *rescaled*, the *simplest* search is closest to $1/f$ (i.e., $\alpha = -1$), and the slope is steeper across raw fixations (i.e., $\alpha = -1.4$). This shift is in a direction toward a brown noise pattern with the pertinent feature of a more predictable long-term pattern. The stronger temporal correlations in these structured conditions are likely due to the extrinsic information preserved in the raw fixations. Likewise, in the baseline scanning task, raw spectral slopes are relatively steep and autocorrelations extremely high; again, these are substantially longer-range correlations than during complex search. Conversely, *raw* fixations in *complex* search patterns are closest to a $1/f$ pattern and whiten when rescaled. This interaction suggests that extrinsic structure dominates and is the primary source of temporal correlations across raw series when stimulus structure is strong. However, intrinsic dynamics dominate the raw series for complex figures when stimulus structure is weak and inadequate as a guide for visual search.

General Discussion and Conclusions

One broad goal of the present work was to illustrate how the study of mental and behavioral processes may be well served through NDS analysis. Using these tools, we examined patterns of behavior that best characterize visual search. First, we set out to understand intrinsic search dynamics and temporal dependencies in minimal constraint conditions. Then we quantified how these dynamics change with display structure. Changing background complexity provided a way to assess how a context constrains and interacts with intrinsic behavior. In a sense, we perturb the search system to learn about its response properties and how these deviate from baseline states. So what have we learned?

An essential property of visual search found in the present study is the pervasive presence of scaling and $\sim 1/f$ power law trends across the sequence of fixations and that search behavior is *not* best described by normal distributions or a characteristic scale. Rather, search scales with contextual complexity as suggested by long-tail PDFs and a variety of signatures of power law scaling. Based on our earlier work (Aks et al., 2002), we expected long-range dependencies (i.e., slow-decay and power law scaling) to emerge across either the sequence of fixations or their differences. This earlier study showed $1/f$ trends with $\alpha = -0.6$ and -1.8, respectively. The striking finding of the present study is the consistency of $1/f$ trends for almost all subjects and across all conditions. This suggests that a common (but highly variable) scanning strategy is used across a wide range of conditions *regardless* of stimulus structure: The $1/f$ pattern is pervasive! It is also important to emphasize that this pattern exists across *fixation* sequences. Because these are a hallmark of attention-based processes (especially in cases in which stimulus structure is not present to guide search behavior), they carry significant implications for the role of $1/f$ patterns in top-down cognitive processes. One is that goal-driven behavior may emerge from self-organizing processes.

When the display's structure is manipulated, there are subtle but reliable shifts in search patterns. Background context affects both spatial and temporal dynamics of search. Changes in the range and scaling region of PDFs reflect spatial shifts, whereas changes in spectral, autocorrelation, and dispersion analyses reflect temporal shifts. Shallower PDF slopes and reduced search range in simpler search trials suggest that scaling and search variability is more constrained relative to search in the more complex and less structured displays. As for temporal correlations, these are weakened in unstructured displays as suggested by the reduced power spectra slopes, autocorrelations, and rescaled range statistics. Extrinsic structure can attenuate (e.g., our complex conditions; Linkenkaer-Hansen et al., 2004) or enhance intrinsic memory (e.g., structure in our simpler displays guides search and extends long-range correlations). Shifts in performance reflect a relative balance of extrinsic and intrinsic influences on search.

Questions for Future Studies

1. How can we improve the separating of extrinsic from intrinsic contributions to search? Our attempt to distinguish extrinsic from intrinsic influences may have left us with more questions than answers. The pervasiveness of $1/f$ patterns, especially in the simplest conditions, was unexpected. One likely account relates to the robustness of intrinsic patterns and how they are revealed even in the residual variability after stimulus structure is removed in the rescaled measures. Further rescaling of fixations to the center of each of the primary (four or five) diamonds in the display would help confirm that intrinsic search dynamics persist regardless of the strength of the stimulus structure.

Whether stimulus structure mimics or masks intrinsic patterns presents an additional challenge to confirming that intrinsic dynamics are $1/f$. Minimal-constraint conditions are useful to uncover intrinsic dynamics (i.e., our homogeneous display), but we also need to know exactly what information our behavioral measures capture. Our search power spectra were closest to $1/f$ ($\alpha = -1$) across raw fixations during complex search. When rescaled, however, $1/f$ patterns emerged in the simplest conditions. Does rescaling reflect a reduced role of stimulus structure and a greater focus on intrinsic $1/f$ dynamics, or does the effect of rescaling depend on the complexity of the display? Perhaps we should revisit the explanations that rescaling isolates saccade amplitude information and that temporal correlations are weakened simply from the loss of the directional information. (Recall, though, that our independent measure of direction produced uncorrelated spectra, steering us to interpret rescaled measures as a way to separate out stimulus structure.) One way to resolve this ambiguity is to use a more direct test of intrinsic versus extrinsic factors. Using our scanning and search tasks, we can compare cases in which diamond structure is visible versus cases in which it is not visible but needs to be held in memory to do the task. Showing the diamond context only at the start of a series of trials would force a memory-dependent search and thus ensure that intrinsic processes are used and help clarify whether $1/f$ patterns reflect these intrinsic dynamics.

2. What accounts for $1/f$ patterns in different regions of the power spectra? One noteworthy finding pertains to the range over which $1/f$ patterns emerge in power spectra and the relationship of this to other findings. Our search fixation series produced $1/f$ patterns either across the full spectra ($\sim$47% raw-x series; $\sim$6% rescaled series) or in the higher frequency range spectra ($\sim$42%

raw-x series; ~78% rescaled series) Similarly, Wagenmakers et al.'s (2004, 2005) short-range autoregressive moving average (ARMA) model mimics $1/f$ trends predominantly in the high-frequency range. On its own, this similarity suggests that search may be generated by short-range processes such as those proposed in GLM models. However, the shapes of the spectra are quite different. Wagenmakers et al.'s model produces a smooth, reverse-sigmoid shape in their power spectra, whereas search fixations, when not $1/f$ across the full spectra, tended to have a more abrupt transition from white to pink, appearing either as a step or even a U shape, as in search results in Figure 5.5. We suspect flattening in the low-frequency regions may be an artifact perhaps due to display constraints or the limited length of our data series. Extending these in future study would help clarify their role. Fortunately, we made use of additional NDS tests of temporal dependence (τ and R/S), and these support our conclusion that the fixation series are best described by genuine long-range patterns.

3. What is the connection between $1/f$ effects and frequency range? Perhaps more important is the divergence of our findings from most RT studies in which $1/f$ effects are prevalent in the *low*-frequency range of power spectra (e.g., Delignières et al., 2005, 2006; Thornton & Gilden, 2005). Gilden (2001) argued that low-frequency patterns reflect cognitive process, whereas high-frequency portions reflect motor response. Might such a two-process account apply only to (coarser) manual RTs? Are eye movements unique with their finer motor precision? Or are eye movements more tightly integrated with the critical sensorimotor interface? These questions hit at the core of conceptions of what constitutes perceptual–cognitive processes. We often characterize perceptual, cognitive, and motor domains as distinct, but assessments of dynamic qualities often point to a far more integrated and coordinated system.

Modeling Long-Range and $1/f$ Behavior

What models generate complex long-range behavior? Which ones best explain complex patterns in visual search? These remain open questions, exacerbated by the fact that NDS tests of visual search are only in their infancy. With many possible models to consider, this is a formidable task. Narrowing to a best explanatory match requires careful scrutiny, with priority placed on a number of pertinent issues: (a) biological plausibility, (b) parallel manipulations assessing whether similar responses occur in human and model behavior, and (c) determining key characteristics of search behavior that emerge over time under these different conditions. A few thoughts along these lines are suggested here, along with an overview of some prospective search models.

Networks and Self-Organization
The most common neural network models of visual search explicitly represent bottom-up (feed-forward) and top-down (feedback) influences in their

design (Itti & Koch, 2001). Others exploit interaction dynamics and emergent self-organizing properties to produce top-down influences such as those that can trigger synchronous oscillations across brain regions (Lumer, Edelman, & Tononi, 1997) and those that give rise to perceptual–cognitive states (Lin & Chen, 2005). Most pertinent to volitional search are models of attentional guidance (Deco, Pollatos, & Zihl, 2002; Deco & Zihl, 2001), and those demonstrating a critical role for neural self-organization (Usher, Stemmler, & Olami, 1995). All of these share the important property that complex behavioral states emerge implicitly from the complex interactions across neural ensembles.

A similar form of distributed control exists for eye movements. In visual search, a network of various brain regions, including the SC in the thalamus and LIP and FEF in the cortex, drives our eyes. Eye movement is often triggered by the joint activation of these distributed sets of neurons, rather than by a small set of maximally activated cells. McIlwain (1991), for example, showed that despite the large receptive and movement fields of SC neurons, inactivating small regions (psychopharmacologically) affects a wide range of eye movements. Such network sensitivity and its spreading effect are a hallmark of a highly integrated network.

Not only do populations of neurons in SC, FEF, and LIP play critical roles in generating saccades, but their cumulative activity can also produce $1/f$ behavior. Similar to a model proposed by Ward (2002), neural activity that accumulates across different cognitive levels can lead to $1/f$ behavior. Within each level, where there are many interacting components acting on different time scales, long-range dependencies emerge. From the interaction of the constituents (neurons, neural populations, microbehaviors, etc.) arises coordinated, and often $1/f$ observed (macro), behavior. System feedback and reentry across these levels of behavior also play an important role in producing complex behavior. The leading theory of population dynamics (e.g., Tononi & Edelman, 1998) presents a compelling case for "recurrent activity loops" as essential to cognition. These cyclical forms of feedback (i.e., reentrant neural activity) flow across cortical and subcortical neural groups. Notably, the temporal characteristics of this activity flow and subsequent behavior may be a signature of neural "avalanche" dynamics and self-organized criticality (Bak, Tang, & Wiesenfeld, 1987; Werner, 2006).

Self-Organized Criticality (SOC)
In our earlier work (Aks, Nokes, Sprott, & Keane, 1998; Aks et al., 2002, 2005), we speculated on the intriguing possibility that an SOC-like mechanism might account for $1/f$ structure in visual search. Similar speculation has been made for many other behaviors – human and otherwise (Bak, 1996). Among its useful characteristics, SOC is widely known for (a) its flexibility, which permits easy adaptation to novel and uncertain conditions, and (b) its biological plausibility (Werner, 2007). Since our early speculation (Aks et al., 1998), and despite much

skepticism and subsequent qualifications of the range over which SOC is thought to generate $1/f$ patterns (Jensen, 1998; Kadanoff, Nagel, Wu, & Zhou, 1989; Werner, 2006), there is an increasing number of demonstrations that SOC is a useful fit to many optimal systems including those far from equilibrium (i.e., far from stable states; Paszuski, Maslov, & Bak, 1996). Cognitive tasks requiring active engagement, such as active forms of visual search, tend to be far from equilibrium. Perhaps the most direct evidence for SOC is the work of Beggs and Plenz (2003, 2004), who reported critical behavior in slices of (intact) cortical tissue of rodents and primates and showed that neural avalanches serve to organize cortical cell assemblies (Plenz & Thiagarajan, 2006). Modeling work draws similar conclusions (e.g., Usher et al., 1995).

One lucrative variant of SOC, described by Kwok and Smith (2005), is a technique that enables a self-organizing neural network (SONN) to achieve optimal performance in combinatorial types of problems including many complex search tasks. This work confirms various claims that $1/f$ intermittency is a signature of an efficient system and shares many "high-priority" characteristics appropriate to modeling search behavior. The SONN model uses an adaptation of Kohonen's (1982) self-organizing feature map, a cost-weighting scheme for updating the network's nodes, and an iterated softmax function (ISF). An ISF is a sigmoid function, with outputs interpreted as continuous probabilities with states between 0 and 1. ISF is similar to the mean-field theory and annealing approach used in neural networks models, and, importantly, enables computations across many time scales. The model behaves as an ongoing competition of neurons in the cost space, and the weights associated with winning neighborhoods are updated with Kohonen's learning rule. Because partial costs are functions of the weights, the competition-updating process forms a feedback loop. The $1/f$ signals in ISF also suggest that the search carries both short- and long-range temporal correlations, thus rendering it sensitive to small fluctuations and at the same time preserving a memory of past states. This strategy is clearly useful in an efficient search of global regions because it has to escape local minima in the short term, while keeping a memory of searched regions over the long term. Like Usher et al. (1995), Kwok and Smith suggested exploitation of $1/f$ dynamics, especially the property of intermittency in neural computations to optimize problem solving, including problems of visual search and foraging.

Search, Foraging, and Collective Behavior

In an early RT study, Posner and Cohen (1984) referred to visual search as a *foraging facilitator* to describe the tendency to seek out new information by inhibiting return to previously visited locations. They suggested that IOR may serve as a memory for previously attended locations to help facilitate finding a target in search. A number of studies claim support: Klein and MacInnes (1999), for example, showed that saccades have a strong (directional) bias away from previously fixated regions. However, much controversy surrounds IOR, including (a) the extent to which IOR exists at all (Horowitz & Wolfe, 1998), (b) whether it depends on the nature of search- or attention-based phenomena (Hooge, Over, van Wezel, & Frenz, 2005), and (c) whether it actually even guides or facilitates search (Horowitz & Wolfe, 2001).

Resolution of these debated issues may be found in studies of animal foraging. The strong behavioral and modeling parallels, together with considerations from a systems perspective, offer compelling reasons to consider animal-behavior research in our attempt to understand visual search. Both visual search and animal foraging produce intermittent behaviors: Rapid (global) behaviors stretch over large regions and are interspersed with sporadic periods of slow, methodical (local) search. Both also produce occasional extreme excursions and long-tailed, power law PDFs and have been described reasonably well by diffusion models (Benichou, Coppey, Moreau, Suet, & Voituriez, 2005; Duchowski, 2005; Smith & Ratcliff, 2004). Different versions of these models can also account for conditions where revisiting locations (i.e., IOR) benefits search. Benichou et al. (2007) demonstrated that intermittent strategies based on a two-phase diffusion model are optimal and proved superior to an alternative (diffusion model) Lévy flight strategy, which is optimal in conditions in which targets are revisited (i.e., analogous to the IOR conditions).

When foraging is a group affair and a consequence of collective behavior (Couzin, Krause, Franks, & Levine, 2005; Sumpter, 2006), it is strikingly analogous to the activity of the brain's neural ensembles, which undoubtedly play an important role in guiding search. We have seen neural network models showing how neural interactions may trigger fortuitous shifts in gaze direction (i.e., SOC, SONN). A similar logic has been applied to particular aspects of search including IOR behavior (Hooge et al., 2005), thus providing a plausible account for our antipersistent patterns (i.e., the tendency for short and long saccades to alternate) as a consequence of intrinsic dynamics arising from interactions across neural populations.

What lessons for neuroscience might be gained by examining collective behavior in animals? Overt behavior is inevitably easier to observe than is neural behavior. Its familiarity and real-world properties also make for easier understanding of collective phenomena and their potential source. Couzin et al. (2005) described how group foraging and other collective (i.e., "swarming") behaviors are driven by *coordination across individuals* making up groups. Many group decisions result from simple interactions among individuals making up a network. Importantly, these individuals need not have access to global (i.e., top-down) information. Rather, local interactions often produce global group responses. These collective decision-making models offer useful predictions and easily generalize to human cognition and visual search. Pertinent are the simple rules described in Couzin et al. (2005) and demonstration that the strength of local interactions may produce unique behaviors. One example of a simple rule that generates complex group behavior with widespread effect is that if weak local interactions dominate, then a taxis response is strong, and the group accrues the most benefit from averaging information across individuals. Strong local interactions instead tend to slow response to environmental stimuli (i.e., gradients). Simple rules such as these, not unlike SOC or SONN rules, present system-level predictions for neural-based activity and subsequent behavior. Future assessments using NDS tools likely will provide insight about foraging and search behavior and whether they share similar mechanisms.

Bridging Structure and Function Into a Unified NDS Theory

Earlier I touched on how complex systems may be understood from the perspective of network theory, how the millions of neurons comprising the brain's network can behave collectively, and how simple rules of interaction can generate complex behavior. That simple rules, such as SOC and SONN, can provide a plausible account for the emergence of complex perceptual–cognitive behavior is of appeal for its parsimony and intuitive threshold and propagation mechanisms. Models of self-organizing, coordinated dynamics bridge neuroscience and many of the interesting scale-free behaviors. Equally compelling but beyond the scope of this chapter is the tight coupling of these behavioral properties with sparse but clustered network structure. Briefly, most nodes in these "small-world" networks have a few interacting connections, but a few (hubs) have hundreds or thousands of connections (Watts & Strogatz, 1998). These hubs share many of the properties found in power law behavior in that they are ubiquitous in the natural world, have an optimal structure to transfer information, produce universal scaling behaviors, and play a critical role in developmental and growth domains (i.e., preferential attachment; Barabási & Albert, 1999).

Perhaps most significant are the recent applications in behavioral neuroscience in which clear empirical bridges are made between network structure and function. Bassett et al.'s (2006) magnetoencephalography study is an excellent example, showing scale-free, long-range properties across a wide range of behavioral states and brain activity (frequency bands: 2–38 Hz). During rest, when intrinsic dynamics dominate, long-range connectivity is strongest at low frequencies (α to δ: <13 Hz), but during a simple motor task, *network activity is reconfigured* so that long-range connectivity is now strongest in high frequencies (β to γ: ~10–70 Hz). New long-range structural connections also emerge (from frontal to parietal cortex) to accommodate the sensory–motor task (i.e., visually cued finger tapping).

Parallels with the findings reported here help clarify ambiguities found in our results. In both studies, long-range, scale-free patterns persist across a wide range of conditions. Bassett et al. (2006) provided compelling evidence that these are due to intrinsic dynamics, suggesting the same is likely to be true of search. Experimental manipulations, in both cases, also produce subtler shifts in these dynamics: high- versus low-frequency activity bands in Bassett et al. and low-frequency spectral whitening in search. These shifts reflect changing dynamics and changes in sensory–motor integration. It would be worthwhile to examine further these links and those elsewhere, including (a) the relation between patterns of synchrony and asynchrony and (b) how shifts in brain activity dynamics and connectivity relate to behavioral dependencies found in perceptual cognitive tasks. Combining neuroscience and behavioral techniques undoubtedly will help clarify the source of many patterns of behavior, including distinguishing and understanding the interplay of extrinsic and intrinsic dynamics. Suffice it to say, such integrated work, effectively using NDS tools and concepts, is one of the critical steps toward unifying theories of mind and behavior – a step likely to bring us closer to some long-awaited answers.

References

Aks, D. J. (2005). *1/f dynamic in complex visual search: Evidence for self-organized criticality in human perception.* Retrieved November 29, 2007, from http://www.nsf.gov/sbe/bcs/pac/nmbs/nmbs.jsp

Aks, D. J., & Enns, J. T. (1992). Visual search for direction of shading is influenced by apparent depth. *Perception and Psychophysics, 52,* 63–74.

Aks, D. J., & Enns, J. T. (1996). Visual search for size is influenced by a background texture gradient. *Journal of Experimental Psychology: Human Perception and Performance, 22,* 1467–1481.

Aks, D. J., Nokes, T., Sprott, J. C., & Keane, E. (1998, November). *Resolving perceptual ambiguity in the Necker cube: A dynamical systems approach.* Paper presented at the Psychonomics Society Meeting, Dallas, TX.

Aks, D. J., & Sprott, J. C. (2003). The role of depth and 1/f dynamics in perceiving reversible figures. *Nonlinear Dynamics, Psychology, and Life Sciences, 7,* 161–180.

Aks, D. J., Zelinsky, G. J., & Sprott, J. C. (2002). Memory across eye movements: 1/f dynamic in visual search. *Nonlinear Dynamics, Psychology, and Life Sciences, 6,* 1–25.

Bak, P. (1996). *How nature works.* New York: Springer-Verlag.

Bak, P., Tang, C., & Wiesenfeld, K. (1987). Self-organized criticality: An explanation of the 1/f noise. *Physical Review Letters, 59,* 381–384.

Barabási, A., & Albert, R. (1999). Emergence of scaling in random networks. *Science, 286,* 509–512.

Bassett, D. S., Meyer-Lindenberg, A., Achard, S., Duke, T., & Bullmore, E. (2006). Adaptive reconfiguration of fractal small-world human brain functional networks. *Proceedings of the National Academy of Sciences, 103,* 19518–19523.

Beer, R. D. (2000). Dynamical approaches to cognitive science. *Trends in Cognitive Science, 4,* 91-99.

Beggs, J. M., & Plenz, D. (2003). Neural avalanches in neocortical circuits. *Journal of Neuroscience, 23,* 1167–1177.

Beggs, J. M., & Plenz. D. (2004). Neural avalanches are diverse and precise activity patterns that are stable for many hours in cortical slice cultures. *Journal of Neuroscience, 24,* 5216–5229.

Beintema, J. A., van Loon, E. M., & van den Berg, A. V. (2005). Manipulating saccadic decision-rate distributions in visual search. *Journal of Vision, 5*, 150–164.

Beltz, B. C., & Kello, C. T. (2004, August). *The effect of cue predictability on long-range dependencies in response times and response durations.* Paper presented at the Proceedings of the 26th Annual Meeting of Cognitive Science, Chicago, IL.

Benichou, O., Coppey, M., Moreau, M., Suet, P. H., & Voituriez, R. (2005). Optimal search strategies for hidden targets. *Physical Review Letters, 94*, 198101–198104.

Bergen, J. R., & Julesz, B. (1983). Parallel versus serial processing in rapid pattern discrimination. *Nature, 303*, 696–698.

Brascamp, J. W., van Ee, R., Pestman, W. R., & Van Den Berg, A. V. (2005). Distributions of alternation rates in various forms of bistable perception. *Journal of Vision, 5*, 287–298.

Brecht, M., Singer, W., & Engel, A. E. (1999). Patterns of synchronization in superior solliculus of anaesthetized cats. *Journal of Neuroscience, 19*, 3567–3579.

Buzsáki, G. (2006). *Rhythms of the brain.* Oxford: Oxford University Press.

Carello, C. M., & Moreno, M. A. (2005). *Why nonlinear methods?* Retrieved November, 29, 2007, from http://www.nsf.gov/sbe/bcs/pac/nmbs/nmbs.jsp

Carpenter, R. H. S. (1981). Oculomotor procrastination. In D. F. Fisher, R. A. Monty, & J. W. Senders (Eds.), *Eye movements: Cognition and visual perception* (pp. 237–246). Hillsdale, NJ: Erlbaum.

Chen, Y., Ding, M., & Kelso, J. A. (2001). Origins of timing errors in human sensorimotor coordination. *Journal of Motor Behavior, 3*, 3–8.

Clauset, A., Shalizi, C. R., & Newman, M. E. J. (2007). Power-law distributions in empirical data [Electronic version]. Retrieved November, 29, 2007, from http://arxiv.org/abs/0706.1062v1

Clayton, K., & Frey, B. B. (1997). Studies of mental "noise." *Nonlinear Dynamics in Psychology and Life Science, 1*, 173–180.

Couzin, I. D., Krause, J., Franks, N. R., & Levin, S. A. (2005). Effective leadership and decision-making in animal groups on the move. *Nature, 433*, 513–516.

Deco, G., Pollatos, O., & Zihl, J. (2002). The time course of selective visual attention: Theory and experiments. *Vision Research, 42*, 2925–2945.

Deco, G., & Zihl, J. (2001). Top-down selective visual attention: A neurodynamical approach. *Visual Cognition, 8*, 118–139.

Delignières, D., Ramdani, S., Lemoine, L., Torre, K., Fortes, M., & Ninot, G. (2006). Fractal analyses for "short" time series: A re-assessment of classical methods. *Journal of Mathematical Psychology, 50*, 525–544.

Delignières, D., Torre, K., & Lemoine, L. (2005). Methodological issues in the application of monofractal analyses in psychological and behavioral analyses. *Nonlinear Dynamics, Psychology, and Life Sciences, 9*, 435–461.

Ding, M., Chen, Y., & Kelso, J. A. (2002). Statistical analysis of timing errors. *Brain Cognition, 48*, 98–106.

Duchowski, A. (2005). Eye-based interaction in graphical systems: Theory and practice [Electronic version]. Retrieved November, 29, 2007, from http://www.vr.clemson.edu/eyetracking/sigcourse

Duncan, J. H., & Humphrey, G. W. (1989). Visual search and stimulus similarity. *Psychological Review, 96*, 433–458.

Edelman, G. M., & Tononi, G. (2000). *Consciousness: How matter becomes imagination.* London: Penguin.

Engel, A. K., & Singer, W. (2001). Temporal binding and the neural correlates of sensory awareness. *Trends in Cognitive Sciences, 5,* 16–25.

Farid, H., & Adelson, T. (2001). Synchrony does not promote grouping in temporally structured displays. *Nature Neuroscience, 4,* 875–876.

Feder, J. (1988). *Fractals.* New York: Plenum Press.

Findlay, J. M., Brown, V., & Gilchrist, I. D. (2001). Saccade target selection in visual search: The effect of information from the previous fixation. *Vision Research, 41,* 87–95.

Findlay, J. M., & Gilchrist, I. D. (2003). *Active vision: The psychology of looking and seeing.* Oxford: Oxford University Press.

Freeman, W. J. (1991). The physiology of perception. *Scientific American, 264,* 78–85.

Freeman, W. J. (2001). *How brains make up their minds.* New York: Columbia University Press.

Gao, J. B., Billock, V. A., Merk, I., Tung, W. W., White, K. D., et al. (2006). Inertia and memory in ambiguous visual perception. *Cognitive Processing, 7,* 105-112.

Gilden, D. L. (1997). Fluctuations in the time required for elementary decisions. *Psychological Science, 8,* 296–301.

Gilden, D. L. (2001). Cognitive emissions of $1/f$ noise. *Psychological Review, 108,* 33–56.

Gilden, D. L., Thornton, T., & Mallon, M. W. (1995). $1/f$ noise in human cognition. *Science, 267,* 1837–1839.

Glimcher, P. (2003). *Decisions, uncertainty, and the brain: The science of neuroeconomics.* Cambridge, MA: MIT Press.

Gong P., Nikolaev, A. R., & van Leeuwen C. (2003). Scale-invariant fluctuations of the dynamical synchronization in human brain electrical activity. *Neuroscience Letters, 336,* 33–36.

Guastello, S. J. (2005). Statistical distributions and self-organizing phenomena: What conclusions should be drawn? *Nonlinear Dynamics in Psychology and Life Science, 9,* 463–478.

Hohle, R. H. (1965). Inferred components of reaction time as functions of fore period duration. *Journal of Experimental Psychology, 69,* 382–386.

Hooge, I. T. C., & Erkelens, C. J. (1998). Adjustment of fixation duration in visual search. *Vision Research, 3,* 1295–1302.

Hooge, I. T. C., Over, E. A. B., van Wezel, R. J. A., & Frens, M. A. (2005). Inhibition of return is not a foraging facilitator in saccadic search and free viewing. *Vision Research, 45,* 1901–1908.

Horowitz, T. S., & Wolfe, J. M. (1998). Visual search has no memory. *Nature, 357,* 575–577.

Horowitz, T. S., & Wolfe, J. M. (2001). Search for multiple targets: Remember the targets, forget the search. *Perception and Psychophysics, 63,* 272–285.

Itti, L., & Koch, C. (2001). Computational modeling of visual attention. *Nature Reviews, 2,* 1–11.

Jensen, H. J. (1998). *Self-organized criticality.* Cambridge, MA: Cambridge University Press.

Kadanoff, L. P., Nagel, S. R., Wu, L., & Zhou, S. (1989). Scaling and universality in avalanches. *Physical Review A, 39,* 6524–6537.

Kapoula, Z., & Robinson, D. A. (1986). Saccade undershoot is not inevitable: Saccades can be accurate. *Vision Research, 26*, 735–743.

Kastner, S., & Pinsk, M. A. (2004). Visual attention as a multilevel selection process. *Cognition, Affect and Behavioral Neuroscience, 4*, 483–500.

Kelso, S. (1995). *Dynamic patterns: The self-organization of brain and behavior.* Cambridge, MA: MIT Press.

Klein, R. M., & MacInnes, W. J. (1999). Inhibition of return is a foraging facilitator in visual search. *Psychological Science, 10*, 346–352.

Kohonen, T. (1982). Self-organized formation of topologically correct feature maps. *Biological Cybernetics, 43*, 59–69.

Kovacs, I., Papathomas, T. V., Yang, M., & Feher, A. (1996). When the brain changes its mind: Interocular grouping during binocular rivalry. *Proceeding of National Academy of Sciences, 93*, 15508–15511.

Kowler, E., Martins, A. J., & Pavel, M. (1984). The effect of expectations on slow oculomotor control – IV. Anticipatory smooth eye movements depend on prior target motions. *Vision Research, 24*, 197–210.

Kwok, T., & Smith, P. L. (2005). Optimization via intermittency with a self-organizing neural network. *Neural Computation, 17*, 2454–2481.

Liebovitch, L. S. (1998). *Fractals and chaos: Simplified for the life sciences.* Oxford: Oxford University Press.

Lin, M., & Chen, T. (2005). Self-organized criticality in a simple model of neurons based on small-world networks. *Physical Review E, 71*, 016133–016135.

Linkenkaer-Hansen, K., Nikouline, V. V., Palva, J. M., Kaila, K., & Ilmoniemi, R. J. (2004). Stimulus-induced change in long-range temporal correlations and scaling behaviour of sensorimotor oscillations. *European Journal of Neuroscience, 19*, 203–211.

Lumer, E. D., Edelman, G. M., & Tononi, G. (1997). Neural dynamics in a model of the thalamocortical system: Layers, loops, and the emergence of fast synchronous rhythms. *Cerebral Cortex, 7*, 207–227.

Mazer, J. A., & Gallant, J. L. (2003). Goal-related activity in V4 during free viewing visual search: Evidence for a ventral stream visual salience map. *Neuron, 40*, 1241–1250.

McGill, W. J. (1963). Stochastic latency mechanisms. In R. D. Luce, R. R. Bush, & E. Galanter (Eds.), *Handbook of Mathematical Psychology* (Vol. I, pp. 309–360). New York: Wiley.

McIlwain, J. T. (1991). Distributed spatial coding in the superior colliculus: A review. *Visual Neuroscience, 6* (1), 3–13.

McPeek, R. M., Skavenski, A. A., & Nakayama, K. (2000). Concurrent processing of saccades in visual search. *Vision Research, 40*, 2499–2516.

Newman, M. E. J. (2005). Power laws, Pareto distributions and Zipf's law. *Contemporary Physics, 46*, 323–351.

Ögmen, H., & Breitmeyer, B. G. (2006). *The first half second: The microgenesis and temporal dynamics of unconscious and conscious visual processes.* Cambridge, MA: MIT Press.

Over, E. A. B., Hooge, I. T. C., Vlaskamp, B. N. S., & Erkelens, C. J. (2007). Coarse-to-fine eye movement strategy in visual search. *Vision Research, 47*, 2272–2280.

Palmer, E. M., Wolfe, J. M., & Horowitz, T. S. (2004). Response time distributions constrain models of visual search [Abstract]. *Journal of Vision, 4*, 674.

Paczuski, M., Maslov, S., & Bak, P. (1996). Avalanche dynamics in evolution, growth and depinning models. *Physical Review E, 53,* 414–443.

Peak, D., & Frame, M. (1994). *Chaos under control: The art and science of complexity.* New York: Freeman.

Pfeifer, R., & Bongard, J. (2007). *How the body shapes the way we think: A new view of intelligence.* Cambridge, MA: Bradford – MIT Press.

Plenz, D., & Thiagarajan, T. C. (2006). The organizing principles of neural avalanches: cell assemblies in the cortex. *Trends in Neurosciences, 30,* 101–110.

Posner, M. I. (1986). *Chronometric exploration of mind.* Oxford, England: Oxford University Press.

Posner, M. I. (2005). Timing the brain: Mental chronometry as a tool in neuroscience. *Public Library of Science Biology, 3,* e51.

Posner, M. I., & Cohen, Y. (1984). Components of attention. In H. Bouma & D. G. Bouwhuis (Eds.), *Attention and performance X* (pp. 55–66). Hillsdale, NJ: Erlbaum.

Press, W. H., Flannery, B. P., Teukolsky S. A., & Vetterling, W. T. (1986). *Numerical recipes.* Cambridge: Cambridge University Press.

Rodriguez, E., George, N., Lachaux, J. P., Martinerie, J., Renault, B., & Varela, F. J. (1999). Perception's shadow: Long-distance synchronization of human brain activity. *Nature, 397,* 430–433.

Shadlen, M. N., & Movshon, J. A. (1999). Synchrony unbound: A critical evaluation of the temporal binding hypothesis. *Neuron, 24,* 67–77.

Shelhamer, M. (2005a). Sequences of predictive saccades are correlated over a span of ~2 s and produce a fractal time series. *Journal of Neurophysiology, 93,* 2002–2011.

Shelhamer, M. (2005b). Sequences of predictive eye movements form a fractional Brownian series – implications for self-organized criticality in the oculomotor system. *Biological Cybernetics, 93,* 43–53.

Shelhamer, M. (2006). *Nonlinear dynamics in physiology: A state-space approach.* Singapore: World Scientific.

Shelhamer, M., & Joiner, W. M. (2003). Saccades exhibit abrupt transition between reactive and predictive; predictive saccade sequences have long-term correlations. *Journal of Neurophysiology, 90,* 2763–2769.

Singer, W. (1993). Synchronization of cortical activity and its putative role in information processing and learning. *Human Perception and Performance, 21,* 901–913.

Singer, W. (1999). Response synchronization: A universal coding strategy for the definition of relations. In M. S. Gazzaniga (Ed.), *The cognitive neurosciences* (Vol. 21, pp. 901–913). Cambridge, MA: MIT Press.

Singer, W., & Gray, C. M. (1995). Visual feature integration and the temporal correlation hypothesis. *Annual Review of Neuroscience, 18,* 555–586.

Skarda, C., & Freeman W. J. (1987). How brains make chaos in order to make sense of the world. *Brain and Behavioral Science, 10,* 161–195.

Smith, P. L., & Ratcliff, R. (2004). Psychology and neurobiology of simple decisions. *Trends in Neurosciences, 27,* 161–168.

Sommer, M. A. (1994). Express saccades elicited during visual scan in the monkey. *Vision Research, 34,* 2023–2038.

Sornette, D. (2004). *Critical phenomena in natural sciences: Chaos, fractals, self-organization and disorder; concepts and tools.* New York: Springer Publishing Company.

Spivey, M. (2007). *The continuity of mind.* Oxford: Oxford University Press.

Sprott, J. C. (2003). *Chaos and time-series analysis.* New York: Oxford University Press.

Stam, C. J., & de Bruin, E. A. (2004). Scale-free dynamics of global functional connectivity in the human brain. *Human Brain Mapping, 22,* 97–109.

Sternberg, S. (1969). The discovery of processing stages: Extensions of Donders' method. *Acta Psychologica, 30,* 276–315.

Stone, A. C. (2006). *Stone Works: Starmores* (Version 1.0 [2]). Albuquerque, NM: Andrew C. Stone & Stone Design.

Sumpter, D. J. T. (2006). Review. The principles of collective animal behaviour. *Philosophical Transactions of the Royal Society B: Biological Sciences, 361,* 5–22.

Thornton, T. L., & Gilden, D. L. (2005). Provenance of correlations in psychological data. *Psychonomic Bulletin and Review, 12,* 409–441.

Tononi, G., & Edelman, G. M. (1998). Consciousness: How matter becomes imagination. *Science, 282,* 1846–1185.

Treisman, A., & Gelade, G. (1980). A feature-integration theory of attention. *Cognitive Psychology, 12,* 97–136.

Usher, M., Stemmler, M., & Olami, Z. (1995). Dynamic pattern formation leads to $1/f$ noise in neural populations. *Physical Review Letters, 74,* 326–329.

Van Loon, E. M., Hooge, I. T., & van den Berg, A. V. (2002). The timing of sequences of saccades in visual search. *Proceedings of Biological Sciences, 269,* 1571–1579.

Van Orden, G. C., Holden, J. G., & Turvey, M. T. (2003). Self-organization of cognitive performance. *Journal of Experimental Psychology: General, 132,* 331–350.

Van Orden, G. C., Holden, J. G., & Turvey, M. T. (2005). Human cognition and $1/f$ scaling. *Journal of Experimental Psychology: General, 134,* 117–123.

Varela, F. (1999). The specious present: A neurophenomenology of time consciousness. In F. J. V. Jean Petitot, B. Pachoud & J. M. Roy (Eds.), *Naturalizing phenomenology: Issues in contemporary phenomenology and cognitive science* (pp. 266–329). Stanford, CA: Stanford University Press.

Varela, F., Lachaux, J. P., Rodriguez, E., & Martinerie, J. (2001). The brainweb: Phase synchronization and large-scale integration. *Nature Reviews Neuroscience, 2,* 229–239.

Varela, F., Thompson, E., & Rosch, E. (1991). *The embodied mind: Cognitive science and human experience.* Cambridge, MA: MIT Press.

Vaughan, J., & Graefe, T. (1977). Delay of stimulus presentation after the saccade in visual search. *Perception and Psychophysics, 22,* 201–205.

Vincent, J. L., Patel, G. H., Fox, M. D., Snyder, A. Z., Baker, J. T., et al. (2007). Intrinsic functional architecture in the anaesthetized monkey brain. *Nature, 447,* 83–86.

Wagenmakers, E. J., Farrell, S., & Ratcliff, R. (2004). Estimation and interpretation of $1/f$ alpha noise in human cognition. *Psychonomics Bulletin and Review, 1,* 579–615.

Wagenmakers, E. J., Farrell, S., & Ratcliff, R. (2005). Human cognition and a pile of sand: A discussion on serial correlations and self-organized criticality. *Journal of Experimental Psychology: General, 134,* 108–116.

Ward, L. M. (2002). *Dynamical cognitive science.* Cambridge MA: MIT Press.

Watts, D. J., & Strogatz, S. H. (1998). Collective dynamics of "small-world" networks. *Nature, 393,* 440–442.

Webber, C. L., Jr., & Zbilut, J. P. (1994). Dynamical assessment of physiological systems and states using recurrence plot strategies. *Journal of Applied Psychology, 76,* 965–973.

Werner, M. D. G. (2006). Brain dynamics across levels of organization [Electronic version]. Retrieved November 29, 2007, from http://cogprints.org/5275/

Werner, M. D. G. (2007). Perspectives on the neuroscience of cognition and consciousness. *BioSystems, 87,* 82–95.

Wolfe, J. M. (1994). Guided search 2.0: A revised model of visual search. *Psychonomic Bulletin and Review, 1,* 202–238.

Wolfe, J. M. (1998a). Visual search. In H. Pashler (Ed.), *Attention* (pp. 13–71). England, London, UK: University College Press.

Wolfe, J. M. (1998b). What can 1,000,000 trials tell us about visual search? *Psychological Science, 9,* 33–39.

Wolfe, J. M., Butcher, S. J., Lee, C., & Hyle, M. (2003). On the contributions of top-down and bottom-up guidance in visual search for feature singletons. *Journal of Experimental Psychology: Human Perception and Performance, 29,* 483–502.

Yates, F. E. (1994). Order and complexity in dynamical systems: Homeodynamics as a generalized mechanics for biology. *Mathematical and Computer Modeling, 19,* 49–74.

Zingale, C. M., & Kowler, E. (1987). Planning sequences of saccades. *Vision Research, 27,* 1327–1337.

6 Embodied and Embedded: The Dynamics of Extracting Perceptual Visual Invariants

PATRICE RENAUD, SYLVAIN CHARTIER,
AND GUILLAUME ALBERT

Perceptual Stability and Lability

Perception provides well-adapted organisms with the vital links they must establish between themselves and their environment. To do this, perception must simultaneously supply stable and reliable reference points about what the environment provides at the behavioral level and allow great flexibility in capturing information. Ideally, perception must be the agent of this compromise between stability and lability at any given time and place, in accordance with the transitory behavioral objectives that organisms target. The complexity and unpredictability of the act of perception, as well as the effect of continuity experienced at the phenomenal level, result from the interplay of these constraints. In this chapter, we present theories and a methodology to probe into the dynamics of perceptual–motor processes as they bear the emergence of perceptual constancy.

Visual Perception and Constancy of Position

Visual perception of space is what guides action in the visible world; it does so by specifying environmental features to organisms that will allow them to achieve their behavioral objectives in a mobile fashion. To fulfill this mission, visual perception must manage to keep the properties of external objects constant, despite the continuously changing projection of the images on the retina of the eye. Perceptual constancy is maintained by transcending the hiatus separating distal and proximal stimuli, that is, by bridging between the physical nature of the perceived object and the physiological stimulation of the retina. To do this, this constancy must allow the organism to maintain contact with the different sources of spatial stability available in the visible world. Texture gradients, occlusions and accretions of objects, continuity and discontinuity of contact between surfaces, linear perspective and parallax (i.e., the differential movement of a pair of points located at different depths, relative to a fixed point) all contribute to maintain constant links between perception and the properties of objects in the visible world (Ebenholtz, 2001; Palmer, 1999; Sedgwick, 2001).

In this regard, an object's spatial position must be considered in relation to that of its observer (*egocentric position*) as well as to the positions of other objects in its vicinity (*exocentric position*). From its egocentric position, an object presents itself in terms of polar coordinates determined by its observer's subjective viewpoint – what we call the *first-person stance*. In this way, the object's relative position corresponds both to a radial direction from the observer's viewpoint and to a distance separating observer from object (Ebenholtz, 2001; Palmer, 1999). The visual system calculates the radial direction of an object by taking into account the direction of eye movement and the position of the retinal image of the object.

Perception of Position Constancy

Indirect Explanation

Perceptual constancy of the position of a static object – the constancy of the object's egocentric position – is obtained by a vector computation in which measurable eye movement cancels measurable displacement of the retinal image of the object. This classical theoretical explanation is called the *taking-into-account* (Helmholtz, 1867/1925).[1] This is an inferential approach based on unconscious deductive processes operating on internal representations of the external world.

This inferential approach has strongly influenced the indirect explanation of perception, which is rooted in the information-processing perspective or computational approach (Rock, 1997). The computational approach, which is still prevalent today in the cognitive sciences, is said to be "indirect" because it is based on internal representations that mediate the perceptual relationship to the environment and necessitates the intervention of an internal monitor that applies transformational rules (Marr, 1982). A percept, in this view, is an output that comes from an act of processing, which starts from a sensory stimulation that is compared to an internal representation and transformed to preserve constancy. According to the indirect approach, this constancy-preserving processing goes through a process that filters and eliminates the internal noise arising from the neurophysiological processes involved, as well as the external noise from visual stimulations that interfere with the extraction of constancy (Handel, 2006). Noise, then, is here conceived first and foremost as an obstacle to true perception, and constancy is a form of statistical regularity. The indirect approach posits that the maximum perceptual information is available to the observer when the elements to be perceived have an equal probability of existence and when their spatial position is totally independent.

Direct Perception of Constancy: Topological Invariance

The familiar, everyday experience we have of the visible world quickly shows that the ideal circumstances for maximum perceptual information according to the computational approach are rarely experienced (Gibson, 1966, 1979; Handel, 2006; Shaw, 2003). In fact, perceptual experience of the visible world inevitably gives rise to correlations between events and objects in themselves and our first-person experience of the world. Our unique idiosyncratic perspective of the world necessarily distorts the perfect Euclidian space used to represent abstractly the geometry of perceptual experience.

This first-person experience of incident light arriving simultaneously from multiple sources and from all directions was both described and explained in considerable detail by the celebrated American psychologist J. J. Gibson (1904–1979), founder of the ecological approach to perception, also known as the direct perception approach. Gibson employed the concept of an *ambient optic array* to describe the conformation of the luminous medium to surfaces and textures found in the environment from the viewpoint of an observer within that environment (Gibson, 1950, 1966, 1979). According to this conception of our experience of the visible, each of the possible positions that an observer can occupy in space specifies an ambient optic array that is structured differently and therefore provides unique information. The shapes, surfaces, and textures of the visible world redeploy incident light according to specific laws, and it is precisely because of these regular and therefore predictable relationships between light and surfaces that perception is possible. The observer has only to directly pick up these singular occurrences of the visible that the immediate environment specifies (Gibson, 1966).

Ecological optics, which is the Gibsonian conception of optics in the service of visual perception embodied and situated in context, explains that the ambient optic array is, in fact, only a slice, a snapshot of the continuous flow of variations in the viewpoint an observer has of the world. These variations result in what is termed *optic flow* (Clancey, 1997; Clark, 1997; Gibson, 1961, 1966, 1979; Warren, 1995, 2004; Warren & Fajen, 2004). Optic flow, which is the actual source of visual perceptual information, is therefore the natural and direct experience of the visible world as it reaches the eyes of an observer who is actively exploring his or her environment. This complex stimulus is made possible by the totality of body movements and not solely eye movements considered in isolation. It is the coordination of multiple degrees of freedom[2] characteristic of the biomechanics of body movements, particularly those of the head and eyes, that gives rise to optic flow (Bernstein, 1967; Kelso, 1995; Mitra, Riley, Schmidt, & Turvey, 1998; Shaw & Turvey, 1999). These interwoven degrees of freedom, and the resulting redundancy, guide the visual system in maintaining perceptual constancy.

To extract the position constancy of objects – in other words, their topological invariance in three-dimensional space – the visual system must consider both the position of the objects and the motion of the observer, which are found simultaneously in optic flow (Gibson, 1950; Kim & Turvey, 1999; Warren, 1995, 2004). The ecological explanation of perceptual invariance in position constancy is in fact based on extraction of higher-order optical information, of which optic flow proves to be the compound. This compound, which presents itself in the form of a vector field, results from the translations and rotations imprinted on the optic flow by the embedded body–head–eye system, which is itself situated in a specific environment (Clancey, 1997; Clark, 1997; O'Regan & Noë, 2001; Warren, 2004). Perceptual invariance extraction comes from effective covariances between information from the *optic flow field* and actions oriented toward a goal (Warren, 2006; Warren & Fajen, 2004). These covariances probably operate on multiple scales in a manner that allows perceptual constancy to persist in space and time. Therefore they are almost certainly the result of self-organizing perceptual–motor processes. These self-organizing processes would arise from the interaction between the degrees of freedom of the perceiving body's biomechanical components and the features of the visible world (Kelso, 1995; Kugler & Turvey, 1987; Van Orden & Holden, 2002; Van Orden, Holden, & Turvey, 2003; Van Orden, Moreno, & Holden, 2003; Warren, 2006).

Fractal Perceptual–Motor Responses

Fractal dynamics, the process side of fractal geometry, presents scale invariance and long-range correlations in complex behaviors taking place in time (Mandelbrot, 1975; Sprott, 2003). Long-range correlations have been observed when a system approaches the critical point associated with a phase transition (Bak & Creutz, 1994; Bak, Tang, & Wiesenfeld, 1987). This criticality is *self-organized*, in the sense that it results from local interactions between components of a given system, without recourse to control exercised by an external agent (Aks, Zelinsky, & Sprott, 2002; Van Orden & Holden, 2002; Van Orden, Holden, et al., 2003; Van Orden, Moreno, et al., 2003).

Fractal processes are to be distinguished from random fluctuations (white noise) or short-range correlations. A fractal process generates a time series with fluctuations organized in a self-similar manner at multiple time scales, and as such can be considered as a scale-free phenomenon. Fractal dynamics have been found in various physiological phenomena (Bassingthwaighte, Liebovitch, & West, 1994; Skarda & Freeman, 1987). They have also been found in many perceptual–motor phenomena (Hausdorff, Peng, Ladin, Wei, & Goldberger, 1995; Hausdorff et al., 1996; Kelso, 1995; Kelso & Zanone, 2002; Mitra et al., 1998; Treffner & Kelso, 1999; Warren, 2006). In particular, it has been shown that postural fluctuations reflect fractal organization and that this organization can be modulated by cognitive factors (Pellechia & Shockley, 2005; Riley,

Balasubramaniam, & Turvey, 1999; Sasaki et al., 2002). The same goes for the organization of ocular fixations in a visual search task (Aks et al., 2002). The ocular movements that constitute the *optokinetic nystagmus* response also present a nonlinear temporal organization distinct from noncorrelated noise (Shelhamer, 1998, 2005). Exploratory visual behavior, as indexed by the line of gaze relative to the spatial position of virtual three-dimensional objects, also exhibits fluctuations organized in terms of long-range correlations with scale invariance (Renaud, Bouchard, & Proulx, 2002; Renaud, Decarie, Gourd, Paquin, & Bouchard, 2003; Renaud, Singer, & Proulx, 2001).

Dynamics of Action–Perception Cycles

As mentioned at the outset of this chapter, visual perception exists to allow adapted motor activity. Reciprocally, as we have seen in the previous sections, motor activity is what allows perception to occur in a flexible dynamics and to result in more than a fixed percept removed from its biological role. The mutuality of action and perception, which is fundamental to the direct perception approach, makes the observer an active agent within his or her environment, and it is from the dynamic of this relationship that forms of higher-level invariant information emerge (Beer, 1995; Gibson, 1979; Kelso, 1995; Kugler & Turvey, 1987; Schöner, Dijkstra, & Jeka, 1998; Schöner & Kelso, 1988; Turvey & Shaw, 1999; Varela, Thompson, & Rosch, 1991; Warren, 2006).

The dynamics of this agent–environment system can be described using a set of *state variables*, as well as by the position this system occupies in the possible *state spaces* defined by these variables (Kelso, 1995; Warren, 2006). The state variables in question are the position and velocity of body segments that the agent involves in the motor activity guided by perception (Mitra et al., 1998; Treffner & Kelso, 1999). The parameters of mass, damping, and stiffness act on the state variables to imprint them with complex trajectories initiated by a *forcing function*.[3] When this function is applied to a nonlinear oscillator, it is possible to observe the effects of a strange attractor, that is, patterns that are highly complex and unpredictable yet which present deterministic regularities. Such patterns are found in the motor acts underlying visual perception, as well as in the subjective effects of these acts of perception.

The coordination dynamics of the degrees of freedom engaged by the agent's motivity are synthesised in the emergence of *order parameters* (also known as collective variables) (Kelso, 1995; Thelen & Smith, 1994). Once stabilized, these order parameters, in turn, influence the entire coordination dynamics of the degrees of freedom. In a mode of circular causality, the agent influences, and in turn is influenced by, his or her own action (Juarrero, 1999; Tschacher & Haken, 2007; Van Orden & Holden, 2002; Van Orden, Holden, et al., 2003; Van Orden, Moreno, et al., 2003). For example, through locomotion, the agent induces variations in his or her optic flow, which let radial and lamellar structures appear, which then guide locomotor activity (Warren, 1995, 2004). Perceptual invariances guiding motor behavior should be considered akin to order parameters.

The coordination dynamics of the degrees of freedom that express motor behavior are also guided by parameters that are nonspecific to the dynamics – namely, the *control parameters*. Control parameters have an effect on the coordination dynamics' changes of phase. Distinct motor coordination patterns may appear when control parameters – pacing, complexity, or any other task performance constraint involving motor control – change (Kelso, 1995; Mitra et al., 1998; Thelen & Smith, 1994; Treffner & Kelso, 1999; Warren, 2006). Although control parameters are related to the independent variables of conventional statistical analysis, they differ in that they act on a set of circular causal factors for which they coordinate the dynamical organization (Van Orden, Holden, et al., 2003; Van Orden, Moreno, et al., 2003). Here, as explained earlier, dynamical organization pertains to the agent–environment coupling at the perceptual–motor level.

It is generally postulated that the agent–environment coupling may be characterized by *low-dimensional dynamics*, in which stable forms associated with specific attractors emerge and then guide the agent's behavior. We have adopted the theoretic model proposed by Warren (2006), in which agent and environment are formalized as the coupling of two interdependent dynamic systems that obey the following laws of motion:

$$\dot{e} = \Phi(e, f)\dot{a} = \Psi(a, i), \tag{6.1}$$

where e is a vector of environmental state variables and f is a vector of external forces applied to them. This first equation expresses the physical laws that regulate our relationship to the environment (Φ). The other equation, which is called the *law of control* (Ψ), is characterized by a, which is a vector of state variables in the agent, and i, a vector of information variables.

Ψa yields the intrinsic dynamics of order parameters embodied in the agent's motor activity (Kelso, 1995; Thelen & Smith, 1994). This is the fundamental coordination of an organism's degrees of freedom, expressed without taking into account environmental contingencies, learning factors, or constraints associated with specific tasks. These contingencies work by shaping these intrinsic dynamics (Kelso, 1995; Kelso & Zanone, 2002).

The information variables vector i is especially important because it interfaces the agent and the environment by mapping, at the visual level, the laws of ecological optics with the position and singular movements that the agent carries out in the environment. Visual perception is therefore largely defined by this mapping, which directly unites agent and environment, without recourse to intermediary representations (Clancey, 1997; Clark, 1997; Gibson, 1966, 1979; Shaw, 2003; Van Orden & Holden, 2002; Van Orden, Holden, et al., 2003;

Van Orden, Moreno, et al., 2003; Warren, 2006). This fundamental embedded-ness acts directly as a set of constraints on perceptual–motor dynamics.

The law of control does not determine as such the resultant behavioral trajectory but rather helps direct it toward a space of solutions where the trajectory can be satisfactorily stabilized (Warren, 2006; Warren & Fajen, 2004). This reorganization in the form of attractors is generally accompanied by a reduction of their complexity. For stabilization to occur, the informational and motor-control terms must be of the same dimension and must be expressed in common variables.

Intentional Dynamics and Invariance Extraction

By reconciling a control law with the aforementioned physical and informational constraints, the agent aims to stabilize his or her perceptual–motor dynamics to achieve a given behavioral goal (Warren, 2006). To the biomechanical and environmental constraints we must therefore add intentional constraints that map out the agent's actions according to the behavioral objectives to be achieved. These intentional constraints are linked to boundary conditions such as those corresponding to the instructions given to a subject in a laboratory experiment (Van Orden & Holden, 2002; Van Orden, Holden, et al., 2003; Van Orden, Moreno, et al., 2003). The intentional content is itself an emergent structure nested within a hierarchy of control parameters (Juarrero, 1999; Van Orden & Holden, 2002; Van Orden, Holden, et al., 2003; Van Orden, Moreno, et al., 2003). Once again, in a circular causal manner, the intentions modulate the control parameters, which in turn maintain (or modify) the intentions.

Intentional constraints produce their effect by causing a pattern of perceptual–motor coordination to persist in time (Kelso, 1995; Van Orden & Holden, 2002; Van Orden, Holden, et al., 2003; Van Orden, Moreno, et al., 2003). To do this, they act on a time scale larger than the time scale on which body movements occur. In this way they modulate the intrinsic dynamics of the order parameters linked both to the flow of information and the flow of motor control. By so doing, they define an attractor capable of guiding motor behavior toward the desired pattern. Thus, in a visual search task, intentional constraints will serve to limit the search space to circumscribe better the location of information that is immediately relevant to the established behavioral objectives.

Intentions self-organize to remain in a critical zone that allows behavioral objectives to be achieved (Bak et al., 1987; Juarrero, 1999; Kelso, 1995; Van Orden & Holden, 2002; Van Orden, Holden, et al., 2003; Van Orden, Moreno, et al., 2003; Warren, 2006). This critical zone must allow the agent's immediate objectives to reconcile the imperatives of flexibility and stability that the perception–action system must achieve. In a visual search task, the agent should be able to change his or her viewpoint in a flexible manner, while maintaining a

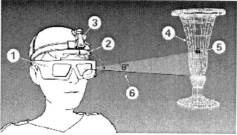

Figure 6.1. Left: Image of the virtual room. Right: 1. Active Nuvision 60GX stereoscopic glasses. 2. IS-900 motion tracker from InterSense. 3. Oculomotor tracking system (ASL model H6). 4. Example of a wired frame virtual object. 5. A virtual measurement point (VMP). 6. A gaze radial angular deviation from the VMP.

constant perceptual link with the environment through topological invariance extraction.

Perceptual Constancy and Visual Search: Predictions and Methods

Perceptual constancy, by definition, must remain accessible at all times to guide the agent adequately through the exploration of the environment, particularly when he or she is performing a visual search. An agent actively exploring a strange room must be able to rely constantly on some form of invariance concerning the position of the objects in this new space, regardless of the particular shape of the search trajectory or the specific objectives of the search. The empirical study that follows illustrates how *nonlinear dynamical systems* (NDS) may serve to grasp the inherent stability and lability of perceptual–motor processes. It banks on the use of standard NDS computational techniques applied to perceptual–motor responses to bring out their underlying fractal organization and how this organization is tied to contextual requirements of a search task.

Participants

Ten subjects, including five men, on average 27.8 years of age, were recruited on campus at the l'Université du Québec en Outaouais to take part in a study involving visual search tasks in a virtual environment.

Protocol and Instructions

The subjects were required to stand still in the middle of a CAVE-type[4] three-screen immersive vault, wearing a pair of polarizing stereoscopic glasses, as well as oculomotor monitoring headgear (see Fig. 6.1). After a 5-min acclimatization period in a virtual environment similar to that of the experimental task and after calibration of the eye-tracking devices, the subjects were given general instructions. They were asked not to touch the glasses and headgear while performing the visual search tasks, not to close their eyes except for the normal blinking to moisten the cornea, and not to move their feet from the position markers on the floor. Next, they were given specific instructions about the first experimental condition (Global Search): *Please actively explore the virtual room that will appear in a few seconds. Locate and memorize the position of the various objects in the room.* To control their visual starting point, subjects were asked to focus on the center of a cross projected onto the vault's central screen. After 15 sec, the cross disappeared, and the subjects found themselves immersed in a virtual environment for a period of 60 sec. This virtual environment simulated a furnished room containing various three-dimensional objects (see Fig. 6.1). After a 2-min rest period, the subjects received final instructions to prepare for the second experimental condition (Focused Search): *You are going to return to the same virtual room. Now please locate the blue objects in this scene and memorize their locations. Concentrate your attention exclusively on these objects for a period of 60 sec.* The subjects were again asked to focus on the cross, and they then found themselves in the same virtual room. Once this second condition was completed, the subjects were asked to look at a picture of the room and place an X on the places where the blue objects were found. This paper-and-pencil procedure was done simply to make sure the subjects really had detected the two blue objects present in the virtual room.

One of the two blue-colored target objects (the bottle on the table to the left in the scene) and one nontarget object serving as a control (the plant at the right of the screen beside the TV set) were individually associated with a *virtual measurement point* (VMP) from which the radial angular deviation of the subject's gaze was calculated (see the next section, "Gaze Measurement Technique," below). At the beginning of each step, the subject was placed at a distance of 2.72 m from the target object and 3.80 m from the nontargeted object. The initial radial angular deviation separating the subject's gaze was 18.5 degrees from the center of the target object and 100.9 degrees from the nontarget object.

Gaze Measurement Technique

Our method performs gaze analysis by way of virtual measurement points (VMPs) placed over virtual objects.[5] The gaze radial angular deviation (GRAD) from VMPs is obtained by combining the six degrees of freedom (DOF) resulting from head movements and the two DOF (x- and y-coordinates) resulting from eye movements tracked by the eye-tracking system (Duchowski et al., 2002; Renaud, 2006; Renaud, Bouchard, et al., 2002; Renaud, Decarie, et al., 2003). Whereas variations in the six DOF developed by head movements define momentary changes in the global scene experienced in the immersive vault, the

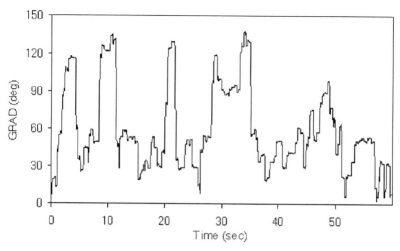

Figure 6.2. Gaze radial angular deviation (GRAD) time series recorded from one subject searching an empty virtual room for a 60-sec period.

two DOF generated by the eye-tracking device allow line-of-sight computation relative to VMPs. The closer this measure approaches to zero, the closer the gaze dwells in the immediate vicinity of the selected VMP. Data are sampled at 60 Hz. The resulting GRAD time series for each subject in each condition contains 3,600 data points from which analyses are performed. Figure 6.2 shows a GRAD data sample from a 1-min active visual exploration in an empty virtual room (i.e., containing no virtual objects, only walls and a floor). The GRAD measurement in this case comes from a VMP placed at exactly the same spot as the target object (without there being any objects visible in this case). These data are reviewed in the "Analytical Strategies" and "Results" sections to illustrate the different analysis techniques employed, as well as to explain the concept of *embodiment* of the *intrinsic dynamics* discussed in the section on the dynamics of action–perception cycles.

Unlike the measurement of ocular fixations and saccades, which are mapped onto a two-dimensional surface, GRAD measurement allows a continuous taking into account of gaze probing in a three-dimensional space relative to the positions of objects arranged in that space. The direction and stability of the visual search behavior are obtained, respectively, through mean GRAD and its standard deviation (GRAD SD). The GRAD velocity is obtained from the absolute value of the signal's first derivative, whereas acceleration comes from the second derivative of the same signal.

Analytical Strategies

Data Preprocessing
GRAD data time series were first filtered to remove any measurement disruptions caused by blinks or signal losses. Data were also detrended, using a linear

regression and subtracting a linear fit. Before performing spectral, correlation dimension, and recurrence plot analyses (see "Analytical Strategies"), GRAD time series were also processed using the Schreiber noise reduction method, which locally averages phase vectors in the phase space of delay coordinates (Schreiber, 1993, 1999).

Spectral Analyses and Self-Similar Patterns

To ascertain the presence of long-range correlations in the variability of the oculomotor responses necessitated by the visual research in virtual immersion, we started by conducting spectral analyses. These were performed on signals obtained from GRAD measurements relative to the VMPs affixed to the selected virtual objects.

Our spectral analyses are based on Fourier series postulates, which assume the decomposability of the time series into sine and cosine waves of variable amplitude and frequency (Sprott, 2003). A signal's *power spectrum* thus represents the relative size of the component waves by expressing their frequency in relation to their strength – in other words, in relation to the mean square of their amplitude. Expressed in a log–log plot, a signal's power spectrum allows us to determine the presence of a power law function, that is, a scale invariance expressed by a polynomial. The power spectrum's scaling exponent in specific cases of scaling invariance will express a signature that meets the criterion $f(cx) \propto f(x)$, where c is a constant. In these typical cases, scaling the function will affect only the constant without altering its general form, hence the self-similarity of the pattern produced by the function.

Analysis of the spectral properties of the signals borrows from acoustical physics and optical physics (Heath, 2000; Sprott, 2003). Thus distribution of spectral strength may be characterized by different types of "colored noises," the strength of which varies inversely to their frequency ($1/f^{\alpha}$). When the signal corresponds to an uncorrelated sequence, we say it is "white" noise and its $\alpha = 0$; the slope of the log–log plot will be zero in this case. When $\alpha = 1$ it is "pink" noise (or "flicker" noise), and the signal's sequence demonstrates highly correlated fluctuations with a shallow slope on the log–log plot. This type of $1/f$ noise, with its long-range correlations, characterizes a dynamic process that is self-similar and invariant on all scales. With a steeper slope, the "brown" noise $1/f^2$ likewise corresponds to a power law with scale invariance but with less extensively correlated fluctuations. When $\alpha < 0$, strength increases with frequency. This is "blue" noise, and the fluctuations are negatively correlated. In this case, a value larger than the mean tends to be followed by a value smaller than the mean. This last type of noise is encountered less frequently and corresponds to fractal anticorrelations.

Figure 6.3 shows the power spectrum of the data shown in Figure 6.2 above. Because perceptual processes begin to organize at around 60 msec (Card, Moran, & Newell, 1983; Newell, Rosenbloom, & Laird, 1989), only the spectral frequencies corresponding to mental activities 60 msec and up (with frequency

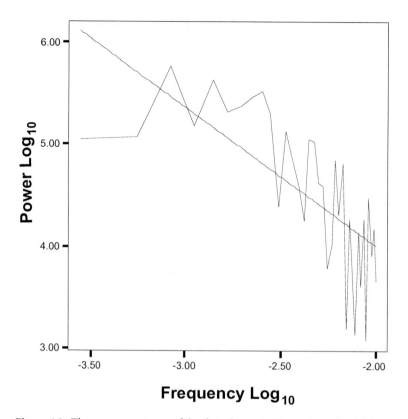

Figure 6.3. The power spectrum of the data shown in Figure 6.2; α is -1.36.

logarithms from 3.56 to 2.00) are considered. The exponent α obtained from the spectrum in Figure 6.3 is -1.36, which corresponds to correlated noise about halfway between pink and brown.

The power law functions found in cognitive phenomena and perception are generally associated with dynamic systems with flexibility that allows adaptive integration of environmental disturbances (Aks et al., 2002; Pressing, 1999; Renaud et al., 2001; Van Orden & Holden, 2002; Van Orden, Holden, et al., 2003; Van Orden, Moreno, et al., 2003). As well, a significant change in the power spectrum of a process with a variable control parameter suggests an adaptive bifurcation in a deterministic system.

Correlation Dimension (D_2)

The evaluation of a power law, using a power spectrum, relies on a conventional linear method limited to the examination of frequencies considered in isolation, which does not allow us to distinguish noise from organized chaos over time. To make this distinction, we must resort to other methods, such as calculating the correlation dimension (D_2). This is a measure of the complexity of the geometric structure of an attractor in the phase space of a dynamic process. The invariant topological properties of the attractor – those that do not vary under the continuous and differential transformations of the system's coordinates – may be extracted by calculating D_2.

This measurement is consistent with nonfractal object: Lines have a dimension of one, whereas a plane has a dimension of two, and so on. Calculation of D_2 is obtained from the Grassberger–Procaccia algorithm (Grassberger & Procaccia, 1983; Grassberger, Schreiber, & Schaffrath, 1991). The idea is to take a given embedded time series x_n and for a given point x_i count the number of other points x_j that are within a distance of ε, then repeat this process for all the points and for various distances of ε. This correlation sum is expressed as:

$$C(\varepsilon) = \frac{2}{N(N-1)} \sum_{i=1}^{N} \sum_{j=i+1}^{N} \Theta\left(\varepsilon - \|\mathbf{x}_i - \mathbf{x}_j\|\right), \qquad (6.2)$$

where N is the number of points in the time series, $\|x\|$ is the Euclidian norm, and $\Theta(x)$ is the Heaviside function expressed by:

$$\Theta(x) = \begin{cases} 0 & \text{for } x < 0 \\ 1 & \text{for } x \geq 0. \end{cases} \qquad (6.3)$$

Consequently, the double sum expressed in Eq. 6.2 counts only the pairs (x_i, x_j), the distance of which is smaller than ε. The sum $C(\varepsilon)$ is expected to scale like a power law for small ε and large N. Therefore a plot of log $C(\varepsilon)$ versus log ε should give an approximate straight line. Figure 6.4 shows the plot obtained with the data shown in Figure 6.2.

$$D_2 = \lim_{\varepsilon \to 0} \lim_{N \to \infty} \frac{d \log C(\varepsilon)}{d \log \varepsilon}. \qquad (6.4)$$

The correlation sum in various embeddings can serve as a measure of determinism in a time series. For pure random noise, the correlation sum satisfies $C(m, \varepsilon) = C(1, \varepsilon)^m$. In other words, if the data are random, they will fill any given embedding dimension. On the other hand, determinism will be shown by asymptotical convergence of D_2 as the embeddings increase (Eq. 6.4). Figure 6.4 shows the asymptotic stabilization of a D_2 obtained from the data shown in Figure 6.2; the mean value of D_2 is of 1.398 ± 0.157 in this case.

False Nearest Neighbors
To choose the minimum embedding for our data correctly, we used the "false nearest neighbors" method (Kennel, Brown, & Abarbanel, 1992; Sprott, 2003). This method involves finding the nearest neighbor, Xl, for each point Xn with a time delay m and quantifying the separation between these points using the formula $Rn(m) = \sqrt{(X_l - Xn)^2 + (X_{l-1} - Xn - 1)^2 + \cdots}$. Calculation is then repeated for $Rn(m+1)$ with $m+1$. If $Rn(m+1)$ is significantly higher

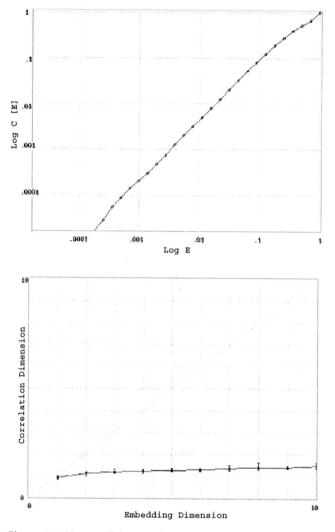

Figure 6.4. Upper: $C(\varepsilon)$ versus log ε. Lower: D_2s versus embedding dimensions. The mean value of D_2 is 1.398 ± 0.157.

than $Rn(m)$, the neighbors are false. Using this method, we established that the minimum embedding for our data was between three and eight.

Recurrence Plot

To verify the stationarity of our data as well as get a better idea of their dynamics, we did a recurrence plot for each time series. This is a simple, practical graphic method based on representation of the dynamics on a two-dimensional plot where each of the axes is labeled with integers one to N from the original time series (Eckmann, Kamphorst, & Ruelle, 1987; Heath, 2000; Sprott, 2003). A point i, j is placed within the $N \times N$ recurrence plot if the distance separating

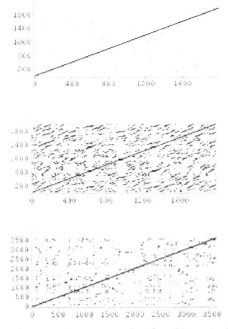

Figure 6.5. Reccurence plots for white noise (upper panel), the Lorenz attractor (center panel), and the signal appearing in Figure 6.2 (lower panel).

its corresponding datum from the next point in the time series is lower than a criterion ε. If the difference separating the two data points is greater than ε, the space is left empty. When the process dynamics go through phase transitions, the pattern drawn in the recurrence plot contains rectangular motifs that fill the graph. When the data are nonstationary, the pattern is nonhomogeneous. Figure 6.5 shows recurrence plots for white noise, the Lorenz attractor, and the signal appearing in Figure 6.2. The recurrence plots based on our data show characteristic patterns of signals coming from stationary dynamic processes and going through phase transitions typical of nonlinear systems.

Surrogate Data Tests
To make sure that D_2 exponents are significantly distinct from exponents coming from correlated noise processes, a surrogate data method introduced by Theiler, Eubank, Longtin, Galdrikian, and Farmer (1992) was used to differentiate statistically each computed D_2 from a sample of D_2s coming from quasirandom processes (McSharry, 2005). For each GRAD time series, we generated 20 surrogate time series by doing a Fourier transform of the original data (the phase of each Fourier component was set to a random value between 0 and 2π) while preserving their power spectrum and correlation function (Sprott, 2003). Figure 6.6 shows one of the surrogate-data time series that were used to test the data appearing in Figure 6.2. These surrogate data correspond to a quasirandom

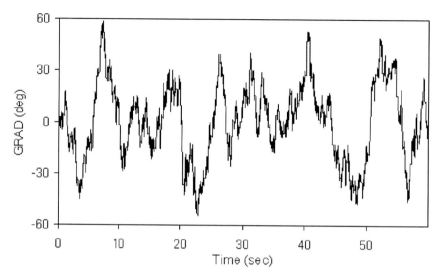

Figure 6.6. One of the surrogate-data time series that were used to test the data shown in Figure 6.2.

trajectory of exploratory visual behavior (GRAD). Using a one-sample t test, we were able to establish that the D_2 calculated from our original data ($D_2 = 1.398 \pm 0.157$) differs significantly from the mean of the 20 D_2 correlation dimensions based on surrogate data ($\bar{X} = 5.336$, $SD = 0.2$, $p < .0001$). Likewise, we established that the 40 D_2 correlation dimensions based on our experimental data (10 subjects × 2 types of searches × 2 types of objects) were all significantly different from the D_2 based on surrogate data ($p < .0001$).

Statistical Analyses
A multivariate analysis of variance was conducted on mean GRAD, GRAD SD, GRAD velocity, GRAD acceleration, and the α values of our spectral analysis, as well as on the D_2 correlation dimensions. These analyses were based on a repeated-measures factorial design, using the within-subjects factors Search (global and focused) and Objects (target and nontarget). The number and duration of ocular fixations, as well as the length of saccades, were also analyzed using a multivariate analysis of variance, but based on a repeated-measurements scheme that did not include the Object factor (see the "Gaze Measurement Technique" section for explanations).

Results and Discussion for Perceptual Constancy and Visual Search

Tables 6.1 and 6.2 contain the means and standard deviations for the set of measurements analysed. Figure 6.7 shows typical signals obtained with one of the subjects under both experimental conditions.

Table 6.1. Means and standard deviations of fixations and saccades according to the search factor

	M		SD	
Measures	Focused search	Global search	Focused search	Global search
Number of fixations	122.70	202.00	43.75	22.99
Fixation duration[a]	.46	.25	.16	.04
Saccade length[b]	5.43	3.92	2.34	.56

[a] Results are in seconds.
[b] Results are in degrees.

Ocular Fixations and Saccades

Results obtained with the ocular fixation (number and time) and saccade measurements revealed distinct visual search patterns when subjects had to search the global virtual environment, compared with when they were asked to do a focused search for a reduced number of objects (see Table 6.1). During the

Table 6.2. Means and standard deviations of measures according to search and object factors

	Global search		Focused search	
Measures	Target object	Nontarget object	Target object	Nontarget object
	M			
GRAD mean[a]	52.78	100.67	31.06	117.74
GRAD SD	26.90	47.08	22.41	22.06
GRAD velocity[b]	.60	.55	.53	.47
GRAD acceleration[c]	.39	.36	.31	.28
Spectral exponent	−1.33	−1.88	−.56	−.74
Correlation dimension	1.45	1.42	1.03	1.35
Correlation dimension SD	.18	.24	.20	.23
	SD			
GRAD mean[a]	2.80	10.28	3.90	5.35
GRAD SD	1.66	2.77	4.66	5.38
GRAD velocity[b]	.16	.13	.11	.10
GRAD acceleration[c]	.10	.09	.06	.05
Spectral exponent	.42	.40	.51	.67
Correlation dimension	.18	.30	.20	.29
Correlation dimension SD	.08	.12	.06	.08

Note: GRAD = Gaze radial angular deviation.
[a] Results are in degrees.
[b] Results are in degrees per second.
[c] Results are in degrees per second squared.

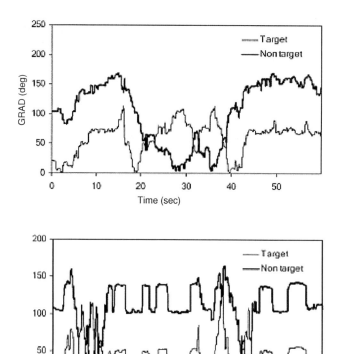

Figure 6.7. Typical signals obtained from one of the subjects under both experimental conditions, global (upper panel) and focused search (lower panel). Target signals are in thin lines and nontarget in bold lines.

focused search, they presented both significantly fewer ocular fixations, $F(1, 9) = 18.62, p < .01$, and fixations that lasted a longer time, $F(1, 9) = 14.67, p < .01$. Ocular saccades in this condition, on the other hand, averaged significantly longer than in the global search condition, $F(1, 9) = 5.20, p < .05$. These results are logically consistent with the effect of the constraints in the task. By limiting the field of exploration to target objects separated from each other by a long distance, the focused search condition encouraged ocular movements of greater amplitude, including fewer moments of rest, which, however, lasted a longer time. The global search gives rise, instead, to an extensive exploration of the entire environment, in which the entire set of objects shares the fixations. Saccades in this condition are generally over short distances to analyze sequentially the content and the position of objects located near each other.

Because they are interpreted through transposition to a bidimensional plane, the fixation and ocular saccade measurements do not allow us to fully grasp the perceptual visual activity through three-dimensional space. For this, we had to use measure of the GRAD, which expresses the visual exploratory activity in relation to the position of the objects in three-dimensional space. This measurement isolates the relationship of the visual search behavior with each object considered separately.

Average GRAD and GRAD Variability

The multivariate repeated-measures analysis of variance shows that the mean GRAD measurement differs significantly depending on the object considered (target and nontarget; $F[1, 9] = 1158.05$, $p < .001$) but not on the type of visual search ($F[1, 9] = 1.19$, ns; see Table 6.2). The mean GRAD calculated for the target object is smaller (see Table 6.2 and Fig. 6.8). We observe a significant interaction effect between the Search and Object factors, however, and this significance becomes clearer in Figure 6.8, $F(1, 9) = 102.30$, $p < .001$. It appears, in fact, that the type of visual search has an impact on performance when the search is focused on a subset of objects. In this case, the average radial angular deviation is not as high with the target object (the blue bottle in the center of the room) as with the nontarget object (the plant on the floor to the left in the scene), which is consistent with the requirements of the task (see Table 6.2 and Fig. 6.8). It is noteworthy that when the subjects focus their attention on the target objects, the nontarget object is outside their visual field. The significance of this finding is discussed later.

The variability of visual search behavior as indexed by GRAD standard deviation provides a more qualified picture (see Fig. 6.8). It suggests that the variability of the visual search process is greater when the research is global than when it is focused, $F(1, 9) = 79.08$, $p < .001$, and it is likewise greater for the nontarget object than for the target object, $F(1, 9) = 124.91$, $p < .001$. A significant interaction effect further reveals that this difference between nontarget and target objects occurs only when the search is performed globally, $F(1, 9) = 410.89$, $p < .001$). The meaning of these results can be found in the distinct modes of motor control exercised by the subjects in the two visual search conditions (see Fig. 6.7), as well as in the differential effect of the objects' positions relative to the subject performing the search. Therefore more labile (because less constrained) motor control allows the subjects to explore more freely, that is, cover a larger and more varied visual space, as they were required to do in the global search condition. The greater constraint imposed in the focused search condition seems, on the other hand, to have contributed to the reduction of this GRAD variability. Also, given its more eccentric position relative to the subject, the nontarget object generated greater angular variations (see Figs. 6.7 and 6.8).

GRAD Speed and Acceleration

The velocity of GRAD rotation was not significantly different between types of visual search, $F(1, 9) = 2.71$, ns. It does differ, however, according to the

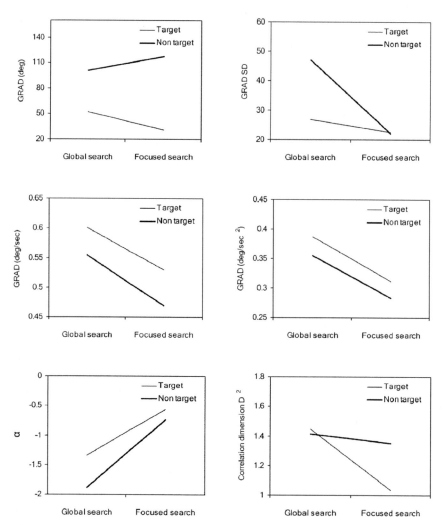

Figure 6.8. Experimental results for average gaze radial angular deviation (GRAD) (upper left), GRAD SD (upper right), GRAD velocity (middle left), GRAD acceleration (middle right), GRAD α (lower left) and GRAD D_2 (lower right). Target signals are in thin lines and nontarget in bold lines.

Object factor and is greater for the target than for the nontarget object, $F(1, 9) = 18.95$, $p < .01$. Interaction between Search and Object factors is not significant, $F(1, 9) = .330$, ns.

As for acceleration of GRAD rotation, we found significant main effects related to the Search and Object factors. Mean acceleration is more pronounced in the global search condition than in the focused search condition (see Fig. 6.8), $F(1, 9) = 6.13$, $p < .05$. Figure 6.7 reveals that velocity seems in fact to be more constant in the focused search condition, in which subjects must operate within tighter search constraints. The predictability of ocular trajectories carried out to keep attention focused on targets already identified probably encourages a more uniform control of the velocity of visual scanning in this condition. As well, the position differential of the objects encouraged a more pronounced mean acceleration relative to the target object, $F(1, 9) = 124.11.13$, $p < .01$. These kinetic effects experienced at the so-called first-person position act on the composition of the optic flow and are particularly constitutive of motion parallax effects (Langer & Mann, 2004; Longuet-Higgins & Prazdny, 1980).

Spectral Analyses: Power Law Exponents

The results from spectral analyses show first of all that the α exponents obtained all correspond to colored noise of the brown, pink, and blue types. This initial finding sheds light on the coordination of visual search behavior around objects in three-dimensional space. In fact, the organization of GRAD oscillations seems distinct from uncorrelated white noise and appears to be more closely related to that of the long-range correlations typical of power laws. The scale invariance and fractal self-similarity that power laws suggest must be linked to perceptual constancy and extraction of topological invariance in the spatial position of objects. Correlation in the distribution of perceptual–motor variance on different scales and the associated fractal similarity may in fact be seen as expressions of mechanisms that ensure a constant link between an agent actively exploring the environment and the objects that appear in it. This crucial link, which is in all likelihood self-organized, is neither on the agent's nor the object's side, but rather in the interaction that arises when these two entities meet. We may therefore consider this noise, at least in part, not as a source of interference to be eliminated in the process of maintaining perceptual constancy but rather as a manifestation of perceptual constancy itself.

Brown noise is found to predominate in the global search condition, whereas the focused search gives rise instead to pink and blue noise (a significant effect of the search factor, $F(1, 9) = 42.62$, $p < .001$; see Fig. 6.8. It may be that the more restrictive search constraints in the focused condition have forced a stricter coordination of the degrees of freedom that constitute the body–head–eye system as oriented toward the position of the visual objects to be located. This more constrained coordination is expressed in higher correlations in the distribution of spectral power. This type of change in spectral power based on search constraints suggests an adaptive bifurcation in the visual search system's phase space.

One significant main effect was likewise obtained for the Object factor, $F(1, 9) = 13.15$, $p < .01$. According to this, the values of α for GRAD as a function of the target object are significantly closer to pink noise than the values for GRAD as a function of the nontarget object, which are closer to brown noise (see Fig. 6.8). Visual search behavior in terms of the target object therefore entails motor coordination with farther-reaching correlations. This result is consistent with the nature of this target, which obviously requires a taking into account that is performed in a more restricted manner and for a longer duration. The effect of interaction between the Search and Object factors is not significant in terms of the spectral analysis results, $F(1, 9) = 2.98$, ns.

Correlation Dimensions (D_2) Analysis

Calculation of D_2 allows us to extend our understanding of the perceptual invariance extraction by more clearly qualifying the processes at work as they unfold over time. By integrating the temporal aspect, D_2 more clearly differentiates between correlated noise and dynamic processes that are fractal. This indicator of dynamic complexity provides more straightforward access to the geometry of the attractors at work in the perceptual–motor processes under discussion here.

The first result to consider was obtained in a preliminary manner in the section concerning the surrogate data test. As mentioned earlier, all the calculated D_2 correlations are clearly distinct from the D_2s coming from surrogate signals that simulate a quasirandom visual exploration process (i.e., respecting the mean, variance, power spectrum, and phases of origin). This means that the specific mode of accomplishing a visual search – the correlational *history* that the original time series comprises – is in itself a distinctive dimension of the perceptual–motor processes at work. This interesting result is, in a certain sense, trivial, however, because it is quite obvious that a quasirandom coordination of the body–head–eye system cannot result in the direction of a precise and effective visual search, when this must be done in three-dimensional space in terms of stationary objects positioned in specific places. Not so trivial, however, is the fact that this perceptual–motor coordination could possibly fall within the fractal geometry of low-dimension strange attractors.

As order parameters, D_2 correlations point in the direction of an emergent property embodied in the motor coordination at the root of visual search. In itself, as we have seen with the data from a visual search in an *empty* room (Fig. 6.2), the intrinsic dynamics of body–head–eye coordination give rise to a highly stabilized order parameter with an organization that clearly seems to be fractal in nature. This intrinsic emergent property, when put into context in the task, takes control, in turn, of the coordination from which it emerges to guide the visual search while preserving stable contact with the environment. The scale invariance revealed by the D_2 correlations, which seem to be distinct from noise, here forms the bridge (like the α values in spectral analyses) to perceptual constancy in the positions of objects. In fact, despite strong and unpredictable variations in translation and rotation of the body–head–eye system, that system's relationship to the positions of the objects to locate is marked by invariance on all spatial and temporal scales. Moreover, this invariance remains available even when the object associated with it is no longer present in the subject's visual field. Thus the nontarget object in the focused search condition, even though it lies outside the visual field of the subject, remains linked to the dynamics of the visual search through a form of fractal invariance. This invariance in the object's spatial position is obtained without a corresponding retinal stimulation and therefore likely derives both from the visual search intrinsic dynamics and the shaping of latter by the task's constraints.

The multivariate repeated-measures analysis of variance conducted on the D_2 correlation dimensions yields, in this sense, significant results for both the Search factors, $F(1, 9) = 5.72$, $p < .05$, and the Object factors, $F(1, 9) = 8.44$, $p < .05$, as well as for the interaction between them, $F(1, 9) = 6.26$, $p < .05$. Figure 6.8 shows that the D_2 correlations that characterize perceptual relationships with the target and nontarget objects are significantly different in the focused search condition, that is, where the subjects had to locate a subset of objects. The fractal complexity of the GRAD attractor that is a function of the target object diminishes significantly in the focused condition – likely to stabilize the motor trajectory searching through the visual space. This stabilization takes place in a double inclusion, as a stabilization within the informational constraints provided by the optic flow and within the intentional constraints brought about by the imperatives of the task that the subject adopts. This double inclusion orientates the law of control, which in turn guides the oculomotor trajectory by modifying the dimensionality of the attractor. Although this dimensionality changes in accordance with the requirements of the task, the perceptual links with the positions of objects remain constant at all times, as the D_2 values we obtained attest. Because our sample is small, the preceding results need to be replicated with more subjects. However, tendencies appear to be strong, even if the overall statistical power needs to be increased.

Conclusion

The preceding results are, in a sense, a reading of the processes of perceptual invariance extraction that is consistent with the direct perception approach (Gibson, 1950, 1966, 1979; Shaw, 2003; Shaw & Turvey, 1999; Turvey & Shaw, 1999). These invariance extraction processes are similar to the fractal dynamics found in various perceptual–motor responses (Aks et al., 2002; Kelso, 1995; Kelso & Zanone, 2002; Mitra et al., 1998; Renaud, Bouchard, et al., 2002; Renaud, Decarie, et al., 2003; Renaud, Singer, et al., 2001; Shelhamer, 1998, 2005; Treffner & Kelso, 1999; Warren, 2006). It was clearly apparent in our results that there are unvarying links between the spatial position of objects and the motor processes on which active visual search is based. These self-organized connections seem to arise intrinsically from the fundamental coordination of the degrees of freedom involved in motor action and then develop under the effect of proprioceptive, visual, and intentional constraints (Kelso, 1995; Van Orden & Holden, 2002;

Van Orden, Holden, et al., 2003; Van Orden, Moreno, et al., 2003; Warren, 2006; Warren & Fajen, 2004). Topological invariance extraction – the cornerstone of visual perception – appears to be simultaneously *embodied* and *embedded*, that is, emerging from the action of an agent situated within the limits of a specific environmental context (Clancey, 1997; Clark, 1997; Shaw, 2003). It does not seem to require an internal instance of control but depends more on spontaneous self-organization that persists in time and space and with dynamics that are not strictly restricted to an immediate visual stimulation. This perceptual self-organization of the mutual agent–environment relationship, although it may seem at first to resemble a noisy and incoherent phenomenon, contains the complex fluctuations and stability necessary for active and adapted perception.

The embeddedness of the perceptual invariance extraction processes is to be found not only in short-term scales but also in the more extended time scales of the biological evolution of species (Sulis, 1995; Swenson & Turvey, 1991; Turvey & Shaw, 1995; Van Orden & Holden, 2002; Varela et al., 1991). Thus the fundamentally adaptive character of maintaining a constant connection with the environment certainly harkens back to very distant biophysical sources. This is why Gibson (1979) connected the concepts of invariance and *affordance.* According to Gibson, the affordances of an object, event, or environment are the opportunities for action that the object, event, or environment offers the observer. These affordances are directed simultaneously toward the agent and the environment as they instantiate at the perception–action level the instantaneous coupling between both entities. The infinite variety of available affordances – their endless landscape, as it were – makes up a single cognitive fabric that is continuously differentiating itself in accordance with invariant combinations of invariances (Gibson, 1979). It is these invariances and higher-level compound invariances that the agent causes to emerge and that guide him in the active first-person exploration of his world.

This is therefore also a philosophical stance, a resolutely nondualistic onto-logical stance that replaces the mind–matter or body–mind dichotomy with organism–environment complementarity (Gibson, 1979; Noë, 2004; Shaw, 2003; Turvey & Shaw, 1999; Varela et al., 1991). It is likewise a nonatomistic stance in which perception is based not on a fragmentary compound of sense-data unified by cognition, but rather on the primacy of direct and holistic lived experience in the world. It is in this sense that the philosopher Maurice Merleau-Ponty, by establishing the connection between phenomenology and gestaltism, opened the door to a conceptual space that reconciles intellectualism and empiricism – a space in which perception establishes our cognitive relationship to the world (Clark, 1997; Dillon, 1997; Freeman, 2001; Merleau-Ponty, 1945, 1946).

The theoretical approach of the nonlinear dynamical system provides the concepts as well as the tools necessary to explore the interaction between perception and action (Gregson & Guastello, 2005; Guastello, 2001, 2006; Guastello & Gregson, 2006). Indeed, because it allows us to explore unpredictability and determinism, circular causality and emergence, complexity and invariance at the same time, NDS proves to be the best approach for probing the empirical and theoretical horizons surrounding our scientific understanding of the agent–environment interaction.

Notes

1. Helmholtz distinguished between two indirect theories of position constancy: the afferent theory, based on muscular feedback originating in the oculomotor nerve, and the efferent copy theory, according to which a copy of the oculomotor command is sent to the cerebral centers responsible for calculating the object's position (Palmer, 1999).
2. In biomechanics, degrees of freedom express the set of separate displacements required to define completely a change of position of the body.
3. A forcing function limits the set of values that is fed as input to a dynamical system.
4. CAVE: cave automatic virtual environment.
5. These VMPs are of course not visible to the subjects in virtual reality immersion.

References

Aks, D. J., Zelinsky, G. J., & Sprott, J. C. (2002). Memory across eye-movements: $1/f$ dynamics in visual search. *Nonlinear Dynamics, Psychology, and Life Sciences, 6*, 1–25.

Bak, P., & Creutz, M. (1994). Fractals and self-organized criticality. In A. Bunde & S. Havlin (Eds.), *Fractals in science* (pp. 27–48). Berlin: Springer-Verlag.

Bak, P., Tang, C., & Wiesenfeld, K. (1987). Self-organized criticality: An explanation of $1/f$ noise. *Physical Review Letters, 59*, 381–384.

Bassingthwaighte, J. B., Liebovitch, L. S., & West, B. J. (1994). *Fractal physiology*. New York: Oxford University Press.

Beer, R. D. (1995). A dynamical systems perspective on agent-environment interaction. *Artificial Intelligence, 72*, 173–215.

Bernstein, N. A. (1967). *The co-ordination and regulation of movements*. Oxford: Pergamon Press.

Card, S. K., Moran, T. P., & Newell, A. P. (1983). *The psychology of human-computer interaction*. Hillsdale, NJ: Erlbaum.

Clancey, W. J. (1997). *Situated cognition: On human knowledge and computer representations*. Cambridge: Cambridge University Press.

Clark, A. J. (1997). *Being there: Putting brain, body, and world together again*. Cambridge, MA: MIT Press.

Dillon, M. C. (1997). *Merleau Ponty's ontology*. Bloomington: Indiana University Press.

Duchowski, A. T., Medlin, E., Cournia, N., Murphy, H., Gramopadhye, A., Nair, S., et al. (2002). 3-D eye movement analysis. *Behavior Research Methods, Instruments, & Computers, 34*, 573–591.

Ebenholtz, S. M. (2001). *Oculomotor systems and perception*. Cambridge: Cambridge University Press.

Eckmann, J.-P., Kamphorst, S. O., & Ruelle, D. (1987). Recurrence plots of dynamical systems. *Europhysics Letters, 4*, 973–977.

Freeman, W. J. (2001). Three centuries of category errors in studies of the neural basis of consciousness and intentionality. In W. Sulis & I. Trofimova (Eds.), *Nonlinear dynamics in life and social sciences* (pp. 275–285). Amsterdam: IOS Press.

Gibson, J. J. (1950). *The perception of the visual world.* Boston: Houghton Mifflin.

Gibson, J. J. (1961). Ecological optics. *Vision Research, 1,* 253–262.

Gibson, J. J. (1966). *The senses considered as perceptual systems.* Boston: Houghton Mifflin.

Gibson, J. J. (1979). *The ecological approach to visual perception.* Boston: Houghton Mifflin.

Grassberger, P., & Procaccia, I. (1983). Characterization of strange attractors. *Physical Review Letters, 50,* 346–349.

Grassberger, P., Schreiber, T., & Schaffrath, C. (1991). Nonlinear time sequence analysis. *International Journal of Bifurcation and Chaos, 1,* 521–547.

Gregson, R. A. M., & Guastello, S. J. (2005). Introduction to nonlinear methodology, part 1: Challenges we face and those that we offer. *Nonlinear Dynamics, Psychology, and Life Sciences, 9,* 371–374.

Guastello, S. J. (2001). Nonlinear dynamics in psychology. *Discrete Dynamics in Nature and Society, 6,* 11–29.

Guastello, S. J. (2006). Motor control research requires nonlinear dynamics. *American Psychologist, 61,* 77–78.

Guastello, S. J., & Gregson, R. A. M. (2006). Introduction to nonlinear methodology, part 2: Domain-specific issues. *Nonlinear Dynamics, Psychology, and Life Sciences, 10,* 159–161.

Handel, S. (2006). *Perceptual coherence: Hearing and seeing.* England: Oxford University Press.

Hausdorff, J. M., Peng, C.-K., Ladin, Z., Wei, J. Y., & Goldberger, A. L. (1995). Is walking a random walk? Evidence for long-range correlations in the stride interval of human gait. *Journal of Applied Physiology, 78,* 349–358.

Hausdorff, J. M., Purdon, P., Peng, C.-K., Ladin, Z., Wei, J. Y., & Goldberger, A. L. (1996). Fractal dynamics of human gait: Stability of long-range correlations in stride interval fluctuations. *Journal of Applied Physiology, 80,* 1448–1457.

Heath, R. (2000). *Nonlinear dynamics: Techniques and applications in psychology.* Mahwah, NJ: Erlbaum.

Helmholtz, H. L. F. von (1925). *A treatise on physiological optics* (Vol. 3, J. P. C. Southall, Trans.). Menasha, WI: Optical Society of America. (Original work published 1867)

Juarrero, A. (1999). *Dynamics in action: Intentional behavior as a complex system.* Cambridge, MA: MIT Press.

Kelso, J. A. S. (1995). *Dynamic patterns.* Cambridge, MA: MIT Press.

Kelso, J. A. S., & Zanone, P. G. (2002). Coordination dynamics and transfer across different effector systems. *Journal of Experimental Psychology: Human Perception Performance, 28,* 776–797.

Kennel, M. B., Brown, R., & Abarbanel, H. D. I. (1992). Determining embedding dimension for phase-space reconstruction using a geometrical construction. *Physical Review A, 45,* 3403–3411.

Kim, N.-G., & Turvey, M. T. (1999). Eye movements and a rule for perceiving direction of heading. *Ecological Psychology, 11,* 233–248.

Kugler, P. N., & Turvey, M. T. (1987). *Information, natural law, and the self-assembly of rhythmic movement.* Hillsdale, NJ: Erlbaum.

Langer, M. S., & Mann, R. (2004). On the computation of image motion and heading in a 3-D cluttered scene. In L. M. Vaina, S. A. Beardsley, & S. K. Rushton (Eds.), *Optical Flow and Beyond* (pp. 289–304). Norwell, MA: Kluwer Academic.

Longuet-Higgins, H. C., & Prazdny, K. (1980). The interpretation of a moving retinal image. *Proceedings of the Royal Society London. Series B, Biological Sciences, 208,* 385–397.

Mandelbrot, B. (1975). *Les objets fractals* [Fractal objects]. Paris: Flammarion.

Marr, D. (1982). *Vision.* New York: Freeman.

McSharry, P. E. (2005). The danger of wishing for chaos. *Nonlinear Dynamics, Psychology, and Life Sciences, 9,* 375–397.

Merleau-Ponty, M. (1945). *Phénoménologie de la perception* [The phenomenology of perception]. Paris: Gallimard.

Merleau-Ponty, M. (1946). *Le primat de la perception et ses conséquences philosophiques* [The primacy of perception and its philosophical consequences]. Lagrasse, France: Éditions Verdier.

Mitra, S., Riley, M. A., Schmidt, R. C., & Turvey, M. T. (1998). Vision and the level of synergies. In L. Harris & M. Jenkin (Eds.), *Vision and action* (pp. 314–331). New York: Cambridge University Press.

Newell, A. P., Rosenbloom, P. S., & Laird, J. E. (1989). Symbolic architectures for cognition. In M. I. Posner (Ed.), *Foundations of cognitive science* (pp. 93–131). Cambridge, MA: MIT Press.

Noë, A. (2004). *Action in perception.* Cambridge, MA: MIT Press.

O'Regan, J. K., & Noë, A. (2001). A sensorimotor account of vision and visual consciousness. *Behavioral and Brain Sciences, 24,* 939–1011.

Palmer, S. E. (1999). *Vision science: Photons to phenomenology.* Cambridge, MA: MIT Press.

Pellechia, G. L., & Shockley, K. (2005). Application of recurrence quantification analysis: Influence of cognitive activity on postural fluctuations. In M. A. Riley & G. C. Van Orden (Eds.), *Tutorials in contemporary nonlinear methods for the behavioral sciences* (pp. 353–400). Retrieved May 30, 2007, from http://www.nsf.gov/sbe/bcs/pac/nmbs/chap3.pdf

Pressing, J. (1999). The referential dynamics of cognition and action. *Psychological Review, 106,* 714–747.

Renaud, P. (2006). Method for providing data to be used by a therapist for analyzing a patient behavior in a virtual environment. *U.S. Patent No. 7128577.* Washington, DC: U.S. Patent and Trademark Office.

Renaud, P., Bouchard, S., & Proulx, R. (2002). Behavioral avoidance dynamics in the presence of a virtual spider. *IEEE Transactions on Information Technology in Biomedecine, 6,* 235–243.

Renaud, P., Decarie, J., Gourd, S. P., Paquin, L. C., & Bouchard, S. (2003). Eye-tracking in immersive environments: A general methodology to analyze affordance-based interactions from oculomotor dynamics. *Cyberpsychology and Behavior, 6,* 519–526.

Renaud, P., Singer, G., & Proulx, R. (2001). Head-tracking fractal dynamics in visually pursuing virtual objects. In W. Sulis & I. Trofimova (Eds.), *Nonlinear dynamics in life and social sciences* (pp. 333–346). Amsterdam: IOS Press.

Riley, M. A., Balasubramaniam, R., & Turvey, M. T. (1999). Recurrence quantification analysis of postural fluctuations. *Gait & Posture, 9,* 65–78.

Rock, I. (1997). *Indirect perception.* Cambridge, MA: MIT Press.

Sasaki, O., Usami, S., Gagey, P. M., Martinerie, J., Le Van Quyen, M., & Arranz, P. (2002). Role of visual input in nonlinear postural control system. *Experimental Brain Research, 147,* 1–7.

Schöner, G., Dijkstra, T. M. H., & Jeka, J. J. (1998). Action-perception patterns emerge from coupling and adaptation. *Ecological Psychology, 10,* 323–346.

Schöner, G., & Kelso, J. A. S. (1988). Dynamic pattern generation in behavioral and neural systems. *Science, 239,* 1513–1520.

Schreiber, T. (1993). Extremely simple nonlinear noise reduction method. *Physical Review E, 47,* 2401–2404.

Schreiber, T. (1999). Interdisciplinary application of nonlinear time series methods. *Physics Reports, 308,* 2–64.

Sedgwick, H. A. (2001). Visual space perception. In E. B. Goldstein (Ed.), *Blackwell handbook of perception* (pp. 128–167). Oxford: Blackwell.

Shaw, R. E. (2003). The agent-environment interface: Simon's indirect or Gibson's direct coupling? *Ecological Psychology, 15,* 37–106.

Shaw, R. E., & Turvey, M. T. (1999). Ecological foundations of cognition: II. Degrees of freedom and conserved quantities in animal–environment systems. *Journal of Consciousness Studies, 6,* 111–123.

Shelhamer, M. (1998). Nonlinear dynamic systems evaluation of "rhythmic" eye movements (optokinetic nystagmus). *Journal of Neuroscience Methods, 83,* 45–56.

Shelhamer, M. (2005). Sequences of predictive eye movements form a fractional Brownian series – implications for self-organized criticality in the oculomotor system. *Biological Cybernetics, 93,* 43–53.

Skarda, C. A., & Freeman, W. J. (1987). How the brain makes chaos in order to make sense of the world. *Behavioral and Brain Sciences, 10,* 161–195.

Sprott, J. C. (2003). *Chaos and time-series analysis.* Oxford: Oxford University Press.

Sulis, W. (1995). Naturally occurring computational systems. In R. Robertson & A. Combs (Eds.), *Chaos theory in psychology and the life sciences* (pp. 103–121). New York: Erlbaum.

Swenson, R., & Turvey, M. T. (1991). Thermodynamic reasons for perception-action cycles. *Ecological Psychology, 3,* 317–348.

Theiler, J., Eubank, S., Longtin, A., Galdrikian, B., & Farmer, J. D. (1992). Testing for nonlinearity in time series: The method of surrogate data. *Physica D: Nonlinear Phenomena, 58,* 77–94.

Thelen, E., & Smith, L. (1994). *A dynamic systems approach to the development of cognition and action.* Cambridge, MA: MIT Press.

Treffner, P. J., & Kelso, J. A. S. (1999). Dynamic encounters: Long memory during functional stabilization. *Ecological Psychology, 11,* 103–137.

Tschacher, W., & Haken, H. (2007). Intentionality in non-equilibrium systems? The functional aspects of self-organized pattern formation. *New Ideas in Psychology, 25,* 1–15.

Turvey, M. T., & Shaw, R. E. (1995). Toward an ecological physics and a physical psychology. In R. L. Solso & D. W. Massaro (Eds.), *The science of the mind: 2001 and beyond* (pp. 143–169). New York: Oxford University Press.

Turvey, M. T., & Shaw, R. E. (1999). Ecological foundations of cognition: I. Symmetry and specificity of animal-environment systems. *Journal of Consciousness Studies, 6,* 95–110.

Van Orden, G. C., & Holden, J. G. (2002). Intentional contents and self-control. *Ecological Psychology, 14,* 87–109.

Van Orden, G. C., Holden, J. G., & Turvey, M. T. (2003). Self-organization of cognitive performance. *Journal of Experimental Psychology: General, 132,* 331–350.

Van Orden, G. C., Moreno, M. A., & Holden, J. G. (2003). A proper metaphysics for cognitive performance. *Nonlinear Dynamics, Psychology, and Life Sciences, 7,* 49–60.

Varela, F., Thompson, E. T., & Rosch, E. (1991). *The embodied mind: Cognitive science and human experience.* Cambridge, MA: MIT Press.

Warren, W. H. (1995). Self-motion: Visual perception and visual control. In W. Epstein & S. Rogers (Eds.), *Perception of space and motion* (2nd ed., pp. 263–325). San Diego, CA: Academic Press.

Warren, W. H. (2004). Optic flow. In L. Chalupa & J. Werner (Eds.), *The visual neurosciences* (pp. 1247–1259). Cambridge, MA: MIT Press.

Warren, W. H. (2006). The dynamics of perception and action. *Psychological Review, 113,* 358–389.

Warren, W. H., & Fajen, B. R. (2004). From optic flow to laws of control. In L. M. Vaina, S. A. Beardsley, & S. K. Rushton (Eds.), *Optic flow and beyond* (pp. 307–337). Norwell, MA: Kluwer Academic.

7 Origins of Order in Cognitive Activity

GEOFF HOLLIS, HEIDI KLOOS, AND GUY C. VAN ORDEN

Origins of Order in Cognitive Activity

Most cognitive scientists have run across *The War of the Ghosts*, a Native American story used by Bartlett (1932) in his classic studies of remembering. British college students read the story twice and recalled it in detail after 15 minutes, hours, days, months, or years "as opportunity offered" (p. 65). The compelling finding was that participants reinterpreted parts of the story, in addition to omitting details. The mystical story was reorganized and changed in the retelling to fit cultural norms of the British participants. In other words, errors in retelling the story were neither random nor arbitrary but fit together within a larger created narrative. The memory errors illustrate the ordinary constructive performance of cognition and the creation of orderly and sensible thought. Despite perpetually moving eyes, swaying body, and ambiguous stimuli, people perceive coherent and orderly objects. Despite the lack of explicit links between events, higher-order cognition fits thought and behavior within larger coherent narratives. However, the origin of such order remains a mystery. What is the basis of orderly thought, memory, speech, and other cognitive abilities?

The origin of order in cognition is the topic of this chapter. We begin with a discussion of how order is explained within a traditional approach of information processing. Taking the shortcomings of this account seriously, we then turn to other disciplines – those that have framed the question of order more successfully. The answers have relied on the concept of self-organization, the idea that order can emerge spontaneously from the nonlinear interaction of a system's components. In the remainder of the chapter, we discuss empirical evidence for self-organization in cognition. The accumulated evidence in reasoning, speaking, listening, reading, and remembering motivates a complex system approach to cognition.

Order and Information Processing

The development of the computer promised a workable metaphor for human cognition. A computer's flow of information processing appears similar to cognition: Information comes in (it is transduced into neural signals), information is manipulated (it is perceived, remembered, reasoned about), and an output is produced (overt behavior takes place). Conveniently, the orderly workings of a computer are transparent. Programs, memory storage, and peripheries are arranged in a systematic way. Thus a reasonable abduction is to equate the workings of cognition with the workings of a computer's software. As Neisser (1968) suggested, "The task of a psychologist trying to understand human cognition is analogous to that of a man trying to discover how a computer has been programmed" (p. 6).

The computer perspective has flourished and still persists. Cognitive activity is often seen as a step-by-step process of detecting, combining, storing, retrieving, and outputting information. In line with this framework, questions pertain to the duration of information processing (e.g., Sternberg, 1969), the capacity of memory systems (e.g., Miller, 1956), low-level versus high-level detection of information (e.g., Marr, 1982), the properties of the central executive (e.g., Allport, 1989), and the specific format of symbolic representations (e.g., Fodor & Pylyshyn, 1981). Accordingly, order is generated through symbol manipulations, "recipes for selecting, storing, recovering, combining, outputting, and generally manipulating [symbols]" (Neisser, 1968, p. 7).

An information processing account envisions the complexities of perceiving, remembering, and thinking as hierarchies of functional components, wherein each component solves a simpler part of cognition. Depending on the requirements of the task, components include instructions to manipulate internal symbols and communicate solutions to other components. Internal symbols such as schemas and representations are themselves the outputs of lower-level components such as edge detectors, acoustic feature detectors, or detectors of other primitive elements. Higher-level executive functions also include instructions that determine planning, selective attention, and deciding among alternatives. Executive functions organize cognition to follow explicit task instructions, for example, by retrieving the appropriate representations and planning the action.

This somewhat compressed summary of the information processing view makes one point clear on the origins of ordered cognition: Overt order in cognitive activities stems from internal components that are themselves ordered. We perceive a stable world because we have stable feature detectors. We perform systematically in a categorization task because we have a stable representation of the category, and we have stable detectors for recognizing category members. And we make errors – for example, when asked to recall an unusual story – because there is a mismatch between the presented stimulus and stable schemas. Behavioral order is equated with intrinsic sources of order – a priori order that exists in the components of cognition. Similar to the functioning of a clock, ordered behavior comes from the interaction of ordered parts.

The obvious advantage of holding this view is that internal components, the ordered parts of the mind, can be described in detail. We can ask such questions as: How do children represent numbers? What is the format of the mental lexicon? How do adults represent cause and effect? This view makes it fairly easy to control behavior. If stable components cause behaviors, particular components can be changed to yield the desired behavior. Merely changing the appropriate component could correct erroneous behavior. Why, then, are we focused on the shortcomings of this account?

Limits of the Information Processing Account

Early on, Neisser (1968) noted puzzling discrepancies between people's behavior and a computer's output. For instance, some computations (e.g., many-digit multiplication) are trivially simple for a computer but exceedingly difficult or impossible for people. Other tasks are immediate and simple for a person (e.g., self-guided locomotion) but exceedingly difficult or impossible for computers. These differences cannot be easily reconciled. Claiming limited capacity in humans could explain poor performance of many-digit multiplications, but it could not explain the relative ease with which even a crawling infant navigates a terrain. Claiming limited complexity in computers could explain a computer's inability to perceive and act in a naturally complex environment, but it could not explain the computer's ease with complex calculations.

Such obvious discrepancies supply a first indication that the computer metaphor has serious limitations for explaining the order in cognition. These and other discrepancies between computations and common sense subsequently were called the *frame problem* (e.g., see Haselager, Bongers, & van Rooij, 2003). However, even if we could set aside the frame problem, important questions remain: How can relatively static components explain the uniqueness of thought? How can ordered components explain context sensitivity? How does order get into the components in the first place? Each of these concerns is addressed in turn.

Uniqueness of Thought

Information processing takes for granted that the same conditions produce the same output time and time again. However, a central finding of empirical cognition is that cognition is always under construction and rarely repeats itself exactly. As Williams James noted: "A permanently existing idea ... is as mythological an entity as the Jack of Spades" (1890, Vol. 1, p. 236). An oncoming thought is almost never a mere repetition of a previous thought, and the same idea communicated more than once by the same person will be conveyed in different sentences each time. To do otherwise creates added idiomatic meaning;

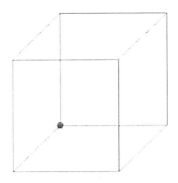

Figure 7.1. Necker cube. Fix your eyes on the dot (green in the original stimulus materials) and watch the cube (red in the original stimulus materials) fluctuate between different orientations.

repetitious speech acts are seen as stubborn, pedantic, sarcastic, or ironic (Gibbs, 1999). Even a repetitive motion, such as swinging a hammer or scratching an itch, will express unique kinematics within each repetition (Berkinblit, Feldman, & Fukson, 1986; Bernstein, 1967). As Neisser explained, "exact repetitions of earlier acts or thoughts are the exception, extremely difficult to achieve, and ascribed to long practice or neurotic defensiveness" (1968, p. 282).

One strategy to address the problem of uniqueness is to add random variation among component outputs, such as adding white noise. Some modern information processing models have sources of randomness built in (e.g., Act-Rational or ACT-R; Anderson, Lebiere, Lovett, & Reder, 1998). Indeed, successive outputs of such models do not just repeat the same solution; they vary from iteration to iteration. However, there is no evidence to support this functional role for random cognitive noise. In fact, no matter how unconstrained the task, variability in repeated measures of cognitive performance is not simply random (Gilden, 2001). Take the perception of a Necker cube as an example (Necker, 1932; see Fig. 7.1). If the display is sufficiently ambiguous, a person's percepts will switch among possible percepts, from one to another and back again, as time passes. If random processes govern switching among percepts, then the time between switches should exhibit white noise. This is not what is found, however. The time series of time between switches displays *pink noise* (Aks & Sprott, 2003), a kind of noise that aliases a deterministic, interdependent system, not random perturbations.

Other information processing models use learning instead of noise to account for the uniqueness of behavior (e.g., Sutton & Barto, 1998). A system that iteratively changes itself based on its interactions with an environment has the potential to display similar, but nonrepeating behavior over time. Learning as the basis for uniqueness is plausible, and it is consistent with the idea of cognition being constructive. However, examples of noniterative, single-trial learning (e.g., Rock, 1957) suggest that there are qualitative differences between human learning and current machine learning. Uniqueness is not always due to incomplete, ongoing, incremental learning. Moreover, although some learning is intuitively asymptotic, massed practice of a precision-aiming motor task

(Wijnants, Bosman, Hasselman, Cox, & Van Orden, 2008), for example, and development of human gait (Hausdorff, Zemany, Peng, & Goldberger, 1999) both seem to asymptote on the pink noise mentioned earlier. Thus although learning might contribute to uniqueness, it does not exhaust the facts of the matter.

Finally, another conventional way to address uniqueness is to supply a unique mental structure for each cognitive act that qualifies as sufficiently unique. Such an approach has lead to a variety of distinctions, including implicit versus explicit processes, declarative versus procedural knowledge, and long-term versus short-term memory. Yet an inherent problem comes with this solution as well. The general basis for any particular distinction is indeterminate (Shallice, 1988; Van Orden, Pennington, & Stone, 2001). How large, or how reliable, or what kind of a difference must exist in behavior before separate mental structures are justified? One can find distinct and uniquely ordered behavior on a long time scale such as planning a vacation or a retirement. One can also find distinct and uniquely ordered behavior on a short time scale such as hammering a nail or scratching an itch. Do all of these distinctions necessitate distinct mental structures? Clearly, accounting for uniqueness by resorting to a priori ordered components raises more questions than it provides answers.

Context Dependence of Cognition

Information processing accounts assume that ordinary perception and cognition originate in atomic components that combine through internalized rules to create cognition. Small or superficial changes in context should therefore not change the cognition. However, cognition is not only unique but is also strongly affected by small changes in context. Adults' performance of strictly mathematical problems changes as a function of their superficial spatial arrangements (Landy & Goldstone, 2007). The well-documented A-not-B search error disappears in infants who are briefly lifted from their sitting position before the toy is hidden at position B (Smith, Thelen, Titzer, & McLin, 1999).

Likewise, children's well-documented difficulty distinguishing between sinking and floating objects disappears when the distribution of experimental objects is altered (Kloos, 2008). Further, well-documented syndromes of brain damage or developmental disabilities change, disappear, or even "reverse" to become an opposite syndrome after changes in the method of observation (Van Orden et al., 2001). For example, the same patient exhibits telegraphic speech under some task conditions, a symptom of agrammatic or Broca's aphasia, and morphological substitutions under different task conditions, a symptom of paraphasia (Hofstede & Kolk, 1994; Kolk & Heeschen, 1992), but these aphasias (symptoms) are sometimes put forward as opposite syndromes, composing a double dissociation.

One way to explain context-dependent cognition is to assume that the stable components of information processing combine in context-unique arrangements for each instance of cognitive activity, as situated expectations for instance (Mandler, 1984). If so, however, there is no reliable basis by which to distinguish between cognitive components and methodological contexts. Where atomic components have been most closely examined, for example, they are reliably different in different task contexts. Atomic components are sufficiently context-sensitive that they are impossible to dissociate from the contexts of their discovery (Goldinger & Azuma, 2003; Van Orden & Kloos, 2005). In other words, no data exist that reliably pick out cognitive components separate from or independent of the contexts in which they are observed.

What is the origin of order in components? Our discussion on the uniqueness of cognition and its context dependence already hints at problems in reducing the global order of behavior to underlying ordered components. A final problem, then, pertains to the question about how order gets into underlying components in the first place. For example, what is the source of order in participants' schemas that affects their recall of *The War of the Ghosts*? What is the source of order in representations about a category or a concept? And what is the source of order in intentional thought and purposeful behavior? Reducing the order of cognitive activity to ordered information processing components leads to a sort of dead end, making it impossible to explain the ultimate origin of order without homunculi or empirically opaque automatic components. Such an approach leaves psychology with no eventual answer for the origins of order (Juarrero, 1999; Kugler & Turvey, 1987; van Gelder & Port, 1995). Consequently, psychology inevitably sees either a stimulus or a homunculus-like executive process as the *prime mover* of behavior (Oyama, 2000; Shaw, 2001).

In the remainder of this chapter, we describe how the complex systems approach has reframed the question of the origin of order. The pivot point of complex systems is self-organization, the emergence of order from unordered parts. We expand on this point to supply answers to the important questions identified by Neisser: "How is the raw material [of constructions] organized? How is the process of construction organized? What determines what is constructed? And what purpose does it serve?" (Neisser, 1968, p. 280)

Emergence of Order in Complex Systems

Questions about order and its origins are asked in a larger sphere than just psychology. Other disciplines have been haunted by similar problems of trying to explain order without having to stipulate its existence a priori in the parts of the system. In contemporary physics and biology, for instance, order has become something to be understood (e.g., Depew & Weber, 1995). Its origins no longer appear so mysterious. The synthesis of shared questions of order has yielded the contemporary science of complexity. It concerns a meta-disciplinary nonlinear dynamical systems view in which the same principled origins of order are expressed in very different material systems. A number of conceptual building blocks lie within this approach, laws that govern the emergence of stable behavior. Of course, additional necessary laws of order in living systems remain to be discovered (Kauffman, 2000).

Cognitive scientists have availed themselves of the complexity view and imported theoretical concepts that come out of it. One of these concepts is self-organization. Applied to cognitive activity, self-organization concerns order in the larger system of organism and environment, order that reduces neither to homunculi nor to stimuli, nor to pieces and bits of a cognitive architecture. Instead, it is based on self-sustaining processes that exploit gradients of uncertainty. In this section, we explain self-ordering and self-sustaining processes in more detail, discussing in particular their relation to traveling waves, constraints, and critical states.

Traveling Waves

Self-perpetuation is a prominent characteristic of physical and biological structures. Convection perpetuates a tornado through its relatively brief life span, for instance. The heart supplies blood and nutrients to the body and itself, allowing its structure to exist through time. Neighboring brain cells supply mutual life support (which is why more cells die in brain trauma than are killed directly). In effect, metabolism is the primary function of the brain and body.

If metabolism is the primary function of a nervous system, then an elegant theory would be one in which cognitive activity emerges out of metabolism. Such a theory would begin to bridge the chasm between laws of physical processes and cognition. Davia (2005) outlined such a theory based on *autocatalytic reactions*, which are fundamental metabolic processes. Autocatalytic reactions are chemical reactions in which a catalyst – an enzyme, for example – accelerates a chemical reaction while remaining unchanged. Enzymes catalyze the biochemical reactions in metabolism that are necessary to sustain life, develop, and reproduce.

Davia (2005) equated enzymes with self-perpetuating structures called *traveling waves* or *solitons*. Traveling waves are the basis in the nervous system for perception and action. To relate metabolism to perception and action, Davia argued that the nervous system functions as an excitable medium. An excitable medium is a landscape containing energy that can be consumed and replenished. A field of grass may be conceived as an excitable medium. It can be grazed but also replenished with nutrients and sunlight. The brain and body, too, may be conceived as excitable media, in which glucose is consumed and resupplied, for instance. Traveling waves are temporally invariant structures that exist as coherent, ordered entities within the space and energy of an excitable medium.

Consider traveling waves in olfactory perception, the dominant mode of perception in most animals. A rabbit, conditioned to respond to banana oil, will exhibit a traveling wave across its olfactory bulb as it inhales banana oil. The wave itself comprises a complex pattern of amplitude-modulated activity; neurons firing at particular amplitudes compose the wave structure. The wave is context sensitive to the extent that learning a new, unrelated association to sawdust will change the amplitude wave profile to banana oil. The pattern of the amplitude wave pertains to what the odor affords for the animal; it is not a representation of smell. For example, if banana oil is a conditioned stimulus that subsequently serves as an unconditioned stimulus, as the same animal acquires the conditioned stimulus sawdust, then the banana oil traveling wave pattern will stay with sawdust, the new conditioned stimulus. Finally, all else being equal, the wave is subject to long-term drift in structure at the pace of hair or fingernail growth. The same findings have been corroborated for other senses; "all the central sensory systems use essentially the same dynamics" (Freeman, 2000, p. 88).

Traveling waves are seen in many forms. Tsunamis are prime examples. They propagate a fixed structure and its associated energy across long distances, even when faced with obstructions. Forest fires are traveling waves that perpetuate their shape outward – at least until confronted with nonflammable terrain or asymmetrically dense, flammable terrain. So is the unwinding of DNA before transcription, as are the movements of a millipede's legs. In the case of the millipede, the traveling wave allows it to move, while also unifying perception and action. This unity poises the millipede to react seamlessly with new movements that may be required.

Traveling waves unify energy and structure in that they perpetuate a fixed form and energy and do not dissipate easily. In classical mechanics, when a force is applied to a physical structure, its energy is quickly dissipated. For traveling waves, this is not true. Consequently, for the millipede, unification of perception and action explains how a reaction can be immediate. Human perception and action can also be immediate. In particular, ultrafast cognition has been observed in which perception or action occur so quickly as to leave little or no time for information processing (e.g., Fabre-Thorpe, Delorme, Marlot, & Thorpe, 2001; Grill-Spector & Kanwisher, 2006; Peterson, 1994; Rauschenberger, Peterson, Mosca, & Bruno, 2003).

Traveling waves maintain their own structure across time and provide a continuous capacity for action (for they are both perpetuating structures of physical material *and* energy). As such, they may provide a basis for cognition without having to refer to fixed static cognitive components (Davia, 2005). Furthermore, traveling waves are demonstrable entities, not hypothetical constructs such as component functions. In biological entities specifically, traveling waves have been observed in enzyme catalysis (Sataric, Zakula, Ivic, & Tuszynski, 1991), DNA (Englander, Kallenbach, Heeger, Krumhansl, & Litwin, 1980; Yakushevich, 2001), heart functioning (Beaumont, Davidenko, Davidenko, & Jalife, 1998), nerve action potential (Aslanidi & Mornev, 1996), the basilar membrane (Duke & Julicher, 2003), the brain (Koroleva & Bures, 1979), muscle contraction (Davydov, 1979), and population dynamics (Odell, 1980), and spontaneous traveling waves in early development organize the auditory cortex, neocortex, hippocampus, spinal cord networks, brainstem nuclei, and the retina (Godfrey & Swindale, 2007).

Constraints

Traveling waves do not reduce to components of the nervous system; they are emergent phenomena that depend instead on the existing balance of constraints. Constraints are accrued through idiosyncratic experience, and constraints are implicit in the immediate context. Constraints are aspects of biology, culture, history, context, or current states that narrow down the possibilities for cognitive activity, prior to its occurrence (see also Mandler, 1997). They are necessary to ensure ordered task performance because there are too many degrees of freedom otherwise (Bernstein, 1967; Turvey, 1990).

Consider adults' memory performance in Bartlett's (1932) *The War of the Ghosts* experiment. The mystical content of the story and its unfamiliar cultural norms provided fewer constraints than what a British story might have supplied to a British reader. The British reader whose experiences did not match those of Native Americans had available many degrees of freedom for interpretation and subsequent recall of the story. Under these circumstances of unfamiliar norms and loosened cultural constraints, participant idiosyncrasies were more fully expressed. Although every participant recalled a coherent story, the way in which this was done varied greatly from one participant to the next. In Bartlett's words, "the particular form adopted [was] due directly to the functioning of individual special interests . . . or to some fact of personal experience, or to some peculiarity of individual attitude which determines the salience or potency of the details in the whole material dealt with" (1932, p. 71).

It is also possible to tighten contextual constraints. A scenario that supplies sufficiently tight constraints should yield performance that is identical across many participants. For example, when presented with a list of words such as "bed," "rest," and "awake," many adults falsely recalled the term "sleep," a related term that was not presented in the list. This memory paradigm is so reliably constraining that participants falsely produced predicted terms on approximately 50% of recall opportunities and falsely recognized such terms at almost the same rate as hit rates for presented terms (Roediger & McDermott, 1995). In the face of this probabilistic outcome, it goes well beyond the facts to invoke causal properties of 50% of participants' sleep schemas. Instead, the methodologically constrained context (providing many words related to the concept of sleep) creates the potential for false-positive sleep memories contingent on idiosyncratic states of mind of participants.

Constraints combine to reduce the degrees of freedom for behavior and thereby increase the likelihood of the behaviors that remain. Note, however, that constraints do not combine additively. Take, for example, the proportion of false positives to target items such as "sleep" after studying a list of related words. Augmenting the list of semantically related words (e.g., "bed," "rest," "awake") with up to three additional semantic relatives does not change the proportion of false positives. However, augmenting the same list with only one word similar in phonology (e.g., "keep") sharply increases the proportion of false positives. Adding three phonologic relatives doubles the proportion of false positives (Watson, Balota, & Roediger, 2003).

In another example of nonadditive and nonlinear effects, participants were presented with a list of homophones such as "paws," after which they were given a surprise recognition task of old and new homophones (e.g., "paws" and "pause," respectively). The proportion of false positives (judging "pause" to be old) was measured. This condition was contrasted with *memory-load* conditions, containing words similar in phonology and spelling to either the old homophone (e.g., "jaws") or to the new homophone (e.g., "cause"). As expected, false positives were highest in the latter condition, when memory-load words shared the phonology of the new homophones (Azuma, Williams & Davie, 2004). However, memory-load words by themselves (e.g., "cause") produced no false-positive effect (e.g., of "pause") above chance. "Cause" on its own did not change the degrees of freedom for responding; but in combination with "paws" it did make false positives to "pause" more likely (cf. Humphreys, Burt, & Lawrence, 2001).

Importantly, constraints do not cause false positives or behavior in general. Behavior does not directly originate in constraints and is not directly determined by constraints. Instead, constraints change the likelihood of behaviors, including false positives, as they change the potential set for responding. Constraints merely narrow this potential set. By contrast, as new capacities become available, constraints are relaxed, and the degrees of freedom for behavior are increased. Braitenberg (1984) illustrated this fact when he imagined robots or vehicles that differed in their capacities for movement, their sensory capacities, their wiring complexity, and their learning capacities. Adding capacities incrementally allowed him to deduce the new behaviors that were brought online.

New capacities reduce constraints and increase the degrees of freedom for behavior. More contexts may become available in the process. Adding constraints reduces the degrees of freedom and the available contexts of constraint. Thus constraints change the possibilities for behavior in general and in particular. When constraints conflict, in fact, they can add new capacities for behavior. Consider Walter's (1953) experiments with robot tortoises in this regard. The robots were programmed with simple fundamental capacities for behavior: to approach a source of light but to avoid any light that is too intense. Situated in sufficiently complex lighted environments, however, tortoises produced rich trajectories of movement over and above and different from merely approaching a source of light. For example, when a light was fixed to the front of a tortoise placed in front of a mirror, the tortoise began "twittering, and jigging like a clumsy Narcissus" (1953, p. 128). The robot experiments of Braitenberg (1984) and Walter (1953), when taken together, illustrate how intrinsic and extrinsic constraints combine to define potentials for behavior.

So far, we have argued that cognition originates in capacities and constraints in the agent and the environment (Clark, 1997; Gibbs, 2006). However, it is the relation between agent and environment that defines the potential for cognitive activity. Agent and environment are causally intertwined in the potential for activity (Turvey, 2004), and unfolding contingencies enact and unfold action trajectories (Van Orden, Kello, & Holden, in press). Capacities and constraints make different behaviors more or less likely, but incidentals realize behavior. In the case of equally likely behaviors, for instance, it is attendant contingencies that decide which behavior will occur.

Gradients of Uncertainty

A useful analogy can be made to a connectionist model. Connectionist models internalize constraints as changing weights among nodes in a crude analogy to synapses and neurons. Behavior then originates in constraint satisfaction (e.g., Grossberg, 1980; McClelland & Rumelhart, 1981). Now imagine an unresolved cloud of active states in a connectionist model. These states could include all the possible ways to see a Necker cube, for example (three-dimensional [3D] cube, two-dimensional [2D] image, and so on). Of all these active states, no single outcome is yet realized. Each face of the Necker cube is merely potential until one or the other is selected by way of the immediate circumstances. Nevertheless, different weights between nodes make some faces more likely to dominate than others (Maia & Cleeremans, 2005). For instance, the flattened 2D Necker cube is a less likely outcome than 3D illusory cubes.

Constraints determine probabilities within the potential set, so that the potential set realizes a gradient of uncertainty. The gradient distinguishes potential states by their likelihood of being realized. Thus it distinguishes possible from impossible actions and the likelihood of possible acts (Fajen, 2005; Warren, 2006). On this basis, we equate the states of gradient potential sets with affordances and effectivities in cycles of action and perception (Davia, 2005; Gibson, 1977; Swenson & Turvey, 1991). *Affordances* are descriptions of the environment directly relevant for action, with reference to an organism and its effectivities; *effectivities* are descriptions of the organism directly relevant for action, with reference to an environment and what it affords (Turvey & Shaw, 1995). To this we would only add that *gradient potential states* are also descriptions of the history of an organism, directly relevant for action, with reference to its immediate future.

Gradients of uncertainty are like energy gradients in physical systems in several ways (however, see Keijzer, 2003; Turvey & Shaw, 1995). Each gradient is a potential set for action that includes the likelihood of respective actions, without fully prescribing the particular action that will occur. In the Necker cube case, two percepts can even be equally likely (i.e., two orientations of a 3D cube). The behavior that is realized is therefore not ultimately determined by the constraints but by the immediate circumstances that enact behavior (Van Orden et al., in press).

Actions as subtle as eye movements or postural sway change the content of uncertainty gradients. Additionally, as the orientation of the perceiver changes, so does the likelihood that any particular act is realized. Facing the doorway will change the likelihood of walking through the doorway, for instance. Actions counter or realize gradients of uncertainty: walking through the door or not. Furthermore, as a cognitive act realizes the instantaneous gradient, it also brings into existence a new or evolved gradient. An action one way or the other changes the uncertainty that pertains to walking through the door or doing something else.

Criticality and Metastability

Cognition is never fully stable in the traditional sense of the term because gradients of uncertainty are perpetually evolving. Try staring at the Necker cube. Perception of the lines changes spontaneously, even though there is no change in the figure. Change occurs because new potentials for action (and perception) are introduced each time an action is taken, even actions as subtle as eye movements. Actions perpetually update potential sets, which ensure a locally unstable system – a system close to a critical state. *Critical states* are states in which oppositional "forces" (constraints that favor one or another available outcome) are precisely balanced against each other. Critical states are thus a kind of boundary between qualitatively different behaviors.

A system that can stay close to critical states over time is metastable. Metastable states support multiple behavioral options, simultaneously, as the potential of attractors: attraction that remains present or potential but that is no longer an attractor (Kelso, 1995). Metastable, or multistable, states are never fully captured by any particular attractor, but instead move among attractors. Just as the connectionist representation of an unresolved Necker cube would be inclusive of different competing percepts, a metastable state is inclusive of different system outcomes. Metastability exists close to critical states, the state in which oppositional constraints are precisely balanced against each other. Near a critical state, metastability can extend sufficiently in time to perpetuate a potential set. This is possible if only relatively small perturbations occur continuously (Jordan, 2003).

Metastability is a central concept for understanding why cognition is so exquisitely context sensitive (Kelso, 1995). Near a critical state, local interactions among component processes are strengthened if they satisfy available contextual constraints. This prunes the available options to those that best suit the context and that best situate the system for future contexts. Criticality is thus a kind of proto-anticipation (Shaw, 2001). In cognition, potential outcomes are a best guess about what will be required in the future (Jordan, 2003). This is particularly clear within language, for example, because context is constitutive of what words mean and how they are pronounced (Elman, 2005; Fowler & Saltzman, 1993; Turvey & Moreno, 2006).

Metastability is a desired property for an organism, a source of flexible and immediate action. Dynamics of the critical state recruit processes to the metastable interaction until local feedback loops extend to the periphery of the system, creating interdependence among all component processes. Interdependence poises processes to act together across the body, as a coherent organism for example. Interdependence also allows that even a small change in constraints, a source of additional minuscule constraint, in favor of one or another behavioral option, will enact behavior immediately. In doing so, action both realizes and destroys the situated gradient of uncertainty that anticipated it (Haken, 2000; Schneider & Kay, 1994).

Criticality and metastability are the source of counterintuitive predictions (Kello, Beltz, Holden, & Van Orden, 2007). Extensive feedback allows each component process to affect every other process. The consequent interdependence shows up as power law behavior, a kind of negotiated compromise between processes' frequency of change and magnitude of change. Frequency and magnitude align themselves in a power law, in that large amplitude change is less frequent, and low amplitude change is more frequent. Power laws have a strong association to fractal behavior, the nested self-similarity of structure. Thus fractal and power law behavior figure prominently in the evidence for self-organized criticality.

Critical states and metastable states also share properties with traveling waves. Traveling waves are themselves self-sustaining potential functions (Iliev, Khristov, & Kirchev, 1994; Infeld & Rowlands, 1990). Traveling waves are special in this regard because they are configurations of matter, energy, or uncertainty in which no fundamental difference exists between the current state and the potential to act.

Self-organization, by itself, would end in an attractor state, whether the attractor is a fixed point, a limit cycle, a taurus, or a strange attractor. By contrast, self-organized criticality does not end in an attractor. Instead it is attracted to metastable states that dance in the neighborhood of attractors without fully realizing them. Rather than being drawn into an attractor, self-organized criticality is drawn toward a critical state, among the possible attractors rather than within a single attractor. Living systems appear to be drawn to such metastable states of criticality. The reason remains unknown (Kauffman, 2000).

Evidence for Self-Organized Order in Cognition

Although it is not entirely clear why living systems are attracted to an inherently unstable state, specific predictions can be made about the consequences of self-organized criticality. We mentioned already the ubiquitous power law and fractal behavior that results from the general coordination among component processes. Other kinds of strongly nonlinear behavior include, for example, *sudden jumps* – qualitative changes in behavior in response to small changes in the balance of constraints. One can also observe *hysteresis*, wherein the balance of constraints that could yield a sudden jump is biased by recent history. Hysteresis is a form of bistable inertia that predisposes cognitive activity to repeat itself until a threshold is crossed, suddenly moving the system to the alternate state of inertia. If such sudden jumps yield thermodynamically favored states, we would expect to see changes in the disorder or *entropy* of behavior. Entropy should increase before the sudden jump, followed by *negentropy* after the jump, a decrease in entropy accompanied by an increase in order. Finally, metastability and criticality imply interdependent components and time scales, yielding scale-free behavior, for example, in the timing and the size of sudden jumps.

In the remaining sections of this chapter, we review evidence that is consistent with the predictions of complexity theory in cognition. Although our organization follows different cognitive activities, the evidence we review is not specific to a particular cognitive activity. Instead, it corroborates fundamental assumptions about strong nonlinearity, emergence, and criticality in cognition overall. It lays the groundwork for reliable analyses, new intuitions, and different questions about cognitive activities.

Reasoning

We start with reasoning, cognitive activity that solves a problem, makes an inference, or creates knowledge. A typical problem with which to study reasoning is the gear-turning task. Participants are presented with a daisy chain of meshed gears and the turning direction of the first gear. They then predict the turning direction of the last gear in the chain. A creative solution to the problem is simply to note whether there is an even or an odd number of gears in the chain. Knowing this, the direction of the last gear follows the simple rule: same direction as the first gear in an odd-numbered chain, and opposite direction as the first gear in an even-numbered chain. Most adults and children discover this more elegant solution after first using a less efficient strategy – namely, tracing the direction of each gear one after the other (Dixon & Bangert, 2002; Dixon & Dohn, 2003; Trudeau & Dixon, 2007).

If the creative solution is self-organizing, a clear prediction can be made about the system's internal entropy before and after the novel solution emerges. One expects to see an increase in entropy before the emergence of the novel strategy. One also expects to see negentropy immediately after the emergence of the novel strategy. The predictions come from viewing the novel strategy as a potential state, before the discovery. In each trial of the gear-turning task, the potential strategy becomes more equal in probability to the gear-tracing strategy. This, in turn, increases uncertainty, which we see as an increase in entropy. At some point, gear counting becomes sufficiently more probable than gear tracing, and the sudden jump to the new strategy occurs. Past that point, the probability of the old strategy plummets, and uncertainty is reduced in the bargain. The dominance of the new strategy is revealed in negentropy.

The prediction has been corroborated in the gear-turning task (Stephen, Dixon, 2008; Stephen, 2007). Detailed motion data were captured for participants' finger movements as they traced gears. Entropy was calculated consistent with the basic formula of Shannon and Weaver (1948) within a recurrence quantification analysis (Webber & Zbilut, 2005). As predicted, entropy in finger movements increased over trials and peaked right before the creative solution emerged. At that point, entropy changed to negentropy, a reduction in entropy with a corresponding increase in information (order). Eye movements showed the same increase in entropy and change to negentropy, parallel with the finger movements (Stephen, 2007).

Repeatedly measuring finger or eye movements during problem solving made it possible to reconstruct the intrinsic dynamics of problem solving; the rise and fall of entropy predicted the emergence of the new solution in the gear-turning task. But what is the logic by which an index of finger or eye movements is transparent to cognitive emergence? It originates in the idea of interdependent processes mentioned earlier. A truly interdependent system allows variation in each component to reflect variation in every other component. Massive interdependence ensures that a well-chosen repeated measurement will contain information about the entire system. In the ideal, one may reconstruct the dynamics of a possibly higher-dimensional system from a one-dimensional time series of repeated measures (Mañé, 1981; Takens, 1981).

No prior studies have successfully captured the coming into existence of a new problem-solving solution, or any other "executive" activity (however, see Kelso, 1995, for emergence of percepts and motor coordination). Should these studies prove reliable, and should they generalize to comparable phenomena, their authors will have established, for the first time, a basis for origins of order in high-level creative cognition. As entropy accumulates, the gear-tracing problem-solving strategy comes apart, so to speak, and makes way for the emergence of the new strategy of counting the gears.

Listening

The key historical issue in speech perception has been categorical perception: how to parse the stream of sounds into meaningful units, whether on the level of phonemes, the level of words, or the level of sentences. No apparent category boundaries exist in speech (Klatt, 1989), and environmental noises, changing speaking rates, as well as coarticulation make it difficult to find invariant acoustic properties that could be used to define such boundaries. Yet even infants ably distinguish between phonemes (Dehaene-Lambertz, Dehaene, & Hertz-Pannier, 2002).

Category boundaries emerge in nonlinear interactions. This is why no one-to-one correspondence exists between acoustical signals and percepts; nonlinear interactions produce many-to-one and one-to-many relations in addition to one-to-one. Consequently, for some regions of the acoustic signal, we can expect, on the one hand, to see no change in the percept despite relatively large changes in the acoustic signal. On the other hand, for other regions of the acoustic signal, we can expect sudden jumps in percept from one category to another, despite only minimal changes in the acoustic signal. The occurrence of sudden jumps can also be expected to vary with the context, constrained by the immediate history of the participant.

Each of these predictions has been confirmed using artificial speech (see Tuller, 2005, for a review). An artificial acoustic continuum was created for the word "say," for example, by inserting an increasingly longer gap of silence after the phoneme /s/. Participants' task was to report whether the acoustic signal sounded like "say" or "stay." Across participants, a short gap of silence (0–20 msec) yielded perception of "say," and a greatly expanded gap of silence (60–80 msec) yielded perception of "stay." These stable regions of the acoustic signal yielded the same percept ("say" or "stay," respectively) despite changes in the gap duration of the acoustic signal.

Intermediate regions (30–50 msec) yielded sudden jumps from one percept to the other. Minimal changes in the acoustic signal induced categorically different percepts. For example, as the gap of silence increased in small increments, a participant abruptly switched from perceiving "say" to perceiving "stay." The sudden jump is highly dependent on context, however, and it does not correspond to a static threshold. For example, when the acoustic signal changes in direction from shorter to longer gaps of silence, the sudden jump will occur at a longer gap than when the acoustic signal changes in the reverse direction, from longer to shorter gaps of silence. In sum, whether the participant heard "say" or "stay" on the previous trial affects what is heard on the subsequent trial. The immediate history of the perceiver matters.

This pattern of context dependency in the say–stay example demonstrates hysteresis. This dynamic originates in ranges of acoustic parameters or input dimensions that are ambiguous (not unlike the Necker cube) and are therefore sensitive to the embedding context. In other words, hysteresis emerges out of a kind of dynamical instability that amplifies available constraints, manifesting as context sensitivity. Thus although hysteresis behavior involves threshold behavior, hysteresis thresholds are not fixed, but rather are emergent properties: The locations of thresholds, or more precisely the locations of critical points, are entirely context dependent.

By changing the available constraints, one can even invert the gradient of uncertainty to turn hysteresis into its opposite, a contrastive effect. In this case, the sudden jump from "say" to "stay" (or vice versa) comes extra early, rather than being delayed. The relative likelihood of the contrastive effect (vs. hysteresis) is increased, for instance, by overexposure to the particular stimulus continuum. In the say–stay example, incrementally changing stimuli in sequence will now pull the category threshold toward the "say" end of the continuum so that the "say" perception looses stability earlier and transitions earlier to "stay" (or vice versa if the order of presentation is reversed).

Sudden jumps, hysteresis, and contrastive effects are not visible when trials are randomized or when participants' performance is averaged over trials to eliminate sequence effects (compare Fechner's method of limits). Once understood, however, these reliable empirical flags of self-organization serve to advance the research program of speech perception. For example, one may write differential equations for emergent order to characterize and explore the intrinsic self-organization of speech perception. By tracking stability within these differential equations, one can flesh out the detailed interplay of context, history, and agent in perception.

Such interplay can even account for the fact that speakers returning from years abroad will have an accent in their native language. Learning nonnative phonemes changes the topology of phoneme perception and production in a native language (Sancier & Fowler, 1997). Clearly, agents are themselves change-able reservoirs of constraint on speech perception, and embodied constraints work in concert with contextual constraints. The critical ratios of constraints that define boundaries in perception "adjust flexibly with factors such as phonetic context, the acoustic information available, speaking rate, speaker, and linguistic experience" (Tuller, 2005, p. 355).

The speech perception examples we have reviewed catalog clear progress toward understanding speech perception. Furthermore, they are not rarified laboratory phenomena. They are laboratory analogues of ordinary, variable, and creative perception. Ordinary perception must recognize the same word produced by males, females, speakers of different ages, and with different dialects and accents "and by the same speaker in markedly different linguistic and intentional contexts, even when the listener has had no prior experience with the other individual's speech patterns. Thus, perceptual stability coexists with perceptual flexibility." (Tuller, 2005, p. 355).

Speaking

Language is more than just parsing a continuous stream of acoustic signals into meaningful units. It requires able communication: the ability to say words and sentences and sustain a conversation with a partner. In what follows, we review evidence for self-organization and criticality in three domains of speech: metastability of producing words, coordination of articulators to pronounce words, and coordination of partners in a conversation.

Power Law Scaling in Repeated Speech
As discussed earlier, the coordination dynamics near critical states (i.e., metasta-bility) express a fractal pattern. Such patterns have a redundancy in their com-position (or self-similarity) that makes them appear similar, no matter how one decomposes the composite whole. For example, power law scaling refers to a fractal pattern in which large-amplitude, low-frequency oscillations embed intermediate amplitude, intermediate frequency oscillations that, in turn, embed low-amplitude, high-frequency oscillations (across an indeterminate number of time scales). Because fractals express self-similarity as a statistical kind of self-affine structure, we should find the same kind of statistical self-affine structure in any way that measurements divide up behavior.

Take, for example, a spoken word. If this behavior is fractal, then no matter where or how we take repeated measures of a spoken word, they should exhibit the same kind of fractal pattern. Kello, Anderson, Holden, and Van Orden (in press) tested this hypothesis by asking adult participants to repeat the word "bucket" over 1,000 times, tracking a metronome beat for when to speak. Each spoken "bucket" was recorded and divided into its syllables "buck" and "ket." Spectographs of "buck" and "ket" were parsed further into 300-Hz frequency bands evenly spaced from 150 Hz to 13,350 Hz. This parsing resulted in 45 component frequency bands per syllable, and the intensity of the acoustic signal was tracked at each of the 45 bands. In total, the speech signal was parsed to yield 45 measurements per syllable and 90 measurements per participant, which were tracked across 1,100 repetitions of "bucket." The point of all this was to create many measurements of a cognitive activity and track them all across many repetitions.

Each participant's 90-measurement series was examined one by one for fractal structure. Fractal scale-free behavior was estimated using spectral analysis, then using relative dispersion analysis, and finally using detrended fluctuation anal-ysis (Holden, 2005). These methods estimate the extent to which data points in a series are correlated over the long term. Each method can yield a frac-tal dimension, in this case dimensions close to the ideal value 1.2, the fractal dimension of metastable dynamics. The important finding was that each of the 90-measurement series of every participant yielded estimates close to the ideal scaling value, just as metastability predicts. This finding is unique because it established fractal patterns in so many simultaneous measurements. It provides strong evidence for metastability in speech production.

Coordination of Articulators
In proper speech, movements of tongue and lips are coordinated in intricate patterns that take years to perfect. If such coordination results from dynamical self-organization, it should obey the laws of coordination dynamics, laws that were first established for the coordination of limbs (Kelso, 1995; Turvey, 1990). For example, a 1:1 limb coupling (e.g., oscillating one index finger at the same

frequency as the other index finger) is more stable than a 2:1 coupling (e.g., oscillating one index finger twice as fast as the other index finger). The more complex 2:1 coordination becomes weaker as frequency of oscillation increases, such that only the simpler mode (1:1) remains stable. If the same principles of coordination hold for speech, then speech errors should also result from failures of coordination.

This prediction was tested in speech production by analyzing the kinematic data of tongue and lip movements during articulation (Goldstein, Pouplier, Chen, Saltzman, & Byrd, 2007). Adults repeated two-word phrases such as "cop top" at varying speeds elicited by a metronome (80-120 beats per minutes). Note that the /p/ sound requires lip constriction, whereas the /k/ and /t/ sounds require tongue constrictions (raised tongue dorsum for /k/, and raised tongue tip for /t/). The lip–tongue coordination in "cop top" therefore follows a 2:1 pattern: Two cycles of lip oscillation (/p/) are completed for every one cycle of tongue dorsum constriction (/k/) or for every one cycle of tongue tip constriction (/t/).

By increasing the frequency of the metronome, Goldstein et al. (2007) induced speech intrusion errors: blends of the intended and intruding articulator movements for the /k/ and /t/ sounds. Tongue dorsum constrictions intruded on tongue tip constrictions to produce a novel combination of articulator movements. Interestingly, the new sound does not occur in English, hence it cannot be explained by some fatigued executive planning faculty. More important, the new sound brought into existence a more stable coordination pattern of lip and tongue movement. Every "word" now had a tongue tip and a tongue dorsum motion at the beginning and a lip motion at the end. As a result, one cycle of lip oscillation was completed for one cycle of tongue dorsum constriction – an anti-phase 1:1 coordination.

Similar results were reported for induced speech errors that did not require any overt repetition of words but instead relied on the visual presentation of primes (Motley & Baars, 1976; see also Pouplier & Goldstein, 2005). Together they strongly reject the idea that speech errors are random, for example, a result of a simple mix-up of articulator motions in the linear sequencing of speech. Instead they show that speech errors, and therefore the system of articulators, follow laws of dynamical stability. At comfortable speeds, coordination of articulators can be more complex, but with increasing speeds, coordination is captured by the most intrinsically stable 1:1 mode.

Coordination in Conversations

More than one person can participate in coordinated cognitive activity. Talking with each other requires substantial coordination and cooperation to sustain the conversation as an ordered structure in time. Indeed speakers in a conversation have a tendency to converge in dialect (Giles, Coupland, & Coupland, 1991), speaking rates (Street, 1984), vocal intensity (Natale, 1975), and pausing frequencies (Cappella, 1981). Thus the conversation itself can be characterized as a self-organizing system (Shockley, Santana, & Fowler, 2003).

However, self-organized criticality goes beyond the coordination of speech activities. It makes the unintuitive prediction that measures of nonspeech activity are coordinated as a conversation takes place. Criticality strictly implies interdependence among component activities across the entire system. As we saw for reasoning with the gear task, a well-chosen repeated measurement should contain information about the entire system. If so, then repeated measures of the nonspeech activity of conversing agents may be coordinated in the course of the conversation.

To test this prediction Shockley et al. (2003) measured bodily sway along the anterior–posterior dimension, at the hip, while participants stood and conversed. Participants' task was to figure out how two subtly different versions of a cartoon differed. Each participant could only see one of the two versions, so a conversation was necessary to find differences between the cartoons cooperatively. Conversing participants either faced each other, or they had their backs turned to each other (facing confederates). In a control condition, the two participants faced each other but conversed with a confederate whom they could not see.

Shockley et al. (2003) found more entrainment of hip movements when participants conversed with each other than when they faced each other but conversed with the confederate. Most important, participants' hip movements were entrained even when the participants could not see each other. The act of conversation between two participants was enough for their respective hip movements to become coordinated. These findings are particularly interesting because hip movements are not directly related to speech, yet hip coordination emerged despite lack of visual feedback. It suggests that a spontaneous coordination between two conversing people can permeate nonlanguage behaviors.

Taken together, findings from speech acts corroborate that interdependent components coordinate cognitive activities. We thus expect unintuitive coordinations of measurements taken across the human body and compared between participants, so long as there is a coordinating event. Information processing and task-specific components do not appear to be the originators of order, whether it is in repeated speech, in speech errors, or in conversations. Rather, the origin of order in speech is coordination, the self-organization of nonspecific component activity in linguistic behavior.

Reading

Reading has long been a kind of poster child for cognition because it includes aspects of perception, language, memory, and so on, and because it is a culturally derived capacity (Huey, 1908). Thus what we learn about reading is likely to generalize to cognition at large. Conveniently, there is also a vast literature on this topic, research that has largely come to focus on questions about the ambiguity of written symbols.

Ambiguities in linguistic discourse exist at all scales of description, from visual features; to letters, phonemes, and syllables; and to the meanings and pronunciations of words, sentences, paragraphs, and narratives (Langacker, 1987). Moreover, multiple scales of ambiguity can accrue, as ambiguity exists among multiple relations, including graphemes and phonemes, spelling bodies and pronunciation rimes, whole-word spellings and pronunciations, morphological structures and meaning, prosody and pragmatics, surface forms and deep forms of phrases, sentences, and narratives, and so on (Van Orden, Pennington, & Stone, 1990). The way in which the system resolves ambiguity is thus an important test of the fundamental workings of the system.

Note that accumulation of ambiguity is a slowly driven process. One requires experience with multiple words and sentences before ambiguity can come into existence. For example, one needs exposure to several kinds of uses of the word "lead" (e.g. lead::metal vs. lead::guide vs. lead::principal vs. lead::ahead, and so on) before "lead" becomes ambiguous in meaning and pronunciation. Thus ambiguity accumulates more slowly than online linguistic experience. Once in place, ambiguity mimics metastability in that both make multiple options for action available. To resolve ambiguity, or to resolve metastability, one needs a sufficiently disambiguating context.

Because ambiguity implies more than one potential outcome, the details of ambiguity define the gradient of uncertainty. Ambiguity works like static friction in a physical system in the sense that it must be resolved or overcome before reading comprehension or performance can occur. Ambiguity resolution is thus a reduction in uncertainty and an increase in information. Comparatively more ambiguity implies greater reductions of uncertainty, an increased likelihood of extended time in the metastable potential set, which is revealed in power law behavior. Thus the degree of ambiguity predicts the extent of power law behavior.

Power Law Behavior in Reading Sentences

Sentence reading can be examined by presenting one word at a time and requiring a key press after each word before the next word is shown. Participants are instructed to read as naturally a possible, but they must press a key after reading a word to see the next word. This method collects self-paced reading times and can be focused on the disambiguating region of an ambiguous sentence – the specific words where the reader confronts the ambiguity.

If reading comprehension is a product of self-organized criticality, we expect to see power law behavior in the frequency distribution of reading times. A power law distinguishes itself from other frequency distributions (see Fig. 1.4A) in the exaggerated or "stretched" slow tails of the distribution. Recall that in a power law, the frequency of an event's occurrence and its magnitude (or amplitude) are aligned in a linear fashion on a log–log scale. In the case of reading times, the frequency of a response time (how often a particular response time occurs) aligns with magnitude of the response time (how slow a response time is). Faster response times are more likely than slower reaction times, with an overall linear relation between likelihood and magnitude on log–log scales. This linear relation is evaluated using the slope of the line that relates likelihood and magnitude. Shallower slopes reflect more extreme values of magnitude – more extremely slow reading times, for instance.

The expected relation between ambiguity and power law behavior was corroborated in an experiment that used increasingly ambiguous sentences (Schultz & Tabor, 2008). For example, the sentence "As the author wrote the story she envisioned *grew rapidly in her* mind" is more ambiguous than the sentence "As the author wrote the story that she envisioned *grew rapidly in her* mind," which in turn is more ambiguous than the sentence "As the author wrote the story *grew rapidly in her* mind." The italicized words are the words in the disambiguating region. Participants' reading times for the words in the disambiguating region were measured and plotted as frequency distributions.

As predicted, the distribution tails at slow reading times became shallower, extending to more extreme slow response times as ambiguity increased. In other words, the slope estimate of the linear relation revealed a direct relation between ambiguity and stretched tails. One implication of this outcome is that the same processes are entailed in all instances of sentence reading. Undifferentiated power law behavior presents no joints at which to carve out isolated workings of particular reading components. Power laws may imply that all sources of constraint on the reading performance are present in all instances of the reading performance; there are no qualitative differences between slow reading responses and fast reading responses in the power law. Different reading tasks may self-organize different dynamics, but tasks and stimulus words do not selectively activate causal properties of reading components.

Power Law Behavior in Reading Words

As discussed earlier, linguistic ambiguity is not limited to sentences but extends in a nested fashion to graphemes, spelling bodies, and whole words. Whole-word ambiguity always nests within it spelling body ambiguity, and spelling body ambiguity always nests grapheme ambiguity, but not vice versa. If a state of ambiguity resembles a critical state, then we expect power law behavior in reading tasks that require disambiguation. Also, if nested structures of linguistic ambiguity comprise fractals, then power law behavior should be more present to the extent that particular words exhibit the fractal nesting.

These predictions were tested using lists of words that differed in the scale at which their spelling was ambiguous: whole-word ambiguity ("lead") versus spelling body ambiguity ("bead") versus grapheme ambiguity ("beat"; Holden, 2002). After a key press, a word appeared on a computer screen, and the participant named it as quickly as possible. As predicted, frequency distributions of naming times differed in their slow tails, in that slow tails were most exaggerated for words with whole-word ambiguity, followed by words limited to spelling body ambiguity, followed by words limited to grapheme ambiguity. Although the modes of the naming time distributions did not change, the slow tails of the distributions were differentially stretched, attendant on differences in word ambiguity.

Scale of ambiguity also exaggerated slow tails when participants decided whether strings of letters were English words (Holden, 2002). The larger the limiting scales of ambiguity, the more stretched were the slow tails of the distribution. Together these results support the idea that linguistic ambiguity itself has fractal structure. Words that represent this structure to a larger degree, such as whole-word ambiguous words, also produce the clearest power law behavior. Interestingly, when response times were combined across the ambiguity conditions, they also combine in a common power law. This is suggestive, although not conclusive, that all reading performances in this case sample a common power law. If so, then the same sources of constraint are present in all reading performances, although they may be differently emphasized in different tasks (see Holden, 2002). Just as in sentence reading (discussed earlier), there is no empirical basis for individuating separate reading processes that act in isolation.

Power Law Versus Lognormal Behavior

Holden (2002) and Schultz and Tabor (2008) manipulated word and sentence properties, the influence of laboratory context on the gradient of uncertainty. In contrast, Holden, Van Orden, and Turvey (2008) conducted analyses to emphasize the influence of participant history. They examined differences among participants in response-time distributions. The task was again a word-naming task, this time using a list of 1,100 words, identical across participants. For a few readers, there was clear evidence of shallow power law behavior in the exaggerated slow tails of their distributions. They produced widely dispersed naming times. For other readers, however, the distribution of word-naming times closely fit a lognormal distribution. Naming times for these readers were more narrowly dispersed. Most readers fell somewhere in between, with naming-time distributions that were well fit by a mix of power law and lognormal behavior.

The difference among readers reflects their propensity for reducing the degrees of freedom in word naming. Holden et al. (2008) speculated that the three kinds of distributions – lognormal dominant, mixed, and power law dominant – map onto the complexity of the reading task for particular readers. The basic idea is that reading is more complex (e.g., less constrained) for some readers than others, which means that more uncertainty exists for some readers than others. For instance, as readers gain experience, they accrue constraints word by word that "grease the wheels" of cognitive dynamics, so to speak. They reduce or eliminate thresholds of ambiguity as word-specific constraints of more and more words dominate performance (yielding lognormally distributed naming times). Thus for some highly experienced readers, word-naming times may simply express a kind of word-naming "inertia," in line with the task-induced intention to read words aloud.

Skilled word naming has long been thought of as an automatic behavior. However, no trustworthy context-free criteria exist for automatic behavior (Fearing, 1970; Tzelgov, 1997). Even a canonical automatic effect such as the Stroop effect (Stroop, 1935) can be reduced or eliminated by only small changes in laboratory method (Bauer & Besner, 1997; Besner & Stolz, 1999a, 1999b; Besner, Stolz, & Boutilier, 1997). These concerns are inconsequential if skilled performance is seen as the interplay of sufficient internalized and external constraints. Sufficiently constrained performances sample response times from a lognormal distribution; otherwise they sample response time from a power law.

In this light, it is noteworthy that the equivalent of "stimulus inertia" in a strictly feed-forward multiplicative system will produce finishing times that are lognormally distributed (as the number of multiplicative steps approaches infinity). This is the multiplicative version of the central limit theorem. Also, one can create a strictly feed-forward system from a feedback system by adding sufficient constraints to make feedback redundant. In other words, a sufficiently constrained complex system will produce finishing times dispersed in the lognormal pattern, as a product of serial multiplicative interactions among random variables (Farmer, 1990).

Remembering

Complex systems exhibit scale invariance, and abundant data suggest that scale invariance occurs in remembering (Brown, Neath, & Chater, 2007). For instance, if people are asked what they did or will do in a week, month, or year's time, they will perform almost identically across the different scales of time. They do not remember better or in greater quantity the events from a recent week than events from a recent year. In these examples, memory appears the same at all time frames for things to be remembered. Memory appears to have no preferred scale; it works the same at all time scales (Chater & Brown, 1999; Maylor, Chater, & Brown, 2001).

Evidence for scale invariance also exists in error data. Patterns of transposition errors in order reconstruction tasks remain constant across many time scales of delay between events, from milliseconds to weeks (Huttenlocher, Hedges, & Prohaska, 1992; Nairne, 1991, 1992; Neath, 1998). Also, the proportion of errors in serial recall tasks for each serial position is invariant to absolute parameters such as interstimulus presentation interval, time between trials, familiarity and meaningfulness of the material, and degree of learning (Braun & Heymann, 1958; McCrary & Hunter, 1953).

Evidence for scale invariance also shows up in the dynamics of serial position curves. A typical finding is that increasing the retention interval on recall tasks abolishes recency effects (Glanzer & Cunitz, 1966; Postman & Phillips, 1965). However, when the spacing between presented items is increased proportionally with the retention interval, the recency effect stays (Bjork & Whitten, 1974). That is, recency effects scale with the ratio of interstimulus interval and retention interval, and the structure of serial position effects holds at many scales of measurement. Further evidence comes from the finding that when items are grouped within a list, items at the beginning and end of each group show improved recall relative to items in the middle of the list in addition to primacy and recency effects present for the entire list (Frankish, 1985, 1989; Hitch, Burgess, Towse, & Culpin, 1996; Ryan, 1969a; 1969b). This sort of nested self-similarity is a hallmark of scale-invariant systems.

Finally, power law forgetting curves may be indicative of scale-free memory. It is well established that the magnitude of the rate of change for forgetting diminishes with time – the type of decay expected from power law forgetting. Power law behavior is characteristic of self-organizing systems, which demon-strate scale invariance in their behavior. Complex systems orient themselves toward states of self-organized criticality, where the potential for action of the system is evenly distributed over all its scales of measurement (Turvey & Moreno, 2006). The result of this organization is power law behavior when the system is perturbed. Note, however, that some have argued that forgetting curves are not actually best described as power laws (Rubin, Hinton, & Wenzel, 1999; Wickens, 1999).

A scale-invariant model of memory would naturally suit the application of complex systems theory to cognition. Brown et al. (2007) described such a model (SIMPLE for scale-invariant memory, perception, and learning) that accounts for many esoteric and fine-grained details of memory performance. Although SIMPLE is not a complex system per se, it is a useful model for building intuitions about how complex systems theory would begin to reframe memory phenomena. For instance, it demonstrates how similar principles can account for various memory phenomena over many time scales and tasks. It emphasizes interference (interactions) among temporal neighbors to account for forgetting. Further, its memory traces are organized at logarithmic distances from a point of reference.

Recent work by Rhodes and Turvey (2007) was inspired by the dynamical implications of the SIMPLE model. They assumed that the minimum units of analysis are organism–environment systems. In that regard, they applied insights from animal foraging behavior to cognition and constructed a dynamical anal-ogy to repeated memory recall. The basic idea was to predict the pattern of times between successive instances of recall. For instance, repeated category recall occurs when a participant reports all the animals he or she can remember or all the world's capital cities. This kind of category recall typically includes briefly interspaced reports of semantically related clusters (e.g., eagle, hawk, pigeon), separated by lengthy time intervals before another report (Bousfield & Sedgewick, 1944).

Animal foraging behavior is also characterized by short path clusters of search activity separated by lengthy search paths, when food is sparsely dispersed at locations that are unknown before foraging. In these conditions, an animal travels an overall search path that strongly resembles a Lévy flight. This is a random walk or diffusion process in which the step sizes are distributed as a power law. Short steps on the search path are common and very long steps are rare. Consequently, the frequency of step sizes is inversely proportional to their length. This search pattern is found in foraging for a variety of species, including humans, and may be optimal for an environment with fractal properties (Viswanathan et al., 2001).

Like foraging behavior, the overall scale-free relation in the recall data is well modeled by Lévy distributions, shallow-sloped inverse power laws with infinite variance. These results allow that memory resembles a sparsely populated landscape with fractal structure. Perhaps memory is an adaptation that is homologous to foraging – for instance, an adaptation to a search domain with fractal properties (Rhodes & Turvey, 2007).

Acting With Purpose

The previous sections all discuss data collected in laboratories, data that concern tasks performed at the behest of a scientist. However, most cognitive activity is self-directed, reflecting the intentions of the actor. What, then, does laboratory performance say about the origin of order in intentional activity? Arguably this is the first question of cognition, the question that qualifies how other details of cognitive performance are interpreted.

A scientist must instruct participants to behave in line with the purpose of the experiment. In this way, participants' intentions become tied to task instructions and the purpose of the laboratory preparation (Vollmer, 2001). In a word-naming task, for example, participants must ensure that they respond with articulated speech, they must be vigilant and attentive to read aloud each word as soon as it appears, and they must keep in mind inherent limits on their behavior – to say aloud only the words presented and only at the time they are presented. In other words, in taking on the purpose of the experiment, a participant situates, or scales, variation in mind and body to stay within constraints made explicit in task instructions.

If intentionality and purposeful behavior are products of self-organized criticality, as Juarrero (1999) has argued, task instructions equal sources of constraint that self-organize a gradient of uncertainty for performance. Purposeful behavior is anticipated in the gradient potential as a metastable state. In turn, we expect the nested fractal pattern of $1/f$ scaling exhibited by metastable states (e.g., a particular power law relationship). In the nested fractal pattern, low-amplitude high-frequency variation is nested within intermediate-amplitude intermediate-frequency variation that, in turn, is nested within large-amplitude low-frequency variation, and so on, to an indefinite number of larger amplitudes and lower frequencies. The resulting fractal pattern is scale-free. Amplitude (magnitude) and frequency of variations, across an indefinite number of time scales, form a line with slope close to -1 on log–log scales, the slope of the scale-free $1/f$ scaling relation.

What laboratory method justifies equating variation in behavioral measurements with variation in the intention to act? First, variation in intentions fluctuates on slower time scales than the pace of measurement trials (as does $1/f$ scaling). Although a participant bears in mind the intention to perform on each and every trial, variation in intentions is seen across trials, on slower time scales. Second, examining variation in the intention to act requires that each measurement trial repeat identical conditions for the intention to act: task demands, stimulus, response, and all else that makes up a laboratory trial. An ideal task is therefore a production task in which participants repeatedly produce lines of one inch in length, for example, or say the same word, or repeatedly estimate the passing of a second. These production tasks entail the same purpose and action on every trial so changes in performance across trials better emphasize fluctuations in the participant's intentions.

In the time-estimation production task, participants press a key to signal that a second has passed, for a total of 1,100 estimates. The relevant data form a pattern of variation in each participant's performance across all of the trials. Spectral analyses of this pattern (and other complementary analyses) reveal the predicted $1/f$ scaling – the fractal pattern of nested variation. That is to say, within and across participants, the spectral analysis yields slopes close to -1, the slope of $1/f$ scaling. As we have explained, the fractal scaling cannot be attributed to changes in experimental task, so it instead reveals the intrinsic fluctuations of acting with purpose. In that regard, production tasks produce the clearest examples of fractal $1/f$ scaling in cognitive performance (Gilden, 2001; Kello et al., in press; Thornton & Gilden, 2005).

The finding of $1/f$ scaling in repeated measures – fractal variation across an indefinite number of time scales – indicates that acting with purpose comprises an indefinite number of psychological dimensions. A reasonable claim is to equate these dimensions with sources of constraint that oscillate across an indefinite range of frequencies (Van Orden, Holden, & Turvey, 2003). Constraints recur across trials and change at their respective natural frequencies to support acting with purpose. Because they combine nonlinearly, resulting in scale-free behavior, they therefore yield the emergent property, $1/f$ scaling. Also, as we have noted for other power law behavior, there are no empirical joints along which to divide intentional behavior. No intelligible means exist to isolate one source of constraint from another (Thorton & Gilden, 2005). The same sources of constraint are present in each instance of intentional behavior.

Variation in intentional behavior exhibits the emergent property of $1/f$ scaling, and so intentional behavior itself is emergent. Acting with purpose originates in metastable cognition, an anticipatory "posture of readiness, like that of a runner poised for a quick start" (Woodward & Schlosberg, 1965, p. 830), or muscles that "become tense in preparation for a task" (Bills, 1943, p. 11). Sources of constraint for purposeful action exist throughout the body, including anticipatory movements and excitations, as well as dynamical processes of the body such as head position, posture, respiration, and digestion. At the extreme, sources of constraints even include the details of capillary red blood flow and local oxidation in muscle tissue. All these constraints combine to reduce the degrees of freedom for cognitive behavior and thus contribute to the fractal variation in cognitive activity.

Summary and New Questions

What are the origins of order in cognitive activity? Or as Neisser (1968) asked, "(1) How is the raw material [of constructions] organized? (2) What determines what is constructed? And (3) what purpose does it serve?" (p. 280). In this chapter, we have addressed these questions, applying concepts of complex systems to cognitive activities. Accordingly, we argued (1) that raw material of cognition self-organizes to stay near critical points, yielding metastable states that anticipate contextually appropriate actions. Furthermore, we argued (2) that potential sets, the system's best guesses about action in the future, are determined by situational and historical constraints, updated each time an action takes place. Finally, we argued (3) that organization serves the purpose of consuming of gradients of uncertainty (creation of information).

We then reviewed evidence for the fundamental assumptions and laws of complex systems within various cognitive activities. We chose the studies for this review to illustrate the breadth of corroboration for fundamental assumptions. This evidence includes, for example, nonlinear disproportionate relations between changes in the environment and changes in behavior, sudden jumps, hysteresis, and contrastive effects, dynamics that obey laws of coordination, and ubiquitous power law behavior and $1/f$ scaling, the signature behaviors of complex systems. Our sample of this evidence comes from reasoning, speaking, reading, remembering, and, most generally, acting with purpose. As with any basic assumptions and their confirmation, the results surveyed here should not be seen as ends in themselves. Valid assumptions are like a license to drive, existence proofs for the legitimacy of the complex systems perspective.

Having corroborated basic assumptions, we now face new questions about cognitive activity. These questions pertain to the control of cognitive activities and their dynamics. Answers to control questions will make explicit otherwise implicit conflicting constraints and uncover the trade-offs that change the qualitative outcomes for perception and action (Kelso, 2003). Control, from this perspective, is not the traditional notion of control, such as control by stimuli or homunculi; rather, control emerges in the interplay of constraints combining agent and environment. This idea of control pertains to human error, for example (Vincente, 1999), and to human creativity.

The question of dynamics concerns changes in the interplay among constraints, over and above simply demonstrating which constraints are in play. It addresses subtler indications of change – quantitative changes in fractal dimension, for example, or the slopes of power laws. To understand details of dynamics will require fleshing out the types and relations among forces at play in cognitive activity, the dynamics at the heart of task difficulty and individual differences, for example, and the conflicts among constraints that bring new capacities for behavior online.

Acknowledgments

We gratefully acknowledge funding from the National Science Foundation to Heidi Kloos (DRL no. 723638) and to Guy Van Orden (HSD no. 0728743; BCS no. 0642716). We also thank Patricia Carpenter, Ray Gibbs, Larry Gottlob, and Damian Stephen for their help with various aspects of the chapter.

References

Aks, D. J., & Sprott, J. C. (2003). The role of depth and $1/f$ dynamics in perceiving reversible figures. *Nonlinear Dynamics, Psychology, and Life Sciences, 7,* 161–180.

Allport, A. (1989). Visual attention. In M. I. Posner (Ed.). *Foundations of cognitive science* (pp. 631–692). Cambridge, MA: MIT Press.

Anderson, J. R., Lebiere, C., Lovett, M., & Reder, L. (1998). ACT-R: A higher-level account of processing capacity. *Behavioral and Brain Sciences, 21,* 831–832.

Aslanidi, O. V., & Mornev, O. A. (1996, July). *Soliton-like regime in the Hodgkin-Huxley equations.* Paper presented to the International Conference on Mathematical Models of Nonlinear Excitation Processes, Tver, Russia.

Azuma, T., Williams, E. J., & Davie, J. E. (2004). Paws + cause = pause? Memory load and memory blends in homophone recognition. *Psychonomic Bulletin & Review, 11,* 723–728.

Bartlett, F. C. (1932). *Remembering.* New York: Cambridge University Press.

Bauer, B., & Besner, D. (1997). Mental set as a determinant of processing in the Stroop task. *Canadian Journal of Experimental Psychology, 51,* 61–68.

Beaumont, J., Davidenko, N., Davidenko, J. M., & Jalife, J. (1998). Spiral waves in two-dimensional models of ventricular muscle: Formation of a stationary core. *Biophysical Journal, 75,* 1–14.

Berkinblit, M. B., Feldman, A. G., & Fukson, O. I. (1986). Adaptability of innate motor patterns and motor control mechanisms. *Behavioral and Brain Sciences, 9,* 585–638.

Bernstein, N. (1967). *The coordination and regulation of movements.* London: Pergamon Press.

Besner, D., & Stolz, J. A. (1999a). Unconsciously controlled processing: The Stroop effect reconsidered. *Psychonomic Bulletin & Review, 6,* 449–455.

Besner, D., & Stolz, J. A. (1999b). What kind of attention modulates the Stroop effect? *Psychonomic Bulletin & Review, 6*, 99–104.

Besner, D., Stolz, J. A., & Boutilier, C. (1997). The Stroop effect and the myth of automaticity. *Psychonomic Bulletin & Review, 4*, 221–225.

Bills, A. G. (1943). *The psychology of efficiency*. New York: Harper & Brothers.

Bjork, R. A., & Whitten, W. B. (1974). Recency-sensitive retrieval processes in long-term free recall. *Cognitive Psychology, 6*, 173–189.

Bousfield, W. A., & Sedgewick, C. H. W. (1944). An analysis of restricted associative responses. *Journal of General Psychology, 30*, 149–165.

Braitenberg, V. (1984). *Vehicles*. Cambridge, MA: MIT Press.

Braun, H. W., & Heymann, S. P. (1958). Meaningfulness of material, distribution of practice, and serial-position curves. *Journal of Experimental Psychology, 56*, 146–150.

Brown, G. D. A., Neath, I., & Chater, N. (2007). A temporal ratio model of memory. *Psychological Review, 114*, 539–576.

Cappella, J. N. (1981). Mutual influence in expressive behavior: Adult–adult and infant–adult dyadic interaction. *Psychological Bulletin, 89*, 101–132.

Chater, N., & Brown, G. D. A. (1999). Scale-invariance as a unifying psychological principle. *Cognition, 69*, 17–24.

Clark, A. (1997). *Being there: Putting brain, body, and world together again*. Cambridge, MA: MIT Press.

Davia, C. J. (2005). Life, catalysis and excitable media: A dynamic systems approach to metabolism and cognition. In J. Tuszynski (Ed.), *The physical basis for consciousness* (pp. 229–260). Heidelberg: Springer-Verlag.

Davydov, A. S. (1979). Solitons, bio-energetica, and the mechanism of muscle contraction. *International Journal of Quantum Chemistry, 16*, 5–17.

Dehaene-Lambertz, G., Dehaene, S., & Hertz-Pannier, L. (2002). Functional neuroimaging of speech perception in infants. *Science, 298*, 2013–2015.

Depew, D. J., & Weber, B. H. (1995). *Darwinism evolving: Systems dynamics and the genealogy of natural selection*. Cambridge, MA: MIT Press.

Dixon, J. A., & Bangert, A. S. (2002). The prehistory of discovery: Precursors of representational change in solving gear-systems problems. *Developmental Psychology, 38*, 918–933.

Dixon, J. A., & Dohn, M. C. (2003). Redescription disembeds relations: Evidence from relational transfer and use in problem solving. *Memory & Cognition, 31*, 1082–1093.

Duke, T., & Julicher, F. (2003). Active traveling wave in the cochlea. *Physics Review Letters, 90*, 158101.

Elman, J. L. (2005). Connectionist models of cognitive development: Where next? *Trends in Cognitive Sciences, 9*, 112–117.

Englander, S. W., Kallenbach, N. R., Heeger, A. J., Krumhansl, J. A., & Litwin, A. (1980). Nature of the open state in long polynucleotide double helices: Possibility of soliton excitations. *Proceedings of the National Academy of Science, 77*, 7200–7226.

Fabre-Thorpe, M., Delorme, A., Marlot, C., & Thorpe, S. (2001). A limit to the speed of processing in ultra-rapid visual categorization of novel natural scenes. *Journal of Cognitive Neuroscience, 13*, 1–10.

Fajen, B. R. (2005). The scaling of information to action in visually guided braking. *Journal of Experimental Psychology: Human Perception and Performance, 31,* 1107–1123.

Farmer, J. D. (1990). A rosetta stone for connectionism. *Physica D, 42,* 153–187.

Fearing, F. (1970). *Reflex action: A study in the history of physiological psychology.* Cambridge, MA: MIT Press. (Original work published 1930)

Fodor, J. A., & Pylyshyn, Z. W. (1981). How direct is visual perception? Some reflections on Gibson's "ecological approach." *Cognition, 9,* 139–196.

Fowler, C., & Saltzman, E. (1993). Coordination and coarticulation in speech production. *Language and Speech, 36,* 171–195.

Frankish, C. (1985). Modality-specific grouping effects in short-term memory. *Journal of Memory and Language, 24,* 200–209.

Frankish, C. (1989). Perceptual organization and precategorical acoustic storage. *Journal of Experimental Psychology: Learning, Memory, and Cognition, 15,* 469–479.

Freeman, W. J. (2000). *How brains make up their minds.* New York: Columbia University Press.

Gibbs, R. (1999). *Intentions and the experience of meaning.* New York: Cambridge University Press.

Gibbs, R. (2006). *Embodiment and cognitive science.* Cambridge, MA: MIT Press.

Gibson, J. J. (1977). *The theory of affordances.* Hillsdale, NJ: Erlbaum.

Gilden, D. H. (2001). Cognitive emissions of $1/f$ noise. *Psychological Review, 108,* 33–56.

Giles, H., Coupland, J., & Coupland, N. (1991). *Contexts of accomodation.* New York: Cambridge University Press.

Glanzer, M., & Cunitz, A. R. (1966). Two storage mechanisms in free recall. *Journal of Verbal Learning and Verbal Behavior, 5,* 351–360.

Godfrey, K. B., & Swindale, N. V. (2007). Retinal wave behavior through activity-dependent refractory periods. *Computational Biology, 3,* 2408–2420.

Goldinger, S. D., & Azuma, T. (2003). Puzzle solving science: The quixotic quest for units in speech perception. *Journal of Phonetics, 31,* 305–320.

Goldstein, L., Pouplier, M., Chen, L., Saltzman, E., & Byrd, D. (2007). Dynamic action units slip in speech production errors. *Cognition, 103,* 386–412.

Grill-Spector, K., & Kanwisher, N. (2006). Visual recognition: As soon as you know it is there, you know what it is. *Psychological Science, 16,* 152–160.

Grossberg, S. (1980). How does the brain build a cognitive code? *Psychological Review, 8,* 1–51.

Haken, H. (2000). *Information and self-organization: A macroscopic approach to complex systems.* Berlin: Springer-Verlag Publishing Company.

Haselager, W. F. G., Bongers, R. M., & van Rooij, I. (2003). Cognitive science, representations and dynamical systems theory. In W. Tschacher & J-P. Dauwalder (Eds.), *The dynamical systems approach to cognition* (pp. 229–241). River Edge, NJ: World Scientific.

Hausdorff, J. M., Zemany, L., Peng, C.-K., & Goldberger, A. L. (1999). Maturation of gait dynamics: Stride-to-stride variability and its temporal organization in children. *Journal of Applied Physiology, 86,* 1040–1047.

Hitch, G. J., Burgess, N., Towse, J. N., & Culpin, V. (1996). Temporal grouping effects in immediate recall: A working memory analysis. *Quarterly Journal of Experimental Psychology, 49A,* 116–139.

Hofstede, B. T. M., & Kolk, H. J. (1994). The effects of task variation on the production of grammatical morphology in Broca's aphasia: A multiple case study. *Brain and Language, 46,* 278–328.

Holden, J. C. (2002). Fractal characteristics of response time variability. *Ecological Psychology, 14,* 53–86.

Holden, J. C. (2005). Gauging the fractal dimension of response times from cognitive tasks. In M. A. Riley & G. C. Van Orden (Eds.), *Contemporary nonlinear methods for behavioral scientists: A tutorial* (pp. 267–318). Retrieved March 1, 2005, from http://www.nsf.gov/sbe/bcs/pac/nmbs/nmbs.jsp

Holden, J. C., Van Orden, G. C., & Turvey, M. T. (2008). Dispersion of response times reveals cognitive dynamics. Manuscript submitted for publication.

Huey, E. B. (1908). *The psychology and pedagogy of reading.* Cambridge, MA: MIT Press.

Humphreys, M. S., Burt, J. S., & Lawrence, S. (2001). Expecting *dirt* but saying *dart*: The creation of a blend memory. *Psychonomic Bulletin & Review, 8,* 820–826.

Huttenlocher, J., Hedges, L. V., & Prohaska, V. (1992). Memory for day of the week: A 5 + 2 day cycle. *Journal of Experimental Psychology: General, 121,* 313–326.

Iliev, I. D., Khristov, E. K., & Kirchev, K. P. (1994). *Spectral methods in soliton equations.* New York: Longman Scientific & Technical.

Infeld, E., & Rowlands, G. (1990). *Nonlinear waves, solitons, and chaos.* Cambridge, MA: Cambridge University Press.

James, W. (1890). *The principles of psychology.* New York: Holt.

Jordan, J. S. (2003). The embodiment of intentionality. In W. Tschacher & J-P. Dauwalder (Eds.), *The dynamical systems approach to cognition* (pp. 201–227). River Edge, NJ: World Scientific.

Juarrero, A. (1999). *Dynamics in action.* Cambridge, MA: MIT Press.

Kauffman, S. A. (1993). *The origins of order.* New York: Oxford University Press.

Kauffman, S. A. (2000). *Investigations.* New York: Oxford University Press.

Keijzer, F. (2003). Self-steered self-organization. In W. Tschacher, & J. -P. Dauwalder (Eds.), *The dynamical systems approach to cognition* (pp. 243–259). River Edge, NJ: World Scientific.

Kello, C. T., Anderson, G. G., Holden, J. G., & Van Orden, G. C. (in press). The pervasiveness of $1/f$ scaling in speech reflects the metastable basis of cognition. *Cognitive Science.*

Kello, C. T., Beltz, B. C., Holden, J. G., & Van Orden, G. C. (2007). The emergent coordination of cognitive function. *Journal of Experimental Psychology: General, 136,* 551–568.

Kelso, J. A. (1995). *Dynamic patterns: The self-organization of brain and behavior.* Cambridge, MA: MIT Press.

Kelso, J. A. (2003). Cognitive coordination dynamics. In W. Tschacher & J. -P. Dauwalder (Eds.), *The dynamical systems approach to cognition* (pp. 45–67). River Edge, NJ: World Scientific.

Klatt, D. H. (1989). *Lexical representation and process.* Cambridge, MA: MIT Press.

Kloos, H. (2008). Will it float? How invariance affects children's understanding of object density. In V. Sloutsky, B. Love, & K. McRae (Eds.). *Proceedings of the 30th annual conference of the Cognitive Science Society*, Washington, DC.

Kolk, H. H. J., & Heeschen, C. (1992). Agrammatism, paragrammatism and the management of language. *Language & Cognitive Processes, 7,* 89–129.

Koroleva, V. I., & Bures, J. (1979). Circulation of cortical spreading depression around electrically stimulated areas and epileptic foci on the neocortex of rats. *Brain Research, 173*, 209–215.

Kugler, P. N., & Turvey, M. T. (1987). *Information, natural law, and the self-assembly of rhythmic movement.* Hillsdale, NJ: Erlbaum.

Landy, D., & Goldstone, R. L. (2007). How abstract is symbolic thought? *Journal of Experimental Psychology: Learning, Memory, and Cognition, 33*, 720–733.

Langacker, R. W. (1987). *Foundations of cognitive grammar.* Stanford, CA: Stanford University Press.

Maia, T. V., & Cleeremans, A. (2005). Consciousness: Converging insights from connectionist modeling and neuroscience. *Trends in Cognitive Sciences, 9*, 397–404.

Mandler, G. (1984). *Mind and body: Psychology of emotion and stress.* New York: Norton.

Mandler, G. (1997). *Human nature explored.* New York: Oxford University Press.

Mañé, R. (1981). On the dimension of the compact invariant set of certain nonlinear maps. In D. A. Rand & L. S. Young (Eds.), *Dynamical systems and turbulence, Warwick, 1980. Lecture notes in mathematics 898* (pp. 230–242). New York: Springer-Verlag.

Marr, D. (1982). *Vision.* New York: Holt.

Maylor, E. A., Chater, N., & Brown, G. D. A. (2001). Scale invariance in the retrieval of retrospective and prospective memories. *Psychonomic Bulletin & Review, 8*, 162–167.

McClelland, J. L., & Rumelhart, D. E. (1981). An interactive activation model of context effects in letter perception: Part 1. An account of basic findings. *Psychological Review, 88*, 375–407.

McCrary, J. W., & Hunter, W. S. (1953). Serial position curves in verbal learning. *Science, 117*, 131–134.

Miller, G. A. (1956). The magical number seven, plus or minus two: Some limits on our capacity for processing information. *Psychological Review, 63*, 81–97.

Motley, M. T., & Baars, B. J. (1976). Laboratory induction of verbal slips: a new method for psycholinguistic research. *Communication Quarterly, 24*, 28–34.

Nairne, J. S. (1991). Positional uncertainty in long-term memory. *Memory & Cognition, 19*, 332–340.

Nairne, J. S. (1992). The loss of positional certainty in long-term memory. *Psychological Science, 3*, 199–202.

Natale, M. (1975). Convergence of mean vocal intensity in dyadic communication as a function of social desirability. *Journal of Personality and Social Psychology, 32*, 790–804.

Neath, I. (1998). *Human memory: An introduction to research, data, and theory.* Pacific Grove, CA: Brooks/Cole.

Necker, L. A. (1932). Observations on some remarkable phenomena seen in Switzerland and an optical phenomenon which occurs on viewing of a crystal or geometrical solid. *Philosophical Magazine, 3*, 329–337.

Neisser, U. (1968). *Cognitive psychology.* New York: Appleton-Century-Crofts.

Odell, G. M. (1980). Biological waves. In L. A. Segal (Ed.), *Mathematical models in molecular and cellular biology* (pp. 523–567). New York: Cambridge University Press.

Oyama, S. (2000). *The ontogeny of information: Development systems and evolution.* Durham, NC: Duke University Press.

Peterson, M. A. (1994). Object recognition processes can and do operate before figure-ground organization. *Current Directions in Psychological Science, 3*, 105–111.

Postman, L., & Phillips, L. W. (1965). Short-term temporal changes in free recall. *Quarterly Journal of Experimental Psychology, 17*, 132–138.

Pouplier, M., & Goldstein, L. (2005). Asymmetries in the perception of speech production errors. *Journal of Phonetics, 33*, 47–75.

Rauschenberger, R., Peterson, M. A., Mosca, F., & Bruno, N. (2004). Amodal completion in visual search: Preemption or context effects? *Psychological Science, 15*, 351–355.

Rhodes, T., & Turvey, M. T. (2007). Human memory retrieval as Lévy foraging. *Physica A, 385*, 255–260.

Rock, I. (1957). The role of repetition in associative learning. *The American Journal of Psychology, 70*, 186–193.

Roediger, H. L., & McDermott, K. B. (1995). Creating false memories: Remembering words not presented in lists. *Journal of Experimental Psychology: Learning, Memory, and Cognition, 21*, 803–814.

Rubin, D. C., Hinton, S., & Wenzel, A. E. (1996). One hundred years of forgetting: A quantitative description of retention. *Psychological Review, 103*, 734–760.

Ryan, J. (1969a). Grouping and short-term memory: Different means and patterns of grouping. *Quarterly Journal of Experimental Psychology, 21*, 137–147.

Ryan, J. (1969b). Temporal grouping, rehearsal, and short-term memory. *Quarterly Journal of Experimental Psychology, 21*, 148–155.

Sancier, M. L., & Fowler, C. A. (1997). Gestural drift in a bilingual speaker of Brazilian Portuguese and English. *Journal of Phonetics, 25*, 421–436.

Sataric, M. V., Zakula, R. B., Ivic, Z., & Tuszynski, J. A. (1991). Influence of a solitonic mechanism on the process of chemical catalysis. *Journal of Molecular Electronics, 7*, 39–46.

Schneider, E. D., & Kay, J. J. (1994). Life as a manifestation of the second law of thermodynamics. *Mathematical and Computer Modeling, 19*, 25–48.

Schultz, A., & Tabor, W. (2008). *Reaction time distributions in sentence processing.* Unpublished manuscript. University of Connecticut.

Shallice, T. (1988). *From neuropsychology to mental structure.* New York: Cambridge University Press.

Shannon, C. E., & Weaver, W. (1948). *The mathematical theory of communication.* Chicago: University of Illinois Press.

Shaw, R. E. (2001). Processes, acts, and experiences: Three stances on the problem of intentionality. *Ecological Psychology, 13*, 275–314.

Shockley, K., Santana, M. V., & Fowler, C. A. (2003). Mutual interpersonal postural constraints are involved in cooperative conversation. *Journal of Experimental Psychology: Human Perception and Performance, 29*, 326–332.

Smith, L. B., Thelen, E., Titzer, R., & McLin, D. (1999) Knowing in the context of acting: The task dynamics of the A-not-B error. *Psychological Review, 106*, 235–260.

Stephen, D. G. (2007, February). *Cognitive representation as a thermodynamic phenomenon.* Invited colloquium, Center for Cognition, Action & Perception, University of Cincinnati, Cincinnati, OH.

Stephen, D. G. & Dixon, J. A. (2008, July). Cognition as the breaking and reforming of constraints. Invited symposium: *Dynamics of mind and body,* XXIX International Congress of Psychology, Berlin.

Sternberg, S. (1969). The discovery of processing stages: Extensions of Donders' method. *Acta Psychologica, 30,* 276–315.

Street, B. V. (1984). *Literacy in theory and practice.* New York: Cambridge University Press.

Stroop, J. R. (1935). Studies of interference in serial verbal reactions. *Journal of Experimental Psychology, 18,* 643–661.

Sutton, R. S., & Barto, A. G. (1998). *Reinforcement learning: An introduction.* Cambridge, MA: MIT Press.

Swenson, R., & Turvey, M. T. (1991). Thermodynamic reasons for perception–action cycles. *Ecological Psychology, 3,* 317–348.

Takens, F. (1981). Detecting strange attractors in turbulence. In D. A. Rand & L. S. Young (Eds.), *Dynamical systems and turbulence, Warwick, 1980. Lecture notes in mathematics 898* (pp. 366–381). New York: Springer-Verlag.

Thornton, T. L., & Gilden, D. L. (2005). Provenance of correlations in psychological data. *Psychonomic Bulletin & Review, 12,* 409–441.

Trudeau, J., & Dixon, J. A. (2007). Embodiment and abstraction: Actions create relational representations. *Psychonomic Bulletin & Review, 14,* 994–1000.

Tuller, B. (2005). Categorization and learning in speech perception as dynamical processes. In M. Riley & G. C. Van Orden (Eds.), *Tutorials in contemporary nonlinear methods for the behavioral sciences* (pp. 353–400). Retrieved March 1, 2005, from http://www.nsf.gov/sbe/bcs/pac/nmbs/nmbs.jsp

Turvey, M. T. (1990). Coordination. *American Psychologist, 45,* 938–953.

Turvey, M. T. (2004). Impredicativity, dynamics, and the perception–action divide. In V. K. Jirsa & J. A. S. Kelso (Eds.), *Coordination dynamics: Issues and trends: Vol. 1. Applied complex systems* (pp. 1–20). New York: Springer-Verlag.

Turvey, M. T., & Moreno, M. A. (2006). Physical metaphors for the mental lexicon. *The Mental Lexicon, 1,* 7–33.

Turvey, M. T., & Shaw, R. E. (1995). Toward an ecological physics and a physical psychology. In R. Solso & D. Massaro (Eds.), *The science of mind: 2001 and beyond* (pp. 144–172). New York: Oxford University Press.

Tzelgov, J. (1997). Specifying the relations between automaticity and consciousness: A theoretical note. *Consciousness and Cognition, 6,* 441–451.

Van Gelder, T., & Port, R. F. (1995). It's about time: An overview of the dynamical approach to cognition. In R. F. Port & T. van Gelder (Eds.), *Mind as motion* (pp. 1–43). Cambridge, MA: MIT Press.

Van Orden, G. C., Holden, J. G., & Turvey, M. T. (2003). Self-organization of cognitive performance. *Journal of Experimental Psychology: General, 132,* 331–350.

Van Orden, G. C., Kello, C. T., & Holden, J. G. (in press). Situated behavior and the place of measurement in psychological theory. *Ecological Psychology.*

Van Orden, G. C., & Kloos, H. (2005). The question of phonology and reading. In M. S. Snowling & C. Hulme (Eds.), *The science of reading: A handbook* (pp. 61–78). Oxford: Blackwell.

Van Orden, G. C., Pennington, B. F., & Stone, G. O. (1990). Word identification in reading and the promise of subsymbolic psycholinguistics. *Psychological Review, 97,* 488–522.

Van Orden, G. C., Pennington, B. F., & Stone, G. O. (2001). What do double dissociations prove? *Cognitive Science, 25,* 111–172.

Vincente, K. J. (1999). *Cognitive work analysis: Toward safe, productive, and healthy computer-based work*. Mahwah, NJ: Erlbaum.

Viswanathan, G. M., Buldryev, S. V., Afanasyev, V., Havlin, S., da Luz, M. G. E., Raposo, E. P., et al. (2001). Levy flights search patterns of biological organisms. *Physica A, 295*, 85–88.

Vollmer, F. (2001). The control of everyday behaviour. *Theory and Psychology, 11*, 637–654.

Walter, G. (1953). *The living brain*. London: Penguin Books.

Warren, W. H. (2006). The dynamics of perception and action. *Psychological Review, 113*, 358–389.

Watson, J. M., Balota, D. A., & Roediger, H. L. (2003). Creating false memories with hybrid lists of semantic and phonological associates: Over-additive false memories produced by converging associative networks. *Journal of Memory & Language, 49*, 95–118.

Webber, C. L., Jr., & Zbilut, J. P. (2005). Recurrence quantification analysis of nonlinear dynamical systems. In M. A. Riley & G. C. Van Orden (Eds.), *Tutorials in contemporary nonlinear methods for the behavioral sciences* (pp. 26–94). Retrieved March 1, 2005, from http://www.nsf.gov/sbe/bcs/pac/nmbs/nmbs.jsp

Wickens, T. D. (1999). Measuring the time course of retention. In C. Izawa (Ed.), *On human memory: Evolution, progress, and reflections on the 30th anniversary of the Atkinson-Shiffrin model*, 245–266. Mahwah, NJ: Erlbaum.

Wijnants, M. L., Bosman, A. M. T., Hasselman, F., Cox, R. F. A., & Van Orden, G. C. (2008). 1/f scaling fluctuation in movement time changes with practice in precision aiming. Manuscript submitted for publication.

Woodward, R. S., & Schlosberg, H. (1965). *Experimental psychology: Revised edition*. New York: Holt, Rinehart & Winston.

Yakushevich, L. V. (2001). *Nonlinear physics of DNA*. Chichester, England: Wiley.

8 Nonlinear Complex Dynamical Systems in Developmental Psychology

PAUL VAN GEERT

Introduction

A good method for obtaining an idea of what a scientific discipline – developmental psychology in this particular case – entails is to browse through introductory student handbooks (Berger, 2003; Bukatko & Daehler, 2001; Cole & Cole, 1993; Kail, 2001; Newman & Newman, 2006; Sigelman & Rider, 2006; Seifert & Hoffnung, 1991; Vasta, Haith, & Miller, 1995). The consulted handbooks either focus on childhood to adolescence or on the human life span. The first chapters typically provide an overview of the "perspectives" on development and comprise a selection of theories ranging from psychodynamically (Freudean) inspired via learning theory to theories of Piaget and Vygotsky. Most handbooks address the nature–nurture problem, discussing the effect of genes and environment on development and present some sort of interactionist or transactionist approach. The main chapters are divided according to two dimensions. One is a content or domain dimension and comprises physical, cognitive, and social aspects of development. The other dimension refers to age and amounts to a distinction in phases or "ages." The standard children-and-youth division encompasses prenatal development and birth; infancy (0–2 years); preschool years (2–6), childhood (6–12), and adolescence (12–21). For each phase or stage, typical developments are described, such as the development of attachment in the first year of life, the development of theory of mind at around 3 years, the emergence of logical thinking (including conservation and other Piagetian themes) around age 5, and so forth. Some handbooks pay attention to individual differences – for instance, individual differences in temperament from birth on – and eventually focus on clinical developmental problems such as autism or hyperactivity.

The main picture revealed through such handbooks is that development, and developmental psychology for that matter, is basically a collection of perspectives and approaches (theories), of influences on development (e.g., genes, environment), of aspects or dimensions (e.g., physical, cognitive), of phenomena (e.g., attachment, conservation), spread out across the life span or part of it, in phases or ages that are defined by tradition, as well as by biology and society. Developmental psychology is apparently not a first-principles-based science. There seems to be no fundamental developmental mechanism, the understanding of which forms the key to a thorough understanding of the emergence of developmental phenomena.

This lack of theoretical sophistication is relatively new. The field started with serious theoretical reflection on the basic mechanisms of development (Piaget's work is a good example of that). However, as it became more and more "empirical," it drifted away from its theoretical origins and became more and more of a descriptive science (van Geert, 1998a). Currently, the focus on theoretical explanation and on finding the nature of the basic developmental mechanisms comes mainly from system-oriented researchers. Examples are the theory of developmental systems, which has its roots in evolutionary biology (Ford & Lerner, 1992; Gottlieb, 2001; Lerner, 2006; Lickliter & Honeycutt, 2003; Oyama, Griffiths, & Gray, 2001; Sameroff, 2000), and the theory of nonlinear, complex dynamical systems, which is the focus of the current chapter.

Anyone who has witnessed a newborn baby grow up into a toddler and then a schoolchild, an adolescent, and an adult has an intuitive appreciation of the fact that developmental processes are prime examples of nonlinear dynamical systems (NDS). However, there is currently little thinking along the lines of complexity, nonlinearity, and dynamical systems among developmentalists (those who call themselves dynamical systems developmentalists form a small minority). In this chapter, I attempt to explain the foundations of a complexity-oriented, NDS approach to human development. Before doing so, however, I first explain what I understand about dynamical systems and how they relate to the assumptions that underlie most of the current developmental studies and theories.

Dynamical Systems and Explanatory Adequacy

Definition

Dynamical systems theory is an approach to the description and explanation of *change*. A simple definition is Weisstein's (1999): "a means of describing how one state develops into another state over the course of time," which can be expressed mathematically as

$$y_{t+1} = f(y_t), \tag{8.1}$$

expressing that the next state (at time $t + 1$) is a function, f, of the preceding state, at time t. In a slightly different notation:

$$\Delta y/\Delta t = f(y), \tag{8.2}$$

stating that the change of a system, denoted by y, over some amount of time, denoted by Δt, is a function f of the state of y. The function f is also referred to as the evolution term or evolution "law." That is, it is important that f specifies some causal principle of change. An important property of the current equation is that it represents recursive relationships. Thus y_t leads to y_{t+1}, and according to the same principle, y_{t+1} generates y_{t+2} and so on.

A system can be described as a set of entities that are related to one another and influence one another, and a state of the system is the set of properties of its components at any particular moment in time. For quite a long time now, mainstream social science, including developmental psychology, has refrained from focusing on change per se. It has been building *static* models and has implicitly assumed that change – for instance, developmental change in an individual – could be approximated by stretching static relationships over the time axis (van Geert & Steenbeek, 2005). A characteristic expression of a static relationship takes the form

$$y_i = f(x_i), \tag{8.3}$$

with y a dependent variable and x an independent variable, which, for any possible value x_i, generates a corresponding value for the dependent variable y.

For the sake of simplicity, take a system no more complex than a single property or variable (e.g., a child's growing lexicon, a child's ability to answer theory of mind problems). A dynamical system describes the current state of the system – that is, the variable's current value – as a function of its preceding state. It does so in a recursive way, taking the result of one step in the process (e.g., the lexicon today) as the starting value generating the next step, the lexicon tomorrow, and so on. The evolution term, f, must represent a theoretically justifiable principle of lexical change; for instance, the principle that the learning of new words at time t depends on the words already known and on the words actually spoken by the person with whom the child communicates at time t. The second principle, the dependence on the words spoken to the child, already illustrates the principle of embeddedness, which is characteristic of dynamical systems models of behavior and which are further elaborated in this chapter.

A static system, on the other hand, describes a particular value of the variable as a function of the value of another variable (or set of such variables). For instance, for any possible age, for any level of the mother's lexical knowledge, or for a combination of age and maternal lexicon, the static system or model will generate a predicted or expected size of the lexicon, without any reference to recursiveness.

Static and Dynamic Models

This distinction between static and dynamic type models has considerable consequences (Howe & Lewis, 2005; van Geert and Steenbeek, 2005). Whereas a dynamic model recursively generates a time series (a state and the next state and the next ...), a static model generates a sample or population of individuals that are in principle independent of one another (an individual with age i and lexicon i, an individual with age j and lexicon j, and so forth). Statements about populations do not necessarily apply to the individuals in the population. For instance, in a sample of drivers, a high level of conscious control of the driving behavior will in general be statistically associated with low driving quality. That is, high levels of conscious control are characteristic of novices, and they tend to have the worst driving behavior. Hence, we will tend to find a negative correlation between controlled driving behavior and driving quality. In an individual driver, however, the relationship might well be the inverse of the relationship in the sample. An experienced driver will tend to increase his or her conscious control on the driving behavior in more complex traffic situations, associated with driving behavior of high-quality driving, for instance, under difficult circumstances. In this example, the difference between the static-association interpretation and the dynamic interpretation (the mechanism behind the increase or decrease of controlled driving in a particular driver) is easy to see.

However, the behavioral sciences, including developmental psychology, often implicitly take a relationship between variables that holds across a sample as a representation of some dynamic rule or principle. For example, a recent study (Duncan et al., 2007) showed that early math skills in five- to six-year-olds have the greatest predictive power for later school achievement, whereas socioemotional behaviors, on the other hand, had little or no predictive power, irrespective of gender and socioeconomic background. From such findings, it is easy to infer that increasing early math achievement (e.g., through preschool teaching programs) will thus lead to better school achievement at a later age, implying also that attempts to increase socioemotional skills should be reduced because they do not relate to academic achievement. However, there exists no logical or direct relationship between the static relationship (how it is associated across a population) and the dynamic relationship (how something can be increased or decreased in individuals). The dynamic relationship – how and to what extent the early growth in math skills contributes to the growth in academic achievement – depends on the mechanisms that govern math learning and academic achievement.

This homology error – taking a relationship holding on one level (e.g., the sample level) as a relationship that also holds on another level (e.g., the level of the life span of the subjects contained in that sample) – is commonly made in the behavioral sciences (Hamaker, Dolan, & Molenaar, 2005; Molenaar, 2004; Musher-Eizenman, Nesselroade, & Schmitz, 2002). It is associated with a relative lack of interest for genuine process models and the assumption that associations between variables across a sample can be used as valid approximations of the dynamic relations that govern the process.

Complexity

A living organism is an ensemble of many closely interacting, interdependent components, the common activity of which is more than a sum of the actions of its components. That is, it is characterized by nonlinearity. It is self-organizing in that its structure and organization result from the interactions between its parts. Although constantly changing, it maintains its coherence over time. In short, it is a complex system (Bar-Yam, 1997; Holland, 1995). Understanding a system, including its growth and development, means to simplify it, but the simplification must conserve the system's characteristic features, one of which is its complexity. For instance, to understand the dynamics of lexical growth in a child, we must postulate a system of interactions at many levels – perceptual, motor, social, cognitive, and linguistic. To put it differently, the simplest possible explanation of lexical dynamics is a system that is complex enough to generate sound-meaning mappings through social interaction. Compare this with a static model of lexical growth that explains lexical knowledge across a sample as a function of variables such as linguistic input, intelligence, and so forth. The simplest possible explanation of lexical knowledge most likely consists of only a few of such variables. Any newly added variable will achieve only a minor gain in explained variance (i.e., in capturing the differences between the individuals, including those differences that covary with age). The notions of simplicity and complexity held by a dynamical model are of an entirely different kind than those held by a static model, and they cannot be traded for each other (not every beard can be shaved by the same razor, even if the razor comes from Occam). Trivial as this remark might seem to students of dynamical systems, it is far from trivial in mainstream (developmental) psychology, where a description of differences between persons is tacitly taken to represent a generalized but nevertheless valid description of differences within persons (i.e., change and development). To explain development as *change*, based on a plausible mechanism of change, we will have to follow a dynamical approach that accounts for a highly characteristic feature of development, namely complexity.

Explanatory Adequacy in Complex, Nonlinear Dynamical Models of Development

The preceding discussion of complexity is closely related to the fact that static models, common in mainstream developmental psychology, and dynamical models are of a different kind and aim at explaining different phenomena. The kind of criteria that make an explanation adequate in one approach is often different from the kind of criteria that make an explanation adequate in the other. Explanatory adequacy refers to the criteria that make an explanation useful – in the sense of testable, for instance – in a particular approach, be it static or dynamic. Let me explain this by means of an example that, again, refers to lexical growth. Students of early lexical development have claimed that the lexicon undergoes a spurt during the second year of life. Ganger and Brent (2004) challenged this idea by putting 38 longitudinal studies of lexical growth to a statistical test. They found out that a quadratic model of lexical growth with time as the only predictor (Eq. 8.4) is statistically superior to a "spurt" model, namely, a sigmoid function which also has time as predictor (Eq. 8.5).

$$L_t = a + bt + ct^2 \tag{8.4}$$

$$L_t = K/(1 + (K/L_0 - 1)e^{-rtK}) \tag{8.5}$$

They concluded the empirical evidence is against the spurt model. However, what the quadratic model – and the sigmoid model, for that matter – really represent is a static model. That is, they are both models describing time samples (levels of the lexicon at different ages) as a function of another variable, namely, the time at which the samples were taken. Indeed, as a sample model, the quadratic model was statistically superior to the sigmoid or spurt model. However, as developmentalists interested in the *mechanism* of lexical growth, sample models are of relatively little use. What we need is a model of lexical *change*. Fortunately, we can infer the models of change present in the statistical models proposed thus far by taking the first derivative of the model equations (the quadratic from Eq. 8.4 and sigmoid from Eq. 8.5, respectively):

$$\Delta L = b + 2ct \tag{8.6}$$

$$\Delta L/\Delta t = r L(K - L). \tag{8.7}$$

The first derivative of the quadratic model describes lexical change as the addition of a constant number of words per unit time plus a number of words per unit time that increases with time. On the other hand, the first derivative of the sigmoid model, which boils down to the logistic growth model that will be introduced later in this chapter, describes lexical change as a process of adding a number of words that depends on the number of words already present in the lexicon and on the number of words not yet known. More precisely, it describes lexical growth as a process of input- and state-based learning, whereas the quadratic model describes lexical growth as mere increase (or decrease for that matter) solely governed by time – more precisely, by the duration of the growth process.

What about the explanatory adequacy of these developmental models? In this context, explanatory adequacy means that the model relies on or refers to causal relationships with a demonstrable plausibility for the field at issue. For instance, the idea that how much you already know determines how you learn, or how much you profit from an experience, refers to a plausible causal mechanism of learning. The idea that learning depends on how much you do not know yet relates to causal mechanisms such as filtering or interpreting one's experiences on the basis of what one knows to make use of what is new or unknown. This principle again relies on plausible causal mechanisms of learning. In short, from a developmental point of view, the sigmoid-based explanation of logistic growth, which encompasses these principles, is considerably more explanatorily adequate than the quadratic because it relates lexical growth to elementary developmental processes. The quadratic model, on the other hand, confines itself to observing that the lexicon increases with time, implicitly claiming that time itself is a causal factor (the claim could be relaxed by taking time as the substitute of a causal factor that linearly changes with time, such as – hypothetically – brain maturation, for instance).

However, the sigmoid model was rejected by Ganger and Brent (2004) on the grounds of unnecessary complexity (in terms of the number of parameters it needed) for explaining the *time sample* characteristics as a function of time. That is, the quadratic model fit the data as well as the sigmoid model did, but it did so with fewer parameters. However, the statistical superiority with regard to time-sample characteristics has no direct bearing on the adequacy of the underlying explanation of change (i.e., of the dynamics of lexical growth). From a developmental point of view, the time-sample model must be rejected as a dynamic explanation of the lexical growth process. Its competitor, the sigmoid or in fact logistic model, is extremely simple but nevertheless comprises an elementary developmental model. In short, statistical simplicity criteria make little sense if they are posited without reference to an underlying plausible model of explanation. The problem relates to a point raised in a quote attributed to Albert Einstein: "Everything should be made as simple as possible, but not simpler."

Development and the Dynamics of Long-Term Change

The Meaning of *Development*

Etymologically, *development* means "unwrapping" or" unfolding," as in the unwrapping or unfolding of a book roll or the unwrapping or unfolding of a flower bud (Thomae, 1959; van Geert, 1986, 1995, 2003). In its basic meaning, development thus carries a notion of an inner logic in the sequence of the unfolding, a notion of potentiality (what is in there must come out), and a notion of finality (the unfolding comes to an end when the folded object is spread out). This historical meaning of development (the term came into use in the photographic sense in the mid-nineteenth century, for instance) of course cannot determine how we see or define development in scientific discourse. However, if we apply the term to some observable phenomenon – and do not use words such as maturation, learning, and so forth instead – we do so because we wish to refer to a phenomenon that is characterized, to a more than trivial extent by these notions of inner logic, potentiality, and finality. Development implies a directed process of change toward or unfolding of a mature state. It is a directed process from an immature to a mature state, implying increasing complexity in terms of a system that differentiates (incorporates more and more elements, features, knowledge . . .) and at the same time integrates (constructs connections between the components).

Readers familiar with dynamical systems will immediately recognize these notions as metaphorical representations of self-organizing dynamics. The inner logic corresponds with the evolution term or the change function that governs the dynamics, and the potentiality and finality refer to self-organization or the systems tendency to move toward a particular attractor state. The notion of increasing developmental complexity refers to theories of complexity and emergence (Casti, 1994; Holland, 1995, 1998; Waldrop, 1992). In short, given its core assumptions, developmental psychology seems like a natural domain of application for the approach of nonlinear, complex dynamical systems. Unfortunately, this is not the image that the majority of the scientific studies convey (see van Geert, 1998a, for a discussion). For instance, the majority of studies in development aim at simplifying our view on developmental processes by conceiving of them as sums of independent factors (e.g., early math knowledge, socioemotional knowledge, socioeconomic background, and so forth) and by estimating direct effects of one variable on another by statistically controlling for the effect of other variables. Although these procedures work well for relationships across samples, they do not correspond with a model of the time evolution of the variables at issue, at the system level where they actually operate, which is the level of the individual person embedded in his or her environment. Complexity is replaced by the simplicity of adding factors, and nonlinearity is replaced by linear additions of effects of variables.

Aspects of Development Through the Human Life Span

In terms of change, the human life span encompasses more than just development. To begin with, change can take place in the form of learning and teaching (being taught by others). Let us, for simplicity, describe learning as having experiences that make a person change in a way that is consistent with those experiences. Teaching can then be described as giving a person experiences that are intended to make him or her change in a particular way. Learning and teaching are closely related to the process of appropriation, of mastering new skills, of assimilating and transmitting knowledge. However, there is also maturation and aging across the life span. They are biologically governed processes of change, with a connotation of rising and falling (deterioration). A somewhat overlooked form of life span change are processes we can call *niche-seeking* and niche construction (i.e., the organism moving toward and eventually actually creating and transforming environments that optimally fit its properties; Clark, 2006; Laland, Odling-Smee, & Feldman, 2000). This is the kind of mechanism that also features in distributed approaches to action and cognition (Clark, 1997; Clark & Chalmers, 1998; Fischer & Granott, 1995).

How does development relate to all this? In my view, development can be seen as the overarching term, covering the notion that these processes – and whatever others one wishes to distinguish – are coordinated in a dynamical way. The coordination entails that development is not just the sum of these processes but, as I stated in the definition of complexity and nonlinearity, that the ensemble of such processes cannot be derived from their summation and that it is nonlinear and self-organizing.

The idea that development forms an encompassing term and, more precisely, an encompassing structure, for a variety of change processes during the life span is one that features prominently in the work of the classic developmentalists. They were the scholars who set the theoretical and empirical stage for the study of development and whose major works date, roughly, from the first half of the 20th century. I am referring to developmentalists such as Piaget, Vygotsky, Werner, Wallon, and others. Although their approaches to development were very different, they had one major thing in common, which is a common view – in abstracto – on the fundamental mechanism of development (for a thorough discussion and justification, see van Geert, 1998b, 2000). The hallmark of development in a complex system is that *all changes of the system occur through information that is moderated through the system. Changes* are both short-term and long-term changes (the related notion of time scales is discussed later). The *system* is a complex system and can refer to different levels of complexity: It can be an individual (an individual child), a social network (a child–educator dyad for instance) or persons interacting in their characteristic environmental niches, including meaningful cultural artifacts. *Information* is used here as a generic term and denotes basically anything that the system can do or that can affect the system. The term *moderated* can take various meanings. It can mean that if the system is an individual, it is the system itself (the embodied brain), that encodes the information in terms of its abilities and then internally adapts its structure in function of this encoding. These are basically the mechanisms that Piaget hinted at with his terms *assimilation* and *accommodation* as the two forms of adaptation. Moderation can also mean that the caring and nurturing environment (educators, parents...) adapts the environment to the system's (e.g., the child's) current level and possibilities, the system changing in function of this adapted information. This is basically the model we find in Vygotsky's theory; for instance, in his notion of the zone of proximal development. Another possibility, discussed earlier, is that the system selects and creates its own niche – its own preferred environment.

Dynamics and Recursiveness of the Developmental Change Function

It is easy to see that the basic developmental function – *all changes of the system occur through information that is moderated through the system* – is a basically recursive or iterative function and is thus directly related to the definition of dynamical system as given earlier. Any theory that takes this function, in any of its many possible forms, as a starting point, must arrive at a dynamical system theory of development. The problem with the classical theories was that although they used a recursive mechanism of change and also appreciated the nonlinearities of the developmental process (take Piaget's stages, for instance), they had no practically feasible means to deduce formally the nonlinear outcomes from the mechanism. In fact, we had to wait until computers became available as easily manageable simulation devices to see how such iterative principles naturally generated nonlinear and self-organizational phenomena. With only a few exceptions, unfortunately, developmental psychologists have so far hardly tried to do their "experimental theory building" (i.e., their simulations of the basic dynamics of development) and are thus still not yet in a position to see the possible links between mechanism and developmental outcome. One approach to simulation is relatively widespread in developmental psychology – namely, connectionist model building (see, for instance, Elman, 2005; Munakata & McClelland, 2003; Schlesinger & Parisi, 2004). However important such connectionist modeling is, it does not in itself answer the question of whether recursive application of one or another formalized version of the basic developmental mechanism indeed generates the kind of dynamics that we see as characteristic of development (van Geert & Fischer, in press).

The Interactional Nature of the Developmental Change Function

In our description of how information that is capable of changing the system is in fact moderated through the system, we have implicitly specified that the dynamics is fundamentally interactional. That is, it involves an interaction between the system and another system, which, for simplicity, can be specified as the system's environment. *Environment* is used as a generic term. For instance, if we conceive of a child's lexicon as a simple one-dimensional system, the lexical system's environment is anything to which the lexicon is dynamically related, such as the child's own cognitive system, but also the linguistic community and the actions of the child's caretakers. Even in the extremely simple dynamical model that I related earlier to the logistic growth model and that specifies the quantitative change in a single variable (for instance, the number of words known by a person), there is an explicit reference in the equation to what is not yet known or appropriated (e.g., the number of words not yet known by the child; this number implies a simple interaction between the child's lexicon and the linguistic environment from which this lexicon is drawn). A much richer notion of interaction emerges if we specify a developmental model as an interaction between components of an overarching system (e.g., motor, sensory, cognition, and language components in addition to "real" context aspects such as caretakers or cultural artifacts).

Intentional Action: An Implicit Component

The developmental change function, *all changes of the system occur through information that is moderated through the system,* aims at understanding long-term change, at the developmental time scale of the life span, in a complex system – for instance, a child in a physical, social, and cultural world. It does not specify where the generically defined "information" comes from, from which source it emerges. The classical developmentalists, Piaget and Vygotsky in particular, addressed this issue by emphasizing the importance of action for development. Action can take many forms, ranging from an individual child's curiosity-driven exploration of manipulable objects to a child's guided participation in an activity he or she cannot yet accomplish alone to the actual teaching and learning that go on in a classroom. This brings us to a different kind of dynamics, which is the short-term dynamics of human action. I call it short term because it involves processes (actions) of considerably shorter duration than those of development.

Action and the Dynamics of Short-Term Change

The Dynamics of Action

Historically speaking, economics provides a good example of how macroscopic (i.e., economic) processes were based on a basic model of human action. The early theory of liberal economics of Adam Smith (1723–1790) conceived of individual human action as a utility-driven and utility-optimizing dynamics. That is, human action is driven by the intention to achieve maximal gain at minimal cost. Gain can be described in terms of actual goods but also in terms of an internal evaluation of the value of the context, of happiness and pleasure, satisfaction, and so on, with cost defined as effort. Human action encompasses the here-and-now events of trading, buying, and manufacturing. The acts of an individual make no sense without complementary acts of other individuals. The whole of such actions across space and time is economy, the dynamics of which emerge from the dynamics of individual actions. The notion that action boils down to motion to or away from certain "objects" – that it is dynamics in the most fundamental sense of the word – dates back (at least) to Hobbes's *Leviathan*:

> The real effect there is nothing but motion, or endeavour; which consisteth in appetite or aversion to or from the object moving. But the appearance or sense of that motion is that we either call delight or trouble of mind. (Hobbes, *Leviathan* I 6)

Let me give some examples of action in a developmental context. A 10-month-old has been put on the lap of a strange person by his mother, and he does whatever he can to get back to her. A four-year-old spots a new toy in the play corner and wants to have it but meets another child who also seems to want it and gets into a fight with the other child. An eight-year-old is given a math assignment by her teacher and tries to solve the sums from her workbook. A 15-year-old gets into an emotional discussion with her mother about staying out late at night with her boyfriend. These examples illustrate the short-term dynamics of action as they are embedded in the long-term dynamics of development. A baby of

10 months, for instance, has already formed the type of attachment that makes her try to escape from a stranger, something she would not have done at an earlier age. A 4-year-old cannot solve the math problems because she does not yet have the skills to do so, and so forth. An important property of the action sequences is that they involve some sort of gradient that is strong enough to release energy for action (see Tschacher & Haken, 2007, who placed action in a thermodynamic perspective). The action of the ten-month-old is aimed at solving the gradient between her position with the stranger and the position close to her mother. The 4-year-old acts to solve the gradient between seeing the new toy and actually playing with it, and so forth. This theory of gradients is highly reminiscent of Lewin's field theory of action (Lewin, 1936, 1946; see also Beach & Wise, 1980; Koch, 1941). The gradients from the examples are associated with the value, or valence, as Lewin called it, of objects, situations, or bodily conditions. Social psychologists tend to speak about evaluations in this regard (Cunningham & Zelazo, 2007), whereas theorists focusing on emotions often tend to speak about appraisals (Frijda, 1986, 1993; Scherer, 1999). Evaluations or appraisals can be specified over a great number of dimensions, involving bodily, physiological, and visceral aspects; social and self-related aspects (Leary, 2007); and cognitive aspects of different kinds. Together these dimensions can be conceived of as a dynamical state space, with a principal component that goes from low or negative hedonic tone (displeasure) to a high or positive hedonic tone (i.e., pleasure; see Cabanac, 2002; Johnston, 2003; Panksepp, 2000; Russell, 2003).

> Pleasure therefore, or delight, is the appearance or sense of good; and molestation or displeasure, the appearance or sense of evil. (Hobbes, *Leviathan* I 6)

The hedonic tone of a person's continuous evaluations has a distinct neurological underpinning (Cunningham & Zelazo, 2007; LeDoux, 1996; Sugrue, Corrado, & Newsome, 2004) and can take various qualities, experienced by the person in the form of emotions. The evaluative state space has specific attractor states, and the nature of these attractors depends on the totality of endogenous (person-specific) and exogenous (environment-specific) properties at any point in time. For instance, the example of the toy specifies an attractor of being close to the toy (in fact being able to play with it) and a gradient (being presently at some distance from the toy), which depends entirely on the current presence of the toy in the child's living space, or *Umwelt*, as von Uexkull used to call it, and on the child's actual interest in the toy. As the child moves through his living space, the attractors of the evaluative state space change continuously, basically because they release actions resulting in resolving gradients and creating new ones in the forms of new opportunities. As noted earlier, this model is highly reminiscent of Lewin's field theory of action. The goals or intentions that guide a person's action are self-organizing attractor states, under the control of the entire dynamic system of organism–environment (Gibbs & Van Orden, 2003; Shaw, 2001; Van Orden, 2002; Van Orden & Holden, 2002).

The dynamics of action are mutually coupled to the dynamics of evaluation (appraisal, hedonic tone). Action serves to optimize evaluation or hedonic tone in the multidimensional evaluation space. In our earlier example, the 4-year-old moves toward the toy, thus decreasing the distance between him and the toy and increasing the hedonic tone along this particular dimension, but as he comes closer, he also comes closer to the other child, his competitor, who might frighten him, leading to a decreasing hedonic tone as he comes closer to that child, eventually resulting in a withdrawal and an exploratory sweep to find an alternative attractive toy without competitors. In a mentalistic perspective, the coupling between action and evaluation is covered by terms such as motivation, goal setting, effort allocation, and so forth.

Steenbeek and van Geert (2005, 2007a, 2008) constructed a dynamical model of dyadic action in children to explain the emergence of action patterns over time and the emergence of differences between children of different sociometric statuses. A central feature of the model is the child's concern or interest in playing with another child versus his concern to play alone with the available toys. It is based on the assumption that the preferred proportion of activities, with the optimal level of pleasure or hedonic tone, depends on the status (or valence) of the play partner versus the attractiveness of the toys. The model yields patterns in time that qualitatively resemble the empirically observed ones and generates distributions of behavioral and emotional variables that are similar to those found in the studied sample (which consisted of dyads composed of a child of average sociometric status with a play partner of either popular, average, or rejected status).

Action and Social Interaction in a Developmental Context

The long-term process of development and the short-term process of action are intimately dynamically related. That is, action creates the conditions in which learning, teaching, maturation, niche-seeking, and so forth take place and thus alters the parameters and properties that constitute the long-term ensemble of development. For instance, if a child experiences that whining and nagging will result in getting the PlayStation he had wanted and that his parents found too expensive, the child will learn that whining and nagging are good means to pursue a goal, according to classical operant learning theory. Development, on the other hand, creates the conditions for actions by changing environments, valences of environments, and the means for realizing one's goals. To really understand how development emerges as long-term dynamics out of the short-term dynamics of coordinated actions of children, adults, and cultural artifacts, one must understand the dynamics of action in the child and the adult in question, as well as how they relate to one another in terms of circular causality (Tschacher & Haken, 2007; Van Orden & Holden, 2002) and how they result in

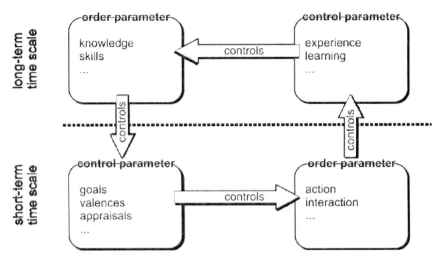

Figure 8.1. Cyclical relationships between order and control parameters on the short-term time scale of action and the long-term time scale of development.

the long-term change of development (Steenbeek & van Geert, 2008; Van Geert & Steenbeek, 2005).

Our current empirical understanding of these dynamics, however, is fragmented and scattered over many small pieces, referring to theories about motivation, teaching, operant learning, conceptual learning, social interaction, attachment, curriculum construction, and so forth, to name just a few possibilities in random order. From a viewpoint of complex dynamical systems, the major question to be solved refers to the fundamental principle(s), if any exist, of the coordination of the many levels implicitly distinguished so far. A major point concerns the coordination of short-term and long-term processes. Using the terminology of control and order parameters, Steenbeek and van Geert (2008) suggested a *circular causality* model of interactions between the short-term time scale of action and the long-term time scale of development. Order parameters on the short-term level of description (i.e., that of action) constitute control parameters at the level of development, giving rise to long-term order parameters (e.g., social status and social power of children in a group) that constitute the control parameters at the short-term level (see Fig. 8.1).

In the next section, I address a question that has occupied developmentalists since the founding of developmental psychology as a scientific discipline – namely, the question of stages. I try to show that the question is more than a descriptive and therefore relatively trivial matter. It touches on a number of issues regarding the fundamental mechanism(s) of development and how they shape the actual unfolding of development over time.

Developmental Phenomena from the NDS Viewpoint

Developmental Stages and the Stage Debate

A typical feature of classical developmental theories (e.g., Piaget, Erikson) is that they view development as occurring in stages. Although the original scholars were less occupied with the stage issue than many current introductory handbooks suggest (see van Geert, 1998a, 1998b, for discussion), they nevertheless saw the course from the initial developmental state to some sort of end state as a stepwise path, or a path moving across various qualitatively distinct states. The current handbook version of Piaget's stages is probably the best-known example. It claims that children begin on a sensorimotor level of thought, that they proceed to a level called preoperational, then concrete operational, and stabilize at a level called formal operational, which is characteristic of adult thinking. What is important is that these stages represent characteristic features of thought, such as preoperational thinking, which is characterized by the fact that thinking is internalized (takes place in the form of internal representation and not as overt action as in the preceding state), but that it is still action-based (does not entail reversibility) and operates on concrete objects (van Geert, 1986, 1987a, 1987b). Reversibility is a property of a cognitive system, implying that every operation has an inverse operation attached to it that cancels out the effect of the first operation; for Piaget, a mature cognitive system is characterized by the formal properties of mathematical groups, notably identity and inverse.

The existence of stages has been heavily criticized, and some scholars saw them as mere bookkeeping categories, distinguished by completely arbitrary boundaries (Boom, 1993; Brainerd, 1978). Recent stage-oriented theorists, in particular the neo-Piagetians, occupy a considerably more sophisticated standpoint (Fischer & Bidell, 2006). They make an analysis of the content structure of thought processes on the basis of general descriptive building blocks, such as representations, relations, systems defined as relations of relations, and so forth. Armed with this descriptive framework, they are able to distinguish "stages" as in fact qualitatively different forms of thought, or skill in general, that are developmentally ordered. The stages are context and domain specific (Case, 1992, 1993; Demetriou & Kyriakides, 2006; Fischer & Bidell, 2006). A child may function on Stage (or level) 1 in Domain A (e.g., simple mathematical operations) and on Level 2 in Domain B (e.g., social relationships). Within a domain, such stages – or one should say levels – can fluctuate with varying context, because context is a part of a person's skill (e.g., a child who faces a particular problem context may function on Level 2 with help and on Level 1 without help). The levels or stages may fluctuate strongly over the short-term time scale: While solving a problem, a child, or a collaborating dyad of two children, may go from mere sensorimotor experimenting to relatively deep conceptual understanding and back in a process that Fischer has called *scalloping* (Fischer & Bidell, 2006; Granott, 2002).

However, irrespective of the domain and context specificity of the levels or stages and of the fact that they may fluctuate strongly over a short time span, there is also a fuzzy but nevertheless convincing ordering in the level or stages. Two-year-olds, for instance, will show a very different mixture and frequency of context- and domain-specific levels than adults and are thus characterized by a different major-stage category than adults are (Dawson-Tunik, Commons, Wilson, & Fischer, 2005). In sum, the current notion of stages reflects the complexity of the developmental system. It views stages or levels all the way down, in a complex, hierarchical, and dynamic organization. In the next section, I discuss to what extent the notion of stage or level really captures the fundamental aspects of the dynamical organization and mechanisms that shape development.

Dynamical Systems and the Notion of Stages

Stages as Attractor States of the Developing System

The notion of stage (e.g., level, phase) reflects an idea of internal coherence, a relatively stable structure of elements such as skills, habits, processes, and so forth that in some way or another support each other's existence. They can be replaced by other relatively stable structures, but they should not be seen as arbitrary collections of features. The notion of stage is thus highly reminiscent of a basic notion from dynamical systems – namely, the notion of attractor. In a multidimensional geometry (e.g., a space consisting of all the dimensions or features necessary to characterize the properties of human thought and action), an attractor can be a single point, a basin, or a (quasi-)cyclical path, with a certain stability. Most points in this geometric space will be unstable, and thus move toward more stable points, which are the system's characteristic modes of operation. We can now take as our starting point the theory of complex systems in general and follow the assumption that such systems tend to self-organize into islands of relative stability rather than remain unconnected collections of features in which any combination of such features is as likely and (un)stable as any other. From this, we can reach the conclusion that stages, defined in the dynamical and complex way explained earlier, should be the default option for a system as complex as human development. The difficult point is, of course, to describe and explain them properly and go beyond a naïve idea of age-dependent, easily specifiable, and uniform modes of thought and action.

(Dis-)Continuous Transitions

Developmental psychologists who took seriously the idea of patterns of stability and coherence and thus adhered, in some way or another, to the notion of stage in the general sense of the word (meaning "relatively stable state, in the sense of attractor") have turned to the issue of discontinuity and continuity in development. The (dis)continuity problem asks whether there is anything between two qualitatively distinct stages or states, A and B. Let me give an example from the field of theory of mind research, which is currently one of the most prolific fields of research in social–cognitive development, with considerable implications for clinical practice. Let B be the typical "other-minds" stance of a child who thinks according to the principles of theory of mind, and A be the "own-mind" stance of a child who has not yet developed a theory of mind (Blijd-Hoogewys, van Geert, Serra, & Minderaa, 2007). For instance, we show a child a candy box and ask him what it contains; the child says "candy," and then we show the child that instead of candy, there are marbles in the box. We then ask the child what his father, who will come in later, will say when asked what the box contains. The B child will say "candy," reasoning from an other-minds stance, lacking the information the child himself has. A child will say "marbles," reasoning from an own-mind stance, identifying his own knowledge with that of somebody else. With this example, I am in no way making the claim that such answers are caused by some internal mechanism called the child's theory of mind. So far our insight into the direct mechanisms of what makes children generate this sort of answer is not deep. Recent studies suggest that executive functioning, notably the ability to inhibit rapid associations, explains part of children's answer tendencies; other studies have pointed at language understanding, the presence of child-aged siblings, and the automatic simulation of an other person's perspective (Gallese & Goldman, 1998; Hughes & Ensor, 2007; McAlister & Peterson, 2007; Pellicano, 2007).

According to the discontinuity view, there is nothing in between the A and B states. A child's problem solving, for instance, when faced with a false-belief experiment, is either A or B, not something in between, as continuity theory would assume. Such discontinuities are the topic of catastrophe or bifurcation theory. In the field of organizational psychology, empirical applications have been pioneered by Guastello (Guastello, 1981, 1987, 1988, 1995). Also, developmental researchers have used the framework of catastrophe theory to answer their questions about developmental (dis)continuity (van der Maas & Molenaar, 1992; van Geert, Savelsbergh, & van der Maas, 1999). By testing for empirical indicators of the so-called catastrophe flags (structural properties of discontinuities in general), they have tried to show that developmental transitions are instances of the so-called cusp catastrophe and thus entail a clear form of discontinuity. Examples of phenomena studied are the transition between nonconservation and conservation understanding in young children (Hartelman, van der Maas, & Molenaar, 1998; van der Maas, 1993; van der Maas & Molenaar, 1992), reasoning (Hosenfeld, van der Maas, & van den Boom, 1997a, 1997b; Jansen & van der Maas, 1997, 2001, 2002; van der Maas, 1993; van der Maas, Jansen, & Raijmakers, 2004), reaching and grasping in infants (Wimmers, Savelsbergh, Beek, & Hopkins, 1998; Wimmers, Savelsbergh, van der Kamp, & Hartelman, 1998), and syntactic development (Ruhland & van Geert, 1998; Van Dijk & van Geert, 2007). The results show that rapid, jumpwise development takes place in a variety of domains. However, it remains unclear whether these changes are real discontinuities in the bifurcation sense. In addition, they seem to occur in some children, but not all. A problem with discontinuities is that the empirical detection depends on the definition given by the researcher (Van Dijk & van Geert, 2007).

(Dis-)Continuities in Embedded–Embodied Agents?

The question is whether this particular branch of bifurcation dynamics is appropriate for dealing with developmental (dis)continuities. The discontinuity approach employed in the developmental studies referred to earlier employed the cusp catastrophe model, which implicitly focuses on simple dynamical systems – namely, those that can be described by means of two control parameters. Control parameters can be estimated as regression functions of any set of parameters, however (Guastello, 1987, 1988; Hartelman et al., 1998). Children are instances of a considerably more complex kind of dynamics. An example of a complex dynamic is Thelen and Smith's model of the dynamics of embedded and embodied action and thought (Smith, 2005; Thelen & Smith, 1994) or Fischer's dynamic skill theory (Fischer & Bidell, 2006). The model of embedded–embodied dynamics claims that thought is a process driven by the continuous dynamic coupling of an organism to an environment. Intelligence is not in the head but in the interface of person and environment. Examples of developmental studies along these lines are those on object permanence in infants and on word learning (Clearfield, Diedrich, Smith, & Thelen, 2006; Jones & Smith, 2002; Kersten & Smith, 2002; Ryalls & Smith, 2000; Samuelson & Smith, 2000; Sandhofer, Smith, & Luo, 2000; Smith, Thelen, Titzer, & McLin, 1999; Spencer, Smith, & Thelen, 2001a; Thelen, Schöner, Scheier, & Smith, 2001; Yoshida & Smith, 2001). In this embodied–embeddedness view, what I earlier called a developmental state is in fact a temporary construction of relationships between the organism's overt and covert actions and components and aspects of the context, related to a descriptive developmental framework. A child's acting and reaching in a so-called A-not-B error problem situation, in which objects are hidden in front of the infant, involves a variety of real-time events, such as visually focusing on the object display, reaching and grasping, refocusing as a result of that, and so forth. Nowhere in this process is an entity called "object concept," which causes the child to act in a particular way (for a similar point, see the discussion on theory of mind earlier in this chapter).

However, the absence of such an entity does not mean that one cannot assign a developmental state or level to this series of actions. The particular properties of this process definitely map onto a descriptive framework of developmental levels and states, but the mapping is not unequivocal. That is, the relationship between an actual process of thought and action and a particular developmental level can be ambiguous or fuzzy. Actual, ongoing processes of thought and action are complex sequences that can involve elements and properties of various developmental levels or states simultaneously. If they do, they are likely to change, more or less rapidly across developmental time, into processes that are more coherent in terms of their functional or formal properties. That is, such processes are likely to move toward more stable and coherent attractor states, the developmental specification of which is relatively unequivocal. Where does this leave us with regard to the (dis)continuity issue? The answer is that a complex developmental system – a child acting in and with the world – maps onto a developmental geometry (a system specifying developmental levels or states) in a complex way. It can create processes that have properties of developmental states that are in themselves mutually incompatible, given their formal properties. Although I realize the dangers of the comparison, actual thought-and-action processes, as conceived by dynamic skill theory or the theory of embodied action and thought, are like quantum physical states in that a kind of superposition principle applies. They can be in different states at the same time (van Geert & Steenbeek, 2005). A more down-to-earth description of the phenomenon involves fuzzy logic, describing a phenomenon by means of continuous membership functions instead of discrete membership functions that apply to mutually exclusive categories (van Geert, 2002). This sort of mixture of properties, which is fairly characteristic of complex dynamical systems, is different from the notion of simple continuity (or discontinuity) that applies to low-dimensional phenomena (phenomena that can be described relatively exhaustively by means of only a few linear dimensions).

This overview suggests that there exist so many kinds of transitional and stagelike phenomena in development that the question "Are there stages in development?" should be considered as unanswerable – or better, should be considered not the right kind of question. The basic issue should be this: Is there any general dynamic principle underlying the process of human development, and if so, what is the pattern of change that results from it? Is it smooth, coarse, continuous, discontinuous, stagelike, or maybe a bit of everything?

The Pattern of Developmental Change

Imagine the following thought experiment. Suppose you have a direct, unlimited, and durable access to all of a child's actions, including his covert thoughts and the components of the context with which the child interacts. Suppose also that you are able to map any point of this long-term time series onto a developmental geometry. Remember that a developmental geometry is a state space consisting of all dimensions, properties, or variables that you need to describe sufficiently the child's actions and capabilities from a developmental viewpoint. Dimensions are quantitative (e.g., the sheer number of words in the lexicon) or of a more structural, qualitative nature. Examples of the latter are descriptions of actions in terms of cognitive structures (e.g., a cognition concerns a relation between representations versus a relation between relations; see Dawson, Fischer, & Stein, 2006; Dawson-Tunik, Commons, Wilson, & Fischer, 2005a; Fischer & Dawson, 2002; Rose & Fischer, 1998). Other examples

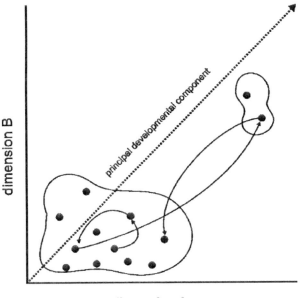

dimension A

Figure 8.2. An imaginary developmental state space, with two descriptive dimensions, A and B, and a principal developmental component. Dots represent positions in the space corresponding with a concrete action or experience in real time; arrows represent successions between actions or experiences. The distribution is bimodal, with a dominant mode on the low end of the developmental component.

concern cognitive strategies in various degrees of developmental complexity, as in Siegler's often-studied balance scale task (Boom & ter Laak, 2007; Jansen & van der Maas, 2001, 2002; Quinlan, van der Maas, Jansen, Booij, & Rendell, 2007; Siegler, 2005; Turner & Thomas, 2002; van der Maas & Jansen, 2003; van Rijn, van Someren, & van der Maas, 2003). An example from language development concerns developmentally ordered syntactic patterns – for instance, patterns of word-order use in learners of German as a foreign language (Pienemann, 2007). What distinguishes learners (or moments in the learning process, for that matter) is the relative frequency with which any of the patterns is used in spontaneous language. Whatever the nature of these dimensions, I consider them primarily as descriptive reference points, comparable to using dimensions of longitude and latitude to describe a particular place on the globe.

If you determine a developing child's position in the descriptive state, you will obtain a point (or cloud, collection of patches, or whatever else is an appropriate description) that moves through the state space and in fact specifies the child's developmental trajectory. The geometry of the state space allows one to specify the distance between any pair of points on the trajectory and thus to specify the rate of change at any point in time (see Fig. 8.2).

What would the graph of the rate of change over time look like? In the preceding section, potential answers to this question have already been suggested. The classical developmental theories predict a stepwise pattern, whereas modern stage theorists would predict a somewhat fuzzy stepwise form, rounded off by the various moments at which context- and domain-specific transitions take place. The majority of developmentalists would probably be inclined to see the many small transitions and likely continuous changes as a summative process averaging out to something that looks relatively linear, leveling off toward adulthood. Another possibility I discuss in this section is that the developmental distance curve will consist of many steps of different magnitudes, statistically distributed according to a power law. The distribution across time would probably also follow a kind of power law, with the distances in time between the major shifts exponentially increasing. Why would this be so?

Are Developmental Transitions Phase Transitions?

One possibility is that what has traditionally been called stages are states that form the natural attractors of the developing system. They are comparable, in that sense, to the phases of physical matter (gaseous, liquid, solid) and depend, in essence, on a single parameter or a confluence of parameters. In the language of synergetics, the developmental stages (if any exist) are the states defined by the developmental system's major order parameter, and they are determined by the system's major control parameters, which are, in all likelihood, the cumulative amount of experience on the one hand, and maturation – in particular, brain maturation – on the other hand (it goes without saying that this is an extremely simplified representation of reality, but what matters here is the principle, not the details). Developmental stages form attractor states in that they are represented by habitual, coherent patterns of performance, skill, or action that self-organize spontaneously in the person's habitual contexts, niches, or living spaces. These patterns consist of mutually supportive and sustaining features. To give a simple example, Piaget's sensorimotor stage defines thought in the form of external action on objects. For instance, reaching to and grasping an object requires the coordination in real time of myriad components or aspects, including the coordination of the muscles in the arm and hand, the coordination of vision and movement, the coordination of vision of the object and vision of the own arm and hand, and so forth. These patterns are not innately given but self-organize through processes that eventually amount to discontinuous changes; a particularly nice example is given in Wimmer's studies of early prehension development (Wimmers, Beek, & Savelsbergh, 1998; Wimmers, Beek, & van Wieringen, 1992; Wimmers, Savelsbergh, van der Kamp, & Hartelman, 1998b). The characteristic feature of these sensorimotor patterns is that their contextual self-organization (e.g., in the form of reaching to and grasping a particular object) emerges on the basis of dominant driving forces or control parameters that are of a sensory and motor nature. See, for instance, dynamic field theory (Erlhagen & Schöner, 2002; Schutte, Spencer, & Schöner, 2003) and in particular its application to infant problem solving (Schutte & Spencer, 2002; Spencer, Smith, & Thelen, 2001b). In addition, the sensory and motor control parameters of infant action are likely to be biologically preadapted to important features of the environment, such as object–person distinctions, numerosity, and so on (Spelke & Kinzler, 2007; Wimmers, Beek et al., 1998; Wimmers, Savelsbergh et al., 1998; Wimmers et al., 1992). A characteristic feature of these sensorimotor patterns is that there is likely to be little influence of control parameters from language or long-term memories in symbolic representational form. The latter type of control parameters emerge later in development, helping the skill and action patterns self-organize in different ways, characteristic of later and higher-developed stages.

The question is whether there is any empirical evidence suggesting that major developmental stages, if any occur, amount to phase transitions. Indirect evidence comes from calculating the relative durations of these stages over the life span. Irrespective of the stage theory under consideration, the durations tend to increase in a logarithmic manner (van Geert, 1994).

Are Developmental Transitions Caused by Self-Organized Criticality?

One might ask if the distribution of stage durations relates to the power law distribution characteristic of self-organizing phenomena (Van Orden, Holden, & Turvey, 2005; Pincus & Guastello, 2005) and, more particularly, to self-organized criticality (Bak, 1996). The phenomenon of self-organized criticality emerges in complex systems, consisting of many components that entertain local relationships. The embodied–embedded brain (or its semantic transformation, the mind) is such a system, consisting of many components (perceptions, thoughts, actions, memories, tools, environments) that are temporally and functionally connected. This complex system is under a certain external "tension": The person has an ongoing stream of experiences. There are problems to solve, goals to achieve. The person does so by means of the complex system of skills, knowledge, and sensory and motor systems. Not every action is successful, and the person adapts, learning from his or her experiences and from being taught by other people. This complex, interconnected system exchanging information with the world is a likely example of a system that shows self-organized criticality. Its attractor states are critical states, that is, states for which any external influence can cause patterns of change with a wide variety of magnitude and duration, dissipating the stress that has been built up in the system. Note the major difference from a phase transition model, in which the attractor states are the phases, whereas in a critical transition model, the attractor states are those where a transition might occur.

The magnitudes and durations of changes are statistically distributed according to a power law distribution, with few large-scale changes and increasing numbers of smaller-scale changes. It is tempting to see development as an example of such a self-organized criticality: a succession of metastable states punctuated by changes of various magnitude (e.g., a relatively small change in a relatively context-specific problem-solving strategy versus an avalanche of changes in many aspects and domains of cognitive performance, the latter characteristic of which would count as a stage transition).

Is there any reason development should show self-organized criticality? To begin with, it has a number of features that are characteristic of such systems. It consists of a great many components (e.g., perceptual, motor, linguistic, cognitive, emotional skills, and combinations thereof; knowledge; memories) with local connectivity. For instance, two perceptual skills share more components than a perceptual and a linguistic skill; some skills are mutually supportive through the effect of their performance, whereas others can be mutually competitive (van Geert, 1991, 1996, 2003). Thus if for some reason something changes in one skill (or of knowledge, ability, action pattern, habit), it is likely to affect other skills (habits, etc.) to the extent that these two developmental components are interrelated. However, the second component, affected by the first, can eventually affect a third one to which it is connected, and so forth. In principle, such changes can remain quite limited, but they can also grow into an avalanche of changes that affects the whole developmental system. If we assume that in a developing system the "weakest," that is, the least adapted or effective skills (habits, knowledge), are eliminated (or altered) more easily than better-adapted or more effective skills, we wind up with a system that closely resembles the Bak–Sneppen model of biological evolution through punctuated equilibria (Bak & Sneppen, 1993; Boettcher & Paczuski, 1996). This model of evolution changes through many events of extinction and speciation, interspersed with periods of stasis.

Although most of the evolutionary changes are small, the evolutionary record counts a few major extinction–speciation events, corresponding with rapid shifts in the structure of the global ecosystem. The pattern of change is clearly reminiscent of the course of human development, with many small and a few major changes. The principle of eliminating or altering the weakest component is also applied in a routine for solving hard optimization problems, called extremal optimization (Boettcher & Percus, 2000). The solution patterns are characterized by shifts following the power law distribution. In a certain sense, (cognitive) development is like solving a hard optimization problem, an adaptation of knowledge and skills to the complexities of reality. It would thus not be surprising that the general dynamic structure of cognitive development follows a pattern very close to that of the extremal optimization process, including the power law distribution of the changes.

Transitions in a Complex System With Developmental Dynamics

Although the similarity between the Bak–Sneppen model of evolution and development is tempting, there is a major difference that might jeopardize the applicability of the self-organized criticality model. In essence, the species ecology of the evolutionary model is a closed system of interacting species; physical environmental circumstances are treated as implicit constants. The environment of a species consists of other species that it feeds on or that feed on it; for an example in biological ecosystems, related to catastrophic changes, see Scheffer and Carpenter (2003). The ecology of a developing system, such as a young child, has more of a dual nature, in that it is in essence an interacting system of an organism in an environment. The developing system consists of the abilities or effectivities of an individual, substantiated in the individual's brain and body, and the affordances and properties of a physical, social, and cultural environment in which the individual lives and acts. This environment is also specifically adapted and adapting to the individual in the form of protection, education, teaching, and so forth. Let us call these subsystems, for convenience, the endo-system and exo-system, respectively. Although development takes place through the dynamic interface between these two coupled systems (action, as described in the section on short-term dynamics), the coacting systems should be treated separately to understand the dynamics of development. Adaptations (changes, alterations, eliminations) of components in the endo-system (the individual) or in the exo-system (the environment as it is accessed by the individual) occur through local and temporal coordinations of components in the two subsystems (i.e., actions). Adaptation does not occur through continuous elimination of weakest elements, all acting simultaneously, as is the case in the species ecology. Thus the first principle of a developmental dynamics is that it occurs through short-term events consisting of couplings or coordination, in time, between the endo- and exo-system.

Whereas the evolutionary (and optimization) dynamics occurred through elimination (or alteration) of the weakest components and correlated changes in the associated components, developmental dynamics occurs through a different mechanism. I found the inspiration for the basic mechanism in the work of Piaget and Vygotsky. They see development as the result of what I have freely termed *conservative* and *progressive* forces. The abstract dynamics of development based on these notions can be explained as follows. Let us begin with the geometric notion of development as specified earlier, that is, the developing system defined as a manifold of dimensions or variables, describing all of its relevant developmental properties. Because all those dimensions can be ordered along a scale of developmental progress (a developmental "ruler"), the developmental state space is thus characterized by a principal component that can be used to specify any kind of developmental progress or succession. At any point in time, a developing system occupies a particular region of the developmental space. This region can be relatively condensed, but it can also be scattered across the state space in diverse ways. For instance, if a child alternates between solving a problem in either a less or more developmentally advanced way (see for instance the examples of the balance scale rules), it occupies two regions in the developmental space between which it shifts randomly. Any point or region

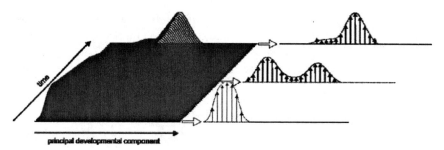

Figure 8.3. Probability functions of developmental levels assigned to potential actions or experiences of a child across time. The probability wave moves from a dominant mode on the left to a bimodal mode in the middle to a dominant mode on the right (see the three probability functions with vectors at the right).

in the developmental state space can be mapped onto the principal component of the space, that is, the general developmental distance introduced above. Any point or region in the space has a certain probability of being "visited" by the developing system. These probabilities can be represented as a vector field, with an activation vector for each point in the developmental principal component or distance dimension. The vector field can specify a single peak, in which case the developmental state of the individual is crisp and unimodal (the classical ideal), or a landscape of peaks, in which case the developmental state of the individual is multimodal, fluctuating, and fuzzy (which is more like reality; see Fig. 8.3).

Development can then be represented as the change of the vector field over time, beginning with a dominant mode in the lower and ending with a dominant mode in the upper regions. The short-term dynamics of development consists of the individual's actions, experiences, and interactions in real time. The idea is that during any such event, the individual functions on a particular level of the developmental distance dimension, that is, his or her actions or experiences are characteristic of this level and invoke knowledge and strategies, contextual support, among others, that are characteristic of this level, and so forth. The level at which an individual operates is a stochastic function of the vector field, with the individual's main modus operandi corresponding with the major peak (or peaks) in the vector field.

The aforementioned conservative and progressive forces, inspired by Piaget and Vygotsky, operate as follows (see van Geert, 1998a, 2000, for an explanation of the model). It is assumed that any activation of components of the developing system in the form of a particular action, experience, or event have a consolidating effect on those components and hence on the developmental level(s) that they represent. The consolidation depends on the functional success of the action or experience in question, that is, on its short-term dynamics in terms of the gradient processes discussed earlier. The consolidation takes place in the form of increasing the vector values at the levels corresponding with the action or experience in question. The consolidation function spreads out to nearby regions and becomes negative (reducing vector values) for regions farther away on the developmental distance dimension. It is actually some sort of familiarity effect, which decreases with increasing distance from the actual, or familiar, level.

The developing system is also driven by a second force – namely, novelty – which is a general term for novelty (new things) per se, inspiring curiosity, interest, goal-related activity, and so forth. *Novelty* is a function that increases with increasing distance from the familiar. Assuming that familiarity and novelty are governed by their own characteristic parameters, there is a point on the developmental distance dimension where the combination of both has a maximal value or optimum (see Fig. 8.3). The vector values corresponding with this point are also upgraded, with an upgrade function that is in principle similar to the conservative upgrade function. A new short-term action or experience will then be a stochastic function of this updated vector field, will cause the vector field to update again, and so forth.

Simulations based on this model of development show that, depending on the values of the main parameters (familiarity and novelty parameters, rate of vector field upgrading, nature of information-activating vector loadings, and so forth), a rich landscape of developmental phenomena can be achieved, ranging from stepwise growth as described in the Piagetian and neo-Piagetian theories, to models of overlapping waves of strategies (Siegler), microgenetic fluctuations in performance, and so forth.

A study by Bassano and van Geert (2007) illustrates the process of the emergence of three successive syntactic generators: the holophrastic, combinatorial, and syntactic generators. The holophrastic generator is basically a "one-word grammar," that is, the set of early grammatical principles that generate utterances with a characteristic word length of one. The combinatorial generator is the developmentally more advanced set of principles that generate combinations of words, typically two per utterance. The syntactic generator is the set of principles that use the syntactic rules of sentence formation typical of mature language. Although the frequency of spontaneously produced sentence types most likely associated with either of these types (one-word, two- to three-word, and four-plus-word sentences) comes and goes in a pattern of continuous waves, there are two periods of increased variability that mark the transitions from a dominant holophrastic to a combinatorial, and from a dominant combinatorial to a syntactic generator. A continuous growth model can explain the pattern of frequencies but not the peaks of variability, which require the conservative–progressive forces model explained earlier (see Fig. 8.4).

Fuzziness, Ambiguity, and the Developmental Construction of Novelty

As developmental psychologists primarily interested in real-life manifestations of development, doing research in naturalistic settings, my collaborators and

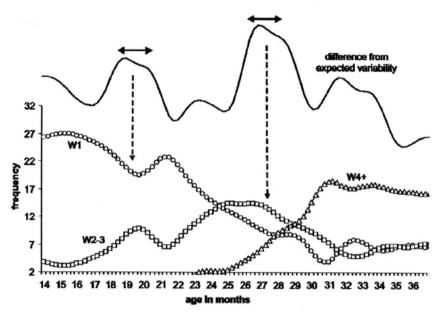

Figure 8.4. Waves of one-word, two- to three-word, and four-plus-word sentences in Pauline, between the ages of 14 and 37 months (based on data from Bassano & Van Geert, 2007). Two peaks of increased variability correspond with assumed transitions between dominant modes of sentence production (holophrastic, combinatorial, and syntactic, respectively).

I are frequently confronted with issues of interpretation of what we see, and also with the fact that what we see today is not necessarily the same as what we will see tomorrow. The standard interpretation of these observations is that they reflect measurement problems – more precisely, problems of reliability caused by superposition of noise on the data. The interpretation issue – for instance, deciding whether an observed phenomenon is in reality an instance of a category A or of a category B – is seen as a problem of signal detection. The noisy signal is either an A or a B, and given the observed properties, we estimate a certain probability that it is an A, for instance. In terms of class membership, the observed phenomenon has either a class membership of 1 with regard to the class A (and by implication a class membership of 0 to B) or vice versa. In fuzzy logic, however, class memberships can have any value between A and B, and the phenomenon can be a bit of A and a bit of B. It is likely that such fuzziness, leading to disagreements among observers who take the possibility of unanimity for granted (among others), is a typical footprint of complex nonlinear dynamical systems.

In language development, for instance, a child is constructing a linguistic system and linguistic categories. There is a time at which no sign exists in the child's language of categories, such as verbs or prepositions (the words the child uses may sound like the words that are verbs or prepositions in the adult's language, but in the child's language, they do not yet have the syntactic properties that such categories need to have). The trajectory toward verbs and prepositions is paved with linguistic forms that are highly fuzzy or ambiguous (some linguists call them "proto"-prepositions or verbs, for instance, or fillers; see Peters, 2001). The problem is not that a particular word of a child spoken in a conversation is "really" a preposition and that the information needed for the observer to make a correct decision is not yet present in the child's performance. The problem is rather that the word is truly ambiguous, truly undecidable from the point of view of the descriptive syntactic system, and that this ambiguity is characteristic for a system at a certain level of syntactic development. It is possible to quantify degrees of ambiguity, among others, by taking observer disagreement as information and to use the changes in ambiguity over time as a time-serial indicator of underlying developmental processes (van Dijk & van Geert, 2005; van Geert & van Dijk, 2002, 2003).

The issue of fluctuation that I discussed in the context of developmental transitions is yet another example of fuzziness and ambiguity in development. If a child fluctuates between various developmental levels over a short period of time, his or her developmental level is ambiguous or, more precisely, bimodal or multimodal, which is a phenomenon that I discussed earlier. It is even possible for a child to display a particular developmental level in his or her verbal behavior that is different from the level expressed in his or her motor actions (Garber & Goldin-Meadow, 2002; Goldin-Meadow, 1997, 2000; Goldin-Meadow & Singer, 2003; Özçaliskan & Goldin-Meadow, 2005). This form of superposition of developmental levels is characteristic of the way complex systems relate to descriptive frameworks, such as developmental level frameworks, that make crisp categorical distinctions to describe a world that is in essence ambiguous, fuzzy, and seemingly contradictory.

Another form of fluctuation concerns the occurrence of relatively isolated spikes or surges in the use of developmentally more advanced forms, superposed onto developmental trajectories that are continuous and even linear. See, for example, our study on the development of spatial prepositions (van Dijk & van Geert, 2007).

A typical developmental form of fluctuation is what one might call initial state fluctuation. Adaptive functions in babies, such as crying and other vocalizations of unease, touching, and smiling, but also physiological reactions to stress, seem to show a broad range of fluctuation in the beginning, zooming in onto a narrower band of fluctuation that seems best adapted to the infant's current environment (de Weerth & van Geert, 1998, 2000; 2002a; de Weerth, van Geert, & Hoijtink, 1999; for reactions to stress, see de Weerth & van Geert, 2002b). The phenomenon has a clear evolutionary and developmental functionality: A newborn does not "know" the environment in which it will be placed and thus profits from a broad range of possibilities at the beginning.

And Where's the Brain?

In this era of brain research and neuroscience, an overwhelming and rapidly growing literature emerges showing how the activity of the brain relates to behavior and performance. The suggestion is that an understanding of how the brain develops is the key to our understanding of development on the level of observable actions. Sometimes the implicit message is that development is driven by brain development and that brain development is like an autonomous trajectory; see, for instance, the discussion on brain-based education in Fischer et al. (2007) and Bruer (2002). The brain is part of the complex system of the individual acting and developing in his or her habitat or environment. The development of the brain has its own self-organizing properties and constraints (Lewis, 2005a, 2005b), but this is not to say that development is unidirectionally driven by the brain any more than the development of the brain is unidirectionally driven by the properties of the environment.

Any attempt to understand how the brain and the environment interact in development must reckon with two things. The first is that there is no direct brain–environment interaction (one needs a science fiction movie for that); the interaction is a theoretical abstraction of what in reality amounts to a conscious, embodied agent trying to accomplish his intentions and goals in a concrete, cultural, and social environment. The second is that the constituents of the game (e.g., the brain, the body, actions evolving in time, context, environments, cultural artifacts, etc.) are not inert components modeled by causal influences from elsewhere but that they have their own dynamic constraints and possibilities, their own self-organizing tendencies given the overall system in which they function and develop.

An interesting illustration of these principles is the phenomenon of brain plasticity, which is the brain's ability to be shaped by experience, resulting in the brain's facilitation of new experiences, which result in further brain adaptation, and so on (Nelson, 1999). The phenomenon of brain plasticity typically invokes a recursive or iterative mechanism characteristic of the mutualistic dynamics of development in general. Brain plasticity is not another word for brain development: Experience can alter brain structure long after brain development is complete (Kolb & Whishaw, 1998).

Brain plasticity is not a constant property of the brain but a typical dynamic property that is nonlinearly dependent on the brain's developmental history. The change in plasticity is not simply linear or curvilinear, as suggested by the notion of a gradual decline in plasticity as the person grows older. Rather, there are nonlinear peaks of plasticity, known as critical periods or sensitive periods. These critical or sensitive periods in which the brain is particularly sensitive to particular experiences are in themselves also self-organizing and dynamical phenomena (Bruer, 2001). They emerge epigenetically from the brain's development and are thus codependent on biological brain growth and the unfolding of experiences, including teaching and learning over developmental time (Knudsen, 2004; Thomas & Johnson, 2006).

A dramatic illustration of how brain plasticity – and development as a whole, for that matter – always passes through the short-term dynamics of action is the development of children after hemispherectomy. Hemispherectomy is the surgical removal of a brain hemisphere, mostly as a last possibility for curing major and highly frequent epileptic insults that cannot be treated pharmacologically (Battro, 2001; Immordino-Yang, 2005; Vargha-Khadem, Carr, Isaacs, & Brett, 1997).

In a recent study, Immordino-Yang (2005, 2007) described the developmental trajectory of Nico and Brooke. Nico lost his right hemisphere at age three, Brooke his left hemisphere at age eleven. Both showed remarkable recovery in that they learned to function extraordinarily well, given the seriousness of the neurological impairment. According to Immordino-Yang (2007), the boys' developmental trajectories show the active role of the learner as well as the organizing role of emotion, which brings us back to the issue of the relationship between the long-term dynamics of development and the short-term dynamics of action and emotional appraisal. Above all, the boys demonstrate the incredible plasticity of the developmental system as well as the fact that self-organizing development occurs through the investment of all the available personal, social, and cultural resources.

Conclusion: The Complex Dynamics of Development

The course of human development over the life span is a prime example of a complex, nonlinear dynamical system. The process of development is recursive and self-organizing. It occurs simultaneously at many levels of organization – for example, the individual person and the person in interaction with others, institutions, and cultures to which the person relates. These levels of organization encompass processes on various time scales.

Unfortunately, the current field of developmental psychology tends to simplify the complexity by taking out most of the features that are fundamental to development as a complex, nonlinear dynamical system. It attempts to linearize the developmental process by focusing on differences among persons in samples as a source of information about underlying processes, and by doing so largely fails in uncovering the mechanisms of developmental change and the properties of the individual developmental trajectories.

In this chapter, I have focused on the interdependence of processes of long-term change in the form of developmental, life-span processes on one hand and short-term processes of action on the other. However, more time scales can be distinguished and should be incorporated into a comprehensive theory of development.

Understanding the long-term developmental changes requires that we take into account that development occurs to a system of an individual embedded in a network of environmental niches and thus that development is a process distributed over the person and the contexts in which that person acts, on the basis of his or her changing concerns and the changing means and tools used to realize them.

To obtain a better understanding of the underlying processes of development, I have discussed three issues that refer to characteristic features of the developmental system as a complex, NDS. The first issue relates to the classical problem of stages and modern views on stages as relatively stable organizations that emerge as soft assemblies in supportive environments and with time can become less dependent on the exact properties or fine-tuning of the supportive environments (e.g., Fischer's approach to stages). The gist of the stage question is not whether there "are" stages, how many there are, and what the ages are at which they occur. The importance of the stage question is that it relates to the possibility of attractor states forming in complex and to the issue of phase transitions and criticality. In this chapter, I have discussed yet another perspective on such developmental attractor states, namely, that of the developmental system as a probability wave over the principal components of the system, including continuous as well as discontinuous changes. The form of change and (dis)continuity provides further information about the nature of the underlying mechanisms that govern developmental change.

The second issue discusses the relationship between the scientific observer of the complex NDS and the system itself and focuses on fuzziness, ambiguity, and multimodality. Instead of discarding such properties as primarily relating to measurement error and lack of information, we should see them as actual fingerprints of complexity, giving us more insight into the processes that we attempt to understand. A final question concerned the relation to brain development and the embodied brain as part of the larger self-organizing system, the development of which is codependent on the behaviors, actions, and contexts it makes possible.

To conclude, the structure of the developmental process far outreaches the triviality of explained variances and associations between variables and will continue to surprise us as long as we keep an open eye to the paradoxical relationship between the magnificent simplicity of its fundamental principles and the complexity of its forms, trajectories, and outcomes.

References

Bak, P. (1996). *How nature works: The science of self-organized criticality.* New York: Springer-Verlag.

Bak, P., & Sneppen, K. (1993). Punctuated equilibrium and criticality in a simple model of evolution. *Physical Review Letters, 71*, 4083–4086.

Bar-Yam, Y. (1997). *Dynamics of complex systems.* Reading, MA: Addison-Wesley.

Bassano, D., & van Geert, P. (2007). Modeling continuity and discontinuity in utterance length: A quantitative approach to changes, transitions and intra-individual variability in early grammatical development. *Developmental Science, 10*, 588–612.

Battro, A. M. (2001). *Half a brain is enough: The story of Nico.* New York: Cambridge University Press.

Beach, L. R., & Wise, J. A. (1980). Decision emergence: A Lewinian perspective. *Acta Psychologica, 45*, 343–356.

Berger, K. S. (2003). *The developing person through childhood and adolescence* (6th ed.). New York: Worth.

Blijd-Hoogewys, E. M. A., van Geert, P. L. C., Serra, M., & Minderaa, R. B. (2008). *Discontinuous paths in the development of theory-of-mind: A nonlinear modeling approach.* Manuscript submitted for publication.

Boettcher, S., & Paczuski, M. (1996). Exact results for spatiotemporal correlations in a self-organized critical model of punctuated equilibrium. *Physical Review Letters, 76*, 348–351.

Boettcher, S., & Percus, A. (2000). Nature's way of optimizing. *Artificial Intelligence, 119*, 275–286.

Boom, J. (1993). *The concept of developmental stage.* Unpublished Doctoral Dissertation, University of Nijmegen.

Boom, J., & ter Laak, J. (2007). Classes in the balance: Latent class analysis and the balance scale task. *Developmental Review, 27*, 127–149.

Brainerd, C. J. (1978). The stage question in cognitive–developmental theory. *Behavioral and Brain Sciences, 1*, 173–182.

Bruer, J. T. (2001). *A critical and sensitive period primer.* Baltimore: Brookes.

Bruer, J. T. (2002). Avoiding the pediatrician's error: How neuroscientists can help educators (and themselves). *Nature Neuroscience, 5*, 1031–1033.

Bukatko, D., & Daehler, M. W. (2001). *Child development: A thematic approach* (4th ed.). Boston: Houghton Mifflin.

Cabanac, M. (2002). What is emotion? *Behavioural Processes, 60*, 69–83.

Case, R. (1992). *Neo-Piagetian theories of intellectual development.* Hillsdale, NJ: Erlbaum.

Case, R. (1993). Theories of learning and theories of development. *Educational Psychologist, 28*, 219–233.

Casti, J. L. (1994). *Complexification: Explaining a paradoxical world through the science of surprise.* New York: HarperCollins.

Clark, A. (1997). *Being there: Putting brain, body and world together again.* Cambridge, MA: MIT Press.

Clark, A. (2006). Language, embodiment, and the cognitive niche. *Trends in Cognitive Sciences, 10*, 370–374.

Clark, A., & Chalmers, D. (1998). The extended mind. *Analysis, 58*, 7–19.

Clearfield, M. W., Diedrich, F. J., Smith, L. B., & Thelen, E. (2006). Young infants reach correctly in A-not-B tasks: On the development of stability and perseveration. *Infant Behavior & Development, 29*, 435–444.

Cole, M., & Cole, S. R. (1993). *The development of children* (2nd ed.). New York: Scientific American Books.

Cunningham, W. A., & Zelazo, P. D. (2007). Attitudes and evaluations: A social cognitive neuroscience perspective. *Trends in Cognitive Sciences, 11,* 97–104.

Dawson, T. L., Fischer, K. W., & Stein, Z. (2006). Reconsidering qualitative and quantitative research approaches: A cognitive developmental perspective. *New Ideas in Psychology, 24,* 229–239.

Dawson-Tunik, T. L., Commons, M., Wilson, M., & Fischer, K. W. (2005). The shape of development. *European Journal of Developmental Psychology, 2,* 163–195.

de Weerth, C., & van Geert, P. (1998). Emotional instability as an indicator of strictly timed infantile developmental transitions. *British Journal of Developmental Psychology, 16,* 15–44.

de Weerth, C., & van Geert, P. (2000). *The dynamics of emotion-related behaviors in infancy.* New York: Cambridge University Press.

de Weerth, C., & van Geert, P. (2002a). Changing patterns of infant behavior and mother-infant interaction: Intra- and interindividual variability. *Infant Behavior & Development, 24,* 347–371.

de Weerth, C., & van Geert, P. (2002b). A longitudinal study of basal cortisol in infants: Intra-individual variability, circadian rhythm and developmental trends. *Infant Behavior & Development, 25,* 375–398.

de Weerth, C., van Geert, P., & Hoijtink, H. (1999). Intraindividual variability in infant behavior. *Developmental Psychology, 35,* 1102–1112.

Demetriou, A., & Kyriakides, L. (2006). The functional and developmental organization of cognitive developmental sequences. *British Journal of Educational Psychology, 76,* 209–242.

Duncan, G., Dowsett, C., Claessens, A., Magnuson, K., Huston, A., Klebanov, P., et al. (2007). School readiness and later achievement. *Developmental Psychology, 43,* 1428–1446.

Elman, J. L. (2005). Connectionist models of cognitive development: Where next? *Trends in Cognitive Sciences, 9,* 112–117.

Erlhagen, W., & Schöner, G. (2002). Dynamic field theory of movement preparation. *Psychological Review, 109,* 545–572.

Fischer, K. W., & Bidell, T. R. (2006). Dynamic development of action, thought, and emotion. In R. M. Lerner & W. Damon (Eds.), *Handbook of child psychology: Vol. 1. Theoretical models of human development* (6th ed., pp. 313–399). New York: Wiley.

Fischer, K. W., Daniel, D., Immordino-Yang, M. H., Stern, E., Battro, A., & Koizumi, H. (2007). Why mind, brain, and education? Why now? *Mind, Brain, and Education, 1,* 1–2.

Fischer, K. W., & Dawson, T. L. (2002). A new kind of developmental science: Using models to integrate theory and research: Comment. *Monographs of the Society for Research in Child Development, 67,* 156–167.

Fischer, K. W., & Granott, N. (1995). Beyond one-dimensional change: Parallel, concurrent, socially distributed processes in learning and development. *Human Development, 38,* 302–314.

Ford, D. H., & Lerner, R. M. (1992). *Developmental systems theory: An integrative approach.* Thousand Oaks, CA: Sage.

Frijda, N. H. (1986). *The emotions: Studies in emotion and social interaction.* Cambridge: Cambridge University Press.

Frijda, N. H. (1993). The place of appraisal in emotion. *Cognition & Emotion, 7,* 357–387.

Gallese, V., & Goldman, A. (1998). Mirror neurons and the simulation theory of mind-reading. *Trends in Cognitive Sciences, 2,* 493–501.

Ganger, J., & Brent, M. R. (2004). Reexamining the vocabulary spurt. *Developmental Psychology, 40,* 621–632.

Garber, P., & Goldin-Meadow, S. (2002). Gesture offers insight into problem-solving in adults and children. *Cognitive Science: A Multidisciplinary Journal, 26,* 817–831.

Gibbs, R. W. J., & Van Orden, G. C. (2003). Are emotional expressions intentional? A self-organizational approach. *Consciousness & Emotion, 4,* 1–16.

Goldin-Meadow, S. (1997). When gestures and words speak differently. *Current Directions in Psychological Science, 6,* 138–143.

Goldin-Meadow, S. (2000). Beyond words: The importance of gesture to researchers and learners. *Child Development, 71,* 231–239.

Goldin-Meadow, S., & Singer, M. A. (2003). From children's hands to adults' ears: Gesture's role in the learning process. *Developmental Psychology, 39,* 509–520.

Gottlieb, G. (2001). *A developmental psychobiological systems view: Early formulation and current status.* Cambridge, MA: MIT Press.

Granott, N. (2002). How microdevelopment creates macrodevelopment: Reiterated sequences, backward transitions, and the Zone of Current Development. In N. Granott & J. Parziale (Eds.), *Microdevelopment: Transition processes in development and learning* (pp. 213–242). New York: Cambridge University Press.

Guastello, S. J. (1981). Catastrophe modeling of equity in organizations. *Behavioral Science, 26,* 63–74.

Guastello, S. J. (1987). A butterfly catastrophe model of motivation in organization: Academic performance. *Journal of Applied Psychology, 72,* 165–182.

Guastello, S. J. (1988). Catastrophe modeling of the accident process: Organizational subunit size. *Psychological Bulletin, 103,* 246–255.

Guastello, S. J. (1995). *Chaos, catastrophe, and human affairs: Applications of nonlinear dynamics to work, organizations, and social evolution.* Mahwah NJ: Erlbaum.

Hamaker, E. L., Dolan, C. V., & Molenaar, P. C. M. (2005). Statistical modeling of the individual: rationale and application of multivariate stationary time series analysis. *Multivariate Behavioral Research, 40,* 207–233.

Hartelman, P. A., van der Maas, H. L. J., & Molenaar, P. C. M. (1998). Detecting and modelling developmental transitions. *British Journal of Developmental Psychology, 16,* 97–122.

Holland, J. H. (1995). *Hidden order: How adaptation builds complexity.* Reading, MA: Perseus.

Holland, J. H. (1998). *Emergence: From chaos to order.* Reading, MA: Helix Books/ Addison-Wesley.

Hosenfeld, B., van der Maas, H. L. J., & van den boom, D. C. (1997a). Detecting bimodality in the analogical reasoning performance of elementary schoolchildren. *International Journal of Behavioral Development, 20,* 529–547.

Hosenfeld, B., van der Maas, H. L. J., & van den Boom, D. C. (1997b). Indicators of discontinuous change in the development of analogical reasoning. *Journal of Experimental Child Psychology, 64,* 367–395.

Howe, M. L., & Lewis, M. D. (2005). The importance of dynamic systems approaches for understanding development. *Developmental Review, 25*, 247–251.

Hughes, C., & Ensor, R. (2007). Executive function and theory of mind: Predictive relations from ages 2 to 4. *Developmental Psychology, 43*, 1447–1459.

Immordino-Yang, M. H. (2005). A tale of two cases: Emotion and affective prosody after hemispherectomy. Doctoral dissertation, Harvard University. *Dissertation Abstracts International*, No. 2005-99022-194.

Immordino-Yang, M. H. (2007). A tale of two cases. Lessons for education from the study of two boys living with half their brains. *Mind, Brain and Education, 1*, 66–83.

Jansen, B. R. J., & van der Maas, H. L. J. (1997). Statistical test of the rule assessment methodology by latent class analysis. *Developmental Review, 17*, 321–357.

Jansen, B. R. J., & van der Maas, H. L. J. (2001). Evidence for the phase transition from rule I to rule II on the balance scale task. *Developmental Review, 21*, 450–494.

Jansen, B. R. J., & van der Maas, H. L. J. (2002). The development of children's rule use on the balance scale task. *Journal of Experimental Child Psychology, 81*, 383–416.

Johnston, V. S. (2003). The origin and function of pleasure. *Cognition & Emotion, 17*, 167–179.

Jones, S. S. J., & Smith, L. B. (2002). How children know the relevant properties for generalizing object names. *Developmental Science, 5*, 219–232.

Kail, R. V. (2001). *Children and their development* (2nd ed.). Englewood Cliffs, NJ: Prentice-Hall.

Kersten, A. W., & Smith, L. B. (2002). Attention to novel objects during verb learning. *Child Development, 73*, 93–109.

Knudsen, E. I. (2004). Sensitive periods in the development of the brain and behavior. *Journal of Cognitive Neuroscience, 16*, 1412–1425.

Koch, S. (1941). The logical character of the motivation concept. II. *Psychological Review, 48*, 127–154.

Kolb, B., & Whishaw, I. Q. (1998). Brain plasticity and behavior. *Annual Review of Psychology, 49*, 43–64.

Laland, K. N., Odling-Smee, J., & Feldman, M. W. (2000). Niche construction, biological evolution, and cultural change. *Behavioral and Brain Sciences, 23*, 131–175.

Leary, M. R. (2007). Motivational and emotional aspects of the self. *Annual Review of Psychology, 58*, 317–344.

LeDoux, J. E. (1996). *The emotional brain: The mysterious underpinnings of emotional life.* New York: Simon & Schuster.

Lerner, R. M. (2006). *Developmental science, developmental systems, and contemporary theories of human development.* Hoboken, NJ: Wiley.

Lewin, K. (1936). *Principles of topological psychology.* New York and London: McGraw-Hill.

Lewin, K. (1946). *Behavior and development as a function of the total situation.* Hoboken, NJ: Wiley.

Lewis, M. D. (2005a). Self-organizing individual differences in brain development. *Developmental Review, 25*, 252–277.

Lewis, M. D. (2005b). Bridging emotion theory and neurobiology through dynamic systems modeling. *Behavioral and Brain Sciences, 28*, 169–245.

Lickliter, R., & Honeycutt, H. (2003). Developmental dynamics: Toward a biologically plausible evolutionary psychology. *Psychological Bulletin, 129*, 819–835.

McAlister, A., & Peterson, C. (2006). Mental playmates: Siblings, executive functioning and theory of mind. *British Journal of Developmental Psychology, 24*, 733–751.

Molenaar, P. C. M. (2004). A manifesto on psychology as idiographic science: Bringing the person back into scientific psychology, this time forever. *Measurement: Interdisciplinary Research & Perspectives, 2*, 201–218.

Munakata, Y., & McClelland, J. L. (2003). Connectionist models of development. *Developmental Science, 6*, 413–429.

Musher-Eizenman, D. R., Nesselroade, J. R., & Schmitz, B. (2002). Perceived control and academic performance: A comparison of high- and low-performing children on within-person change patterns. *International Journal of Behavioral Development, 26*, 540–547.

Nelson, C. A. (1999). Neural plasticity and human development. *Current Directions in Psychological Science, 8*, 42–45.

Newman, B. M., & Newman, P. R. (2006). *Development through life: A psychosocial approach*. Belmont, CA: Thomson Wadsworth.

Oyama, S., Griffiths, P. E., & Gray, R. D. (2001). *Cycles of contingency: Developmental systems and evolution*. Cambridge, MA: MIT Press.

Özçaliskan, S., & Goldin-Meadow, S. (2005). Gesture is at the cutting edge of early language development. *Cognition, 96*, B101–B113.

Panksepp, J. (2000). The riddle of laughter: Neural and psychoevolutionary underpinnings of joy. *Current Directions in Psychological Science, 9*, 183–186.

Pellicano, E. (2007). Links between theory of mind and executive function in young children with autism: Clues to developmental primacy. *Developmental Psychology, 43*, 974–990.

Peters, A. (2001). Filler syllables: What is their status in emerging grammar? *Journal of Child Language, 28*, 229–242.

Pienemann, M. (2007). Variation and dynamic systems in SLA. *Bilingualism: Language and Cognition, 10*, 43–45.

Pincus, D., & Guastello, S. J. (2005). Nonlinear dynamics and interpersonal correlates of verbal turn-taking patterns in a group therapy session. *Small Group Research, 36*, 635–677.

Quinlan, P. T., van der Maas, H. L. J., Jansen, B. R. J., Booij, O., & Rendell, M. (2007). Re-thinking stages of cognitive development: An appraisal of connectionist models of the balance scale task. *Cognition, 103*, 413–459.

Rose, S. P., & Fischer, K. W. (1998). Models and rulers in dynamical development. *British Journal of Developmental Psychology, 16*, 123–131.

Ruhland, R., & van Geert, P. (1998). Jumping into syntax: Transitions in the development of closed class words. *British Journal of Developmental Psychology, 16*, 65–95.

Russell, J. A. (2003). Core affect and the psychological construction of emotion. *Psychological Review, 110*, 145–172.

Ryalls, B. O., & Smith, L. B. (2000). Adult's acquisition of novel dimension words: Creating a semantic congruity effect. *Journal of General Psychology, 127*, 279–326.

Sameroff, A. J. (2000). Developmental systems and psychopathology. *Development and Psychopathology, 12*, 297–312.

Samuelson, L. K., & Smith, L. B. (2000). Grounding development in cognitive processes. *Child Development, 71*, 98–106.

Sandhofer, C. M., Smith, L. B., & Luo, J. (2000). Counting nouns and verbs in the input: Differential frequencies, different kinds of learning? *Journal of Child Language, 27*, 561–585.

Scheffer, M., & Carpenter, S. R. (2003). Catastrophic regime shifts in ecosystems: Linking theory to observation. *Trends in Ecology & Evolution, 18*, 648–656.

Scherer, K. R. (1999). Appraisal theory. In T. Dalgleish & M. J. Power (Eds.), *Handbook of cognition and emotion* (pp. 637–663). New York: Wiley.

Schlesinger, M., & Parisi, D. (2004). Beyond backprop: Emerging trends in connectionist models of development: An introduction. *Developmental Science, 7*, 131–132.

Schutte, A. R., & Spencer, J. P. (2002). Generalizing the dynamic field theory of the A-not-B error beyond infancy: Three-year-olds' delay- and experience-dependent location memory biases. *Child Development, 73*, 377–404.

Schutte, A. R., Spencer, J. P., & Schöner, G. (2003). Testing the dynamic field theory: Working memory for locations becomes more spatially precise over development. *Child Development, 74*, 1393–1417.

Seifert, K. L., & Hoffnung, R. J. (1991). *Child and adolescent development* (2nd ed.). Boston: Houghton Mifflin.

Shaw, R. (2001). Processes, acts, and experiences: Three stances on the problem of intentionality. *Ecological Psychology, 13*, 275–314.

Siegler, R. S. (2005). Children's learning. *American Psychologist, 60*, 769–778.

Sigelman, C. K., & Rider, E. A. (2006). *Life-span human development* (5th ed.). Belmont, CA: Thomson Wadsworth.

Smith, L. B. (2005). Cognition as a dynamic system: Principles from embodiment. *Developmental Review, 25*, 278–298.

Smith, L. B., Thelen, E., Titzer, R., & McLin, D. (1999). Knowing in the context of acting: The task dynamics of the A-not-B error. *Psychological Review, 106*, 235–260.

Spelke, E. S., & Kinzler, K. D. (2007). Core knowledge. *Developmental Science, 10*, 89–96.

Spencer, J. P., Smith, L. B., & Thelen, E. (2001). Tests of a dynamic systems account of the A-not-B error: The influence of prior experience on the spatial memory abilities of two-year-olds. *Child Development, 72*, 1327–1346.

Steenbeek, H., & van Geert, P. (2005). A dynamic systems model of dyadic interaction during play of two children. *European Journal of Developmental Psychology, 2*, 105–145.

Steenbeek. H., & van Geert, P. (2007). A dynamic systems approach to dyadic interaction in children: emotional expression, action, dyadic play, and sociometric status. *Developmental Review, 27*, 1–40.

Steenbeek. H., & van Geert, P. (2008). The empirical validation of a dynamic systems model of interaction: Do children of different sociometric statuses differ in their dyadic play interactions? *Developmental Science, 11*, 253–218.

Sugrue, L. P., Corrado, G. S., & Newsome, W. T. (2004). Matching behavior and the representation of value in the parietal cortex. *Science, 304*, 1782–1787.

Thelen, E., & Smith, L. (1994). *A dynamic systems approach to the development of cognition and action*. Cambridge: MIT Press.

Thelen, E., Schöner, G., Scheier, C., & Smith, L. B. (2001). The dynamics of embodiment: A field theory of infant perseverative reaching. *Behavioral & Brain Sciences, 24*, 1–86.

Thomae, H. (1959). Entwicklungsbegriff und entwicklungstheorie [The concept of development and developmental theory]. In R. Bergius & H. Thomae (Eds.), *Handbuch der Psychologie, Band 3: Entwicklungspsychologie [Handbook of psychology, part 3, developmental psychology]* (pp. 3–20). Göttingen: Verlag für Psychologie.

Thomas, M. S. C., & Johnson, M. H. (2006). The computational modeling of sensitive periods. *Developmental Psychobiology, 48*, 337–344.

Tschacher, W., & Haken, H. (2007). Intentionality in non-equilibrium systems? The functional aspects of self-organized pattern formation. *New Ideas in Psychology, 25*, 1–15.

Turner, G. F. W., & Thomas, H. (2002). Bridging the gap between theory and model: A reflection on the balance scale task. *Journal of Experimental Child Psychology, 81*, 466–481.

van der Maas, H. L. (1993). *Catastrophe analysis of stagewise cognitive development.* Unpublished doctoral dissertation, Faculty of Psychology, University of Amsterdam.

van der Maas, H. L. J., & Jansen, B. R. J. (2003). What response times tell of children's behavior on the balance scale task. *Journal of Experimental Child Psychology, 85*, 141–177.

van der Maas, H., Jansen, B., & Raijmakers, M. (2004). *Developmental patterns in proportional reasoning.* New York: Cambridge University Press.

Van Der Maas, H. L., & Molenaar, P. C. (1992). Stagewise cognitive development: An application of catastrophe theory. *Psychological Review, 99*, 395–417.

Van Dijk, M., & van Geert, P. (2005). Disentangling behavior in early child development: Interpretability of early child language and its effect on utterance length measures. *Infant Behavior & Development, 28*, 99–117.

Van Dijk, M., & van Geert, P. (2007). Wobbles, humps and sudden jumps: A case study of continuity, discontinuity and variability in early language development. *Infant and Child Development, 16*, 7–33.

van Geert, P. (1986). The concept of development. In P. van Geert (Ed.), *Theory building in developmental psychology* (pp. 3–50). Amsterdam: North Holland.

van Geert, P. (1987a). The structure of developmental theories: A generative approach. *Human Development, 30*, 160–177.

van Geert, P. (1987b). The concept of development and the structure of developmental theories. In W. J. Baker & M. E. Hyland (Eds.), *Current issues in theoretical psychology: Selected/edited proceedings of the founding conference of the International Society for Theoretical Psychology held in Plymouth, U.K., 30 August–2 September, 1985* (pp. 379–392). Oxford: North-Holland.

van Geert, P. (1991). A dynamic systems model of cognitive and language growth. *Psychological Review, 98*, 3–53.

van Geert, P. (1994). *Dynamic systems of development. Change between complexity and chaos.* Hertfordshire, England: Harvester Wheatsheaf.

van Geert, P. (1995). Dimensions of change: A semantic and mathematical analysis of learning and development. *Human Development, 38*, 322–331.

van Geert, P. (1998a). A dynamic systems model of basic developmental mechanisms: Piaget, Vygotsky, and beyond. *Psychological Review, 105*, 634–677.

van Geert, P. (1998b). We almost had a great future behind us: The contribution of nonlinear dynamics to developmental-science-in-the-making. *Developmental Science, 1*, 143–159.

van Geert, P. (2000). The dynamics of general developmental mechanisms: From Piaget and Vygotsky to dynamic systems models. *Current Directions in Psychological Science, 9*, 64–68.

van Geert, P. (2002). Developmental dynamics, intentional action and fuzzy sets. In N. Granott & J. Parziale (Eds.), *Microdevelopmental clues: Transition processes in development and learning* (pp. 319–343). Cambridge: Cambridge University Press.

van Geert, P. (2003). Dynamic systems approaches and modeling of developmental processes. In J. Valsiner & K. J. Conolly (Eds.), *Handbook of developmental psychology* (pp. 640–672). London: Sage.

van Geert, P. L. C., & Fischer, K. W. (in press). Dynamic systems and the quest for individual-based models of change and development. In J. P. Spencer, M. S. C. Thomas, & J. McClelland (Eds.), *Toward a new grand theory of development? Connectionism and dynamic systems theory re-considered.* Oxford: Oxford University Press.

van Geert, P. L. C., Savelsbergh, G., & van der Maas, H. (1999). Transitions and non-linear dynamics in developmental psychology. In G. Savelsbergh, H. van der Maas, & P. L. C. van Geert (Eds.), *Non-linear developmental processes* (pp. 11–20). New York: Elsevier Science.

van Geert, P., & Steenbeek, H. (2005). Explaining after by before. Basic aspects of a dynamic systems approach to the study of development. *Developmental Review, 25*, 408–402.

van Geert, P., & van Dijk, M. (2002). Focus on variability: New tools to study intra-individual variability in developmental data. *Infant Behavior & Development, 25*, 340–374.

van Geert, P. L.C., & van Dijk, M. (2003). Ambiguity in child language: the problem of inter-observer reliability in ambiguous observation data. *First Language, 23*, 259–284.

Van Orden, G. C. (2002). Nonlinear dynamics and psycholinguistics. *Ecological Psychology, 14*, 1–4.

Van Orden, G. C., & Holden, J. G. (2002). Intentional contents and self-control. *Ecological Psychology, 14*, 87–109.

Van Orden, G. C., Holden, J. G., & Turvey, M. T. (2005). Human cognition and $1/f$ scaling. *Journal of Experimental Psychology: General, 134*, 117–123.

van Rijn, H., van Someren, M., & van der Maas, H. (2003). Modeling developmental transitions on the balance scale task. *Cognitive Science: A Multidisciplinary Journal, 27*, 227–257.

Vargha-Khadem, F., Carr, L. J., Isaacs, E., & Brett, E. (1997). Onset of speech after left hemispherectomy in a nine-year-old boy. *Brain: A Journal of Neurology, 120*, 159–182.

Vasta, R., Haith, M. M., & Miller, S. A. (1995). *Child psychology: The modern science* (2nd ed.). Oxford: Wiley.

Waldrop, M. M. (1992). *Complexity: The emerging science at the edge of order and chaos.* London: Penguin.

Weisstein, E. W. (1999). *CRC concise encyclopedia of mathematics.* Boca Raton, FL: Chapman & Hall/CRC.

Wimmers, R. H., Beek, P. J., & Savelsbergh, G. J. P. (1998). Developmental changes in action: Theoretical and methodological issues. *British Journal of Developmental Psychology, 16*, 45–63.

Wimmers, R. H., Beek, P. J., & Van Wieringen, P. C. (1992). Phase transitions in rhythmic tracking movements: A case of unilateral coupling. *Human Movement Science, 11*, 217–226.

Wimmers, R. H., Savelsbergh, G. J. P., Beek, P. J., & Hopkins, B. (1998). Evidence for a phase transition in the early development of prehension. *Developmental Psychobiology, 32*, 235–248.

Wimmers, R. H., Savelsbergh, G. J. P., van der Kamp, J., & Hartelman, P. (1998). A developmental transition in prehension modeled as a cusp catastrophe. *Developmental Psychobiology, 32*, 23–35.

Yoshida, H., & Smith, L. B. (2001). Early noun lexicons in English and Japanese. *Cognition*, B63–B74.

9 Developmental Psychopathology: Maladaptive and Adaptive Attractors in Children's Close Relationships

ERIKA S. LUNKENHEIMER AND THOMAS J. DISHION

Introduction

Routine, day-to-day interactions form the fabric of our interpersonal experience. A mother and her toddler, for example, might have a number of difficult moments in any given day as they jointly navigate the child's newly developing autonomy (e.g., the child wants to play with a forbidden toy). On the other hand, the majority of the day will typically be spent speaking about more neutral topics, such as eating, cleaning up, and getting dressed. Historically, clinical researchers have focused on more atypical, maladaptive interactions between children and their parents or peers, with the goal of reducing these aversive interactions. These maladaptive interactions are important. For example, negative interpersonal interchanges, in moderation, may allow for reflection and insight, offering important opportunities for adaptive change in relationships (Dunn & Brown, 1994; Lunkenheimer, Shields, & Cortina, 2007). However, they are also rare: Even with the most problematic children, observational researchers code only about 5% to 10% of family and peer interactions as aversive (Dishion, Duncan, Eddy, & Fagot, 1994). In contrast, adaptive neutral or positive interactions are not only more common, but we are more likely to observe them in the home and laboratory contexts. Further, an important goal of preventive intervention programs is to promote and build on existing adaptive interaction patterns in close personal relationships. Thus both adaptive and maladaptive interactions in close relationships should be of interest to clinical and developmental psychopathology researchers.

In this chapter, we argue that a nonlinear dynamical systems (NDS) framework offers an efficient and theoretically sound analysis of both adaptive and maladaptive interactions in children's close relationships, thereby improving our understanding of the development of psychopathology in children and adolescents. Moreover, NDS analysis of close relationships informs the design of efficient and effective preventive and clinical interventions, which most often target children's relationships. We first briefly review the study of maladaptive relationship influence in developmental psychopathology, focusing on coercion and peer deviancy research with regard to parent–child and child–peer relationships, respectively. We then address how NDS theory and principles (attractors in particular) add to the field of developmental psychopathology by informing research on relationship influence. Next, we address NDS methods and review empirical research that has used NDS methods to analyze maladaptive attractors to date. Subsequently, we offer new directions for the study of attractors in developmental psychopathology, proposing the notions that adaptive attractors and the study of attractors across contexts may hold untapped value for developmental and intervention scientists. Finally, we suggest some implications of NDS theory and methods for clinical interventions with children and their parents and peers.

Developmental Psychopathology

According to the principles of developmental psychopathology, human behavior is determined by multiple influences at various layers of the ecology (e.g., self, family, neighborhood, culture) that interact continually and dynamically (Cicchetti, 1993; Garmezy & Rutter, 1983; Sameroff, 1995). Developmental phenomena are thus conceptualized systemically because they are contextually dependent and organized hierarchically through integrated intrapersonal, interpersonal, and higher-order systemic processes. For example, one could imagine the process of a parent dealing with her child's behavior problem at school as embedded within many potential historical and environmental contexts, such as her own school involvement when she was a child, the culture of teacher–parent interactions at that particular school, and how she and her partner coparent in disciplining the child's behavior. In conceptualizing these sorts of contextual factors and their interrelations, the systemic approach to developmental psychopathology has been shaped by many theories, including general systems theory (Sameroff, 1995; von Bertalanffy, 1968), developmental systems theory (Ford & Lerner, 1992), the ecological framework (Bronfenbrenner, 1986), the transactional model (Sameroff & Chandler, 1975), the organizational approach (Cicchetti & Schneider-Rosen, 1986; Sroufe & Rutter, 1984), and the epigenetic view (Gottlieb, 1991).

A primary aim in developmental psychopathology is the study of individual differences in children's adaptive and maladaptive developmental trajectories, and the mechanisms that produce continuity and discontinuity in those trajectories. Therefore, when studying relationship influences, developmental psychopathologists examine how interactions in interpersonal relationships act as the mechanisms that contribute to children's adaptive versus maladaptive development. Research targeting these mechanisms has often involved the study of negative, aversive interactions in family and peer relationships, because these relationships act as the primary contexts for child development.

A prominent example of this research is the study of parent–child coercion. Coercion theory (Patterson & Reid, 1970) originated in the study of reciprocally aversive behaviors between mother and child and is based on a social learning perspective. Early analyses of parent–child interactions revealed that both participants were being mutually shaped to engage in aversive behavior through a combination of classical and operant conditioning. For example, a mother scolding a child for misbehavior can lead to the child's angry shouting. If the mother backs out of the interaction to stop the child's shouting, both participants are shaped by this behavior. The mother has been shaped to "give up" when the child becomes aversive, and the child has been shaped to become aversive again the next time the mother scolds or nags. The parent's negative reinforcement contributes to a positive feedback cycle whereby parent–child interactions become increasingly aversive and difficult to manage, leading to the escalation of children's underregulated, aggressive behaviors and the elevation of parental rejection over time (Patterson & Bank, 1989). This reciprocal causality between parent and child must be understood to inform how children emerge from such family interactions with serious antisocial behavior problems (Patterson, Reid, & Dishion, 1992) and effectively intervene with families to solve these problems (Patterson, 1982). According to coercion theory, these maladaptive interaction patterns between parents and children can also generalize across contexts to children's relationships with siblings, teachers, and peers.

Research linking parent–child coercion and children's problem behaviors over time (Patterson, 1986; Patterson, Capaldi, & Bank, 1991) has illustrated the importance of relationship influence on children's developmental psychopathology. Global ratings of parent–child relationship quality have predicted the development of disruptive behavior problems in early and middle childhood (Criss, Shaw, & Ingoldsby, 2003; Deater-Deckard, Atzaba-Poria, & Pike, 2004; Harrist, Pettit, Dodge, & Bates, 1994; Mize & Pettit, 1997). Aversive transactions of mutually negative affect have been observed across adolescence (Conger & Ge, 1999), with parents' and adolescents' expressed negativity predicting increases in the other's negativity in subsequent assessments (Kim, Conger, Lorenz, & Elder, 2001). In fact, experimental research has shown that mothers of conduct-disordered children express more negative affect with their own children than with unfamiliar conduct-disordered children, indicating that emotions and behaviors are entrenched in past relationship history (Anderson, Lytton, & Romney, 1986).

The social learning perspective and the role of negative reinforcement in coercion theory originally prompted a methodological focus on contingency (i.e., action–reaction) patterns in microsocial interaction. Thus developmental psychopathologists have also studied relationship influence by examining contingency patterns in real time (in seconds or minutes) in relation to child development. For example, Dumas, LaFreniere, and Serketich (1995) examined group differences in sequential chains of affect and behavior in early mother–child interactions involving socially competent, anxious, or aggressive children (2.5–6 years). Competent children and their mothers showed more positive, reciprocal chains, with firm limit setting in the face of coercive attempts. Aggressive children made more coercive control attempts, and their mothers responded with indiscriminant affect and failures in limit setting, as coercion theory would predict. Cole, Teti, and Zahn-Waxler (2003) examined self-initiated and contingent affect in mother–child interactions at age 5 in relation to change in children's conduct problems between 5 and 7 years of age. Mothers' contingent angry emotional responses were uncommon but still contributed to stability in children's behavior problems over time, whereas mothers' positive contingent responses predicted reduced levels of child problems.

Research on peer relationships in adolescence has also illustrated the effects of maladaptive, real-time interactions in close relationships on developmental outcomes. Dishion, Andrews, and Crosby (1995) examined adolescent friendship interactions and their influence on adolescents' problem behavior. Initial coding of hundreds of interaction patterns with a topographic coding system (e.g., converse, negative engagement, positive engagement, and directives) revealed that a vast majority (more than 70%) could be described as simply "converse," or neutral verbal conversation. This pattern was not particularly useful for understanding individual differences in the development of serious antisocial behavior in adolescence (Dishion, Andrews, et al., 1995). Thus a new coding system was designed that captured the salient features of the conversation topics used in adolescent friendships. Two topics were identified, deviant talk and normative talk, and two reactions were also identified, "laugh" and "pause." With only these four codes, Dishion and colleagues explained considerable variation in adolescent outcomes such as drug use (Dishion, Capaldi, Spracklen, & Li, 1995), delinquency (Dishion, Spracklen, Andrews, & Patterson, 1996), and violence (Dishion, Eddy, Haas, & Li, 1997) with a process they called *deviancy training.*

For example, in testing the peer deviancy training model of how adolescents' involvement with deviant peers affects their development, Dishion et al. (1996) examined whether friends' contingent, positive reactions (e.g., laughter) to the target child's deviant talk influenced the development of problem behavior. Contingencies between two proximal behaviors (i.e., lag 1 contingencies from t_n to t_{n+1}) across the interaction can be quantified by a Z score (Gottman & Roy, 1990). When two behaviors reliably covary in time, the Z score index is greater than 1.96. Using this approach, findings supported the hypothesis that friends mutually influenced one another through laughter contingent on deviant talk (Dishion et al., 1996). In general, adolescents tended to match their level of deviant talk to the relative rate of reinforcement, a principle referred to as *matching law* (see McDowell, 1988). These deviant interactions predicted increases in adolescents' self-reported delinquent behavior over a 2-year period, providing support for the ongoing importance of proximal interactions into adolescence.

As these examples illustrate, we have learned a good deal about the role of maladaptive relationship influence in developmental psychopathology to date, and we have the theories to guide further research in the realms of coercive family process and deviant peer interactions. This is fitting, because intervention programs target the reduction of aggressive, antisocial behaviors, and thus a comprehensive model for the development of such behaviors is essential. However, interventions also aim to increase adaptive relationship patterns, and thus developmental psychopathology research also relies on an understanding of adaptive and normative developmental processes. The field's predominant focus on the continuity of maladaptive processes has diverted needed attention away from its emphasis on change, discontinuity, and adaptation for the purposes of prevention (Granic & Patterson, 2006).

Despite the evidence that contingent, dyadic interaction sequences play a role in the development of child psychopathology, there are also methodological limitations in the sequential analysis of microsocial interactions. First, as previously stated, the low base rate of negative behaviors expressed during observational assessments (Dishion et al., 1994) makes the study of positive and neutral behaviors a needed complement to this research. Second, the quantitative framework of sequential analysis may be limited by the manner in which codes are defined (e.g., on a dyadic or individual level), and the number of events within a sequence will affect the magnitude of the Z score representing relationships among these events (Bakeman & Quera, 1995). Third and most important, sequential analysis misses some important properties of a relationship as an evolving and changing system. An operative assumption in sequential analysis is that the contingency between partners' behaviors is stationary or linear, meaning that it remains the same during the course of an observation. However, it is the changing patterns of interaction over time that are of interest when studying a close relationship as a system. For instance, subtle, gradual adjustments such as a wink, smile, or roll of the eyes can lead to the emergence of a new interaction pattern that repeats itself and can have meaning for a close relationship that goes far beyond the tit-for-tat details. It is precisely these sorts of nonlinear interaction patterns that may help illuminate the individual differences in development that developmental psychopathologists study.

Finally, there is a vital, overarching feature of relationship processes that developmental psychopathologists have not yet fully captured: the interrelations among different developmental scales (Granic & Hollenstein, 2003; Granic & Patterson, 2006; Lewis, 2000), whether they are time scales (from real time in seconds to developmental time in years) or nested scales of the ecological context (from the molecular to the cultural). These scales are interdependent; for instance, more macroscopic patterns in the family such as family routines (e.g., a mother working the night shift) might shape more microscopic parent–child dynamics (e.g., the child's behavior problems with his father at bedtime), which in turn might contribute to changes at the macroscopic level (e.g., marital discussion that results in new parental work schedules). If we then analyze parental work status and child behavior problems as two separate variables with a linear relationship, we have missed this fluid interdependency across time and relational context. Although extant research has provided evidence for a link between processes on different scales (e.g., real and developmental time), we need to move beyond representing these scales as separate entities and work toward the direct analysis of their interrelationship.

Application of NDS Theory to Developmental Psychopathology

The application of NDS theory to the study of relationship influence in developmental psychopathology allows for the direct analysis of dynamic interrelations across scales of time and context. This is because NDS theory conceptualizes developmental phenomena as dynamic systems governed by the principle of self-organization (discussed in detail later). By treating a close relationship as a dynamic system that self-organizes, we have a theoretical foundation with which to understand the structure, organization, and patterning of the relationship within and across time and context. An NDS approach also offers corresponding empirical tools for researchers to analyze more effectively the whole of the relationship as a system. These tools allow for the direct study of the interrelations between real and developmental time, for example, or the study of nonlinear pattern shifts during the course of a given interaction. Consequently, a major benefit of an NDS approach to developmental psychopathology is that it provides researchers with the opportunity to study individual differences in these structural and organizational patterns to determine how these facets of the relationship influence trajectories of child development.

The application of NDS theory to developmental phenomena draws on dynamic and nonlinear systems theories in disciplines such as biology, physics, and mathematics. Many developmental theorists and scientists have paved the way for the application of NDS to developmental psychopathology by arguing for related systemic and process-based accounts of developmental phenomena (Gottlieb, 1997; Kantor & Smith, 1975; Sameroff & Chandler, 1975; Schneirla, 1957; Werner, 1948, 1957). Thus, in many respects, an NDS approach to development builds on a body of successful interdisciplinary behavioral science approaches.

In describing developmental phenomena from an NDS perspective, Thelen and Smith (1994, 1998) argued that developmental changes are, at their core, qualitatively discontinuous or novel and that such novelty emerges from within the system itself through processes of *self-organization*. In other words, the interactions within a complex system produce pattern and order without explicit instruction to do so. A system may be bound at various levels; for example, the self is a system that encompasses multiple intrapersonal processes (e.g., emotional, cognitive, biological) geared toward development. Any given dyad (e.g., parent and child) is also a system, as are broader ecological contexts (e.g., a school district) and more microscopic internal processes (e.g., the neurological substrates of language production). Although self-organizing, these developmental systems are also *open systems* because they draw in information from the surrounding environment to increase this internal order or organization. This is in contrast to a *closed system* in which information is not absorbed from the surrounding environment.

Many different components make up a dynamic, developmental system, and they operate interdependently and continually on scales of both ecology (i.e., from the molecular to the cultural) and time (i.e., from milliseconds to years; Thelen & Smith, 1998). Although theoretically these diverse components could interact in millions of potential ways, the actual number of ways in which they relate to one another is constrained. Through self-organization, hierarchical integration emerges, with certain integrative variables (termed *order parameters*) organizing the behavior of the system into a small number of preferred states or adaptive modes of behavior. These behavioral states that the system settles into are called *attractors*, in that the system is "attracted to" a particular state under certain conditions. In this way, microlevel components of the system organize and constrain macrolevel organizational processes, and vice versa.

Initially, microlevel elements of the system couple and then attract behavior away from other potential states in real time. Therefore attractors are these patterns of interactions between elements of the system that become stable over developmental time. Open, living systems are characterized by multistability, in which there are multiple possible attractors in the system, some deeper or shallower than others. The deeper or more stable the attractor, the more likely that behavior will enter it, remain there, and prove resistant to perturbations from the environment. By definition, attractors should represent relatively frequent events because they are the key dynamics underlying a developmental process. Attractors are also contextually dependent (Granic & Patterson, 2006) because they are situated in a complex, multilayered ecology of development and are shaped by a history of prior interactions between the given elements. Therefore self-organization in real time and developmental time scales regulate and constrain each other: Individual elements and dyadic patterns between elements are products of past recurring dyadic interactions, which then go on to constrain future dyadic behavioral repertoires (Cicchetti & Toth, 1997; Dumas & LaFreniere, 1995).

Relationships as Nonlinear Dynamical Systems

Interpersonal relationships are self-organizing in that they produce ordered patterns that can be characterized using multiple NDS principles, as illustrated in this volume and elsewhere (Dumas, Lemay, & Dauwalder, 2001; Lewis, 2000; Pincus & Guastello, 2005). At present, we focus specifically on how attractors can be used to characterize relationship patterns. As applied to a relationship, an attractor is a systemic tendency for a dyad to get "stuck" in an exchange pattern that unfolds over time (Fogel, 1993; Fogel & Thelen, 1987). With repetitive exposure, these interactions may become deeper and deeper behavioral attractors, in the context of which it becomes more difficult to induce or experience change (Hollenstein, Granic, Stoolmiller, & Snyder, 2004; Lewis, 2000). Individual and dyadic systems therefore become more entrenched and organized, and less activation is needed to trigger these attractors over time (Granic, 2000).

Correspondingly, the relationship system involves the coupling of elements within microsocial interactions, as in when a parent's particular behavioral state (e.g., hostility) is coupled with a particular behavioral state of his or her child (e.g., withdrawal). For example, a father comes home from work exhausted and stressed, sees that his child's room is a mess, and tells him in an irritated tone to clean it up. The child responds to this aversive tone by ignoring his father and continuing to play his video game. The father becomes angry and yells at his son that he never listens to him. The son becomes equally angry and locks himself in his room for the rest of the night. These behaviors or elements of the system repeatedly interact to reproduce this sequence, which then serves as one of the attractor states that organizes the behavioral repertoire of this dyad over time. Another relevant example, as discussed previously, is the coupling of deviant talk and laughter in maladaptive adolescent peer interactions (Dishion et al., 1996). This attractor then shapes the available range of behaviors within the adolescent peer relationship in which deviant behavior is the preferred and rewarded state.

As illustrated by these examples, proximal, real-time microsocial interaction processes in interpersonal relationships are the engines of human development (Bronfenbrenner & Morris, 1998; Fogel & Thelen, 1987). In fact, many researchers have espoused the notion that development is essentially relational in nature (Diamond & Aspinwall, 2003; Fogel, 1993; Laible & Thompson, 2000). The relationship between the child and his or her environment is an active, self-organizing system in which stability is found not only in the individual but also in the processes by which traits are upheld by transactions between the child and the context (Sameroff & MacKenzie, 2003). A transaction between individuals involves a novel qualitative or quantitative change (Sameroff & Chandler, 1975), but subsequently this new dynamic between elements evolves into an attractor over time (Thelen & Smith, 1994). Thus real-time, microlevel interaction processes drive the formation of attractors, which characterize the macrolevel organization of the system, or the relationship within which the interaction lies (Dumas et al., 2001; Pincus, 2001).

Accordingly, one can see how the attractor principle is especially useful for our study of relationship influence in developmental psychopathology. Unfortunately, the lack of appropriate methodologies has caused these processes to remain understudied in the field at large (Hinshaw, 2002). With this in mind, we now address some burgeoning NDS analytic methods and discuss how they have been applied to the study of attractors in developmental psychopathology.

NDS Analytic Methods in Developmental Psychopathology

An NDS approach provides an important methodological alternative to the study of microsocial interactions of relationship processes (Granic & Hollenstein, 2003; Granic & Patterson, 2006). Thelen and Smith (1994, 1998) defined interlinking steps in an NDS-based methodological strategy for the study of developmental phenomena:

1. Identify the collective variable of interest: An observable phenomenon that captures the interrelatedness of diverse systemic elements must be identified. For example, with regard to the development of self-regulation, one might study the most prevalent exchange pattern in the inter-coordination of biological arousal, cognitive appraisal, and emotional expression.

2. Describe the attractors of the system: Look at how the system operates with respect to the collective variable at a descriptive level. For example, map the real-time trajectory of parent–child coregulatory patterns to understand their relative stability and instability across various contexts and developmental stages. High stability across contexts or developmental time would indicate an attractor.

3. Map the individual developmental trajectories of the collective variable: Determine whether individual variation in the collective variable over repeated assessments (or in the case of dyadic research, between-dyad variation in attractor states) is associated with developmental pathways. For example, consider whether a pattern of joint attention and engagement in parent–child interaction could contribute to individual differences in children's language development.

4. Identify phase transitions in development: Phase transitions occur when the underlying pattern of interaction shifts to another pattern under predictable conditions. When one can predict phase transitions in social interaction, both the method with which an interaction dynamic can be changed and the relevant control parameters become clearer. For example, if a talk–listen exchange pattern in a parent–adolescent dyad predictably shifts into a hostile exchange attractor when discussing problems within their relationship, it is a predictable phase transition, and appraised conflict is the control parameter.

5. Identify control parameters: As discussed in the previous step, the control parameters are the nonlinear agents or mechanisms of change in the system (see Thelen & Ulrich, 1991). Identification of the control

parameter is the critical step in determining whether a pattern can be changed through intervention.

6. Manipulate control parameters to generate phase transitions experimentally: Following from the prior step, we must subsequently test whether hypothesized mechanisms of change do, in fact, produce the expected shift in behavior. For some time, it has been acknowledged that the behavioral sciences lack rigor with respect to intervention experiments that test hypothesized relationships (Cook & Campbell, 1979; Dishion & Patterson, 1999).

These steps offer a research strategy with respect to NDS methods that, if followed, would facilitate great improvements over more traditional methodologies. As illustrated in these guidelines, one aims first to identify an attractor within microlevel behaviors and then link this attractor to longer-term developmental trajectories. This necessarily involves the measurement of behaviors on at least two time scales: real time (e.g., in seconds or minutes) and developmental time (e.g., over weeks or years). Several innovations in the visualization and measurement of microsocial interactions have been developed that allow for the study of developmental processes across different time scales. For example, one may use Fourier analysis to illustrate cyclic patterns in time series data (Newtson, 1994, 1998), Karnaugh maps to represent event frequencies of combinations of binary variables (Dumas et al., 2001), or dynamic growth modeling to match simulations derived from logistic difference equations to observed longitudinal data (van der Maas & Molenaar, 1992; van Geert, 1994, 1995). In this chapter, we focus on one particular methodology, state space grids (SSGs; Lewis, Lamey, & Douglas, 1999) because it holds significant promise. For a broader review of the application of NDS methods to developmental psychopathology, see Granic and Hollenstein (2003).

According to NDS theory, a *state space* is a concept used to reflect the range of behaviors or possible states for a given system. Behavior moves along a trajectory in the state space in real time, and this trajectory is pulled toward certain attractors (stable behavioral patterns) and away from others. Lewis et al. (1999) developed the SSG, a graphical approach that uses observational data and quantifies the data according to two ordinal variables that define the state space for any particular system (see Fig. 9.1 for an example). For instance, these two behavioral variables might consist of parent positive affect on the x-axis and child positive affect on the y-axis, each coded at three levels (e.g., low, medium, and high), resulting in a 3 by 3– cell grid. Each point on the trajectory that moves throughout the grid then represents dyadic information about the joint affect of parent and child (e.g., parent is low positive, and child is high positive) in that particular time interval. Alternatively, instead of levels of a particular behavior, cells may represent different behaviors such as positive affect, negative affect, neutral conversation, and directives (see Fig. 9.2).

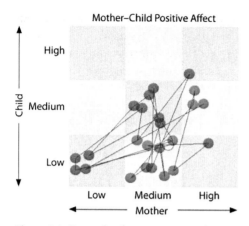

Figure 9.1. Example of a state space grid.

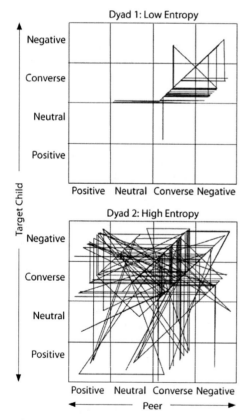

Figure 9.2. State space grids: High (upper) and low (lower) entropy friendship dyads in adolescence.

Investigators working within an NDS framework have used SSGs to look at several structural features of relationship interactions to date, described in more detail later in the chapter. For example, the analysis of behavioral rigidity and its converse, flexibility, is of interest to developmental psychopathologists because these features have been linked to mental health outcomes (Hollenstein, Granic, Stoolmiller, & Snyder, 2004). The extent to which the interaction is organized and predictable versus chaotic and unpredictable is captured through an SSG-based computation of *entropy* (Attneave, 1959; Dishion, Nelson, Winter, & Bullock, 2004). Both rigidity and entropy are related to the concept of an *attractor;* for example, a dyadic attractor could consist of a rigid interaction pattern during which the dyad's behavior remains in only one or two affective states. However, despite the advantages of using SSGs to study attractors, the field of developmental psychopathology has yet to converge on the exact nature of an attractor, its computation, or a formal stochastic test (Lewis, 2000).

Several researchers have successfully used SSGs to identify dynamic patterns of parent–child flexibility and rigidity as key factors in the early emergence of psychopathology in children and adolescents (Granic, 2000; Granic, Hollenstein, Dishion, & Patterson, 2003). For example, Hollenstein et al. (2004) examined the effect of dyadic parent–child rigidity at the beginning of the kindergarten year on the development of children's externalizing and internalizing behavior problems across kindergarten and first grade. Externalizing problems are disruptive problems of underregulation, such as hyperactivity, impulsivity, emotional lability, and aggression, whereas internalizing problems are problems of maladaptive overregulation, such as anxiety, fear, and depression (Achenbach, 1990). These researchers found that parent–child rigidity predicted the child's inclusion in the "consistently high" and "increasing" externalizing groups and the "consistently high" internalizing group of children during the course of four assessments. Further, the effect of rigidity remained after controlling for the content of the interaction. These findings point to the utility of SSGs for illuminating the effects of real-time dynamic interaction structure on change in child development over time.

Granic and Dishion (2003) were the first to apply SSGs to the analysis of adolescent peer deviancy training. They used a time series approach to the identification of attractors. That is, if two individuals become stuck in a deviant talk attractor, the amount of time they spent discussing that topic should get increasingly longer during an observation session; thus the "duration of bouts" was used as an index of an attractor. These authors derived a slope score from the length of deviant talk bouts over the course of the session, with a positive slope indicating that bout length increased throughout the session. This slope score not only differentiated problem from nonproblem youth as measured concurrently but also predicted individual differences in adolescent outcomes 3 years later, such as authority conflict (arrests, school expulsions, etc.) and drug abuse. This was the first study to link individual differences in the display of an attractor to individual differences in adolescent development over the course of several years.

Following up on this work, Dishion et al. (2004) applied SSGs to the analysis of adolescent friendship interactions in the Oregon Youth Study by examining deviant talk bouts and entropy in dyadic exchanges. The construct of entropy is drawn from Shannon's work in information theory (Shannon & Weaver, 1949). Transitions in events are conceptualized as units of information, and the information system can range from being organized and predictable to complex and uncertain. The general idea is that less information is needed to predict reactions from the actions in a low-entropy dyad compared with a high-entropy dyad. Dishion et al. (2004) used Attneave's (Attneave, 1959; Krippendorff, 1986) computation of Shannon entropy, in which entropy (H) is computed simply by considering the distribution of conditional probabilities within an action–reaction transition matrix. Therefore, an organized dyad would have a transition matrix low in entropy (H), and its SSG would show a few cells that were heavily used and many other cells that remained empty (see Fig. 9.2 upper). Conversely, an unpredictable dyad would have a transition matrix high in entropy where all conditional cells would be equivalently probable (see Figure 9.2 lower).

Dishion et al. (2004) attempted to explain variation in antisocial behavior of 200 men at age 24 by observing 30 min of interaction with their friends when study participants were age 13. After controlling for the boys' prior antisocial behavior, they found that the duration of deviant talk bouts significantly predicted antisocial behavior 10 years later. Although entropy did not show a main effect, the interaction term between entropy and deviant talk was significant. As one would expect, adolescents who were both organized in their interaction patterns (low entropy) and engaged in high levels of deviant talk content were those who showed the highest levels of antisocial behavior as young adults. Thus as a result of a dyadic friendship system that was organized around deviance, individual outcomes were highly problematic.

Figure 9.2 shows the SSGs for two dyads from this study. Each grid displays the interactions of the friendship dyad throughout the 30-min observation session, using the codes *positive engagement* (e.g., compliment, praise), *directives* (e.g., command, requests), *negative engagement* (e.g., criticism, blame), and *converse* (e.g., calm talk, discussions). A visual inspection of these SSGs reveals an obvious difference between the dyads in the organization of the dyadic exchange. Even though both interactions had approximately the same number of events, one dyad restricted interactions to one area of the grid, whereas the other appeared more disorganized and complex. Friends who had long, uninterrupted conversations in the converse–converse area of the grid were the most likely to be quantified as having a low-entropy interaction. However, it should be noted that this dynamic structural facet of the interaction did not convey the content of their exchange. These findings elucidate that to understand the influence of close relationship interactions on development, it is important to study the interplay between their content and their dynamic structure.

In summary, these studies demonstrate the possibilities available through the use of an NDS approach, and specifically, how important the study of attractors in close personal relationships is to our understanding of children's maladaptive developmental trajectories. Clearly, negative interactions appear to have a distinct and powerful organizing function (Granic & Dishion, 2003), and both the content and structure of these interactions are important for determining future problem behaviors (Dishion et al., 2004). However, these studies also raise questions about how dynamic systems indices of positive and neutral aspects of microsocial interaction relate to individual differences in children's developmental psychopathology. In addition, the analysis of dynamic interaction patterns as they evolve and change across relationship contexts is implicated in the study of flexibility and rigidity, yet this research has rarely been conducted. The remainder of this chapter addresses these issues by offering some new directions for the study of attractors in developmental psychopathology and by examining the possible application of NDS principles and methods to the study of adaptive attractors for the purposes of intervention.

New Directions in the Study of Attractors

Adaptive Attractors

As previously described, there are multiple potential attractors in the behavioral landscape of a relationship, as delineated by the NDS principle of multistability. Thus rather than focus on only aversive exchanges in family interactions, which are low base rate by nature, one can look more broadly at all interactions in the family and how aversive interactions are related to positive, neutral, or other significant behaviors. This is an extremely important point. Considering that negative interactions make up only about 5% to 10% of all coded family or peer interactions even within clinical populations (Patterson, 1982), it is difficult to study repeated, aversive patterns except in the most dysfunctional family systems.

Researchers have been calling for closer study of positive parent–child interactions and their role in distinguishing children's normative and atypical developmental trajectories for some time (e.g., Gardner, 1987, 1992; Pettit, Bates, & Dodge, 1997). Research indicates that conduct-problem children spend less time in joint play and conversation with their parents than do nonproblem children (Gardner, 1987). However, when they do engage in contingent, positive interactions, these interactions are protective against the development of problem behaviors (Cole et al., 2003). For example, Lunkenheimer, Olson, and Kaciroti (2007) found that the time-lagged coregulation of positive affect between parents and their 3-year-old children, specifically children's positive responses to their mothers and fathers, predicted lower levels of externalizing behavior problems across the transition to school.

We know even less about how more neutral attractors, such as the converse–converse attractor mentioned previously, contribute to individual differences

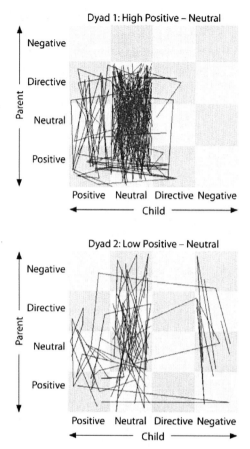

Figure 9.3. Parent–preschooler dyads that are high (upper) and low (lower) in the proportional duration of positive–neutral interaction.

in child development. Lunkenheimer, Dishion, and Winter (2008) have found preliminary evidence to support the notion that positive and neutral attractors play a role in children's adaptive and maladaptive developmental outcomes. In a study involving yearly assessments with parents and their children beginning at age 2 years, parent–child dyads were observed interacting in the home during a variety of tasks (e.g., free play, clean-up, inhibition tasks) and were coded for positive, neutral, negative, and directive behaviors. These behaviors were then mapped onto an SSG. These researchers tested whether the proportional duration of time the dyad spent engaged in joint positive and neutral affect at child age 2 years predicted child outcomes at age 4. Figure 9.3 provides examples of a parent–child dyad that spent a high proportion of the interaction in this quadrant (upper panel) and another dyad that spent a proportionally low time there (lower panel). The proportional duration of dyadic positive–neutral interaction predicted children's language ($\Delta R^2 = .03$, $p < .001$), inhibitory control ($\Delta R^2 = .03$, $p < .001$), and externalizing behavior problems ($\Delta R^2 = .01$, $p < .01$) across this formative developmental period (Lunkenheimer et al., 2008). Although preliminary, these findings point to the need for more NDS analysis of positive and neutral attractors and their role in children's developmental psychopathology.

Attractors Across Contexts

Another important new direction for NDS approaches to the study of close relationships and developmental psychopathology is to pursue a more comprehensive overview of attractors across contexts. In other words, how do the particular content or goal of the interaction (e.g., problem solving vs. play) and the particular relationship in question (e.g., parent vs. peer vs. teacher) influence the development of attractor patterns and their associated outcomes? Although NDS theorists have argued for the importance of understanding attractors across contexts (Thelen & Smith, 1994, 1998), we have little empirical evidence to date with which to answer these questions. Perhaps the predominant focus on maladaptive attractors has made it difficult to assess the consistency and pervasiveness of relationship dynamics across contexts in the child's life because we typically see few of these interactions in observational research sessions. The study of adaptive attractors in close relationships may offer a broader window for examining how organizational properties of close relationships transfer across various relationship or environmental contexts in the child's life.

The evidence that has been gathered thus far suggests that attractors may shift depending on the goal of an interpersonal interaction. Granic and Lamey (2002) introduced perturbations to mother–child problem-solving interactions and considered the change in interaction structure in reaction to the perturbation for children defined as comorbid (having both externalizing and internalizing problems) versus those who were "pure" externalizers. They found that when the interaction changed from a problem-solving interaction to one in which the dyad had to "wrap up" and produce a solution, dyads that included comorbid children shifted from a permissive to a mutually hostile attractor. This shift did not occur for parents and children in the externalizing dyads, who remained permissive throughout the interaction despite the change in goal.

An NDS index of a relationship (e.g., entropy) may be significantly correlated across various interaction tasks, although from a conceptual perspective these tasks may be quite different. Consider, for instance, that a parent and adolescent are asked to solve an interpersonal conflict regarding the time the youth comes home in the evening. During this discussion, the dyad shifts in unison between negative and neutral bouts that are punctuated by humor. Indeed, humor functions as a release valve to promote a shift out of the negative–negative attractor to a more constructive discussion. Then, later, the dyad is asked to plan a family celebration. This particular task results in circular positive–neutral exchanges, with no negative bouts. The attractors derived from these two interactions look quite different, the first being more flexible (as they engaged in a wider array of affective states) and the second relatively rigid. However, both interactions are low in entropy in that even when the dyad shifted states, they did so in unison, much like two dancers shifting from the fox trot to the tango. More important, despite the fact that these interactions pull for different sorts of attractors, each is appropriately tailored to the specific goal of the interaction.

Therefore, in the study of developmental psychopathology, it is crucial to assess attractors in the context of varying interaction goals, and similarly in the context of various relationships. This is especially important in light of the field's emphasis on the role of self-regulation in individual differences in children's normative and atypical developmental trajectories (Cicchetti & Toth, 1997; Cole, Michel, & Teti, 1994; National Institute of Child Health and Human Development [NICHD], 2004). Ultimately, individuals are considered flexible or "well regulated" when they respond to changing interpersonal contexts in diverse ways, and rigid when they apply the same interpersonal strategy across interpersonal contexts, regardless of whether it is optimal. For example, if we were to learn that a child with behavior problems typically engages in a rigid, maladaptive attractor with her mother, but not with her father or teacher, it might inform our basic understanding of the problem: The mechanism underlying her behavior might be her relationship with her mother rather than generalized self-regulatory difficulties. In an applied example, imagine if this maladaptive attractor presents itself when the mother and child are discussing her academic performance, but not her artwork or her peer relationships; a clinician's awareness of these distinctions could offer points of entry in designing an intervention to improve their relationship. Incorporating these and other considerations, an improved relationship science would make sense of the contextual differences in peer and family relationships and provide a comprehensive framework for studying relationship influence within and across these contexts.

Implications for Intervention Science

A critical concern for developmental psychopathologists is the application of knowledge of basic developmental processes toward intervention, in an effort to change developmental outcomes. Although relationship dynamics are not the only cause of child psychopathology, they may be particularly critical to the solution in the context of family treatment (Dishion & Patterson, 2006). Typical family intervention strategies often involve the treatment of multiple aspects of the family system simultaneously in an effort to alter or ameliorate the child's difficulties. For instance, a family therapist might have a mother practice her positive reinforcement skills with her child, while also addressing how the father can support the mother's efforts during that interaction. Thus even though researchers often rely on linear approaches to test the effects of family processes, an NDS framework comes closer to what therapists actually do in treatment sessions by more accurately representing the embedded nature of family relationships and the fluid, real-time interactions they attempt to alter in treatment.

One way NDS theory may be applied to improve interventions in children's close relationships is through the identification of "control parameters." As previously mentioned, in NDS theory, control parameters are the nonlinear agents or mechanisms of change in the system. With respect to intervention, control parameters are the constructs and dynamics we seek to identify that both predict salient developmental outcomes for children and serve as possible intervention targets. A better understanding of both adaptive and maladaptive interaction dynamics through NDS research could lead to the identification of control parameters that both improve the treatment of maladaptive interactions and promote adaptive interactions in prevention-oriented interventions.

Several treatment studies suggest that changing relationship dynamics in families reduces children's problem behavior, thus providing evidence for how specific aspects of intervention and family process may act as control parameters. Intervening systematically in parent–child relationships to improve parent management practices has been shown to reduce child problem behavior (Forgatch & DeGarmo, 1999; Gardner, Burton, & Klimes, 2006; Gardner, Shaw, Dishion, Burton, & Supplee, 2007; Martinez & Forgatch, 2001). Research has also shown that reductions in parent–adolescent coercion (Dishion, Patterson, & Kavanagh, 1992) and improvements in parental monitoring (Dishion, Nelson, & Kavanagh, 2003) are associated with reductions in adolescent problem behavior. More impressively, therapists' skills in guiding change in parenting practices have been linked to changes in observed parenting and reductions in child problem behavior (Forgatch, Patterson, & DeGarmo, 2005).

Recent work has taken this a step further by examining the role of parents' positive behavioral support as a mediator of the effects of early intervention on children's behavior problems (Dishion et al., in press) and school readiness (Lunkenheimer, Dishion, Shaw, et al., in press). These studies incorporated proactive parenting behaviors (e.g., praise, positive reinforcement) and neutral behaviors that served to maintain interactive engagement such as conversation about routine matters and verbal acknowledgments of another's statement. In both studies, intervention had a modest but significant effect on child outcomes through its impact on parents' positive behavior support. Successfully engaging parents in positive parenting practices may help increase the frequency of seemingly routine parent–child interactions such as conversation and play, which are formative to the development of school readiness factors such as language and self-regulation (Baldwin, 1995; Hart & Risley, 1995). This work illustrates the need for more research on the role of adaptive dyadic attractors as potential control parameters in preventive interventions, especially with respect to children in formative developmental periods.

Another important way an NDS perspective can be useful to intervention science is its application to the technologies of change in actual clinical practice. It became evident some time ago that simple knowledge of the behavioral principles underlying a clinical problem was not sufficient for helping people change (Patterson, 1985). It is rare that clients arrive in clinics with a strong sense of how they want to change or a willingness to give up the interaction dynamics within which their troubles are embedded (DiClemente & Prochaska, 1998). Thus an emerging trend in intervention science is to focus on strategies to enhance motivation to change (Miller & Rollnick, 2002). Dishion and colleagues developed the ecological approach to family intervention and treatment (EcoFIT) program, which is designed to both prevent and treat maladaptive outcomes in children and adolescents using motivational interviewing strategies. The core of the program is the Family Check-Up (Dishion & Stormshak, 2007), which begins with a videotaped microsocial observational assessment in the home. In the subsequent feedback session, the therapist reviews the videotaped parent–child interactions with the parent and engages the parent in a discussion about his or her motivation to change aspects of these interactions. The therapist builds on the parent's existing strengths while also addressing maladaptive parent–child interaction patterns. NDS-based visual stimuli such as the SSG could be a powerful source of information for parents in this respect, enhancing motivation and also providing directions for change. In this way, NDS could help improve the efficiency of family interventions.

In conclusion, an NDS approach to the role of children's close relationships in developmental psychopathology has proved beneficial for modeling prominent theories in the field. Additionally, this approach has spawned promising methodological techniques to test those theories, especially with respect to maladaptive interaction patterns. However, we have much farther to go. The integrated study of adaptive and maladaptive attractors in microsocial interaction can inform basic research in children's normative as well as atypical developmental pathways, and offer potential avenues for preventive intervention efforts. Understanding the roles of positive and neutral interaction attractors in child development, examining attractors across the contexts of varying interaction goals and relationship types, and applying NDS principles to the analysis of change mechanisms in intervention will bolster the utility of NDS theory to developmental and intervention science.

References

Achenbach, T. M. (1990). Conceptualization of developmental psychopathology. In M. Lewis & S. M. Miller (Eds.), *Handbook of developmental psychopathology* (pp. 3–14). New York: Plenum Press.

Anderson, K. E., Lytton, H., & Romney, D. M. (1986). Mothers' interactions with normal and conduct-disordered boys: Who affects whom? *Developmental Psychology, 22,* 604–609.

Attneave, F. (1959). *Applications of information theory to psychology: A summary of basic concepts, methods, and results.* Oxford, England: Holt.

Bakeman, R., & Quera, V. (1995). Log-linear approaches to lag-sequential analysis when consecutive codes may and cannot repeat. *Psychological Bulletin, 118,* 272–284.

Baldwin, D. A. (1995). Understanding the link between joint attention and language. In C. Moore & P. J. Dunham (Eds.), *Joint attention: Its origins and role in development* (pp. 131–158). Hillsdale, NJ: Erlbaum.

Bronfenbrenner, U. (1986). Ecology of the family as a context for human development: Research perspectives. *Developmental Psychology, 22,* 723–742.

Bronfenbrenner, U., & Morris, P. A. (1998). The ecology of developmental processes. In W. Damon (Series Ed.) & R. M. Lerner (Vol. Ed.), *Handbook of child psychology: Vol. 1. Theoretical models of human development* (5th ed., pp. 993–1028). New York: Wiley.

Cicchetti, D. (1993). Developmental psychopathology: Reactions, reflections, projections. *Developmental Review, 13,* 471–502.

Cicchetti, D., & Schneider-Rosen, K. (1986). An organizational approach to childhood depression. In M. Rutter, C. E. Izard, & P. B. Read (Eds.), *Depression in young people: Developmental and clinical perspectives* (pp. 71–134). New York: Guilford Press.

Cicchetti, D., & Toth, S. L. (1997). Transactional ecological systems in developmental psychopathology. In S. S. Luthar & J. A. Burack (Eds.), *Developmental psychopathology: Perspectives on adjustment, risk, and disorder* (pp. 317–349). New York: Cambridge University Press.

Cole, P. M., Michel, M. K., & Teti, L. O. (1994). The development of emotion regulation and dysregulation: A clinical perspective. *Monographs of the Society for Research in Child Development, 59,* 73–100.

Cole, P. M., Teti, L. O., & Zahn-Waxler, C. (2003). Mutual emotion regulation and the stability of conduct problems between preschool and school age. *Development and Psychopathology, 15,* 1–18.

Conger, R. D., & Ge, X. (1999). Conflict and cohesion in parent-adolescent relations: Changes in emotional expression from early to midadolescence. In M. J. Cox & J. Brooks-Gunn (Eds.), *Conflict and cohesion in families: Causes and consequences* (pp. 185–206). Mahwah, NJ: Erlbaum.

Cook, T. D., & Campbell, D. T. (1979). *Quasi-experimentation design and analysis issues for field settings.* Boston: Houghton Mifflin.

Criss, M. M., Shaw, D. S., & Ingoldsby, E. M. (2003). Mother–son positive synchrony in middle childhood: Relation to antisocial behavior. *Social Development, 12,* 379–400.

Deater-Deckard, K., Atzaba-Poria, N., & Pike, A. (2004). Mother– and father–child mutuality in Anglo and Indian British families: A link with lower externalizing problems. *Journal of Abnormal Child Psychology, 32,* 609–620.

Diamond, L. M., & Aspinwall, L. G. (2003). Emotion regulation across the life span: An integrative perspective emphasizing self-regulation, positive affect, and dyadic processes. *Motivation and Emotion, 27,* 125–156.

DiClemente, C. C., & Prochaska, J. O. (1998). Toward a comprehensive, transtheoretical model of change: Stages of change and addictive behaviors. In W. R. Miller & N. Heather (Eds.), *Treating addictive behaviors (Applied clinical psychology)* (2nd ed. pp. 3–24). New York: Plenum Press.

Dishion, T. J., Andrews, D. W., & Crosby, L. (1995). Antisocial boys and their friends in early adolescence: Relationship characteristics, quality, and interactional process. *Child Development, 66,* 139–151.

Dishion, T. J., Capaldi, D., Spracklen, K. M., & Li, F. (1995). Peer ecology of male adolescent drug use. *Development and Psychopathology, 7,* 803–824.

Dishion, T. J., Duncan, T. E., Eddy, J. M., & Fagot, B. I. (1994). The world of parents and peers: Coercive exchanges and children's social adaptation. *Social Development, 3,* 255–268.

Dishion, T. J., Eddy, M., Haas, E., & Li, F. (1997). Friendships and violent behavior during adolescence. *Social Development, 6,* 207–223.

Dishion, T. J., Nelson, S. E., & Kavanagh, K. (2003). The family check-up with high-risk young adolescents: Preventing early-onset substance use by parent monitoring. *Behavior Therapy, 34,* 553–571.

Dishion, T. J., Nelson, S. E., Winter, C. E., & Bullock, B. M. (2004). Adolescent friendship as a dynamic system: Entropy and deviance in the etiology and course of male antisocial behavior. *Journal of Abnormal Child Psychology, 32,* 651–663.

Dishion, T. J., & Patterson, G. R. (1999). Model building in developmental psychopathology: A pragmatic approach to understanding and intervention. *Journal of Clinical Child Psychology, 28,* 502–512.

Dishion, T. J., & Patterson, G. R. (2006). The development and ecology of antisocial behavior in children and adolescents. In D. Cicchetti & D. J. Cohen (Eds.), *Developmental Psychopathology, Vol. 3: Risk, disorder, and adaptation* (2nd ed., 503–541). Hoboken, NJ: Wiley.

Dishion, T. J., Patterson, G. R., & Kavanagh, K. A. (1992). An experimental test of the coercion model: Linking theory, measurement, and intervention. In J. McCord & R. E. Tremblay (Eds.), *Preventing antisocial behavior: Interventions from birth through adolescence* (pp. 253–282). New York: Guilford Press.

Dishion, T. J., Shaw, D. M., Connell, A., Gardner, F., Weaver, C., & Wilson, M. (in press). The Family Check-Up with high-risk indigent families: Preventing problem behavior by increasing parents' positive behavior support in early childhood. *Child Development.*

Dishion, T. J., Spracklen, K. M., Andrews, D. W., & Patterson, G. R. (1996). Deviancy training in male adolescents' friendships. *Behavior Therapy, 27,* 373–390.

Dishion, T. J., & Stormshak, E. A. (2007). *Intervening in children's lives: An ecological, family-centered approach to mental health care.* Washington, DC: American Psychological Association.

Dumas, J. E., & LaFreniere, P. J. (1995). Relationships as context: Supportive and coercive interactions in competent, aggressive, and anxious mother–child dyads. In J. McCord (Ed.), *Coercion and punishment in long-term perspectives* (pp. 9–33). New York: Cambridge University Press.

Dumas, J. E., LaFreniere, P. J., & Serketich, W. J. (1995). "Balance of power": A transactional analysis of control in mother-child dyads involving socially competent, aggressive, and anxious children. *Journal of Abnormal Child Psychology, 104,* 104–113.

Dumas, J. E., Lemay, P., & Dauwalder, J. (2001). Dynamic analyses of mother–child interactions in functional and dysfunctional dyads: A synergetic approach. *Journal of Abnormal Child Psychology, 29,* 317–329.

Dunn, J., & Brown, J. (1994). Affect expression in the family, children's understanding of emotions, and their interaction with others. *Merrill-Palmer Quarterly, 40*, 120–137.

Fogel, A. (1993). Two principles of communication: Co-regulation and framing. In J. Nadel & L. Camaioni (Eds.), *New perspectives in early communicative development* (pp. 9–22). London: Routledge.

Fogel, A., & Thelen, E. (1987). Development of early expressive and communicative action: Reinterpreting the evidence from a dynamic systems perspective. *Developmental Psychology, 23*, 747–761.

Ford, D. H., & Lerner, R. M. (1992). *Developmental systems theory: An integrative approach.* Thousand Oaks, CA: Sage.

Forgatch, M. S., & DeGarmo, D. S. (1999). Parenting through change: An effective prevention program for single mothers. *Journal of Consulting & Clinical Psychology, 67*, 711–724.

Forgatch, M. S., Patterson, G. R., & DeGarmo, D. S. (2005). Evaluating fidelity: Predictive validity for a measure of competent adherence to the Oregon Model of Parent Management Training. *Behavior Therapy, 36*, 3–13.

Gardner, F. (1987). Positive interaction between mothers and children with conduct problems: Is there training for harmony as well as fighting? *Journal of Abnormal Child Psychology, 15*, 283–292.

Gardner, F. (1992). Parent–child interaction and conduct disorder. *Educational Psychology Review, 4*, 135–163.

Gardner, F., Burton, J., & Klimes, I. (2006). Randomised controlled trial of a parenting intervention in the voluntary sector for reducing child conduct problems: Outcomes and mechanisms of change. *Journal of Child Psychology and Psychiatry, 47*, 1123–1132.

Gardner, F., Shaw, D. S., Dishion, T. J., Burton, J., & Supplee, L. (2007). Randomized prevention trial for early conduct problems: Effects on proactive parenting and links to toddler disruptive behavior. *Journal of Family Psychology, 21*, 398–406.

Garmezy, N., & Rutter, M. (Eds.). (1983). *Stress, coping, and development in children.* Baltimore: Johns Hopkins University Press.

Gottlieb, G. (1991). Epigenetic systems view of human development. *Developmental Psychology, 27*, 33–34.

Gottlieb, G. (1997). Commentary: A systems view of psychobiological development. In D. Magnusson (Ed.), *The lifespan development of individuals: Behavioral, neurobiological, and psychosocial perspectives: A synthesis* (pp. 76–103). New York: Cambridge University Press.

Gottman, J. M., & Roy, A. K (1990). *Sequential analysis: A guide for behavioral researchers.* New York: Cambridge University Press.

Granic, I. (2000). The self-organization of parent-child relations: Beyond bidirectional models. In M. D. Lewis & I. Granic (Eds.), *Emotion, development, and self-organization: Dynamic systems approaches to emotional development* (pp. 267–297). New York: Cambridge University Press.

Granic, I., & Dishion, T. J. (2003). Deviant talk in adolescent friendships: A step toward measuring a pathogenic attractor process. *Social Development, 12*, 314–334.

Granic, I., & Hollenstein, T. (2003). Dynamic systems methods for models of developmental psychopathology. *Development and Psychopathology, 15*, 641–669.

Granic, I., Hollenstein, T., Dishion, T. J., & Patterson, G. R. (2003). Longitudinal analysis of flexibility and reorganization in early adolescence: A dynamic systems study of family interactions. *Developmental Psychology, 39,* 606–617.

Granic, I., & Lamey, A. V. (2002). Combining dynamic systems and multivariate analyses to compare the mother–child interactions of externalizing subtypes. *Journal of Abnormal Child Psychology, 30,* 265–283.

Granic, I., & Patterson, G. R. (2006). Toward a comprehensive model of antisocial development: A dynamic systems approach. *Psychological Review, 113,* 101–131.

Harrist, A. W., Pettit, G. S., Dodge, K. E., & Bates, J. E. (1994). Dyadic synchrony in mother–child interaction: Relation with children's subsequent kindergarten adjustment. *Family Relations, 43,* 417–424.

Hart, B., & Risley, T. R. (1995). *Meaningful differences in the everyday experience of young American children.* Baltimore: Brookes.

Hinshaw, S. P. (2002). Process, mechanism, and explanation related to externalizing behavior in developmental psychopathology. *Journal of Abnormal Child Psychology, 30,* 431–446.

Hollenstein, T., Granic, I., Stoolmiller, M., & Snyder, J. (2004). Rigidity in parent–child interactions and the development of externalizing and internalizing behavior in early childhood. *Journal of Abnormal Child Psychology, 32,* 595–607.

Kantor, J. R., & Smith, N. W. (1975). *The science of psychology: An interbehavioral survey.* Chicago: Principia Press.

Kim, K. J., Conger, R. D., Lorenz, F. O., & Elder, G. H. (2001). Parent–adolescent reciprocity in negative affect and its relation to early adult social development. *Developmental Psychology, 37,* 775–790.

Krippendorff, K. (1986). *Information theory: Structural models for qualitative data.* Thousand Oaks, CA: Sage.

Laible, D. J., & Thompson, R. A. (2000). Attachment and self-organization. In M. D. Lewis & I. Granic (Eds.), *Emotion, development, and self-organization: Dynamic systems approaches to emotional development* (pp. 298–323). New York: Cambridge University Press.

Lewis, M. D. (2000). The promise of dynamic systems approaches for an integrated account of human development. *Child Development, 71,* 36–43.

Lewis, M. D, Lamey, A. V., & Douglas, L. (1999). A new dynamic systems method for the analysis of early socioemotional development. *Developmental Science, 2,* 457–475.

Lunkenheimer, E. S., Dishion, T. J., Shaw, D. S., Connell, A., Gardner, F., Wilson, M., et al. (in press). Collateral benefits of the Family Check-Up on early childhood school readiness: Indirect effects of parents' positive behavior support. *Developmental Psychology.*

Lunkenheimer, E. S., Dishion, T. J., & Winter, C. (2008, March). *Positive parent-child interaction in high-risk families and growth in children's self-regulation from ages 2 to 4.* Paper presented at the International Conference on Infant Studies, Vancouver, Canada.

Lunkenheimer, E. S., Olson, S. L., & Kaciroti, N. (2007, March). *Parent-child co-regulation of affect in early childhood and children's behavior problems across the transition to school.* Paper presented at the Biennial Meeting of the Society for Research in Child Development, Boston, Massachusetts.

Lunkenheimer, E. S., Shields, A. M., & Cortina, K. S. (2007). Parental coaching and dismissing of children's emotions in family interaction. *Social Development, 16*, 232–248.

Martinez, C. R., Jr., & Forgatch, M. S. (2001). Preventing problems with boys' noncompliance: Effects of a parent training intervention for divorcing mothers. *Journal of Consulting and Clinical Psychology, 69*, 416–428.

McDowell, J. J. (1988). Matching theory in natural human environments. *Behavior Analyst, 11*, 95–109.

Miller, W. R., & Rollnick, S. (2002). *Motivational interviewing: Preparing people for change.* New York: Guilford Press.

Mize, J., & Pettit, G. S. (1997). Mothers' social coaching, mother–child relationship style, and children's peer competence: Is the medium the message? *Child Development, 68*, 312–332.

Newtson, D. (1994). The perception and coupling of behavior waves. In R. R. Vallacher & A. Nowak (Eds.), *Dynamical systems in social psychology* (pp. 139–167). San Diego, CA: Academic Press.

Newtson, D. (1998). Dynamical systems and the structure of behavior. In K. M. Newell & P. C. M. Molenaar (Eds.), *Applications of nonlinear dynamics to developmental process modeling* (pp. 199–220). Mahwah, NJ: Erlbaum.

National Institute of Child Health and Human Development (NICHD). Early Child Care Research Network. (2004). Affect dysregulation in the mother-child relationship in the toddler years: Antecedents and consequences. *Development and Psychopathology, 16*, 43–68.

Patterson, G. R. (1982). *Coercive family process.* Eugene, OR: Castalia.

Patterson, G. R. (1985). Beyond technology: The next stage in developing an empirical base for training. In L. L. Abate (Ed.), *Handbook of family psychology and therapy* (pp. 1344–1379). Homewood, IL: Dorsey.

Patterson, G. R. (1986). Performance models for antisocial boys. *American Psychologist, 41*, 432–444.

Patterson, G. R., & Bank, L. (1989). Some amplifying mechanisms for pathologic processes in families. In M. R. Gunnar & E. Thelen (Eds.), *Systems and development* (pp. 167–209). Hillsdale, NJ: Erlbaum.

Patterson, G. R., Capaldi, D., & Bank, L. (1991). An early starter model for predicting delinquency. In D. J. Pepler & K. H. Rubin (Eds.), *The development and treatment of childhood aggression* (pp. 139–168). Hillsdale, NJ: Erlbaum.

Patterson, G. R., & Reid, J. B. (1970). Reciprocity and coercion: Two facets of social systems. In C. Neuringer & J. L. Michael (Eds.), *Behavior modification in clinical psychology* (pp. 133–177). New York: Appleton-Century-Crofts.

Patterson, G. R., Reid, J. B., & Dishion, T. J. (1992). *Antisocial boys.* Eugene, OR: Castalia.

Pettit, G. S., Bates, J. E., & Dodge, K. A. (1997). Supportive parenting, ecological context, and children's adjustment: A seven-year longitudinal study. *Child Development, 68*, 908–923.

Pincus, D. (2001). A framework and methodology for the study of non-linear, self-organizing family dynamics. *Nonlinear Dynamics, Psychology and Life Sciences, 5*, 139–174.

Pincus, D., & Guastello, S. J. (2005). Nonlinear dynamics and interpersonal correlates of verbal turn-taking patterns in group therapy. *Small Group Research, 36,* 635–677.

Sameroff, A. J. (1995). General systems theories and developmental psychopathology. In D. Cicchetti & D. J. Cohen (Eds.), *Handbook of Development and Psychopathology* (pp. 659–695). New York: Wiley.

Sameroff, A. J., & Chandler, M. (1975). Early influences on development: Fact or fancy? *Merrill-Palmer Quarterly, 21,* 267–294.

Sameroff, A. J., & MacKenzie, M. J. (2003). Research strategies for capturing transactional models of development: The limits of the possible. *Development and Psychopathology, 15,* 613–640.

Schneirla, T. C. (1957). The concept of development in comparative psychology. In D. B. Harris (Ed.), *The concept of development: An issue in the study of human behavior* (pp. 78–108). Minneapolis: University of Minnesota Press.

Shannon, C. E., & Weaver, W. (1949). *The mathematical theory of communication.* Urbana: University of Illinois Press.

Sroufe, L. A., & Rutter, M. (1984). The domain of developmental psychopathology. *Child Development, 55,* 17–29.

Thelen, E., & Smith, L. B. (1994). *A dynamic systems approach to the development of cognition and action.* Cambridge, MA: MIT Press.

Thelen, E., & Smith, L. B. (1998). Dynamic systems theories. In W. Damon (Ed.), *Handbook of child psychology: Vol. 1. Theoretical models of human development* (5th ed., pp. 563–633). New York: Wiley.

Thelen, E., & Ulrich, B. D. (1991). Hidden skills: A dynamic systems analysis of treadmill stepping during the first year. *Monographs of the Society for Research in Child Development, 56* (1, Serial No. 223).

Van Der Maas, H., & Molenaar, P. (1992). Stagewise cognitive development: An application of catastrophe theory. *Psychological Review, 99,* 395–417.

Van Geert, P. (1994). *Dynamic systems of development: Change between complexity and chaos.* New York: Prentice Hall/Harvester Wheatsheaf.

Van Geert, P. (1995). Dimensions of change: A semantic and mathematical analysis of learning and development. *Human Development, 38,* 322–331.

von Bertalanffy, L. (1968). *General systems theory.* New York: Braziller.

Werner, H. (1948). *Comparative psychology of mental development.* New York: International Universities Press.

Werner, H. (1957). The concept of development from a comparative and organismic view. In D. B. Harris (Ed.), *The concept of development: An issue in the study of human behavior* (pp. 125–148). Minneapolis: University of Minnesota Press.

10 Psychopathology

WOLFGANG TSCHACHER AND ULI JUNGHAN

Introduction

Using nonlinear dynamical systems (NDS) theory and methodologies within psychopathology research is a relatively recent development, with roots in various disciplines ranging, at least, from biology to psychiatry and psychology. Some early work on schizophrenia and catatonia (Danziger & Elmergreen, 1954; Gjessing, 1932) already elaborated mathematical models of psychopathological conditions, by which these authors approximated what would later be known as the dynamical disease approach (Mackey & Glass, 1977; Wehr & Goodwin, 1979). Gestalt psychiatry (Goldstein, 1934/1995; Matussek, 1952) may be viewed as a predecessor of contemporary complexity theory as it applied the holistic concepts of Gestalt psychology to mental disorders. Fields within biology such as chronobiology (Winfree, 1980) provided additional, independent developments that were more explicitly based on dynamical systems theory.

Psychopathology theory and research has focused on a number of properties of NDS, such as stability, deterministic chaos, and complexity. From a phenomenological point of view, these properties appear to have little in common. In a majority of applications the focus was put on the asymptotic stability of systems dynamics because stability and homeostasis are easily accessible in empirical research. Chaos theory, on the other hand, has placed an emphasis on the nonpredictability and erratic nature of some nonlinear systems (Freeman, 1992; Guastello, 1995). Complexity theory addressed still another phenomenon, the reduction of degrees of freedom that characterizes self-organizing systems; if certain prerequisites are given (i.e., if complex systems dwell in an environment far from thermodynamic equilibrium), in which collective parameters entrain the behavior of the microscopic elements of a system (Haken, 1977).

Homeostatic, chaotic, and self-organizing dynamics, however, have a shared denominator in that they all are signatures of clearly defined subgroups of NDS. In the psychopathology literature, not all of these signatures have equally contributed to an understanding of impaired psychological functioning. Chaos theory has offered a number of intriguing hypotheses about the erratic nature of courses of mental disorders (e.g., schizophrenia). To date, however, measurements in quantitative empirical research in this field have rarely been of a quality to allow for chaos assessment in a strict sense. It seems that deterministic chaos will remain difficult to detect in real-world measurements of mental or neurocognitive processes. Because of this apparent limitation, the field has focused on those further properties of NDS that can be detected more easily, such as stability and self-organization. In our view, such features are the most likely to support progress in psychopathology research.

NDS theory has had an impact not only on the research-oriented empirical scientists in the larger field of psychology, but also on a large group of clinical practitioners and social scientists. The two most influential approaches here are autopoiesis theory (Maturana & Varela, 1980) and social systems theory (Luhmann, 1984). Autopoiesis theory considers complex systems that are capable of sustaining and continuously recreating themselves. Such systems are autonomous ("structurally closed") with respect to their environment. The methodology of autopoiesis theory has remained largely qualitative and has neglected to endorse quantitative hypothesis testing altogether; its applications, particularly to psychology, have therefore remained restricted to phenomenology and epistemology. Luhmann's theory of social systems adapted the concept of autopoiesis in the framework of an encompassing theory of various self-referential social systems (such as science, art, economy, religion, etc.). Again, different social systems are sharply contrasted from each other because their "codes" (i.e., their logics of functioning) are seen as incommensurably distinct. Luhmann's encompassing sociological approach has, for theoretical reasons, refused to consider the individual person as a dynamical system of its own right, which does not invite a dynamical systems conception of psychopathology in the first place. Autopoiesis theory and Luhmann's sociological systems approach have both developed sophisticated theoretical frameworks of NDS theory, yet their impact has remained restricted to philosophical discourses about, and constructivistic therapeutic applications for, the field of psychopathology.

Therefore only the dynamical disease concept and complexity theory are considered in more detail in this chapter. The former is described in the next section, which is followed by a presentation of the complexity approach.

The Dynamical Disease Approach

The dynamical disease approach is a direct application of dynamical systems theory to disorders of mental functioning, as well as to the wider context of somatic disorders and medical conditions (Bélair, Glass, an der Heiden, & Milton, 1995). The concept *dynamical disease* implies that underlying overt symptoms we may find the processing of a dynamical system. Disease is thus equivalent to a significant change of a system's dynamical regime, such that pathological behavior evolves out of healthy behavior by way of a phase transition between two dynamical regimes. The expectation is that rather than the system per se, it is only the dynamics which is pathologically altered.

Among the somatic disorders that have been conceived as dynamical diseases are diverse conditions such as cardiac disorders and epilepsy. The motivations of such conceptions have often been phenomenological. For example, strikingly different cardiac rhythms (such as atrial fibrillation and normal heartbeat) can sometimes occur in a working heart in the absence of any specific external trigger; dynamically, the heart has become a bistable system. Cardiac arrhythmia is characterized by the (unwanted) shifting between dynamical regimes of the heart. Analogous dynamics can be found in epilepsy: Seizures often involve large areas of the brain with synchronous neural activity, which can be accompanied by dramatic symptoms such as convulsions and loss of consciousness. Seizures may arise unprovoked in an otherwise neurologically unimpaired individual, and this individual can then revert to normal functioning without no or minimal aftereffects.

In psychiatry, mainly bipolar depression and schizophrenia have been viewed from this dynamical angle (Ciompi, 1989; Emrich & Hohenschutz, 1992; Gottschalk, Bauer, & Whybrow, 1995; Tschacher & Kupper, 2007). Depression and schizophrenia belong to the most disabling and economically costly of all disorders, even when severe somatic diseases such as cancer and cardiac illnesses are considered. The societal burden of schizophrenia is especially weighty. The origin of schizophrenia is still unknown, although an abundance of empirically grounded theories have been accumulated to date. Whereas much is known about the symptoms, course, and therapeutic factors of treatment, as yet no generally accepted theory of schizophrenia exists. The best theories to date are rather encompassing, but also opaque, frameworks such as stress-vulnerability theory (stressors can trigger schizophrenia when a certain predisposition makes an individual susceptible) and the psychobiosociological approach (all of these domains together can, and usually do, cause schizophrenia). There is a bulk of knowledge on the phenomenology of schizophrenia: Symptoms typically fluctuate, and different symptoms may predominate at different points in the course of the illness. Several subtypes of schizophrenia exist that produce typical clinical pictures; in paranoid schizophrenia, for instance, delusional ideas and hallucinations are in the foreground; in the disorganized type of schizophrenia, flat and incoherent affect, disorganized speech, and negative symptoms predominate, whereas none of the positive symptoms of the paranoid type are seen. There have been many attempts to find a common factor or a basic dimension for all types of schizophrenia. One century ago, the Swiss psychiatrist Bleuler (who coined the term *schizophrenia* for what was known before as dementia praecox) suggested as basic symptoms the loosening of associations and disordered, ambivalent affectivity. In the mid-20th century, chance findings led to the development of reasonably efficient drugs, the neuroleptics; their mechanism of action favored the dopamine theory of schizophrenia: A dysbalance of neurotransmitters, especially dopamine, in cortical brain centers is likely connected to the disease. No neurobiological theory, however, can account for all available data. More recently, some researchers have doubted that one should speak of schizophrenia at all; given the heterogeneity of manifestations, one should rather consider a spectrum of psychobiological conditions, the "schizophrenias."

The application of dynamical systems theory in psychology and psychiatry seems especially promising because virtually all psychiatric disorders exhibit, as a common characteristic, sudden or periodic shifts in cognitive, emotional, or behavioral functioning that can favorably be modeled using dynamical concepts. Thereby the emergence of psychopathological symptoms is governed by the same mechanisms that have been the basis of normal cognitive and emotional functioning. In other words, there is continuity between dysfunction and mental health even if the system's phenomenological behavior may be altered completely. Instances of pathology may occur in an utterly healthy system as soon as it dwells, because of unfavorable control parameter settings, in a dysfunctional region of phase space.

Several examples of a dynamical disease approach to psychopathology, and schizophrenia in particular, may be found in the literature. Tschacher, Scheier, and Hashimoto (1997) investigated whether psychotic episodes could be understood as manifestations of a nonlinear, possibly chaotic system (i.e., whether schizophrenic psychoses should be considered dynamical diseases). They classified empirical time series data, which were gained by observers' daily ratings of a patient's severity of symptoms. The goal of modeling these courses of psychosis was to disentangle the different dynamical sources of variation in the time series, specifically: *linear autoregressive noise, moving average dynamics, white noise,* and *colored noise* dynamics. Linear autoregressive noise means that any state of a system (e.g., the level of psychotic symptoms of a patient in any one day) is linearly correlated with one or more previous states; more or less noise ("random shocks") is added on top of the linear component. Moving average dynamics is realized when the state of a system is linearly correlated with one or more previous random shocks. White noise simply means there is no correlation between contiguous states. Colored noise is any mixture of autoregressive and moving average dynamics.

This classification was an effort to estimate attributes of the disease courses on the basis of the rating data. Purely stochastic systems without any serial structure (white noise) posed a first null hypothesis. Such modeling would view psychotic behavior as largely under the control of high-dimensional unspecified stimuli. In other words, the system states of a random system are determined by the random shocks alone, so the system may be viewed as a merely passive recipient of environmental inputs. The dynamics of a random system do not result from the system's intrinsic properties: We would not speak of a dynamical disease in this case at all. Nonlinear and chaotic dynamics, on the other hand, would point to the existence of an internally controlled, possibly low-dimensional system unfolding relatively autonomously from environmental fluctuations. Empirical evidence of these latter systems (always conceding a certain, additional level of stochasticity) was considered suggestive of the dynamical disease concept of schizophrenia. This was the case in the earlier mentioned somatic examples (heart fibrillation; epileptic seizure), in which marked deterministic dynamics unfolded over time, largely independent of environmental random shocks. In short, the model selection was among random systems (no dynamical disease), linear systems (deterministic but trivial systems underlying the disease), and nonlinear systems (deterministic nontrivial systems, maybe chaotic).

Fourteen patients' daily manifestations of psychotic symptoms were recorded independently for each patient. The inclusion criterion was availability of recordings over at least 200 consecutive days (one patient was monitored for almost 800 days). The resulting time series were embedded in an m-dimensional state space. The forecastability (i.e., predictability) of the measured psychotic dynamics was assessed using a nonparametric algorithm (Sugihara & May, 1990) for up to 10 days of forecasts. The forecastabilities for each patient were then statistically compared with surrogate data that were constructed from the original data to represent three types of dynamics. The first comparison involved random dynamics (i.e., the original data would not corroborate the dynamical disease hypothesis). The second comparison involved linear autoregressive dynamics (i.e., the original data would point to a trivial linear dynamical disease), which would, by definition, not allow the existence of attractors other than limit cycles (i.e., oscillatory behavior) or fixed-point attractors. Finally, the third comparison involved linearly correlated noise with the same Fourier spectrum as the original time series, which would indicate that the original data were still only additive compositions of several linear systems (i.e., colored noise). This third comparison was implemented because such dynamics have been shown to closely mimic the signs of chaos in fractal analysis. Whenever the forecastability contained in the time series significantly exceeded the forecastability of the three surrogate types, it was concluded that the patients' time series could not be explained by linear assumptions alone. This would leave open, by way of falsification, the possibility of nonlinear, maybe chaotic, dynamics. This method may illustrate how the strong assumptions of the chaos theory approach may be partially integrated in a stochastic dynamical disease study.

The results of these comparisons demonstrated that 8 of 14 of these individuals showed a nonlinear time course in their symptoms. This provided some initial support for the validity of the concept of dynamical diseases in the area of schizophrenia research (Tschacher et al., 1997).

A different approach to unravel the underlying dynamics in schizophrenia-related impairment was chosen by Paulus, Geyer, and Braff (1996), who aimed to quantify the complexity of behavioral patterns in a sample of 22 schizophrenia patients compared with 16 healthy control subjects. The participants in this study were engaged in a simple choice task. They were asked to predict 500 right or left appearances of a stimulus, producing individual binary response sequences for each participant. Of these sequences and subsequences, dynamical entropy and the fluctuation spectrum were calculated to estimate the degree of interdependency between consecutive responses made by each individual. The entropy used was a variant of Shannon's information entropy. Compared with control subjects, the response sequences generated by schizophrenia patients showed a higher degree of interdependency and at the same time were less consistent in the selection and ordering of responses because of the contribution of highly perseverative and unpredictable subsequences. These findings could not be explained by the existence of subgroups within schizophrenia patients with either highly predictable or unpredictable response sequences. Moreover, the schizophrenia patients did not differ from comparison subjects in the probability of response switches, response balance, or response duration and hence were not simply aberrant on all measures. These findings suggest that this differential change in the complexity of stimulus response sequences in schizophrenia point to a circumscribed dysfunction (i.e., altered dynamics) of the internal capacity to organize stimulus sequences.

Yet another type of behavior was investigated in a study by Leroy, Pezard, Nandrino, and Beaune (2005). They aimed to quantify the dynamical properties of linguistic production in individuals with schizophrenia. It is well known from clinical observation that the discourse of patients suffering from this disorder in certain states is characterized by the occurrence of specific linguistic signs such as neologism (invention of words not contained in the accepted lexicon) or associative loosening (the flow of speech is governed by free or superficial associations instead of coherent content). It has been argued that these individuals display a disorganization of semantic systems (Paulsen et al., 1996). Moreover, these language impairments in schizophrenia have been linked to dysfunction in working memory, attention, conceptual sequencing failures, and other cognitive dysfunctions (Docherty, Hall, Gordinier, & Cutting, 2000; Sullivan, Shear, Zipursky, Sagar, & Pfefferbaum, 1997). In this vein, Leroy et al. (2005) hypothesized that temporal organization of speech would be impaired and that this dysfunction could be modeled by nonlinear dynamics. More precisely, according to the described speech and memory deficits, they assumed that the complexity of recalled semantic material would be diminished in individuals with schizophrenia. In addition, they expected to find a specific temporal organization in the recall of verbal material in their patients.

To test these assumptions, they used an experimental paradigm in which 10 subjects with schizophrenia and matched healthy control subjects read a short story aloud and then were immediately asked to recall its plot. The narratives were tape-recorded, and transcripts of the tapes were used for further analysis. Two entropy indices (Lempel–Ziv entropy and Shannon entropy) derived from the linguistic analyses of these speech samples were then compared with those from shuffled surrogate data. By this means, it could be demonstrated that temporal organization was a significant feature of speech in both schizophrenia and control subjects. Significant differences between schizophrenia patients and healthy control subjects were only found for the ability to *maintain* what in linguistic terms is called a discourse plan, not with respect to the overall capacity to *generate* such a discourse plan. In other words, schizophrenia patients and healthy individuals were equally capable of creating meaningful speech sequences to master the recall task, but schizophrenia patients displayed a deficit in their organization of the semantic material. These findings fit well into the concept of schizophrenia as a dynamical disease, because they suggest that characteristic psychopathology symptoms (e.g., disordered thought) may emerge from a change in the mode of neuronal organization (phase transition) rather than from some stable brain dysfunction.

To date the dynamical disease concept has predominantly been related to the field of schizophrenia research, but some interesting approaches have been reported for other psychiatric disorders as well. Pezard, Nandrino, Renault, Massioui, and Varela (1996) applied a nonlinear systems approach to the analysis of data from electroencephalograms (EEG) of depressed patients and related these to psychopathological symptoms. From their analyses, they identified different EEG dynamics in both first-episode depressed individuals and subjects with recurrent depression compared with healthy control subjects. To achieve this, they repeatedly performed EEG recordings in individuals with first-episode depression, a history of previous depression episodes and healthy control subjects while they were engaged in a simple attention task (discriminating two tones). The EEG data were used to compute the underlying brain dynamics by comparing original data with surrogate data and calculating the respective entropy measure. The group of first-episode patients displayed a convergence of their measures toward those of the control group that went along with a reduction of depressive symptoms over a 3-week period. This shift toward "normality" could not be observed in the subjects with recurrent depressive episodes. Thus the application of the dynamical diseases concept to major depression allowed for a clinically meaningful discrimination between different courses of depressive disorders and carries the potential of guiding the refinement of clinical strategies to treat these two groups of patients.

The findings from the work just described support the validity of the concept of dynamical diseases in the area of psychopathology research. At the same time, because direct evidence for deterministic chaos in relatively short empirical time series is difficult to obtain, the cited and related findings (Hoffman & McGlashan, 1993; Paulus & Braff, 2003) are likely to be among the most appropriate approaches used in dynamical systems research to test the chaos hypothesis of schizophrenia and other psychiatric diseases.

The Complexity Theory Approach

The complexity approach explicitly addresses the phenomenon of self-organization. The striking analogies between the behavior of certain physical systems and mental processes (e.g., Haken, Kelso, & Bunz, 1985), together with the explanatory power of mathematical models of synergetics (Haken, 1977; Haken & Tschacher, unpublished manuscript), provide the platform for the complexity theory approach to psychopathology.

Synergetics is an interdisciplinary field of research that deals with systems composed of many components. By means of their interaction, these components can self-organize and thereby produce new qualitative features on macroscopic scales (these self-organized patterns are described by so-called order parameters). In other words, synergetics studies the emergence of new qualities. Its main question is whether there are general principles that govern the behavior of complex systems when such qualitative changes occur. In a large class of systems, it has been shown that these emergent situations become accessible to unifying mathematical and conceptual approaches. The core of synergetic modeling is *circular causality*. On one hand, the behavior of a system close to instability points is described and determined by a few quantities, the order parameters. According to synergetics, these order parameters enslave (i.e., determine) the behavior of the many individual components. This implies an enormous information compression, because it suffices to describe the order parameters instead of all the components. On the other hand, the individual components react on the order parameters and, in this way, even generate the order parameters. Thus the relationship between order parameters and components is based on circular causality, which consequently explains the rapid, avalanche-like generation of self-organized patterns once the critical instability points are accessed. A similar perspective is taken by the theory of dissipative systems (Nicolis & Prigogine, 1977). Prigogine's approach emphasized the thermodynamic considerations of self-organization, because increase of order through pattern formation means reduction of entropy. Haken (1977), however, argued that the concept of entropy is ill defined in nonlinear open systems. For our present purposes, the theoretical disagreements are of minor importance. The practical and theoretical implications of both approaches, synergetics and dissipative systems theory, are analogous, at least for psychopathology.

Self-organization is, according to this view, an essential aspect of information processing in cognitive systems because self-organizing dynamics are a natural model of the ability of a cognitive system to form patterns or, conversely, to recognize and perceive patterns. Within the history of psychology, this ability to form and recognize patterns has been investigated first by the gestalt school (Köhler,

1940; Wertheimer, 1912). In modern cognitive science and neuroscience, such cognitive processes and functions are again the focus of study, under modern theoretical rubrics, including neurocognitive binding, perceptual grouping, or cognitive coordination (Dennett & Kinsbourne, 1992; Phillips & Silverstein, 2003). In all of the various theoretical formulations, it is essential that from the interaction of many components of a cognizing system, new emergent variables (gestalts) arise.

Concerning psychopathology, the complexity theory approach suggests that mental disorders, or symptoms in the context of such disorders, are characterized by an impairment of gestalt pattern formation. This impairment likely resides in a specific neurocognitive dysfunction. Gestalt applications to psychopathology have a long history, most notably again in endeavors to understand schizophrenia better. Pioneers of gestalt psychiatry were Matussek (1952) and Conrad (1958), who suggested that the core symptoms of schizophrenia originate from dysfunctional processing of the gestalt patterns afforded by stimuli. In neuropsychological research, these ideas were operationalized and subsequently implemented by various tasks requiring perceptual organization. In this section, first a brief reference is made to a few of the many studies in this field. Then we focus on three paradigms that were recently investigated in our own laboratory.

A classical example of gestalt perception is apparent motion. Apparent motion is the perception of motion when physical motion of the stimuli presented is absent. A familiar example is the stroboscopic effect used in cinematography. Although only a rapid succession of still images is displayed on the screen, smooth, uninterrupted motion (a "movie") is seen. Since the early days of experimental psychology, the phenomenon of apparent motion has influenced the development of psychological theory. In particular, gestalt theory posited apparent motion as a demonstration of the holistic aspects of perception (*phi phenomenon*, Wertheimer, 1912). Schizophrenia research using apparent motion paradigms has been performed as early as by Saucer and Deabler (1956), who found a decrease in the organizational ability in schizophrenics. Chambers and Wilson (1968) reported differences between schizophrenia patients and control subjects in an apparent motion discrimination task in which the more severely disordered patients had greater difficulty detecting apparent motion. After that, however, apparent motion paradigms disappeared from the agenda of psychopathology research.

A different area of gestalt perception is perceptual grouping, the binding together of items to a group of items. Through this process, perception becomes much easier and more efficient, because several details of a perceptual array can be treated as a whole and processed in parallel. Silverstein, Kovacs, Corry, and Valone (2000) found that the capability of schizophrenia patients to detect contours was reduced. Contours were groupings offered by regularly arranged patches embedded in noisy backgrounds (i.e., additional patches distributed randomly). A majority of additional studies have shown impairments of perceptual organization in schizophrenia (Kéri, Kelemen, Benedek, & Janka, 2005; Silverstein & Uhlhaas, 2004; Uhlhaas & Silverstein, 2005), indicating that many persons with schizophrenia appear to have difficulties perceiving such gestalt properties. Place and Gilmore (1980) implemented a line-counting task to assess the influence of perceptual grouping on cognitive performance measured by counting errors. Grouping was realized by the orientation of the lines (i.e., some of the lines were displayed at identical angles). Cognitive performance in schizophrenia patients, in contrast to healthy control subjects, was not affected by the level of perceptual grouping of the lines. This finding showed that, in some rare contexts, the ability to ignore grouping information may prove advantageous. Consistent with other research, schizophrenia patients were better at ignoring context when necessary for a task. These general findings can be reversed, however, in prodromal stages of schizophrenia (i.e., before the occurrence of overt symptoms). Then persons may even experience enhanced perceptual grouping instead of deficiency (Parnas et al., 2001), which resembles the observations of prodromal gestalt excesses reported by Conrad (1958).

In addition to differences between schizophrenia patients and control groups, several studies have reported significant correlations between perceptual organization and dimensions of psychopathology, such as the disorganization syndrome (Silverstein et al., 2000), positive symptoms (Goodarzi, Wykes, & Hemsley, 2000) and negative symptoms (Doniger, Silipo, Rabinowicz, Snodgrass, & Javitt, 2001). The correlations showed that disorganization as well as negative symptoms are associated with decreased perceptual organization, whereas positive symptoms are linked to excessive perceptual organization. Both decreases as well as excesses may prove dysfunctional.

In neuroscience, perceptual organization is viewed as a neurocognitive binding process by which the brain, before conscious processing, integrates multiple sensory inputs to bind together perceptual configurations. Synchronous neuronal dynamics presumably underlies such binding processes, whereby self-organized neuronal synchrony is supposed to act as "neuronal glue" by which different brain regions are coordinated (Singer & Gray, 1995; Varela 1995). Neurocognitive binding has since been embedded in a dynamical systems framework, because resulting patterns show the characteristic properties of dynamical attractors, the asymptotically stable states described by NDS theory (Haken, 1996; Kelso, 1995; Tschacher & Dauwalder, 2003). This can be demonstrated especially in the perception of ambiguous stimuli in which an identical stimulus pattern can be processed in two or more qualitatively different ways: The stimuli give rise to two or more attractors. In such cases of multistability, with time passing, a viewer frequently observes notable "flips" between perceptions, transitions – between the various attractors. These transitions show the characteristics of nonlinear phase transitions, which may be modeled mathematically (Haken et al., 1985). Kruse, Carmesin, Pahlke, Strüber, and Stadler (1996) performed an empirical investigation of phase transitions in the context of apparent motion.

Empirical Examination of Perceptual Organization and Schizophrenia

We focus here on three examples of perceptual organization with a focus on schizophrenia. Transitions in the perception of ambiguous stimuli were observed in subjects using various neurocognitive tasks inspired by the gestalt psychology tradition. We summarize data on patients diagnosed as suffering from schizophrenia spectrum disorder and a sample of healthy control subjects matched to patients with respect to sex and age. The psychopathological states of the patients were determined using standardized clinical interviews (Positive and Negative Syndrome Scale (PANSS; Kay, Fiszbein, & Opler, 1987). The PANSS yields an estimate of five factors of psychopathology – namely, the positive, negative, excitement, depression, and cognitive factors. The positive factor includes symptoms characteristic of florid psychosis, such as the following: delusions, hallucinatory behavior, and unusual thought content. The negative factor includes deficit symptoms of schizophrenia commonly manifested as emotional and social withdrawal. The excitement factor consists of items such as excitement, hostility, tension, and impulsivity. The depression factor consists of the PANSS items depression, anxiety, guilt feelings, somatic concern, and preoccupation. Finally, the cognitive factor incorporates signs of cognitive disorganization, such as conceptual disorganization, disorientation, and difficulty in abstract thinking.

We first present the studies of each paradigm and subsequently summarize the empirical findings. We refer in this summary to results reported in a series of articles (Tschacher & Kupper, 2006; Tschacher, Schuler, & Junghan, 2006; Tschacher, Dubouloz, Meier, & Junghan, 2008).

Apparent Motion

The simplest paradigm that evokes apparent motion consists in presenting a stimulus (e.g., a black disc), alternately in positions x and y of the visual field. Over a wide range of interstimulus intervals and frequencies of flashing, the viewer perceives the stimulus not as appearing alternately at positions x and y, but as wandering back and forth between x and y. Clearly the perceptual quality of movement is actively added to the objective physical stimuli by the viewer's information processing system. As was introduced earlier, apparent motion represents an emergent property of perception.

It can be shown that apparent motion is ecologically significant for the functioning of visual perception. The reason is this: Visual scanning of scenes is commonly performed in successions of single fixations and intermittent fast

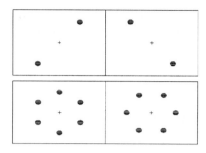

Figure 10.1. Top panel, the stimulus patterns (A, left; B, right) presented alternately in the stroboscopic apparent motion paradigm. Bottom panel, the stimulus patterns (A, left; B, right) presented alternately in the circular apparent motion paradigm.

saccadic eye movements. Nevertheless, the optical scene is subjectively seen as stationary during scanning, although the eyes may move repeatedly. The reason for perceived stationarity despite massive retinal translations is the reafference system (von Holst & Mittelstaedt, 1950), a feedback loop by which the brain compensates for bodily motion and for eye movements. Viewing *real* locomotion, with eyes moving in a saccadic fashion, and viewing *apparent* motion in a laboratory paradigm can hence be considered similar from the standpoint of neurocognitive processing. Consequently, we may investigate apparent motion perception as a valid model for perception of motion in natural settings; any dysfunction in the former should entail general problems with visual perception.

As introduced earlier, we implemented a situation of multistability in which perception may flip repeatedly between different attractors, so that the stability of attractors can be assessed. First, transition rates can be measured in fixed periods of time, and, second, the response to control parameter variation can be assessed. Stability of perceptual gestalts, therefore, becomes an observable marker of perceptual organization and neurocognitive binding (Tschacher et al., 2008). Multistability was established by various apparent motion paradigms.

One paradigm known as stroboscopic apparent motion (SAM) was introduced by von Schiller (1933) to exemplify apparent motion evoked by stimulus patterns flashed alternately. In addition to the perception of apparent motion, which is reported by all viewers, transitions between different kinds of apparent motion frequently occur (*gestalt flips*). Transitions are perceived spontaneously (i.e., in the absence of environmental or stimulus changes). Thus the SAM paradigm induces multistability. In the present experiment, the SAM paradigm was realized by showing two stimulus patterns (A and B) alternately and repeatedly without interstimulus intervals (Fig. 10.1 top). Each SAM stimulus pattern consisted of two black discs of 1 cm in diameter shown against a white background. The discs were placed at the corners of an imaginary rectangle with horizontal sides of approximately 8 cm and vertical sides of approximately 9 cm.

Each presentation of the stimulus pattern A or B lasted 500 msec (i.e., the flashing frequency was 2 Hz). One run of successive presentations A-B-A-B-A-... lasted 60 sec. Three such runs were presented to each subject. For each subject, the number of SAM transitions was counted to assess the global stability of spontaneously arising SAM gestalt perceptions (i.e., SAM transition rate). Taking the research findings on apparent motion, and generally on perceptual organization, as points of departure, it was expected that apparent motion is affected in schizophrenia.

A further paradigm was developed on the basis of the SAM paradigm. It has previously been established that the probability of perceiving either vertical or horizontal apparent motion closely depends on the aspect ratio of the display (aspect ratio = horizontal side : vertical side). Hence, the aspect ratio constitutes a control parameter of SAM perception. Large aspect ratios (i.e., the horizontal sides of the imaginary rectangle in Figure 10.1, top panel, exceed its vertical sides) are associated with a higher probability of perceiving vertical apparent motion. When the aspect ratio is reduced toward zero, a spontaneous gestalt flip from vertical apparent motion to horizontal apparent motion occurs. Each run of this paradigm started with an aspect ratio of 2.1 (horizontal extension, 18.6 cm; vertical extension, 9 cm). The aspect ratio was then gradually reduced to zero by keeping the vertical extension constant while reducing the horizontal extension step by step with each successive frame. Each run lasted 30 sec (i.e., 60 single frames were presented with a flashing frequency of 2 Hz as in the SAM paradigm). A total of six runs were presented. Subjects recorded the times at which gestalt flips occurred by key presses (*time to SAM transition*).

The final apparent motion paradigm introduced a circular configuration of six discs as in Figure 10.1 (bottom). The CAM (circular apparent motion) paradigm provokes spontaneous gestalt transitions in the same way as the SAM paradigm. The alternating attractors here are clockwise and counterclockwise CAM, and sometimes the experience of discs moving back and forth (oscillatory apparent motion). The variable *CAM transition rate* was defined as described earlier in the SAM paradigm by counting the numbers of CAM transitions during the time of presentation (three runs of 60 sec each).

In tests for group differences in apparent motion variables, no significant differences were found between participants with schizophrenia spectrum disorder and the control group. It was found, however, that the patient group was very heterogeneous with regard to apparent motion perception. In all three apparent motion paradigms, outpatients consistently displayed higher levels of gestalt stability than the control group, and inpatients showed lower stability than the control group (more information and discussion on the details of subgroup specificity is provided in the cited publication by Tschacher et al., 2008, using latent class modeling). In an encompassing multivariate analysis of variance (MANOVA) test, the hypothesis of a general relationship between all apparent motion variables (as dependent responses) and all psychopathology variables (PANSS dimensions, the independent variables) was assessed. The overall test was significant ($p < .01$), indicating an association between apparent motion and psychopathology. The results of multiple regression analyses furthermore showed which of the dimensions of psychopathology were significantly

Table 10.1. Summary of the statistical analyses for psychopathology dimensions predicting pattern formation variables

	Whole model tests	Stepwise regression tests
	Explained variance (R^2)	Significant psychopathology predictor (direction of contribution)
SAM transition rate	.29	Positive (+)
		Depression (−)
Time to SAM transition	.48**	Negative (+)
CAM transition rate	.37*	Cognitive (+)
		Excitement (−)
		Negative (−)
MIB rate	.49**	Positive (+)
		Depression (−)
		Excitement (+)
MIB duration	.26	Positive (+)
Perceived causality	.46**	Positive (+)
		Cognitive (−)

Note. SAM, stroboscopic apparent motion; CAM, circular apparent motion; MIB, motion induced blindness.
$^*p < .05; ^{**}p < .01; ^{***}p < .001.$

associated with these effects. In the SAM and CAM tasks, the weights of predictors indicated that psychopathology dimensions contributed differentially to gestalt perception. The positive factor and the cognitive factor were both linked to reduced gestalt stability (i.e., increased transition rates), whereas the negative, excitement, and depression factors were related to high stability of gestalt perception (i.e., decreased transition rates and delayed time to SAM transition) (Table 10.1).

Apparent Blindness

Pattern formation in perception generally leads to the emergence of new, additional variables. In some important cases, however, the opposite may be true: several *negative illusions* have been described in which areas or aspects of a stimulus field go unnoticed even though they are clearly present. For example, the phenomenon of *change blindness* is the inability of viewers to observe changes in those parts of a scene on which they are not focused (Milner & Goodale, 1995): When reading text from a monitor, readers frequently fail to notice changes in the unattended regions, even if all letters, except those in the line that is being read, are exchanged for meaningless pseudo-letters. An amazing demonstration of *inattentional blindness* was reported by Simons and Chabris (1999); they instructed subjects observing a ball game to count the number of passes among members of the team wearing white outfits, finding that even highly unusual

Figure 10.2. The motion-induced blindess stimulus pattern. The discs (in the paradigm, yellow) representing the points of an invisible triangle are stationary. The distractor pattern of crosses (in the paradigm, blue) rotates in clockwise direction around the center of the pattern.

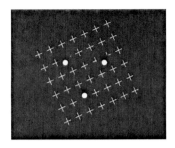

events (a black gorilla walking through the middle of this scene) may go utterly unnoticed. *Perceptual filling-in* (Ramachandran & Gregory, 1991) occurs when a homogeneous gray square peripheral to the center of vision is displayed against a background of twinkling two-dimensional noise of black and white dots. On steady eccentric fixation, the square vanishes and is filled in by the twinkling noise from the surround.

Tschacher et al. (2006) focused on a similar phenomenon, *motion-induced blindness* (MIB), described by Bonneh, Cooperman, and Sagi (2001), in a small sample of normal observers. Bright-yellow stationary dots are presented as target stimuli on a screen. At the same time, a distracter pattern (e.g., a cloud of low-contrast blue dots) rotates next to the targets. It was found that a large majority of observers experienced that the salient target dots disappeared and reappeared repeatedly for periods of several seconds, depending on the movement of the distracter pattern.

We conceptualized MIB as representing the opposite of the gestalt process, with higher levels of MIB occurring when the gestalt process is weaker. This view was supported by recent findings of Hsu, Yeh, and Kramer (2004) who found that MIB (as well as perceptual filling-in) was enhanced by poor perceptual grouping between targets and distracters. Graf, Adams, and Lages (2002) correspondingly showed that MIB can be induced by illusory surfaces originating from Kanizsa elements. Both studies point to the close complementary connection between gestalt reversals and MIB.

In our trial, MIB was chosen as a further indicator of the functioning of the neurocognitive binding system. We again hypothesized that MIB, reflecting a class of neurocognitive binding, is affected by schizophrenia. Target stimuli consisted of three stationary yellow discs 0.3 cm in diameter (Fig. 10.2). The bright target stimuli were presented on a black background together with a low-luminance grid of blue crosses. The grid rotated clockwise 20 times during each run, equaling 120 degrees per second.

Subjects were instructed to fixate visually on the middle of the display and report verbally whether they perceived any change in the target stimuli. After the preparatory run, most participants cited one or more disappearances either of a single target or of multiple targets. After being informed about the possible disappearance of targets, the subjects were instructed to press the keyboard space bar when any of the yellow discs disappeared and not to release it until all three targets had reappeared. The variable *MIB rate* was defined as the number of reported disappearances. *MIB duration* was defined as the total time in seconds during which the MIB phenomenon was reported.

MIB rates differed significantly between participants with schizophrenia spectrum disorders and the control subjects. The control group showed higher rates of the MIB illusion, whereas the patients perceived MIB less often. Correspondingly, the total durations of MIB were longer in the control participants, yet this second difference failed to reach statistical significance (Table 10.1). MIB was experienced during approximately 23% of total stimulus exposure time in the control group and 18% in the patient group. These values accord with the results of Bonneh et al. (2001), who reported 25% invisibility in their two-dimensional paradigm, and with Graf et al. (2002), who found 17%. A finding in line with the results of the apparent motion study was derived in a MANOVA test in which both MIB variables were used as dependent responses and psychopathology dimensions as independent variables. The overall test was significant, indicating an association between MIB and psychopathology. More specifically, the positive and excitement factors were both linked to enhanced MIB perception, whereas the depression factor was related to fewer incidences of the illusion (Table 10.1).

Apparent Causality

Most schizophrenia-spectrum patients report that their phenomenological appraisals of self, other, and environment have undergone marked changes in the course of the disorder. Many of these changes affect agency and causality, the issue of who causes actions and events, and how events are causally linked. Patients' views on the relationships between causes and effects often deviate markedly from what other people think. This is especially true when positive symptoms are manifest; a person with delusional ideation, for example, believes in causal links that may seem highly unusual to external observers. In addition to paranoid and delusional ideas, a person may sense an immediate link between himself or herself and external events (Lindner, Thier, Kircher, Haarmeier, & Leube, 2005). In such *ideas of reference*, a person perceives causal relationships between himself or herself and the social environment when in fact there are none. The disorganization syndrome of schizophrenia is characterized by altered causality as well, yet in a different manner; associations, particularly causal associations, are reduced in disorganized cognition. Such results are consistent with the Bleulerian notion of a weakening of associations as well as the premises of gestalt psychiatry.

The research on *theory of mind* (ToM) points in a similar direction (Brüne, 2005). ToM is defined as the ability to "mentalize," to monitor and infer one's own and others' mental states. If a person's causal attributions are deficient or lacking, the mentalizing ability of this person will by necessity be compromised. As a general consequence, social skills and interactive behavior as well as the phenomenology of patients are likely to be affected (Sass & Parnas, 2003). It has been found that ToM was impaired in patients with positive symptoms (Frith & Corcoran, 1996) and disorganization symptoms (Sarfati, Hardy-Baylé, Brunet, & Widlocher, 1999).

The phenomenology of schizophrenia as well as the findings on ToM deficiencies indicate that notions of causality are altered in schizophrenia, with ensuing impact on social cognition and behavior. The origins of these deficiencies, however, remained undetermined. ToM research typically addresses higher cognition, such as mental modules that process abstract information, as, for instance, meta-representational information (thinking about what others think). ToM research therefore has relied to a great extent on the verbal descriptions and interpretations that are provided by study participants (Russell, Reynaud, Herba, Morris, & Corcoran, 2006). This renders localization of the origin of ToM problems encountered by schizophrenia patients quite difficult. The locus of deficiencies may be anywhere in higher cognition (e.g., in linguistic skills; in inductive reasoning), but also in basic cognition (e.g., memory, attention, vigilance) or even in perception (e.g., preattentional binding processes; Tschacher et al., 2006). To date, ToM research has not unambiguously disentangled the multiple mental processes of varying cognitive complexity levels, on which the mentalizing ability likely rests. We do not yet know why ToM is dysfunctional in patients.

The Belgian gestalt psychologist Michotte (1962) developed an empirical research program for the investigation of low-level causality perception using simple psychophysical paradigms. In Michotte's prototypical *launch experiment*, some geometric object A moves toward object B, which is stationary. After collision, object A is stationary and B moves away from A, evoking an immediate perception that the first motion caused the second: "A pushed B." Michotte viewed this phenomenal causality attribution as an example of a gestalt perception illusion akin to apparent motion. Michotte's experimental setup thus has the potential to clarify high-level causal attributions by investigating "early," preattentional causality perception. A variant of Michotte's experiments was used in this trial to study visual motion perception in the presence of additional, auditory stimuli (Sekuler, Sekuler, & Lau, 1997). In our paradigm, two identical discs move, from opposite sides of a monitor, steadily toward and then past one another (Fig. 10.3). Their coincidence generates an ambiguous, bistable percept: The discs appear to either "stream through" or to "bounce off" one another. At around the time of coincidence, a click sound of 40-msec duration was presented from two speakers next to the monitor. The probability of a bouncing perception (i.e., perception of causal interaction between the discs) is low in general but is elevated when a sound is presented near the time of "collision" of the discs (Scheier, Lewkowicz, & Shimojo, 2003).

Figure 10.3. Screen display (schematic) for the perceived causality paradigm. Two discs move horizontally toward each other with constant speed, coincide in the screen center, and continue moving until they are again separated by their initial distance. An auditory stimulus is presented at the time of coincidence.

In Tschacher and Kupper (2006), this phenomenon was used to investigate basic causality perception in schizophrenia spectrum disorder. Causality perception was again conceptualized as a neurocognitive binding process, by which the brain – prior to conscious processing – integrates multiple sensory inputs to create perceptual configurations (Dennett & Kinsbourne, 1992). For each subject, the probability of "bounce" responses was computed across all evaluated runs (*perceived causality*).

The test for overall group differences regarding perceived causality showed a tendency for lower perceived causality in schizophrenia patients. As in the apparent motion paradigms, considering the heterogeneity within the schizophrenia group was necessary. There was a significant effect for contrasts between inpatients and outpatients (the two subgroups within the patients sample) and healthy persons, showing that perceived causality was significantly lowered in outpatients. These findings pointed toward preattentional binding processes being a cause of impaired ToM in a large subgroup of patients. With respect to perceived causality, again a significant and strong association with psychopathology was found, with 46% of total variance of perceived causality explained by differences in psychopathology (Table 10.1). A stepwise regression analysis suggested that perceived causality was increased in the presence of positive symptoms and attenuated by cognitive symptoms.

Gestalt Studies, Complexity, and Schizophrenia

What follows is a summary and discussion of the results from each of the gestalt studies of schizophrenia discussed as an illustration of how the complexity theory approach may be applied to theoretical questions regarding the nature of psychopathology.

Cognitive Pattern Formation

In all whole-model tests performed on the introduced variables in three domains of gestalt functioning, significant associations were found in the respective MANOVA tests. This corroborates and completes the general picture that derives from evaluations of the gestalt approach to schizophrenia. It is thus likely that low-level gestalt impairments are present in, and maybe causally related to, the dimensions of schizophrenia symptoms. In other words, complexity theory can help explain the cognitive impairments present in schizophrenia.

The results of multiple regression analyses showed that the dimensions of psychopathology are differentially associated with perception and cognitive functioning. This is detailed in the overview provided by Table 10.1. As can be seen, the positive symptom factor was most clearly associated with less stable gestalts. Patients' depression, an affective dimension of the disease, was conversely connected to gestalt formation. This means the analysis of cognitive impairments must bear in mind that dimensions of psychopathology may have opposing effects, which may even cancel each other out. In multivariate analysis, however, the explained variance is large, which again corroborates the complexity theory approach.

Patients Versus Healthy Control Subjects

Contrary to expectations, not all group comparisons between participants with schizophrenia spectrum disorder and the control group were significant. Post hoc, it is likely that this reflects the profound heterogeneity within the schizophrenia group. It may not be advisable to speak of schizophrenia as a psychopathological entity at all; rather, one should distinguish between the stages in the course of the illness each patient is in. The cognitive function of gestalt formation is clearly not a trait marker of schizophrenia. Instead, it may serve as a "stage marker" of schizophrenia (Tschacher, 2004). This emphasizes the importance of viewing the schizophrenias as dynamical diseases, diseases that can only be understood by reflecting on their temporal dimension.

General Discussion and Conclusions

Two approaches to psychopathology were deemed promising: the dynamical disease approach and the complexity theory approach. Dynamical systems research in the psychopathology field has relied to a large extent on these two approaches. Both have a large overlap of shared methodology and theory, especially with respect to the mathematical tools and concepts. These approaches diverge, however, in the main topics they address. The dynamical disease approach is focused predominantly on characteristics of the temporal courses of diseases. The modeling of time series in longitudinal research is its natural goal. The complexity theory approach has put the emphasis on the phenomenon of pattern formation and self-organization. We argued that pattern formation and its companion, pattern recognition, are core issues in much of information processing and cognition. Recent years of research in cognitive science have shown that the once prevalent notion of cognition as symbol processing (popularly coined, the computer metaphor of the mind) was ill designed because it cannot account for the self-organizing aspects of cognition, that is, for the constructive, emergent features of information processing (Tschacher & Dauwalder, 2003). For instance, Glenberg and Robertson (2000) proposed that memory is not adequately conceived as a "storehouse" of single items that may be retrieved from a store or register. Rather, remembering is a constructive process with properties that closely resemble those of pattern formation processes as studied by synergetics. Similarly, cognitive categories and schemata are not sufficiently understood as additive collections of attributes (Edelman, 1992). Again, processes of pattern formation and reduction of complexity are necessary to account for these neurocognitive structures.

We found that altered gestalt perception is specific for schizophrenia in the sense that the cognitive function of preattentional neurocognitive pattern formation is focally affected by the disorder. More precisely, it is stage specific in that both the up- and down-regulation of gestalt-like neurocognitive binding is found in schizophrenia depending on the stage of the disorder. Enhancement of gestalt perception is found in prodromal and incipient schizophrenia, which was characterized by Conrad (1958) as the *trema* stage. Reduction of gestalt perception is found in chronic schizophrenia, especially in patients with poor premorbid adaptation (Silverstein & Uhlhaas, 2004).

As anticipated, a considerable proportion of variance in the various paradigms was associated with psychopathology dimensions in the patient sample. Multiple regression analyses pointed to a differential association, that is, positive symptoms enhanced the perceptual effects, whereas depression, negative symptoms, and cognitive disorganization tended to reduce gestalt formation. This differential association between psychopathology and the patients' ability to coordinate features is congruent with the gestalt hypothesis of schizophrenia (Uhlhaas & Silverstein, 2005).

Perceived causality was likewise found to be closely related to psychopathology, especially positive symptoms and the cognitive (disorganization) factor. Positive symptoms were associated with increased perceived causality, and disorganization with attenuated perceived causality. Fundamental symptom domains of schizophrenia spectrum disorder are thus associated with perceived causality in a meaningful way. Our interpretation of results is that causality perception may underlie positive and cognitive symptoms in patients. Likely, perceived causality studied with the present paradigm is a fundamental preattentional cognitive function that occurs independently of conscious, linguistic, or metacognitive processing. The findings therefore suggest that adult patients showing deficient ToM may already be compromised at this early and fundamental stage of perceptual organization. These findings, together with the previous work on cognitive coordination and perceptual grouping, show that a dynamical systems approach with a focus on complexity can account for a significant portion of the variance in schizophrenia psychopathology. Disturbances of perceptual organization may well be a key cognitive symptom in many schizophrenia-spectrum patients.

There are many approaches to, and theories of, psychopathology. Why, then, should we bother with another one, the NDS view? Is it just another theory in a complex field? We have pointed out that there is something special about the NDS approach and that there are specific reasons to take this approach seriously. In the remainder of this chapter, we wrap up our argument by a threefold outlook, because there are theoretical, therapeutic, and philosophical reasons to pursue and elaborate further the dynamical systems approach.

Theoretical Implications

NDS theory is a unifying theory and methodology, which can be applied to diverse problems. This theory is intrinsically interdisciplinary in nature, because its foundation is not confined to any one substrate or scientific discipline. It may be applied on different levels of cognitive functioning – for instance, at the level of preattentional perceptual grouping (as in apparent motion perception) or at the level of concept formation as in causality attributions. Notwithstanding the level and field of application, the core concepts of dynamical systems theory remain the same: pattern formation, stability and attractors, complexity reduction, and self-organization. These core constructs have been modeled mathematically (Frank & Beek, 2003; Haken, 1977) and provide a large variety of methods. These methods are especially helpful for longitudinal research, an aspect of psychopathology that has hitherto been largely neglected.

One may note that the present scientific debate of linear–computational versus NDS psychology is not entirely new to the larger field of psychology. About a century ago, an analogous, even identical, debate was carried out in this then-young scientific field – namely, between associationist psychology and gestalt psychology. It is not surprising that today's psychology and neurocognitive science implement "old" gestalt psychological paradigms to a growing extent (without necessarily referring to the original references).

Therapeutic Implications

The dynamical systems approach to psychopathology throws a different light on mental disorders. Mental states, disordered or not, are viewed as attractors, as dynamical invariants that are constantly in flux, rather than as constants or lesions. A psychopathological state is not fundamentally different from a healthy state in this respect. It is hoped that this view on psychopathology will prove to be instrumental in supporting and developing new clinical interventions.

In our investigation into mental pattern formation, we have repeatedly found that especially low-level, preattentional processes are easily described by the complexity theory approach. It is unclear so far which of these low-level cognitive processes and deficits can be modified by cognitive remediation therapy. Higher-order cognitive processes are based not on external stimuli but on a pre-processed version of these. Higher-order cognition depends on preattentional stages of cognition, which attach holistic, gestalt-like attributes to single-stimulus items. The ease and elegance by which such pre-processing occurs is crucial for cognitive performance in subsequent functions, such as the conscious allocation of attention, memory processes, reasoning, or planning. This aspect of cognition may be targeted by cognitive remediation therapy (Wykes et al., 2003; Wykes & van der Gaag, 2001).

A focus on perceptual organization can, for instance, lead to the instigation of novel approaches for the psychological treatment. Disturbances of perceptual organization differ from other cognitive deficits found in schizophrenia in that they are not strictly performance deficits, such as reduced attention, reduced memory abilities, or reduced planning skills. Rather, deregulated perceptual organization can take both the form of *gestalt deficit*, (i.e., underresponsiveness to holistic stimulus features) and of *gestalt excess* (i.e., overresponsiveness). Because disturbances of perceptual organization are likely to be markedly different in subgroups of patients, a selective indication approach to cognitive remediation is appropriate (e.g., remediation for gestalt excesses and remediation for gestalt deficits). Gestalt excess may be at the basis of the well-described cognitive symptom of "jumping to conclusions" in schizophrenia (Garety et al., 2005; Moritz & Woodward, 2005). Gestalt excess may be responsive to both more cognitive, informational, and practice-oriented remediative interventions. Cognitive procedures can inform patients about their possible tendencies to make premature judgments and practice modified responses to their perceptions. Presumably, the secondary cognitive and emotional processing of gestalt excess perceptions, in the form of fear, paranoid thinking, or avoidance, may be more suitable targets for intervention than the gestalt excess per se. For example, auditory hallucinations often acquire the shape of imperative commands. Trower et al. (2004) have shown that compliance with hallucinated commands (which can be severely destructive to the patient and his or her social environment) can be considerably reduced using cognitive therapy. In a further randomized controlled study, patients' chronic drug-refractory symptoms were treated by cognitive–behavioral therapy (Valmaggia, van der Gaag, Tarrier, & Sloof, 2005). They found that the physical characteristics (e.g., loudness of hallucinated voices) and cognitive interpretation of auditory hallucinations (attribution of control; amount of preoccupation) was reduced in the active treatment group. Therapy for gestalt deficits, on the other hand, could be accomplished through practice-oriented interventions. In applying pattern-recognition exercises (e.g., using abstract visual patterns and materials from social perception; Brenner, Hodel, Genner, Roder, & Corrigan, 1992), the subgroup of schizophrenia patients with a gestalt deficit must generally be supported in expecting, and searching, causal structures and meaning.

Philosophical Implications

Gestalt perception is of considerable importance to most mental processes in that it sets the stage for subsequent steps, such as the allocation of attention, memory processes, and executive functioning. From a first-person perspective, gestalt formation organizes the experienced world, rendering it reliable and familiar, while categorizing information in a way that supports recognition and action. According to our general hypothesis, this process is affected in schizophrenia spectrum disorders, but also in other psychopathological states. Parnas et al. (2001, p. 172) recognized in schizophrenia "a deficiency in the automatic *pre-reflective* intentionality." From a third-person perspective, pattern formation is a well-known and mathematically accessible function of material complex systems.

The relationship between mind and matter (especially, the brain) belongs to the hard and long-standing questions of philosophy. Interestingly, this relationship is addressed by the basic process of emergence, which in the context of synergetics is described as circular causality: From the very many degrees of freedom of a complex system, order parameters arise that in turn "enslave" the complex system in an avalanche-like manner. This basic circularity can explain the rapid emergence of novel patterns in a complex system. Tschacher and Haken (2007) proposed that the emergence of patterns in a self-organizing system has a further, retrograde, effect not only within the system, but also on control parameters, that is, those environmental parameters that caused pattern formation in the first place. For this process, they coined the term *second circularity*. Because of this process, one may ascribe functionality to self-organized patterns because the emerging patterns are capable of reducing the control parameters. This may serve as a formulation of *intentionality* in complex systems. Haken and Tschacher (unpublished manuscript) have formalized this idea and proposed a mathematical application to neural networks showing that the axonal pulse rate of a neural population increases until it saturates, while at the same time the effective control parameter (e.g., the concentrations of certain neurotransmitters that have activated the neurons) is reduced. Thus it can be formally shown that complexity reduction by pattern formation appears to serve a purpose in all complex systems as soon as they are being driven by nonequilibrium parameters. Because the brain is such a complex system, we consider the analogy of this formulation of second circularity to intentional behavior mediated by the brain an interesting and, in our view, compelling result of NDS theory.

Most psychologists and neuroscientists hold, with respect to the mind–body question, a concept of emergent materialism, that is, they would consider mind to be an emergent property of a brain. The theory of second circularity in this context puts forward an argument that emergent mental properties *do indeed matter*, that emergent mind is more than just an epiphenomenon. We believe such philosophical topics are essential for psychopathology, which is a field that must eventually integrate the perspectives of both mind *and* brain. Thus because complexity theory is applicable to both sides of the mind–body gap, and may even put forward ways to bridge this gap, it deserves a special status among the elementary theories of psychopathology.

Acknowledgments

Studies cited in this chapter were supported by the Swiss National Foundation grant 32-55954. The authors thank the staff and directors of Soteria Bern and two day hospitals. We are grateful for the help provided by Daniela Schuler, Priscilla Dubouloz, Rahel Meier, Simon Grossmann, and Zeno Kupper.

References

Bélair, J., Glass, L., an der Heiden, U., & Milton, J. (1995). Dynamical disease: Identification, temporal aspects and treatment strategies of human illness. *Chaos: An Interdisciplinary Journal of Nonlinear Science, 5*, 1–7.

Bonneh, Y. S., Cooperman, A., & Sagi, D. (2001). Motion-induced blindness in normal observers. *Nature, 411*, 798–801.

Brenner, H. D., Hodel, B., Genner, R., Roder, V., & Corrigan, P. W. (1992). Biological and cognitive vulnerability factors in schizophrenia: Implications for treatment. *British Journal of Psychiatry, 161* (Suppl.), 154–163.

Brüne, M. (2005). "Theory of mind" in schizophrenia: A review of the literature. *Schizophrenia Bulletin, 31*, 21–42.

Chambers, J. L., & Wilson, W. T. (1968). Perception of apparent motion and degree of mental pathology. *Perceptual and Motor Skills, 26*, 855–861.

Ciompi, L. (1989). The dynamics of complex biological–psychosocial systems. Four fundamental psycho-biological mediators in the long-term evolution of schizophrenia. *British Journal of Psychiatry, 155* (Suppl.), 15–21.

Conrad, K. (1958). *Die beginnende Schizophrenie* [Early schizophrenia]. Thieme: Stuttgart.

Danziger, L., & Elmergreen, G. L. (1954). Mathematical theory of periodic relapsing catatonia. *Bulletin of Mathematical Biophysics, 16*, 15–21.

Dennett, D. C., & Kinsbourne, M. (1992). Time and the observer: The where and when of consciousness in the brain. *Behavioral and Brain Sciences, 15*, 183–247.

Docherty, N. M., Hall, M. J., Gordinier, S. W., & Cutting, L. P. (2000). Conceptual sequencing and disordered speech in schizophrenia. *Schizophrenia Bulletin, 26*, 723–35.

Doniger, G. M., Silipo, G., Rabinowicz, E. F., Snodgrass, J. G., & Javitt, D. C. (2001). Impaired sensory processing as a basis for object-recognition deficits in schizophrenia. *American Journal of Psychiatry, 158*, 1818–1826.

Edelman, G. M. (1992). *Bright air, brilliant fire – on the matter of the mind.* New York: Basic Books.

Emrich, H., & Hohenschutz, C. (1992). Psychiatric disorders: Are they "dynamical diseases"? In W. Tschacher, G. Schiepek, & E. J. Brunner (Eds.), *Self-organization and clinical psychology* (pp. 204–212). Berlin: Springer-Verlag Publishing Company.

Frank, T., & Beek, P. (2003). A mean field approach to self-organization in spatially extended perception-action and psychological systems. In W. Tschacher & J.-P. Dauwalder (Eds.). *The dynamical systems approach to cognition* (pp. 159–179). Singapore: World Scientific.

Freeman, W. J. (1992). Chaos in psychiatry. *Biological Psychiatry, 31*, 1079–1081.

Frith, C. D., & Corcoran, R. (1996). Exploring "theory of mind" in people with schizophrenia. *Psychological Medicine, 26*, 521–530.

Garety, P. A., Freeman, D., Jolley, S., Dunn, G., Bebbington, P. E., Fowler, D. G., Kuipers, E., & Dudley, R. (2005). Reasoning, emotions, and delusional conviction in psychosis. *Journal of Abnormal Psychology, 114*, 373–384.

Gjessing, R. (1932). Beiträge zur Kenntnis der Pathophysiologie des katatonen Stupors. *Archive der Psychiatrie, 96*, 319–393.

Glenberg, A. M., & Robertson, D. A. (2000). Symbol grounding and meaning: A comparison of high-dimensional and embodied theories of meaning. *Journal of Memory and Language, 43*, 379–401.

Goldstein (1995). *The organism: A holistic approach derived from pathological data in man* (original title: *Der Aufbau des Organismus*). New York: Zone Books. (Original work published 1934)

Goodarzi, M. A., Wykes, T., & Hemsley, D. R. (2000). Cerebral lateralization of global-local processing in people with schizotypy. *Schizophrenia Research, 45*, 115–121.

Gottschalk, A., Bauer, M. S., & Whybrow, P. C. (1995). Evidence of chaotic mood variation in bipolar disorder. *Archives of General Psychiatry, 52*, 947–959.

Graf, E. W., Adams, W. J., & Lages, M. (2002). Modulating motion-induced blindness with depth ordering and surface completion. *Vision Research, 42*, 2731–2735.

Guastello, S. (1995). *Chaos, catastrophe, and human affairs: Applications of nonlinear dynamics to work, organizations, and social evolution.* Hillsdale, NJ: Erlbaum.

Haken, H. (1977). *Synergetics – an introduction: Nonequilibrium phase-transitions and self-organization in physics, chemistry and biology.* Berlin: Springer-Verlag Publishing Company.

Haken, H. (1996). *Principles of brain functioning.* Berlin: Springer-Verlag Publishing Company.

Haken, H., Kelso, J. S., & Bunz, H. (1985). A theoretical model of phase transitions in human hand movements. *Biological Cybernetics, 51*, 347–356.

Haken, H., & Tschacher, W. (unpublished manuscript). A model of intentionality based on neural activity.

Hoffman, R. E., & McGlashan, T. H. (1993). Parallel distributed processing and the emergence of schizophrenic symptoms. *Schizophrenia Bulletin, 15*, 119–140.

Hsu, L. C., Yeh, S. L., & Kramer, P. (2004). Linking motion-induced blindness to perceptual filling-in. *Vision Research, 44*, 2857–2866.

Kay, S. R., Fiszbein, A., & Opler, L. A. (1987). The Positive and Negative Syndrome Scale (PANSS) for schizophrenia. *Schizophrenia Bulletin, 13*, 261–276.

Kelso, J. S. (1995). *Dynamic patterns: The self-organization of brain and behavior.* Cambridge, MA: MIT Press.

Kéri, S., Kelemen, O., Benedek, G., & Janka, Z. (2005). Lateral interactions in the visual cortex of patients with schizophrenia and bipolar disorder. *Psychological Medicine, 35*, 1043–1051.

Köhler, W. (1940). *Dynamics in psychology.* New York: Liveright.

Kruse, P., Carmesin, H.-O., Pahlke, L., Strüber, D., & Stadler, M. (1996). Continuous phase transitions in the perception of multistable visual patterns. *Biological Cybernetics, 75*, 321–330.

Leroy, F., Pezard, L., Nandrino, J. L., & Beaune, D. (2005). Dynamical quantification of schizophrenic speech. *Psychiatry Research, 133*, 159–171.

Lindner, A., Thier, P., Kircher, T. T., Haarmeier, T., & Leube, D. T. (2005). Disorders of agency in schizophrenia correlate with an inability to compensate for the sensory consequences of actions. *Current Biology, 15*, 1119–1124.

Luhmann, N. (1984). *Soziale Systeme: Grundriß einer allgemeinen Theorie*. Frankfurt: Suhrkamp.

Mackey, M. C., & Glass, L. (1977). Oscillation and chaos in physiological control systems. *Science, 197*, 287–289.

Maturana, H., & Varela, F. (1980). *Autopoiesis and cognition: The realization of the living*. Dordrecht: Reidel.

Matussek, P. (1952). Untersuchungen über die Wahrnehmung. 1. Mitteilung. *Archive für Psychiatrie und Zeitschrift für Neurologie, 180*, 279–319. (English: In Cutting J., & Sheppard, M. (Eds.). (1987). *Clinical roots of the schizophrenia concept. Translations of seminal European contributions on schizophrenia* (pp. 87–103). Cambridge: Cambridge University Press.)

Michotte, A. (1962). *The perception of causality*. Andover, MA: Methuen.

Milner, G., & Goodale, N. (1995). *The visual brain in action*. Oxford: Oxford University Press.

Moritz, S., & Woodward, T. S. (2005). Jumping to conclusions in delusional and non-delusional schizophrenic patients. *British Journal of Clinical Psychology, 44*, 193–207.

Nicolis, G., & Prigogine, I. (1977). *Self-organization in nonequilibrium systems: From dissipative structures to order through fluctuations*. New York: Wiley-Interscience.

Parnas, J., Vianin, P., Saebye, D., Jansson, L., Volmer-Larsen, A., & Bovet, P. (2001). Visual binding abilities in the initial and advanced stages of schizophrenia. *Acta Psychiatrica Scandinavica, 103*, 171–180.

Paulsen, J. S., Romero, R., Chan, A., Davis, A. V., Heaton, R. K., & Jeste, D. V. (1996). Impairment of the semantic network in schizophrenia. *Psychiatry Research, 63*, 109–121.

Paulus, M. P., & Braff, D. L. (2003). Chaos and schizophrenia: Does the method fit the madness? *Biological Psychiatry, 53*, 3–11.

Paulus, M. P., Geyer, M. A., & Braff, D. L. (1996). Use of methods from chaos theory to quantify a fundamental dysfunction in the behavioral organization of schizophrenic patients. *American Journal of Psychiatry 153*, 714–717.

Pezard, L., Nandrino, J.-L., Renault, B., Massioui, F. E., Allilaire, J.-F., & Varela, F. J. (1996). Depression as a dynamical disease. *Biological Psychiatry, 39*, 991–999.

Phillips, W. A., & Silverstein, S. M. (2003). Convergence of biological and psychological perspectives on cognitive coordination in schizophrenia. *Behavioral and Brain Sciences, 26*, 65–138.

Place, E. J., & Gilmore, G. C. (1980). Perceptual organization in schizophrenia. *Journal of Abnormal Psychology, 89*, 409–418.

Ramachandran, V. S., & Gregory, R. L. (1991). Perceptual filling in of artificially induced scotomas in human vision. *Nature, 350*, 699–702.

Russell, T. A., Reynaud, E., Herba, C., Morris, R., & Corcoran, R. (2006). Do you see what I see? Interpretations of intentional movement in schizophrenia. *Schizophrenia Research, 81*, 101–111.

Sarfati, Y., Hardy-Bayle, M. C., Brunet, E., & Widlocher, D. (1999). Investigating the-ory of mind in schizophrenia: Influence of verbalization in disorganized and non-disorganized patients. *Schizophrenia Research, 37,* 183–190.

Sass, L. A., & Parnas, J. (2003). Schizophrenia, consciousness, and the self. *Schizophrenia Bulletin, 29,* 427–444.

Saucer, R. T., & Deabler, H. L. (1956). Perception of apparent motion in organics and schizophrenics. *Journal of Consulting Psychology, 20,* 385–389.

Scheier, C., Lewkowicz, D. J., & Shimojo, S. (2003). Sound induces perceptual reorgani-zation of an ambiguous motion display in human infants. *Developmental Science, 6,* 233–241.

Sekuler, R., Sekuler, A., & Lau, R. (1997). Sound alters visual motion perception. *Nature, 385,* 308.

Silverstein, S. M., Kovacs, I., Corry, R., & Valone, C. (2000). Perceptual organiza-tion, the disorganization syndrome, and context processing in chronic schizophrenia. *Schizophrenia Research, 43,* 11–20.

Silverstein, S. M., & Uhlhaas, P. J. (2004). Gestalt psychology: The forgotten paradigm in abnormal psychology. *American Journal of Psychology, 117,* 259–277.

Simons, D. J., & Chabris, C. F. (1999). Gorillas in our midst: Sustained inattentional blindness for dynamic events. *Perception, 28,* 1059–1074.

Singer, W., & Gray, C. M. (1995). Visual feature integration and the temporal correlation hypothesis. *Annual Review of Neuroscience, 18,* 555–586.

Sugihara, G., & May, R. (1990). Nonlinear forecasting as a way of distinguishing chaos from measurement error in time series. *Nature, 344,* 734–741.

Sullivan, E. V., Shear, P. K., Zipursky, R. B., Sagar, H. J., & Pfefferbaum, A. (1997). Patterns of content, contextual, and working memory impairments in schizophrenia and nonamnesic alcoholism. *Neuropsychology, 11,* 195–206.

Trower, P., Birchwood, M., Meaden, A., Byrne, S., Nelson, A., & Ross, K. (2004). Cognitive therapy for command hallucinations: Randomised controlled trial. *British Journal of Psychiatry, 184,* 312–320.

Tschacher, W. (2004). How specific is the gestalt-informed approach to schizophrenia? *Gestalt Theory, 26,* 335–344.

Tschacher, W., & Dauwalder, J.-P. (Eds.). (2003). *The dynamical systems approach to cognition.* Singapore: World Scientific.

Tschacher, W., Dubouloz, P., Meier, R., & Junghan, U. (2008). Altered perception of apparent motion in schizophrenia spectrum disorder. *Psychiatry Research, 159,* 290 – 299.

Tschacher, W., & Haken, H. (2007). Intentionality in non-equilibrium systems? The functional aspects of self-organized pattern formation. *New Ideas in Psychology, 25,* 1–15.

Tschacher, W., & Kupper, Z. (2006). Perception of causality in schizophrenia spectrum disorder. *Schizophrenia Bulletin, 32,* S106–S112.

Tschacher, W., & Kupper, Z. (2007). A dynamics-oriented approach to psychopathology. *Nebraska Symposium on Motivation, 52,* 85–122.

Tschacher, W., Scheier, C., & Hashimoto, Y. (1997). Dynamical analysis of schizophrenia courses. *Biological Psychiatry, 41,* 428–437.

Tschacher, W., Schuler, D., & Junghan, U. (2006). Reduced perception of the motion-induced blindness illusion in schizophrenia. *Schizophrenia Research, 81,* 261–267.

Uhlhaas, P. J., & Silverstein, S. M. (2005). Perceptual organization in schizophrenia spectrum disorders: A review of empirical research and associated theories. *Psychological Bulletin, 131*, 618–632.

Valmaggia, L. R., van Der Gaag, M., Tarrier, N. M. P., & Sloof, C. J. (2005). Cognitive behavioural therapy for refractory psychotic symptoms of schizophrenia resistant to atypical antipsychotic medication. *British Journal of Psychiatry, 186*, 324–330.

Varela, F. J. (1995). Resonant cell assemblies: A new approach to cognitive function and neuronal synchrony. *Biological Research, 28*, 81–95.

von Holst, E., & Mittelstaedt, H. (1950). Das Reafferenzprinzip. Wechselwirkung zwischen Zentralnervensystem und Peripherie [The reafference principle: Mutual relationship between central nervous system and periphery]. *Naturwissenschaften, 37*, 464–476.

von Schiller, P. (1933). Stroboskopische Alternativversuche [Stroboscopic alternation trials]. *Psychologische Forschung, 17*, 179–214.

Wehr, T. A., & Goodwin, F. K. (1979). Rapid cycling in manic-depressives induced by tricyclic antidepressants. *Archives of General Psychiatry, 36*, 555–559.

Wertheimer, M. (1912). Experimentelle Studien über das Sehen von Bewegungen [Experimental studies on visual perception of motion]. *Zeitschrift für Psychologie, 61*, 161–265.

Winfree, A. T. (1980). *The geometry of biological time.* New York: Springer-Verlag Publishing Company.

Wykes, T., Reeder, C., Williams, C., Corner, J., Rice, C., & Everitt, B. (2003). Are the effects of cognitive remediation therapy (CRT) durable? Results from an exploratory trial in schizophrenia. *Schizophrenia Research, 61*, 163–174.

Wykes, T., & van Der Gaag, M. (2001). Is it time to develop a new cognitive therapy for psychosis–cognitive remediation therapy (CRT)? *Clinical Psychology Review, 21*, 1227–1256.

11 Coherence, Complexity, and Information Flow: Self-Organizing Processes in Psychotherapy

DAVID PINCUS

The *True* Nature of Psychotherapy

What is psychotherapy? This simple question can stimulate hours of discussion, producing more new questions for each new answer. For example, one may ask if there is a single answer to what psychotherapy is, or if in fact psychotherapy is always different for each unique client. Probing deeper, one may also wonder if scientifically informed "theories" of psychotherapy really add to the "truth" of what therapy is for any given client, or whether truth is actually derived through a constructive process. Such questions raise the question of the merits of "truth" versus "utility," as even the most scientifically controlled or "manualized" approaches to treatment encourage the therapist to accommodate any approach to fit the values, goals, and unique situations of the client. It appears that defining psychotherapy is a difficult matter, creating practical and scientific questions that are worthy of deep exploration.

Psychotherapy has a great tradition of such deep self-examination. For example, Frank and Frank (1991) have influenced two generations of therapists with the well-reasoned yet apparently controversial suggestion that modern psychotherapy is based more on applied rhetoric than on scientific discovery. The psychotherapy field has generally been forced to conclude that factors common across approaches are better predictors of treatment outcome than are the use of a specific technique (Orlinsky & Howard, 1995), particularly the quality of the therapist–client relationship (Orlinsky, Grawe, & Parks, 1994). Unfortunately, this clear and ubiquitous set of findings has not deterred the proliferation of more than 400 purportedly distinct "theories" of psychotherapy (Garfield, 1995). Each of these new theories may be characterized by considerable overlap with other approaches (past and present) and a difficulty in demonstrating any true scientific advancement beyond showing that the treatment is generally effective.

This situation has led many prominent researchers to turn away from the quest for the final new approach, toward the ways in which the therapeutic relationship and other common factors of therapy may be better understood and enhanced to make therapy more effective. These investigations have led down more philosophical avenues, examining such things as the social roles of clients, the cultural aspects of science, and the role of the therapist from cultural and historical perspectives. For example, Orlinsky and Howard (1995) wrote:

> The modern scientific psychotherapies can be seen as modes of healing that have been reinvented to suit the secular, rational, and technological culture that predominates among the middle and elite strata of urban industrial society. [p. 5].... a *professional service* that provides *personal help* in the sphere of *private life* under the symbolic authority and guidance of *scientific knowledge* [italics in original] ... This combination of professional service with personal attachment ... is a defining and distinctive feature of modern psychotherapy. (p. 9)

Psychotherapy is a strange profession indeed. Session after session the therapist's job is to create in 50-minute segments the most unique and open relationship that each client is likely to experience in his or her life. It is no wonder that the vast majority of therapists see scientific principles as antithetical to this process (Crane, Wampler, Sprenkle, Sandberg, & Hovestadt, 2002; Garfield, 1998). On the job, the psychotherapist must serve such disparate functions as diagnostician, source of emotional support, coach, referee, leader, follower, and healer. This interpersonal balance of psychotherapy continually unfolds over numerous scales of time, from exchange to exchange, emotion to emotion, session to session, from beginnings to ends to new beginnings. Therapists are pulled by competing biopsychosocial forces throughout, as they attempt to stay present and aware of these processes, within the client, within themselves, and among the two.

The common thread that could tie together these questions about the science and the practice of psychotherapy is the therapeutic relationship. A number of key questions remain in this regard, such as: Which interpersonal processes are therapeutic? When are they most therapeutic? Which interpersonal processes are destructive? When are they most destructive? Which specific techniques or heuristics might therapists use to intervene in the direction of healthy functioning? How may we use this ubiquitous *interpersonal space* in which we do our work to assist our clients in *moving from here to there*?

Many of the deeper basic science questions have remained as well, such as: Why does this interpersonal process exist in the first place? What purpose does it serve in human relationships in general? Perhaps some individual clinicians have achieved momentary states of wisdom in this regard. For the great majority of us, however, we get a rare and fuzzy glimpse at the apparent meaning of interpersonal processes only now and then. At the same time, the optimistic among us await the scientific development of a single objectively testable theory of psychotherapy that may unite the field under a single paradigm. The more cynical among us watch with amusement as the development of integrative approaches attempt to keep pace with the development of "new theories."

This chapter is written in the spirit of optimism, suggesting that self-organization is just such a general theory that may assist in providing a deeper, scientifically grounded understanding of the complex biopsychosocial processes involved in psychotherapy. To provide some foundation to this rather grand suggestion, the following review rests on five more specific theoretical propositions stemming from self-organization theory: (a) Order emerges naturally from the exchange of information among individuals (i.e., agents) involved in psychotherapeutic interactions; (b) this emergent self-organizing interpersonal system is open, interacting with neighboring systems across scales of time (i.e., moment-to-moment, week-to-week) and biopsychosocial space (i.e., from physiological systems, through self-systems, and up to larger-scale social networks); (c) mindfulness practices act to open, balance, and reintegrate self-organizing biopsychosocial systems by utilizing natural processes of recursion within these systems; (d) the most commonly studied interpersonal processes (i.e., control, closeness, and conflict) are emergent structures, arising from patterned flows of information exchange, and feeding back to regulate subsequent flows over time in a circular manner across scales; and (e) self-organizing interpersonal information flows and emergent regulating structures naturally evolve toward the edge of chaos, with shifts toward rigidity and complexity reflecting evolutionary demands (see Fig. 11.1 for this general model which will be used throughout this chapter).

The analysis of these propositions begins with an integrative review of traditional theories of interpersonal process through the lens of nonlinear dynamical systems (NDS) and self-organization theory in particular. Next, the contemporary empirical and theoretical developments using NDS to understand psychotherapy process are reviewed. Finally, some general conclusions are drawn, and avenues for future research are suggested. The goal here is not to do away with the rich diversity in approaches to therapy. Rather, the aim is to frame such approaches as *approaches*, rather than as *theories*, and to tie these approaches together through a deeper understanding of self-organizing interpersonal processes in psychotherapy.

With these goals in mind, five specific questions pertaining to depth, breadth, and clinical relevance are addressed: (a) How may we begin to integrate the various theories and approaches to psychotherapy within a common scientific framework? (b) How and why do interpersonal systems emerge? (c) Why do these systems always seem to involve a mixture of both coherence and complexity? (d) What is the significance of ubiquitous relational processes such as control, closeness, and conflict? (e) What is the true meaning of interpersonal patterns?

From Roots to Branches: Historical Development of the Process-Oriented Psychotherapies

With more than 400 supposedly different ways to do the same rather complex job, it seems that the last thing the field needs is yet another approach: *chaos therapy* anyone? No? Yet development within the field of psychotherapy has been

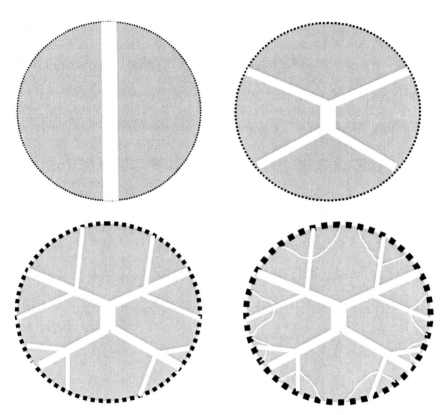

Figure 11.1. A conceptual illustration of self-organizing interpersonal dynamics. The white space within each circle represents areas in which interpersonal information may flow. Gray areas indicate areas that are off-limits to discussion, or *out of bounds*. Information flowing along the vertical dimension represents control-oriented information. Information flowing along the horizontal dimension represents closeness. The dashed outer boundaries around each circle define the group as a whole, with branches representing openness of the group to flows of information. The thickness of this external boundary represents the robustness, or integrity, of the group. Each bifurcation point (branch node) represents a resolved conflict with regard to control or closeness among the group members. Moving from top left to bottom right, one observes an evolutionary progression in group process over time.

defined by this very type of ongoing expansion and division, with the splintering and relabeling of distinct rhetorical concepts, from old to new, to newer, newest, and invariably back to old. As Frank and Frank (1991) observed, no school of psychotherapy has ever disbanded because of a lack of clinical effectiveness. Thus our first task here is to appreciate the tangled wisdoms that have already appeared, rather than simply plaster NDS jargon on old concepts and call them new.

There is a common assumption that, within interpersonal processes, there exist patterns of events that repeat themselves, and produce a general structure of some sort. Next, assume that these patterns may be shifted through a variety of techniques toward the goal of improved biopsychosocial functioning. Indeed, notions of interpersonal patterning are ubiquitous in applied psychology, despite the often fragmented and indirect nature in which they tend to be understood. To begin the grand task of weaving together the common threads among clinical approaches, I focus on the rigid patterning that is associated with conflict.

Conflict, emerging across all scales from small to large, from internal conflicts ("I hate myself"), to marital conflicts ("I hate you"), to world wars ("We hate them"). Furthermore, experimental research has demonstrated that conflicts are not only ubiquitous across scales but that they are prone to spreading across these scales along with rigidity and flexibility corresponding to conflict and conflict resolution respectively (Matz & Wood, 2005; McGregor, Zanna, Holmes, & Spencer, 2005; McKimmie, et al., 2003). It is easy to identify real-world examples of such processes, such as the political despots from whom internal conflicts have contributed to wars on the lager scales (e.g., Hitler's neuroticism and World War II). The associations among conflict, rigidity, and dysfunction across individual and social scales may help to explain why conflict is so important within the various schools of psychotherapy.

Psychoanalysis: The First Word in Conflict

Freud's (1905) theory of personality and psychotherapy was built upon the conflict dynamic. Specifically, analysis suggests that there is an ongoing conflict within all individuals between the *id* and *superego*, competing psychic structures representing biological drives and internalized social norms, respectively. It was this enduring conflict dynamic according to Freud that was the developmental engine of the psyche. Internal conflict resolution was believed to spur healthy growth and psychosocial flexibility, whereas unresolved conflicts were believed to result in fixations, characterized by stagnation, rigidity, and an overreliance on primitive defense mechanisms employed to block conflicting information from consciousness. Although not explicit or formal, notions of information flow, coevolutionary processes across individuals, complex regulation across scales, structural coherence, integration versus fragmentation, and other aspects of self-organization may be gleaned rather easily between the lines of Freud's original texts.

Following Freud's original theory of psychoanalysis, his conflict model has been expanded, divided, revised, and subdivided by others, resulting in the myriad analytically informed schools that exist today, including psychodynamic, object-relations, ego, humanist, existential, attachment based, emotion-focused, interpersonal, and family systems (see Fig. 11.2). Although many of the original details and points of emphasis from analytic theory have been revised, most of

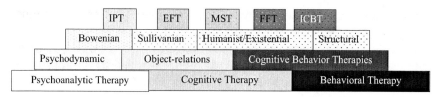

Figure 11.2. A conceptual diagram representing an evolution in psychotherapeutic approaches. Older, foundational approaches are located at the bottom of the pyramid. Newer, more integrative approaches are at the top. The gray-scale represents the underlying research model's focus on nonobservable phenomena (i.e., thoughts). The dotted backgrounds of the third level represents the nonscientific constructivist influence that permeated many of the approaches of the 1950s to the 1970s. This pyramid contains only a very narrow subset of the full number of approaches and the complex patterns of influence among approaches. IPT = interpersonal therapies; EFT = emotion-focused therapies; MST = multisystemic therapies; FFT = functional family therapy; ICBT = integrative cognitive–behavioral therapies.

the basic systemic concepts have remained. For example, the psychodynamic clinicians have focused heavily on the repetitive relational processes associated with the particular internal conflicts of clients (Luborsky & Crits-Christoph, 1998). The object-relations clinicians (i.e., Bowlby, 1982) have focused on the ego and its recursive self-relations (i.e., autonomy and coping) and outward other relations (i.e., objects and intimacy needs). Furthermore, self-relations and other relations are proposed to be either balanced (flexible and complex), or unbalanced (extreme and rigid). The humanists (i.e., Rogers, 1951) have focused more explicitly on the inherent potential for growth and flexibility within individuals and the factors that promote integration and growth, such as empathy (i.e., shared understanding and connection) and mindful acceptance (i.e., nonjudgment and congruence). Similarly, the existentialists (i.e., May, 1977) have focused on experiential awareness that may bring healing through connection to larger values, bringing flexible meaning to an inherently chaotic world.

Horney's (1966, 1970) psychodynamic model provides a good starting point to examine the systemic commonalities among these analytically based approaches. Horney (1970) suggested that individuals may use three primary strategies to meet interpersonal needs: (a) *moving toward*, accepting and accommodating the needs of others to gain intimacy or closeness with others; (b) *moving against*, pushing others to accommodate one's need to establish dominance or control; and (c) *moving away*, a strategy of self-protection through withdrawal and avoidance. Healthy individuals are defined by their ability to apply flexibly any of the three strategies depending on the goodness of fit with the particular interpersonal context, whereas dysfunctional individuals rigidly cling to one approach without regard to its usefulness. Furthermore, the rigid strategy of dysfunctional individuals is thought to take on a quasi-adaptive function (leading to short-term relative fitness), whereby the problem is employed as its own solution. Rigid overuse of one particular strategy becomes self-sustaining through positive circular feedback over time.

For example, if an individual rigidly uses a moving-toward strategy to get close to others, he or she will tend to subjugate assertiveness and autonomy for the sake of acceptance by others. When the strategy works, garnering social approval, the strategy gets stronger, and when the strategy is ineffective, the individual is motivated to work even harder to please others on the next possible occasion. The same process of self-fulfilling prophecy happens regardless of the strategy used, as those who move against find themselves constantly under attack from others and those who move away find themselves constantly alone. Over time, rigidity leads to rigidity leads to rigidity, as short-term interpersonal adaptations aimed at avoiding a *narcissistic injury* (Kohut, 1977) block the development of more flexible longer-term adaptive strategies.

In each case the internal conflict is maintained by the circular regulatory mechanism involving the use of the problem to solve the problem. Within the individual, rigid flows of self-other information emerge across time and within psychosocial space: putting oneself down to stop feeling exploited, striking first to reduce attacks, and abandoning others so as not to be abandoned. Within these psychodynamic models, one may glean a first piece of clinical wisdom that may be retained in the study of interpersonal processes from an NDS perspective. Hypothetical Proposition (1): *the fundamental process underlying conflict is rigidity, which may spread across the intersection of the psyche across time and scales of biopsychosocial space.*

Sullivan and Rogers: Interpersonal Process and Humanism

The 1950s brought the ideas of two clinical theoreticians to the forefront of popular therapy, with approaches that have come to be considered distinct from their psychoanalytic roots: Carl Rogers's *Humanism* (i.e., client-centered therapy; 1951) and Harry Stack Sullivan's (1953) *interpersonal psychiatry.* Rogers (1957) was the first to place theoretical focus on the common factors of psychotherapy. Specifically, Rogers identified (a) *empathy*: understanding the experience of the client in an *as if* manner (Rogers, 1957, p. 829); (b) *unconditional positive regard*: unfettered esteem for and nonjudgment of your client as a human being; and (c) *congruence*: a state of mindful self-acceptance and self-integrity. Subsequent research by Rogers (and others; for a review, see Orlinsky & Howard, 1986) has indeed confirmed the necessity of these common factors to treatment outcome.

Rogers's (1951) humanistic theory of personality suggests that psychopathology is the result of conflicts between the phenomenological *self* as subjectively perceived by the client, and the *organism*; the client in a more objective sense and as typically perceived by others. Self versus organism conflicts were thought to be created during early interactions with caregivers involving empathic failures, misattuned caregiving responses, leading to internalized *conditions of worth* within the developing child that were self-sustaining over time. Herein, one finds a strong linkage with earlier psychodynamic models of conflict.

Such self-conflicting parent–child misattunements include statements such as: "You're not tired, you just had a nap," "You're not hungry, you just ate," or "Why are you sad? We're having fun." In sufficient quantity, these empathic failures are believed to build up internal conflicts within the child, blocking certain internal experiences and leading to a lack of self-understanding (i.e., "maybe I'm not really sad?") and in the worst case conditions of worth (i.e., "if I am sad, I'm no good"). The objective sadness of the organism is at conflict with the subjective experience of the self, such that certain experiences bring conflict and incongruence (a lack of structural integrity) within the self. Within the process of therapy, accurate empathy and radical acceptance on the part of the congruent therapist is believed to create an ideal interpersonal context that would allow for self-repair (Rogers, 1951). When viewed from an NDS perspective, it is clear that the same psychodynamic principles describing the spread of unresolved conflict and rigidity remain within these humanist traditions.

However, a paradox lies within the fact that humanist and other more modern approaches to therapy embrace these same principles with respect to conflict, balance, and change, while rejecting psychodynamic traditions as a whole. Within contemporary psychotherapeutic practice, one would be hard-pressed to find any approach that has not adopted these humanistic principles, or an empirical study that has not found them to be beneficial when balanced with some change-oriented activity (Orlinsky & Howard, 1995). Indeed, even the most recent trends in behavioral therapy (for a review, see S. C. Hayes, Follette, & Linehan, 2004) have converged with the work of process-oriented psychotherapy researchers (Lynch, Chapman, Rosenthal, Kuo, & Linehan, 2006; Sexton, Alexander, & Mease, 2004), resulting in the common notion that successful psychotherapy ultimately involves a balance between stability and complexity, acceptance and change.

Yet these traditions remain in isolation from one another. Lacking a comprehensive scientific framework to couch this process of balance within the behavioral traditions and still refusing to merge with the nonbehavioral therapeutic traditions, these clinicians have instead relied on dialectical philosophy as a metaphor to guide treatment development and explain efficacy. This appears a rather extreme maneuver in and of itself, particularly considering the radical empirical foundations underlying the development of behaviorism in psychology. Lynch et al. (2006) described dialectical philosophy as applied to behavioral therapy in the following manner:

> The process by which a phenomenon, behavior, or argument is transformed is the dialectic, which involves three essential stages: (1) the beginning, in which an initial proposition or statement (thesis) occurs; (2) the negation of the beginning phenomenon, which involves a contradiction or "antithesis;" and (3) the negation of the negation, or the synthesis of thesis and antithesis. Essentially, tension develops

between thesis and antithesis, the synthesis between the two constitutes the next thesis, and the process is repeated ad infinitum. Dialectical philosophy also posits that
reality is composed of interrelated parts that cannot be defined without reference to
the system as a whole. Similarly, a whole system is composed of parts and cannot be
defined without reference to its parts. The system and its parts constantly are in a state
of change or flux, and changes in one influence changes in the other. When applied
to the understanding of human suffering, this ontological principle of interrelatedness and wholeness leads to a systemic and contextual conceptualization of behavior.
(pp. 461–462)

In addition to the lack of integration with the psychodynamic traditions, it is
also apparent from this passage that the contemporary behavioral approaches
have made an ironic connection to dialectical philosophy rather than using an
equivalent yet empirically oriented approach grounded in self-organization.

The modern psychodynamic approaches, typically renamed as *interpersonal*
approaches to therapy, rely implicitly on the same general principles of change.
For example, the acceptance–change *dialectic* is clearly exemplified through
the use of *process comments* in Teyber's (2005) interpersonal model of therapy.
Process comments involve the therapist engaging the client in a discussion of the
here and now unfolding of interpersonal processes within the therapist–client
relationship. In this manner, the therapist and client may actively cocreate the
interpersonal reality in which they are operating. For example, the therapist
may model congruence in the here and now: "When I hear you asking that
question, it pulls me to want to give you reassurance and care." In this example,
the therapist is being honest and focusing attention on an interpersonal pull or
attractor within the session, while at the same time maintaining psychosocial
distance from the attractor through mindful acceptance. Process comments may
serve a number of other functions as well, such as allowing a therapist to deliver
a challenge to the client that would otherwise be likely to bring about conflict or
resistance: "How sure are you right now that what you're telling me is really the
whole story? Because I'm feeling a strong pull to challenge what you are saying
right now."

Ultimately, each of these examples involves opening up the interactive space
to allow for more flexibility in the exchanges of information between therapist
and client. It is one thing to tell clients that they may break down information
boundaries and discuss anything that they may be experiencing. It is another
thing altogether to do this actively within the relational space. The term *emotionally corrective experience* (Alexander & French, 1980; Teyber, 2005) is used
to describe novel exchanges that may emerge from such process comments. The
term describes the breaking down of rigid, emotion-laden information boundaries that have served to spread the internal conflicts of a client across time and
biopsychosocial space. Intrinsic to such notions one may generate a second theoretical proposition that is informed by NDS and builds on the former proposition
regarding the equivalence of conflict and rigidity: *Psychotherapy works through*

the resolution of conflicts, which open up the boundaries that regulate a client's biopsychosocial flows of information.

From the perspective of self-organization theory, this proposition may explain why mindfulness-based approaches have become so popular over the past decade across the various approaches to therapy and why such approaches tend to be so effective (Baer, 2003; Eifert & Forsyth, 2005). Mindfulness practices in therapy come originally from the Buddhist traditions of meditation and involve "intentionally bringing one's attention to the internal and external experiences occurring in the present moment" (Baer, 2003, p. 125). Mindfulness, be it interpersonal in the form of process comments or internal in the form of non-judgmental self-reflection, may in theory obtain its power through recursion, which assists in the resolution of conflicting flows of biopsychosocial information. Mindfulness involves turning one's flows of information on one's flows of information. Therein the self becomes loosely involved with the self, and within the relationship, the individuals loosely relate about their relations. As such, a third theoretical proposition may be proposed: *Mindfulness practices act to open, balance, and reintegrate self-organizing biopsychosocial systems by utilizing natural processes of recursion within these systems.*

At the same time as Rogers was converting notions of internal conflict into the humanistic perspective, Sullivan was translating the relational aspects of analysis into a tradition that would become the foundation for family therapy (i.e., Minuchin & Fishman, 1974), group therapy (i.e., Yalom, 1985), and the modern interpersonal approaches to therapy. Sullivan's basic premise is that psychopathology is primarily a manifestation of one's degree of positive connection to others, rather than some internal process. This idea is most clearly reflected in his definition of personality as "the relatively enduring pattern of recurrent interpersonal situations" that occur over the life span (Sullivan, 1953, p. 111). Sullivan's focus on interpersonal needs closely resembles psychodynamic premises (i.e., Horney, 1970), as well as the earlier analytic theory of Adler (1930), which was also a balance model involving needs for power and affiliation. Despite these equivalencies, Sullivan was the first to suggest that personality is largely driven by the social environment rather than vice versa. Furthermore, Sullivan focused on the interactive nature of person and situation, including the self-regulating flexibility that comes from conflict resolution, be it social, individual, or, more likely, mixed. Sullivan's ideas were later formalized for research purposes within the interpersonal circumplex models (Leary, 1957; Wiggins, 1979), which have continued to be of influence in social psychology research.

The Conjoint Therapies: Adventures in Avalanche Control

Whereas each of the individual therapy traditions outlined in the previous subsections has dealt with the spread of internal conflict up to the interpersonal domain, Sullivan's interpersonal psychiatry provided a foundation for the development of the conjoint therapies, which focused on the converse: resolving interpersonal conflicts help the individual. Perhaps the clearest example of this notion of group dynamics flowing downward into individuals is within the various approaches to family therapy. The traditional belief espoused within these approaches is that individual pathology may be more accurately conceptualized as a symptom of larger-scale problems of family relations. In a classic example, a child is pulled toward misbehavior by the family system because the misbehavior serves to distract the family from underlying marital conflicts. Some contemporary family therapists have challenged this unidirectional explanation and emphasized the practical need to consider systems across scales, from family to individual and back (Diamond, Diamond, & Liddle, 2000).

Unfortunately, innovations such as these are slow and hard to come by in the field of family therapy because of the radical constructivist traditions on which the field was founded (Nichols & Schwartz, 2005). Indeed, there is still a rather strong antiscience streak within the family therapy community, which serves to magnify the split between empirical research on the one hand, and clinical theory on the other (Diamond et al., 2000; Sprenkle & Blow, 2004). As a result, family systems theory has seen little change over the past 30 to 40 years (Nichols & Schwartz, 2005).

Nevertheless, the term "*systemic*" continues to be a powerful buzzword used by professional guilds in family therapy – for example, in mission statements to guide professionals and as a pedagogical requirement for training in accredited programs (see, for example, the Commission on Accreditation for Marriage and Family Therapy Education, 2005). Yet there is almost no mention within the field of family therapy of contemporary systems concepts (i.e., NDS) or research involving NDS theory or methods. Indeed, the term "*systemic*" is typically treated as equivalent to "*relational*" or to convey a value for diversity within psychotherapy. As such, modern family therapy is paradoxical at its core; it is devoted to its founding within the general systems concepts of the 1960s and 1970s (von Bertallanffy, 1950; also see Davidson, 1983, for a summary of general systems theory) but is almost completely cut off from the contemporary systems models that have grown from these earlier concepts.

However, when one removes the politics and constructivist influences of the past, rational analysis of the various family systems concepts suggests that the underlying theoretical mechanisms are actually equivalent across the various family systems theories between these family theories and the individual therapy traditions and also a number of theories from social psychology. The distinctions among approaches, rather, tend to lie in modality (i.e., how many people are seen at once) and technique. For example, Bowen's (1978) analytically based approach to family therapy focuses largely on *differentiation*, which is equivalent to the original analytic term *individuation*, each of which describes the process by which family members become decoupled along the familiar dimensions of closeness and control. Bowen's approach also relied on the central concept of relational *triangles*, stable interpersonal structures involving three group members whereby conflict between two individuals could be *detoured* (see Minuchin & Fishman, 1974, for the overlapping concept of detouring). For example, a parent may find a dysfunctional yet quasi-adaptive manner of managing intimacy-related marital conflicts by pulling one of the children into the role of confidant (increasing the child's level of closeness and control within that parent-child relationship). The upside for the family system is avoidance of marital conflict, whereas the downside is the positioning of the child into a developmentally inappropriate regulatory function within the family. Vital interpersonal boundaries to both the child and the family's longer-term adaptations have been crossed. Specifically, both parents will be limited in their abilities to provide the necessary structure (e.g., control) and support (e.g., closeness; see Baumrind, 1983, for independently derived parenting styles comprising these equivalent dimensions) for that child.

The predominant style of therapy from the Bowenian tradition is for the therapist to join the system, enter into a stabilizing triangle with conflicting individuals, and act within that triangle to discharge carefully the stored up information behind the unresolved conflict. Conflict resolution is accomplished by using the therapist as a mutually agreed upon go-between for information exchange. In the interest of theoretical integration, it is worthwhile to point out that in addition to the overlapping concept of *detouring* from structural family therapy (Minuchin & Fishman, 1974), the triangles suggested to provide conflict balance by Bowen are essentially identical (although less precise) to Heider's (1958) balance theory from social psychology.

Minuchin's (Minuchin & Fishman, 1974) structural family therapy is the other major family therapy tradition apart from Bowen's (see Nichols & Schwartz, 2005), which is primarily distinguishable based on technique rather than theory per se. Structural family therapy focuses more directly on the information boundaries and subsystems within families. For example, in the family situation outlined earlier, a structural family therapist would suggest that the boundaries around the family's *executive subsystem* are too diffuse (with respect to both power and intimacy) and the intimacy boundary (i.e., emotional cutoff) between the parents is too rigid, whereas a Bowenian therapist would describe the situation in equivalent terms such as differentiation of the child from the parental relationship or as the family system being *enmeshed*. Minuchin's approach typically involves activating the family to increase flows of information in a particular area, flooding a dysfunctional boundary, while at the same time creating other more functional boundaries to damn up dysfunctional flows. For example, after joining with the family system, a structural family therapist may frame the relationship between the parent and child as a metaphorical *affair* and challenge the detached spouse to end these transgressions and fight to save the marriage. Structural family therapy tends to involve more heated exchanges among family members and more complex maneuvering from the therapist.

Each of these two dominant approaches to family therapy appears to be focusing on self-organizing dynamics within families. Each approach seeks to shift structural boundaries to the flow of information to bring the regulatory functions of closeness and control into balance and to move related conflicts toward resolution. For example, one may use Bak's (1996) NDS model of self-organized criticality to understand the commonality among different approaches to resolving family conflicts. Bak (1996) suggested that information discharge in self-organizing systems is optimally poised within a critical region at the *edge of chaos*. Family conflict may be viewed as an example of such a process of information discharge. Just as avalanches involve discharges of matter in physical systems at criticality, family conflict may serve to discharge information in order to maintain an adaptive mix of coherence and complexity. When viewed in this manner, one finds that the fundamental differences among schools of family therapy may be integrated based on the methods used to promote movement of the family toward criticality, allowing for subsequent self-regulation and growth.

Bowenian therapists typically release such *information avalanches* by acting as a go-between in a therapeutically created triangle, leading to increased mindful reflection (i.e., less emotional reactivity) among conflicting family members. Structural family therapists (e.g., Minuchin & Fishman, 1974) tend to build up structural boundaries where needed (to hold appropriate information in place) and to apply strategic *blasts of psychosocial dynamite* in other areas to break down boundaries and release pent-up information in a more sudden manner. Ultimately, then, the theories of family therapy are equivalent to the individual-therapy theories, despite their differences in scale and method of intervention. They all work toward conflict resolution, shifting the biopsychosocial flows of information. Such a view is consistent with empirical studies of family process, which thus far have generally showed that it is balance of supportive and structuring by the therapist that best predicts positive outcomes (Friedlander, Wildman, Heatherington, & Skowron, 1994). With respect to theory to guide future research a fourth theoretical proposition may be offered: *Relational phenomena involving closeness and control serve a regulatory function within self-organizing interpersonal systems, maintaining the structural coherence of boundaries that guide information flows within the group. Conflict processes act to increase the level of rigidity and constraint in these boundaries.*

Group psychotherapy (Yalom, 1985) when viewed through an integrative and systemic lens, relies on equivalent mechanisms of conflict resolution as well. The similarities are so complete, in fact, that one could easily conceptualize the individual process-oriented approaches to therapy as special cases of group therapy, comprising a therapist-client group of two. Indeed, Yalom's (1985) descriptions of group therapy process focus on the group as a place in which clients' interpersonal conflicts will naturally emerge, where they may be safely resolved to the benefit of each member and as a place where new and more flexible interpersonal behaviors may be safely practiced and generalized.

Yalom's approach is more conceptually based than research based out of necessity, because the large theoretical and empirical gaps in the traditional understanding of small-group processes (Bednar & Kaul, 1994). As such, Yalom's approach includes 11 therapeutic factors (e.g., altruism, the instillation of hope, interpersonal learning, etc.) that have been identified as important factors through self-report surveys of group members. These factors are not designed to be independent, mutually exclusive, or integrated under a common theory of group process. Again, the priority has been on practicality rather than science.

Within Yalom's approach, the artful task of the therapist is to act through the leadership role within the group to create a climate that enhances each of these 11 factors. In doing so, the group climate becomes a microcosm in which members have opportunities to practice novel interpersonal strategies leading to what is akin to a set of emotionally corrective experience across the members. Group cohesion, or a sense of *we-ness*, is identified as a key group-level precondition to interpersonal experimentation according to Yalom (1985). Cohesion may be considered analogous to the therapeutic alliance of individual therapy.

The group therapist uses the leadership role to artfully direct the force of cohesion toward the goal of allowing for constructive conflict within the group. In this manner, control and closeness become more flexible among members, and open conflict is increasingly tolerable. The primary technique again is the use of process comments. With increasingly flexible relations with respect to control and closeness among members, social and internal conflicts may be resolved, as members relate in ways to which they are not typically accustomed. If this process goes well, the group develops a social climate that is flexible enough to withstand and supportively confront even the most pathologically rigid interpersonal behavior of its members.

Although Yalom (1985) did not use NDS concepts explicitly, he did suggest that interactive flexibility is necessary within the group: "A freely interactive group, with few structural restrictions, will, in time, develop into a social micro-cosm of the participant members" (p. 28). Therefore, in terms of observable patterns of interaction, therapy groups develop ideally in such a way as to allow for the exchange of information between as many different members as possible. This ability for therapeutic groups to form strong external boundaries, to endure repeated and escalating conflicts, and to become increasingly open internally over time is arguably the main set of factors that distinguish them from other relationships. This process of increasing coherence and complexity is also a good fit for empirical modeling using self-organization theory.

Pavlov's Buddha? Contemporary Cognitive–Behavioral Therapies

Before concluding this review of interpersonal processes traditions in psychotherapy, it is worthwhile to point out that similar notions of conflict and rigidity may be found within cognitive–behavioral therapy (CBT) traditions of psychotherapy as well. Admittedly, direct references to interpersonal processes and conflict tend to be relatively rare in CBT. This may be largely attributable to the historical desire for CBT practitioners to distinguish themselves from their less empirically oriented psychodynamic counterparts from the past. However, one could make the case that the only theoretical difference between contemporary CBT and the psychodynamic therapies is the size or scale at which each approach operates. CBT is a highly specific, detailed, and structured approach to therapy in which one closely examines specific thought processes or behaviors. In contrast, psychodynamic therapies take a broader perspective, examining more vague patterns of self and other in mental, emotional, and behavioral processes. Again, one finds a difference in approach, more than underlying theory. Indeed, one may even suggest that this difference essentially boils down to the therapist's perspective, near versus far.

Through the lens of NDS, it becomes clear that traditional cognitive therapies have always focused on the identification and modification of rigid and extreme belief systems (Ellis, 1977) through the use of methods aimed at opening these beliefs to novel flows of information (i.e., Beck, 1970). More recent acceptance-based cognitive approaches have made a subtle shift, aiming to change one's relations with cognition (i.e., de-fusion), essentially decoupling the broader self from any particular thought, through the use of acceptance and mindfulness-based techniques (Eifert & Forsyth, 2005; S.C. Hayes, Strosahl, & Wilson, 1999). Sharing the goal of increasing flexibility with traditional cognitive therapy, these approaches present a more clear-cut process orientation, aiming to modify one's hold on beliefs, rather than to modify directly the beliefs themselves. Like modern interpersonal therapies, the focus is on process rather than content.

Similarly, the CBT approaches have shared the goal of helping individuals open up relatively closed and ineffective behavioral habits through the use of effective problem-solving skills (i.e., Meichenbaum, 1975), experiential exposure (Barlow, Allen, & Choate, 2004), and values clarification (S. C. Hayes et al., 2004). Implicit across all approaches and innovations to CBT, however, is the primary goal of opening relatively closed and rigid systems to new sources of information to increase flexibility and self-regulation. In this respect, all of the traditions of therapy converge.

Lauterbach (1996) provided one clear example of the study of conflict from a cognitive–behavioral perspective. Defining internal conflict as *conceptual* in nature and involving an "incompatibility between beliefs, values, and attitudes" (p. 214), Lauterbach (1996) grounded psychodynamic notions of conflict within an integrative model comprised of Heider's (1958) notions of balance and Festinger's (1957) notions of cognitive dissonance, a similar integration undertaken by a number of contemporary social psychologists (i.e., Matz & Wood, 2005). Using a comprehensive measurement paradigm that reflects this *balance perspective*, Lauterbach (1996) found some promising results. For example, more conflicted individuals are more likely to have psychosomatic illnesses and more severe psychiatric symptom profiles. Furthermore, levels of internal conflict tend to decrease in lockstep with symptom severity over the course of psychotherapy. Empirical studies from social psychology have repeatedly demonstrated similar results, that internal conflict involves rigidity, psychopathology, and general biopsychosocial dysregulation (Eid & Dieiner, 1999; Gallo, Smith, & Ruiz, 2003; O'Connor, 2002; Schultz & Searleman, 2002; Shaver & Brennan, 1992).

Despite the lack of explicit focus on conflict and rigidity (not to mention no understanding of NDS) within the clinical approaches to CBT the concepts are assumed implicitly throughout. For example, cognitive therapies have traditionally focused on the identification and restructuring of rigid dysfunctional beliefs (i.e., Ellis, 1977). Although there are many methods of cognitive restructuring, each essentially focuses on bringing new information to an existing dysfunctional belief system. This new information is intended to increase the flexibility of rigid and nonadaptive beliefs, allowing the client greater flexibility in coping responses as well as more flexible means of affective regulation.

The Nonlinear Elephant in the Office: The Common NDS Assumptions of Therapy Process

None of the approaches reviewed thus far makes any specific reference to self-organization or related concepts from NDS. Yet practical concerns have drawn each approach to include a central focus on: (a) rigidity and flexibility; (b) control, closeness, and conflict as organizing parameters underlying interpersonal processes; (c) interactions among the individual and interpersonal scales; and (d) the use of mindfulness and related techniques to resolve such conflicts to improve balance and integrity across these scales. The lack of internally consistent and empirically testable systemic grounding to these approaches has allowed them to evolve over the history of psychotherapy as if they were distinct theories, rather than different approaches to working with a common underlying biopsychosocial process. Yet each of the seemingly distinct clinical traditions shares a number of common systemic mechanisms believed to underlie psychotherapeutic process (a): Context-specific constellations of interpersonal control and closeness emerge naturally and automatically from interpersonal information exchanges. (b) These emergent processes serve a regulatory function within self-organizing interpersonal systems, maintaining the structural coherence of boundaries that guide the information flows within the group from which they have emerged. (c) Conflict processes emerge from imbalances in the constellations of control and closeness among group members, acting to increase the level of rigidity and constraint with respect to information flows. (d) The resulting rigidity of conflict may spread beyond the individual psyche to neighboring systems, across scales of both size (down to biology and up to culture) and time (from moments to years). (e) Process-oriented therapies aim to resolve conflicts (increasing flexibility) through techniques that open these relational boundaries, allowing the client more complex yet integrated flows of psychosocial information. The common theoretical thread here is self-organizing flows of information, which helps to provide a deeper explanation of the ongoing questions and unexamined assumptions of psychotherapy process.

This chapter began with a reevaluation of mainstream psychotherapy theory using self-organization as an integrative theoretical framework. Indeed, clinicians and researchers have been able to develop a good degree of knowledge without the benefit of NDS theory or methodologies, which have only arrived to the clinical psychology literature within the last 10 years or so. At this point, I turn to the next step in the study of process, clinical theory that is both empirically testable and also explicitly nonlinear and systemic, using NDS concepts literally rather than as metaphor.

Interpersonal Processes in Psychotherapy

Pincus (2001; Pincus & Guastello, 2005) has developed an integrative model of interpersonal processes known as the 5-R model, based on much of the same clinical theory reviewed earlier, along with the initial theoretical concepts of several authors who had already been suggesting that family systems theories could be updated through the use of NDS principles (Butz, Chamberlain, & McCown, 1997; Elkaim, 1981; Koopmans, 1998, 2001; Ward, 1995). The basic assumption of this model is that interpersonal relationships serve an information processing function, regulating flows of information over time. Arising from this basic information regulatory function are the various complex and phenomenological aspects of interpersonal reality, which serve as the contexts for meaning within biopsychosocial health.

The name "5-R" refers to the five domains most frequently cited as targets of treatment by the various approaches to family therapy: *rules, roles, relationships, realities,* and *response patterns* (Pincus, 2001), which also overlap with control, closeness, and conflict (i.e., 3-Cs; Pincus & Guastello, 2005). Again, with the basic function of interpersonal process as regulation of information flows, *rules are defined as the boundaries that channel such flows.* For example, the initial conditions in psychotherapy are marked by a brief discussion by client and therapist as to the rules that will govern their working relationship. In the case of process-oriented treatments, these rules may be described as a combination of a relatively closed external boundary on the flows of information (i.e., confidentiality) with increasingly permeable and fluid internal boundaries to allow for new and potentially adaptive relational strategies (i.e., detailed exploration of hidden and emotionally painful topics). This combination of extreme professionalism along with extreme intimacy is unique among modern relationships (Orlinsky & Howard, 1995) and arguably provides the necessary relational context that provides for the optimally structured yet open relationship to emerge.

As opposed to norms, which are used in social psychology to describe expectations for appropriate behaviors, rules are more broadly viewed as the boundary conditions around interactive behavior (see Fig. 11.1). They are hypothetically overdetermined, maintaining their coherence not only through expectations but also through an array of cognitive processes such as attitudes, momentum (i.e., habit), as well as the interactive responses of other members' interactants (i.e., a disapproving look). In other words, rules are reflected in cognitive processes such as expectations but may not be reduced to individual cognition. Instead, rules emerge from the collective behavior of interacting individuals.

The next R in the model, *roles*, is defined as the unique constellation of rules that may be ascribed to an individual within an interpersonal process. Control is a central dimension within any role distinction, emerging quickly and automatically within groups (Bales, 1999) and theoretically forming the basis for some of the driver–slave dynamics that may regulate flows of information within the relationship.

It is through roles that individual- and group-level self-organizing dynamics may hypothetically interface. For example, a relatively healthy individual would be expected to have internal boundaries (self-relations) that are flexibly integrated, combining coherence and complexity; Marks-Tarlow (1999) developed this theme in a theoretical account of the self-organization of the self. Such an integrated yet flexible individual would be able to assume more flexible role relations with others. Koopmans (2001) described such a process of spreading conflict through social roles through a process he refers to as *N-binds*. N-binds represent in an updated NDS-based conceptualization of double binds a well-known concept from the history of family therapy. Interpersonal binds involve mixed social messages from which there is no escape. Benign examples occur everyday, such as when a casual yet disliked acquaintance asks you what's the matter because "You look really upset." If you are upset, but admit it to this person, you will have entered a vulnerable and uncomfortable position of intimacy. If you are not upset (the more typical scenario), you are in a position of having to make the subtle suggestion that he or she is wrong and somewhat insensitive. If the question annoys you, so that now you *are* in a bad mood when you were otherwise fine, you are now really trapped! Similar traps happen within intimate relationships as well, such as if a romantic partner says during a conflict, " . . . but I still love you." If you protest, you are denying a positive statement (at the level of content at least). If you accept the statement, you are going along with the notion that your transgressions warranted an evaluation of your love-worthiness. At a minimum, N-binds may represent a particularly strong process whereby conflict spreads across scales through contradictory flows of information pertaining to roles.

Working in the opposite direction, relational processes that break down rigid interpersonal boundaries and allow new flexible boundaries to emerge would be expected to cascade down into the self-system, bringing flexible flows of information to the individual consciousness. Indeed, the current model suggests that one would expect self-similar dynamics to emerge across scales from individual to group and back. This suggestion may help to make deeper sense of the recent line of social psychology research outside of the NDS paradigm that have demonstrated the bidirectional flows of conflict and conflict resolution across these scales (De Dreu & van Knipperberg, 2005; Matz & Wood, 2005; McGregor et al., 2005, McKimmie et al., 2003; O'Connor & Dyce, 1997). The notion of self-similarity in flows of information also provides an empirically grounded explanation for the psychodynamic phenomena of *identification* (i.e., internalizing the conflicted dynamics of parents) and *recapitulation* (i.e., recreating past conflicts in the present; Teyber, 2005).

The third *R* in the model stands for relationships, which may be defined as *constellations of two or more roles involved in the exchange of information* (Pincus, 2001). Along with gradations in control, closeness may be considered to be a universal dimension of relationships (see Fig. 11.1). The current model proposes that conflict emerges from imbalances on these two dimensions, leading to the emergence of rigidity. This explanation helps to ground the empirical findings reviewed earlier, which have consistently demonstrated that imbalances in either of these dimensions is associated with spreading biopsychosocial dysfunction (see Leary, 1957, and Wiggins, 1979, for circumplex models containing these two dimensions). This updated NDS-based interpersonal model also helps to make sense of the ubiquitous notion in psychotherapy that conflict and conflict resolution are necessary for psychosocial growth and that egalitarian and flexible relations are ideal for facilitating such growth within the therapeutic context.

The fourth R, *realities*, is defined as shared, group-relevant information structures. Theoretically, they are the same as social realities described by Festinger, Schachter, and Back (1950). Realities are the most abstract of the 5-Rs and are determined primarily through cognitive processes in which typical interaction patterns are perceived and stored in long-term memory. As coherent structures of flowing information within and among individuals, this self-organized conceptualization of realities helps to make sense of the power of the group context to radically transform the personalities of individuals within a group (i.e., Zimbardo, Maslach, & Haney, 2000). In addition to roles, this conceptualization also helps to inform the notion of how emotionally corrective experiences actually work within the psychodynamic traditions. When a new and more flexible response pattern emerges within the therapeutic relationship, this new pattern may unleash intense emotion along with an irreversible increase in the flexibility of the self and other schemata of a client. Therapy works not just through insight or information flows within the brain but changes that spread across emotional boundaries into the therapy relationship and beyond.

The fifth and final R in the model stands for *response patterns*, the observable repetitive back-and-forth patterns of interaction within therapy. These patterns hypothetically serve as the raw material for clinical inference within treatment and at the same time may be operationalized for empirical study. For example, NDS methodologies may be used to extract turn-taking or other behaviorally defined patterns during treatment for both quantitative (i.e., entropy) and qualitative analysis (clinically meaningful exchanges). Because the 5-R model suggests that higher-order relational processes emerge through self-organizing mechanisms from information flows, the complexity of response patterns should reflect the complexity of these higher-order relational processes. Areas of conflict, for example, should result in rigid patterns of interaction, a phenomenon supported both by clinical wisdom and empirical research, yet heretofore lacking in theoretical grounding.

NDS Methodologies

It is not sufficient to take the grand theories of the past, add NDS jargon to them, and then contend that these theories have been improved in some meaningful way. Unfortunately, this type of theory building does happen on occasion. For the theoretical mechanisms underlying psychotherapy to become truly refined through the use of NDS principles, those principles must be used to make specific predictions, and those predictions must be investigated using methodologies capable of assessing NDS concepts. It is through NDS-informed methodology that one may ascertain whether a nonlinear model is applicable to a given phenomenon at all, and, if so, how applicable it may be.

The widespread adoption of new methodologies in psychology is notoriously slow, and methods that are able to capture the richness and complexity of psychotherapy research have been particularly hard to come by (see Snyder & Kazak, 2005, for a recent review in the context of family therapy). There are some noteworthy exceptions, however. For example, extensive research has been completed using nonlinear differential equations to model marital interactions (Gottman, Murray, Swanson, Tyson, & Swanson, 2002). Within this area, empirical research into nonlinear reciprocal patterns of influence within couples (i.e., how strongly does negativity from a wife pull for negativity from a husband) has been used to develop models of marital stability over time.

Another set of techniques referred to under the rubric of *state-space grids* (Lewis, Lamey, & Douglas, 1999) has been used to investigate interpersonal interaction patterns in terms of rigidity versus flexibility (Granic, Hollenstein, Dishion, & Patterson, 2003; Hollenstein, Granic, Stoolmiller, & Snyder, 2004). State space grids are essentially a method of graphing the sequential behaviors of two individuals during an interaction. One individual's behavior is tracked along the x-axis and the other's behavior along the y-axis, forming a two-dimensional square grid. For example, one could track three possible behaviors (i.e., positive, negative, and neutral) between a parent and child by coding each behavior in sequence across the grid. There is nothing inherently grounded in NDS within this aspect of the approach, which is quite similar to traditional sequential analysis techniques such as Markov chains and other methods based on the examination of transition probabilities within a matrix (Bakeman & Gottman, 1997).

However, Lewis et al. (1999) suggested that the movement across the grid may be used as a way of assessing attractors underlying interpersonal processes. Within this context, state space grids have been used to investigate such things as the presence and strength of fixed-point attractors in the course of anxiety and depressive disorders (Katerndahl & Wang, 2007) and the complexity in movement in parent–child interactions (Hollenstein et al., 2004).

Tschacher, Scheier, and Grawe (1998) examined coherence within the therapeutic alliance using principle components analyses and Shannon entropy values from self-report measures acquired over the course of therapy. Tschacher et al. (1998) found that the number of factors and entropy values each decreased in sync over the course of therapy, suggesting that coherence in therapist–patient viewpoints increases as the therapeutic alliance is formed across sessions. Furthermore, the degree of coherence was a significant predictor of treatment outcomes.

The methodology most relevant to the current theoretical discussion is known as *orbital decomposition* (OD; Guastello, 2000; Guastello, Hyde, & Odak, 1998; Pincus, 2001; Pincus & Guastello, 2005). OD is an NDS approach designed to measure the complexity within hierarchical patterns within a categorical time series, such as a series of utterances within a small-group discussion that have been coded in some objective manner. In this respect, the method is a specific example from the broader class of symbolic dynamics procedures (see Guastello et al., 1998, for further discussion). It is this ability to identify and isolate longer, hierarchical patterns, and to produce direct measures of entropy within these patterns that most clearly distinguishes the technique from other approaches (i.e., state space grids).

Although it is grounded in mathematics, conceptually OD is a rather simple approach to understand. One begins with a series or *string* of utterances, for example, made within a small group. For instance, one may track the interaction within a family therapy session simply in terms of who speaks in what order. In a typical 50-minute session, one may find that there are approximately 300 turns at speech taken, which may be recorded based on who spoke (T = Therapist, F = Father, M = mother, C = child). The entire coded conversation, then, is a time series of categorical data in the form of T-F-M-F-T-C-F-M, for example. Next, the researcher records all possible pairs within the time series (i.e., strings of Length 2), for example: T-F, F-M, M-F and so on, followed by triples (i.e., T-F-M, F-M-F), quadruples, and so on. A variety of empirically based rules of thumb may be used to determine the ideal length of strings at which one will obtain the optimal analysis of the discussion (Pincus & Perez, 2006). Once this optimal string length is identified, a variety of indices of entropy may be derived on the basis of the recurrence structures within the patterns in the discussion.

For example, a discussion comprising almost exclusively T-F-C repetitions would be a relatively rigid conversation, whereas a more-or-less equal distribution of all possible patterns would produce higher measures of entropy (i.e., Shannon entropy and fractal dimension). An estimate of Lyapunov dimensionality may be calculated on the basis of the number of distinct, immediately recurring patterns (analogous for periodic orbits within a strange attractor; see Guastello, 2000, for a full explanation of the derivation of this methodology). In addition to measures of entropy, which may be used as the outputs of any variety of statistical prediction equations (Pincus & Guastello, 2005), one may analyze highly repetitive patterns or long patterns in a more clinical or qualitative manner as well (Pincus, 2001). Numerous other quantitative analyses may be added to these basic procedures, such as estimates of structural integrity within the relationships, measures of transients within the relationship dynamics (i.e., qualitative transitions to the underlying relational processes), or quantitative assessments of the contribution of each group member to overall structure and integrity of the discussion (Pincus & Perez, 2006).

Empirical Validation of the 5-R Model

In an initial empirical test of the 5-R model, Pincus (2001) used OD and found evidence for self-organization (i.e., low-dimensional chaotic patterning and high levels of pattern repetition) within a clinic-referred family discussion using measures of Shannon entropy (equal to 8.68) and Lyapunov dimension (1.7). This result has been replicated (Pincus, 2005) across multiple sessions of family therapy using tests of the inverse power law (IPL) model (R^2 ranging from .86 to 1.00, mean = .93). This result suggests that the turn-taking dynamics of family therapy sessions was fractal and was exhibiting complex self-organizing dynamics at the edge of chaos.

Similar results were observed in a study of group-therapy process (Pincus & Guastello, 2005), with a significant fit ($R^2 = .95$) between the distribution of patterned recurrences in turn-taking dynamics during a group-therapy session and an IPL model. Furthermore, Pincus and Guastello (2005) found that a multivariate regression model including measures of conflict, control, and closeness accounted for 48% of the variance within this IPL model. Together these results suggest that the turn-taking responses of the group were reflecting an underlying self-organizing process with a fractal temporal structure. The results also suggest that control, closeness, and conflict among members were behaving as emergent structures within that process, consistent with the predictions of self-organization theory applied to interpersonal process, particularly the 5-R model.

The gold standard, however, in science is the experiment, which provides the best possible evidence for cause. The results reviewed earlier may be considered to be quasi-experimental inasmuch as they involve controlled regression analyses on time-dependent order parameters (i.e., entropy and structure). Nevertheless, systemic models need not sacrifice rigor for holism. With these empirical goals in mind, Pincus (2005) conducted a series of studies on experimentally created groups using a similar paradigm as the family and group therapy studies outlined earlier. The specific aim was to determine whether the controlled induction of internal conflict within a single member of an experimentally created group is sufficient to reduce the entropy in turn-taking dynamics of the group as a whole. Results from a single-group experimental design (e.g., ABA design) suggested just that: with significant drops in entropy in group dynamics following the induction of conflict within a single group member (Pincus, Fox, Perez, Turner, McGeehan, 2008).

A series of six experimental replications (24 discussions in all), furthermore, were consistent with these results. Levels of induced conflict within group members and subsequent conflict resolution among the members (ABAB designs) accounted for approximately 20% of the variance in the entropy of response patterns. Higher levels of conflict induction within group members was associated with significant drops in entropy in group dynamics, and higher levels of subsequent conflict resolution were associated with significant increases in entropy. Furthermore, the turn-taking dynamics of all groups fit strongly the IPL model (R^2 ranging from .86 to .99, mean $= .94$ across the 24 discussions, Pincus, 2005).

These results suggest that conflict creates structural changes within hierarchical self-organizing interpersonal dynamics. Conflict narrows information flows within the individual's cognitive, behavioral, and emotional systems, leading to rigid personality dynamics (i.e., all-or-nothing thinking). Furthermore, individual conflicts spread to the group level, causing a narrowing of the information flows at the broader level of interpersonal relationships. When viewed from the broader evolutionary context of self-organization, it seems that conflict is a necessary evil within the adaptive processes of biopsychosocial systems. In the short term, conflict narrows information flows to protect the structural integrity of the hierarchical systems (i.e., self-relations and interpersonal relations), whereas conflict resolutions appear to be a precursor to adaptive growth. Altogether, this research supports a fifth theoretical proposition: *Self-organizing interpersonal information flows naturally evolve toward the edge of chaos, with shifts toward rigidity and complexity reflecting evolutionary demands on biopsychosocial systems.*

Related Empirical Results Using the NDS Perspective

A number of studies examining various relational contexts with variations in nonlinear modeling and methods have found similar results as those informed by the psychotherapy-oriented 5-R model. Within the domain of group therapy, Burlingame, Fuhriman, and Barnum (1995) measured fluctuations in the number of therapeutic statements over the course of a 16-week group therapy process and found that the complexity (using fractal dimensions) increased over the course of the therapy, peaking at around the two-thirds mark (around Session 10) and then decreasing. This group therapy pattern was similar to the results of Badalamenti and Langs (1992), who found increasing complexity (using Shannon entropy) in verbal utterances over the course of individual (dyadic) treatment. Together these results suggest that interactive complexity tends to increase over time as therapeutic relationships evolve. Yet while interactive complexity appears to increase over the course of therapy, the shared understandings among therapist and client with respect to goals, procedures, and expected outcomes tend to become more coherent (Tschacher et al., 1998). Together these results suggest that the self-organizing coherence in psychotherapy process involves an open and positive coordination in the therapeutic expectations, which facilitate open and flexible behavioral exchanges among members.

An overlapping line of research has examined more precisely the putative adaptive route through chaos to increasing self-organized flexibility that may occur for clients during the course of therapy. Hayes and Strauss (1998) have had some success in finding what appear to be bifurcations during the course of cognitive therapy for depressed individuals. The hallmarks they observed were sudden disorganization (and worsening) in depressive symptoms immediately preceding improvements in functioning. Subsequent research has found that sudden gains are rather common in successful therapy, occurring in about 40% of cases in both CBT and psychodynamic treatments for depression and resulting in better treatment outcomes when compared with clients without sudden gains (Tang, Luborsky, & Andrusyna, 2002).

The most extensive research applying NDS to psychosocial processes has been carried out within the context of marital interactions (Gottman et al., 2002). The general research results in this area have suggested that interactive rigidity within marital conversation is predictive of marital dissatisfaction and divorce. More specifically, Gottman et al. (2002) have been able to predict marital dissolution with a 94% rate of accuracy using a differential equation model based on matches and mismatches in couples' interactive response styles. In general, they have found that regulated couples appear to respond to one another with a positive-to-negative ratio equal to or greater than 5 to 1. On the contrary, a dysregulated cascade toward marital dissatisfaction and potential separation ensues when the response styles of couples lead to negativity that falls below this 5-to-1 level. Related empirical studies have demonstrated that this process of conflict-driven instability is reflected at the smaller biological scales as well. For example, physiological linkage (i.e., rigidity in the mirrored stress responses of couples) accounts for approximately 60% of the variance in self-reported levels of marital dissatisfaction (Levinson & Gottman, 1983). Furthermore, the most toxic variety of rigid interactions, contempt (e.g., "thumbing your nose" at another person), puts the object of that contempt at risk for heart disease at levels comparable to poor diet and smoking (Gottman et al., 2002).

Guastello, Pincus, and Gunderson (2006) extended Levinson and Gottman's (1983) results on physiological linkage in marital satisfaction, demonstrating that such linkage occurs during routine interactions among strangers getting to know one another and is associated with social sensitivity as well as conflict. Furthermore, Guastello et al. (2006) found that, in addition to a relatively simple nonlinear model for ups and downs of physiological arousal within individuals, linkage also occurs in the exchange of entropy across individuals, with the entropy levels of one individual predicting the entropy levels of the other individual at a lag of 20 seconds. The nonlinear regression model was based on the Lyapunov exponent. The exchanges of physiological entropy were usually symmetrical, although a few were asymmetrical with one individual driving the complexity in physiological responses of the other (e.g., driver–slave dynamics). Importantly, many of the linkages within the dyads would have been missed if only a linear analysis were used.

With respect to theory, these initial results suggest that the self-organizing processes found between individual and interpersonal scales extend further down into the physiologies of individuals engaged in relationships with others. These results are consistent with the latest wave of clinical approaches espousing a perspective typically referred to as *interpersonal neurobiology* (i.e., Siegel, 2006). In addition to inspiring new perspectives for clinical work, such results may provide a theoretical foundation for future NDS-informed approaches to health psychology (i.e., Pincus & Sheikh, in press).

Although the use of NDS in child psychopathology research is not the focus of the current chapter, it is worth mentioning the recent interest that has been paid to updating classic models of reciprocity and social learning using NDS (see for example, Granic & Patterson, 2006). For example, Granic et al. (2003) examined the dynamics of videotaped parent–child interactions in a group of one hundred forty-nine 9- to 10-year-old boys over a span of several years and found a significant increase in that the number of interactive states and transitions among those states during the 12- to 13-year age range. These results suggest that the complexity of family dynamics may undergo a *phase shift* (an irreversible systemic reorganization toward greater organizational flexibility) in response to the maturational influences of an individual child as he or she reaches adolescence. On a systemic level, this naturally occurring process may be equivalent to the type of adaptations that appear to be occurring over the course of psychotherapy.

Research using similar NDS models and methods has also found that rigidity in parent–child interactions predicts developmental trajectories toward psychopathology during the transition from kindergarten to first grade (Hollenstein et al., 2004), and similarly that rigidity in peer dynamics was predictive of enduring psychopathology during the transition from early adolescence to young adulthood (Dishion, Nelson, Winter, & Bullock, 2004). This interpersonal process-oriented NDS research extends the traditional psychopathology research results reviewed earlier, suggesting again that rigidity is connected to psychopathology, spreading both within and among individuals. Inasmuch as these NDS studies have tracked the development of these psychosocial processes as they occur naturally, over the course of critical periods of development, the case for self-organizing processes underlying healthy and unhealthy psychosocial development appears strong.

Although Gottman (1991; Gottman, et al., 2002) uses fixed-point attractors rather than the broader concepts involved in self-organization to interpret his results, it is rather simple to apply these results to a model involving self-organizing biopsychosocial processes. Specifically, when conflicting flows of interpersonal information cross critical thresholds (e.g., less than a 5:1 ratio for positive to negative statements), rigidity may spread across scales of time and size, making the system less flexible, adaptive, and robust against turbulent flows from neighboring systems in which the relationship is nested.

Fredrickson and Losada (2005) have used chaos theory to support their findings that a similar ratio (greater than 2.9:1.0) underlies positive versus negative mental health processes over time. In their study, they obtained daily records of subjective positive and negative emotional experiences from 188 participants over the course of 28 days. The ratio of 2.9:1.0 served as the cut point dividing healthy from unhealthy participants. The ratings over time in this study were not analyzed to produce measures of flexibility. Rather, the 2.9:1.0 results were interpreted in relation to the results of a prior math modeling study of group dynamics, with the similar ratio found in this context taken as evidence of a universal principle of biopsychosocial balance.

In this prior study, Losada (1999) had run a simulation model of team performance using the Lorenz (1993) equations for meteorological chaos. Using empirically derived parameters from real groups within the simulation model, Losada (1999) found that values above the 2.9:1.0 ratio among parameters produced a more chaotic result than values below this ratio. Using these and other similar results from related research (including the work of Gottman et al., 2002), Fredrickson and Losada (2005) suggested that chaos theory may be used as a general theory to understand human biopsychosocial growth. They further suggested that the output of such theory will be general mathematical laws that may be used to assess and promote such growth.

Subsequent research will surely examine these bold suggestions in greater detail. In particular, future studies should determine whether such systems truly involve deterministic chaos (e.g., few variables producing unpredictable behavior as in meteorological models), or complexity through self-organization (e.g., many variables becoming coupled to produce ordered emergent processes). Each theory has been used to support the notion that more open processes are healthy, and more closed processes are not. The primary difference may be seen as the underlying mechanism involved, which is major distinction that needs to be made. Therefore subsequent studies aiming to differentiate between the two models will need to use empirically derived measures of entropy rather than the results of simulations from an a priori simulation model. Specifically, if equations such as those of Lorenz are used in a psychosocial application, one is predisposed toward finding chaotic dynamics.

Summary and Conclusions

Conceptualizing interpersonal processes from an NDS perspective, one may suggest some deeper answers to the five theoretical questions posed at the outset of this chapter. We began with a question: How may the various theories of psychotherapy become integrated within a single testable theoretical framework? It is suggested that self-organization theory may be used as a general framework for weaving together the various empirical and applied approaches to psychotherapy. When viewed as self-organizing flows of information, nested between the biological scales and broader society, interpersonal processes appear to be open self-organizing systems that adapt through self-regulating feedback mechanisms, leading to complex synchronization phenomena within and among individuals.

Second question: How and why do interpersonal systems emerge? Self-organizing interpersonal processes are an inevitable and naturally occurring set of emergent phenomena. Self-organization arises automatically once human beings begin to engage in a process of exchange information. They arise because we talk, and we talk because they arise.

Such processes serve an adaptive regulatory function for individuals, as well as the emergent systems in which the individuals are nested. Furthermore, one might suggest that once a sufficient number of linkages are made among two or more individuals (i.e., constellations of closeness and control across different domains), an emergent order with respect to flows of information exchange over time will naturally emerge and begin to evolve. This emergent order is commonly known as a *relationship*, whereas the subsequent flows of information are called *conversations*. When you talk to people, you develop relationships with them, which determine the subsequent ways that you talk with them and so on. This is why psychotherapy is known as "talk therapy" and invariably relies on the method of conversation.

Our third question was: Why do psychosocial systems invariably display a mixture of coherence and complexity? Self-organizing interpersonal systems are both coherent and complex because such a balance allows for optimal systemic evolution. Coherence provides stability, structure, and supportive coregulation. Complexity allows for novel adaptations and robustness against the inevitable turbulent flows that spill over from neighboring biopsychosocial systems.

Fourth question: What is the evolutionary significance of control, closeness, and conflict? It is suggested here that control and closeness are emergent structures within interpersonal systems, aspects of the relationship that serve regulatory functions, holding the system together. Generally speaking, one would expect that a flexible and balanced combination of control and closeness within relationships would be the healthiest state, reflecting flexible and adaptive structure-making processes within the relationship. At the same time, special situations would require a different mix of these two coherence-making processes. For example, parents need to provide higher levels of both structure and support for younger versus older children. These systems would be expected to appear more rigid and predictable in their behavioral outputs, and yet provide a better fit for the relatively rigid internal dynamics of the young children. War, or other extreme threat contexts, would provide other examples in which some measure of rigidity would be ideal.

Conflict is theoretically a second-order emergent property arising from discrepant and constraining flows of information, within or among individuals and often both. It is suggested that these conflicting flows typically involve a lack of coordination with respect to closeness and control. For example, when one person wants more distance than the other or when two or more individuals want to be in charge at the same time, conflict will emerge. Short-term conflict and rigidity may serve an adaptive function by increasing the structural integrity of the interpersonal system as it prepares to accommodate and evolve more complex flows of information (i.e., a new and adaptive mode of role taking by one or more members). Chronic unresolved conflict conversely, may be the hallmark of pathology, at both individual and also interpersonal levels. Furthermore, it is possible that some systems evolve toward a reliance on chronic unresolved conflict as a source of structure, rather than mutual closeness or reciprocal control. In these situations, conflict may appear to be the only thing holding the relationship together.

Question five: What is the meaning of interpersonal patterns? Interpersonal patterns are the ubiquitous observable sign of the self-organizing processes that characterize human relationships. Humans who examine their own or others' relationships will perceive repeating patterns in their modes of connection and synchronization with others. Interpersonal approaches to therapy most clearly focus on these patterns, allowing them to emerge within a safe and open therapeutic relational context. Next, these approaches focus on the therapeutic relationship itself in a recursive manner to allow for conflict resolution and adaptation in the client's biopsychosocial systems.

Self-organization appears to hold great promise in guiding the future clinical developments and research into interpersonal process in psychotherapy. The theory is specific enough to allow for research predictions and simulations, yet broad enough to account for the unique aspects of each individual psychotherapy encounter. In addition, the theory allows for relationships to be modeled in a number of ways, depending on the goals of the study. For example, when viewed in terms of microprocesses such as turn taking in conversations, the evidence has been quite consistent in suggesting that verbal behaviors produce recurrence structures consistent with an IPL model. In this context, models such as the 5-R model hold promise for understanding the connections between structural rigidity in the flows of information at the moment-by-moment inter-actions and the broader relational processes that emerge from those interactions (i.e., conflict, closeness, and control). Ultimately, the application of an NDS concept such as self-organization may allow clinical psychology to switch from a process of microparadigms that compete simultaneously, splintering over time rather than ever truly being replaced or refined. Perhaps psychotherapy research will discover its first laws in just over 100 years of its existence as a scientific discipline? Perhaps there will be the first true paradigm, a truly integrated the-ory of psychopathology and psychotherapy that still allows for as many unique approaches as there are clinicians?

Each of these approaches may be considered to be a creative means of working with interpersonal processes. None of them need be a *theory* per se, but rather a set of approaches to be used for case conceptualization and treatment planning. Self-organization could be the actual *theory*, which may be modeled in a number of respects depending on the goals of the researcher or clinician. For example, on a larger time scale, it may be useful to model self-organizing interpersonal processes in terms of catastrophes (i.e., cusp) – for example, if one wishes to capture a phase change in the dynamics of a group after an evolutionary phase shift (Byrne, Mazanov, & Gregson, 2001; Guastello, 2000, 2002, 2005). Or at a smaller scale, one may wish to examine the biological synchronization that underlies interpersonal self-organization processes.

These regulatory processes may also be captured in terms of more qualitative indices as well, such as Gottman et al.'s (2002) predictive models of marital stability using regulation of positive and negative affect. Finally, it may be use-ful to analyze interpersonal process such as family dynamics, through the use of attractor dynamics. For example, rigid boundaries or conflict avoidance dynam-ics could be represented as a relatively high surface or repellor on the family's behavioral manifold. Open conflict or diffuse boundaries could be represented as fixed points; and mismatches in these dynamics among members could be represented as saddles (e.g., attractor on one side and repellor on the other). This type of conceptualization could be done qualitatively, on the basis of clin-ical information gleaned from sessions, or more quantitatively, such as by con-structing attractor manifolds based on patterned behavioral outputs coded from videotape. Simulation models could be generated and examined on the basis of attractors as well.

The common thread through each of these analytic strategies is self-organization, and so each analytic approach does not need to become a "the-ory" with its own cults of personality, disciples, and "certified" practitioners. Self-organization theory suggests that interpersonal processes emerge natu-rally as information is exchanged among humans, that these processes serve a regulatory function for the affects, cognition, behaviors, and physiologies of interactants. Furthermore, the research reviewed here suggests that structural rigidity, integrity, phase shifts, and other measures of process may be useful in understanding relational evolution. On a more specific level, the five theoretical propositions listed at the outset of this chapter, and the five additional principles developed throughout, may be used as guides for continuing research from this perspective.

In homage to the power of process, let us finish with a recursive examination of both the content and process of self-organization on the broader scientific and clinical contexts. The systemic nature of the NDS perspective allows inter-personal processes to be understood through a diverse set of theoretical and clinical models, allowing for an artistic richness in epistemology and approach, while retaining the ability for a more integrated search for empirical discovery and justification. One is left with a coherent scientific framework that allows clinicians to be infinitely creative. On the broadest level, the NDS approach may then serve to reintegrate research and practice in psychotherapy.

References

Adler, A. (1930). *The neurotic constitution: Outlines of a comparative individualistic psychology and psychotherapy* (B. Glueck & J. E. Lind, Trans.). New York: Dodd, Mead.

Alexander, F., & French, T. M. (1980). *Psychoanalytic therapy: Principles and applications.* Lincoln: University of Nebraska Press.

Badalamenti, A. F., & Langs, R. J. (1992). The thermodynamics of psychotherapeutic communication. *Behavioral Science, 37,* 152–180.

Baer, R. A. (2003). Mindfulness training as a clinical intervention: A conceptual and empirical review. *Clinical Psychology: Science and Practice, 10,* 125–143.

Bak, P. (1996). *How nature works: The science of self-organized criticality.* New York: Springer-Verlag.

Bakeman, R., & Gottman, J. M. (1997). *Observing interaction: An introduction to sequential analysis* (2nd ed.). New York: Cambridge University Press.

Bales, R. F. (1999). *Social interaction systems: Theory and measurement.* New Brunswick, NJ: Transaction.

Barlow, D. H., Allen, L. B., & Choate, M. L. (2004). Toward a unified treatment for emotional disorders. *Behavior Therapy, 35,* 205–230.

Baumrind, D. (1983). Familial antecedents of social competence in young children. *Psychological Bulletin, 94,* 132–142.

Beck, A. T. (1970). Cognitive therapy: Nature and relation to behavior therapy. *Behavior Therapy, 1,* 184–200.

Bednar, R. L., & Kaul, T. J. (1994). Experiential group research: Can the canon fire? In A. E. Bergin & S. L. Garfield (Eds.), *Handbook of psychotherapy and behavior change* (4th ed., pp. 631–663). New York: Wiley.

Bowen, M. (1978). *Family therapy in clinical practice.* New York: Aronson.

Bowlby, J. (1982). *Attachment and loss: Vol. 1. Attachment* (2nd ed.). New York: Basic Books. (Original work published 1969)

Burlingame, G. M., Fuhriman, A., & Barnum, K. R. (1995). Group therapy as a nonlinear dynamical system: Analysis of therapeutic communication for chaotic patterns. In F. D. Abraham and A. R. Gilgen (Eds.), *Chaos theory in psychology* (pp. 87–105). Westport, CT: Greenwood Press.

Butz, M. R., Chamberlain, L. L., & McCown, W. G. (1997). *Strange attractors: Chaos, complexity, and the art of family therapy.* New York: Wiley.

Byrne, D. G., Mazanov, J., & Gregson, R. A. M. (2001). A cusp catastrophe analysis of changes to adolescent smoking behavior in response to smoking prevention programs. *Nonlinear Dynamics, Psychology, and Life Sciences, 5,* 115–137.

Commission on Accreditation for Marriage and Family Therapy Education. (2005). American Association of Family Therapy, COAMFTE Page. Retrieved December 18, 2007, from http://www.aamft.org/about/COAMFTE/index_nm.asp

Crane, D. R., Wampler, K. S., Sprenkle, D. H., Sandberg, J. G., & Hoverstadt, A. (2002). The scientist-practitioner model in marriage and family therapy doctoral programs: Current status. *Journal of Marital and Family Therapy, 28,* 75–83.

Davidson, M. (1983). *Uncommon sense.* Los Angeles: Tarcher.

De Dreu, C. K. W., & van Kippenberg, D. (2005). The possessive self as a barrier to conflict resolution: Effects of mere ownership, process accountability and self-concept clarity on competitive cognitions and behavior. *Journal of Personality and Social Psychology 89,* 345–357.

Diamond, G. M., Diamond, G. S., & Liddle, H. A. (2000). The therapist–parent alliance in family-based therapy for adolescents. *Journal of Clinical Psychology, 56,* 1037–1050.

Dishion, T. J., Nelson, S. E., Winter, C. E., & Bullock, B. M. (2004). Adolescent friendship as a dynamic system: Entropy and deviance in the etiology and course of male antisocial behavior. *Journal of Abnormal Child Psychology, 32,* 651–663.

Eid, M., & Deiner, E. (1999). Intraindividual variability in affect: Reliability, validity, and personality correlates. *Journal of Personality and Social Psychology, 76,* 662–676.

Eifert, G. H., & Forsyth, J. P. (2005). *Acceptance and commitment therapy for anxiety disorders: A practitioner's treatment guide to using mindfulness, acceptance, and values-based behavior change strategies.* Oakland, CA: New Harbinger.

Elkaim, M. (1981). Non-equilibrium, chance and change in family therapy. *Journal of Marital and Family Therapy, 7,* 291–297.

Ellis, A. (1977). Rejoinder: Elegant and inelegant RET. *The Counseling Psychologist, 7,* 73–82.

Festinger, L. (1957). *A theory of cognitive dissonance.* Evanston, IL: Row, Peterson.

Festinger, L., Schachter, S., & Back, K. (1950). *Social pressures in informal groups.* Stanford, CA: Stanford University Press.

Frank, J. D., & Frank, J. B. (1991). *Persuasion and healing: A comparative study of psychotherapy* (3rd ed.). Baltimore: Johns Hopkins University Press.

Frederickson, B. L., & Losada, M. F. (2005). Positive affect and the complex dynamics of human flourishing. *American Psychologist, 60,* 678–686.

Friedlander, M. L., Wildman, J., Heatherington, L., & Skowron, E. A. (1994). What we do and don't know about the process of family therapy. *Journal of Family Psychology, 8,* 390–416.

Freud, S. (1905). Three essays on the theory of sexuality. In J. Strachey (Trans. and Ed.) *The complete psychological works, vol. 7.* New York: Norton, 1976.

Gallo, L. C., Smith, T. W., & Ruiz, J. M. (2003). Attachment style: Circumplex descriptions, recalled developmental experiences, self-representations, and interpersonal functioning in adulthood. *Journal of Personality, 71*, 141–181.

Garfield, S. L. (1995). *Psychotherapy: An eclectic-integrative approach* (2nd ed.). New York: Wiley.

Garfield, S. L. (1998). The future and the scientist-practitioner split. *American Psychologist, 53*, 1231–1232.

Gottman, J. M. (1991). Chaos and regulated change in families: A metaphor for the study of transitions. In P. A. Cowan & M. Hetherington (Eds.), *Family transitions* (pp. 247–272). Hillsdale, NJ: Erlbaum.

Gottman, J. M., Murray, J. D., Swanson, C., Tyson, R., & Swanson, K. R. (2002). *The mathematics of marriage: Dynamic nonlinear models*. Cambridge, MA: MIT Press.

Granic, I., Hollenstein, T., Dishion, T. J., & Patterson, G. R. (2003). Longitudinal analysis of flexibility and reorganization in early adolescence: A dynamic systems study of family interactions. *Developmental Psychology, 39*, 606–617.

Granic, I., & Patterson, G. R. (2006). Toward a comprehensive model of antisocial development: A dynamic systems approach. *Psychological Review, 113*, 101–131.

Guastello, S. J. (2000). Symbolic dynamic patterns of written exchanges: Hierarchical structures in an electronic problem-solving group. *Nonlinear Dynamics, Psychology, and Life Sciences, 4*, 169–189.

Guastello, S. J. (2002). *Managing emergent phenomena: Nonlinear dynamics in work organizations*. Mahwah NJ: Erlbaum.

Guastello, S. J. (2005). Statistical distributions and self-organizing phenomena: What conclusions should be drawn? *Nonlinear Dynamics, Psychology, and Life Sciences, 9*, 463–478.

Guastello, S. J., Hyde, T., & Odak, M. (1998). Symbolic dynamic patterns of verbal exchange in a creative problem solving group. *Nonlinear Dynamics, Psychology, and Life Sciences, 2*, 35–58.

Guastello, S. J., Pincus, D., & Gunderson, P. R. (2006). Electrodermal arousal between participants in a conversation: Nonlinear dynamics and linkage effects. *Nonlinear Dynamics, Psychology, and Life Sciences, 10*, 341–375.

Hayes, A. M., & Strauss, J. L. (1998). Dynamic systems theory as a paradigm for the study of change in psychotherapy: An application to cognitive therapy for depression. *Journal of Consulting and Clinical Psychology, 66*, 939–947.

Hayes, S. C., Strosahl, K. D., & Wilson, K. G. (1999). Acceptance and commitment therapy: An experiential approach to behavior change. New York: Guilford Press.

Hayes, S. C., Follette, V. M., & Linehan, M. M. (2004). *Mindfulness and acceptance: Expanding the cognitive-behavioral tradition*. New York: Guilford.

Heider, F. (1958). *The psychology of interpersonal relations*. New York: Erlbaum.

Hollenstein, T., Granic, I., Stoolmiller, M., & Snyder, J. (2004). Rigidity in parent-child interactions and the development of externalizing and internalizing behavior in early childhood. *Journal of Abnormal Child Psychology, 32*, 595–607.

Horney, K. (1966). *Our inner conflicts*. New York: Norton.

Horney, K. (1970). *Neurosis and human growth*. New York: Norton.

Katerndahl, D., & Wang, C. (2007). Dynamic covariation of symptoms of anxiety and depression among newly-diagnosed patients with major depressive episode, panic disorder, and controls. *Nonlinear Dynamics, Psychology, and Life Sciences, 11*, 349–367.

Kohut, H. (1977). *The restoration of the self.* New York: International Universities Press.

Koopmans, M. (1998). Chaos theory and the problem of change in family systems. *Nonlinear Dynamics, Psychology, and Life Sciences, 2,* 133–148.

Koopmans, M. (2001). From double bind to N-bind: Toward a new theory of schizophrenia and family interaction. *Nonlinear Dynamics, Psychology, and Life Sciences, 5,* 289–325.

Lauterbach, W. (1996). The measurement of personal conflict. *Psychotherapy Research 6,* 213–225.

Leary, T. (1957). *Interpersonal diagnosis of personality: A functional theory and methodology for personality evaluation.* New York: Ronald Press.

Levinson, R. W., & Gottman, J. M. (1983). Marital interaction: Physiological linkage and affective exchange. *Journal of Personality and Social Psychology, 49,* 85–94.

Lewis, M. D., Lamey, A. V., & Douglas, L. (1999). A new dynamic systems method for the analysis of early socioemotional development. *Developmental Science, 2,* 457–475.

Lorenz, E. N. (1993). *The essence of chaos.* Seattle: University of Washington Press.

Losada, M. (1999). The complex dynamics of high performance teams. *Mathematical and Computer Modeling, 30,* 179–192.

Luborsky, L., & Crits-Christoph, P. (1998). *Understanding transference: The Core Conflictual Relationship Theme method* (2nd ed.). Washington, DC: American Psychological Association.

Lynch, T. R., Chapman, A. L., Rosenthal, M. Z., Kuo, J. R., & Linehan, M. M. (2006). Mechanisms of change in dialectical behavior therapy: Theoretical and empirical observations. *Journal of Clinical Psychology, 62,* 459–480.

Marks-Tarlow, T. (1999). The self as a dynamical system. *Nonlinear Dynamics, Psychology, and Life Sciences, 3,* 311–345.

Matz, D. C., & Wood, W. (2005). Cognitive dissonance in groups: The consequences of disagreement. *Journal of Personality and Social Psychology, 88,* 22–37.

May, R. (1977). *The meaning of anxiety* (Rev. ed.). New York: Norton.

McGregor, I., Zanna, M. P., Holmes, J. G., & Spencer, S. J. (2001). Compensatory conviction in the face of personal uncertainty: Going to extremes and being oneself. *Journal of Personality and Social Psychology, 80,* 472–488.

McKimmie, B. M., Terry, D. J., Gogg, M. A., Manstead, A. S. R., Spears, R. & Doosje, B. (2003). I'm a hypocrite, but so is everyone else: Group support and the reduction of cognitive dissonance. *Group Dynamics: Theory, Research, and Practice, 7,* 214–224.

Meichenbaum, D. H. (1975). Self-instruction methods. In F. H. Kanfer & A. P. Goldstein (Eds.), *Helping people change: A textbook of methods* (pp. 357–391). New York: Pergamon.

Minuchin, S., & Fishman, C. H. (1974). *Family therapy techniques.* Cambridge, MA: Harvard University Press.

Nichols, M. P., & Schwartz, R. C. (2005). *Family therapy: Concepts and methods* (5th ed.). New York: Allyn & Bacon.

O'Connor, B. P. (2002). The search for dimensional structure differences between normality and abnormality: A statistical review of published data on personality and psychopathology. *Journal of Personality and Social Psychology, 83,* 962–982.

O'Connor, B. P., & Dyce, J. (1997). Interpersonal rigidity, hostility, and complementarity in musical bands. *Journal of Personality and Social Psychology, 72,* 362–372.

O'Connor, B. P., & Dyce, J. A. (2001). Rigid and extreme: A geometric representation of personality disorders. *Journal of Personality and Social Psychology, 81*, 1119–1130.

Orlinsky, D. E., Grawe, K., & Parks, B. K. (1994). Process and outcome in psychotherapy. In E. Bergin & S. L. Garfield (Eds.), *Handbook of psychotherapy and behavior change* (4th ed., pp. 270–376). New York: Wiley.

Orlinsky, D. E., & Howard, K. I. (1986). Process and outcome in psychotherapy. In S. L. Garfield & A. E. Bergin (Eds.), *Handbook of psychotherapy and behavior change* (3rd ed., pp. 311–382). Hoboken, NJ: John Wiley & Sons.

Orlinsky, D. E., & Howard, K. I. (1995). Unity and diversity among psychotherapies: A comparative perspective. In B. Bongar & L. E. Buetler (Eds.), *Comprehensive textbook of psychotherapy: Theory and practice* (pp. 3–23). New York: Oxford University Press.

Pincus, D. (2001). A framework and methodology for the study of non-linear, self-organizing family dynamics. *Nonlinear Dynamics, Psychology, and Life Sciences, 5*, 139–174.

Pincus, D. (2005, August). *Bad apples: The relationship between individual-level and group level dynamics.* Paper presented at the annual meeting for the Society for Chaos Theory in Psychology & Life Sciences, Denver, CO.

Pincus, D., Fox, K. M., Perez, K. A., Turner, J. S., & McGeehan, A. R. (2008). Nonlinear dynamics of individual and interpersonal conflict in an experimental group. *Small Group Research, 39*, 150–178.

Pincus, D., & Guastello, S. J. (2005). Nonlinear dynamics and interpersonal correlates of verbal turn-taking patterns in group therapy. *Small Group Research, 36*, 635–677.

Pincus, D., & Perez, K. (2006, August). *Orbital decomposition for analyzing conversation patterns: An example using contiguous family therapy sessions.* Workshop presented at the annual meeting for the Society for Chaos Theory in Psychology & Life Sciences, Baltimore, MD.

Pincus, D., & Sheikh, A. A. (in press). Imagery for pain relief: A scientifically grounded guide book for clinicians. New York: Routledge.

Rogers, C. (1951). *Client-centered therapy.* Boston: Houghton Mifflin.

Rogers, C. (1957). The necessary and sufficient conditions of therapeutic personality change. *Journal of Consulting and Clinical Psychology, 60*, 827–832.

Schultz, P. W., & Searleman, A. (2002). Rigidity of thought and behavior: 100 years of research. *Genetic, Social, and General Psychology Monographs, 128*, 165–207.

Sexton, T. L., Alexander, J. F., & Mease, A. L. (2004). Levels of evidence for the models and mechanisms of therapeutic change in family and couple therapy. In M. J. Lambert (Ed.), *Bergin & Garfield's handbook of psychotherapy and behavior change* (5th ed., pp. 590–546). New York: Wiley.

Shaver, P. R., & Brennan, K. A. (1992). Attachment style and the 'Big Five' personality traits: Their connections with each other and with romantic relationship outcomes. *Personality and Social Psychology Bulletin, 18*, 535–545.

Siegel, D. J. (2006). An interpersonal neurobiology approach to psychotherapy. *Psychiatric Annals, 36*, 248–256.

Snyder, D. K., & Kazak, A. E. (2005). Methodology in family science: Introduction to the special issue. *Journal of Family Psychology, 19*, 3–5.

Sprenkle, D. H., & Blow, A. J. (2004). Common factors and our sacred models. *Journal of Marital and Family Therapy, 30*, 113–129.

Sullivan, H. S. (1953). *The interpersonal theory of psychiatry.* New York: Norton.

Tang, T. Z., Laborsky, L., & Adrusyna, T. (2002). Sudden gains in recovering from depression: Are they also found in psychotherapies other than cognitive-behavioral therapy? *Journal of Consulting and Clinical Psychology, 70,* 444–447.

Teyber, E. (2005). *Interpersonal process in therapy: An integrative model* (5th ed.). Belmont, CA: Brooks-Cole.

Tschacher, W., Scheier, C., & Grawe, K. (1998). Order and pattern formation in psychotherapy. *Nonlinear Dynamics, Psychology, and Life Sciences, 2,* 195–216.

Von Bertalanffy, L. (1950). An outline of general system theory. *British Journal of the Philosophy of Science, 1,* 134–165.

Ward, M. (1995). Butterflies and bifurcations: Can chaos theory contribute to our understanding of family systems? *Journal of Marriage and the Family, 57,* 629–638.

Wiggins, J. S. (1979). A psychological taxonomy of trait-descriptive terms: The interpersonal domain. *Journal of Personality & Social Psychology, 37,* 395–412.

Yalom, I. (1985). *The theory and practice of group psychotherapy.* New York: Basic Books.

Zimbardo, P. G., Maslach, C., & Haney, C. (2000). Reflections on the Stanford prison Experiment: Genesis, transformations, consequences. In T. Blass (Ed.), *Obedience to authority: Current perspectives on the Milgram paradigm* (pp. 193–237). Mahwah, NJ: Erlbaum.

12 The Dynamics of Human Experience: Fundamentals of Dynamical Social Psychology

ROBIN R. VALLACHER AND ANDRZEJ NOWAK

Introduction

There is an important but largely unrecognized paradox at the core of social psychology. On the one hand, everyone (psychologist and layperson alike) acknowledges the inherent dynamism characterizing human experience, from microprocesses of mind to macro processes of society. Social judgments are embedded in the rapid and ever-changing flow of thought, diverse emotions supplant one another on multiple time scales, social interactions revolve around the complex and time-dependent exchange of motoric and verbal acts, relationships evolve and undergo constant transformation on different dimensions, and collective phenomena at the level of groups and societies occur against the backdrop of a complex and constantly changing field of forces. The dynamism inherent in personal and interpersonal experience is reflected in the seminal contributions of such pioneers as James (1890), Mead (1934), Cooley (1902), Lewin (1936), and Asch (1946) and is apparent today in the coupling of the word "dynamic" with the various literatures that define the field. Thus psychologists theorize about personality dynamics, dynamics of attitude change, interpersonal dynamics, and group dynamics, as if these topics each represented a particular manifestation of an underlying proclivity for evolution and change on the part of people.

The very ubiquity of dynamism, however, renders it a poor candidate for generating theories in social psychology. Theories, after all, are couched in terms of invariant properties representing stable *signals* that are obscured by the *noise* associated with personal, interpersonal, and societal processes. The stream of consciousness, for example, may be a true reflection of phenomenal experience, but its turbulent nature seems antithetical to fundamental properties that transcend particular individuals and their moment-to-moment mental states. To discern regularities and invariant properties characterizing social processes, theorists and researchers commonly ignore the ever-changing undercurrent of mind and action, focusing instead on those elements of thought and behavior that admit to stability and structure. Within social psychology especially, the emphasis is typically on higher-order units of mental and behavioral phenomena (e.g., traits, schemata, stereotypes, global evaluations, norms, roles) that presumably lend stability and coherence to phenomenal experience. The turbulent flow of lower-level elements (thoughts, feelings, utterances, movements) is not denied, but it is effectively rendered irrelevant to "true" understanding and meaningful prediction.

We suggest that the gulf between the reality of experiential turbulence and the focus on stability in theory construction is unnecessary. Dynamism and structure should instead be viewed as complementary aspects of experience that together provide the basis for cognitive, emotional, and behavioral accommodation in people's daily lives. The general notion is that the flow of lower-level elements gives rise to higher-order structures, which in turn constrain the dynamics of lower-level elements. This reciprocal causal relationship between lower-level and higher-level units of experience is a central tenet in dynamical social psychology (cf. Nowak & Vallacher, 1998; Vallacher & Nowak, 2007; Vallacher, Read, & Nowak, 2002), a recently developed paradigm for the field that represents an adaptation of the concepts, principles, and tools developed within dynamical systems and complexity science. Our aim in this chapter is to outline the essential features of dynamical social psychology and illustrate the relevance of this perspective for a wide variety of personal, interpersonal, and collective processes.

We will not try to describe every version of the dynamical perspective, nor every application of this general approach. This may have been possible in the 1990s (see, e.g., Eiser, 1994; Goldstein, 1996; Guastello, 1995; Kaplowitz & Fink, 1992; Vallacher & Nowak, 1994a) when the dynamical perspective was more a promissory note than an established paradigm. Since that time, however, there has been a proliferation of many innovative research strategies – some forwarding formal models implemented in computer simulations, others offering empirical means for capturing the dynamics of personal, interpersonal, and societal processes – that have been used to investigate a wide array of phenomena. Our plan instead is to highlight the crucial elements of the dynamical perspective that find expression in otherwise distinct theories, research strategies, and topical agendas.

We begin by describing the basic concepts from the study of nonlinear dynamical systems that are directly relevant to the subject matter of social psychology. These concepts have considerable intuitive appeal but are nonetheless difficult to appreciate within canonical approaches to social psychological phenomena. We then describe dynamical minimalism (Nowak, 2004), an approach that provides a workable entrée into the nature and expression of dynamic processes at different levels of social reality. This approach is illustrated with respect to two lines of research – one emphasizing the emergence of group-level properties from the self-organization of individual agents, the other exploring the proclivity of individuals to coordinate their respective behavioral and mental dynamics in service of forming dyads and social groups. We conclude by reflecting on the trajectory of dynamical social psychology thus far and offering caveats concerning the relevance of this approach to the unique features of human experience.

The Dynamical Perspective

Intrinsic Dynamics

People's cognitive and affective states, overt behavior, goal-directed actions, and social relations evolve and change in the absence of external influence. The internally generated nature of psychological processes was central to the early formulations of social psychology and has clear, almost self-evident intuitive appeal for laypeople. Yet contemporary social psychological theory and research rarely focuses on the intrinsic dynamics of personal and interpersonal phenomena (cf. McGrath & Kelley, 1986; Nowak & Vallacher, 1998). Instead, research typically concentrates on the prediction of outcome variables (operationalized as dependent measures) from the knowledge of other factors (independent variables). To be sure, external causation is relevant to social processes, and the focus on outside forces has generated important insight into social psychological phenomena. External factors, though, do not exert their effect by acting on an empty or passive system. Rather, they interact with the intrinsic dynamics associated with the process in question.

The centrality of intrinsic dynamics is observable at different levels of social reality, from basic intrapersonal processes to macro-level societal phenomena. At the level of the mind, the temporal pattern of cognitive and affective elements in the stream of thought (James, 1890) often provides a better characterization of a person's mental makeup than do the summary aspects of the person's mental process (e.g., overall attitude, final decision) that are more commonly the focus of investigation (Vallacher & Nowak, 1994b). Research has shown, for example, that simply thinking about an attitude object (e.g., another person) in the absence of external influence or new information tends to promote more extreme (polarized) evaluations of the object over time (e.g., Tesser, 1978).

In a related vein, research on social judgment has shown that internally generated thoughts and feelings about a target person commonly reflect elaborate (but identifiable) patterns of change that convey important information about the person's judgment. A judgment that is neutral when collapsed over time, for instance, can have very different meanings and implications, depending on the intrinsic dynamics of the judgment process (Vallacher, Nowak, & Kaufman, 1994). When neutrality reflects relatively little variation in evaluation occurring on a relatively slow time scale, the summary judgment might indeed reflect a truly neutral sentiment (or detachment). But if neutrality reflects oscillation between highly positive and highly negative judgments on a rapid time scale, the summary judgment signifies heightened involvement and ambivalence rather than neutrality per se.

Intrinsic dynamics are also central to the characterization of personal action. Actions typically have a hierarchical structure, in that the performance of an action entails the coordinated interplay of more basic actions or subacts. The act of going to work, for example, may involve getting dressed, leaving the house, driving a car, parking the car, and entering a building. Each of these lower-level acts can, in turn, be decomposed into yet more basic lower-level elements. Driving, for example, consists of starting the car, turning the steering wheel, making turns, and braking. Each level in an action hierarchy is associated with a different time scale, with the lower-level acts taking place in shorter intervals of time (cf. Newtson, 1994). Going to work occurs on a longer time scale than does driving, for example, and the time scale for driving is longer than that for each instance of turning the steering wheel.

The intrinsic dynamics of action, in other words, span the levels of action in an overall action hierarchy. Thus a person's behavior may appear to be a continual succession of momentary movements when defined in low-level, mechanistic terms but take on the appearance of switching between qualitatively different actions, each occurring on a longer time scale, when defined in higher-level terms. Interestingly, there is evidence that the embedded time scales in an action hierarchy often have a fractal structure (Newtson, 1994). Research on action identification (cf. Vallacher & Wegner, 1987) has enumerated a variety of factors that dictate the level at which an action is regulated. Research has also demonstrated that people reliably differ in their default level of action identification across a wide variety of action domains (Vallacher & Wegner, 1989), and that individuals who characteristically think about their actions in lower-level terms are predisposed to the emergence of higher-level action understanding. Emergence takes place when such individuals are exposed to cues (e.g., social feedback) that suggest higher-level meaning for the actions (Wegner, Vallacher, Kiersted, & Dizadji, 1986) or when they reflect on their actions, allowing the lower-level action elements to self-organize into a higher-level act identity that provides subjective integration for these elements (Vallacher & Nowak, 1997).

Social interaction involves the coordination of individuals' behavior over time and thus can be investigated with respect to intrinsic dynamics. Relevant research has focused on the interpersonal coordination of relatively low-level actions, such as speaking (e.g., Condon & Ogston, 1967; Dittman & Llewellyn, 1969) and limb movement (e.g., Beek & Hopkins, 1992; Kelso, 1995; Newtson, 1994; Turvey, 1990). In one common approach, two individuals are simply asked to swing their legs while sitting down across from one another (Beek & Hopkins, 1992). In particular, one person swings his or her legs in time to a metronome, and the other person tries to match those movements. Two forms of coordination have been revealed in this research: *in-phase*, with the individuals swinging their legs in unison, and *anti-phase*, with the individuals swinging their legs with the same frequency but in the opposite direction. Individuals are able to maintain anti-phase coordination only up to a certain frequency of movement, at which point they switch to in-phase coordination. When the frequency is then decreased, at some value they are able to coordinate anti-phase again, but this tempo is significantly lower than the point at which they originally started to coordinate in-phase. Such *hysteresis* indicates that movement coordination can be analyzed as a nonlinear dynamical system (cf. Hock, Kelso, & Schoner, 1993; Kelso, 1995).[1] Modes of coordination more complex than in-phase and anti-phase have also been identified in this line of research (cf. Baron, Amazeen, & Beek, 1994; Rosenblum & Turvey, 1988; Turvey, 1990; Turvey & Carello, 1995).

Interpersonal dynamics are not limited to the coordination of speech and motor movements; they also include the temporal coordination of higher-level actions (e.g., plans, goals) and internal states (moods, judgments, etc.). There is relatively little research on this form of interpersonal dynamics, but there is reason to believe that the quality of a social relationship is reflected in the ability of partners to coordinate in-phase with respect to their respective higher-level actions, opinions, and feelings (e.g., Baron et al., 1994; Guastello, Pincus, & Gunderson, 2006; McGrath & Kelly, 1986; Nowak, Vallacher, & Zochowski, 2002, 2005; Tickle-Degnen & Rosenthal, 1987). Indeed, the ebb and flow of sentiment, information exchange, and action may convey deeper insight into the nature of a relationship than might global indices such as the average sentiment, the amount of information exchanged, or the summary action tendencies. Thus people who feel positively about one another are said to "be in synch" or "on the same wavelength" with respect to their internal states. In a later section, "Dynamics of Interpersonal Synchronization," we present a formal model of social coordination (implemented in computer simulations) that has implications for classic and contemporary issues in interpersonal relations.

At the level of societal phenomena, tracking the temporal trajectory associated with the emergence of norms and public opinion may provide greater insight into the society's future makeup and likely response to external threat than simply knowing what the societal norms and opinions are at a single point in time (cf. Nowak, Szamrej, & Latané, 1990). When norms and opinions develop incrementally over a long period of time, for example, the society tends to display resistance to external threats or even to new information that might promote better economic conditions. But societal change in political and economic ideology can also occur in a rapid, nonlinear manner (e.g., Nowak & Vallacher, 2001; Nowak, Vallacher, Kus, & Urbaniak, 2005), with a trajectory that resembles phase transitions in physical systems (Lewenstein, Nowak, & Latané, 1993). Societies undergoing such nonlinear transitions are vulnerable to subsequent rebounds of the earlier ideologies and highly responsive to threats and new information, and they can experience a period of sustained oscillation between conflicting worldviews (Nowak & Vallacher, 2001).

Attractors in Psychological Systems

Psychological systems display intrinsic dynamics, but they also demonstrate stability and remarkable resistance to change. People encounter vast amounts of information relevant to social judgment and interpersonal relations each day, much of which is mutually contradictory. Yet people typically manage to form and maintain relatively coherent patterns of thought and behavior in their social lives. Two people in a romantic relationship, for example, are likely to experience a wide variety of thoughts and feelings about one another, but over time each person's mental state will tend to converge on positive sentiment toward the other. Despite the ever-changing nature of intrapersonal and interpersonal experience, then, people's mental, affective, and behavioral states tend to converge on relatively narrow sets of specific states or on patterns of change between specific states. These states or patterns of change are referred to as *attractors*.

Beyond implying the convergence of intrinsic dynamics on a small set of states or a pattern of change between states, the presence of an attractor implies resistance of the system to external perturbation. When a system is at its attractor, it tends to maintain that state despite forces and influences that have the potential to destabilize that state. An external influence may prove capable of moving the system to any other state, but the system will return fairly quickly to one of its attractors. Several well-documented phenomena imply the existence of an attractor. Self-regulation, for example, is defined in terms of resistance to temptations and distractions, impulse control, and the maintenance of states corresponding to salient personal standards and values (cf. Carver & Scheier, 1999, 2002; Vallacher & Nowak, 1999). In similar fashion, self-esteem maintenance (Tesser, Martin, & Cornell, 1996), self-verification (Swann, 1990), and psychological reactance (Brehm & Brehm, 1981) all reflect a tendency of mental systems to converge on a particular state (e.g., a level of self-esteem) and to resist outside forces that threaten to dislodge the person's judgments and beliefs from that state.

Across different domains of science, three basic types of attractors have been identified: fixed-point attractors, periodic (including multiperiodic) attractors, and deterministic chaos (cf. Eckmann & Ruelle, 1985; Nowak & Lewenstein, 1994; Schuster, 1984). Each type is likely to have relevance for understanding different intrapersonal and interpersonal processes, although work designed to establish such relevance is in its nascent stage.[2]

Fixed-Point Attractors

A *fixed-point attractor* describes the case in which the state of the system converges to a stable value. It is similar, then, to the notion of equilibrium or homeostasis (cf. Cannon, 1932; Miller, 1944). A fixed-point attractor corresponds, for example, to a desired end-state or goal (cf. Carver & Scheier, 1999, 2002; Vallacher & Nowak, 1997, 2007). This is evident when a person maintains a belief, an evaluation of someone, or an action tendency despite forces or sources of information that challenge these tendencies. In principle, though, attractors are not limited to goals, intentions, or other desired states. Conceivably, a person might display a pattern of antagonistic behavior in his or her social relations, despite concerted efforts to avoid behaving in this manner. In similar fashion, a person with low self-esteem may initially embrace flattering feedback from someone, but over time he or she may discount or reinterpret this feedback, displaying instead a pattern of thought that converges on a negative self-evaluative state (Swann, Hixon, Stein-Seroussi, & Gilbert, 1990). In intergroup relations, meanwhile, warring factions may exhibit conciliatory gestures when prompted to do so, but revert to a pattern of antagonistic thought and behavior when outside interventions are relaxed (Coleman, Vallacher, Nowak, & Bui-Wrzosinska, 2007). When a system's dynamics are governed by a fixed-point attractor, in short, the system will consistently evolve to a particular state, even if this state is not hedonically pleasant, and will return to this state despite being perturbed by forces that might promote a more pleasant state.

A psychological system may have more than one attractor, with each corresponding to a distinct equilibrium state. Which of these multiple attractors governs a system's dynamics in a particular instance depends on the initial states or starting values of the system's evolution. The set of initial states converging on each attractor represents the *basin of attraction* for that attractor. This implies that for a person or a group characterized by multiple fixed-point attractors, the process in question can display different equilibrium tendencies, each associated with a distinct basin of attraction. Within each basin, very different initial states will follow a trajectory that eventually converges on the same stable value. But by the same token, even a slight change in the system's initial state will promote a large change in the system's trajectory if this change represents a state that falls just outside the original basin of attraction and within a basin for a different attractor. In conflict situations, for example, there are often two dominant responses, one corresponding to aggression and one corresponding to conciliation. Very slight differences in the circumstances associated with the conflict can thus promote dramatically different behaviors, with no option for a response that integrates the two tendencies (e.g., Coleman et al., 2007).

The essence of the attractor concept and its relevance for personal and social processes can be captured in a simple metaphor. Figure 12.1 portrays a ball on a hilly landscape. The ball represents the current state of the system and the valleys (A and B) represent different fixed-point attractors for the system. The evolution of the system toward an attractor is represented by the ball rolling down a hill and coming to rest in the bottom of a valley. Each attractor in Figure 12.1 has an associated basin of attraction, represented by the width of

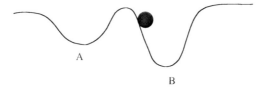

Figure 12.1. A dynamical system with two fixed-point attractors. From Vallacher and Nowak (2007). Reprinted by permission of Guilford Press.

the valley. The basin of attraction for Attractor A in Figure 12.1 is wider than the basin for Attractor B. This means that a wider range of states will evolve toward Attractor A than toward Attractor B. Attractors can also vary in their respective strength, represented by the corresponding depth of the two valleys in Figure 12.1. Attractor B, then, is considerably stronger than Attractor A. This means that it is more difficult for external influence to change the current state of the system when the system is within the basin of attraction for Attractor B as opposed to Attractor A.

The existence of multiple fixed-point attractors in a system expresses the intuition that people can have different (perhaps even mutually contradictory) goals, values, self-concepts, and patterns of social behavior. A person may have two or more standards for self-regulation, for example, with each providing for action guidance and self-control under different sets of conditions. The person's behavior may reflect an achievement standard under one set of conditions, but reflect an affiliation standard under a different set of conditions. Similarly, a person may have multiple self-views (e.g., Markus & Nurius, 1986), each representing a coherent and stable way of thinking about him or herself. One of these self-views is likely to become salient when a specific set of self-relevant information is primed or made salient by virtue of context or role expectations. What appears to be inconsistency or conflict in personality, meanwhile, can be viewed as the existence of multiple attractors, each associated with a different basin of attraction for thought, feeling, and action (cf. Nowak et al., 2002). One set of conditions might promote a trajectory that evolves toward compassion and warmth, for example, while another might promote dominance and competition.

Because the strength of an attractor and the size of its basin of attraction are potentially independent, different combinations of these basic properties may have unique implications for psychological processes (cf. Nowak et al., 2002, 2005). Consider the two attractors in Figure 12.1. Attractor A has a wide basin of attraction but is relatively weak. This means that a relatively small force may change the state of the system (i.e., move the ball up the gradual slope). However, the system is likely to return to the attractor (i.e., it will roll back into the valley) even if these changes are relatively large. In contrast, Attractor B is relatively strong but has a narrower basin of attraction. In this case, considerable influence is required to promote even a slight impact on the system (i.e., move the ball up the steep slope), but if this effect is achieved, the system will not return to the attractor (i.e., it will escape the valley).

To illustrate this difference, consider a romantic couple that has two attractors: a strong attractor associated with positive feelings and a weak attractor associated with negative feelings. Let us assume the couple has a wider range of attraction for positive feelings than for negative feelings. The partners are likely to evolve toward positive feelings if they begin an interaction within a broad range of affective states (e.g., neutral to very positive), but they may end up feeling negative about one another if they begin an interaction within a different (more restricted) range of affective states (e.g., mildly to highly negative). In other words, a broader range of initial states are likely to promote a communication trajectory that results in an exchange of warm sentiments as opposed to critical comments. However, if the couple routinely starts out with negative feelings, the negative attractor, despite having a narrow basin, may dictate the trajectory for feelings expressed in the couple's interactions. It is conceivable, too, that the couple has a wider basin of attraction for negative feelings, in which case anything short of a highly positive initial state could dissolve into a negatively toned exchange (see Gottman, Murray, Swanson, Tyson, Swanson, 2002; Gottman, Swanson, & Swanson, 2002).

Latent Attractors

A system may be characterized by multiple attractors, but when the system is at one of these attractors, the others may not be visible to observers (perhaps not even to the actors themselves). The existence of these potential states of the system might not even be suspected. These *latent attractors* may be highly important in the long run, however, because they determine which states are possible for the system when conditions change. By specifying possibilities for a system that have yet to be observed or experienced, the concept of latent attractor goes beyond the traditional notion of equilibrium (e.g., Abraham & Shaw, 1992). Critical changes in a system might not be reflected in the observable state of the system, but rather in the creation or destruction of a latent attractor representing a potential state that is currently invisible to all concerned.

The implications of latent attractors have recently been explored in the context of social relations characterized by seemingly intractable conflict (Coleman, Bui-Wrozinska, Vallacher, & Nowak, 2006; Coleman et al., 2007; Nowak, Vallacher, Bui-Wrzosinska, & Coleman, 2007). Consider intergroup relations, for example. Although factors such as objectification, dehumanization, and stereotyping of outgroup members are preconditions for the development of intractable conflict (Coleman, 2003; Deutsch, 1973), their immediate impact may not be apparent. Instead, these factors may gradually create a latent attractor to which the system can abruptly switch in response to a provocation that seems relatively minor, even trivial. But by the same token, efforts at conflict resolution that seem fruitless in the short run may have the effect of creating a latent positive attractor for intergroup relations, thereby establishing a potential relationship to which the groups can switch if other conditions permit. The existence of a latent positive attractor can promote a rapid de-escalation of conflict, even between groups with a long history of seemingly intractable conflict.

Periodic Attractors

Rather than converging on a stable value over time, some systems display sustained rhythmic or oscillatory behavior. A temporal pattern conforming to this tendency is referred to as a periodic or limit-cycle attractor. Periodicity is clearly associated with many biological phenomena, such as circadian rhythms and menstrual cycles (cf. Glass & Mackey, 1988), but this dynamic tendency may also underlie important psychological phenomena (Gottman, 1979). Moods, for example, have been shown to have a periodic structure, often corresponding to a weekly cycle (e.g., Brown & Moskowitz, 1998; Larsen, 1987; Larsen & Kasimatis, 1990). Investigation of the intrinsic dynamics associated with both social judgment (Vallacher, Nowak, & Kautman, 1994) and self-evaluation (Vallacher, Nowak, Froehlich, & Rockloff, 2002), meanwhile, has demonstrated that the stream of thought often oscillates between positive and negative assessments, sometimes in accordance with remarkably fast time scales. Periodic structure has also been shown to characterize human action (Newtson, 1994) and is a feature of social interaction as well (e.g., Beek & Hopkins, 1992; Gottman, 1979; Nezlek, 1993).

It may be difficult to distinguish a periodic attractor from the existence of multiple fixed-point attractors. In both cases, the system displays movement between different states over time. The distinction centers on the regularity of the movement between states and the role of external factors in producing such movement. A periodic attractor represents a repetitive temporal pattern, with the values of the dynamical variable repeating after a time T, $x_i(t) = (t + T)$, where T is the period of motion. Even in the absence of noise or external influence, the state of the system undergoes constant change. For a pattern of change to qualify as a periodic attractor, then, it must represent a pattern on which the system converges, and to which it returns after small perturbations. In a daily cycle of activity, for example, a sleepless night might temporarily disrupt the pattern (e.g., oversleeping the next few days), but eventually the pattern will be restored.

A system characterized by fixed-point attractors, in contrast, displays a tendency to stabilize on a particular state or set of states. Because such attractors capture all trajectories within their respective basins, a disturbance, noise, or an external influence operating on the system is necessary to move the system from one stable state to another. A person with self-regulatory standards for both confrontation and compromise, for example, will display one of these tendencies as long as the context surrounding the person is within the basin of attraction for that tendency. If the two attractors differ in the size of their respective basins, and if contexts are avoided that attract the person's mental, emotional, or behavioral state toward the smaller basin, the person may operate for long periods of time in line with the stronger attractor. Likewise, a romantic couple may have fixed-point attractors for both positive and negative affective states, but whether they display periodic movement between them will depend on the starting conditions associated with their interactions. Thus even if the couple seems to oscillate between positive and negative states, each of these states provides at least temporary stability. In periodic evolution, stability is not afforded by any particular state but rather by the pattern of changes between states.

The distinction between periodic and fixed-point attractor dynamics was observed in a study investigating the temporal trajectories of affective states on the part of bipolar depressive individuals (Johnson & Nowak, 2002). Time series analysis of mood and other symptoms revealed that many of these patients seemed to oscillate between a normal and a depressed state. The results showed, however, that patients whose temporal dynamics did not reflect fixed-point attractor tendencies were at highest risk for suicide and were hospitalized more often for their depression. These risks were equally low for individuals whose moods oscillated around a single attractor, even one corresponding to a depressed state, and those whose moods switched between two distinct attractors reflecting a normal state and a depressed state. These results suggest an interesting connection between attractor dynamics and self-regulatory tendencies. Self-regulation implies approach and stabilization with respect to some states and avoidance and de-stabilization of other states. The stable states represent fixed-point attractors for a person's mental and emotional dynamics. From this perspective, the lack of fixed-point attractors for one's internal state signals a breakdown in the capacity for self-regulation.

Deterministic Chaos

The best known, and arguably the most popular insight concerning nonlinear dynamical systems centers on *deterministic chaos* (cf. Schuster, 1984). Indeed, many researchers and scholars – especially those from fields other than mathematics and physics – commonly discuss the primary insights from the work on nonlinear dynamics as chaos theory (see Chapter 1 of this volume). When investigating a chaotic system, anything short of infinite precision in the knowledge of a system at one point in time can undermine knowledge of the system's future states. This decoupling between determinism and practical predictability occurs because all initial inaccuracies are amplified by the system's intrinsic dynamics, so that the inaccuracies grow exponentially over time. After some finite (often quite short) time, exponential growth ensures that the size of the error will exceed the possible range of states of the system's behavior.

Chaos represents an ever-present possibility in nonlinear dynamical systems (cf. Goldstein, 1996; Nowak & Lewenstein, 1994). In fact, chaos has been demonstrated in many biological and physical phenomena. One cannot rule out the possibility, then, that human thought and behavior may sometimes follow a chaotic trajectory. After all, social psychology is replete with nonlinear phenomena, such as threshold functions, inverted-U relations, and complex interactions among causal variables (Nowak & Vallacher, 1998; Vallacher & Nowak, 1997). But despite this potential, unequivocal evidence for deterministic chaos in human thought and behavior remains to be documented. Human dynamics invariably contain some degree of randomness, and human behavior is often unpredictable. However, it can be quite difficult to determine the degree to which such unpredictability reflects deterministic chaos, the stochastic nature of the laws governing human nature, or the multitude of influences unaccounted for by measurement that can be treated as noise.

Attractor Dynamics in Perspective

Attractor dynamics are highly relevant to personal and interpersonal processes. Beyond capturing basic intuitions underlying many social psychological phenomena, framing such phenomena in terms of attractors may allow for a significant simplification in the description of a system's dynamics. Instead of describing moment-to-moment changes in a system's state, one can describe the structure of attractors in the system and the patterns of transition between the attractors. Short-lived reversible changes of the state of the system correspond to transitions between attractors. Deep and lasting changes, on the other hand, usually correspond to changes in the structure of attractors.

Dynamical Minimalism

In the traditional approach to theory construction, the complexity of human thought and behavior is assumed to reflect complex interactions among a large number of variables. In marked contrast, the approach of *dynamical minimalism* (Nowak, 2004) assumes that very complex properties can be produced by simple rules specifying the interactions among very simple elements. Complexity emerges in this fashion when the elements are nonlinear and interact over time (cf. Holland, 1995). Complex cognitive phenomena (e.g., pattern recognition, error correction, generalization), for example, can be observed in a simple network of binary elements, where each element reacts to the input it receives from other elements (e.g., Hopfield, 1982).

Dynamical minimalism is concerned with identifying the simplest, yet realistic, set of assumptions capable of producing a phenomenon of interest. The theories that result from this approach then provide simple explanations that still capture the nuance and complexity of human experience. In formal models, this is tantamount to identifying the simplest mathematical rules to express what is known about a phenomenon. As noted earlier, many well-documented relationships in social psychology (e.g., threshold phenomena, inverted-U relations, and statistical interactions) are nonlinear in nature and thus have the potential for self-organization and emergence, provided the variables are embedded in a larger system that evolves over time (cf. Nowak & Vallacher, 1998; Vallacher & Nowak, 1997). In effect, the approach of dynamical minimalism achieves parsimony in theory construction but does so without stripping the phenomenon of its subtlety and nuance.

This approach provides a new way of thinking about the relation between micro and macro levels of description. Mainstream models commonly assume reductionism, such that the rules observed at one level of description correspond to the rules operating at another level. Thus the properties at a macro level of description can be reduced to the properties of elements at a micro level of description. The relation between poverty and crime in a social system, for example, might be explained by reducing this relation to the relation between frustration and crime at the level of individuals in the society.

Dynamical models do not assume isomorphism among levels of description. In fact, the rules specifying the interaction among a system's elements are likely to generate quite different rules at higher levels of system behavior (see Durkheim, 1938, for an early appreciation of this idea). The emergence of new properties is illustrated in the *society of self* model of self-structure (Nowak, Vallacher, Tesser, & Borkowski, 2000). This model assumes very simple rules by which self-relevant information is integrated in service of self-concept formation. Specifically, each element of information (e.g., episodic memory, physical feature, self-perceived trait) adopts the prevailing valence (positive vs. negative) of related elements. When iterated over time, this simple rule generated interesting but largely unexpected consequences at the global level of self-understanding. Thus the self-structure became differentiated into locally coherent regions (e.g., social roles, areas of competence) of contrasting valence, each of which displayed resistance to discrepant information (e.g., negative social feedback). Global self-esteem, characterized by relatively high self-certainty, also emerged at the macro level from the simple rule of influence among elements at the micro level.

Such emergence would seem to represent a paradox for theory construction. If properties at a macro level cannot be derived from properties of the system's lower-level elements, how can knowledge of the lower-level elements provide an explanation of the higher-level properties? The resolution of this paradox centers on the role of computer simulations in dynamical minimalism. Computer models enable one to specify the properties of system elements and the rules of interaction among these elements. As the elements interact over time in accordance with these rules, dynamics appear at the system level that were not assumed or programmed for the elements themselves. By means of computer simulation, then, a theory constructed at a basic level of psychological reality (e.g., moment-to-moment thought process, dyadic social interaction) can be tested at a higher level of psychological reality (e.g., social judgment, group norms).

Dynamical minimalism relies on computer simulations for another reason. The basic elements comprising a system are often uninteresting, even trivial, and the interactions among them may have only minor impact on the system's global properties. But some properties of system elements may have significant impact on the system's higher-order properties as the elements interact over time. In advance, it may not be obvious which properties are trivial and which are essential for the emergence process. Dynamical minimalism is intended to make this distinction and to construct a model that incorporates only the properties that are critical for the emergence of macro-level phenomena. With computer simulations, one can systematically vary the assumptions regarding the properties of elements and their interactions, and then observe which assumptions promote meaningful changes at the macro level. Those properties that have trivial consequences at the macro level can be eliminated from the model. In this way, computer simulations enable one to distill the minimal set of components necessary to capture the essence of a phenomenon.

We hasten to add that computer simulations cannot substitute for empirical verification of the theoretical model. Computer simulations are critical in identifying the properties that are central to the model and investigating the consequences of these properties for the functioning of the system in question. Knowledge of these consequences provides the basis for framing hypotheses that can then be investigated in empirical research. The interplay of simulation and empirical research is exemplified in the formulation and testing of dynamic social impact theory (Nowak et al., 1990). Computer simulations were used to derive predictions concerning spatial–temporal patterns of social change processes. The hypotheses were later investigated through archival data concerning patterns of voting and entrepreneurship in Poland following the fall of Communism in the 1990s (Nowak et al., 2005). The relationship between computer simulations and empirical research is sometimes reversed. Empirical studies can serve to refine a model, which is then implemented in computer simulations. The results of the simulations, in turn, can generate new hypotheses to be tested in empirical research. Indeed, the mutual feedback loops among theory, computer simulation, and empirical research is central to the approach of dynamical minimalism.

The Dynamics of Social Influence

People can function as individuals, but most of the time they prefer not to. There is a strong drive for people to form bonds with one another, whether for purely social reasons or to achieve ends that require collective action. Individuals are assembled into groups by one of two basic processes. Social interdependence, first of all, reflects the idea that the decisions and actions of one individual have consequences for the decisions and actions of other individuals. Social interdependence is central to game theoretic approaches in psychology (cf. Thibaut &

Kelley, 1959). The Prisoner's Dilemma game (PDG) is perhaps the best-known exemplar of this approach, and it has been the focus of various dynamical models (e.g., Axelrod, 1984; Messick & Liebrand, 1995). Social influence is the other basic process by which individuals are assembled into dyads and groups. Widely considered to be the core process of social experience (cf. Vallacher, Nowak, & Miller, 2003), social influence refers to any change in an individual's thoughts, feelings, or behavior that occurs as the result of the real or imagined presence of others (cf. Allport, 1968). It subsumes a wide array of phenomena, including obedience to authority, conformity, imitation and modeling, bystander intervention in emergencies, social loafing, stage fright, persuasion, and groupthink. Despite this diversity, there is evidence that the essence of social influence can be described in terms of three crucial factors: the number, strength, and immediacy of the sources of influence (Latané, 1981). Empirical research (see Latané, 1981) has shown that the magnitude and nature of social influence represents a multiplicative function of these sources.

Modeling Social Influence Dynamics

Nowak et al. (1990) used cellular automata to model the dynamics of social influence. In this approach, each individual has three properties: an opinion on a topic, a degree of persuasive strength, and a position in a social space. As a simplifying assumption, individuals are typically assumed to have one of two opinions on an issue (e.g., pro vs. con). The group consists of n individuals located on a two-dimensional grid, with each cell corresponding to an individual, as portrayed in Figure 12.2. The color of the cell specifies the individual's current opinion (light gray denotes pro, dark gray denotes con), and the height of the cell represents the individual's strength (e.g., expertise, confidence, charisma). In the model, each individual interacts with other group members to discuss the issue and ascertain the degree of support for each position. As a result of this assessment, each individual adopts the opinion that is most prevalent. The strength of influence of each opinion is expressed by the following formula:

$$I_i = \left(\sum_1^N \left(\frac{s_j}{d_{ij}^2} \right)^2 \right)^{1/2},$$

where I_i denotes total influence, s_j represents the strength of each individual, and d_{ij} represents the distance between individuals i and j. The opinions of those who are closest to the individual and have the greatest strength are weighted most heavily by him or her. An individual's own position is also considered and is weighted most heavily by virtue of immediacy (0 distance). Finally, influence grows with the square root of the number of people exerting influence.

In each round of the computer simulations, one individual is chosen (usually at random), and influence is computed for each opinion in the group. A simple

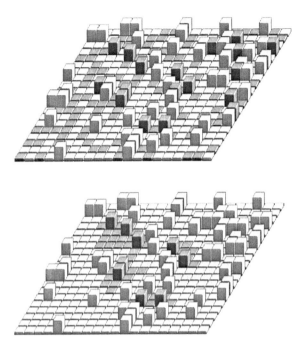

Figure 12.2. Distributions of opinions in the simulated group, initial (upper) and final (lower). From Vallacher and Nowak (2007). Reprinted by permission of Guilford Press.

updating rule is employed: The individual changes his or her opinion to match the prevailing opinion if the resultant strength for this opinion position is greater than the strength of the individual's current position. This process is performed for each individual in the group. This simple procedure is repeated until there are no further changes in opinion. This usually involves several rounds of simulation, because an individual who had previously changed his or her position to match that of his or her neighbors may revert to the original position if the neighbors change their opinions. Figure 12.2 illustrates representative results of the computer simulations. Initially, as depicted in Figure 12.2 (upper), there is a majority of 60% (light gray) and a minority of 40% (dark gray), with the majority and minority opinions randomly distributed in social space. The majority and minority groups have the same relative proportions of strong and weak members (tall vs. short cells). As depicted in Figure 12.2 (lower), an equilibrium is reached after six rounds of simulated discussion. Note that the majority has grown (to 90%) at the expense of the minority (now 10%). The minority opinion has survived, however, by forming clusters of like-minded people. These clusters are primarily formed around strong individuals.

These two group-level outcomes are routinely observed in computer simulations of this process (cf. Latané, Nowak, & Liu, 1994): *polarization* and *clustering*. Each is reminiscent of well-documented social processes. Empirical research on group dynamics (e.g., Myers & Lamm, 1976), for example, has shown that the average attitude in a group becomes polarized in the direction of the prevailing attitude as a result of group discussion. Polarization reflects the greater influence of the majority opinion. Note that in the initial (random) configuration, depicted in Figure 12.2 (upper), the average proportion of neighbors holding a particular opinion (pro or con) reflects the proportion of this opinion in the total group. This means that the average group member is surrounded by more majority than minority members. Consequently, more minority members are converted to the majority position than vice versa. Some majority members are converted to the minority position, however, because they happen to be located close to an especially strong minority member or because more minority members happen to be at this location.

Clustering is also pervasive in social experience. Clustering has been documented for such diverse facets of social life as attitudes, political beliefs, religions, clothing fashions, and farming techniques. Attitudes, for example, tend to cluster in residential neighborhoods (Festinger, Schachter, & Back, 1950). The clustering of opinions reflects the relatively strong influence exerted by an individual's neighbors. As long as opinions are distributed randomly, the sampling of opinions through social interaction provides a realistic portrayal of the distribution of opinions in the larger society. When opinions are clustered, however, the same sampling process produces a very biased result because the opinions of one's nearby neighbors are weighted the most heavily. This means that the prevalence of one's own opinion is likely to be overestimated. Hence, opinions that are in the minority in global terms can form a local majority. This enables individuals with a minority opinion to maintain this opinion in the belief that it actually represents a majority position.

Three basic factors prevent unification of the group around the majority opinion (Latané & Nowak, 1997; Lewenstein et al., 1993; Nowak, Lewenstein, & Frejlak, 1996). Minority clusters survive, first of all, because individuals differ in their relative strength. Strong individuals (e.g., leaders) stop minority clusters from decaying by counteracting the greater number of majority opinions. Individual differences in strength, moreover, tend to become correlated with opinions. This correlation emerges because the weakest minority members tend to adopt the majority position, so that the average strength of the remaining minority members will increase over time at the expense of the majority. This scenario provides insight into why individuals who advocate minority positions are commonly more influential than those who advocate majority positions (cf. Moscovici, Lage, & Naffrechoux, 1969).

The second factor relevant to the survival of minority clusters is nonlinearity in attitude change. When individuals move incrementally toward the opinions of their interaction partners, there is a tendency for groups to become unified in their support of the majority opinion (Abelson, 1979). In the Nowak et al. (1990) model, however, attitudes change in a nonlinear fashion corresponding to a threshold function. In other words, individuals maintain their current opinion until social influence reaches a critical level, at which point they switch from one categorical position (e.g., con) to the other (pro). Under a linear change rule, opinions are normally distributed and tend to become unified over time. A nonlinear change rule, in contrast, promotes a bimodal distribution and can prevent complete unification, enabling minority opinion to survive in clusters. There is empirical evidence that a normal distribution tends to develop for relatively unimportant attitudes, but that a bimodal distribution tends to be observed when attitudes have high personal importance (Latané & Nowak, 1994).[3] One implication of this finding is that achieving consensus in a group may necessitate that individuals temporarily decrease the subjective importance of the topic.

The third factor that preserves minority clusters concerns the geometry of the social space in which individuals interact (Nowak, Latané, & Lewenstein, 1994). People do not communicate equally with all members of a group, nor do social interactions take place at random. The cellular automata model can be used to approximate different communication patterns with various geometries of social space. When no geometry exists and social interactions occur randomly, minority opinion decays rapidly and the group converges on the majority position. Other geometries, each representing a different communication pattern, have predictable consequences for the fate of minority opinions. In real social settings, of course, several different geometries are likely to coexist and shape the emergence of opinion structure. The ubiquity of e-mail, telephones, shopping malls, and parks add many dimensions to the effective geometry in which interactions take place. The combination of geometries in everyday life no doubt plays an important role in shaping the distribution of public opinion.

Social Influence Dynamics in Perspective

Sometimes people's attempt to influence one another represents only a concern with forwarding personal agendas. But social influence also plays a role in social life that is critical to collective well-being. It binds separate individuals into a social group that experiences a shared psychological state and a common platform for action. In the process of social interaction, individuals adjust their opinions, mood, or behavior to achieve consensus and a shared reality. Even when there is wide diversity of opinion and individuals initially disagree with one another, sustained social interaction tends to promote uniformity in opinions. The group-level product of local social interactions, however, does not simply reflect the central tendency of members' individual initial opinions. To the contrary, social interaction often promotes the emergence of an opinion that is typically more extreme than the average of group members' opinions.[4] Because of individual differences in strength (e.g., persuasiveness), minority opinions are likely to be preserved, albeit at a lower proportion, especially if the issue under discussion has high subjective importance for group members.

For the most part, the adoption of a common psychological state through social interaction is adaptive. It provides the consensus and social coordination necessary for social life and group action (cf. Caporeal & Baron, 1997). But there are also noteworthy downsides associated with the tendency for groups to achieve uniformity. Considerable research in social psychology has shown, for example, that social influence in groups can promote mindless conformity to inaccurate assessments of reality (cf. Asch, 1955; Sherif, 1936). The emphasis on like-mindedness in groups can also lead to decisions and recommendations for action that reflect a concern for reaching consensus rather than a concern for developing the best policy. Under the spell of "groupthink" (Janis, 1982), for example, people expend considerable mental energy on achieving and maintaining opinion unanimity and group solidarity. Once a group has achieved a common psychological state, moreover, an individual who expresses a contrary view is likely to experience enormous pressure to change. Those who do not cave in to group pressure run the risk of being ostracized (Schachter, 1951). The rejection of deviates has clear and important implications for many social phenomena, from peer pressure among adolescents to deliberations in jury trials in which a guilty verdict carries the death sentence (e.g., Hastie, Penrod, & Pennington, 1983).

Dynamics of Interpersonal Synchronization

The dynamical account of social influence describes how the state (e.g., attitude) of a single individual depends on the state of other individuals. Because many psychological processes are defined in terms of intrinsic dynamics, however, individuals are best conceptualized as displaying patterns of change rather than as a set of states. With this in mind, social influence can be approached as the coordination over time of individual dynamics. This observation provides the foundation for a recently developed model of *synchronization* (Nowak, Vallacher, & Zochowski, 2002, 2005), a phenomenon that characterizes coupled dynamical systems (Kaneko, 1993; Shinbrot, 1994). In this model, individuals in an interaction or a relationship are not represented as static or passive entities, but instead as separate systems capable of displaying rich dynamics. The synchronization of individuals' dynamics produces a higher order system with its own dynamic properties. Each individual attempts to achieve synchronization by adjusting his or her internal state or overt behavior in response to the state or behavior of the individual with whom he or she is interacting. In other words, individuals in social interaction modify their respective thoughts, feelings, or action tendencies to promote coordination over time in these features of experience.

Positive correlation or in-phase relation represents the most basic form of synchronization. In social interaction, this means that the overt behaviors, attitudes, or emotions of one person induce similar behaviors or states in the other person at the same time. This form of synchronization is epitomized by imitation, mimicry, and empathy. But one can identify other forms of synchronization and their counterparts in different contexts for social interaction (Newtson, 1994). For example, turn taking in conversation represents negative correlation (anti-phase relation) between individuals in their respective talking and listening (i.e., when one person speaks, the other is silent). Negative correlation can also be observed in antagonistic relationships, such that the sadness or despair of one person induces satisfaction or happiness in the other person and vice versa. More complex forms of synchronization can also be observed that reflect nonlinear relationships and higher-order interactions between the partners' respective behaviors and internal states (cf. Nowak & Vallacher, 1998; Nowak, Vallacher, & Zochowski, 2002).[5] Because positive correlation represents the most funda-mental and arguably the most common form of coordination, it has provided the primary focus to date in our model of synchronization dynamics.

A Model of Synchronization Dynamics

Coupled logistic maps are useful for modeling the synchronization of people in social interaction (Nowak & Vallacher, 1998; Nowak, Vallacher, & Borkowski, 2000; Nowak et al., 2002, 2005). A logistic equation, which is the simplest dynam-ical system capable of displaying complex (e.g., chaotic) behavior (Feigenbaum, 1978; Schuster, 1984), is used to represent the dynamics of each individual. To model synchronization, the behavior of each person not only depends on his or her preceding state but also to a certain extent on the preceding state of the other person. The coupling of individuals' dynamics is specified in the following equation:

$$x_1(t+1) = \frac{r_1 x_1(t)(1 - x_1(t)) + \alpha r_2 x_2(t)(1 - x_2(t))}{1 + \alpha}$$

$$x_2(t+1) = \frac{r_2 x_2(t)(1 - x_2(t)) + \alpha r_1 x_1(t)(1 - x_1(t))}{1 + \alpha}.$$

The dynamical variable (x) can be interpreted as intensity of behavior, and the control parameter, r, can be interpreted as corresponding to internal states, such as personality traits, moods, and values, that shape the person's pattern of behavior (i.e., changes in x over time). To the value of the dynamical variable representing one individual's behavior (x_1), one adds a fraction (α) of the value of the dynamical variable representing the behavior of the other individual (x_2). The magnitude of α represents the strength of coupling and can be viewed as reflecting mutual influence. This might reflect the intensity of communication or degree of mutual imitation in social interaction. When α is 0, there is no coupling (e.g., no influence or communication) on the behavior level, whereas when α is 1, each person's behavior is determined equally by his or her preceding behavior and the influence of the other person. Intermediate values of α represent moderate values of coupling.

Modeling Behavioral Synchronization

The respective control parameters of two individuals are rarely identical when they first interact with one another. Further, the degree of influence and interdependence differs across interactions and relationships. To capture this variability in real-world interactions and relationships, Nowak and Vallacher (1998) systematically varied the similarity of partners' control parameters (r), representing their internal states and their degree of coupling (α), representing their mutual influence (e.g., communication, imitation). Each simulation began with a random value of x for each person, drawn from a uniform distribution that varied from 0 to 1. We let the simulations run for 300 steps, allowing each system to converge on its pattern of intrinsic dynamics and both systems to synchronize. For the next 500 simulation steps, we recorded the values of x for each system and the degree of synchronization of the two systems.

In general, the results demonstrated that the degree of behavioral synchronization increased both with α and similarity in r. At each level of coupling, synchronization increased for greater similarity in partner's internal states. Likewise, at each level of similarity in internal states, synchronization increased with stronger degrees of coupling. The implications of these results are straightforward. If two people have similar control parameters (internal states), relatively little coupling is necessary for them to achieve a high degree of synchronization in their behavior. If the partners have different internal states, however, high mutual influence (communication, mutual reinforcement, constant monitoring, etc.) is required to maintain the same level of synchronization. In the context of a close relationship, this suggests that constant and intense communication may be a sign that the partners are not well coordinated with respect to relevant internal states (e.g., temperament, values, desires). When the partners are similar with respect to these internal states, however, they can devote their energy to common pursuits rather than to constant clarification, monitoring, and influence.

Modeling Internal Synchronization

Some internal parameters, such as emotions and moods, vary a great deal across time and settings. If a particular context induces a common emotion or mood in a dyad or group, synchronization is easy to achieve. Other internal states, however, are considerably more stable and less likely to vary across different contexts. Habits, attitudes, values, and personality traits, for example, are generally considered enduring (cross-situational) features of a person's psychological makeup. Yet even these internal parameters are subject to variability and even modification. This potential for change can be understood and modeled in terms of synchronization dynamics (see Nowak, Vallacher, & Zochowski, 2005). The core idea is that individuals are motivated to achieve coordination in their internal parameters (cf. Caporeal & Baron, 1997; Chartrand & Bargh, 1999; Marsh, Richardson, & Baron, 2006). In their efforts to satisfy this fundamental motive, individuals vary their internal parameters in a direction that leads to increasing synchronization. When synchronization is achieved, the value of the control parameter is engraved as an attractor for that internal state. In effect, people develop stable internal states through social synchronization (e.g., Vallacher, Nowak, & Zochowski, 2007).

To model this process, we simply assume that the value of each person's control parameter drifts somewhat in the direction of the value of the other person's control parameter on each simulation step. How quickly the control parameters begin to match depends on the rate of this drift and on the size of the initial discrepancy between the values of the respective control parameters. It is not necessary that each person knows the exact value of the other person's control parameter. Indeed, people's internal states are often difficult to infer (cf. Jones & Davis, 1965; Kelley, 1967; Nisbett & Ross, 1980; Wegner & Vallacher, 1977). The model assumes only that each person remembers the other person's most recent behaviors (i.e., the most recent values of x) as well as his or her own most recent behaviors. Each person compares his or her own behavior with that of the other person, and then adjusts his or her internal parameter so as to promote increased similarity with the other person's behavior pattern, until there is a match (cf. Zochowski & Liebovitch, 1997, 1999). If the other person's behavior is more complex than the person's own pattern of behavior, for example, the person slightly increases the value of his or her own control parameter. Conversely, the person slightly decreases the value of his or her own control parameter if the other person's behavior is less complex than his or her own. In short, the individuals estimate one another's internal state by monitoring the evolution of each other's behavior.

We performed simulations to investigate the convergence of behavior and internal states under both relatively weak and relatively strong coupling ($\alpha = .25$ and $.7$, respectively). Figure 12.3 displays the results of these simulations. The y-axis corresponds to the magnitude of difference between the two systems in their behavior or internal states, and the x-axis corresponds to time, as reflected in the number of iterations. Consider first the results observed under weak coupling (Fig. 12.3 upper). The systems demonstrate convergence of behavior in a relatively slow and nonlinear manner. Note, however, that the control parameters also show a clear tendency toward convergence. When a match in internal states is achieved, moreover, full synchronization of behavior is also obtained. Now consider the results observed under strong coupling (Fig. 12.3 lower). Although there is immediate synchronization of behavior, the control parameters fail to synchronize, even after 1,000 iterations.

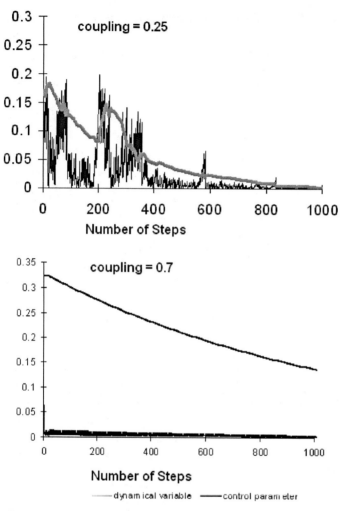

Figure 12.3. Convergence of behavior and internal states under (upper) weak coupling and (lower) strong coupling. From Nowak, Vallacher, and Zochowski (2002). Reprinted by permission of Guilford Press.

The differential results obtained for weak and strong coupling have interesting implications for interpersonal relations. Even for people with very different internal parameters, strong coupling promotes full synchronization of behavior. Further, once this synchrony is achieved, the two people may be totally unaware that their internal states are different. Hence, if the coupling were to be reduced in magnitude (or removed altogether), the dynamics of the two people would immediately diverge. This suggests that people who employ very strong influence (e.g., reinforcement, monitoring) to obtain coordination of behavior may effectively hinder synchronization of their respective internal parameters. More generally, in interpersonal relations, there may be an optimal level of influence and control over one another's behavior (cf. Vallacher et al., 2003). When influence is too weak, synchronization may fail to develop, but when it is strong it can prevent the development of a relationship based on mutual understanding and empathy. Intermediate levels of mutual influence would seem to be most effective for the development of synchronization on a deep level. From this perspective, the most advantageous degree of coupling (e.g., influence and control) is the minimal amount necessary to achieve synchronization.

These implications resonate with extensive research in social psychology suggesting that behavior attributed to external causes is less likely to promote psychological change than is behavior attributed to internal causes. People are remarkably resistant to changing their attitudes and desires, for example, if they believe that their behavior was in response to direct orders, rewards, threats, and other external influences (cf. Bem, 1967; Lepper & Greene, 1978). Indeed, salient external influences may activate mechanisms to counter the influences, creating an internal state that is opposite of the intended effect of the influence (cf. Brehm & Brehm, 1981; Vallacher et al., 2003).

The Trajectory of Dynamical Social Psychology

Social psychology has advanced enormously as a science since its inception a century ago. Yet the insights that established the agenda for the discipline have stood the test of time and still have yet to be fully appreciated in contemporary research. In different but equally compelling ways, such pioneers as James (1890), Cooley (1902), Mead (1934), Lewin (1936), and Asch (1946) brought attention to the multiplicity of interacting forces operating in individual minds and in social groups and the potential for sustained patterns of change resulting from such complexity. They also recognized the converse of dynamism and complexity: an inherent tendency toward stability and simplicity, reflected in the individual's press for mental coherence and in the penchant for groups to achieve coordination in members' thoughts, feelings, and actions.

The surface paradox between complexity and dynamism on the one hand, and simplicity and stability on the other hand, proved problematic for mainstream social psychology during much of the 20th century. The canonical paradigm in this period reduced dynamics to a one-step process involving a purported cause, operationalized as an independent variable at an arbitrary Time 1, and its effect, operationalized as a dependent variable that was assessed at an arbitrary Time 2. The inherent complexity of experience, with multiple variables interacting in myriad ways over time to generate a stream of thought or action, was difficult if not impossible to investigate with recourse to available statistical techniques (e.g., regression, correlation, analysis of variance). By looking "where the light is better," social psychology fostered an image of human experience that was long on simplicity and stability but short on complexity and dynamism. A concern with the complex and dynamic features of interpersonal processes never fully disappeared from social psychology, but neither were these twin towers of experience fully exploited in theory and research as the field moved beyond these initial insights to stake its claim as a legitimate area of scientific inquiry.

With the dawn of a new century, social psychology shows signs of coming full circle, returning to the deep intuitions concerning human experience articulated by the field's founding fathers. This reemergence of appreciation for complexity and dynamism was made possible by developments in the understanding of nonlinear dynamical systems in the 1970s and 1980s and the application of these developments to the subject matter of social psychology within the past two decades (1990s and 2000s). These advances have enabled researchers to explore the inherent dynamism and complexity of interpersonal processes, while recognizing the tendencies toward stability and simplicity in these domains. Indeed, the dynamical perspective in social psychology is defined in terms of these opposing facets of human experience, with theories providing for their reconciliation in a theoretically meaningful manner.

Dynamical social psychology recaptures the foundational insights of the field with a degree of scientific rigor that simply was not available until recently. The understanding of NDS in the physical sciences and mathematics has generated a rich source of methods and formalisms that has enabled social psychology to have its cake and eat it, too. Computer simulations enable psychologists to capture the complexity of social processes and document the emergence of higher-order properties from the interaction of basic elements in a mental or social system. Innovative means of collecting and analyzing time series data provide rigorous yet deep insight into the intrinsic dynamics of mental, affective, behavioral, and interpersonal processes. Formal models enable researchers to identify the parameters that are critical for understanding the fundamental nature of psychological and social processes. The approach of dynamical minimalism is based on the reciprocal interplay of each of these means. Consequently, it provides a paradigm by which social psychology can advance as a precise science while preserving (and refining) the basic insights that launched the field over a century ago.

Dynamical social psychology is an ironic discipline. It is ideally suited to capture the dynamics of human experience, yet it is grounded in concepts and methods that provide meaningful integration with the natural sciences. These disciplines have established the importance of intrinsic dynamics, nonlinear phenomena, self-organization, and the significance of complexity: phenomena that resonate with deep intuitions into human experience. Psychologists in recent years have become increasingly cognizant that these features of systems in nature have counterparts in mental, interpersonal, and collective experience. Indeed, it would be odd for a contemporary psychologist to discount the potential for emergence or to ignore the role of computer simulations and time series in illuminating how minds, groups, and societies work.

We hasten to add a word of caution, however. Social reality should not be confused with physical reality. Individuals are not interchangeable in the way that atoms are, and groups are more than self-organized ensembles of simple particles. People have values and beliefs, moments of self-reflection and sudden impulse, universal concerns and idiosyncratic tendencies. Further, one of the basic rules of human functioning is people's capacity and penchant for reflecting on their operating rules and attempting to override them. People live in a symbolically constructed world and thus do not respond in a reflexive way to the objective features of the environment. These unique yet defining features of human experience cannot be chalked up to the recognition that people are dynamic and complex. This makes the task of dynamical social psychology more daunting than discovering the differential equations that govern intrapersonal, interpersonal, and collective dynamics. The dynamical models developed in the natural sciences may be a good first approximation, but the properties that separate us from other systems in the world must ultimately be incorporated into theory and research. It is an ironic testament to the dynamical perspective that a coherent theory of social psychology should be assembled from elements that are both universal within nature and at the same time unique to human experience.

Notes

1. The double threshold for phase transitions characterizing hysteresis has been modeled in terms of cusp catastrophes (see Guastello, 1995, 2002).
2. In phase space, there may exist another set of points that have the opposite effect of attractors. Such points, referred to as *repellors*, represent unstable equilibria of the system, such that the smallest departure from their exact values will result in the system rapidly escaping from the region surrounding the point. Whereas attractors may be described as states which systems "seek" over long periods of time, repellors correspond to states which systems selectively "avoid." Quite often, we can learn a great deal about a system by characterizing its repellor states. This notion has been used, for example, to describe how neural networks avoid particular memories (Vallacher & Nowak, 1999).
3. From the perspective of catastrophe theory, importance functions as a bifurcation factor (Byrne, Mazanov, & Gregson, 2001; Clair, 1998; Mazanov, & Byrne, 2006).
4. This phenomenon underlies the so-called risky shift observed in laboratory studies of group decision making (e.g., Myers & Lamm, 1976).
5. In a related vein, Guastello et al. (2006) have shown that entropy in the electrodermal response of one person predicted entropy of an interaction partner at a 20-sec lag, controlling for autocorrelation.

References

Abelson, R. P. (1979). Social clusters and opinion clusters. In P. W. Holland & S. Leinhardt (Eds.), *Perspectives in social network research* (pp. 239–256). New York: Academic Press.

Abraham R. H., & Shaw, C. D. (1992). *Dynamics, the geometry of behavior* (2nd ed.). Reading, MA: Addison-Wesley.

Allport, G. W. (1968). The historical background of modern social psychology. In G. A. Lindzey & E. Aronson (Eds.), *The Handbook of Social Psychology* (Vol. 1, pp. 1–46). Reading. MA: Addison-Wesley.

Asch, S. E. (1946). Forming impressions of personalities. *Journal of Abnormal and Social Psychology, 41*, 258–290.

Asch, S. E. (1955). Opinions and social pressure. *Scientific American, 19*, 31–35.

Axelrod, R. (1984). *The evolution of cooperation.* New York: Basic Books.

Baron, R. M., Amazeen, P. M., & Beek, P. J. (1994). Local and global dynamics of social relations. In R. R. Vallacher & A. Nowak (Eds.), *Dynamical systems in social psychology* (pp. 111–138). San Diego, CA: Academic Press.

Beek, P. J., & Hopkins, B. (1992). Four requirements for a dynamical systems approach to the development of social coordination. *Human Movement Science, 11*, 425–442.

Bem, D. J. (1967). Self-perception: An alternative interpretation of cognitive dissonance phenomena. *Psychological Review, 74*, 183–200.

Brehm, S. S., & Brehm, J. W. (1981). *Psychological reactance: A theory of freedom and control.* New York: Academic Press.

Brown, K. W., & Moskowitz, D. S. (1998). Dynamic stability of behavior: The rhythms of our interpersonal lives. *Journal of Personality, 66*, 105–134.

Byrne, D. G., Mazanov, J., & Gregson, R. A. M. (2001). A cusp catastrophe analysis of changes to adolescent smoking behaviour in response to smoking prevention programs. *Nonlinear Dynamics, Psychology, and Life Sciences, 5*, 115–137.

Cannon, W. B. (1932). *The wisdom of the body.* New York: Norton.

Caporeal, L. R., & Baron, R. M. (1997). Groups as the mind's natural environment. In J. A. Simpson (Ed.), *Evolutionary social psychology* (pp. 317–344). Hillsdale, NJ: Erlbaum.

Carver, C. S., & Scheier, M. F. (1999). Themes and issues in the self-regulation of behavior. In R. S. Wyer, Jr. (Ed.), *Advances in social cognition* (Vol. 12, pp. 1–105). Mahwah, NJ: Erlbaum.

Carver, C. S., & Scheier, M. F. (2002). Control processes and self-organization as complementary principles underlying behavior. *Personality and Social Psychology Review, 6*, 304–315.

Chartrand, T. L., & Bargh, J. A. (1999). The chameleon effect: The perception-action link and social interaction. *Journal of Personality and Social Psychology, 76*, 893–910.

Clair, S. (1998). A cusp catastrophe model for adolescent alcohol use: An empirical test. *Nonlinear Dynamics, Psychology, and Life Sciences, 2*, 217–241.

Coleman, P. T. (2003). Characteristics of protracted, intractable conflict: Towards the development of a meta-framework – I. First paper in a three-paper series. *Peace and Conflict: Journal of Peace Psychology, 9*, 1–37.

Coleman, P. T., Bui-Wrzosinska, L., Vallacher, R. R., & Nowak, A. (2006). Protracted conflicts as dynamical systems. In A. K. Schneider & C. Honeyman (Eds.), *The negotiator's fieldbook: The desk reference for the experienced negotiator* (pp. 61–74). Chicago: American Bar Association Books.

Coleman, P. T., Vallacher, R. R., Nowak, A., & Bui-Wrzosinska, L. (2007). Intractable conflict as an attractor: A dynamical systems approach to conflict escalation and intractability. *American Behavioral Scientist, 50*, 1454–1475.

Condon, W. S., & Ogston, W. D. (1967). A segmentation of behavior. *Journal of Psychiatric Research, 5,* 221–235.

Cooley, C. H. (1902). *Human nature and the social order.* New York: Scribner.

Deutsch, M. (1973). *The resolution of conflict: Constructive and destructive processes.* New Haven, CT: Yale University Press.

Dittman, A. T., & Llewellyn, L. G. (1969). Body movement and speech rhythm in social conversation. *Journal of Personality and Social Psychology, 11,* 98–106.

Durkheim, E. (1938). *The rules of sociological method.* Chicago: University of Chicago Press.

Eckmann, J. P., & Ruelle, D. (1985). Ergodic theory of chaos and strange attractors. *Review of Modern Physics, 57,* 617–656.

Eiser, J. R. (1994). *Attitudes, chaos, and the connectionist mind.* Oxford: Blackwell.

Feigenbaum, M. J. (1978). Quantitative universality for a class of nonlinear transformations. *Journal of Statistical Physics, 19,* 25–52.

Festinger, L., Schachter, S., & Back, K. (1950). *Social pressures in informal groups.* Stanford, CA: Stanford University Press.

Glass, L., & Mackey, M. C. (1988). *From clocks to chaos: The rhythms of life.* Princeton, NJ: Princeton University Press.

Goldstein, J. (1996). Causality and emergence in chaos and complexity theories. In W. Sulis & A. Combs (Eds.), *Nonlinear dynamics and human behavior* (pp. 161–190). Singapore: World Scientific.

Gottman, J. M. (1979). Detecting cyclicity in social interaction. *Psychological Bulletin, 86,* 338–348.

Gottman, J., Swanson, C., & Swanson, K. (2002). A general systems theory of marriage: Nonlinear difference equation modeling of marital interaction. *Personality and Social Psychology Review, 4,* 326–340.

Gottman, J. M., Murray, J. D., Swanson, C. C., Tyson, R., & Swanson, K. R. (2002). *The mathematics of marriage.* Cambridge: MIT Press.

Guastello, S. J. (1995). *Chaos, catastrophe, and human affairs: Applications of nonlinear dynamics to work, organizations, and social evolution.* Mahwah, NJ: Erlbaum.

Guastello, S. J. (2002). *Managing emergent phenomena: Nonlinear dynamics in work organizations.* Mahwah, NJ: Erlbaum.

Guastello, S. J., Pincus, D., & Gunderson, P. R. (2006). Electrodermal arousal between participants in a conversation: Nonlinear dynamics and linkage effects. *Nonlinear Dynamics, Psychology, and Life Sciences, 10,* 365–399.

Hastie, R., Penrod, S. D., & Pennington, N. (1983). *Inside the jury.* Cambridge, MA: Harvard University Press.

Hock, H. S., Kelso, J. A. S., & Schoner, G. (1993). Bistability and hysteresis in the organization of apparent motion pattern. *Journal of Experimental Psychology: Human Perception and Performance, 19,* 63–80.

Holland, J. H. (1995). *Emergence: From chaos to order.* Reading, MA: Addison-Wesley.

Hopfield, J. J. (1982). Neural networks and physical systems with emergent collective computational properties like those of two-state neurons. *Proceedings of National Academy of Sciences, 79,* 2554–2558.

James, W. (1890). *Principles of psychology.* New York: Holt.

Janis, I. L. (1982). *Groupthink.* Boston: Houghton Mifflin.

Johnson, S. L., & Nowak, A. (2002). Dynamical patterns in bipolar depression. *Personality and Social Psychology Review, 6,* 380–387.

Jones, E. E., & Davis, K. E. (1965). From acts to dispositions: The attribution process in person perception. In L. Berkowitz (Ed.), *Advances in experimental social psychology* (Vol. 2, pp. 220–266). New York: Academic Press.

Kaneko, K. (Ed.). (1993). *Theory and applications of coupled map lattices.* Singapore: World Scientific.

Kaplowitz, S. A., & Fink, E. L. (1992). Dynamics of attitude change. In R. L. Levine & H. E. Fitzgerald (Eds.), *Analysis of dynamic psychological systems* (Vol. 2, pp. 341–369). New York: Plenum Press.

Kelley, H. H. (1967). Attribution in social psychology. *Nebraska Symposium on Motivation, 15,* 419–422.

Kelso, J. A. S. (1995). *Dynamic patterns: The self-organization of brain and behavior.* Cambridge, MA: MIT Press.

Larsen, R. J. (1987). The stability of mood variability: A spectral analytic approach to daily mood assessments. *Journal of Personality and Social Psychology, 52,* 1195–1204.

Larsen, R. J., & Kasimatis, M. (1990). Individual differences in entrainment of mood to the weekly calendar. *Journal of Personality and Social Psychology, 58,* 164–171.

Latané, B. (1981). The psychology of social impact. *American Psychologist, 36,* 343–356.

Latané, B., & Nowak, A. (1994). Attitudes as catastrophes: From dimensions to categories with increasing involvement. In R. R. Vallacher & A. Nowak (Eds.), *Dynamical systems in social psychology* (pp. 219–249). San Diego, CA: Academic Press.

Latané, B., & Nowak, A. (1997). The causes of polarization and clustering in social groups. *Progress in Communication Sciences, 13,* 43–75.

Latané, B., Nowak, A., & Liu, J. (1994). Measuring emergent social phenomena: dynamism, polarization and clustering as order parameters of social systems. *Behavioral Science, 39,* 1–24.

Lepper, M. R., & Greene, D. (Eds.). (1978). *The hidden costs of reward.* Hillsdale, NJ: Erlbaum.

Lewenstein, M., Nowak, A., & Latané, B. (1993). Statistical mechanics of social impact. *Physics Review A, 45,* 703–716.

Lewin, K. (1936). *Principles of topological psychology.* New York: McGraw-Hill.

Markus, H., & Nurius, P. (1986). Possible selves. *American Psychologist, 41,* 954–969.

Marsh, K. L., Richardson, M. J., & Baron, R. M. (2006). Contrasting approaches to perceiving and acting with others. *Ecological Psychology, 18,* 1–37.

Mazanov, J., & Byrne, D. G. (2006). A cusp catastrophe model analysis of changes in adolescent substance use: Assessment of behavioural intention as a bifurcation variable. *Nonlinear Dynamics, Psychology, and Life Sciences, 10,* 445–470.

McGrath, J. E., & Kelley, J. R. (1986). *Time and human interaction: Toward a psychology of time.* New York: Guilford Press.

Mead, G. H. (1934). *Mind, self, and society.* Chicago: University of Chicago Press.

Messick, D. M., & Liebrand, V. B. G. (1995). Individual heuristics and the dynamics of cooperation in large groups. *Psychological Review, 102,* 131–145.

Miller, N. E. (1944). Experimental studies of conflict. In J. M. Hunt (Ed.), *Personality and the behavior disorders* (pp. 431–465). New York: Ronald.

Moscovici, S., Lage, E., & Naffrechoux, M. (1969). Influence of a consistent minority on responses of a majority in a color perception task. *Sociometry, 32*, 365–379.

Myers, D. G., & Lamm, H. (1976). The group polarization phenomenon. *Psychological Bulletin, 83*, 602–627.

Newtson, D. (1994). The perception and coupling of behavior waves. In R. R. Vallacher & A. Nowak (Eds.), *Dynamical systems in social psychology* (pp. 139–167). San Diego, CA: Academic Press.

Nezlek, J. B. (1993). The stability of social interaction. *Journal of Personality and Social Psychology, 65*, 930–941.

Nisbett, R., & Ross, L. (1980). *Human inference: Strategies and shortcomings of social judgment.* Englewood Cliffs, NJ: Prentice Hall.

Nowak, A. (2004). Dynamical minimalism: Why less is more in psychology. *Personality and Social Psychology Review, 8*, 183–192.

Nowak, A., Latané, B., & Lewenstein, M. (1994). Social dilemmas exist in space. In U. Schulz, W. Albers, & U. Mueller (Eds.), *Social dilemmas and cooperation* (pp. 114–131). Heidelberg: Springer-Verlag.

Nowak, A., & Lewenstein, M. (1994). Dynamical systems: A tool for social psychology? In R. R. Vallacher & A. Nowak (Eds.), *Dynamical systems in social psychology* (pp. 17–53). San Diego, CA: Academic Press.

Nowak, A., Lewenstein, M., & Frejlak, P. (1996). Dynamics of public opinion and social change. In R. Hegselman & H. O. Pietgen (Eds.), *Modeling social dynamics: Order, chaos, and complexity* (pp. 54–78). Vienna: Helbin.

Nowak, A., Szamrej, J., & Latané, B. (1990). From private attitude to public opinion: A dynamic theory of social impact. *Psychological Review, 97*, 362–376.

Nowak, A., & Vallacher, R. R. (1998). *Dynamical social psychology.* New York: Guilford Press.

Nowak, A., & Vallacher, R. R. (2001). Societal transition: Toward a dynamical model of social change. In W. Wosinska, R. B. Cialdini, D. W. Barrett, & J. Reykowski (Eds.), *The practice of social influence in multiple cultures* (pp. 151–171). Mahwah, NJ: Erlbaum.

Nowak, A., Vallacher, R. R., & Borkowski, W. (2000). Modeling the temporal coordination of behavior and internal states. In G. Ballot & G. Weisbuch (Eds.), *Applications of simulation to the social sciences* (pp. 67–86). Oxford: Hermes Science.

Nowak, A., Vallacher, R. R., Bui-Wrzosinska, L., & Coleman, P. T. (2007). Attracted to conflict: A dynamical perspective on malignant social relations. In A. Golec & K. Skarzynska (Eds.), *Understanding social change: Political psychology in Poland.* Hauppague, NY: Nova Science.

Nowak, A., Vallacher, R. R., Kus, M., & Urbaniak, J. (2005). The dynamics of societal transition: Modeling nonlinear change in the Polish economic system. *International Journal of Sociology, 35*, 65–88.

Nowak, A., Vallacher, R. R., Tesser, A., & Borkowski, W. (2000). Society of self: The emergence of collective properties in self-structure. *Psychological Review, 107*, 39–61.

Nowak, A., Vallacher, R. R., & Zochowski, M. (2002). The emergence of personality: Personal stability through interpersonal synchronization. In D. Cervone & W. Mischel. (Eds.), *Advances in personality science* (pp. 292–331). New York: Guilford Press.

Nowak, A., Vallacher, R. R., & Zochowski, M. (2005). The emergence of personality: Dynamic foundations of individual variation. *Developmental Review, 25*, 351–385.

Rosenblum, L. D., & Turvey, M. T. (1988). Maintenance tendency in coordinated rhythmic movements: Relative fluctuations and phase. *Neuroscience, 27*, 289–300.

Schachter, S. (1951). Deviation, rejection and communication. *Journal of Abnormal and Social Psychology, 46*, 1990–207.

Schuster, H. G. (1984). *Deterministic chaos.* Vienna: Physik Verlag.

Sherif, M. (1936). *The psychology of social norms.* New York: Harper.

Shinbrot, T. (1994). Synchronization of coupled maps and stable windows. *Physics Review E, 50*, 3230–3233.

Swann, W. B., Jr. (1990). To be adored or to be known? The interplay of self-enhancement and self-verification. In E. T. Higgins & R. M. Sorrentino (Eds.), *Handbook of motivation and cognition: Foundations of social behavior* (Vol. 2, pp. 408–448). New York: Guilford, Press.

Swann, W. B., Hixon, J. G., Stein-Seroussi, A., & Gilbert, D. (1990). The fleeting gleam of praise: Cognitive processes underlying behavioral reactions to self-relevant feedback. *Journal of Personality and Social Psychology, 59*, 17–26.

Tesser, A. (1978). Self-generated attitude change. In L. Berkowitz (Ed.), *Advances in experimental social psychology* (Vol. 11, pp. 85–117). New York: Academic Press.

Tesser, A., Martin, L., & Cornell, D. (1996). On the substitutability of self-protective mechanisms. In P. M. Gollwitzer & J. A. Bargh (Eds.), *The psychology of action* (pp. 48–68). New York: Guilford Press.

Thibaut, J. W., & Kelley, H. H. (1959). *The social psychology of groups.* New York: Wiley.

Tickle-Degnen, L., & Rosenthal, R. (1987). Group rapport and nonverbal behavior. *Review of Personality and Social Psychology, 9*, 113–136.

Turvey, M. T. (1990). Coordination. *American Psychologist, 4*, 938–953.

Turvey, M. T., & Carello, J. (1995). Some dynamical themes in perception and action. In R. F. Port & T. van Gelder (Eds.), *Mind as motion: Explorations in the dynamics of cognition* (pp. 373–402). Cambridge, MA: MIT Press.

Vallacher, R. R., & Nowak, A. (Eds.). (1994a). *Dynamical systems in social psychology.* San Diego, CA: Academic Press.

Vallacher, R. R., & Nowak, A. (1994b). The stream of social judgment. In R. R. Vallacher & A. Nowak (Eds.), *Dynamical systems in social psychology* (pp. 251–277). San Diego, CA: Academic Press.

Vallacher, R. R., & Nowak, A. (1997). The emergence of dynamical social psychology. *Psychological Inquiry, 8*, 73–99.

Vallacher, R. R., & Nowak, A. (1999). The dynamics of self-regulation. In R. S. Wyer, Jr. (Ed.), *Advances in self-regulation* (Vol. 12, pp. 241–259). Mahwah, NJ: Erlbaum.

Vallacher, R. R., & Nowak, A. (2007). Dynamical social psychology: Finding order in the flow of human experience. In A. W. Kruglanski & E. T. Higgins (Eds.), *Social psychology: Handbook of basic principles* (2nd ed, pp. 734–758). New York: Guilford Press.

Vallacher, R. R., Nowak, A., Froehlich, M., & Rockloff, M. (2002). The dynamics of self-evaluation. *Personality and Social Psychology Review, 6*, 370–379.

Vallacher, R. R., Nowak, A., & Kaufman, J. (1994). Intrinsic dynamics of social judgment. *Journal of Personality and Social Psychology, 66*, 20–34.

Vallacher, R. R., Nowak, A., & Miller, M. E. (2003). Social influence and group dynamics. In I. Weiner (Series Ed.) & T. Millon & M. J. Lerner (Vol. Eds.), *Handbook of psychology: Vol. 5. Personality and social psychology* (pp. 383–417). New York: Wiley.

Vallacher, R. R., Nowak, A., & Zochowski, M. (2007). Dynamics of social coordination: The synchronization of internal states in close relationships. In P. Hauf & F. Forsterling (Eds.), *Making minds: The shaping of human minds through social context* (pp. 31–46). Amsterdam: John Benjamins.

Vallacher, R. R., Read, S. J., & Nowak, A. (Eds.). (2002). The dynamical perspective in social psychology. *Personality and Social Psychology Review, 6,* 264–388.

Vallacher, R. R., & Wegner, D. M. (1987). What do people think they're doing? Action identification and human behavior. *Psychological Review, 94,* 1–15.

Vallacher, R. R., & Wegner, D. M. (1989). Levels of personal agency: Individual variation in action identification. *Journal of Personality and Social Psychology, 57,* 660–671.

Wegner, D. M., & Vallacher, R. R. (1977). *Implicit psychology: An introduction to social cognition.* New York: Oxford University Press.

Wegner, D. M., Vallacher, R. R., Kiersted, G., & Dizadji, D. (1986). Action identification in the emergence of social behavior. *Social Cognition, 4,* 18–38.

Zochowski, M., & Liebovitch, L. S. (1997). Synchronization of the trajectory as a way to control the dynamics of the coupled system. *Physical Review E, 56,* 3701.

Zochowski, M., & Liebovitch, L. S. (1999). Self-organizing dynamics of coupled map systems. *Physical Review E, 59,* 2830.

13 Group Dynamics: Adaptation, Coordination, and the Emergence of Leaders

STEPHEN J. GUASTELLO

Introduction

This chapter describes three interrelated topics in group or team behavior that have been developed substantially from the nonlinear dynamical systems (NDS) perspective: adaptive behavior, coordination, and the emergence of leadership. Explanations for all three phenomena would have a great deal of practical relevance. Ironically, there is a growing awareness of the need for NDS concepts within the conventional group dynamics literature that is dominated by linear models and linear relationships. In their comprehensive review of factors related to team performance, Kozlowski and Ilgen (2006) remarked that "teams are complex dynamic systems that exist in a context, develop as members interact over time, and evolve and adapt as situational demands unfold" (p. 78). Others have also made reference to emergent phenomena in groups (Burke, Stagl, Salas, Pierce, & Kendall, 2006; Marks, Mathieu, & Zaccaro, 2001; Tasa, Taggar, & Seijts, 2007). These authors have not mentioned any of the empirical work or theoretical principles of NDS, however, although the connection should be glaring and the relevant NDS contributions were already on record at the time of their writing, if not earlier. Thus the goal of this chapter is to recount the progress within the NDS paradigm in each of these areas.

The current use of the term *emergence* within the linear community is consistent with Sawyer's (2005) exposition, however: Interactions among individual group members give rise to a supervenient group-level outcome that is not explicable as simply the result of individual actions. The resulting group-level outcome has a downward influence on the actions of group members. The formation of the group-level outcome is a self-organizing process and is the downward influence.

Adaptive Behavior

Conventional Approaches

The interest in the adaptive behavior of groups is focused on groups' ability to respond effectively to rapidly changing environments. The words *group* and *team* are used interchangeably in this chapter inasmuch as the groups that were studied did function as teams, at least when they were functioning effectively. Burke et al. (2006) developed 21 propositions for research on team adaptation, each of which was accompanied by a substantial amount of research in the conventional linear mode. The 21 propositions can be aggregated into seven principles – individual differences, cognition–action stages, multiple feedback loops, self-management, psychological safety, communication and leadership, team orientation – which are explained subsequently. They are followed by the concept of the complex adaptive system (CAS), which is strongly tied to NDS principles and reasoning.

Individual situation awareness, general intelligence, creativity, and task knowledge all contribute to group-level situation awareness and eventual task effectiveness (Burke et al., 2006). This is the bottom-up phase of self-organization and emergence.

There is a sequence of group cognitive and action stages that begins with situation awareness and continues with the formation of mental models, plans, and actions. Each subsequent stage will have a better result in proportion to the quality of the previous stage (Burke et al., 2006). Two recent studies seem to indicate that the situation is more complex, however. In one (Omodei, McLennan, & Wearing, 2005), firefighters worked with a computer simulation of an emergency under conditions in which they were led to believe that the situation status information was reliable versus unreliable. Those who worked in the unreliable condition performed better overall than those who worked with reliable information. The explanation is that the decision makers with the unreliable or incomplete data spend less time analyzing it and more time formulating decisions and strategies. In another experiment that involved the use of a simulator of an automated airplane cockpit (Bailey, Scerbo, Freeman, Mikulka, & Scott, 2006), those who knew they had an unreliable system were able to detect 91% of system errors correctly, compared with 80% with a reliable system. Apparently the belief that the automated system was unreliable engendered greater attentiveness. In both cases, a deficiency in one aspect of the cognitive process, which is shared by humans and machines, was compensated for by another aspect of the process.

Group-level action, which involves interacting with the environment, generates information that has the potential to alter situation awareness, mental models, plans, and subsequent actions (Burke et al., 2006). This is essentially the double-loop learning model that Argyris and Schon (1978) introduced and that was interpreted as an example of a self-organized system (Guastello, 2002). This system of feedback loops could occur whether all the team members worked on all tasks or were associated with specific parts of the process.

The foregoing phenomena are enhanced to the extent that the group can work relatively free from the influence of any upper management (Burke et al., 2006). This principle makes use of the frequently reported finding that autonomous work groups outperform those that have a traditional top-down supervisory structure within. The idea of an autonomous work group originated with sociotechnical systems theory. The central premise of sociotechnical systems theory is that work should be rationalized from the point of view of the people who are doing the work, rather than from the viewpoint of the work itself. The best way to divide work among people is to put together a group of people who have all the necessary capabilities, present them with the whole job, and let the forces of self-organization take over (DeGreene, 1991). The optimal arrangement of people and tasks will ensue. The self-organizing properties of the situation will give the group the flexibility that it needs to adapt to a changing environment.

The foregoing phenomena are enhanced in proportion to the level of psychological safety in the work group (Burke et al., 2006). Psychological safety is a climate of trust and mutual respect that fosters interpersonal risk taking. It also characterizes an important aspect of the interactions among agents, which in turn give rise to the supervenient group-level effect (Sawyer, 2005). Different types of interactions among agents are explored throughout this chapter.

The use of mutual performance monitoring, backup plans, leadership input, and communication quality all lead to coordinated execution of the adaptive response. This principle sounds good, but NDS would give it a big "maybe," because there are some important exceptions that are not adequately represented in the conventional literature. The NDS perspective on communication, leadership, and coordination is addressed in the later section of this chapter.

The foregoing phenomena are enhanced if the group has a "team orientation," which Burke et al. (2006) characterize as the members' willingness to forego personal interests in service of the collective. This particular point is revisited later in conjunction with social loafing, group self-efficacy, and Stag Hunt coordination.

Groups, Organizations, and Complex Adaptive Systems

In the long history of organizational psychology, knowledge about specific phenomena was often guided by a mental model of what an organization actually is. The mental model of the organization has evolved during the last century from the bureaucracy, to the humanized versus dehumanized work environments, the organization as a living system, and the organization as a CAS. The CAS concept can be applied to any living system, although Dooley (1997) first articulated it as the new dominant mental model of organizations; see Anderson (1999), Guastello (2002), and Dooley (2004) for later developments. The perspective incorporates NDS concepts to study patterns of behavior. In doing so, it frames new questions regarding how the system recognizes signals and events in the environment, harnesses its capabilities to make effective responses, changes its internal configurations as new adaptive responses require, and interacts with the external environment.

Although Dooley (1997) framed the CAS concept in terms of organizations, there is no loss of meaning by substituting the word "group" for "organization," especially when one considers that small work organizations and single work teams are often one and the same. The central themes of the CAS are schema and agents, agent interaction, problem solving and conflict, supervenience of internal order, and agent fitness. I discuss each of these themes further in what follows.

Schema and Agents

Group members scan the environment and develop schemata (Dooley, 1997). A *schema* (*pl.* schemata) is essentially the same as a mental model, although its history in psychology is much older and places some additional emphasis on the actions that could be taken in response to the mental models of the situation (Newell, 1991). Schemata define rules of interaction with other agents that exist within the team or outside the team's boundaries (Dooley, 1997). A group's schemata are often built from existing building blocks, which are inevitably brought into the group when members arrive. Here we see the role of particular individual differences, for example, job knowledge, that Burke et al. (2006) introduced.

A group's schemata can be indeterminate, observer dependent, and contradictory (Dooley, 1997). The integration of individual perspectives on a work situation is not always smooth. Although the individual schemata self-organize into one or more supervenient mental models, there can be individual differences remaining that could provide enough entropy for further modification of the schemata.

Schemata change through mutation, recombination, and acquisition of new ideas from outside sources. Change occurs in response to both changing environments and changing internal conditions. Indeed there are numerous sources of entropy (described in Chapter 1) that could arise from changes in client populations, the workforce, demands for products and new markets, and governmental regulations (K. D. Bailey, 1994; Bigelow, 1982; Guastello, 2002). The processes of mutation and recombination suggest an analogy between the dynamics of genetics or genetic algorithms and creative problem solving.

When schemata change, requisite variety, robustness, and reliability are ideally enhanced (Dooley, 1997). *Reliability* denotes error-free action in the usual sense. *Robustness* denotes the ability of the system to withstand unpredictable shock from the environment. *Requisite variety* refers to Ashby's (1956) Law: For the effective control of a system, the complexity of the controller must be at least equal to the complexity of the system that is being controlled. *Complexity* in this context refers to the number of system states, which are typically conceptualized as discrete outcomes.

Agent Interaction

As team members interact, there is a flow of information and resources (Dooley, 1997). In the early stages of team life, the interaction patterns are often volatile, but they eventually self-organize to enhance collective efficiency, which is in part a reduction in the entropy and uncertainty in how the flows will occur. The performance of the system can be enhanced by manipulating the levels of decentralization, diversification, and specialization of members' roles. The use of symbolic tags (e.g., job titles) facilitates the formation of subunits or specific functions.

Problem-Solving and Conflict

Team members interact in the course of solving work-related problems and making and executing plans, as described by Burke at al. (2006). The associated feedback loops sometimes result in the need to change schemata. The potential intellectual conflict could involve differences between a current schema and a view of external reality, different views of external reality, different views of current schema, or different alternative schemata. The problem-solving strategies could be dialectic or teleological. The *dialectic* strategy compares contradictory ideas and usually seeks to resolve their conflict. The *teleological* mode relates to the design or purpose and how a system's purpose would unfold or evolve over time (Dooley, 1997; Van de Ven & Poole, 1995). Teleological discussions require the group to recognize that its current situation is not a static one but a slice of a drama that has been changing over time, perhaps not smoothly so. A collective understanding – mental model – of things evolves over time and helps matters greatly, although some individuals are substantially more skilled in this regard than others (Guastello, 2002).

Irreversibility and Emergent Order

If it is indeed a complex *adaptive* system, it remains poised on the edge of chaos ready to reorganize itself in response to new demands. The sequence of states through which it reorganizes are relatively unpredictable, although at some point it should be possible to envision possible future scenarios and states; again some people are better at it than others. A team's particular sequence of stages is often subject to initial conditions that contribute to the global unpredictability of the system. The states of team organization are irreversible once they have taken hold and stabilized (Dooley, 1997). Although teams can redeploy old schemata, the effect is not the same because of the history that accumulated, events that occurred, and time that has elapsed.

The dynamics of agent interaction and problem solving give rise to the development of schemata. Once adopted, they are expected to have a supervenient effect on the further actions of the agents. The presence of the supervienient effect presents another reason why group events are irreversible: A schema is deployed or changed against a context that could contain little history or precedent, as in a group's early stages of life, but the same schema might have a different impact within a context in which a supervenient effect was occurring.

Agent Fitness

A final feature of the CAS involves agent fitness. The notion of fitness arises from computational evolution or genetic algorithm studies. A team might generate a lot of work-related ideas or schemata for its internal operation, but some ideas and schemata will be better than others according to some criteria. *Fitness* is the rating of how good they are. Similarly, agents have a level of fitness that projects their longevity with the group. It is not the same as a performance rating, but something closer to a person–job fit. More precisely it is the subjective response on the part of the agents to their levels of discrepancy between personal schemata and group schemata. Many global issues could be involved, and the various discrepancies culminate in an agent's level of satisfaction with the team situation.

According to Dooley (1997), the probability of a change in a team's schema is a nonlinear function of satisfaction. Here we have the basis for a new episode of self-organization that is generated by the levels of fitness, discrepancy, or satisfaction. Importantly, the top-down driving effect is not immutable once it is installed unless there is a rigid one-way flow of information in the group. In the more likely scenarios, we have the potential for sufficient entropy and upward information flow to destabilize or change the top-down driver in some fashion. Rosser et al. (1994) characterized the bottom-up destabilization phenomenon as a "revolt of the slaved variables," and it can be very apparent in hierarchically organized work groups (Guastello & Johnson, 1999).

Coordination: Intersection Type

Coordination occurs in a work team when two or more people do the same task, or complementary tasks, at the same time. Coordination is often a vital element for a group's work objectives, especially when the rewards for task completion are assigned to the group as a whole. Brannick, Roach, and Salas (1993) operationalized coordination as the time delay between a group member's action and another member's contingent action. Daily (1980) measured it as the quality of communication between members of a group. Guastello and Guastello (1998), who worked from the NDS perspective, operationalized coordination as a group task (card game) wherein members were required to take correct actions in the correct sequence. The conventional explanations for how coordination occurs and sustains in a work team rests primarily on the principle of shared mental models.

NDS perspectives on coordination involve three related principles. One is the fundamental role of *self-organization*. The second is the *game theory perspective*, which on the one hand gives rise to evolutionarily stable states (ESS) that in turn have a supervenient impact on team behavior, and on the other hand specifies local rules of interaction that distinguish a few different types of coordination phenomena. The third aspect of NDS appears in the time series for *coordination acquisition* wherein we can observe chaos in the early or incomplete sequences, and self-organization as group learning consolidates. Both explicit and implicit learning is involved.

The importance of the learning component should not be underestimated in light of the expressed concerns in the team performance literature. Kozlowski and Ilgen (2006) concluded, however, that a viable theory and research base for collective learning was not yet available. NDS has a lot to contribute here.

Shared Mental Models

Studies indicate that the coordination among work group members is greatly enhanced if the members have a shared mental model of their tasks, proce-dures, and group processes (Banks & Millward, 2000; Cannon-Bowers, Salas, & Converse, 1990, 1993; Druskat & Pescosolido, 2002; Kozlowski & Ilgen, 2006; Stout, Cannon-Bowers, Salas, & Milanovich, 1999). Shared mental models may be induced by cross-training the group members in each others' roles, or by discussions and presentations of groups' task models (Marks, Sabella, Burke, & Zaccaro, 2002; Matthieu, Heffner, Goodwin, Salas, & Cannon-Bowers, 2000). They also require consistent organizational support if the group is not a free-standing group (Druskat & Pescosolido, 2002).

Another manifestation of the principle behind shared mental models can be found in some older studies on experimental cultures. Those studies showed that decision norms can persist in a group even as group members are system-atically replaced. Norms persist even after all the original group members have been replaced (Insko et al., 1980; Jacobs & Campbell, 1961; Weick & Gilfillan, 1971). Conformity pressure supports the persistence of norms. In real societies, knowledge of events that occurred before birth dissipates over time but does so gradually to above-chance levels (Rubin, 1998).

Nonlinear Dynamics of Coordination

One productive area of psychology in which the notion of self-organization has been productively applied is in the understanding of the coordination among muscle groups and limbs in any moving organism (Jirsa & Kelso, 2004; Turvey,

1990). Turvey (1990) made an important observation: It takes far fewer degrees of freedom to account for all the combinations of coordinated limb movements by assuming a system of internal information flows, such as a self-organizing process would indicate, compared with a system that relies on an external puppeteer pulling all the strings. In other words, the system works efficiently and excellently with no leader or deus ex machina involved. It is also evident that none of the information flows involved here are verbal in nature. Cognitive processes can be involved in some types of movement, however; indeed the latest round of research is addressing those phenomena (Jirsa & Kelso, 2004).

Animal models for coordination also support the premise that leadership is not required, and at the same time, obviate any requirement for verbal communication. A flock of birds maintains its structure and its travel itinerary through use of only three rules: (a) Avoid colliding with flockmates, (b) maintain the general heading of the flock, and (c) stay close to one's flockmates (Reynolds, 1987). In complex physical environments, there is one additional rule: Do not crash into buildings, trees, or other fixed objects. The flock has no leader; any apparent leadership role among birds is the result of rotating turns in positions within the flock. Similar dynamics have been observed with schools of fish (Semovski, 2001) and continue to be studied in the context of collective intelligence (Sulis, 1999).

None of the foregoing should be interpreted as meaning that leaders cannot emerge from coordination-intensive groups; that point is addressed later on in this chapter. Nor should the foregoing remarks be interpreted as meaning that verbal communication plays no role in team coordination. Rather, the NDS experiments needed to be defined in a manner that isolated the role of verbalization.

Game Theory
The central premise behind game theory (von Neumann & Morgenstern, 1953; Zagare, 1984) is that when interacting agents are faced with options, they will choose options that maximize their own outcomes. The outcomes associated with the options are expressed as *utilities,* and the utilities of any option depend on the options that are selected by the other agents. Typical experiments do not allow participants to talk while gaming to prevent the discussion from altering the perceived game utilities (Friedman, 1994). Furthermore, no leaders are appointed the typical experiments.

The NDS connection to game theory began with Nash equilibria and *dominant strategies* that agents acquire after many repeated interactions. If games are played by a population of agents (e.g., in a computer simulation) iteratively in a "tournament," a strategy usually dominates in the form of an ESS. The ESS will be close to the Nash equilibrium for a simple one-exchange game (Maynard-Smith, 1982). If we add some complexity to the possible game options and the utilities and give up the assumption of strict competitiveness, however, the ESS cannot be guessed from any knowledge of the Nash equilibria. Rather the ESS becomes highly dependent on initial conditions as they pertain to options and utilities (Samuelson, 1997). Thus ESS experiments are needed to identify real behavior patterns from games that emulate real-world problems and decisions.

Coordination, meanwhile, can be observed within the context of game theory when agents simultaneously select a cooperative response, as opposed to a competitive or indifferent response (Camerer & Knez, 1997; Friedman, 1994). Indeed it is the case that some game structures are not strictly competitive. For example, Prisoner's Dilemma attracted a great deal of attention in psychology and economics because of its counterpoint between cooperative and competitive response options (e.g., Axelrod, 1984; Friedman, 1994; Rapoport, 1967). It is thus a *mixed motivation* game. Two types of *strictly cooperative* games that are considered in this chapter are the Intersection and Stag Hunt.

In an Intersection game, the decision to participate in a group activity is not assumed. The objective is to select an action that facilitates the individual's utilities, which can only occur if the group's utilities are facilitated (Crawford, 1991; Guastello, Bock, Caldwell, & Bond, 2005; Guastello & Bond, 2007a; Guastello & Guastello, 1998). A critical feature of the Intersection game is that the agents must figure out what the correct actions are and in what order they must be taken to facilitate the group's outcome. The game got its name from the four-way stop intersection on roadways. Each motorist approaching the intersection must figure out which rule is in play for moving through the intersection, which is not always immediately predictable from having memorized the state driver's manual, when one's turn occurs, and to take one's turn instead of sitting there waiting. Intersection is thought to characterize many forms of work performance in industry, military operations, hospital emergency rooms, and the performing arts.

Learning Processes
There is literature on organizational learning that dates back to Cyert and March's (1963) behavioral theory of the firm: Organizations execute strategies to maximize profits in much the same manner as the rat runs to where the cheese is located. A more contemporary view characterizes an organization's ability to learn as part of what it does to adapt to situations in the sense of what a CAS does, and often through use of teleological discussion (Seo, Putnam, & Bartunek, 2004). Learning in another sense is equivalent in meaning to evolutionary organizational change rather than revolutionary change. In short there is no systematic agreement about what organizational learning is or how it occurs (Lewin, Weigelt, & Emery, 2004). Thus Kozlowski and Ilgen (2006) called for a theory of group learning that explains how collective learning effects emerge from individual efforts. Here NDS has a great deal to contribute with regard to the dynamics of learning at the individual and group level and with the likelihood of a scaling relationship of some sort between levels.

Distributed
Intelligence

Nonlinear
Dynamical p 402
Systems

Group Dynamics   411

The earliest connections among NDS, learning, and motivation took the form of catastrophe models (Baker & Frey, 1980; Frey & Sears, 1978; Guastello, 1981, 1995), which characterized learning as a discontinuous process with an underlying bifurcation structure. Indeed Newell (1991) reported that although the power law function for simple learning or motor skill acquisition processes was firmly lodged in the psychological literature, it did not account for the fact that discontinuities are inherent in more complex learning phenomena. Discontinuities occur in automaticity processes wherein the elementary perception-cognition-action elements consolidate into larger, smoother units of behavior (Guastello, 2006).

A particular learning curve can be represented as a slice of the catastrophe response surface; the full response surface describes the full range of possible learning trajectories, including the possibility that some agents never learn. Learning curves differ with respect to the sharpness of their ascent over time; the underlying catastrophe model suggests that the bifurcation manifold accounts for the sharpness of inflection. It would appear, therefore, that the conventional two-dimensional representations of the learning curve obfuscate the reasons for the differences in the shapes of the learning curves by not projecting them into three dimensions.

Another aspect to NDS and learning pertains to the variability in the learning curve, which is usually higher during the acquisition period. Hoyert (1992) examined the behavioral response patterns of pigeons in a fixed-interval schedule of reinforcement. Although the general shape of the scallops was the same as those reported during the previous 50 years, there were epochs of variability and internal patterning that could not be explained by the schedule of reinforcement alone. A phase diagram (plot of ΔX against X for a time series) of the pigeons' responses closely resembled the phase diagrams of chaotic patterns, thus indicating that the microlevel variability was deterministic rather than random variation or measurement error. Analyses using structural equations showed that the variability between intervals could be better accounted for by nonlinear models than by linear models.

The (possible) presence of chaos suggests an eventual transition to a self-organized structure. The learning curve has been characterized as a phase transition whereby a self-organized structure is thought to occur when the asymptote is attained (Vetter, Stadler, & Haynes, 1997). Furthermore, the neuron patterns in the (human) brain respond in a chaotic pattern in the presence of novel stimuli, but the neural patterning becomes more regular once learning has occurred (Freeman, 2000; Grigsby & Stevens, 2000). The entrained patterns qualify as basins of attraction (Bar-Yam, 1997). These and other pieces of evidence (Guastello, 1995; Li, Krauth, & Huston, 2006; Pascual & Rodriguez, 2006; Yuan & McKelvey, 2004) establish learning as an NDS phenomenon. It would follow that coordination acquisition would be no different; it would follow a learning curve globally, with an epoch of chaos in the early stages and self-organization culminating in a fixed point later on – if learning is successful. Otherwise, the self-organization and asymptotic stability would not occur.

Implicit Learning

The foregoing examples of learning and NDS processes were mostly confined to the explicit more of learning. Groups acquire coordination as an implicit learning process, however, which is an unconscious learning effect that takes place when an agent is trying to explicitly learn something else (Frensch & Runger, 2003; Seger, 1994). In coordination learning (Intersection type), the explicit learning goal is to figure out the correct sequence of actions that lead to successful task completion. The implicit learning objective is to learn how to respond correctly to actions and nonverbal signals given by other players. Guastello and Guastello (1998) demonstrated experimentally that coordination within a group of four agents that was acquired while learning one task transferred to subsequent tasks performed by the same group when the coordination rule is different.

Although implicit learning is usually regarded as an individual process, the study of group coordination indicated that implicit learning could also take the form of a group process. This group or organizational form of learning has become known as *situated learning* in some contexts (Dobson et al., 2001; Yuan & McKelvey, 2004).

Intersection Experiments

The Intersection game was operationalized as a card game in a series of experiments (Guastello, Bock, et al., 2005; Guastello & Bond, 2007a; Guastello & Guastello, 1998). Participants were organized into groups of four. They were dealt five cards from a limited standard deck. Their objective was to play the cards in the correct order to acquire points (utilities), although they had to figure out what the correct sequence was. Four points were awarded to the group if a series of four cards was played correctly, one point if three out of four cards were played correctly, and no points otherwise. One round of the game consisted of eight hands of five cards. After one round, the participants were told that the rule changed, and they had to figure out the new rules. There were four rounds altogether, including rounds that switched to a rule that was equal in difficulty to the first rule and a rule that was more difficult.

The following mathematical model for performance over time was established empirically from the foregoing experiments (Guastello, Bock, et al., 2005; Guastello & Bond, 2007a; Guastello & Guastello, 1998):

$$z_2 = q_1 z_1 \exp(\theta_2 z_2) + \theta_3, \quad \theta_2 < 0 \tag{13.1}$$

$$z_2 = \exp(\theta_2 z_2) + \theta_3, \quad \theta_2 > 0, \tag{13.2}$$

where z_i are a time series of performance measures and θ_i are nonlinear regression weights. Equation 13.1 is the primary function that was extracted from the data. The term $\theta_1 z_i$ denotes a bifurcation effect whereby some groups attain coordination more decisively than others. The term θ_2 is comparable to a Lyapunov exponent and is usually negative, denoting asymptotic stability at a fixed point.

Equation 13.2 is a secondary function that was extracted from the residuals of Eq. 13.1 and appears in conditions in which coordination is particularly challenging; θ_2 is positive denoting chaos. For further elaboration of this nonlinear statistical modeling system, see Guastello (1995, 2002, 2005a). A substantial amount of variance was explained by knowing the dynamical process that was occurring (average $R^2 = .41$) compared with the conventional linear explanation (average $R^2 = .14$).

There was transfer of coordination learning from the first round of the game to the second with the rule of equal difficulty, as evidenced by an overall higher mean of points accumulated by the groups. This point was true whether or not the experimental groups were allowed to talk (Guastello, Bock et al., 2005; Guastello & Bond, 2007a; Guastello & Guastello, 1998). The transfer substantiated the implicit nature of coordination learning.

In the experimental conditions in which verbalization was varied, verbalizing groups performed better overall than groups that were not allowed to talk, and their learning curves indicated sharper coordination acquisition. In one of the experiments (Guastello, Bock, et al., 2005), one, two, or three of the participants were replaced at the beginning with the third round of the game with a participant who had no prior experience with the game up to that point. The transfer of learning effect persisted when one or two participants were changed; changing three out of four was tantamount to starting the coordination acquisition process over again. Interestingly, the ability to talk did not help or hinder the assimilation of new personnel; new personnel apparently had to learn something critical in the nonverbal channel for coordination to occur at all.

Gorman et al. (2006) found, on the other hand, that group performance can be enhanced by exchanging personnel with members of other groups who were already trained and coordinated on the same type of task. The situation surrounding those personnel changes appears to be different and might possibly be explained by an elevated sense of interpersonal awareness among the members of the reformed group. More research is required to know for sure why the differences in results occurred.

Even though leadership is not required to produce coordination, leaders can still emerge from coordination-intensive groups. In the third study from the NDS series (Guastello & Bond, 2007a), participants completed a questionnaire at the end of the study in which they were asked which of the members in their group acted most like the leader and who acted second-most like the leader. There were also asked a number of other leadership-related questions about who contributed to the group in what way. The response options allowed to indicate that no one behaved like the leader or made a particular type of contribution.

There were 13 groups that were allowed to talk during the coordination game and 13 groups that were not allowed to talk. Clear leaders emerged from both types of groups, and importantly, the verbalizing groups did not produce more or stronger leaders than the nonverbal groups. The talking and nontalking groups did vary on other points covered in the questionnaire, however.

Despite the alleged advantages of shared mental models, the NDS studies showed that coordination occurred without discussion, cross-training, verbal communication, or leaders. Furthermore, group members had to arrive at the shared mental model through their own individual observations and interactions with other group members. Similarly, verbalization had its advantages, but it did not have a critical effect on the assimilation of new personnel, and it was not a requirement for coordination to occur. Of course, businesses are not likely to prevent their personnel from talking about the work, but there are times when communication is impossible because of combinations of technological faults and geographic dispersal.

Coordination: Stag Hunt Type

Stag Hunt is a game in which the agents choose between working with the group or working on their own. In other words, an agent can join a group of hunters to hunt stag or go off alone to hunt rabbits. The likelihood of a hunter joining the group depends on a comparison of the group's efficacy versus personal efficacy. The expected performance of the group depends on the combined skill and efforts of all the hunters as evaluated by the particular agent. If the agent is savvy enough to determine the extent to which the whole is greater than the sum of its parts, so much the better for that agent.

The agents' levels of individual involvement are observable in the course of the tournament. One can measure either the level of participation or the performance of the group over time as evolutionary outcomes. The group outcomes can tolerate some individual differences in contributions, but if too few agents take the group action once they join, the overall performance of the group suffers. Two other strands of group research from the conventional medium, social loafing and self-efficacy theory are relevant here.

Social Loafing

Social loafing is a phenomenon in which a group of people is supposedly working together for a common goal and sharing a common reward, but some people work a lot harder than others (Geen, 1991; Latané, Williams, & Harkins, 1979). The potential for a disparity in input seems to be greater in larger groups. Possible explanations for the phenomenon include output equity, the free-rider effect, evaluation apprehension, and lack of a performance standard.

Output equity is the result of an agent's attempt to work only as hard as other people; if an agent expects the other agents to loaf, that agent will also loaf. The free-rider effect is similar, but it is an expectation of a disparity in contributions. Here the agent expects one person in the group to solve the problem, although most will not do so, so it is beneficial to be part of the group of which the star performer is a member.

The evaluation apprehension explanation also has merit according to various experimental reports (Geen, 1991). In this scenario, the individual does not expect to perform well and thus sees a benefit in becoming anonymous in a larger group. The same effect could work in the opposite direction as the group becomes larger: As the size of the group or organization increases, the agent's contribution becomes a smaller percentage of the total, leading to the re-action, "Why bother? It doesn't make any difference anyway" (Comer, 1995). Given the ambiguities regarding how the other agents are expected to perform, agents might loaf because they really do not know what expectations for their performance would apply (Geen, 1991).

Social loafing can be reduced in work groups by organizing a larger group into smaller units and then identifying some "coordinator roles" to connect the subunits. This solution helps make each person's contribution more visible and proportionately larger (Comer, 1995). The solution also involves making a hierarchical structure within the work group. Yet other work shows that a lot of work time can be lost waiting for information to travel up and down a hierarchy (Guastello, 2002). In those cases, what might appear to be social loafing is not at all related to people not wanting to work; it is the result of people waiting for the work to flow in their direction.

Self-Efficacy

The concept of self-efficacy plays a central role in social cognitive theory (Bandura, 2001) and in the performance of challenging tasks. It is partially the result of past performance (and personal evaluations thereof), motivation, and belief in one's ability to control one's own behavior and to control aspects of the situation. It is sometimes the sole determinant of which competitor will win a wrestling match, or of similar situations (Bandura & Locke, 2003). Not only does self-efficacy contribute to constructive reactions that people have to the discrepancies between current situations and their self-set goals, it contributes to proactive responses as well.

Teams also need self-efficacy. A meta-analysis of 42 effect sizes for the relationship between team self-efficacy and team performance produced a corrected mean $r^2 = .17$ (Gully, Incalcaterra, Joshi, & Beaubein, 2002). Tasa et al. (2007) illustrated that group self-efficacy might self-organize from the individual agents' experiences by comparing individuals' perceptions of group self-efficacy with feedback the group received about their collective work at several points in time. There was no explicit use of nonlinear theory involved in that experiment, however, and the principles of self-organization and emergence would only be apparent to people who were accustomed to nonlinear thinking already.

Evolutionary Stag Hunt Games

Stag Hunt games are thought to comprise a significant number of team experiences during an emergency response situation. There are some differences between the economic game of Stag Hunt, a real stag hunt, a situation involving an analogous game against a natural disaster, and an analogous game against a disaster that involved a sentient attacker. In a real stag hunt or game against a sentient attacker, there are learning dynamics by both the humans and the prey or protagonist; natural disasters and hypothetical stag are indifferent to the humans' responses. *Subgame perfect* means that, at each choice point within the game, the options are always the same, and utilities associated with the players' choices are always the same. In real-world Stag Hunt situations, the choices facing the group members are always to participate in the group decision to define a strategic option versus not participating. Other than that dichotomy, however, the possible strategic options are plentiful, and the utilities associated with them vary each time the group faces a decision.

Guastello and Bond (2004) devised an experimental task that centered on a board game ("The Creature That Ate Sheboygan") in which an emergency response (ER) team worked cooperatively together, but competitively against an adversary. Four ER Teams of four participants (undergraduates) plus one Attacker could move game tokens for police, fire, helicopter, and military ground troops to reduce the Attacker's defenses and eventually finish him off. There were 17 turns within a game, three games per experimental session, and two sessions. Two of the groups worked under conditions of a communication outage during one of the sessions, meaning that they could no longer talk to each other while working.

The performance of both the ER Team and the Attacker varied over time in several important ways. First, the ER Teams and the Attackers improved their performances over time. Thus evolutionarily stable states are partially the result of learning effects and thus not linked to the outcomes of single games or exchanges in a simple fashion. Furthermore, the Attackers learned how to perform better over two consecutive sessions of three games, which presented an added challenge to the ER Teams; this is a feature that distinguishes emergencies that involve sentient attackers from those involving natural disasters. ER Teams showed both improvements and drops in performance as they played more games.

Second, the communication outages did not hinder the ER Teams' performance, but Attackers did better under those conditions. This finding suggests that although team members might be sufficiently well coordinated with each other to overcome communication impairments, the communication impairments could hinder counteradaptive responses to the adaptive responses of the Attacker.

Videotapes of the games indicated that the number of team members who participated in the decision associated with each move depended on the number of points accumulated by the Attacker on the previous turn. This analysis was performed only on groups without the communication outages because of the difficulty in interpreting the tapes. ER Team members tended to disengage when the going got tough. This result supported the basic Stag Hunt effect that the efficacy of the group affects the utilities of individual participation and, furthermore, that group self-efficacy can fluctuate over time.

The nonlinear model for participation was:

$$h_2 = \exp(\theta_1 m_1) + \theta_2, \tag{13.3}$$

where h_2 was the number of team members participating on a given turn, m_1 was the Attacker's cumulative score on the previous turn, which was itself nonlinear over time, and θ_i were nonlinear regression weights.

Dynamics and Group Size

A second, larger-scale experiment (Guastello & Doyle, 2007) considered whether there existed an optimal group size as evidenced in the performance curves for the ER Teams. For creative problem-solving groups, a group that is large enough would generate a critical mass of useful strategic ideas (Dennis & Valacich, 1993; Guastello, 2002). From a coordination standpoint, however, a group that is too large would either take too long to make a decision or produce a situation in which some members work a lot harder than others would (Comer, 1995).

Groups of 4, 6, 9, and 12 undergraduates (four groups each) played the same board game against an adversary who worked alone. There was a significant main effect for team performance as a function of group size, whereby ER Teams performed best and attackers the worst with team sizes of nine people (Guastello & Doyle, 2007).

Performance trends were analyzed for nonlinear properties using the same statistical approach that was used in other coordination studies reported here. For the ER Teams,

$$h_2 = \exp(\theta_1 h_1) + \theta_2 \exp(\theta_3^* m_1), \tag{13.4}$$

where h_2 was the ER Teams' cumulative performance on a given turn, h_1 was the ER teams' cumulative performance on the previous turn, m_1 was the Attacker's cumulative score on the previous turn, and θ_i were nonlinear regression weights. All games from teams of the same size were spliced end to end to form longer times series of 100 to 250 observations. θ_1 was the Lyapunov exponent associated with teams' performance trends, and θ_3 was the Lyapunov exponent associated with Attackers' performance trends. The same equation was used for Attackers' time series, except that m_2 replaced h_2 on the left side of the equation.

The teams' performance dynamics were chaotic, and the fractal dimension of the series was unaffected by group size (average $D_L = 1.52$). Chaos was signified by a positive Lyapunov exponent and was interpreted as an indicator of adaptive capability. Teams' performance on a given iteration was negatively affected by the attacker's performance in the previous turn ($R^2 = .86-.90$). The performance dynamics of the adversary were not affected by the progress made by the teams on the previous iteration ($R^2 = .67-.75$). Their chaosticity level was generally higher than the teams', although it was less when the adversaries played against teams of 12 ($D_L = 2.00$, compared with $D_L = 2.67$ for smaller groups).

The results indicated that the groups are affected by signs of their own self-efficacy, whereas individuals are not as affected. The attackers seemed to have lost adaptivity when the team size increased to 12.

Self-Organization and Leadership Emergence

The phenomenon in which leaders emerge from leaderless groups was first reported more than 50 years ago (e.g., Ansbacher, 1951; Bass, 1949, 1954). The traditional research paradigm lent itself to measuring individual traits before the start of the group activity and comparing them against indicators of leadership after the group activity (Cattell & Stice, 1954; Zaccaro, 2007). The *process* of emergence remained a black box, however, until recently with help of NDS concepts and analyses (Guastello, 1998, 2002, 2007a, 2007b; Guastello & Bond, 2007b; Guastello, Craven, Zygowicz, & Bock, 2005; Zaror & Guastello, 2000).

Landmarks

The intervening decades of leadership research produced several important land-marks. The profile of traits that characterized emerging and successful leaders that were usually found in business settings (Cattell & Stice, 1954) was found to be robust across 40 years and the major English-speaking countries (Rieke, Guastello, & Conn, 1994). The leadership profile, interestingly, was opposite of the profile for creative professionals with regard to imagination, spontaneity, self-sufficiency, and openness to experience. It was not until the early dawn of the CAS that some other possibilities were considered, perhaps because people had started to change: Simonton (1988) proposed that creativity *is* leadership because successful creative products induce people to think differently in impor-tant ways. Similarly, *transformational* leadership is a style that emphasizes the intellectual aspects of leadership in addition to the social aspects (Bass, 1985). Cattell and Stice (1954) had also identified a distinct secondary form of leader, the technical leader, but the idea of secondary or technical leaders did not filter through the rest of leadership research in any obvious way. Creative thinking and the ability to lead groups into doing it has become all the more necessary in a business environment in which adaptive responses need to be made relatively quickly (Sternberg, 2007).

The counterpoint to transformation leadership is *transactional* leadership (Bass, 1985), which is probably what most leadership encounters involve. The previous landmark of transactional leadership was established by Fleishman and Harris (1962), in the form of two factors: structure of the work and consideration of individual needs. This important finding gave rise to the notion that there was one best way to lead, which was by maximizing one's performance on both factors (Blake & Mouton, 1964). The counterpoint to the notion of one best way to lead is that different situations require different strategies from the leaders (Vroom & Jago, 2007), and if there is one best way of leading, it would be through the versatile use of styles and techniques to help the group to attain its goals (House & Mitchell, 1975).

Kozlowski and Ilgen (2006) summarized some meta-analyses in their review of team effectiveness that capture the relative impact of some leadership variables from the traditional linear perspective. In short, structure and consideration, which are factorially independent, produce a total R^2 of .31 for predicting group performance, in static situations of course. For the distinction between transformational versus transactional leadership under conditions of peak the average r^2 values were .36 versus .10 respectively (pp. 107–108). Finally, if one were to consider studies in which ratings of leadership effectiveness and transformational leadership behaviors were all produced by the group members, the average r^2 is higher, .53 (p. 108).

One body of research indicates that the particular leaders that emerge in a given situation will be predicated on the type of task (Barge, 1996; Guastello, Craven, et al., 2005; House & Mitchell, 1975; Kolb, 1992; Neuman & Wright, 1999; Zander, 1994), task complexity, information requirements, performance verifiability (Hirokawa, 1990), and the group's preferences for dominant, considerate, or radical thinking on the part of their leaders (Bales, 1999). Yet another body indicates that the individuals who emerge as leaders in one type of situation are likely to emerge as leaders in other situations (Zaccaro, 2007). In the NDS perspective, the fundamental dynamics are the same for all types of situations, although they play out differently for different types of task situations. It appears from several viewpoints that the quality of the communications between the would-be leader and members is more important than the sheer quantity of communication (Bass, 1990; Bonito & Hollingshead, 1997; Bottger, 1984; Fisher, 1986; Graen & Uhl-Bien, 1995; Guastello, 1995; Guastello, Craven, et al., 2005).

According to Avolio (2007), a greater range of variables needs to be explored with regard to the situational differences in leadership emergence or effectiveness. The variables would include cognitive elements, individual leader–follower behavior, historical context, proximal content, and distal context. The NDS

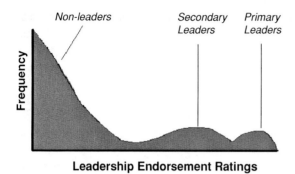

Leadership Endorsement Ratings

Figure 13.1. Probability density function for leadership emergence, from Guastello (2007). Reprinted with permission from the American Psychological Association.

perspective on leadership emergence is not inconsistent with these views: The process of leadership emergence actually involves the emergence of an entire social structure in which the leader is particularly prominent (Bales, 1999; Guastello, 2007b).

Rugged Landscape Model

The nonlinear theory behind leadership emergence (Guastello, 1998, 2002, 2007a, 2007b; Guastello & Bond, 2007b; Guastello, Craven, et al., 2005; Zaror & Guastello, 2000) was grounded in the rugged landscape model of self-organization (Kauffman, 1993, 1995). As leaderless groups interact while performing a task, their members become differentiated into primary leaders, secondary leaders, and the majority of the group who remain nonleaders after the differentiation process has occurred. The resulting frequency distribution would take the form that is shown in Figure 13.1. The horizontal axis corresponds to K in Kauffman's $NK[C]$ function (see Chapter 1) and represents the number of traits that are associated with the social niche that a person occupies when the group self-organizes. The majority of group members comprise the large mode at the left. The large mode is unstable, meaning that members of this subgroup could wander into a leadership mode if the values of control parameters pulled them toward one of the stable attractors. The vertical axis, N, is the number of cases associated with a value of K, in both the $NK[C]$ function and in any general frequency distribution.

The K traits are observed as social contributions or schemata in work-related conversations, such as asking questions, giving answers, initiating a new path of discussion, facilitating the expression of ideas by others, following a line of reasoning started by someone else, and so on, in which leaders tend to have wider repertoires of conversational behavior than nonleaders. According to Graen and Uhl-Bien (1995), the building block of leadership is the dyadic relationship between the leader and each of the members, and the quality of the social exchange and reciprocity among them. A high-quality interaction would be characterized by four principles – loyalty, respect, contribution, and positive affect – that comprise a single indicator of leader–member exchange (Liden & Maslyn, 1998). High ratings on leader–member exchange have been associated with work outcomes such as individuals' work performance, job satisfaction, satisfaction with supervision in particular, increased role clarity and reduced role conflict, and leader–member agreement (Gerstner & Day, 1997). When enough interactions have occurred, some people will attract more interactions than others, hence leaders and other roles will emerge from the group (Graen & Uhl-Bien, 1995). Thus local interactions give rise to global phenomena (Zaror & Guastello, 2000). Not only does a leader emerge, but a whole social structure emerges with leaders being particularly visible (Bales, 1999).

The constellation of K traits is just one of three control parameters that are apparently involved in the process (Guastello, 1998; Guastello & Bond, 2007b; Guastello, Craven, et al., 2005; Zaror & Guastello, 2000). Group interactions can range from light socialization to task-specific insights and problem solving. According to Kauffman's model, the C factor signifies the complexity of interaction of agents within a (virtual) ecological niche. In this context, ruggedness would take the form of distinct role separations among the participants in a group from which leaders emerge, and thus in the distinctiveness of the modes of density in Figure 13.1.

Asymmetries in members' interaction patterns eventually occur whereby some group members become more central to the group's interaction pattern than do other members. When this asymmetry occurs, group members will have self-organized into roles that exhibit broad leadership or secondary leadership. Secondary leadership might reflect particular social contributions such as technical contributions or conflict resolution (Cattell & Stice, 1954). Bales (1950) distinguished between task leaders and process leaders in the early stages of his group process theory. Bales (1999) explicated later that many possible group structures, in addition to leadership emergence, form, dissolve, and reorganize.

Swallowtail Catastrophe Model

The presence of self-organizing processes might suggest an inverse power law or a catastrophe as a descriptive probability density function. The swallowtail catastrophe model is an excellent fit for leadership emergence data and better suited than an inverse power law (Guastello, 2005b). In fact, the peculiar distribution shown in Figure 13.1 is actually unique to the swallowtail catastrophe model.

The swallowtail model (Fig. 13.2) distinguishes two stable states and a large unstable state. The unstable state is separated from the two stable states by a substantial antimode in which relatively few observations are found. The antimodes are created by the model's underlying bifurcation structure. Because

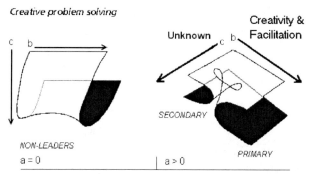

Broad Range of Traits Corresponding to Kauffman's K ⟶
Control of Conversation and Task

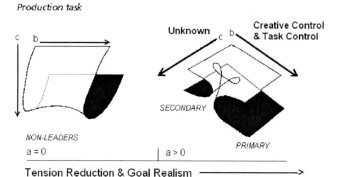

Tension Reduction & Goal Realism ⟶

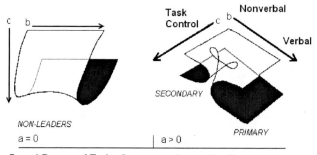

Broad Range of Traits Corresponding to Kauffman's K ⟶
Control of Conversation

Figure 13.2. Swallowtail catastrophe models for leadership emergence. Top: creative problem-solving groups; center: production groups; lower: coordination-intensive groups. Adapted from Guastello, Craven, et al. (2005) and Guastello and Bond (2007b), with permission of the Society for Chaos Theory in Psychology & Life Sciences.

the response surface is four-dimensional, it must be presented in two three-dimensional sections. The equation for the swallowtail response surface is:

$$\mathrm{d}f(y)/\mathrm{d}y = y^4 - cy^2 - by - a, \tag{13.5}$$

where y is the dependent measure, that is an index of leadership, and a, b, and c are control parameters.

The separation among the stable and unstable states is produced by a bifurcation mechanism that gives rise to the three control parameters. Control parameter a, also known as the *asymmetry* parameter, governs the broad distinction between two subsections of the swallowtail response surface. For low values of a, data points, which represent people in the system, will either fall within a single mode associated with nonleaders, or be sent to an undefined place somewhere else. At higher values of a, "somewhere else" is the other subsection of the surface where it is possible to see two possible stable states (attractors), and points can move around the surface between the stable and unstable states.

Control parameters b and c determine whether a point will fall into one of the two distinct stable states or in the shaded and unstable region between them. Control b is also known as the *bifurcation* parameter, and it denotes the extent to which points move from the ambiguous area of the surface (rear) to the stable states that signify leadership roles (unfolded portion, front).

Control c is also known as the *bias* or *swallowtail* parameter. The bias parameter distinguishes between the primary and secondary leadership roles. Points can also move between the two stable states so long as the asymmetry parameter remains high. If a drops too far in value, however, the point makes a discontinuous shift back to the unstable state on the left-hand (in Fig. 13.2) portion of the surface.

Research Design

Participants in the studies conducted thus far have involved college students who were recruited from the usual sources and assigned by the experimenters to groups with average sizes of 4 to 14 people. Three experimental tasks have been used to date. One was a creative problem-solving task that involved sorting out the social and economic problems of a small island nation; the average group sizes were 8 or 14 people (Guastello, 1998; Guastello, Craven, et al., 2005; Zaror & Guastello, 2000). One was a simplistic production task that involved coloring in two to four dozen copies of a line drawing under time pressure; the average group size was 7 people (Guastello, Craven, et al., 2005). The third was a coordination-intensive task that involved the Intersection card game with a group size of 4 people (Guastello & Bond, 2007b).

In each type of task situation, participants completed a brief questionnaire at the end of the game that asked who was most like the leader and who was second-most like the leader. The ratings that were given to each person were summed over the ratings that were received from all the participants in the group. Thus for a group of 8 people the scores ranged from 0 to 16. The questionnaire continued with additional items that used the same response format. Those items assessed conversation behaviors that originated with the work of Benne and Sheats (1948) – information seeking, information giving, tension reduction, clarifying responses and ideas, gatekeeping, initiating a stream of discussion, and following the ideas of others – and questions about various aspects of leadership style that had become salient in the leadership literature since that time. The questionnaires appear in the original articles (Guastello & Bond, 2007a; Guastello, Craven, et al., 2005). The questions were aggregated into a smaller number of constructs with the use of factor analysis. The constructs that exhibited a significant effect in swallowtail models appear in Figure 13.2. The study of coordination-intensive tasks involved an experimental condition in which participants could not talk to each other; thus the instruction for all participants in that study were amplified to allow for the possibility that no one behaved like the leader or exhibited any of the other characteristics that were mentioned on the questionnaire.

The swallowtail model was tested using the nonlinear regression model in Eq. 13.6:

$$\text{pdf}(z) = \xi \exp[\theta_1 z^5 + \theta_2 z^4 + \theta_3 c z^3 + \theta_4 b z^2 + \theta_5 a z], \tag{13.6}$$

where z is the leadership measurement and a, b, and c are the control parameters. θ_i and ξ are nonlinear regression weights. Pdf(z) is the cumulative probability of z within the distribution, that is, a probit transformation of z. The potential control variables resulted from a principal components analysis of the questionnaire (without the leadership variable) and from experimental manipulations that were also introduced.

Creative Problem-Solving Groups

In the swallowtail model for creative problem-solving groups (Guastello, Craven, et al., 2005), the asymmetry parameter was defined by a large group of social contributions, not unlike what one would expect from Kauffman's K parameter: clarifying responses and ideas, gatekeeping, initiating, following, harmonizing, facilitating the ideas of others, controlling the conversation, task orientation, consideration of the other players' interest (as defined by their roles in the game), and concern for the quality of the game outcomes. This group of behaviors was defined collectively as *controlling the conversation* (Guastello, Craven, et al., 2005).

The bifurcation parameter was composed of four variables, which were collectively defined as *creativity*: giving information, creative ideas, competitive behavior, and concern for the game outcomes. Here the latter two variables indicated a strong immersion in the creative role-play. Although another variable, *tension reduction*, was identified in the components analysis of the questionnaire data, it had no effect when tested as any of the control parameters. The bias factor for creative problem-solving groups remains unknown at this time. An R^2 of .74 was produced nonetheless, and were obtained for all regression weights were statistically significant ($p < .05$).

Production Groups

The study of production groups involved a game in which the group members had to plan some work then produce two, three, or four dozen units of work in a fixed amount of time (Guastello, Craven, et al., 2005). The groups that were assigned the goal of producing two dozen units actually produced more work than the groups that we assigned three or four dozen units. Hence the variable *goal realism* entered the study: The two-dozen condition was scored as high realism and the other two conditions were scored as low-realism.

The results of the study showed that goal realism and tension reduction both contributed to the asymmetry parameter for leadership emergence in production groups. Two variables contributed to the bifurcation parameter, which contributes to the strength of the separation of the two modes for primary and secondary leaders: *task control* and *creative control*. Creative control was a combination of creative ideas and controlling the conversation during the first phase of the game. Task control was a combination of task orientation, clarifying responses and ideas, gatekeeping, following, and controlling the conversation. The bias parameter, which would sort participants into primary or secondary leaders, also remains unknown for production groups. An R^2 of .62 was obtained for the swallowtail model with the available control variables for production groups.

Coordination-Intensive Groups

The study of the emergence of leaders in coordination-intensive groups used an experimental manipulation in which half the groups were allowed to talk, but the other half were not (Guastello & Bond, 2007a). Once again the potential control parameters were identified through the principle components analysis of the postsession questionnaire. This time it was possible to find all three parameters that contributed to the swallowtail response surface for leadership emergence in coordination-intensive groups (Guastello & Bond, 2007b). Parameter a was a *general participation* factor that was about as broad in scope as the a parameter that was obtained for creative problem-solving groups. Parameter b was whether the group worked *verbally or nonverbally*; people in verbalizing groups were more often distinctively associated with the primary leadership mode of the response surface. Parameter c was task control, which consisted of asking questions, controlling the card play, task orientation, and competitive behavior. An R^2 of .61 was obtained for the swallowtail model.

Summary

Specific NDS concepts and analyses produced new research questions concerning adaptive behavior, coordination, and leadership emergence that would not have been asked under the ordinary linear framework. Ironically, the newfound interest in adaptation within the linear community was addressed more deeply by the nonlinear community a decade earlier. Nonlinear dynamics, furthermore, offers a metric for quantifying adaptation levels and makes use of the concepts of attractors, bifurcations, chaos, turbulence, catastrophe, and self-organization for explaining groups' responses to situations. The same group of concepts appear to be necessary for explaining learning phenomena at the group level, if not also at the organizational level. Although a collective learning theory for humans has not yet solidified, the combination of basic dynamics, the group phenomena studied here, plus collective intelligence (as described in Chapter 2) should bring such a theory into focus relatively soon.

The primary results for team coordination phenomena from the nonlinear paradigm are the specific roles of nonverbal and verbal communication, explicit and implicit learning at the group level of analysis, at least two distinct forms of coordination, explicit and implicit learning at the group level, the impact of group self-efficacy on performance over time, and nonlinear models that are substantially more accurate than linear models that are based on conventional concepts. The empirical results show that the nonlinear models explain phenomena more accurately than linear models by a substantial margin.

One primary result for leadership emergence from the nonlinear paradigm is that an entire social structure emerges that produces primary and secondary forms of leadership. The swallowtail catastrophe model captures the dynamics in three types of groups. There are three control parameters in the model, which always have the same function. The control parameters are different variables in each type of group, although there are some recurrent themes. One recurrent theme is that primary leaders exhibit a broad repertoire of social skills and contributions to the group's activities. Another is that control over the task, or important aspects of it, is intrinsic to being recognized as the leader. The models exhibit a good degree of accuracy for predicting what they are intended to predict. Once again, the empirical results show that the nonlinear models explain phenomena more accurately than linear models, as given in various meta-analyses, by a substantial margin.

There are many opportunities for further research. For instance, only one type of creative problem-solving, production, or coordination-intensive group has been tested thus far, and it would be reasonable to determine whether similar results would be obtained for other examples of the same three types of tasks and in real-world situations. Varying the situations could help to identify the missing bias parameters and support the generalizability of the others that have been found already. Research on leadership emergence in Stag Hunt tasks is now in progress.

The experiments to date have involved teams that were assembled for the purpose of the experiments, and thus the teams did not have any meaningful prior history with each other. Real-world groups often have deep and complex histories, all of which could affect the social structures and leaders that emerge. Future NDS research should explore historical context variables within a group for their dynamical impact. The same case could be made for more examples of real-world coordination research as well.

References

Anderson, P. (1999). Complexity theory and organization science. *Organization Science, 10*, 216–232.

Ansbacher, H. L. (1951). The history of the leaderless group discussion technique. *Psychological Bulletin, 48*, 383–391.

Argyris, C., & Schon, D. (1978). *Organizational learning: A theory of action perspective.* Reading, MA: Addison-Wesley.

Ashby, W. R. (1956). *Introduction to cybernetics.* New York: Wiley.

Avolio, B. J. (2007). Promoting more integrative strategies for leadership theory-building. *American Psychologist, 62*, 25–33.

Axelrod, R. (1984). *The evolution of cooperation.* New York: Basic Books.

Bailey, K. D. (1994). Talcott Parsons, social entropy theory, and living systems theory. *Behavioral Science, 39*, 25–45.

Bailey, N. R., Scerbo, M. W., Mikulka, P. J., & Scott, L. A. (2006). Comparison of a brain-based adaptive system and a manual adaptive system for invoking automation. *Human Factors, 48*, 693–709.

Baker, J. S., & Frey, P. W. (1980). A cusp catastrophe, hysteresis, bimodality, and inaccessibility in rabbit eyelid conditioning. *Learning and Motivation, 10*, 520–535.

Bales, R. F. (1950). *Interaction process analysis: A method for the study of small groups.* Cambridge, MA: Addison-Wesley.

Bales, R. F. (1999). *Social interaction systems.* New Brunswick, NJ: Transaction.

Bandura, A. (2001). Social cognitive theory. An agentic perspective. *Annual Review of Psychology, 52*, 1–26.

Bandura, A., & Locke, E. A. (2003). Negative self-efficacy and goal effects revisited. *Journal of Applied Psychology, 88*, 87–99.

Banks, A. P., & Millward, L. J. (2000). Running shared mental models as a distributed cognitive process. *British Journal of Psychology, 91*, 513–531.

Bar-Yam, Y. (1997). *Dynamics of complex systems.* Reading, MA: Addison Wesley.

Barge, J. K. (1996). Leadership skills and the dialectics of leadership in group decision making. In R. Y. Hirokawa & M. S. Poole (Eds.), *Communication and group decision making* (2nd ed., pp. 301–342). Thousand Oaks, CA: Sage.

Bass, B. M. (1949). An analysis of the leaderless group discussion. *Journal of Applied Psychology, 33*, 527–533.

Bass, B. M. (1954). The leaderless group discussion. *Psychological Bulletin, 51*, 465–492.

Bass, B. M. (1985). *Leadership and performance beyond expectations.* New York: Free Press.

Bass, B. M. (1990). *Bass & Stogdill's handbook of leadership: Theory, research and managerial applications* (3rd ed.). New York: Free Press.

Benne, K. D., & Sheats, P. (1948). Functional roles of group members. *Journal of Social Issues, 4*, 41–49.

Bigelow, J. (1982). A catastrophe model of organizational change. *Behavioral Science, 27*, 26–42.

Blake, R., & Mouton, J. S. (1964). *The managerial grid: Key orientation for achieving production through people.* Houston, TX: Gulf.

Bonito, J. A., & Hollingshead, A. B. (1997). Participation in small groups. In B. R. Burleson (Ed.), *Communications Yearbook* (Vol. 20, pp. 227–261). Thousand Oaks, CA: Sage.

Bottger, P. C. (1984). Expertise and air time of actual and perceived influence in problem-solving groups. *Journal of Applied Psychology, 69*, 214–221.

Brannick, M. T., Roach, R. M., & Salas, E. (1993). Understanding team performance: A multimethod study. *Human Performance, 6*, 287–308.

Burke, C. S., Stagl, K. C., Salas, E., Pierce, L., & Kendall, D. (2006). Understanding team adaptation: A conceptual analysis and model. *Journal of Applied Psychology, 91*, 1189–1207.

Camerer, C., & Knez, M. (1997). Coordination in organizations: A game-theoretic perspective. In Z. Shapira (Ed.), *Organization decision making* (pp. 158–188). New York: Cambridge University Press.

Cannon-Bowers, J., Salas, E., & Converse, S. (1990). Cognitive psychology and team training: Training shared mental models of complex systems. *Human Factors Bulletin, 33*, 1–4.

Cannon-Bowers, J., Salas, E., & Converse, S. (1993). Shared mental models in expert team decision making. In N. J. Castellan (Eds.), *Individual and group decision making: Current issues* (pp. 221–246). Hillsdale, NJ: Erlbaum.

Cattell, R. B., & Stice, G. F. (1954). Four formulae for selecting leaders on the basis of personality. *Human Relations, 7*, 493–507.

Comer, D. R. (1995). A model of social loafing in real work groups. *Human Relations, 48*, 647–667.

Crawford, V. P. (1991). An "evolutionary interpretation" of Van Huyk, Batalio, and Beil's experimental results on coordination. *Games and Economic Behavior, 3*, 25–59.

Cyert, R. M., & March, J. G. (1963). *A behavioral theory of the firm.* Englewood Cliffs, NJ: Prentice-Hall.

Daily, R. C. (1980). A path analysis of R & D team coordination and performance. *Decision Sciences, 11*, 357–369.

DeGreene, K. (1991). Emergent complexity in person-machine systems. *International Journal of Man-Machine Studies, 35*, 219–234.

Dennis, A. R., & Valacich, J. S. (1993). Computer brainstorms: More heads are better than one. *Journal of Applied Psychology, 78*, 531–537.

Dobson, M. W., Pengally, M., Sime, J-A., Albaladejo, S. A., & Garcia, E. V., et al. (2001). Situated learning with co-operative agent simulations in team training. *Computers in Human Behavior, 17*, 547–573.

Dooley, K. J. (1997). A complex adaptive systems model of organization change. *Nonlinear Dynamics, Psychology, and Life Sciences, 1*, 69–97.

Dooley, K. J. (2004). Complexity science models of organizational change and innovation. In M. S. Poole & A. H. Van de Ven (Eds.), *Handbook of organizational change and innovation* (pp. 354–373). New York: Oxford University Press.

Druskat, V. U., & Pescosolido, A. T. (2002). The content of effective teamwork mental models in self-managing teams: Ownership, learning and heedful interrelating. *Human Relations, 55*, 283–314.

Fleishman, E. A., & Harris, E. F. (1962). Patterns of leadership behavior related to employee grievance and turnover. *Personnel Psychology, 15*, 43–56.

Fisher, B. A. (1986). Leadership: When does the difference make a difference? In R. Y. Hirokawa & M. S. Poole (Eds.), *Communication and group decision-making* (pp. 197–218). Beverly Hills, CA: Sage.

Freeman, W. J. (2000). *Neurodynamics: An exploration of mesoscopic brain dynamics.* New York: Springer-Verlag.

Frensch, P. A., & Runger, D. (1983). Implicit learning. *Current Directions in Psychological Science, 12*, 13–18.

Frey, P. W., & Sears, R. J. (1978). Model of conditioning incorporating the Rescorla–Wagner associative axiom, a dynamic attention process, and a catastrophe rule. *Psychological Review, 85*, 321–340.

Friedman, J. W. (Ed.). (1994). *Problems of coordination in economic activity.* Boston: Kluwer Academic.

Geen, R. G. (2001). Social motivation. *Annual Review of Psychology, 42*, 377–399.

Gerstner, C. R., & Day, D. V. (1997). Meta-analytic review of leader-member exchange theory: Correlates and construct issues. *Journal of Applied Psychology, 82*, 827–844.

Gorman, J. C., Cooke, N. J., Pedersen, H. K., Winner, J., Andrews, D., & Amazeen, P. G. (2006). Changing team composition after a break: Building adaptive command-and-control teams. *Proceedings of the Human Factors and Ergonomics Society, 50th Annual Meeting* (pp. 487–491). Baltimore: Human Factors and Ergonomics Society.

Graen, G. B., & Uhl-Bien, M. (1995). Relationship-based approach to leadership: Development of leader-member exchange (LMX) theory of leadership over 25 years: Applying a multi-level multi-domain perspective. *Leadership Quarterly, 6*, 219–247.

Grigsby, J., & Stevens, D. (2000). *Neurodynamics of personality.* New York: Guilford Press.

Guastello, S. J. (1981). Catastrophe modeling of equity in organizations. *Behavioral Science, 26*, 63–74.

Guastello, S. J. (1995). *Chaos, catastrophe, and human affairs: Nonlinear dynamics in work, organizations, and social evolution.* Mahwah, NJ: Erlbaum.

Guastello, S. J. (1998). Self-organization and leadership emergence. *Nonlinear Dynamics, Psychology, and Life Sciences, 2*, 303–316.

Guastello, S. J. (2002). *Managing emergent phenomena: Nonlinear dynamics in work organizations.* Mahwah, NJ: Erlbaum.

Guastello, S. J. (2005a). Nonlinear models for the social sciences. In S. A. Whelan (Ed.), *The handbook of group research and practice* (pp. 251–272). Thousand Oaks, CA: Sage.

Guastello, S. J. (2005b). Statistical distributions and self-organizing phenomena: What conclusions should be drawn? *Nonlinear Dynamics, Psychology, and Life Sciences, 9*, 463–478.

Guastello, S. J. (2006). *Human factors engineering and ergonomics: A systems approach.* Mahwah, NJ: Erlbaum.

Guastello, S. J. (2007a). Nonlinear dynamics and leadership emergence. *Leadership Quarterly, 18*, 357–369.

Guastello, S. J. (2007b). Comment: How leaders really emerge. *American Psychologist, 62,* 606–607.

Guastello, S. J., Bock, B. R., Caldwell, P., & Bond, R. W., Jr. (2005). Origins of coordination: Nonlinear dynamics and the role of verbalization. *Nonlinear Dynamics, Psychology, and Life Sciences, 9,* 175–208.

Guastello, S. J., & Bond, R. W., Jr. (2004). Coordination in Stag Hunt games with application to emergency management. *Nonlinear Dynamics, Psychology, and Life Sciences, 8,* 345–374.

Guastello, S. J., & Bond, R. W., Jr. (2007a). The emergence of leadership in coordination-intensive groups. *Nonlinear Dynamics, Psychology, and Life Sciences, 11,* 91–117.

Guastello, S. J., & Bond, R. W., Jr. (2007b). A swallowtail catastrophe model for the emergence of leadership in coordination-intensive groups. *Nonlinear Dynamics, Psychology, and Life Sciences.*

Guastello, S. J., Craven, J., Zygowicz, K. M., & Bock, B. R. (2005). A rugged landscape model for self-organization and emergent leadership in creative problem solving and production groups. *Nonlinear Dynamics, Psychology, and Life Sciences, 9,* 297–334.

Guastello, S. J., & Doyle, M. (2007, August). *Performance dynamics in Stag Hunt games as a function of group size.* Paper presented to the 17th Annual International Conference of the Society for Chaos Theory in Psychology & Life Sciences, Orange, CA.

Guastello, S. J., & Guastello, D. D. (1998). Origins of coordination and team effectiveness: A perspective from game theory and nonlinear dynamics. *Journal of Applied Psychology, 83,* 423–437.

Guastello, S. J., & Johnson, E. A. (1999). The effect of downsizing on hierarchical work flow dynamics in organizations. *Nonlinear Dynamics, Psychology, and Life Sciences, 3,* 347–377.

Gully, S. M., Incalcaterra, K. A., Joshi, A., & Beaubein, J. M. (2002). A meta-analysis of team efficacy, potency, and performance: Interdependence and level of analysis as moderators of observed performance relationships. *Journal of Applied Psychology, 87,* 819–832.

Hirokawa, R. Y. (1990). The role of communication in group decision-making efficacy: A task contingency perspective. *Small Group Research, 21,* 190–204.

House, R. J., & Mitchell, T. R. (1975). Path-goal theory of leadership. In K. N. Wexley & G. A. Yukl (Eds.), *Organizational behavior and industrial psychology* (pp. 177–186). New York: Oxford University Press.

Hoyert, M. S. (1992). Order and chaos in fixed-interval schedules of reinforcement. *Journal of the Experimental Analysis of Behavior, 57,* 339–363.

Insko, C. A., Thibaut, J. W., Moehle, D., Wilson, M., Diamond, W. D., et al. (1980). Social evolution and the emergence of leadership. *Journal of Personality and Social Psychology, 39,* 431–448.

Jacobs, R. C., & Campbell, D. T. (1961). The perpetuation of an arbitrary tradition through several generations of a laboratory microculture. *Journal of Abnormal and Social Psychology, 62,* 649–658.

Jirsa, V. K., & Kelso, J. A. S. (Eds.). (2004). *Coordination dynamics: Issues and trends.* New York: Springer Publishing Company.

Kauffman, S. A. (1993). *The origins of order: Self-organization and selection in evolution.* New York: Oxford University Press.

Kauffman, S. A. (1995). *At home in the universe: Self-organization and selection in evolution.* New York: Oxford University Press.

Kolb, J. A. (1992). Leadership of creative teams. *Journal of Creative Behavior, 26,* 1–9.

Kozlowski, S. W. J., & Ilgen, D. R. (2006). Enhancing the effectiveness of work groups and teams. *Psychological Science in the Public Interest, 7,* 77–124.

Latané, B., Williams, K., & Harkins, S. (1979). Many hands make light the work: The cases and consequences of social loafing. *Journal of Personality and Social Psychology, 37,* 822–832.

Lewin, A. Y., Weigelt, C. B., & Emery, J. D. (2004). Adaptation and selection in strategy and change. In M. S. Poole & A. H. Van de Ven (Eds.), *Handbook of organizational change and innovation* (pp. 108–160). New York: Oxford University Press.

Li, J. S., Krauth, J., & Huston, J. P. (2006). Operant behavior of rats under fixed-interval reinforcement schedules: A dynamical analysis via the extended return map. *Nonlinear Dynamics, Psychology, and Life Sciences, 10,* 215–240.

Liden, R. C., & Maslyn, J. M. (1998). Multidimensionality of leader-member exchange: An empirical assessment through scale development. *Journal of Management, 24,* 43–72.

Marks, M. A., Mathieu, J. E., & Zaccaro, S. J. (2001). A temporally based framework and taxonomy for team processes. *Academy of Management Review, 26,* 356–376.

Marks, M. A., Sabella, M. J., Burke, C. S., & Zaccaro, S. J. (2002). The impact of cross-training on team effectiveness. *Journal of Applied Psychology, 87,* 3–13.

Matthieu, J. E., Heffner, T. S., Goodwin, G. F., & Salas, E., & Cannon-Bowers, J. A. (2000). The influence of shared mental models on team process and performance. *Journal of Applied Psychology, 85,* 273–283.

Maynard-Smith, J. (1982). *Evolution and the theory of games.* Cambridge, UK: Cambridge University Press.

Neuman, G. A., & Wright, J. (1999). Team effectiveness: Beyond skills and cognitive ability. *Journal of Applied Psychology, 84,* 376–389.

Newell, K. M. (1991). Motor skill acquisition. *Annual Review of Psychology, 42,* 213–237.

Omodei, M. M., McLennan, J., & Wearing, A. J. (2005). How expertise is applied in real-world decision environments: Head-mounted video and cued recall as a methodology for studying routines of decision making. In T. Betsch & Haberstroh, S. (Eds.), *The routines of decision making* (pp. 271–288). Mahwah, NJ: Erlbaum.

Pascual, M. A., & Rodriguez, M. A. (2006). Learning by operant conditioning as a nonlinear self-organized process. *Nonlinear Dynamics, Psychology, and Life Sciences, 10,* 341–364.

Rapoport, A. (1967). Optimal policies for the Prisoners' Dilemma game. *Psychological Review, 74,* 136–148.

Rieke, M. L., Guastello, S. J., & Conn, S. (1994). Leadership and creativity. In S. Conn & M. L. Rieke (Eds.), *16PF fifth edition technical manual* (pp. 183–212). Champaign, IL: Institute for Personality and Ability Testing.

Reynolds, C. W. (1987). Flocks, herds, and schools: A distributed behavioral model. *Computer Graphics, 21,* 25–34.

Rosser, J. B., Jr., Folke, C., Gunther, F., Isomaki, H., Perrings, C., & Puu, T. (1994). Discontinuous change in multilevel hierarchical systems. *Systems Research, 11*, 77–94.

Rubin, D. C. (1998). Knowledge and judgments about events that occurred prior to birth: The measurement of the persistence of information. *Psychonomic Bulletin & Review, 5*, 397–400.

Samuelson, L. (1997). *Evolutionary games and equilibrium selection.* Cambridge, MA: MIT Press.

Sawyer, R. K. (2005). *Social emergence: Societies as complex systems.* New York: Cambridge University Press.

Seger, C. A. (1994). Implicit learning. *Psychological Bulletin, 115*, 163–196.

Semovski, S. V. (2001). Self-organization in fish school. In W. Sulis & I. Trofimova (Eds.), *Nonlinear dynamics in the life and social sciences* (pp. 398–406). Amsterdam: IOS Press.

Seo, M.-G., Putnam, L. L., & Bartunek, J. M. (2004). Dualities and tensions of planned organizational change. In M. S. Poole & A. H. Van de Ven. (Eds.), *Handbook of organizational change and innovation* (pp. 73–107). New York: Oxford University Press.

Simonton, D. K. (1988). Creativity, leadership, and change. In R. J. Sternberg (Ed.), *The nature of creativity: Contemporary psychological perspectives* (pp. 386–426). Cambridge, MA: MIT Press.

Sternberg, R. J. (2007). A systems model of leadership: WICS. *American Psychologist, 62*, 34–42.

Stout, R. J., Cannon-Bowers, J., Salas, E., & Milanovitch, D. M. (1999). Planning, shared mental models, and coordinated performance: An empirical link is established. *Human Factors, 41*, 61–71.

Sulis, W. (1999). A formal theory of collective intelligence. In W. Tschacher & J.-P. Dauwalder (Eds.), *Dynamics, synergetics, and autonomous agents* (pp. 83–104). Singapore: World Scientific.

Tasa, K., Taggar, S., & Seijts, G. H. (2007). The development of collective efficacy in teams: A multilevel and longitudinal perspective. *Journal of Applied Psychology, 92*, 17–27.

Turvey, M. T. (1990). Coordination. *American Psychologist, 45*, 938–953.

Van de Ven, A. H., & Poole, M. S. (1995). Explaining development and change in organizations. *Academy of Management Review, 20*, 510–540.

Vetter, G., Stadler, M., & Haynes, J. D. (1997). Phase transitions in learning. *Journal of Mind and Behavior, 18*, 335–350.

von Neumann, J., & Morgenstern, O. (1953). *Theory of games and economic behavior.* Princeton, NJ: Princeton University of Press.

Vroom, V. H., & Jago, A. G. (2007). The role of the situation in leadership. *American Psychologist, 62*, 17–24.

Weick, K., & Gilfillan, D. (1971). Fate of arbitrary traditions in a laboratory microculture. *Journal of Personality and Social Psychology, 17*, 179–191.

Yuan, Y., & McKelvey, B. (2004). Situated learning theory: Adding rate and complexity effects via Kauffman's NK model. *Nonlinear Dynamics, Psychology, and Life Sciences, 8*, 65–102.

Zaccaro, S. J. (2007). Trait-based perspectives of leadership. *American Psychologist, 62*, 6–16.

Zagare, F. C. (1984). Game theory: Concepts and applications. *Quantitative Applications in the Social Sciences Paper Series,* No. 41. Newbury Park, CA: Sage.

Zander, A. (1994). *Making groups effective* (2nd ed.). San Francisco: Jossey-Bass.

Zaror, G., & Guastello, S. J. (2000). Self-organization and leadership emergence: A cross-cultural replication. *Nonlinear Dynamics, Psychology, and Life Sciences, 4,* 113–119.

14 Organizational Psychology

KEVIN J. DOOLEY

Introduction

It has been almost 100 years since Frederick Taylor introduced his concept of scientific management (Taylor, 1911). Taylor's work was significant in three important ways. First, it recognized business organizations as specialized social entities that were different from other social and economic structures and therefore worthy of study and a specialized science. Second, by conceptualizing organizations as mechanistic in nature, his work provided the foundational assumptions for the majority of organization psychology theory developed during the 20th century – the organization as a rational, deterministic, teleological system. Organizations were to be understood by their goals and their strategy for getting there, by their components (human and physical resources) and how they fit together (organizational structure), and how individuals outside of the machine (managers) made decisions and "managed" others to achieve their strategic goals. Third, Taylor opened the door for the continued appropriation of the physical sciences into the domain of organizational science.

Despite its dominance, Taylor's view of a centrally controlled, mechanistic, rational organization has been challenged since its inception. Humanism in its various forms has always had a strong contingency of support (Dingley & Durkhelm, 1997), and more recently organizations have been conceptualized as political (Morgan, 1986), organic (Burns & Stalker, 1961), postmodern (Boje, 2001), and even anarchic (Cohen, March, & Olsen, 1972). With the emergence of complexity science, however, we have an opportunity to bring together these disparate "modern" views of organizations. To the extent that complexity science offers a theoretical umbrella that brings coherence to the "thousand blooming flowers" in the garden of organizational psychology (Van Maanen, 1995), it facilitates significant advancement of both theory and practice.

Because there are numerous books, book chapters, and articles that address how organizations can be viewed as complex adaptive systems (e.g., Anderson 1999; Axelrod & Cohen, 1999; Begun, 1994; Begun, Dooley, & Zimmerman,

2003; Boisot, 1995; Dooley, 1997; Dooley, 2004a; Dooley, Johnson, & Bush, 1995; Eve, Horsfall, & Lee, 1997; Goldstein, 1994; Guastello 1995, 2002; Kelley & Allison, 1999; Lissack, 1999; Maguire & McKelvey, 1999; Marion, 1999; McDaniel & Driebe, 2001; Olson & Eoyang, 2001; Preismeyer, 1992; Stacey, 1992; Zimmerman, Lindberg, & Plsek, 1998), this chapter takes a slightly different approach toward a review of the topic by addressing three related but more specific questions: First, I attempt to answer the question: *Why do organizational scientists need complexity science?* To answer this question, I revisit three famous organizational theories: Burn and Stalker's concept of *mechanistic versus organic organizations* (1961), Cohen et al.'s (1972) *garbage can model* (GMC), and Perrow's (1984) *Normal Accident Theory*. At a surface level, all three appear to resonate strongly with concepts from complexity science, so the question becomes: What additional perspectives or nuances does complexity science give us that we would not otherwise have? Second, I review recent literature to identify *which complexity science ideas have been most used by organizational theorists.* Answering this question will help us understand the current status of the field. Third, I make some predictions as to *where organizational complexity science is likely to see the most development in years to come.*

Why Do We Need Complexity Science?

Complexity science emerged to the world in the late 1980s. For those who seek to find such connections, one can find numerous parallels between organizational psychology conceptualized before this date and complexity science. For example, Schelling's work (1978) on crowd behavior demonstrates how the micro-motives of individuals (agents) interplay at local levels to create emergent behavior that is not directly controlled or predictable from a top-down view. Thompson's (1967) concept of complexity buffering recognizes that managers actively seek out ways to block the effects of uncertainty within their environment by creating routines and schedules that are overtly stable and predictable. Weick's work (1995) extended March and Simon's (1958) concept of the (bounded) rational manager by claiming that we often act before we think and by highlighting the role of managers as sensemakers and sensegivers.

Organizational theorists and practitioners were introduced to complexity science through three different, loosely connected bodies of work: (a) chaos and nonlinear dynamics, via Gleick's (1987) book of the same name; (b) self-organization, emergence, and far-from-equilibrium dynamics via Prigogine and Stenger's (1984) *Order Out of Chaos*; and (c) fractals, via Mandelbrot's (1982) book and a host of computer programs that created stunning visualizations of fractal systems. People who were concerned about how to plan, structure, and execute organizational processes and systems were intrigued by chaos because it suggested to them that there were limits to prediction and planning and at the same time hinted that randomness was in fact the result of simple (but nonlinear) behavior (Eoyang, 1997; Hayles, 1991; Kellert, 1994). People who were concerned about how organizations change, and how to change organizations, were drawn to the concept of far-from-equilibrium dynamics because, like chaos theory, it suggested that the outcome of a change process was unpredictable but that change could be induced, and perhaps "steered" in the right direction by attention to how individuals in the organization interact with one another and create collective action (Goldstein, 1988; Guastello, Dooley, & Goldstein, 1995; Leifer, 1989).

Although the initial reaction among organizational psychologists to complexity science was enthusiastic, it was also confined to a relatively small group of people. In the ensuing 20 years, applications of complexity science have diffused and matured, have come to interest an increasing number of researchers and practitioners, and have benefited from the parallel emergence of the Internet and the growing importance of "network-based" thinking. We have reached the chasm, however; for organizational complexity science to continue to develop and grow it must appeal to a much broader and more "practical" (from a paradigm perspective) population of potential users. Thus the relevant question becomes this: How has complexity science enriched our theoretical repertoire? The three aforementioned organizational theories resonate strongly with complexity science, and I discuss here how complexity science can enhance these theories.

Mechanistic Versus Organic Organizations

Burns and Stalker's *Management of Innovation* (1961) posed the following question: Are there particular forms of organizing that are more appropriate for innovation, given a particular type of organizational environment? In classic organizational theory, *environment* equates to the organization's market (customers, suppliers, competitors, and technology) and other endogenous effects beyond the control of the firm. In the same vein as Ashby's (1958) Law of Requisite Variety, which states that a control system must have the same or greater level of complexity as the system it is controlling, Burns and Stalker suggested that traditional *mechanistic* forms of organizing are appropriate in environments that are stable, whereas *organic* forms of organizing are more appropriate for volatile environments.

> The organic form is appropriate to changing conditions which give rise constantly to fresh problems and unforeseen requirements for action which cannot be broken down or distributed automatically arising from the functional roles defined within a hierarchic structure. (p. 121)

Burns and Stalker went on to characterize the organic form: distributed knowledge and authority; local and lateral interactions leading to constantly changing tasks; the loosening of bureaucratic constraints; a "network structure of control, authority, and communication" (p. 121); and task over obedience, expertise over rank. As such, the organic form appears similar to what has popularly been defined as a complex adaptive system. A closer examination provides a more nuanced view, however. In an attempt to deconstruct Burns and Stalker's book, Boje (1999) argued that the mechanistic–organic duality is misleading. Rather than being treated as extremes along a continuum, the two are treated as ideals, opposite in nature, for example, one is the dual of the other; thus the reason that firms do not completely succeed is because they are not mechanistic or organic enough. Moreover, the language used to frame the concept of the organic organization is mechanistic in nature – a manager is still in control: scanning the environment to see whether it is stable or volatile, and then designing the system so that it is mechanistic or organic. Thus according to Boje, Burns and Stalker treated the organic as a special case of the mechanistic.

The lens of complexity science offers a different perspective. Like much traditional organizational theory, Burns and Stalker's model is prescriptive – there is a performance dimension, and the model states which combination of environment and organizing structure is most likely to enhance performance. Conversely, complexity science is descriptive in nature – it recognizes that both "mechanistic" and "organic" structures can be described as complex adaptive systems but makes no judgment about whether one form is preferable over the other. Even the most bureaucratic structures can be usefully described as consisting of teleological agents with local actions and interactions that create emergent behavior at the firm level. Likewise, complexity science highlights the reality that mechanistic and organic traits exist concurrently, often in contradiction with one another at the same level, and constraining and enabling one another at different levels of scale and time. Thus complexity science offers theoretical coherence, synthesizing the thesis and antithesis of mechanistic and organic.

Second, complexity science does not admit the "puppeteer" model in which managers sit outside of and manipulate a social system at will. Instead, complexity science posits that managers are part of the same system as all employees, but like everyone else, they have different linkages, resources, and motivations. It frames the problem as one of coevolution of organization and environment, rather than organization reacting to environment. A complexity science lens focuses attention on the micro-actions of all organization members and how these might yield networks that appear more or less mechanistic or organic, and how these traits evolve and change over time due to evolutionary, teleological, dialectic, and life-stage forces (Poole, Van de Ven, Dooley, & Holmes, 2000).

The Garbage Can Model

Like the concept of the organic firm, Cohen et al.'s GCM (1972) deals with environmental uncertainty. In some ways, the GCM is an extreme, anarchical form of the organic – one in which behavior at the firm level may appear irrational. The GCM was derived from anomalies in explaining the behavior of university departments and is framed as dealing with organizational systems that have an extreme level of loose coupling; power and decisions are diffuse; goals are not necessarily shared; and even participation in the organization is limited and ad hoc.

In traditional organization theory, decision makers (e.g. managers) identify problems, make decision alternatives explicit, and choose action in some bounded rational manner. In the GCM, problems, solutions, decisions, and decision makers are decoupled from each other and exist as concurrent streams. Solutions are not derived as answers to problems but rather exist by themselves, fueled by individual ideologies, biases, and concerns. Decision makers seek out problems for which they can apply their solutions; as many solutions may exist which do not yet have a problem, these exist in a "garbage can" waiting possible retrieval later in time. Decision makers themselves are not stable per se. Their interest in a problem depends on their attention, which can be divided in numerous ways and change over time.

This model appears completely resonant with a complexity science lens. While agents in a complex adaptive system are typically considered to be goal seeking, there is no assumption that these goals are shared. Likewise, the "simple rules" that agents employ moment by moment in a complex adaptive system do not presuppose that problems and solutions are closely linked or that an agent's involvement in a system is constant. The insight that a complexity lens provides is that the GCM is not a special case but rather a different take on reality, as valid and useful as the original mechanistic–organic duality. In other words, a complexity science lens demands that we assume elements of the GCM may be present in different parts of the organization, at different times, in varying amounts. The problem is not that with the content of the GCM model but rather its usage. By treating the GCM as only valid for anarchic organizations, its usefulness has been limited and stagnated. A complexity science lens highlights the more general validity of the GCM and provides both a conceptual and computational framework for its advancement.

Normal Accidents

Perrow's (1984) *normal accident theory* posits that accidents (e.g., catastrophes) are normal and to be expected in systems that are complex. Perrow's definition of complexity goes beyond Burn and Stalker's and Cohen et al.'s and encompasses both structure and interactions between the human and the technological or organizational system. System complexity is defined in two dimensions. Complex systems have complex interactions, meaning that task sequences may not be visible or comprehensible; they may be cyclical or nonlinear; and they may have causal effects that are lagged, nonlinear, and can act at a distance. Complex systems also are tightly coupled, whereby little slack (time, attention, resources, alternative paths) is available to respond to failures.

Tensions exist between those who advocate the normal accident model and others who believe that humans can significantly alter the chance of system failure (a.k.a. high reliability organization theory; see Weick & Sutcliffe, 2001). For the former, systemwide failure is made less likely, but never eliminated, by designing systems that have less complexity, that is, simple and visible causal mechanisms; for the latter, systemwide failure can be avoided by human systems that are resilient, pay attention to details, constantly challenge existing mental models by seeking anomalous and disconfirming information, and do not settle for simple explanations of complex phenomena (La Porte & Consolini, 1991).

Perrow's model also seems to resonate well with a complexity science lens. A complex adaptive system is assumed to have the potential for complex interactions, although such complexity may be temporally local or situational. Likewise, a complex adaptive system may be tightly coupled, but it may not be. Thus complexity science operates as a description that can encompass but is not solely defined by the conditions under which normal accidents are supposed to occur.

To appreciate the "conceptual bridging" that complexity science enables, consider the following. According to normal accident theory, failure to perform is due to tight coupling between elements of the system. According to the GCM, failure to perform is due to loose or the complete lack of coupling between elements of the system. So is failure to perform due to tight coupling or loose coupling? The conflict arises because the models make different assumptions about the nature of agents in the system. Normal accident theory assumes all of the elements of the system have the same goals; the GCM assumes the opposite. A complexity lens conceptualizes the degree to which goals are shared as a variable that differs amongst agents and over time, and thus would treat each model as extremes of the same continuum. Indeed, Kauffman's (1995) NK model posits that moderate amounts of complexity are most robust, whereas no coupling and extreme coupling can lead to much poorer adaptive response.

Another dimension where complexity science can provide nuance and additional understanding to normal accident theory is by discussing the generative mechanisms that lead complex systems to be susceptible to failure. For example, systems with complex interactions and tight coupling can be described as being in a state of self-organized criticality, which Bak (1996) and others' works on inverse power laws addresses. Like normal accident theory, self-organized criticality posits that catastrophes are rare but to be expected in complex systems. Likewise, the mathematics of nonlinear dynamical systems (NDS) provides a theoretical and analytical framework for modeling the actual dynamics of such complex systems. For example, catastrophe theory models (Guastello, 1995) link system parameters with nonlinear changes in performance, which can include sudden failure and sensitivity to small perturbations.

What Complexity Science Gives Us

These three examples have demonstrated at least three ways in which complexity science adds to our existing theories of organizations. First, complexity science "lies above" existing organizational theories. It unifies dualities such as mechanistic versus organic, loose versus tight coupling, control versus emergence, and thoughts versus actions. For theories with assumptions that are already resonant with a complexity science lens, complexity science can provide a way to view the theory within a broader ontological context. Second, complexity science "lies below" existing organizational theories. It provides a host of generative mechanisms that explain the "how" of causation and thus enables existing theories to go beyond surface-level descriptions. It also suggests that causation can take many forms that are not simple – nonlinear, time varying, and mutual. Third, complexity science provides a methodological framework with which to study and enhance further existing organizational theories. Tools such as agent-based modeling, cellular automata, and NDS can help researchers model the complexity in real systems both inductively and deductively.

How Has Complexity Science Been Used to Study Organizations?

A study of the current use of complexity science in organizational psychology identifies that complexity science is being pursued by three interest groups. First are those interested in change – how and why and when does an organization change, and how can organization be changed in purposeful ways? Second, given that an organization is a complex adaptive system, how does this mental model change the way workers and managers should "act"? Here the interest is in behavior – what do managers or workers do if they view their organization as a complex adaptive system? Whereas the first group is cognizant that change cannot be completely controlled, the second group still shows overtones of the control paradigm. Third, given that an organization is complex, how should it be designed and operated so as to be both efficient and robust in lieu of uncertainty? These individuals view complexity science as a design science, and both the metaphor and mathematics of networks is predominant here.

The use of complexity science in organizational psychology is still at an early stage of development. Two specialty journals have emerged and remained in existence for a significant period of time: *Nonlinear Dynamics, Psychology, & Life Science* (*NDPLS*), and *Emergence: Complexity and Organization* (*E:CO*). *NDPLS* covers the breadth of social, life, and economic sciences so its focus on organizational psychology is only partial. Most of the organizational-related contributions have been empirical and have focused on individual and small-group issues (Guastello, 2004), such as leadership emergence (e.g., Guastello & Bond, 2007), communication in small groups (e.g., Dooley, Corman, McPhee, & Kuhn, 2003), and local adaptation (e.g., Haslett & Osborn, 2003).

E:CO is dedicated wholly to the application of complexity science to organizations. Contributions are conceptual (not empirical), and cover a broad range of interests. As the journal title suggests, the one unifying thread is the concept of emergence and all of it philosophical, theoretical, and practical implications. A detailed content analysis of *E:CO* articles is beyond the scope of this chapter; however, to get a sense of the conceptual biases of articles presented there, I performed a computerized text analysis of their titles using centering resonance analysis (Corman, Kuhn, McPhee, & Dooley, 2002). Several insights were gained. First, complex science is framed as a "perspective"; thus there is the recognition of the limitations of any theoretical frame, as well as the drawing of boundaries between traditional organizational science and complexity-based organizational science. Second, the term *organizational theory* is much more common than *social science*, indicating that authors are concentrating their conceptualizations on the unique entity of "organization." Third, several areas of emphasis appear: knowledge and learning (Fioretti & Visser, 2004), narrative (Shumate, Bryant, & Monge, 2005), social networks, leadership (Hazy, 2006), emergence (Goldstein, 2004), and change. However these concepts are not strongly linked to one another; they are only related to one another semantically because of their connection to organization and complexity. Although this result is somewhat driven by the appearance of several special issues (on narrative, knowledge, and leadership), it also indicates a lack of conceptual continuity in the discourse – authors are still connecting existing ideas to complexity rather than integrating terms that are already a part of the accepted complexity discourse. A similar analysis of *NDPLS* articles (Dooley, 2004b) indicated the same type of "loose coupling" between articles, indicating that a strong coherent semantic frame had not emerged in discourse on complexity and organizations.

Although a significant number of articles on complexity and organizations have been published outside of these two journals, their numbers are not concentrated, and there is a distinct lack of presence in the "top-tier" management, operations, marketing, and information systems journals, indicating a lack of deep penetration. Conversely, there is strong emergence of perspectives that are resonant with complexity science: network sciences (Barabasi, 2002), including small worlds, "tipping points," and social capital; innovation in open source collaborations; distributed intelligence; adaptive processes; and an increase in the number of theories that consider environmental or task complexity as a contingency factor.

Examination of the relevant publications demonstrates that organizational researchers primarily draw from four areas of complexity science. *Generative mechanisms*: These studies involve examination of system dynamics such as cyclicality, chaos, and colored noise (inverse power law). The purpose here is to explain the "how" of a complex system, to explore the causal structure in a deeper, more fundamental manner. Explanations can be deductive, in which analytical models are formulated a priori and conclusions drawn (e.g., Alfaro

& Sepulveda, 2006; Feichtinger & Kopel, 1993; Rasmussen & Mosekilde, 1998; Riggle & Madey, 1997; Wu & Zhang, 2007), or inductive, in which empirical (statistical) models are used to diagnose dynamics and thereby characterize the underlying system (e.g., Cheng & Van de Ven, 1996; Dooley & Van de Ven, 1999; Guastello, 2005). Various authors have also discussed the general implications of chaos (e.g., Eoyang, 1997; Levy, 1994; McDaniel, 1997; Smilor & Feeser, 1991; Thietart & Forgues, 1996). More recently, McKelvey and colleagues (McKelvey & Adriani, 2006) have examined the implications of power law distributions in organizational data.

Emergence and self-organization: Emphasis is on how "simple rules" and local agent interactions create complex, unpredictable behavior at a global level. The purpose of this work is to explore the differences between this mental model and the traditional mental model of organizations as rational and deterministic. McKelvey's (2004a) view of complexity science as "order-creation science" is the dominant meme here. In these applications, researchers use complexity science as a template, mapping the domain's "reality" into a complexity framework. This leads to the deduction, "If the system is complex adaptive and therefore is self-organizing and emergent, here are the implications with respect to topic X." The utility of these applications is directly related to how much care was taken to create an accurate mapping. Applications have been broad, covering organizational design (Maguire, 1999; Mitelton-Kelly, 2003; Siggelkow & Levinthal, 2003; Siggelkow & Rivkin, 2005), strategy (MacIntosh & MacLean, 1999; Merry, 1999; Mintzberg & Waters, 1995; Stacey, 1995), innovation and learning (Allen, 2001; Brown & Eisenhardt, 1997; Hirooka, 2006; McCarthy, Tsinopoulos, Allen, & Rose-Anderssen, 2006; Nonaka & Takeuchi, 1995), firm creation (Chiles, Meyer, & Hench, 2004; Lichtenstein, Carter, Dooley, & Gartner, 2007; Lichtenstein, Dooley, & Lumpkin, 2006; McKelvey, 2004b), organizational fields (Boisot & Child, 1999; Meyer, Gaba, & Colwell, 2005), organizational change (Lichtenstein, 1997, 2000), sensemaking (Axley & McMahon, 2006; McDaniel, Jordan, & Fleeman, 2003), decision making (Anderson & McDaniel, 2000), careers (Lichtenstein & Mendenhall, 2002), and action (Anderson, Issel, & McDaniel, 2003; Letiche, 2006). Within this community there is also an increased interest in the role of narrative, both for describing complex systems (Tsoukas, 1998; Tsoukas & Hatch, 2001) and for explaining how they work (Boje, 1991; Shumate et al., 2005). Leadership is also a favorite topic (Guastello, Craven, Zygowicz, & Bock, 2005; Hazy, 2006; Marion & Uhl-Bien, 2001, 2003; McKelvey, 2002; Osborn, Hunt, & Jaunch, 2002; Plsek & Wilson, 2001; Regine & Lewin, 2000), which I discuss in the next section.

Adaptive search: Kauffman's NK model and variants thereof have been popular among organizational researchers interested in how organizational structure and systems search for optimality over time (Levinthal, 1997; Levinthal & Warglien, 1999; McKelvey, 1999; Oliver & Roos, 1999; Rivkin, 2000; Rivkin & Siggelkow, 2002, 2003; Sinha & Van de Ven, 2005; Yuan & McKelvey, 2004). There are direct links to the practical concepts of modular versus integral designs, and thus the topic extends beyond management researchers into applied areas such as innovation (Ethiraj & Levinthal, 2004), operations and supply chain management (Choi, Dooley, & Rungtusanatham, 2001; Surana, Kumara, Greaves, & Raghavan, 2005) and information systems (Sherif, 2006).

Computational mechanisms: The framework of complex adaptive systems enables a computational framework for researchers to simulate complex systems to develop theory and insight; in fact, Holland's (1995) definition of complex adaptive systems is a high-level specification for an agent-based computer language. The broad contributions of agent-based models are covered elsewhere in this book.

Predictions About Future Developments in Organizational Science

One pattern that jumps out from the review of literature in organizational science is the severe lack of empirical studies. Any quantitative work has been limited almost exclusively to deductive studies involving analytical models or simulation. Whereas empirical studies of nonlinear dynamics are present in studies of individual and small-group phenomena, they are lacking at the organizational level. There are at least three reasons for this. First, organizational phenomena tend to be higher dimensional, thus lower dimensional dynamics such as periodicity and chaos are more difficult to observe. Second, empirical methods involved with complex systems are complex themselves, thus requiring specialized training and knowledge which is not widespread. Third, we have, to date, attempted to adapt empirical methods to (complex) theory; we have not adopted conventional methods such as survey analysis to the study of complexity-related issues. It is possible that increased interest in process-based research can simultaneously benefit development of complexity science organizational research.

Organizational psychology applications have been opportunistic, emerging in areas where existing work was resonant with complexity. For example, the issues specialization and differentiation have long been givens within the study of organizational design. Thus it is not surprising that Kauffman's NK model of adaptation across a rugged landscape would become popular. Likewise topics such as organizational change or learning are natural applications of complexity science, because both are core concepts in the science. To move significantly forward, however, organizational complexity science must be more than just "above and below" existing theories; it must go beyond. For that reason, I predict that the largest growth of application will be in areas where traditional models of linear and deterministic models are woefully inadequate. Three areas come to mind.

First, the topic of leadership has already received considerable attention by researchers in the area, and this is likely to continue and expand significantly, particularly the issue of complexity and leadership. Two special issues of journals have already been devoted to this topic (in *E:CO* and *Leadership Quarterly*), and a number of other collective research efforts are moving forward, inspired in part by a series of workshops sponsored by the Center for Creative Leadership, which brought together leadership and complexity scholars. Traditional leadership scholarship focuses on the personality of the manager-as-leader, and the extra-ordinary things that they do. Complexity science focuses attention away from the individual and toward process and network. *Leadership*, a noun, becomes *leading*, a verb, and mutual interaction between agents supplants leader–follower exchange. Because of traditional leadership scholarship's focus on managers, and executives specifically, it ignores the majority of people in the organization, much like Taylorism. Leadership theories based on complexity science have the potential to reengage the whole.

A second area in which applications of complexity science may accelerate is in interorganizational relations, specifically organizational alliances, customer rela-tions, logistics and distribution, and supply chain management. Network theory has already become a popular framework for theories concerning strategic alliances, because there is recognition that the network effects can be as large as or even dominate the effects within the dyad itself. The rise of consumer-generated media such as blogs and discussion boards creates emergent, self-organizing communities of customers whose word-of-mouth can influence other customers – positively and negatively. Within operations of the firm, the Internet and reductions in transportation costs have significantly increased the variety, and thus the complexity, of distribution channels, and catastrophes such as Hurricane Katrina force theorists and practitioners for ways to make logistical networks more reliable in response to unforeseen events. Firms also recognize the importance of their "supply networks," especially as in increasing portion of a product or service's value is provided by suppliers, often separated by an ocean. In all of these cases, the behavior of the system is characterized by its underlying network; conversely, existing theories in marketing, operations and supply chain management, and information systems are based on simple assumptions of centralized control, simple causality, and determinism. These areas are ripe for what complexity science can offer.

Third, the post – September 11 world is sensitive to planning for catastrophic events, natural or otherwise. Existing research in emergency response has long recognized that successful disaster response depends on balancing strict control and improvisation. However, the number of researchers in this domain has always been limited, and so its theoretical base is not deep. With an increase in the amount of research being done in this area, there is a good opportunity for complexity science to serve as a unifying framework to bridge the old and new. Emergency response is characterized by loosely coupled networks interacting in highly uncertain environments; goals may not be completely shared, and information is incomplete and often erroneous. Control has both centralized and decentralized components, and no one is unimportant; for example, "victims" often play significant roles in rescue and recovery. Because emergency response is difficult to experiment with in the physical realm, simulation can greatly expand the variety of mental models that we can draw from regarding successful recovery.

Overall, future application of complexity science to organizations will grow to the extent that the community of thought begins to build on itself. The adaptive search and agent-based modeling subcommunities are good examples here; both have a group of researchers who continue to collaborate with one another and build on each other's work. In other areas, existing works stand more independently, and so there is little movement beyond the definitional. The lack of empiricism is another example of this lack of building on; rather than test existing ideas, researchers continue to theorize from the armchair.

Where will inspiration for complexity-based organizational psychology come from in the future? Previous work has drawn from the mathematics of nonlinear dynamical systems; agent-based and other computational models, and far-from-equilibrium models of emergence and self-organization. All of the concepts and models being used existed by 1995; nothing "new" from complexity science is being used by any significant number of organizational researchers, and one may reasonably question whether anything new from complexity science has really been invented since then anyway. We may have reached a point of diminishing returns with appropriating the complexity science concepts of physics and biology. Instead, future breakthroughs in complexity science may need to come from social scientists and organizational theorists. After all, organizations are the most complex entities we know of.

Summary

Over the past 20 years, complexity science has provided many benefits to existing thought in organizational science. Organizational science resides both above existing theories, providing a unified explanatory framework that gives coherence and adds nuance to organizational theories with assumptions that are resonant with complexity science and below those existing theories, providing possible generative mechanisms that explain causation at a deep, fundamental level. Organizational science also provides a conceptual and methodological framework with which to study real, complex systems.

Use of complexity science in organizational research appears to be still at an early stage of development. It can be classified as falling into one of the following four areas: generative mechanisms, self-organization and emergence, adaptive search, and computational models. Applications have tended to be opportunistic, first appearing in areas in which current assumptions were most well aligned with complexity assumptions. The important pieces of work have tended to be disconnected with one another, and a unified semantic framework has not emerged. Further advancements are expected to come in areas in which the classical linear, deterministic model is most afar from reality – leadership, supply networks, and emergency response. Future work should also attempt to build on what is there already and further develop the empirical side of the science.

References

Alfaro, M., & Sepulveda, J. (2006). Chaotic behavior in manufacturing systems. *International Journal of Production Economics, 101*, 150–158.

Allen, P. M. (2001). A complex systems approach to learning, adaptive networks. *International Journal of Innovation Management, 5*, 149–180.

Anderson, P. (1999). Complexity theory and organization science. *Organization Science, 10*, 216–232.

Anderson, R., Issel, L., & McDaniel, R., Jr (2003). Nursing homes as complex adaptive systems: Relationship between management practice and resident outcomes. *Nursing Research, 52*, 12–21.

Anderson R., & McDaniel R. Jr. (2000). Managing health care organizations: Where professionalism meets complexity science. *Health Care Management Review, 25*, 83–92.

Ashby, R. (1958). Requisite variety and its implications for the control of complex systems. *Cybernetica, 1*, 1–17.

Axelrod, R., & Cohen, M. (1999). *Harnessing complexity: Organizational implications of a scientific frontier.* New York: Free Press.

Axley, S., & McMahon, T. (2006). Complexity: A frontier for management education. *Journal of Management Education, 30*, 295–315.

Bak, P. (1996). *How nature works: The science of self-organized criticality.* New York: Copernicus Press.

Barabasi, A. (2002). *Linked: The new science of networks.* Cambridge, MA: Perseus.

Begun, J. W. (1994). Chaos and complexity: Frontiers of organizational science. *Journal of Management Inquiry, 3*, 329–335.

Begun, J., Dooley, K., & Zimmerman, B. (2003). Health care organizations as complex adaptive systems. In S. M. Mick & M. Wyttenbach (Eds.), *Advances in health care organization theory* (pp. 253–288). San Francisco: Jossey-Bass.

Boisot, M. H. (1995). *Information space: A framework for learning in organizations, institutions and culture.* Routledge: London.

Boisot, M., & Child, J. (1999). Organizations as adaptive systems in complex environments: The case of China. *Organization Science, 10*, 237–252.

Boje, D. (1991). Organizations as storytelling networks: A study of story performance in an office supply firm. *Administration Science Quarterly, 36*, 106–206.

Boje, D. (1999). *Five centuries of mechanistic–organic debate.* Retrieved May 20, 2007, from http://business.nmsu.edu/~dboje/between.html

Boje, D. (2001). TAMARA manifesto. *Tamara: Journal of Critical Postmodern Organization Science; 1*, 15–25.

Brown, S. L., & Eisenhardt, K. M. (1997). The art of continuous change: Linking complexity theory and time-paced evolution in relentlessly shifting organizations. *Administrative Science Quarterly, 42*, 1–34.

Burns, T., & Stalker, G. (1961). *The management of innovation.* London: Tavistock Press.

Cheng, Y.-T., & Van de Ven, A. H. (1996). Learning the innovation journey: Order out of chaos? *Organization Science, 7,* 593–614.

Chiles, T., Meyer, A., & Hench, T. (2004). Organizational emergence: The origin and transformation of Branson, Missouri's musical theaters. *Organization Science, 15,* 499–520.

Choi, T., Dooley, K., & M. Rungtusanatham (2001). Supply networks and complex adaptive systems: Control versus emergence. *Journal of Operations Management, 19,* 351–366.

Cohen, M., & March, J., & Olsen A. (1972). Garbage can model of organizational choice. *Administrative Science Quarterly, 17,* 1–25.

Corman, S., Kuhn, T., McPhee, R., & Dooley, K. (2002). Studying complex discursive systems: Centering resonance analysis of organizational communication. *Human Communication Research, 28,* 157–206.

Dingley, J., & Durkhelm, M. (1997). Morality and management. *Journal of Business Ethics, 16,* 1–18.

Dooley, K. (1997). A complex adaptive systems model of organization change. *Nonlinear Dynamics, Psychology, & Life Sciences, 1,* 69–97.

Dooley, K. (2002). Organizational complexity. In M. Warner (Ed.), *International encyclopedia of business and management* (pp. 5013–5022). London: Thompson Learning.

Dooley, K. (2004a). Complexity science models of organizational change. In S. Poole & A. Van De Ven (eds.), *Handbook of organizational change and development* (pp. 354–373). Oxford: Oxford University Press.

Dooley, K. (2004b, July). *The semantic evolution of Nonlinear Dynamics, Psychology, and Life Sciences.* Paper presented to the annual conference of the Society for Chaos Theory in Psychology and Life Sciences Conference, Milwaukee, Wisconsin.

Dooley, K., Corman, S., McPhee, R., & Kuhn, T. (2003). Modeling high-resolution broadband discourse in complex adaptive systems. *Nonlinear Dynamics, Psychology, and Life Sciences, 7,* 61–86.

Dooley, K., Johnson, T., & Bush, D. (1995). TQM, chaos, and complexity. *Human Systems Management, 14,* 1–16.

Dooley, K., & Van de Ven, A. (1999). Explaining complex organizational dynamics. *Organization Science, 10,* 358–372.

Ethiraj, S., & Levinthal, D. (2004). Modularity and innovation in complex systems. *Management Science, 50,* 159–173.

Eoyang, G. (1997). *Coping with chaos: Seven simple tools.* Cheyenne, WY: Lagumo Press.

Eve, R. A., Horsfall, S. & Lee, M. (Eds.). (1997). *Chaos, complexity, and sociology: Myths, models, and theories.* Thousand Oaks, CA: Sage.

Feichtinger, G., & Kopel, M. (1993). Chaos in nonlinear dynamical systems exemplified by an R & D model. *European Journal of Operational Research, 68,* 145–159.

Fioretti, G., & Visser, B. (2004). A cognitive interpretation of organizational complexity. *Emergence: Complexity and Organization, 6,* 11–23.

Gleick, J. (1987). *Chaos: Making of a new science.* Harmondsworth, England: Penguin Books.

Goldstein, J. (1988): A far-from-equilibrium systems approach to resistance to change. *Organizational Dynamics, 17,* 16–26.

Goldstein, J. (1994). *The unshackled organization: Facing the challenge of unpredictability through spontaneous reorganization.* Portland, OR: Productivity Press.

Goldstein, J. (2004). Emergence then and now: Concepts, criticisms, and rejoinders. *Emergence: Complexity and Organization, 6,* 66–71.

Guastello, S. (1995). *Chaos, catastrophe, and human affairs.* Mahwah, NJ: Erlbaum.

Guastello, S. (2002). *Managing emergent phenomena.* Mahwah, NJ: Erlbaum.

Guastello, S. (2004). Progress in applied nonlinear dynamics: Welcome to NDPLS Volume 8. *Nonlinear Dynamics, Psychology, and Life Sciences, 8,* 1–16.

Guastello, S. (2005). Statistical distributions and self-organizing phenomena: What conclusions should be drawn? *Nonlinear Dynamics, Psychology, and Life Sciences, 9,* 463–478.

Guastello, S. J., & Bond, R. W., Jr. (2007). The emergence of leadership in coordination-intensive groups. *Nonlinear Dynamics, Psychology, and Life Sciences, 11,* 91–117.

Guastello, S., Craven, J., Zygowicz, K., & Bock, B. (2005). A rugged landscape model for self-organization and emergent leadership in creative problem solving and production groups. *Nonlinear Dynamics, Psychology, and Life Sciences, 9,* 297–334.

Guastello, S., Dooley, K., & Goldstein, J. (1995). Chaos, organizational theory, and organizational development. In A. Gilgen, & F. Abraham (Eds.), *Chaos theory in psychology* (pp. 267–278). Westport, CT: Praeger.

Haslett T., & Osborne C. (2003). Local rules: Emergence on organizational landscapes. *Nonlinear Dynamics, Psychology, and Life Sciences, 7,* 87–98.

Hayles, N. K. (1991). Introduction: Complex dynamics in science and literature. In N. K. Hayles (Ed.), *Chaos and order: Complex dynamics in literature and science* (pp. 1–36). Chicago: University of Chicago Press.

Hazy, J. K. (2006). Measuring leadership effectiveness in complex socio-technical systems. *Emergence: Complexity and Organization, 8,* 58–77.

Hirooka, M. (2006). Complexity in discrete innovation systems. *Emergence: Complexity and Organization, 8,* 20–34.

Holland, J. H. (1995). *Hidden order.* Reading, MA: Addison-Wesley.

Kauffman, S. (1995). *At home in the universe.* Oxford: Oxford University Press.

Kellert, S. (1994). *In the Wake of Chaos.* Chicago: University of Chicago Press.

Kelly, S., & Allison, M. (1999). *The complexity advantage: How the science of complexity can help your business achieve peak performance.* New York: McGraw-Hill.

La Porte, T., & Consolini, P. (1991). Working in practice but not in theory: Theoretical challenges of high-reliability organizations. *Journal of Public Administration Research and Theory, 1,* 19–47.

Leifer, R. (1989). Understanding organizational transformation using a dissipative structure model. *Human Relations, 42,* 899–916.

Letiche, H. (2000). Self-organization, action theory and entrainment. *Emergence: Complexity and Organization, 2,* 24–37.

Levinthal, D. A. (1997). Adaptation on rugged landscapes. *Management Science, 43,* 934–950.

Levinthal, D. A., & Warglien, M. (1999). Landscape design: Designing for local action in complex worlds. *Organization Science, 10,* 342–357.

Levy, D. (1994). Chaos theory and strategy: Theory, application and managerial implications. *Strategic Management Journal, 15,* 167–178.

Lichtenstein, B. (1997). Grace, magic and miracles: A "chaotic logic" of organizational transformation. *Journal of Organizational Change Management, 10,* 393–411.

Lichtenstein, B. (2000). Self-organized transitions: A pattern amid the chaos of transformative change. *Academy of Management Executive, 14,* 128–141.

Lichtenstein, B., Carter, N., Dooley, K., & Gartner, W. (2007). Dynamics of organizational emergence: Pace, punctuation, and timing in nascent entrepreneurship. *Journal of Business Venturing, 22,* 236–261.

Lichtenstein, B., Dooley, K., & Lumpkin, T. (2006). An emergence event in new venture creation: Measuring the dynamics of nascent entrepreneurship. *Journal of Business Venturing, 21,* 153–175.

Lichtenstein, B., & Mendenhall, M. (2001). Nonlinearity and responsibility: Emergent order in 21st century careers. *Human Relations, 55,* 5–32

Lissack, M. R. (1999). Complexity: The science, its vocabulary, and its relation to organizations. *Emergence: Complexity and Organization, 1,* 110–126.

MacIntosh, R., & MacLean, D. (1999). Conditioned emergence: A dissipative structures approach to transformation. *Strategic Management Journal, 20,* 297–321.

Maguire, S. (1999). Strategy as design: A fitness landscape framework. In M. Lissack & H. Gunz (Eds.), *Managing complexity in organizations: A view in many directions* (pp. 67–104). Westport, CT: Quorum.

Maguire, S., & McKelvey, B. (1999). *Complexity and management: Moving from fad to firm foundations. Emergence: Complexity and Organization, 1,* 19–61.

Mandelbrot, B. (1982). *The fractal geometry of nature.* San Francisco, WH: Freeman and Co.

March, J. G., & Simon, H. (1958). *Organizations.* New York: McGraw-Hill.

Marion, R. (1999). *The edge of organization: Chaos and complexity theories of formal social systems.* Thousand Oaks, CA: Sage.

Marion, R., & Uhl-Bien, M. (2001). Leadership in complex organizations. *Leadership Quarterly, 12,* 389–418.

Marion, R., & Uhl-Bien, M. (2003). Complexity theory and Al-Qaeda: Examining complex leadership. *Emergence: Complexity and Organization, 5,* 56–78.

McCarthy, I., Tsinopoulos, C., Allen, P., & Rose-Anderssen, C. (2006). New product development as a complex adaptive system of decisions. *Journal of Product Innovation Management, 23,* 437–456.

McDaniel, R., Jr. (1997). Strategic leadership: A view from quantum and chaos theories. *Health Care Management Review, 22,* 21–37.

McDaniel, R., Jr., & Driebe. D. (2001). Complexity science and health care management. In M. D. Fottler, G. T. Savage & J. D. Blair (Eds.), *Advances in health care management* (pp. 11–36). Oxford: Elsevier Science.

McDaniel, R., Jr., Jordan, M., & Fleeman, B. (2003). Surprise, surprise, surprise! A complexity science view of the unexpected. *Health Care Management Review, 28,* 266–278.

McKelvey, B. (1999). Avoiding complexity catastrophe in coevolutionary pockets: Strategies for rugged landscapes. *Organization Science, 10,* 294–321.

McKelvey, B. (2002). Complexity and leadership. In M. Lissack (Ed.), *The interaction of complexity and management* (pp. 85–90). Westport, CT: Quorum Books.

McKelvey, B. (2004a). Complexity science as order creation science: New theory, new method. *Emergence: Complexity and Organization, 6*, 2–27.

McKelvey, B. (2004b). Toward a complexity science of entrepreneurship. *Journal of Business Venturing, 19*, 313–341.

McKelvey, B., & Andriani, P. (2006). Why Gaussian statistics are mostly wrong for strategic organization. *Strategic Organization, 3*, 219–228.

Merry, U. (1999). Organizational strategy on different landscapes: A new science approach. *Systemic Practice and Action Research, 12*, 257–278.

Meyer, A., Gaba, V., & Colwell, K. (2005). Organizing far from equilibrium: Nonlinear change in organizational fields. *Organization Science, 16*, 456–473.

Mintzberg, H., & Waters, J. A. (1985). Of strategies, deliberate and emergent. *Strategic Management Journal, 6*, 257–72.

Mitleton-Kelly, E. (2003). Ten principles of complexity and enabling structures. In E. Mitleton-Kelly (Ed.), *Complex systems and evolutionary perspectives of organizations: The application of complexity theory to organizations* (pp. 23–50). London: Elsevier.

Morgan, G. (1986). *Images of organization*, Newbury Park, CA: Sage.

Nonaka, I., & Takeuchi, H. (1995). *The knowledge creating company: How Japanese companies create the dynamics of innovation.* New York: Oxford University Press.

Oliver, D., & Roos, J. (1999). *Striking a balance: Complexity and knowledge landscapes.* London: McGraw-Hill.

Olson, E., & Eoyang, G. (2001). *Facilitating organizational change: Lessons from complexity science.* San Francisco: Jossey-Bass.

Osborn, R. N., Hunt, J. G., & Jauch, L. R. (2002). Toward a contextual theory of leadership. *Leadership Quarterly, 13*, 797–837.

Perrow, C. (1984). *Normal accidents: Living with high-risk technologies.* New York: Basic Books.

Plsek, P. E., & Wilson, T. (2001). Complexity, leadership, and management in healthcare organizations. *British Medical Journal, 323*, 746–749.

Poole, M., Van de Ven, A., Dooley, K., & Holmes, M. (2000). *Organizational change and innovation processes: Theory and methods for research.* Oxford: Oxford Press.

Priesmeyer, H. R. (1992). *Organizations and chaos.* Westport, CT: Quorum Books.

Prigogine, I., & Stengers, I. (1984). *Order out of chaos: Man's new dialogue with nature.* New York: Bantam.

Rasmussen, D., & Mosekilde, R. (1988). Bifurcations and chaos in a genetic management model. *European Journal of Operational Research, 35*, 80–88.

Regine, B., & Lewin, R. (2000). Leading at the edge: How leaders influence complex systems. *Emergence: Complexity and Organization, 2*, 5–23.

Riggle, C., & Madey, G. (1997). An analysis of the impact of chaotic dynamics on management information flow models. *European Journal of Operational Research, 103*, 242–254.

Rivkin, J. W. (2000). Imitation of complex strategies. *Management Science, 46*, 824–844.

Rivkin, J. W., & Siggelkow, N. (2002). Organizational sticking points on NK landscapes, *Complexity, 7*, 31–43.

Rivkin, J. W., & Siggelkow, N. (2003). Balancing search and stability: Interdependencies among elements of organizational design. *Management Science, 49*, 290–311.

Schelling T. (1978). *Micromotives and macrobehavior.* New York: Norton.

Sherif, K. (2006). An adaptive strategy for managing knowledge in organizations. *Journal of Knowledge Management, 10,* 72–80.

Shumate, M., Bryant, J. A., & Monge, P. (2005). Storytelling and globalization: The complex narratives of netwar. *Emergence: Complexity and Organization, 7,* 74–84.

Siggelkow, N., & Levinthal, D. (2003). Temporarily divide to conquer: Centralized, decentralized, and reintegrated organizational approaches to exploration and adaptation. *Organization Science, 14,* 650–669.

Siggelkow, N., & Rivkin, J.W. (2005). Speed and search: Designing organizations for turbulence and complexity. *Organization Science, 16,* 101–122.

Sinha, K. K., & Van de Ven, A. (2005). Designing work within and between organizations. *Organization Science, 15,* 389–408.

Smilor, R. W., & Feeser, H. R. (1991). Chaos and the entrepreneurial process: Patterns and policy implications for technology entrepreneurship. *Journal of Business Venturing, 6,* 165–172.

Stacey, R. D. (1992). *Managing the unknowable: Strategic boundaries between order and chaos in organizations.* San Francisco: Jossey-Bass.

Stacey, R. D. (1995). The science of complexity: An alternative perspective for strategic change. *Strategic Management Journal, 6,* 477–96.

Surana, A., Kumara, S., Greaves, M., & Raghavan, U. (2005). Supply-chain networks: A complex adaptive systems perspective. *International Journal of Production Research, 43,* 4235–4265.

Taylor, W. W. (1911). *The principles of scientific management.* New York: Harper.

Thietart, R., & Forgues, B. (1995). Chaos theory and organization. *Organization Science, 6,* 19–31.

Thompson, J. (1967). *Organizations in action.* New York: McGraw-Hill.

Tsoukas, H. (1998). Introduction: Chaos, complexity and organization theory. *Organization, 5,* 291–313.

Tsoukas, H., & Hatch, M. J. (2001). Complex thinking, complex practice: The case for a narrative approach to organizational complexity. *Human Relations, 54,* 979–1013.

Van Maanen, J. (1995). Style as theory. *Organizational Science, 6,* 133–143.

Weick, K. (1995). *Sensemaking in organizations.* Thousand Oaks, CA: Sage.

Weick, K., & Sutcliffe, K. (2001). *Managing the unexpected.* San Francisco, CA: Jossey-Bass.

Wu, Y., & Zhang, D. (2007). Demand fluctuation and chaotic behaviour by interaction between customers and suppliers. *International Journal of Production Economics, 107,* 250–259.

Yuan, Y., & McKelvey, B. (2004). Situated learning theory: Adding rate and complexity effects via Kauffman's NK model. *Nonlinear Dynamics, Psychology, and Life Sciences, 8,* 65–102.

Zimmerman, B., Lindberg, C., & Plsek, P. (1998). *Edgeware: Insights from complexity science for health care leaders.* Irving, TX: VHA.

15 Complexity, Evolution, and Organizational Behavior

PETER ALLEN

Introduction

The many approaches and ideas that have been developed in exploring the relationship between complexity and organizational behavior have been reviewed recently by Maguire, McKelvey, Mirabeau, and Oztas (2006), in the *Handbook of Organizational Studies*. I do not attempt to summarize this wide-ranging review but instead try to put forward a personal view of the way that complexity allows us to understand evolutionary processes and, in particular, the emergence and characteristics of organizations. This is because organizations are the result of evolutionary processes, shaped by history and playing some role within a larger system. Their current structure and form are something that has emerged as the result of the particular historical processes that have been involved and of course, this evolution is still ongoing and will lead to further transformations as the complex system adapts and changes to its changing context.

The context of an organization is, of course, its physical, economic, and technological environment, as well as other organizations, individuals, and the cultural and social realities of the moment. As Tsoukas and Chia (2002) said, "Firstly, organization is the attempt to order the intrinsic flux of human action, to channel it towards certain ends by generalizing and institutionalizing particular cognitive representations. Secondly, organization is a pattern that is constituted, shaped, and emerging from change" (p. 567). The coevolution of an organization with its context is therefore about the continual to and fro of modification as the "inside" and the "outside" of the organization restructure over time, blurring the separation and indeed, sometimes radically redefining the boundary. Thus organizations may separate into different specialist arms or outsource work that was previously done in-house. A supply chain may become the relevant competitive unit rather than the firm, and indeed, we may see that evolution is governed by an ecology of interacting entities, none of which control the changes that are occurring.

452

In a recent review of complexity and organizational change Burnes (2005) pointed out that there is in fact a large consensus that organizations are facing unprecedented levels of change and that their ability to manage change is therefore of great importance (Brown & Eisenhardt, 1997; Cooper & Jackson 1997; Dawson. 2003; Dunphy, Griffiths, & Benn, 2003; Greenwald, 1996; Johnson & Scholes, 2002; Kanter, Kao, & Wiersema, 1997; Kotter, 1996; Peters, 1997; Romanelli & Tushman, 1994). However, despite the gravity of the situation organizational change has proved to be difficult, with up to 80% failure rate (Beer & Nohria 2000; Brodbeck 2002; Bryant 1998; Burnes 2004, 2005; Clarke 1999; Harung Heaton, & Alexander 1999; Huczynski & Buchanan 2001; Stickland 1998; Styhre 2002; Zairi, Letza, & Oakland, 1994). This suggests that the traditional way of looking at and planning organizational change and evolution is somewhat flawed, and that perhaps complexity can offer us some help in improving this performance.

Despite the ubiquitous nature of evolutionary processes, we still tend to understand and make sense of what is occurring by looking at successive "snapshots" of the organization at different moments. Understanding these changes becomes related to seeing these as successive "stable" (temporarily) regimes of operation. These arise and persist (temporarily) when the interactions between their heterogeneous elements are such as to lead to a flow of resources from the environment, necessary to maintain the elements and their coordination. Clearly, any structure or organization can either persist by finding an environment that will maintain it, or it must adapt itself to draw sustenance from where it is. Ultimately then, it is the second law of thermodynamics that dictates that the persistence of any coherent structure requires supporting flows of energy and matter, and to a necessary coevolution of structure and flows.

The importance of the openness of an organization to its environment points to the absolutely fundamental significance of the idea of the "fit" between an organization and its environment. The immediate implication is that the "fitness" of any organization or structure is a measure of its ability to elicit, capture or merit resources from its environment. To maintain "fitness" in a changing environment, then, it will be necessary for the organization to be capable of actively transforming itself over time.

The ability to transform itself creates a second level of explanation of organizational behavior. The first level is that it must be such as to obtain resources from the current environment. The second is that it must also be capable of changing itself in such a way as to respond to the changing environment. This environment may well consist, among other things, of other organizations with similar objectives, and so we can directly see that there will be two directions of change: (a) the ability to out compete similar organizations or (b) the ability to discover other "niches" that can still command resources, but which escape the competition.

In this chapter, I use complex systems ideas to show how we can understand organizational behavior and reveal the elements and characteristics that lead to successful organizations. I consider evolutionary drive, ignorance and learning, and evolutionary computation models for fisheries, emergent markets, and manufacturing strategies.

Evolutionary Drive

Evolutionary drive was put forward some years ago (Allen & McGlade, 1987a) as the underlying mechanism that describes the change and transformation of complex systems. In this view, evolution is driven by the interplay over time of processes that create microdiversity at the elemental level of the system and the selection operated by the collective dynamic that results from their interaction together with that of the system with its environment.

This coevolution is seen as a continuous, ongoing process and not one that has already "run its course," as in the case of "evolutionary stable strategies" (Maynard-Smith, 1979). Because of the ignorance of individuals as to the pay-offs that will occur over time for a given behavior, there are always new aspects of microdiversity that can occur, so that coevolution never reaches an "optimal" as in the game theory approach. Instead, we see this multilevel exploration and retention process as an ongoing process that is occurring in real time, enabling the system to respond to currently undefined changes in the environment. History is still running. Each behavioral type is in interaction with others, and therefore evolutionary improvements may lead to greater synergy or conflict between behaviors, and in turn to lead to a chain of responses without any obvious end. If there is no end, then the most that can be said of the behavior of any particular individual or population is that its continued existence proves *only that it has been "good enough," but not that it is optimal.*

This brings evolutionary drive very close to the ideas of creative destruction and evolutionary economics expressed initially by Schumpeter (1942/1975), Foster and Kaplan (2001), Metcalfe (1998, 1999), as well as to the views of Tsoukas and Chia (2002) who see organization as an emergent and passing outcome of an ongoing evolution, as captured by Fig 15.1. We shall therefore establish the basis of the complex evolutionary processes that give rise to the emergence and development of organizations and the behaviors and identities of the participating elements and individuals.

My aim here is to show that successful organizations require underlying mechanisms that continuously create internal microdiversity of ideas, practices, schemata, and routines – not that they will all be taken up, but so that they may be discussed, possibly tried out, and then either retained or rejected. It is this that will drive an evolving, emergent system that is characterised by qualitative, structural change. These mechanisms also explain exaptation (Gould, 2002;

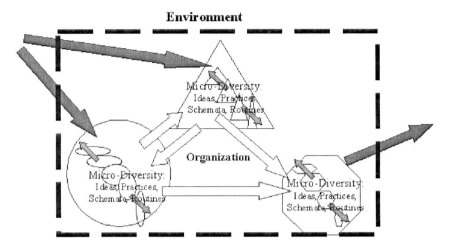

Figure 15.1. A multilevel coevolution occurs between the internal microdiversity of elements because of their differential performance within the organization and environment.

Gould & Vrba, 1982) because the microdiversity preexists the "uses" and "niches" that they later embody.

It firmly anchors success in the future on the tolerance of seemingly unnecessary perspectives, views, and ideas, because it is through the future implementation of some of these that survival will be achieved. If we define the diversity within an organization as the different functional types that are present – the number of different boxes in a systems diagram – then this system diversity is in fact driven by the existence of microdiversity within the functional types – at the level below. In other words, the organizational behavior and the functional types that comprise it *now*, have been created from the competitive or cooperative interactions of the microdiversity that occurred within them in the *past*.

Ignorance and Learning

Let us now consider the practical reality of the way that evolution occurs. Initially, we may suppose that we have the simplest possible system of interacting elements that are of the same type, but differ from each other in detail. Nobody knows whether these differences will make a difference – maybe they are just random variations around a reasonable average. Consider, however, that there is in fact a "fitness" landscape that actually reflects better and worse "fit" to the environment for the different variations. In biology, the variation is caused by genetic variation that leads to phenotypic heterogeneity, so that the fitness landscape will provide differential survival and reproduction rates, thus amplifying the fitter, and suppressing the less fit. In this way, the existence of

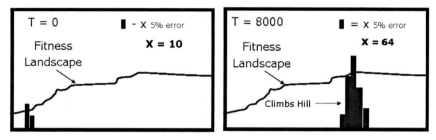

Figure 15.2. Microdiversity production will lead to many nonviable types, but the population will still evolve greater fitness and climb the fitness landscape.

mechanisms that provoke genetic and phenotypic variation will automatically produce the exploration of the fitness landscape. Within organizations, however, evolutionary change will require the differences in performance of the different individuals, ideas, practices, or routines, to be noticed and then for what works well to be deliberately reinforced, and what works less well to be discouraged. However, in a competitive market it will be true that differential performance will also serve to amplify automatically the fitter firms and suppress the less fit. Of course, "fitter" will be defined now by customers and investors through the choices they make. In any case, it is necessary to have multiple possible ideas, routines, practices, and behaviors inside organizations to provide a spread of behaviors on which differential dynamics can act. Differential dynamics are really the "selection" term of Darwin, operated by the environment, through either the upper echelons of the organization or the customers and investors of the marketplace. The organization chooses among various possible practices, routine, and so on; the market chooses between various possible products and services made by firms – and the only thing that is certain is that if there is no diversity to make choices available, then nothing can happen. Evolution can occur only if there is something that will generate heterogeneity spontaneously. This is, in fact, ignorance, or a lack of commonly agreed on norms of how things should be done that allows creative individual beliefs about what may work. Individual freedom and nonconformity are the secret power behind learning and evolution.

We can devise a simple computer program to demonstrate this idea by considering a population that initially sits at a low point of a fitness landscape and then has random variation of individual fitness. These are equally distributed left and right, but those that are of higher fitness are amplified slightly compared with those of lower fitness, and so gradually the population will "climb" the fitness landscape as in Figure 15.2.

This experiment tells us that the population increases in fitness – climbs the hill – because of processes of "exploration" in character space. Ignorance and error making are robust sources of such exploration. Clearly random changes in the design of any complicated entity will mean that most experiments are simply

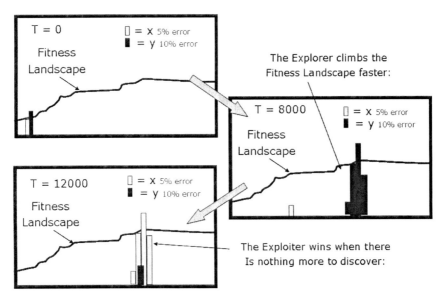

Figure 15.3. If we have two populations with different rates of "exploration," then we find that the relative success changes from early exploration to late exploitation.

nonviable, and only half (randomly) of those that remain are "better." This effectively tells us that there is an "opportunity cost" to behavioral exploration. This is illustrated with the "before" and "after" pictures of Figure 15.2 with a species climbing the fitness landscape by simply making random "errors" in its reproduction.

In a second experiment we can examine "how much" diversity creation (error making) wins in the discovery of better performance. In this experiment, we launch two populations simultaneously at the foot of the fitness hill and see how successfully they climb it. Here Population 1 is assumed to have a 5% exploration rate in character space, whereas Population 2 has 10%. However, we also make the assumption that of these "random" experiments, only 2% are actually viable, which means that there is a considerable "opportunity" cost in exploring rather than making perfect copies. Initially, Population 2 wins, because, despite its cost in nonviable individuals, diffusing faster is rewarded by the fitness slope but later when the hill is climbed, faster diffusion in no longer rewarded and Population 1 dominates. This sequence of events is shown in Figure 15.3.

Our model shows that when we are in a new domain and there is much to learn, then high rates of exploration pay off. However, when we are in a mature system that has already been thoroughly explored, there is no point wasting effort on further exploration. Of course, we can only know whether there are opportunities by actually engaging in exploration, but clearly, unless there is some structural change, the value of exploration falls with sector maturity, and this will lead exploration behavior to switch to exploitation.

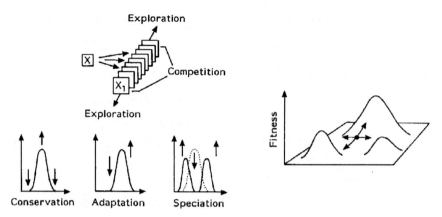

Figure 15.4. The coupled effects of mechanisms producing individual heterogenity and differential performance in the collective dynamics leads to evolutionary drive.

The production of individual heterogeneity leads to differential performance of the collective dynamics, leading to the amplification of some individual types and the suppression of others (Fig. 15.4). This in turn leads to changing performance at the level of the organization as a whole, and to a changing role in the larger environment. The performance of the organization within the wider environment changes as a result, and this will tend to amplify organizations in which internal learning is working well, and to suppress those where it is not. This also means that where there is selection at the lower level in favor of behaviors that do not improve the organizational performance as a whole, then these will tend to be eliminated as a result of competition in the environment. Evolutionary drive will automatically lead to the selection of organizations in which there is an alignment between the selection processes at the individual level and at the organizational level.

In human systems, the typical development of economic sectors and markets, as shown by Hirooka (2003), both expresses and results from the fact that initially search is rewarded, and therefore the bundling of components attracts investments (Fig. 15.5). However, as the sector becomes well established, the payoffs to new types of products falls, and so investment falls. It then switches to some other area that may seem to offer better opportunities. This is exactly what our simple theoretical model above predicts.

The presence of firms with different levels of exploration and exploitation (error making and accuracy) will automatically lead to evolution selecting whichever is most appropriate. So evolution will be driven by the amount of diversity generation to which it leads.

Evolution selects for an appropriate capacity to evolve, and this will be governed by the balance between the costs of experimental "failures" (the nonviable individuals created) and the improved performance capabilities discovered by the exploration. This is what holds "total diversity generation" in check.

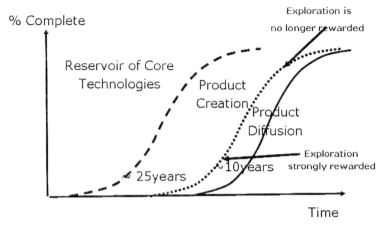

Figure 15.5. The evolution of any industrial sector (here consumer electronics) may be explained by a similar dynamics, where investment gradually switches from exploration to exploitation.

Complexity and Evolutionary Drive

Having examined some simple examples, we find a clear outcome. Evolutionary drive tells us that evolution is driven by the noise to which it leads. Providing that microscopic diversity (noise) is produced in systems of interacting populations, the dynamics resulting from the interactions will lead to the retention and amplification of some and to the suppression of others. Not only that, the selection process operated by the "level above" will automatically select for individuals and groups that retain the ability to create microdiversity. This process will select for evolvability as well as for particular types of microdiversity at a given time. The implication is that there will never be a completely clear understanding of any evolving system at a given time, because it will always contain microdiverse elements that may or may not turn out to be successful. The understanding that we can have of reality is obtained by creating a "system" of interacting entities that are sufficiently correct to describe the current situation but inadequate to predict the future structural evolution that may occur.

We understand situations by making creative, but simplifying, assumptions. We define the domain in question (the boundary) and by establishing some rules of classification (a dictionary) that allow us to say what things were present when. We thus describe things strategically in terms of words that stand for classes of object. The "evolutionary tree" is an abstraction concerning types of things rather than things themselves. To go further in our thinking and to get more information about an actual situation, we then consider only the present, and, say, what is this system made of *now*, and how is it operating *now*. This is "operational" not strategic. It therefore assumes structural stability and takes us away from open, evolutionary change, to the effects of running a fixed set of

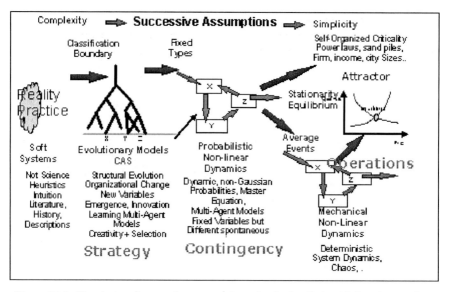

Figure 15.6. The choice of successive assumptions that lead to "scientific" understanding of a situation.

processes. If the events considered are discreet, then the running is according to a probabilistic dynamics, and we have what is called stochastic nonlinear dynamics, where different regimes of operation are possible, but the underlying elements never change nor learn, nor tire of their behaviors. If we assume that we can use average rates instead of probabilities for the events, then we arrive at deterministic, system dynamics. This is in general, nonlinear dynamics and may involve cycles, chaos, or equilibria, but what happens is certain, simple, and easy to understand.

In Figure 15.6, we show how successive assumptions are made to "understand" the real situation. On the left-hand side, we have the "cloud" of reality and practice. Here, we are in the realm of nonscience, in which people try to sum their experiences informally and come up with heuristic rules and folklore of various kinds to deal with the problems of the real world.

Science begins by deciding on a boundary within which explanation will be attempted, in the context of the environment outside. The second assumption is that of classification. The elements present within the boundary are classified into types, so that potentially, previously established behavior and responses of similar types can be used to predict behavior (Table 15.1). In examining any system of interest over some long time, however, it will be found that the components and elements present in the system have in fact changed over time. Qualitative evolution has occurred in which some types of component have disappeared, others have changed and transformed, and still others have appeared in the system initially as innovations and novelties. This possibility

Table 15.1. *The general complexity framework*

Number	Assumption made	Resulting model
1	Boundary assumed	Some local sense-making possible – no structure supposed
2	Classification assumed	Strategic, open-ended evolutionary – structural change occurs; statistical distributions part of evolutionary process, can be multimodal
3	Average types	Operational, probabilistic, nonlinear equations, master equations, Kolmogorov equations – assumed structurally stable; statistical distributions can be multimodal or power laws
First Pathway		
4	Statistical attractors	Self-organized criticality, power law distributions
Second Pathway		
4	Average events, dynamics of average agents	Deterministic mechanical equations, system dynamics – assumed structurally stable; no statistical distribution.
5	Attractors of nonlinear dynamics	Study of attractors, catastrophe theory; nonlinear dynamics with point, cyclic or chaotic/strange attractors

of transformation and evolution is the domain of the complex system that coevolves with its environment.

If we are interested in understanding the behavior of the existing system, then we can simply take the inventory and description now and consider the "working" of the components. This will lead to probabilistic, coupled equations describing their interactions. These will be probabilistic in the absence of detailed knowledge of the precise, mechanical operation of the parts. This probabilistic dynamics will give rise to a dynamics of average values, of variances and higher moments, as a result of the coupled processes. Because there may be different possible attractor bases for the dynamics, the statistical distribution will reflect this, being multimodal and not a simple Gaussian or normal distribution. The dynamical system will itself generate the distribution and all its moments, including the variance, and so there will be no simplification into an "average" dynamic with a given random variance. Instead, all the moments will really play a role in defining the evolution of the distribution. These types of probabilistic dynamics are described by *Master* or *Kolmogorov equations* (Barucha-Reid, 1960) governing Markov processes and the change in the probability distributions as a result of the nonlinear interactions.

There are now two routes to simplification: (a) Consider the stationary solution of the probabilistic nonlinear dynamics – the Master or Kolmogorov equation and (b) consider the dynamics of the average, mean, or first moment of the probability distribution and assume that this can be uncoupled from the higher moments. This leads to deterministic system dynamics – a mechanical representation of the system. We can then study the attractors of this simplified system and find point, cyclic, or chaotic attractor dynamics as the long-term outcome.

This succession of models arises from making successive, simplifying assumptions, and therefore models on the right are increasingly easy to understand, and picture, but increasingly far from reality. The operation of a mechanical system may be easy to understand, but that simplicity has assumed away the more complex sources of its ability to adapt and change. A mechanical model is more like a "description" of the system at a particular moment but does not contain the magic ingredient of microdiversity that constitutes evolutionary drive. The capacity to evolve is generated by the behaviors that are averaged (and hence removed) by Assumptions 3 and 4 – that of average types and average events. Organizations or individuals that can adapt and transform themselves do so as a result of the spontaneous generation of microdiversity within its microcontextualities, although without knowing which novelties will prove successful or how the larger system will be affected. This captures for us the meaning of Prigogine's phrase concerning complexity – "From Being to Becoming" (Prigogine, 1981) between a reality that is dead, a fixed mechanical representation, instead of the unpredictable, living reality of our experience, a reality that is continually "becoming."

Modeling Human Systems

Behaviors, practices, routines, and technologies are invented, learned, and transmitted over time between successive actors and firms, and I discuss here how the principles of evolutionary drive can be used to understand them as well in human systems as in the biological.

A Fisheries Example

A detailed model was developed of Canadian Atlantic fisheries (Allen, 1994, 2000; Allen & McGlade, 1987b), as shown in Figure 15.7. This consists of a spatial model with 40 zones over which up to eight fleets of fishermen roam, attempting to make a living by finding and catching different fish populations. The fishermen's movements are informed by their "mental maps" of potential profit, and this is based on the information they have from other fishermen. Clearly, members of their own fleet will exchange information, but this may not be true for other fleets. The model therefore describes fishing as a result of the acquisition and exploitation of knowledge about where profits are being made by other fishermen. Thus there is a spatial positive feedback mechanism that structures fishing patterns. Of course, in deciding which zone to go to, fishermen

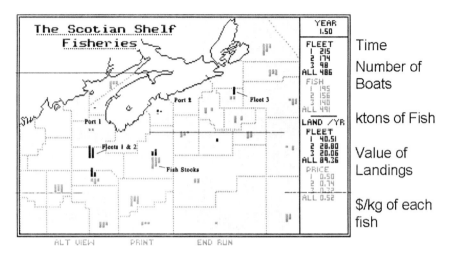

Figure 15.7. The dynamic, spatial model of learning fishing fleets, based on real data, showing that economically optimizing fishermen are unsuccessful.

take into account the distances involved to go there, and to return to port and the cost of fuel.

In addition to these effects, however, our equation takes another very important factor into account. This factor R expresses how "rationally," how "homogeneously," or with what probability a particular skipper will respond to the information he is receiving. For example, if R is small, then whatever the "real" attraction of a zone i, the probability of going to any zone is roughly the same. In other words, "information" is largely disregarded, and movement is "random." We have called this type of skipper a *stochast*. Alternatively if R is large, then it means that even the smallest difference in the attraction of several zones will result in every skipper of that fleet going, with a probability of 1.00, to the most attractive zone. In other words, such deciders put complete faith in the information they have and do not "risk" moving outside of what they *know*. These "ultra rationalists" we have called *Cartesians*. The movement of the boats around the system is generated by the difference at a given time between the number of boats that would like to be in each zone, compared with the number that actually are there. As the boats congregate in particular locations of high catch, so they fish out the fish population that originally attracted them. They must then move on the next zone that attracts them, and in this way there is a continuing dynamic evolution of fish populations and of the pattern of fishing effort.

The fishery simulation models show us that it is not true that fleets seeking profit with the highest possible economic rationality win. Indeed, the models show that it is important *not* to seek profit too ardently. Over time, higher profits are actually generated by behavior that does not seek profit maximally at any moment. The reason is because to fish for any length of time, it will be necessary not only to exploit current information about fish stocks, but to generate new, currently unknown fish stocks, and exploit them. As a result, exploitation alone is inadequate and some mix of exploration and exploitation are required. Thus the ability to learn is more important over time than is the ability to exploit efficiently. Essentially it means that there has to be exploration and then a selection using the new information generated by the exploration.

Just as in the biological model discussed earlier, humans need to generate microdiversity in their knowledge, and then make decisions based on the positive pieces of information, while being careful not to continue with exploratory behavior. This model also shows us that there is no such thing as an optimal strategy. As soon as any particular strategy becomes dominant in the system, it will always be vulnerable to the invasion of some other strategy. More important, we see that the knowledge generation of fleets arises from their ability and willingness to explore. So instead of this corresponding to ultra efficiency and rationality, it actually arises from the opposite – a lower level of rationality, and a freedom to take creative action.

Emergent Market Structure

The ideas developed in the earlier sections can also show us how important dynamic capabilities are for firms in the marketplace. Here we see how these dynamic capabilities are what is responsible for structuring of economic markets, because competition creates ecologies of firms, creating and filling interacting market niches. The fundamental process can be explored initially using a simple model in which we consider the possible growth and decline of several firms that are attempting to produce and sell goods in the same market. The potential customers of course will see the different products according to their particular desires and needs, and in the simple case examined here, we shall simply consider that customers are differentiated by their revenue and therefore have different sensitivities to price.

This model has been discussed in Allen and Varga (2007), and so we shall not give much of the detail here. Inputs and labor are necessary for production, and the cost of these added to the fixed and start-up costs produces goods that are sold by sales staff who must "interact" with potential customers to turn them into actual customers. The potential market for a product is related to its qualities and price, and although in this simple case we have assumed that customers all like the same qualities, they have a different response to the price charged. The price charged is made up of the cost of production (variable cost) to which a mark-up is added. The mark-up needs to cover the fixed and start-up costs as well as the sales staff wages. Depending on the quality and price, therefore, there are different-sized potential markets coming from the different customer segments.

When customers buy a product, they cease to be potential customers for a time that is related to the lifetime of the product. This may be longer for high-quality than for low-quality goods, but of course, many goods are bought to follow fashion and style rather than through absolute necessity. Indeed, different strategies would be required depending on whether this is the case, and so this is one of the many explorations that can be made with the model.

The model calculates the relative attractiveness of a product (of given quality and price) for a customer of a given type (poor, medium, or rich) and subsequently calculates the "potential market" for each firm at each moment. Sales staff must interact with these potential customers to turn them into customers. When a sale is made, then the potential customer becomes a customer and disappears from the market for a time that depends on the product's lifetime. The revenue from the sales of a firm is used to pay the fixed and variable costs of production, and any profit can be used either to increase production or to decrease the bank debt if there is any. In this way, the firm tries to finance its growth and to avoid going near its credit limit. If a firm exceeds its credit limit, then it is declared bankrupt and is closed down.

An important issue that arises in the modeling concerns the rationality of the managers involved in the new market. In traditional economic theories, firms might be expected to use the "profit" experienced as the driving force behind their strategies. The problem is, however, that in launching a new product the initial situation will be one of investment, not profit. Thus, if the model regulates production on the basis of the (negative) profit currently experienced, then it will shut down. Clearly this would be a foolish model, and so a more realistic model would link production to the *expected profit over some future time.* This would also be an oversimplification for two reasons. First, the manager of Firm A cannot calculate expected profits without knowing the pricing strategy of competing Firms B, C, D, and so on, and they in their turn cannot decide what their expected profits will be without knowing the strategy of Firm A. Secondly, whatever Firms A, B, C, and so on do choose as a strategy, and whatever expectations they have, many of them clearly get it wrong because a large fraction in fact make losses and go bankrupt. This tells us that firms do not calculate expected profits rationally at all, because this is impossible. Instead, they simply believe in a strategy and then discover heuristically whether it works as they thought. The market is therefore the arena for learning, in which beliefs are either reinforced or destroyed. A wise manager will be ready to modify his or her beliefs and strategy as rapidly as possible to avoid bankruptcy. Our model shows that it is the economies and diseconomies of production and distribution that will determine the number, size, and scale of the niches that may be discovered.

We can use our model to explore the effect of different learning strategies of firms (Fig. 15.8). The strategy space in view here is that of what percent profit to charge and what quality of product to make. Obviously, a lower mark-up will

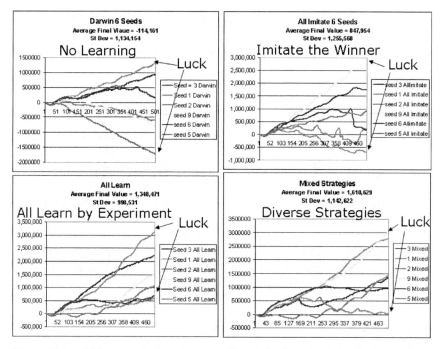

Figure 15.8. Multiple simulations show that Darwinian learning is ineffective, and the best overall performance is achieved by firms with learning mechanisms.

provide larger market share and lead to economies of scale, but these may not come soon enough to avoid bankruptcy. Alternatively, a firm can have a very high mark-up and make much profit on each unit it sells. However, its sales may be too small to allow survival.

Our model can allow us to study the effects of different learning strategies of managers. We distinguish four different types:

1. Darwinian Learning: In this case, we launch firms with random strategies, and if a firm goes bankrupt, we replace it with a new firm, with a random strategy. In this way, in theory the performance of the market will improve as unsuccessful strategies are eliminated, and only successful ones remain after a long time.

2. All Imitate: Here, firms are launched initially with random strategies, but firms move to imitate whichever strategy is winning. In this way, in theory, the resulting market should evolve to a collection of firms all using a very successful strategy.

3. All Learn: In this case, after being launched with random strategies, firms each explore the effects on profits of changing quality and mark-up. They then move up the profit slope – if possible. In this way, they demonstrate the effect of a learning strategy.

4. Mixed Strategies: Here, after a random launch, we have two Darwinists, two imitators, and two learners. This leads to an evolution of the market structure gradually exploring and changing as profit and loss select for the winners and losers.

The model demonstrates the degree to which luck plays an important role, because for these four learning strategies, results depend considerably on the particular random strategies initially chosen and on the subsequent failures and random launchings that occurred. For different random sequences, very different market evolutions occur. If we use the model to calculate the total profits of all firms present and allow for the cost of bankruptcies, then we can plot the performance of the emerging markets over time. The model shows us that for the Darwinian learning strategy, average market value achieved by the process, including the cost of bankruptcies, is actually negative. In other words, Darwinism, applied to market evolution, using bankruptcy as the selection process is so costly on average that the industry as a whole takes a loss. There is, in fact, enormous variance in the performance of the market as a whole, with some simulations showing very effective organization by chance and others with very negative performance following a different sequence of choices.

The next block of simulations looks at the performance of the market when the players all imitate any winning strategy. This does perform better than Darwinian learning on average, with an average final value of more than 800,000 compared with 114,000. The strategy seems to provide the most unstable trajectories, however, with some examples of market crashes and severe setbacks in the general pattern of improvement.

The most consistently successful performance comes from the "learning" strategy, where firms adopt an "experimental" strategy of probing their "profit" landscape and moving in the direction of increase. The fourth set of mixed strategies produces the largest average value of market performance but has very wide variance.

These simulations show us that organizational behaviors are linked through the market interactions in which they participate and that the best behavior of a firm is in fact that of "learning" what price and quality are successful in the market. In turn this requires that the firm can adapt its product and produce it competitively and that it also conducts experiments with quality and mark-up to find out how to improve its performance within the market.

Evolution of Manufacturing Organizations

The study of organizational change and strategy can be looked at by reflecting on the organizations in terms of their constituent practices and techniques. The changing patterns of practices and routines that are observed in the evolution of firms and organizations can be studied using the ideas of evolutionary drive. We would see a "cladistic diagram" (a diagram showing evolutionary history)

Table 15.2. Fifty-three characteristics of manufacturing organizations

1. Standardization of parts	27. Total Quality Management sourcing
2. Assembly time standards	28. 100% inspection sampling
3. Assembly-line layout	29. U-shaped layout
4. Reduction in craft skills	30. Preventive maintenance
5. Automation	31. Individual error correction
6. Pull production system	32. Sequential dependency of workers
7. Reduction of lot size	33. Line balancing
8. Pull procurement system	34. Team policy
9. Operator-based machine maintenance	35. Toyota verification scheme
10. Quality circles	36. Groups vs. teams
11. Employee innovation prizes	37. Job enrichment
12. Job rotation	38. Manufacturing cells
13. Large-volume production	39. Concurrent engineering
14. Mass subcontracting by subbidding	40. ABC costing
15. Exchange of workers with suppliers	41. Excess capacity
16. Training through socialization	42. Flexible automation of product versions
17. Proactive training program	43. Agile automation for different products
18. Product range reduction	44. In-sourcing
19. Automation (machine-paced shops)	45. Immigrant workforce
20. Multiple subcontracting	46. Dedicated automation
21. Quality systems	47. Division of Labor
22. Quality philosophy	48. Employees are system tools
23. Open-book policy with suppliers	49. Employees are system developers
24. Flexible multifunctional workforce	50. Product focus
25. Setup time reduction	51. Parallel processing
26. Kaizen change management	52. Dependence on written rules
	53. Further intensification of labor

showing the history of successive new practices and innovative ideas in an economic sector. It would generate an evolutionary history of both artifacts and the organizational forms that underlie their production (McCarthy, 1995; McCarthy, Leseure, Ridgeway, & Fieller, 1997; McKelvey, 1982, 1994). Let us consider manufacturing organizations in the automobile sector.

Using the characteristics in Table 15.2 as our "dictionary" we can also identify 16 distinct organizational forms: (a) ancient craft system, (b) standardized craft system, (c) modern craft system, (d) neocraft system, (e) flexible manufacturing, (f) Toyota production, (g) lean producers, (h) agile producers, (i) just in time, (j) intensive mass producers, (k) European mass producers, (l) modern mass producers, (m) pseudo-lean producers, (n) Fordist mass producers, (o) large-scale producers, and (p) skilled large-scale producers.

Cladistic theory calculates backward the most probable evolutionary sequence of events (see Fig. 15.9). Again, in agreement with the ideas of evolutionary drive, we shall look at this as being the result of micro-explorations, and then a differential amplification of systems with emergent capabilities. We

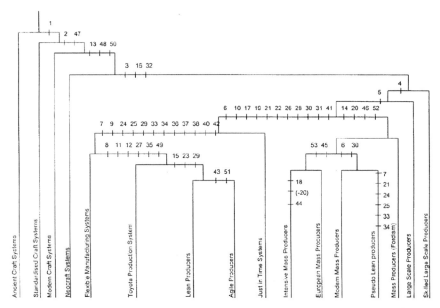

Figure 15.9. The cladistic diagram for automobile manufacturing organizational forms.

have studied the evolution of the automobile production industry by conducting a survey of manufacturers, and obtaining their estimates of the pairwise interactions between each pair of practices. In this approach, the microscopic explorations consist in the attempts to connect in new practices to an existing system, with the object of improving performance and creating positive emergent capabilities. As has been previously reported, we can understand and make retrospective sense of the evolution of the automobile industry.

We have then been able to develop an evolutionary simulation model, in which a manufacturing firm attempts to incorporate successive new practices at some characteristic rate. The "receptivity" of the existing complex determines which new practice will in fact be amplified or suppressed if it tries to "invade."

Figure 15.10 shows us one possible history of a firm over the entire period of the development of automobile production. The particular choices of practices introduced and their timing allows us to assess how their performance evolved over time and also to assess whether they would have been eliminated by other firms. As a result of the different firms experimenting over time, there is an incredible range of possible structures that can emerge, depending simply on the order in which practices are tried. Yet, each time a new practice is adopted within an organization, it changes the "invadability" or "receptivity" of the organization for any new innovations in the future. This illustrates the "path dependent evolution" that characterizes organizational change. Successful evolution is about the "discovery" or "creation" of highly synergetic structures of interacting practices.

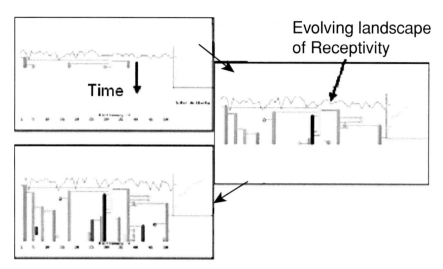

Figure 15.10. Successive moments ($t = 3,000$, $10,000$ and $15,000$) in the evolution of a particular firm. The evolutionary tree of the organization emerges over time.

The model starts off from a craft structure. New practices are launched with small initial values (actually 5). Sometimes the behavior declines to zero and disappears, and sometimes it grows up to a size of 20 or so, becoming a significant part of the "formal" structure that then changes which innovative behavior can invade next. The model shows how the 16 organizational forms have increasingly high synergy as they change in the direction of lean and agile Japanese practices. Overall performance is a function of the synergy of the practices that are tried successfully. The particular emergent attributes and capabilities of the organization are a function of the particular combination of practices that constitute it. Different simulations lead to different structures, and there are a very large number of possible "histories." This demonstrates a key idea in complex systems thinking. The explorations or innovations that are tried out at a given time cannot be logically or rationally deduced because their overall effects cannot be known ahead of time. Therefore the impossibility of prediction gives the system "choice."

The competition among firms' exploratory pathways through time means that those who for one reason or another fail to find synergetic combinations of practice will be eliminated. Once again, we find the principle of evolutionary drive, where the micro-explorations involving the testing of new practices leads to microscopic diversity among firms, and in turn these are either amplified or suppressed by the economic competition.

Conclusions

From the discussions and models presented here we can derive some key points about organizational behavior and its evolution. Organizational behavior must be such as to allow organizational evolution, or the organization will fail. The rules that allow organizational evolution are as follows:

1. The presence of mechanisms that produce internal heterogeneity, which will involve freedom, ignorance, and underlying error making, exploratory processes.
2. Differential performance needs to be detected and evaluated with respect to their alignment with higher-level goals. This will then provide the selection process that will amplify or suppress different elements of individual behavior.
3. The relative performance of the organization within the wider environment needs to be constantly reviewed and evaluated to see how the selection criteria are changing and how this may affect the capabilities and competences that the organization needs.
4. For successful organizations, as Chia and Tsoukas (2002) pointed out, aggregate descriptions will always be short-term emergent properties of an evolving system.

Successful management must behave as evolution does and make sure that mechanisms of exploration and experiment are present in the organization. Although they will not be profitable in the short term, they are the only guarantee of survival into the longer term. In reality, the organizations that we observe and describe formally at any given moment are "structural attractors" (Allen, Strathern, & Baldwin, 2005), which, if they persist over time, will change qualitatively as successive organizational forms emerge.

In classical science, a new theory must be capable of being falsified, and therefore must produce testable predictions, which if not falsified lead to genuine cumulative knowledge. In complex systems, however, clean predictions are no longer possible, and the knowledge evolves under less severe selection criteria. In ecological and human systems, emergent structural attractors can occur simply because their particular emergent capabilities or behavior succeeds in getting resources from the environment. Fashion, lifestyles, art, artifacts, and communities of practice can emerge and survive providing there is a clientele for them. They are not about being "true or false" but simply about whether there is a "market" for them. Living systems create a world of connected, coevolved, multilevel structures that may be temporally self-consistent but will evolve and change over time. In our fishing example, the organizational behavior of a successful fleet will be heterogeneous, having explorers and exploiters, who share information and allow the fleet to discover new fish concentrations and therefore to have a future beyond current information. In a marketplace, we find that our firms need to experiment with their strategy to find out how to improve profits in the moving constellation of other firms. Luck plays a role, but learning will do better than just hoping. Similarly in our study of automobile manufacturing, we can actually break down organizational behavior into its "atomic" components of working practices, skills, and techniques. Complexity tells us that as well as the "organization you see" – the set of practices – there also have to be additional agents that decide to try out new practices and determine which ones these should be. This is really the role of management, although hopefully it uses information from throughout the organization. However, the main point is that although a particular bundle of practices is what is observable at any given time, a successful evolution will require, in addition, the presence of agents that suggest new practices, discuss how to bring them in and implement them, and evaluate how they are performing.

Organizational behavior can be many things, but none of them will survive long if they are not capable of evolving and adapting over time. Complexity science provides the scientific framework in which we can understand how and why organizational behavior can be evolutionary. It is the natural result of evolutionary drive – a multilayered coevolution of the various levels of description and interaction that emerge in open, nonlinear systems.

Acknowledgement

This work was supported by the ESRC RES-000-23-0845 Aerospace project with Sheffield University.

References

Allen, P. M. (1994). Evolutionary complex systems: Models of technology change. In L. Leydesdorff & P. van den Besselaar (Eds.), *Chaos and economic theory* (pp. 1–19). London: Pinter.

Allen, P. M. (2000). Knowledge, ignorance and learning. *Emergence, 2*, 78–103.

Allen, P. M., & McGlade, J. M. (1987a). Evolutionary drive: The effect of microscopic diversity, error making & noise. *Foundation of Physics, 17*, 723–728.

Allen, P. M., & McGlade, J. M. (1987b). Modelling complex human systems: A fisheries example. *European Journal of Operational Research, 30*, 147–167.

Allen, P. M., Strathern, M., & Baldwin, J. S. (2005). Models of self-organisation and evolution in socio-economic systems. *European Journal of Economic and Social Systems, 18*, 171–199.

Allen, P. M., & Varga L. (2006). Complexity: The co-evolution of epistemology, axiology and ontology. *Nonlinear Dynamics, Psychology, and Life Sciences, 11*, 19–50.

Barucha-Reid, A. T. (1960). *Elements of the theory of Markov processes and their applications.* New York: McGraw-Hill.

Beer M., & Nohria, N. (Eds.). (2000). *Breaking the code of change.* Boston: Harvard Business School Press.

Brodbeck, P. W. (2002). Implications for organization design: Teams as pockets of excellence. *Team Performance Management: an International Journal, 8*, 21–38.

Brown, S. L., & Eisenhardt K. M. (1997). The art of continuous change: Linking complexity theory and timepaced evolution in relentlessly shifting organizations. *Administrative Science Quarterly, 42*, 1–34.

Bryant, A. (1998). Beyond BPR: Confronting the organizational legacy. *Management Decision, 36*, 25–30.

Burnes, B. (2004). *Managing change* (4th ed.). Harlow, Essex, England: FT/Prentice Hall.

Burnes, B. (2005). Complexity theories and organizational change. *International Journal of Management Reviews, 7,* 73–90.

Clarke, M. (1999). Management development: A new role in social change. *Management Decision, 37,* 767–777.

Cooper, C. L., & Jackson S. E. (Eds.). (1997). *Creating tomorrow's organizations today: A handbook for future research in organizational behavior.* Chichester, England: Wiley.

Dawson, P. (2003). *Reshaping change: A processual perspective.* London: Routledge.

Dunphy, D., Griffiths, A., & Benn S. (2003). *Organizational change for corporate sustainability.* London: Routledge.

Foster, R., & Kaplan, S. (2001). *Creative destruction.* New York: Doubleday.

Gould, S. J. (2002). *The structure of evolutionary theory.* Cambridge, MA: Belknap.

Gould, S. J., & Vrba, E. S. (1982). Exaptation – a missing term in the science of form. *Paleobiology, 8,* 4–15.

Greenwald, J. (1996). *Reinventing Sears. Time, 23* December, 53–55.

Harung, H. S., Heaton, D. P., & Alexander, C. N. (1999). Evolution of organizations in the new millennium. *Leadership and Organization Development Journal, 20,* 198–207.

Hirooka, M. (2006). *Innovation dynamism and economic growth.* Cheltenham, England: Edward Elgar.

Huczynski, A., & Buchanan, D. (2001). *Organizational behaviour* (4th ed.). Harlow Essex, England: FT/Prentice Hall.

Johnson, G., & Scholes, K. (2002). *Exploring corporate strategy* (6th ed.). Harlow Essex, England: FT/Prentice Hall.

Kanter, R. M., Kao J., & Wiersema, F. (Eds.). (1997). *Innovation: Breakthrough thinking at 3M, DuPont, GE. Pfizer, and Rubbermaid.* New York: Harper Business.

Kotter, J. P. (1996). *Leading change.* Boston: Harvard Business School Press.

Maguire, S., McKelvey, B., Mirabeau L., & Oztas, N. (2006). *Complexity science and organization studies.* In S. Clegg, C. Hardy, W. Nord, & T. Lawrence (Eds.), *Handbook of organization studies* (2nd ed., pp. 165–214). London: Sage.

Maynard-Smith, J. (1979). Game theory and the evolution of behaviour. *Proceedings of the Royal Society of London, B, 205,* 475–488.

McCarthy, I. (1995). Manufacturing classifications: Lessons from organisational systematics and biological taxonomy. *Journal of Manufacturing and Technology Management – Integrated Manufacturing Systems, 6,* 37–49.

McCarthy, I., Leseure, M., Ridgway K., & Fieller, N. (1997). Building a manufacturing cladogram. *International Journal of Technology Management, 13,* 2269–2296.

McKelvey, B. (1982). *Organizational systematics.* Berkeley: University of California Press.

McKelvey, B. (1994). Evolution and organizational science. In J. Baum & J. Singh, *Evolutionary dynamics of organizations* (pp. 314–326). Oxford: Oxford University Press.

Metcalfe, J. S. (1998). *Evolutionary economics and creative destruction.* London: Routledge.

Metcalfe, J. S (1999). *Restless capitalism, returns and growth in enterprise economics* [CRIC Technical Report]. Manchester, England: University of Manchester.

Peters, T. (1997). *The circle of innovation: You can't shrink your way to greatness.* New York: Knopf.

Prigogine (1981). *From being to becoming.* New York: Freeman.

Romanelli, E., & Tushman, M. L. (1994). Organizational transformation as punctuated equilibrium: An empirical test. *Academy of Management Journal, 37,* 1141–1166.

Schumpeter, J. A. (1975). *Capitalism, socialism and democracy.* New York: Harper. (Original work published 1942).

Stickland, F. (1998). *The dynamics of change: Insights into organisational transition from the natural world.* London: Routledge.

Styhre, A. (2002). Non-linear change in organizations: Organization change management informed by complexity theory. *Leadership and Organization Development Journal, 23,* 343–351.

Tsoukas, H., & Chia R. (2002). On organizational becoming: Rethinking organizational change. *Organization Science, 13,* 567–582.

Zairi, M., Letza, S., & Oakland, J. (1994). Does TQM impact on bottom line results? *TQM Magazine, 6,* 38–43.

16 Agent-Based Modeling Within a Dynamic Network

TERRILL L. FRANTZ AND KATHLEEN M. CARLEY

Introduction

The study of nonlinear and complex adaptive systems is well supported by both agent-based modeling (ABM) and dynamic network analysis (DNA) techniques (Carley, 2003; Dooley & Corman, 2002). When applied, separately or jointly, to research design, ABM and DNA are powerful techniques that have recurrently led to the progress of social theory over recent decades. Both have also been technological forces leading to the acceptance of computer simulation as a sound and revolutionary research methodology (Bankes, 2002); a methodology that has come to be heralded as the *third way of doing research* (Axelrod, 2006; Elliott & Kiel, 2004; Ostrom, 1988). This revolution is being further fueled by the escalating dissatisfaction with traditional research methods (Elliott & Kiel, 2004) and the ubiquity of inexpensive computing power. The growing number of success stories of applying ABM, DNA, and computer simulation to social research is rapidly escalating the broad acceptance of these tools by researchers – as evidenced by numerous supportive, scholarly articles recently published in prominent academic publications (Davis, Eisenhardt, & Bingham, 2007; Harrison, Lin, Carroll, & Carley, 2007; Henrickson, 2004).

The success of these techniques reflect the realization that in human systems the complex behaviors of individuals acting within a group are not only critical to the microlevel dynamics, but that the stability, adaptability, and evolution of the entire system can be heavily influenced by these behaviors. At the microlevel, the individuals' actions take place within an operating environment consisting of multiple and multiple types, of social and interrelated network structures. Whether studying economic markets (Kaizoji, 2002; White, 2004), terrorist groups (Carley, Reminga, & Kamneva, 2003), or a government organization such as NASA (Schreiber & Carley, 2005), understanding human behavior and the way local activity is further constrained and enabled by the networks in the environment is essential to understanding the overall group behavior. By applying ABM and DNA constructs to the design of a computer model and simulation, researchers can create a computationally based, theory-grounded, and suitably valid laboratory in which to experiment and test new social theory in an effective and cost-efficient manner.

ABM employs the use of artificial agents, typically representing humans, acting and interacting in a virtual group (i.e., an organization, community, or society). The behavior of these agents can be nondeterministic, and their inter-action within the group can result in the coevolution of complex, social, and cultural group-level dynamics. During their lifetime, these agents may move through and interact with the environment, reproduce, consume resources, age, learn, and even die. Moreover, agents are typically adaptive; they can vary individually in their information-processing capabilities, intelligence, activity frequency, and complexity. By taking the ABM approach, researchers can gener-ate a series of detailed forecasts about the behavior of a system. Depending on the assumptions built into the model, the results might be interpreted as predictions about organizing in general or about organizing in a particular context. ABM is different from alternative simulation design approaches, because the agents' behavior is characterized as a microtechnique, in which the resulting dynamics are based specifically on the interactive behaviors related to specific individuals. Other types of simulation modeling methods, such as system dynamics, are more macro-oriented, with the population itself being assigned a behavior. By using ABM, researchers can understand and spotlight the general factors and non-linear dynamics that affect either the individual or the group behavior (Carley, 1995a; Carley & Prietula, 1994; Masuch & Warglien, 1992). The ABM method-ology is especially prominent because of its successful history of advancing the development of human group theory by focusing on the nonlinear dynamics taking place (Marschak, 1955; McGuire & Radner, 1986; Radner, 1993).

DNA is an extension of the traditional social network analysis (SNA) method-ology. That is to say, DNA is a more powerful approach than the basic framework in which a researcher represents and studies the relationships among a group of people. Like SNA, DNA provides researchers with a quantitative-based toolkit in which to study the qualitative relationships within a group. However, DNA builds on SNA ideas and techniques by recognizing that the real world is made up of and influenced by many networks of abundant types that exist at many levels, rather than being influenced by a single, isolated network. For example, from the DNA perspective, a person's *friendship* network coexists with their *advice* network, which often consists of different people and relationship structures. DNA fully integrates this multinetwork perspective in its constructs and analysis perspective.

The increasing use of ABM and DNA for social research demands that psy-chology and social science researchers learn and become increasingly comfort-able with these sophisticated techniques. To succeed in the future, researchers will need to understand numerous concepts that may prove to be an intellec-tual challenge and, at a minimum, certainly will be time-consuming to grasp.

Recognizing this, the aim of this chapter is to introduce psychologists and social researchers to these contemporary concepts and methods. In terms of the organization of this chapter, we next provide a summary of the histories of ABM and DNA to situate the reader for the remainder of the chapter; this is followed by presenting computer simulation as a research strategy. Next, we present ways in which computer simulation has been applied specifically to social research, followed by a discussion on how to construct an agent-based simulation. We then describe a comprehensive simulation model of a goal-seeking, task-oriented organization that uses the ABM and DNA frameworks and then introduce specific software that can readily bring these advanced techniques to any researcher's desktop computer. Next, we identify some limitations of ABM and DNA. Finally, we discuss a few high-level implications of this new, third way of doing science.

History of Social Simulation and Network Analysis

Although their disconnected histories have now entwined, the origins of ABM and DNA have had very different trajectories. Forward progress in ABM has experienced an uninterrupted forward path, whereas the progress in network analysis experienced a start-then-stop path. In this section, we present these disconnected histories and describe how they paved the way for their present-day conjunction into becoming a powerful simulation design approach.

Computational Sociology: From Artificial Life to Agent-Based Modeling

In the 1940s, while they were working on the development of the hydrogen bomb, mathematician John von Neumann and his colleagues had a flurry of ideas that spawned three branches of scientific innovation: artificial life, cellular automata, and game theory. Their dazzling idea of creating an artificial, virtual environment within a computer for the purpose of testing scientific ideas arose as a direct outcome of the development of the bomb; the idea of taking a computational approach to the generation of lifelike behavior in a virtual environment was merely a side project. During this time, while working on self-reproducing automata, the group also began to work on abstracting the underpinnings of natural self-reproduction and during the development of this, it was conceived that the entities could be described in a cell-space format, which was the beginning of cellular automata. The abundant and innovative ideas conceived by von Neumann and his counterparts were quickly followed by developing their idea of using pure mathematical analysis to study tactical and decision-making problems in conflict situations; this field is now known as game theory. Building on the initial ideas of game theory, it was academic Albert William Tucker who conceived of the now-infamous Prisoner's Dilemma game merely to resolve the difficulty of explaining the new game-theoretic perspective to his psychology students.

The plethora of ideas spawned by the von Neumann group were followed by even more innovative ideas in the 1950s, but they came from other scientific communities. Economist George Zipf (1949) tied mathematical ideas to empirical observation by proposing that for most cities, the distribution of the population follows a power law, and biologist Ludwig von Bertalanffy launched general systems theory (GST). Early on, von Bertalanffy referred to GST's applicability to human organizations, these being viewed as an open system. Also during this decade, future Nobel laureate Herb Simon (Simon, 1952, 1957; Simon & Guetzkow, 1955) started to take portions of existing social theories and recount them mathematically. He constructed quantitative and demonstrative nonlinear models of numerous theories involving group formation, the competition of groups for members, individuals' attention between two activities, and the communication processes in small groups.

In the 1960s, Cyert and March (1963) published a theoretical model of the dynamics of an organization presented by an assemblage of computations. Toward the end of the decade, business-focused Jay Forrester (1969) demonstrated to managers, via computer simulation, how structure determines behavior by applying a feedback perspective to GST. Forrester followed this by extending GST and demonstrating its applicability beyond business decision making (Forrester, 1958) to theory development, which advanced the methods of systems dynamics to academic research (Forrester, 1969). Around the same time, Herbert Simon (1962) brought to the fore the perspective that complex systems often have a hierarchical form and that there are common properties of the subsystem hierarchy across different systems. One such universal characteristic of subsystems and their hierarchies is the idea of near-decomposability: Interactions within one subsystem are stronger than the interactions between the subsystems. In a follow-up lecture, Simon (1969) advanced the notion of using computers as a tool in the social sciences and computer simulation as a new source of knowledge.

The 1970s brought forward the introduction of Conway's Game of Life (Gardner, 1970), which used the cellular automata landscape and was the first documented attempt at applying the agent-based model to social science (Epstein & Axtell, 1996) to demonstrate the relevance of the initial state of an evolutionary system. Also during the period, future Nobel laureate Thomas Schelling (1971) developed new theories about racial segregation using cellular automata. Schelling used a checkerboard in which squares were occupied by pieces of different colors. The movements of each piece were determined by the color of the composition of its neighboring squares. As Schelling showed, simple rules for the actors based on their local environments could generate complex and interesting global patterns of segregation. Schelling also described the beach problem (also known as the El Farol Bar; Arthur, 1994), which modeled individuals of a city going to the beach on Saturdays and how they would decide to go if they thought the beach would not be too crowded; this experiment illustrated the dynamic of decentralized versus centralized decision making.

In the 1980s, Axelrod (1984) constructed two momentous agent-based computer simulations demonstrating that (a) in the Prisoner's Dilemma game, the tit-for-tat strategy is optimal to the individual and (b) the emergence of cooperation within a group is improved when interactions are controlled by the individual rather than being controlled by a central authority (Axelrod, 1984). Later in the same decade, Reynolds (1987) developed the well-known Boids computer program, which demonstrated that the organized behavior of a flock of birds can be entirely reproduced by a set of three simple rules of behavior that are executed by each bird; the motion of the group appears to be centrally controlled, but it is actually not.

In the 1990s, Arthur (1994) used computer simulations to explore the hypothetical beach problem. He conjectured that individuals have a working hypothesis contained in their mental model and learn whether the operating hypothesis works; if not, they may discard the ineffective hypothesis in favor of another hypothesis. He suggests that individuals hold on to a belief not necessarily because it is correct, but because it does not fall beyond a threshold. Epstein and Axtell developed Sugarscape (1996), which, like Schelling's simulation, is a hybrid of cellular automata and agent-based simulation. Sugarscape models a virtual society and its corresponding economy. Its agents navigate in an economy constructed in a 50 × 50 lattice and behave according to a few simple rules. Their objective is to consume a single commodity, sugar, from their environment and move around the environment seeking it out and then consuming it. The environment also abides by some simple rules, such as how quickly the sugar grows back after being consumed and how much pollution an agent produces in a cell. From this perspective, Epstein and Axtell were able to demonstrate the emergence of a class system in a society. These and many more ideas and innovations over the last half-century have cleared the way for the plethora of virtual experiments being conducted today.

Mathematical Sociology: From the Social Network to the Metanetwork

The earliest evidence of research explicitly investigating the connections between people (see Freeman, 2004) can be found in studies such as the dynamics of crowd behavior (LeBon, 1897/1998) and social interactions among pairs and triads (Simmel, 1908/1971). However, most academics point to the 1930s as the beginning of social network analysis, which is when medical doctor Jacob Moreno (1934) published *Who Shall Survive?*, which documented the social relations of children in a schoolyard. Moreno was the first to use matrix and node-link diagrams to report observed relational information. By the end of the decade, Moreno was publishing the journal *Sociometry* (now defunct), and he was being joined by prominent others. In particular, mathematician Paul Lazars-feld began the practice of actually quantifying the observed relationships and assigning probabilities to future relationships occurring in the group (Moreno & Jennings, 1938).

However, sociometry was promptly to enter its "dark ages" (Freeman, 2004) in the 1940s, '50s, and '60s, as the initial enthusiasm behind it waned somewhat. Nevertheless, throughout this period, there was a small group of academics advancing and applying these novel ideas. The study of phenomena such as the relative position of an individual in a group (Homans, 1950), patterns of acquaintanceship, and influences among relations (see Pool & Kochen, 1978) all continued to advance the methods of sociometry. Notably, in the early 1950s mathematician Frank Harary (see Harary & Norman, 1953) recognized that his expertise in graph theory would be a useful tool for sociometry, and he successfully began to pitch the idea to social scientists. Coincidentally, it was at this time that linguist Eugene Garfield (1955) began to study the links between citations of scientific publications; he recognized the links were not only a social concept, but analogously, that relations can be also formed between ideas and that they can be mapped into a network.

In the 1960s, the contemporary notion of social network analysis began to form as the methodology began to escape from its dark period when sociologist Harrison White began investigating the mathematical aspect of social structure by using the techniques from sociometry. He shared his insights and the methods with his Harvard University students, who then gradually spread them through-out the scientific community by holding conferences, teaching, and applying the methods to their own research. Many of these students are now elders in the field of social network analysis (see Freeman, 2004). In what has since become an infamous article, social psychologist, Stanley Milgram (1967) reported the small-world problem in an empirical study that determined the average path length among people was around six; thus the social network concept and pop-ular phrase *six degrees of separation*.

By the 1970s, the methods of social network analysis began to gain a foothold in the research community. Granovetter (1973) found that close friends likely have the same information as you and that your more socially distant friends will likely have information that you do not already hold. So if you happen to be searching for leads to a new job, instead of polling your close friends, you should instead poll your acquaintances. By publishing his popular book, *Getting a Job*, Granovetter started to introduce the notion of social networks into the broader, nonresearch community. Over the next decade and into the 1990s, and with the dawn of the ubiquitous computer, much of the noticeable progress in this field was in the development of computer software because there was now a practical way to operationalize the computation of measures on larger, more real-world social networks; in addition, there were countless numbers of academics improving the techniques, developing measures, and moving the ideas of social network analysis forward and outward. Late in the decade, Krackhardt and Carley (1998) represented networks in multiple and multimode form, namely: precedence (P), representing a temporal ordering of the tasks; commitment (C), indicating which resources are required for each task; assignment (A), identifying which people are to be working on which tasks; network (N), showing the people one knows, and skill (S) indicating the resources or skills to which a person has access. The PCANS model of the structure of an organization, which conceptualizes an organization as consisting of individuals, tasks, and resources that can be thought of and represented as multiple, multimode social networks.

At the turn of the century, perhaps fueled by the growth of the Internet and the World Wide Web (WWW), the interest in social network analysis exploded. Sociologist Duncan Watts (1999) published a book titled *Small Worlds: The Dynamics of Networks Between Order and Randomness,* which formally brought the network perspective to the masses. During this period, nonsociologists began to be interested in networks as well. Computer scientists Faloutsos, Faloutsos, and Faloutsos (1999) discovered that there was a power law relationship among the network of computers forming the Internet, which sparked the interests of the physics community, discovering that the WWW also had a power-law among its hyperlinks (Barabási & Albert, 1999). This was followed by research into the robustness of such networks to error and attack (Albert, Jeong, & Barabási, 2000).

By 2005, the concept of a social network was in the popular lexicon and even part of the pop culture. For example, the notion of a network distance measure, which when applied in a collaboration network was long within the folklore of mathematicians (e.g., the Erdos number), warped into fun pop culture activities, such as the Six Degrees of Kevin Bacon (pun on six degrees of separation), the Kevin Bacon game (Watts, 1999), the Six Degrees of Lois Weisberg (Gladwell, 1999), and even a popular theater play. This explosion into the pop culture can be explained by the ubiquity of the WWW and popular nonscientific books written on simple concepts such as *Six Degrees: The Science of a Connected Age* (Watts, 2004) and *Linked: How Everything Is Connected to Everything Else and What It Means* (Barabasi, 2003).

The Convergence of Agent-Based Modeling and Dynamic Network Analysis

Carley and Prietula (1994) demonstrated that to obtain interesting and detailed organizational predictions, one had to incorporate a model of agents, organizational structure and situation, and task. In particular, task places an extremely strong constraint on individual and organizational behavior. Carley (2002) built on the prior ideas of the PCANS model and developed the metamatrix construct. She conceptualized the multimode, multilevel notion of social networks that can richly represent a social organization beyond the traditional social network view of a single network representing a single type of relationship. The metamatrix can capture a more complete snapshot of a situation. Because it stays within the realm of network analysis, the network measures can be applied to actor and nonactor data. Next, Carley (2003) conceived of the DNA perspective, which extends SNA by applying the metamatrix construct to network analysis and treating such ties as probabilistic, and combining these networks with multi-agent modeling.

Since the development of the metamatrix and the development of combining DNA with multiagent simulation in 2003, the ability to create rich, intercon-nected models of group behavior has taken hold as a viable systems technique. This technique has been used for studying the dynamics of organizational per-formance, leadership, and terrorist organizations. The metamatrix has since been expanded to include individuals and group mental models and belief sys-tems. A rich model of organization has been developed using these techniques, which will be described later in this chapter.

Agent-Based Simulation as a Research Strategy

Agent-based simulation is particularly suited for research in the social sciences that seeks to explain collective, social phenomena arising from individual behav-iors. A well-designed simulation provides a platform to study the distinct micro- and macro-behaviors, their interaction and the collective outcomes, all in one unified experiment. Simulation is not classical experimentation and not classi-cal mathematic analysis (Schultz & Sullivan, 1972); instead simulation can be considered a model in and of itself, just as a mathematical equation is generally accepted as a model (Dawson, 1962). Broadly, computer simulation is especially valuable for research situations in which experimentation or analytical tech-niques are not feasible (Schultz & Sullivan, 1972). In this section, we present various articulations on the uses of computer simulation as a research strategy, from the perspective of several researchers.

Developing a simulation model, with its inherent requirement for precision, brings to bear the frequent imprecision of behavioral theories constructed from traditional methods; the requirement for precision forces a rigor unfounded in traditional research techniques. A simulation also demonstrates the internal consistency of a theory by enabling a demonstrable confirmation that the results can be produced according to the theory (Repenning, 2002; Sastry 1997). These simulations provide an operational laboratory (Repenning, 2002) that facilitates the uncovering of various aspects of a theory that may not be readily apparent.

Glibert (1996) drew a distinction between conventional research strategies and computer simulation: Conventional strategies can be characterized as taking a variable-centered or case-based approach; computer simulation, in contrast, is a process-centered approach. He suggests that computer simulation methods can even explore complex nonlinear dynamics that other mathematical approaches cannot because of the complex simultaneous interaction between microlevel and macrolevel processes. He advises that simulation may not necessarily reduce the complexity in the models, but it will at least make partial elements and dynamics of the model entirely viewable.

In general, the simulation methodology can be used for prediction, the construction of proofs, discovery, explanation, critique, prescription, and empirical strategies, but when used for prediction, the findings must be strictly restricted to the phenomena modeled and corroborated with empirical evidence. They can prove through demonstration proof that phenomena can indeed occur, even if such a phenomenon may have minuscule probability of occurring in the real world; simulations can uncover dynamics that may not be readily apparent empirically. Simulations can be used to aid in explaining phenomena that are typically only observed and can be used to analyze and perhaps critique behavioral theories arising from the traditional research techniques. Moreover, simulations can be used to aid in the development of strategies for empirical research and experiments (Axelrod, 1997; Harrison et al., 2007).

From another perspective, Axelrod and Tesfatsion (2006) enumerated four forms of goals of ABM researchers: (a) *empirical understanding*, how can observed regularities be explained; (b) *normative understanding*, using ABM as a laboratory to devise good social design and policies; (c) *heuristic*, to garner greater insight into the causes of social phenomena; and (d) *methodological advancement*, by developing improved ABM tools and tactical methods.

Put another way, Axtell (2000) made the case for agent-based computation in the social sciences by pointing out three distinct uses for the technique: (a) It provides a tool for presenting complex computational results, even a novel Monte Carlo analysis, (b) It can deal with the unsolvable mathematics of complex systems, and (c) In some cases, it can be used to write down equations for some processes is just not viable. Simulation also, unlike the traditional methods of social science, can answer the following questions: (a) What happened? (b) How did it happen?, and (c) Why did it happen? Simulations can help to answer the what-if question (Dooley, 2002).

Applied Agent-Based Simulations

A powerful characteristic of ABM is that it provides a viewpoint and framework that can be applied effectively in a wide variety of research programs. Agent-based models can be classified into three types, consistent with their behavioral complexity: (a) artificial life, (b) structural, and (c) cognitive agent. Although all three types are still vigorously being applied to research, the cognitive agent is being aggressively used in the human–organizational research setting and is the type we describe in more detail later in this chapter.

Artificial life models can be characterized by a large number of rule-based agents that move in a grid that learn in a binary fashion that result in the agents evolving. A well-known example of application of this type model is Sugarscape (Epstein & Axtell, 1996). In this classic simulation, agents behaved in a lockstep fashion by moving around on a 50 × 50 lattice. The agents' goal is to accumulate sugar that is inventoried across the grid landscape. The experiments using this type of model demonstrated that collective behaviors do indeed arise from the interaction of individuals who follow a few simple rules.

The structural type of agent-based simulation characteristically specifies the agents' behavior from a combination of equations and rules. The agents can learn and communicate through social networks and may have communication technologies, such as e-mail. An example application of this genre is the OrgAhead simulation (Lee & Carley, 2004), which is an organizational learning model designed to test different forms of organizational reporting structure. In the model, each member of the organization receives information from a subordinate or from the environment, makes a decision based on the information, and, based on what he or she knows, provides superiors with a local decision. At the top, an organizational decision is made on the basis of the information that was collectively passed up through the organizational ranks. This simulation model allows for experiments focused on the exploration of organizational structures, the effect of individual learning and forgetting, and numerous other organizational phenomena. As a structural type agent-based model, OrgAhead agents do not move around on a landscape, as is often the case in a cellular automata simulation.

The third type is the cognitive-agent model; an example is the Construct model, which is presented thoroughly later in this chapter. In short, these cognitive-agent models involve agents that follow complex rules, can learn, and carry out knowledge-intensive and sometimes physical tasks. These cognitive agents can modify their social network, and, in turn, their network can affect their behavior. Agent-based models of the cognitive-agent type have been used for research in areas as varied as organizational design, cultural dynamics, diffusion of ideas, and personnel turnover (Dal Forno & Merlone, 2004), to name just a few.

One complexity-rich application of the cognitive-agent approach of broad research interest is for the study of organizational leadership (Dal Forno & Merlone, 2006; Hazy, 2007). As early as 1994, a simulation of the leader–follower relationship that demonstrated the dynamics of first mover advantage was published (Hubler & Pines, 1994). The study showed that the first to signal leadership was at an advantage because it was more efficient for the others to comply rather than to compete. Simulation experiments (Schreiber, 2006; Schreiber & Carley, 2004a) have also showed that different leadership styles have an impact on the team configurations and thus on the group performance. In another study (Anghel, Toroczkai, Bassler, & Korniss, 2004), it was shown that a small number of popular agents in a social network can influence a large portion of the other agents. Hazy (2007) provided a comprehensive survey of these various simulations and leadership studies, and, in a more recent paper (Hazy, 2008), he proposed a theory of leadership in complex systems, derived from taking the computational modeling approach, that can ultimately lead to further operational simulations for studying the underlying nonlinear dynamics.

Another broad-based research area that demonstrates how agent-based models can be applied is in the field of computational organization theory (COT), which uses computer simulation to develop and test organization theory. For example, a simulation by Carley and Ren (2001) aptly demonstrated the nonlinear dynamics of adaptability and performance in organizations. Numerous other models of organizational behavior have been developed over the years; a thorough review of the state of such computational modeling and simulations in organization science identified 29 specific computer simulations that were introduced between 1989 and 2003; the authors made a particular point that the richness of the models has increased over the same years (Ashworth & Carley, 2004, 2007). Since the time of the report, the number of applications has continued to grow in number, sophistication, and topical reach.

Designing an Agent-Based Dynamic Network Simulation

The mission of constructing an agent-based simulation involves two nontrivial, resource-intensive tasks: (a) designing a concrete representation of the theoretical or conceptual model and (b) developing software to embody the model and perform the simulation. The challenge that these tasks present should not be underestimated. Both are technically intricate; very different skill sets and experience are necessary to complete both tasks effectively. In this section, we discuss only the task of designing the model. Software is discussed in a later section. Herein, we discuss only a few of the key aspects of the design task, because it is a complex activity with many dimensions that are too numerous and exacting to be covered wholly in this short section.

A critical decision that a modeler must make when designing an ABM, as with any other model-building exercise, is to balance suitably the *complexity* with the *simplicity* of the model. There is a vital trade-off between keeping the model simple with only few features and increasing the model's veridicality, relative to the complexity of the real world. This is a delicate balance that the designer must strike by using careful judgment that comes from extensive prior experience, repetitive trial and error, or utilizing the expertise of others. If it is too complex, the researchers cannot adequately explain the model to the consumers of the research, nor possibly fully understand the model themselves. Moreover, the aforementioned simulation software necessary to implement a complex model may never reach the point of actually being operational.

Although we can describe the elements of ABM in numerous ways (see Epstein, 1999), for present purposes, we tend toward parsimony and characterize

ABM as having two broad and essential components: the *agent behavior* and the *environment*. An agent is an entity that interacts with its environment by using input from its various sensors that can obtain information from the environment. An agent senses bits of information from the environment, makes a decision to determine its behavior(s), then takes the action(s); actions in turn, affect the environment that the agent senses once again. An agent is probably not designed to have complete control over its environment, but the agent usually does influence the environment in which it navigates.

The key issue is the behavioral nature of the agent; it can merely be a simple, *reactive* agent or a somewhat more complex, cognitively *intelligent* agent. A *reactive* agent is deterministic in its behavior; it makes the exact same decision when faced with the same situation each and every time. Conversely, an *intelligent* agent will have at least some stochastic aspect to its behavior. The intelligent agent makes decisions using a probabilistic distribution of its possible behaviors when faced with any given situation. Indeed, each respective intelligent agent may behave very differently each time when it is faced with an identical situation. In general, the reactive agent models are characteristically simpler than intelligent agent models; the intelligent agent is also outfitted, in some manner, to learn from past experience and adapt its future behavior accordingly.

The environment in which the agent behaves can be thought of and represented as a metanetwork of evolving relations that can constrain or enable individual behavior. Processes at both the individual and group level affect adaptation and change in these dynamic, environmental metanetworks. Behavioral conflicts can ensue across the agents, when individual perceptions of the structure of the environmental network vary and when change occurs at different rates in different parts of the shared environment. An agent model that does not include individual cognition, a view of the metanetwork of relations, and the process of change at both the individual and group level may be unable to replicate the observed behaviors associated with the group; these are important aspects of designing an effective agent-based, dynamic network simulation. In the remainder of this section, we present more detail about the design of each of the two vital components: agent behavior and the environment.

A Constructural Model of Agent Behavior

As an illustrative, working example of a definition of an agent-based simulation, we describe a theory-rich model of agents operating within a human, task-performing organization. The intended purpose of this model is to simulate the dynamics of a goal-seeking organization at the aggregated organization level. This model reflects the recognition that human agents' behavior is substantially influenced by external factors (other agents and the environment) and that the external factors are, in turn, affected by the agent. This model uses the simplicity of cellular automata models, such as Boids (Reynolds, 1987) and Holland's adaptation (1995), but establishes a model of the much more complex human behavior, which requires greater and more multidimensional environmental feedback. Agents in this model regularly interact with the environment and socialize with other agents, and subsequently integrate feedback resulting from the decisions made and actions taken by the other agents. By establishing these simple rules of agent adaptive behavior and the use of environmental feedback, this model provides an invaluable, generic laboratory for numerous social research programs owing to diverse objectives beyond its initial purpose.

Herein, we describe the *construct model*, which has been used extensively for social theory generation and testing since the early 1990s and continues to evolve and be refined. As with what we briefly described earlier in a generalized form, the construct model provides a robust representation of agent behavior within a group that has its roots in symbolic interactionism (Blumer, 1969), structural interactionism (Stryker, 1980), and structural differentiation theory (Blau, 1970). These theories are combined into a social modeling theory called constructuralism (Carley, 1991a), which is embodied in the construct model. Among its many applications, for example, the construct model can be used to simulate the diffusion of beliefs and ideas through groups as constrained and enabled by the social structure of the group and the communications technology available. The model has been used extensively for analysis in industry, nonprofits, emergency response, higher education, military, and government. The model has been scientifically validated numerous times (Carley & Hill, 2001; Schreiber & Carley, 2004b, 2007) and has also been compared with and validated against real observations, such as Kapferer's Zambia Tailor Shop data (Carley, 1990).

The construct model couples the information processing perspective with the viewpoints of the social information processing theorists (Rice & Aydin, 1991; Salancik & Pfeffer, 1978), who contend that the knowledge people have is dependent on what information they have access to through their social network. The model recognizes that people interact within a dynamic, social, or organizational network and are information-seeking agents. They interact through complex discourse (Dooley, Corman, McPhee, & Kuhn, 2003) to exchange information and frequently seek out others who have information that they do not yet hold and are sought out by others seeking their information, or knowledge. This interaction dynamic is played out numerous times within a group or formal organization. When coupled with the routine group membership changes (e.g., hiring and firing in an organization), the emerging microinteraction dynamics illustrate complex dynamics. We describe more details of this agent behavior in four parts: (a) the information processing aspect of the agent, (b) the agent as being an intelligent and adaptive being, (c) the agent as holding a mental model of its environment, and (d) the transactive memory aspect of the agent.

Agent as Information Processor

The Carnegie School of Organizational Theory (Cyert & March, 1963; March & Simon, 1958; Simon, 1957) proposed an information processing perspective in which individual decisions, and thus behavior, could be explained in terms of what information was available to whom, cognitive limits to information processing abilities, organizational (social and cultural) limits to access to information, the quality of the information, and so forth. Simon (1945), March and Simon (1958), and Cyert and March (1963) examined the decision-making components of group action. According to the information processing perspective of organization theory (Cyert & March, 1963; Galbraith, 1973, 1977; March & Simon, 1958), individual behavior and organizational decisions can be explained in terms of what information is available to whom, who holds specific information, and what the person's cognitive limits are, which can ultimately result in complex, collective decisions (Iwanaga & Namatame, 2002). In a group, agents interact as a matter of routine, and in the course of their interaction, they exchange information; this is to say that they exchange knowledge among one another as they interact, either through person-to-person communications or through various forms of broadcast media (Dooley & Corman, 2004).

Agent as Intelligent Adaptive Agents

An intelligent adaptive agent is one that makes decisions on the basis of information, but that information changes over time in response to the environment. Thus the agent learns responses and may improve performance. Models in this arena include those using simulated annealing, genetic programming, genetic algorithms, and neural networks. Some of these analyses focus on the evolution of industries and the sets of organizations within a market, rather than adaptation within a single organization (Axelrod, 1987; Axelrod & Dion, 1988; Crowston, 1994, 1998; Holland, 1975; Holland & Miller, 1991; Padgett, 1997). Others explore issues of organizational performance and experiential learning (Carley, 1992; Lin & Carley, 1998; Mihavics & Ouksel, 1996; Verhagan & Masuch, 1994) or expectation-based learning (Carley, 1999).

The construct model reflects that group dynamics are due to, and may even emerge from, the level of adaptiveness of the agents within the group. This process has been referred to by a variety of names, including colearning (Shoham & Tennenholtz, 1994), synchronization, and concurrent interaction (Carley, 1991b). For Carley (1991a), concurrent interaction and the coevolution of self and society is necessary for the emergence of social stability and consensus. For Shoham and Tennenholtz (1994), colearning occurs when several agents simultaneously try to adapt to one another's behavior so as to produce desirable group-level results. Collectively, the findings from these models indicate that emergent social phenomena (such as the emergence of hierarchy) and the evolutionary dynamics (patterns of change) depend on the rate at which the agents age, learn, and move, constraints on access and other group processes.

Agent Holds a Mental Model

Individuals' mental models can be characterized as the information known by the individual and the pattern of relationships among these pieces of information (Carley & Palmquist, 1992). A mental model is not just all the information that is in an individual's head. Rather, a mental model is a structure of information that is created and can be called up or used in specific contexts. Individuals have many mental models about themselves, others, objects, the world, tasks, and so forth. These mental models include social, historical, cultural, environmental, personal, and task knowledge and are specialized on the basis of varying contexts and needs. From a group perspective, an individual's mental model includes the individual's perception of the sociocognitive structure – the sets of relations that an individual perceives as existing between other pairs of individuals (Krackhardt, 1987, 1990) and their understanding of others' knowledge and beliefs (Carley, 1986). Problem solving involves searching through the set of salient mental models. As such, mental models influence not only what decisions individuals make but also their perceptions of others' decisions. According to this perspective, cognition mediates between structure and outcome; that is, it is the individual's perception of social structure (as encoded in the individual's mental model) that influences behavior, attitudes, evaluations, and decisions, and not the structure itself (Carley & Newell, 1994). Individuals' mental models are thought to develop as they interact with other individuals.

Agent Has Transactive Memory

The individual navigates within an intricate web (Davis, 1973) of relationships. The interconnection of their thoughts, or cogitative interdependence, is what has been termed *transactive memory* (Wegner, Giuliano, & Hertel, 1985). Network approaches have formalized the representation of transactive memory as an individual's knowledge of who knows who, who knows what, who has access to what resources, who is assigned to or is doing what tasks, and who is where. In other words, transactive memory is the individual's perception of environment, which can be represented in the form of a collection of interrelated networks. People in close relationships with one another will often know much about what the other knows, while not knowing the actual fact itself. For example, a married couple often segregates the knowledge of minute details of their monthly bill-paying routine; one spouse handles the bills and maintains the details, whereas the other distances himself or herself. (Wegner, Erber, & Raymond, 1991). The bill-distant spouse will know that the detail-oriented other will know certain details and may seek information from them, as opposed to asking their neighbor for the same information. We all depend on information that others hold that we do not. Perhaps our dependency is caused by our limitations in our absorptive capacity (Cohen & Levinthal, 1990) or out of specialization and the segregation of tasks; regardless, the system of transactive memory refers to knowing what others know.

The Environment as a Metanetwork

The second primary component of an agent-based simulation design, beyond the agent behavior, is the environment within which an agent exists and navigates. An effective construct to represent such an environment, both conceptually and tangibly in the software architecture, is to assemble multiple, relational networks that capture the various elements of the environment; this is the perspective of DNA as previously discussed. By representing environment as metanetwork, the designer can take advantage of the numerous techniques that are part and parcel of DNA. This approach has proved useful, manageable, and effective in numerous simulations developed for academic and governmental research, as well as in real-world policy making. In this section, we present the basic ideas underlying the previously mentioned basic social network analysis (SNA) and the more advanced DNA, then discuss how the network-styled constructs are applied to representing the environment in an agent-based simulation.

Social Network Analysis

SNA is a methodology that is fixated on the notion of relationships among defined entities. Most often, these relationships are an interaction of some sort, but could very well result from an attribute of the entity as well. SNA provides quantitative and visual techniques that enable a rich analysis of relational data. The technique enables researchers to quantify the network of relationships among the entities. By studying the topological structure and other characteristics of the network, much can be exposed about the social phenomena that may not be readily uncovered using traditional sociological methods. The network perspective also gives the researcher an invaluable tool set for studying change in the group over time. The essence of the network perspective is the node and tie structure that associates an entity as a node and represents the disposition of a relationship between two nodes with a tie; this lends itself well to visualization (see Fig. 16.1) as well as extensive mathematical analysis of the data. The visualization feature usually represents the nodes as circles and the tie as a line drawn between and connecting the two nodes or circles.

The classic objectives of the network analysis are to compute node-level measures, identify the nodes that have the most or the least prestige, identify social groups, identity-connected paths among various nodes, and characterize the network by global measures. The most prominent local measures are those that indicate the centrality of a particular node. The three most often used measures of centrality are *degree, closeness,* and *betweenness.* Degree is a measure

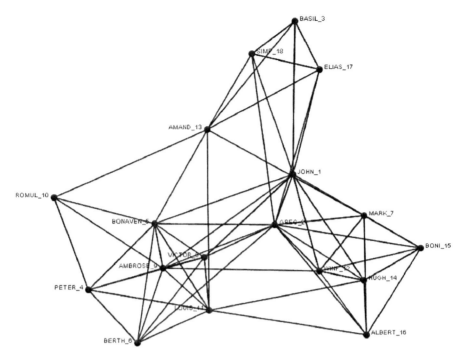

Figure 16.1. A node-link representation of a social network, consisting of a single type of node.

of how many immediate ties each individual node has. Closeness is a measure of how close, or minimally distant, the individual node is to each of all other nodes in the same network. Betweenness is a measure that quantifies the extent to which an individual node is in the shortest path between all pairs of other nodes. For each of these centrality measures, there is a corresponding network-level centralization measure that is essentially the arithmetic mean of the values for all of the nodes in the network. SNA also can be an invaluable means for studying subgroups; in social psychology and sociology, the notion of subgroups and cliques are widely studied, and SNA provides algorithms and heuristics for identifying cohesive group structures within a social network. For a rich discussion from the NDS perspective of network formation using a method for orbital decomposition, see Guastello (2002).

In particular, attention has been paid to network models that are described in terms of the relationships or ties among human individuals (Krackhardt & Brass, 1994; Nohria & Eccles, 1992). Researchers distinguish between the group structure (in a formal organization, the organizational chart dictating who reports to whom) and the informal organizational structure (the emergent set of adversarial and friendship relations among the individuals in the organization). Network models have been used to successfully examine issues such as organizational adaptation (Carley & Svoboda, 1996), power (Burt, 1976, 1992; Burt &

Cook, 2001; Krackhardt, 1990), diffusion (Burt, 1973; Carley, 1995b; Carley & Wendt, 1991; Granovetter, 1973), changing jobs (Granovetter, 1974), structuration (DiMaggio, 1986), innovation (Burt, 1980), and turnover (Krackhardt, 1991; Krackhardt & Porter, 1985, 1986). These studies demonstrate that the structure of relations can affect individual and group behavior. Moreover, the informal structure often has as much or more influence on behavior than does the formal structure.

Dynamic Network Analysis

A significant constraint of traditional SNA, however, is its incapacity to work with multimode and multiple networks. An extension to SNA is now emerging; the field of DNA (Carley, 2003) builds on the single-network paradigm of SNA by having the capacity of working with multiple networks simultaneously and dynamically. DNA allows researchers to represent and work with richer social networks that more closely reflect the group dynamics being studied. Two of the key advances from traditional SNA to DNA are the introduction of the metamatrix and the combining of social networks with cognitive science and multiagent systems (Carley, 2003). The construct of a metamatrix extends the PCANS (Krackhardt & Carley, 1998) approach, which is a representative model of organizations that includes combined networks consisting of people, resources, and tasks. Traditional SNA techniques do not recognize that the people in the social networks are active and adaptive agents that are capable of taking action, learning, and changing their social networks.

Researchers using DNA recognize that networks can consist of nodes of various types and networks that go beyond the human-to-human relationship. Entities may include intelligent agents (such as humans, robots), events, knowledge, resources, task, and so on. For example, a network can be fashioned from people and the various knowledge they have (the nodes are referred to as *concepts*). By melding the representational constructs with the dynamical aspects, DNA provides a straightforward platform that incorporates both the agent-based model and the social network paradigms. In essence, the DNA models allow for node and tie changes (add, remove, modify) that easily captures the dynamic nature of the phenomena being modeled. For example, people are born and can die; a node can be added and removed. Knowledge can be created by innovation or discovery, and it can be removed by forgetting. Agents can gain knowledge and lose it, just as a tie between an agent and a knowledge concept can be added and removed. In a metamatrix, multiple entity types beyond people and knowledge can be represented – for example, tasks, organizations, and events. Each entity type in the set of entity types in a particular metamatrix can be associated with any other entity type. For example, in an agent, knowledge, and task metanetwork, there are six types of networks possible: agent × agent, agent × knowledge, agent × task, knowledge × knowledge, knowledge × task, and task × task. In a metanetwork, there may be several networks of each combined type as is shown by Figure 16.2.

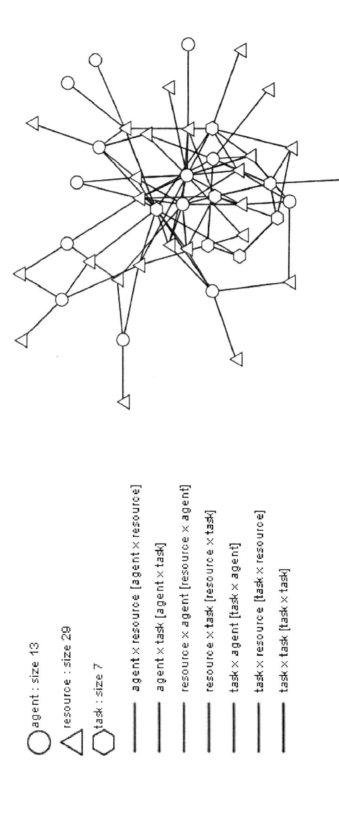

agent : size 13

resource : size 29

task : size 7

agent × resource [agent × resource]

agent × task [agent × task]

resource × agent [resource × agent]

resource × task [resource × task]

task × agent [task × agent]

task × resource [task × resource]

task × task [task × task]

Figure 16.2. A node-link representation of a metanetwork, consisting of three types of nodes.

Along with the multinetwork representation capabilities of DNA come a plethora of additional, multinetwork metrics that serve to quantify richly the organizational-level dimensions of a complex organization. *Cognitive load* is a measure that combines agent, knowledge, task, and resource networks to compute a value that can serve as a strong indicator of who the group's emergent leaders are (Carley & Ren, 2001) by indicating the amount of effort expended by each member to perform his or her assigned tasks. Another DNA measure, *cognitive expertise,* is a metric indicating how much *unique* knowledge one member of the organization has over another member by using the agent-to-knowledge network. The *communication* measure is an indication of the knowledge similarity between two members. Another measure, which indicates what information an actor lacks that is necessary for that actor to complete an assigned task, is called *agent knowledge*; this utilizes the actor-to-task, actor-to-knowledge, and task-to-knowledge networks. The *agent knowledge waste* measure indicates how much of the knowledge an agent holds but is not necessary for the tasks to which the actor is assigned.

The Environment as a Metanetwork

An effective and straightforward construct in which to envision and represent the environment, both conceptually and within software architecture, is the metamatrix, or metanetwork. The metanetwork is a characteristic feature of DNA, as previously discussed, that can be described simply as multiple networks with node entities of various types, such as human agents, tasks, resources, knowledge, and beliefs. In the same manner of the PCANS model (Krackhardt & Carley 1998), also mentioned earlier, this multinetwork perspective provides a formalized data structure to represent richly the various entities and relations forming an environment in which an agent coexists. The actors' assigned tasks, their available resources, the resources required for a task, and the temporal precedence of the task execution all can be captured easily and wholly in the metanetwork construct. Further, real-world changes, such as birth and death of an actor, the reassignment of tasks, and so on, are all simple matters to capture and represent within the metanetwork representation. Although these examples pertain to an agent-based model of an organization, the metanetwork, as a construct to represent the environment, can easily be used effectively in a wide variety of characteristically different applications beyond the domain of human agents.

Simulation Software Platforms and Tools

Although the conceptual underpinnings and techniques of ABM and DNA are becoming evident to an ever greater number of researchers, the software required to take full advantage of these methods can sometimes be momentous to develop. The high cost of computer hardware or timeshare usage that was a genuine barrier to operationalizing simulations before the 1970s has now been overcome (Dawson, 1962), but now the still-immense resource costs of software development can be considered *the* greatest obstacle. Fortunately, there are now numerous software toolkits available to researchers that at least take care of some of the core computer science aspects associated with developing operational simulations. Although these toolkits can provide a ready-platform for use and in some cases require no programming, there remains a great deal of effort required to learn how to navigate skillfully within these software platforms. One powerful example of these software tools is SWARM, which is a multiagent simulation for studying complex systems, developed at the Santa Fe Institute (Minar, Burkhart, Langton, & Askenazi, 1996). Its basic unit is the *swarm*, which is a group of agents that abide by identical rules. SWARM is primarily used for individual-based modeling in ecology research, but it has been used successfully to study the self-organizing behavior of agents of many other life-forms. Like many other tools and platforms, SWARM productively insultates the researcher from many of the device- and lexical-level software programming issues. Numerous ready-to-use SNA software tools are available, with the most popular being UCINET (Borgatti, Everett, & Freeman, 1992). UCINET provides a complete platform for analyzing and viewing network data set, although it is limited to working with only single networks.

We provide a brief description of two software programs used extensively by the authors for operationalizing the CONSTRUCT agent-based model and analyzing the resulting dynamic networks, as described throughout this chapter. CONSTRUCT (Carley, 1990; Hirshman, Carley, & Kowalchuck, 2007; Schreiber & Carley, 2004b) is a program that provides a platform for researchers to experiment with the metamatrix data using virtual simulation. It embodies and implements the agent-based dynamic network model, based on the construct model described in this chapter. To analyze the networks, we use the Organization Risk Analyzer (ORA; Carley, Columbus, DeReno, Reminga, & Moon, 2007; Carley & Reminga, 2004), which is a program that computes traditional SNA and DNA metrics on single and metanetwork data. ORA is the only software that handles both traditional SNA techniques and the more advanced DNA methods. It provides powerful renditions of traditional node-link and advanced visualizations and facilitates editing of the metanetwork data. ORA can be used to identify key nodes, assess changes in networks, identify vulnerabilities in networks, suggest missing data, and assess the impact of node and link extraction. ORA provides several other aids for advanced analysis, including error detection and what-if analysis using agent-based simulation based on the construct model using CONSTRUCT software. Both CONSTRUCT and ORA are developed by the Center for Computational Analysis of Social and Organizational Systems

(CASOS) at Carnegie Mellon University and are freely available on the WWW to researchers without license.

Limitations

Although computer simulation is becoming imperative to the development of new theory, its progression is not unabated. A major issue with computer simulation is that the validation of the model design and underlying agent behavior mechanisms is a daunting challenge (Burton, 1998; Keller-McNulty et al., 2006; Prietula & Carley, 1994; Robinson, 1997). The complexity of the human dimension, coupled with the difficulty in controlling comparable real-world experiments and actual situations, makes the challenge of stringent validation practically insurmountable. Frequently the models are used to provoke thought and discussion rather than in a strict predictive capacity, so that the requirements for the depth of validation may be somewhat less in this case, but some level of validation is still critical nonetheless. When validation is achievable, it is normally possible only in part; hence one must be careful not to use a model outside the scope to which it has been properly validated.

Chang and Harrington (2006) provided three introspective issues with the computational methodology at this juncture: (a) Often there is a lack of attention to relating the model to reality (e.g., the appropriateness of interpreting an agent as a person); (b) the bounded rationality of an agent is assumed; and (c) all too often, the law of parsimony can be violated as the capability to develop more complex models arises accompanied by the difficulty in explaining complex results to the layperson.

The emergence of simulation methods means that computer science and software engineering are now a large part of the research process. Thus researchers need at least to be comfortable with and able to work in multidisciplinary teams. Another challenge posed by these methods and the associated increase in complexity is that the models themselves are more difficult to describe and explain, thus greater attention to precise explanation of the capabilities is now necessary.

Harrison, Lin, Carroll, and Carley (2007) raised several concerns, limitations and shortcomings pertaining to simulation-based research: (a) Pragmatically, simulations can easily suffer from complexity creep because many times models are habitually added on to, to the point of becoming overly complex and difficult to interpret; (b) the artificial nature of simulations situates the model for a requirement to be grounded to empirical research; (c) the craft of simulation modeling and design is highly complex and requires interdisciplinary skills that can be difficult to garner; (d) software bugs are ubiquitous, and simulation software and design is not isolated from the challenges; (e) accurate translation of theory to computer code can be challenging and difficult to validate; and (f) inferences from simulation studies the real world must be performed with precise care for accurate and proper deduction.

Implications for Researchers

Researchers can look forward to the continued development and advancement of computer simulation as a methodology, and to ABM and DNA as interconnected, supporting techniques to this advance. As the operational challenges of implementation lessen and acceptance of the findings that these methods generate grows, researchers in the social sciences will benefit progressively more from this evolutionary, "third way," of doing social research; these methods will increasingly provide a powerful means to take a fresh look at many extensive social research questions.

To a particular research program, this greater power comes at a high cost, however. The personnel and technological start-up costs for these methods can be exorbitant; there is a great deal of education, skill training, experimental trial and error, and prerequisite quantitative and computer science skills that are necessary to conduct validated and effectual research. Fortunately, however, once the start-up phase is complete, the cost of maintaining these technologies is exceptionally low. The incremental outlay for each virtual experiment a researcher conducts can become trivial and be markedly minimal across entire research programs, relative to conducting real-world, human-based studies. Costs aside, it may take quite some time for traditionally grounded scholars to get to the point of fully accepting these innovative techniques and embracing this third way. In the meantime, simulation-oriented researchers will need to continue to be explicit by vigorously justifying and explaining these methods to traditionally oriented researchers. For the early adopters, this will likely continue to be a burden in the near term, but ultimately the use of ABM simulations and DNA will, over time, happily coexist with the traditional time-tested methods; there is just too much science to be gained by using these powerful techniques for them to be ignored.

Researchers who embrace ABM and DNA must recognize the trade-offs between the cost of doing simulation well and the cost of doing ethnographic empirical studies well. Indeed, very different skill sets are necessary to execute these disparate methods. Thus researchers will likely need to form teams of support from various disciplines to carry out a fully validated and effective research program. With the simulations, computer expertise is essential, and for the external validity of the research, a solid grounding in traditional methods and with human subjects is essential. It is likely that the assortment of diverse perspectives of the team members will present many challenges to working in harmony – a situation that will need to be overcome to be an effective unit. Although the ready-made software platforms for simulation are broadly available and can be used by non–computer science professionals, there is the potential to make material mistakes in the implementation and design of a model, and thus the research, if the model designer is not expert enough to be able to understand fully the impact of the smallest design and implementation decisions. This carries great implication to a researcher's decision to apply ABM and DNA methods.

Beyond this immediate focus, there will likely be continued technological innovations that may seem far-fetched today but may indeed come to the fore. For example, fast approaching are multimedia computer simulations in which one or more of the agents is controlled by an actual human in real time. With this technology, the behavior of an agent, instead of being mandated by software rules, is managed by an actual human. Currently, these interactive, agent-based simulations are used as recreational games or applied to education (Keys & Bell, 1977; Keys & Wolfe, 1990) and experiential learning (Bowen, 1987; Kolb, 1984), but using them directly for research purposes is likely on the near-term horizon.

To keep abreast of the rapid changes and further advancements in the field, we suggest making use of the swelling amount of information freely available on the Internet. For example, the Web site maintained by the Society for Chaos Theory in Psychology & Life Sciences (2008) features a resources page that has links to several ABM sites, such as Axelrod and Tesfatsion's (2007) online guide containing information about ABM, including pertinent background, modeling techniques, and tips for getting started. For the latest information about SNA, the International Network for Social Network Analysis (2007) has a Web site with many useful resources. Finally, as mentioned in the previous section of software and tools, the Web site maintained by the Center for Computational Analysis of Social and Organizational Systems (CASOS) (2008) has a multitude of resources pertaining to ABM, SNA, and DNA, including papers and indispensable software tools.

References

Albert, R., Jeong, H., & Barabási, A. (2000). Error and attack tolerance of complex networks, *Nature, 406*, 378–482.

Anghel, M., Toroczkai, Z., Bassler, K. E., & Korniss, G. (2004). Competition in social networks: Emergence of a scale-free leadership structure and collective efficiency. *Physical Review Letters, 92*, 058701–068704.

Arthur, W. B. (1994). Inductive reasoning and bounded rationality. *The American Economic Review, 84*, 406–411.

Ashworth, M., & Carley, K. M. (2004, June). *Toward unified organization theory: Perspectives on the state of computational modeling.* Paper presented to the North American Association for Computational Social and Organization Science 2004 Conference, Pittsburgh, PA.

Ashworth, M., & Carley, K. M. (2007). Can tools help unify organization theory? Perspectives on the state of computational modeling. *Computational and Mathematical Organization Theory, 13*, 89–111.

Axelrod, R. (1984). *The evolution of cooperation.* New York: Basic Books.

Axelrod, R. M. (1987). The evolution of strategies in the iterated prisoner's dilemma. In W. Davis (Ed.), *Genetic algorithms and simulated annealing* (pp. 32–41). London: Pitman.

Axelrod, R. M. (1997). Advancing the art of simulation in the social sciences. In R. Conte, R. Hegselmann, & P. Terna (Eds.), *Simulating social phenomena* (pp. 21–40). Berlin: Springer Publishing Company.

Axelrod, R. M. (2006). Agent-based modeling as a bridge between disciplines. In Leigh Tesfatsion & Kenneth L. Judd (Eds.), *Handbook of computational economics, Vol. 2: Agent-based computational economics* (pp. 1565–1584). Amsterdam: North-Holland.

Axelrod, R. M., & Dion, D. (1988). The further evolution of cooperation. *Science, 242*, 1385–1390.

Axelrod, R. M., & Tesfatsion, L. (2006). Guide for newcomers to agent-based modeling in the social sciences. In Leigh Tesfatsion & Kenneth L. Judd (Eds.), *Handbook of computational economics, Vol. 2: Agent-based computational economics*, pp. 1647–1659. Amsterdam: North-Holland.

Axelrod, R. M., & Tesfatsion, L. (2007). On-line guide for newcomers to agent-based modeling in the social sciences. Retrieved February 3, 2008, from http://www.econ.iastate.edu/tesfatsi/abmread.htm

Axtell, R. (2000). *Why agents? On the varied motivations for agent computing in the social sciences.* Center on Social and Economic Dynamics, Working Paper No. 17. Washington, DC: Brookings Institution Press.

Bankes, S. (2002). Agent-based modeling: A revolution? *Proceedings of the National Academy of Sciences, 99* (Suppl. 3), 7199–7200.

Barabasi, A.-L. (2003). *Linked: How everything is connected to everything else and what it means.* New York: Plume.

Barabási, A.-L., & Albert, R. (1999). Emergence of scaling in random networks. *Science, 286*, 509–512.

Blau, P. M. (1970). A formal theory of differentiation in organizations. *American Sociological Review, 35*, 201–218.

Blumer, H. (1969). *Symbolic interactionism: Perspective and method.* Englewood Cliffs, NJ: Prentice-Hall.

Borgatti, S., Everett, M., & Freeman, L. C. (1992). *UCINET IV, Version 1.0.* Columbia, MD: Analytic Technologies.

Bowen, D. D. (1987). Developing a personal theory of experiential learning: A dispatch from the trenches. *Simulation & Gaming, 18*, 192–206.

Burt, R. S. (1973). The differential impact of social integration on participation in the diffusion of innovations. *Social Science Research, 2*, 125–144.

Burt, R. S. (1976). Positions in networks. *Social Forces, 55*, 93–122.

Burt, R. S. (1980). Innovation as a structural interest: Rethinking the impact of network position in innovation adoption. *Social Networks, 4*, 337–355.

Burt, R. S. (1992). *Structural holes: The social structure of competition.* Cambridge, MA: Harvard University Press.

Burt, R. S., & Cook, K. (Eds.). (2001). *Social capital: Theory and research.* New York: Aldine.

Burton, R. (1998). Validating and docking: An overview, summary and challenge. In M. Prietula, K. Carley, & L. Gasser (Eds.), *Simulating organizations: Computational models of institutions and groups* (pp. 215–228). Cambridge, MA: American Association for Artificial Intelligence/MIT Press.

Carley, K. M. (1986). An approach for relating social structure to cognitive structure. *Journal of Mathematical Sociology, 12*, 137–189.

Carley, K. M. (1990). Group stability: Socio-cognitive approach. In A. E. Lawler, B. Markovsky, C. Ridgeway, & H. Walker (Eds.), *Advances in group processes, Vol. 7* (pp. 1–44). Greenwich, CT: JAI Press.

Carley, K. M. (1991a). A theory of group stability. *American Sociological Review, 56,* 331–354.

Carley, K. M. (1991b). Designing organizational structures to cope with communication breakdowns: A simulation model. *Industrial Crisis Quarterly, 5,* 19–57.

Carley, K. M. (1992). Organizational learning and personnel turnover. *Organizational Science, 3,* 2–46.

Carley, K. M. (1995a). Computational and mathematical organization theory: Perspective and directions. *Computational & Mathematical Organization Theory, 1,* 39–56.

Carley, K. M. (1995b). Communication technologies and their effect on cultural homogeneity, consensus, and the diffusion of new ideas. *Sociological Perspectives, 38,* 547–571.

Carley, K. M. (1999). On the evolution of social and organizational networks. *Research in the Sociology of Organizations, 16,* 3–30.

Carley, K. M. (2002). Smart agents and organizations of the future. In L. A. Lievrouw & S. Livingstone (Eds.), *The handbook of new media, social shaping and consequences of ICTS* (pp. 206–220). London: Sage.

Carley, K. M. (2003). Dynamics network analysis. In R. Breiger, K. Carley, & P. Pattison (Eds.), *Dynamic social network modelling and analysis: Workshop summary and papers* (pp. 133–145). Washington, DC: The National Academies Press.

Carley, K. M., Columbus, D., DeReno, M., Reminga, J., & Moon, I. (2007). *ORA user's guide 2007* (Technical Report, CMU-ISRI-07-115). Pittsburgh, PA: Carnegie Mellon University, School of Computer Science, Institute for Software Research.

Carley, K. M., & Hill, V. (2001). Structural change and learning within organizations. In A. Lomi & E. R. Larsen (Eds.), *Dynamics of organizations: Computational modeling and organizational theories* (pp. 63–92). Menlo Park: MIT Press.

Carley, K. M., & Newell, A. (1994). The nature of the social agent. *Journal of Mathematical Sociology, 19,* 221–262.

Carley, K. M., & Palmquist, M. (1992). Extracting, representing and analyzing mental models. *Social Forces, 70,* 601–636.

Carley, K. M., & Prietula, M. J. (1994a). ACTS theory: Extending the model of bounded rationality. In K. M. Carley & M. J. Prietula (Eds.), *Computational organization theory* (pp. 55–88). Hillsdale, NJ: Erlbaum.

Carley, K. M., & Reminga, J. (2004). *ORA: Organization risk analyzer* (Technical Report CMU-ISRI-04-106). Pittsburgh, PA: Carnegie Mellon University, School of Computer Science, Institute for Software Research International.

Carley, K. M., Reminga, J., & Kamneva, N. (2003, June). *Destabilizing terrorist networks.* Paper presented to the NAACSOS conference, Pittsburgh, PA.

Carley, K. M., & Ren, Y. (2001). *Tradeoffs netween performance and adaptability for C3I architectures.* Working Paper, Center for Computational Analysis of Social and Organizational Systems. Pittsburgh, PA: Carnegie Mellon University.

Carley, K. M., & Svoboda, D. (1996). Modeling organizational adaptation as a simulated annealing process. *Sociological Methods Research, 25,* 138–168.

Carley, K. M., & Wendt, K. (1991). Electronic mail and scientific communication: A study of the soar extended research group. *Knowledge Creation, Diffusion, Utilization, 12,* 406–440.

Center for Computational Analysis of Social and Organizational Systems (2008). Retrieved February 3, 2008 from http://www.casos.cs.cmu.edu

Chang, M. H., & Harrington, J. (2006). Agent-based models of organizations. In Leigh Tesfatsion & Kenneth L. Judd (Eds.), *Handbook of computational economics, Vol. 2* (pp. 1274–1337). Amsterdam: Elsevier.

Cohen, W. M., & Levinthal, D. A. (1990). Absorptive capacity: A new perspective on learning and innovation. *Administrative Science Quarterly, 35*, 128–152.

Crowston, K. (1994). Evolving novel organizational forms. In K. M. Carley & M. J. Prietula (Eds.), *Computational Organization Theory* (pp. 19–38). Hillsdale, NJ: Erlbaum.

Crowston, K. (1998). An approach to evolving novel organizational forms. *Computational & Mathematical Organization Theory, 2*, 29–47.

Cyert, R. M., & March, J. G. (1963). *A behavioral theory of the firm*. Oxford: Blackwell.

Dal Forno, A., & Merlone, U. (2004). Personnel turnover in organizations: An agent-based simulation model. *Nonlinear Dynamics, Psychology, and Life Sciences, 8*, 205–230.

Dal Forno, A., & Merlone, U. (2006). The emergence of effective leaders: An experimental and computational approach. *Emergence: Complexity and Organization, 8(4)*, 36–51.

Davis, J. P., Eisenhardt, K. M., & Bingham, C. B. (2007). Developing theory through simulation methods. *Academy of Management Review, 32*, 480–499.

Davis, M. S. (1973). *Intimate relations*. New York: Free Press.

Dawson, R. E. (1962). Simulation in the social sciences. In H. S. Guetzkow (Ed.), *Simulation in social science: Readings* (pp. 1–15). Englewood Cliffs, NJ: Prentice-Hall.

DiMaggio, P. J. (1986). Structural analysis of organizational fields: A block model approach. *Research in Organizational Behavior, 8*, 335–370.

Dooley, K. (2002). Simulation research methods. In J. Baum (Ed.), *Companion to organizations* (pp. 829–848). London: Blackwell.

Dooley, K., & Corman, S. (2002). Agent-based, genetic, and emergent computational models of complex systems. In L. D. Kiel (Ed.), *Encyclopedia of life support systems (EOLSS)*. Oxford, UK: UNESCO/EOLSS.

Dooley, K., & Corman, S. (2004). Dynamic analysis of new streams: Institutional versus environmental effects. *Nonlinear Dynamics, Psychology, and Life Sciences, 8*, 403–428.

Dooley, K. J., Corman, S. R., McPhee, R. D., & Kuhn, T. (2003). Modeling high-resolution broadband discourse in complex adaptive systems. *Nonlinear Dynamics, Psychology, and Life Sciences, 7*, 61–86.

Elliott, E., & Kiel, L. D. (2004). Agent-based modeling in the social and behavioral sciences. *Nonlinear Dynamics, Psychology, and Life Sciences, 8*, 121–130.

Epstein, J. M. (1999). Agent-based computational models and generative social science. *Complexity, 4*, 41–60.

Epstein, J. M., & Axtell, R. (1996). *Growing artificial societies: Social science from the bottom up*. Cambridge: MIT Press.

Faloutsos, M., Faloutsos, P., & Faloutsos, C. (1999). On power-law relationships of the Internet topology. *Proceedings of the conference on applications, technoloiges, architectures and protocols for computer simulation, SIGCOMM* (pp. 251–262). New York: Association for Computing Machines.

Forrester, J. (1958). Industrial dynamics: A major breakthrough for decision makers. *Harvard Business Review, 36*, 37–66.

Forrester, J. (1969) *Urban dynamics*. Cambridge: MIT Press.

Freeman, L. C. (2004). *The development of social network analysis*. Vancouver: Empirical Press.

Galbraith, J. R. (1973). *Designing complex organizations*. Reading, MA: Addison-Wesley.

Galbraith, J. R. (1977). *Organization design*. Reading, MA: Addison-Wesley.

Gardner, M. (1970). Mathematical games: The fantastic combinations of John Conway's new solitaire game "Life." *Scientific American, 223*, 120–123.

Garfield, E. (1955). Citation indexes for science. *Science, 122(3159)*, 108–111.

Gilbert, N. (1996). Simulation as a research strategy. In K. G. Troitzsch, U. Mueller, G. N. Gilbert, & J. E. Doran (Eds.), *Social Science Microsimulation* (pp. 448–454). Berlin: Springer Publishing Company.

Gladwell, M. (1999, January 11). Six degrees of Lois Weisberg. *The New Yorker*, 52–63.

Granovetter, M. S. (1973). The strength of weak ties. *American Journal of Sociology, 78*, 1360–1380.

Granovetter, M. S. (1974). *Getting a job: A study of contacts and careers*. Cambridge, MA: Harvard University Press.

Guastello, S. J. (2002). *Managing emergent phenomena: Nonlinear dynamics in work organizations*. Mahwah, NJ: Erlbaum.

Harary, F., & Norman, R. Z. (1953). Graph theory as a mathematical model in social science. *Research Center for Group Dynamics, Monograph No. 2*. Ann Arbor: University of Michigan.

Harrison, J. R., Lin, Z., Carroll, G. R., & Carley, K. M. (2007). Simulation modeling in organizational and management research. *Academy of Management Review, 32*, 1229–1245.

Hazy, J. K. (2007). Computer models of leadership: Foundations for a new discipline or meaningless diversion? *The Leadership Quarterly, 18*, 391–410.

Hazy, J. K. (2008). Toward a theory of leadership in complex systems: Computational modeling explorations. *Nonlinear Dynamics, Psychology, and Life Sciences, 12*, 281–310.

Henrickson, L. (2004). Trends in complexity and computation in the social sciences. *Nonlinear Dynamics, Psychology, and Life Sciences, 8*, 279–302.

Hirshman, B. R., Carley, K. M., & Kowalchuck, M. J. (2007). *Specifying agents in Construct* (Technical Report, CMU-ISRI-07-107). Pittsburgh, PA: Carnegie Mellon University, School of Computer Science, Institute for Software Research.

Holland, J. H. (1975). *Adaptation in natural and artificial systems*. Ann Arbor: University of Michigan Press.

Holland, J. H. (1995). *Hidden order: How adaptation builds complexity*. Cambridge: Perseus.

Holland, J. H., & Miller, J. (1991). Artificial adaptive agents in economic theory. *American Economic Review Papers and Proceedings, 81*, 365–370.

Homans, G. C. (1950). *The human group*. NY: Harcourt.

Hubler, A., & Pines, D. (1994). Prediction and adaptation in an evolving chaotic environment. In G. Cowan, D. Pines & D. Meltzer (Eds.), *Complexity: Metaphors, models and reality, Vol. XIX* (pp. 343–382). Reading, MA: Addison-Wesley.

International Network for Social Network Analysis (2007). Homepage. Retrieved February 3, 2008 from http://www.insna.org

Iwanaga, S., & Namatame, A. (2002). The complexity of collective decision. *Nonlinear Dynamics, Psychology, and Life Sciences, 6*, 137–158.

Kaizoji, T. (2002). Speculative price dynamics in a heterogeneous agent model. *Nonlinear Dynamics, Psychology, and Life Sciences, 6*, 217–229.

Keller-McNulty, S., Bellman, K. L., Carley, K. M., Davis, P. K., Ivanetich, R., et al. (2006) *Defense modeling, simulation, and analysis: Meeting the challenge.* Washington, DC: National Academy Press.

Keys, J. B., & Bell, R. R. (1977). A comparative evaluation of the management of learning grid applied to the business policy learning environment. *Journal of Management, 3*, 33–39.

Keys, J. B., & Wolfe, J. (1990). The role of management games and simulations in education and research. *Journal of Management, 16*, 307–336.

Kolb, D. A. (1984). *Experiential learning: Experience as the source of learning and development.* Englewood Cliffs, NJ: Prentice Hall.

Krackhardt, D. (1987). Cognitive social structures. *Social Networks, 9*, 109–134.

Krackhardt, D. (1990). Assessing the political landscape: Structure, cognition, and power in organizations. *Administrative Science Quarterly, 35*, 342–369.

Krackhardt, D. (1991). The strength of strong ties: The importance of philos in organizations. In N. Nohira & R. Eccles (Eds.), *Organizations and networks: Theory and practice* (pp. 216–239). Cambridge, MA: Harvard Business School Press.

Krackhardt, D., & Brass, D. (1994). Intra-organizational networks: The micro side. In S. Wasserman & J. Galaskiewicz (Eds.), *Advances in the social and behavioral sciences from social network analysis* (pp. 209–230). Beverly Hills, CA: Sage.

Krackhardt, D., & Carley, K. M. (1998). A PCANS model of structure in organization. In *Proceedings of the 1998 International Symposium on Command and Control Research and Technology (June 1998), Monterrey, CA* (pp. 113–119). Vienna, VA: Evidence Based Research.

Krackhardt, D., & Porter, L. W. (1985). When friends leave: A structural analysis of the relationship between turnover and stayers' attitudes. *Administrative Science Quarterly, 30*, 242–261.

Krackhardt, D., & Porter, L. W. (1986). The snowball effect: Turnover embedded in communication networks. *Journal of Applied Psychology, 71*, 50–55.

LeBon, G. (1897/1998). *The crowd.* New Brunswick, NJ: Transaction.

Lee, J.-S., & Carley, K. M. (2004). *OrgAhead: A computational model of organizational learning and decision making* (Technical Report CMU-ISRI-04-117). Carnegie Mellon University, School of Computer Science, Institute for Software Research International.

Lin, Z., & Carley, K. M. (1998). Organizational response: The cost performance tradeoff. *Management Science, 43*, 217–234.

March, J. G., & Simon, H. A. (1958). *Organizations.* New York: Wiley.

Marschak, J. (1955). Elements for a theory of teams. *Management Science, 1*, 127–137.

Masuch, M., & Warglien, M. (1992). *Artificial intelligence in organization and management theory.* Amsterdam: Elsevier.

McGuire C. B., & Radner, R. (1986). *Decision and organization.* Minneapolis: University of Minnesota Press.

Mihavics, K., & Ouksel, A. M. (1996). Learning to align organizational design and data. *Computational & Mathematical Organization Theory, 1*, 143–155.

Milgram, S. (1967). The small-world problem. *Psychology Today, 1*, 60–67.

Minar, N., Burkhart, R., Langton, C., & Askenazi, M. (1996). *The Swarm simulation system: A toolkit for building multi-agent simulations.* Working papers No. 96-06-042. Sante Fe: Santa Fe Institute.

Moreno, J. (1934). *Who shall survive?* Washington, DC: Nervous and Mental Disease Publishing.

Moreno, J., & Jennings, H. H. (1938). Statistics of social configurations. *Sociometry, 1,* 342–374.

Nohria, N., & Eccles, R. (1992). *Networks and organizations: structure, form, and action.* Boston: Harvard Business Press.

Ostrom, T. (1988). Computer simulation: The third symbol system. *Journal of Experimental Social Psychology, 24,* 381–392.

Padgett, J. F. (1997). The emergence of simple ecologies of skill. In B. Arthur, S. Durlauf, & D. Lane (Eds.), *The economy as a complex evolving system, II* (pp. 199–222). Reading MA: Addison-Wesley.

Pool, I. S., & Kochen, M. (1978). Contacts and influence. *Social Networks, 1,* 5–51.

Prietula, M. J., & Carley, K. M. (1994). Computational organization theory: Autonomous agents and emergent behavior. *Journal of Organizational Computing, 4,* 41–83.

Radner, R. (1993). The organization of decentralized information processing. *Econometrica, 6,* 1109–1146.

Repenning, N. P. (2002). A simulation-based approach to understanding the dynamics of innovation implementation. *Organization Science, 14,* 109–127.

Reynolds, C. (1987). Flocks, herds, and schools: A distributed behavioral model. *Computer Graphics, 21,* 25–34.

Rice, R. E., & Aydin, C. (1991). Attitudes toward new organizational technology: Network proximity as a mechanism for social information processing. *Administrative Science Quarterly, 2,* 219–244.

Robinson, S. (1997). Simulation model verification and validation: Increasing the users' confidence. In S. Andradcttir, K. J. Healy, D. H. Withers, & B. L. Nelson (Eds.), *Proceeding of the 1997 Winter Simulation Conference* (pp. 53–59). San Diego, CA: Society for Computer Simulation.

Salancik, G. R., & Pfeffer, J. (1978). A social information professing approach to job attitudes and task design. *Administrative Science Quarterly, 23,* 224–253.

Sastry, M. A. (1997). Problems and paradoxes in a model of punctuated organizational change. *Administrative Science Quarterly, 42,* 237–275.

Schelling, T. (1971). Dynamic models of segregation. *Journal of Mathematical Sociology, 1,* 143–186.

Schreiber, C. (2006). *Human and organizational risk modeling: Critical personnel and leadership in network organizations* (Technical Report CMU-ISRI-06-120). Carnegie Mellon University, School of Computer Science, Institute for Software Research International.

Schreiber, C., & Carley, K. M. (2004a). *Key personnel: Identification and assessment of turnover risk.* CASOS working paper. Pittsburgh, PA: Carnegie Mellon University.

Schreiber, C., & Carley, K. M. (2004b). *Construct – A multi-agent network model for the co-evolution of agents and socio-cultural environments* (Technical Report CMU-ISRI-04-109). Pittsburgh, PA: Carnegie Mellon University, School of Computer Science, Institute for Software Research International.

Schreiber, C., & Carley, K. M. (2005). *Ineffective organizational practices at NASA: A dynamic network analysis* (Technical Report, CMU-ISRI-05-135). Pittsburgh, PA: Carnegie Mellon University, School of Computer Science, Institute for Software Research International.

Schreiber, C., & Carley, K. M. (2007, March). *Agent interactions in construct: An empirical validation using calibrated grounding.* Paper presented to the 2007 BRIMS Behavior Representation in Modeling Simulation Conference, Norfolk, VA.

Schultz, R., & Sullivan, E. M. (1972). Developments in simulation in social and administrative science. In H. S. Guetzkow, P. Kotler, & R. L. Schultz (Eds.), *Simulation in social and administrative science; overviews and case-examples* (pp. 3–47). Englewood Cliffs, NJ: Prentice-Hall.

Shoham, Y., & Tennenholtz, M. (1994). *Co-learning and the evolution of social activity* (Technical Report No. STAN-CS-TR-94-1511). Stanford, CA: Stanford University, Department of Computer Science.

Simmel, G. (1908/1971). *On individuality and social forms.* Chicago: University of Chicago.

Simon, H. A. (1945). *Administrative behavior: A study of decision-making processes in administrative organization.* New York: Macmillan.

Simon, H. A. (1952). A formal theory of interaction in social groups. *American Sociological Review, 17,* 202–211.

Simon, H. A. (1957). *Models of man: Social and rational; Mathematical essays on rational human behavior in a social setting.* New York: Wiley.

Simon, H. A. (1962). The architecture of complexity. *Proceedings of the American Philosophical Society, 106,* 467–482.

Simon, H. A. (1969). *The sciences of the artificial.* Cambridge, MA: MIT Press.

Simon, H. A., & Guetzkow, H. (1955). A model of short- and long-run mechanisms involved in pressures toward uniformity in groups. *Psychological Review, 62,* 56–68.

Society for Chaos Theory in Psychology & Life Sciences. (2008). Chaos and complexity resources for students and teachers. Retrieved February 3, 2008, from http://www.societyforchaostheory.org/tutorials/

Stryker, S. (1980). *Symbolic interactionism: A social structure version.* Menlo Park, CA: Benjamin/Cummings Publishing.

Verhagen, H., & Masuch, M. (1994). TASCCS: A synthesis of double-AISS and plural-SOAR. In K. M. Carley & M. J. Prietula (Eds.), *Computational organization theory* (pp. 39–54). Hillsdale, NJ: Erlbaum.

Watts, D. J. (1999). *Small worlds: The dynamics of networks between order and randomness.* Princeton, NJ: Princeton University Press.

Watts, D. J. (2004). *Six degrees: The science of a connected age.* New York: Norton.

Wegner, D. M., Giuliano, T., & Hertel, P. (1985). Cognitive interdependence in close relationships. In W. J. Ickes (Ed.), *Compatible and incompatible relationships* (pp. 253–276). New York: Springer-Verlag.

Wegner, D. M., Erber, R., & Raymond, P. (1991). Transactive memory in close relationships. *Journal of Personality and Social Psychology, 61,* 923–929.

White, H. C. (2004). *Markets from networks: Socioeconomic models of production.* Princeton, NJ: Princeton University Press.

Zipf, G. (1949). *Human behavior and the principle of least effort: An introduction to human ecology.* Cambridge, MA: Addison-Wesley.

17 Epilogue: Psychology at the Edge of Chaos

MATTHIJS KOOPMANS

> I liked numbers because they were solid, invariant; they stood unmoved in a chaotic world.
>
> Oliver Sacks, *Uncle Tungsten: A Chemical Boyhood*, p. 26

Introduction

It is rewarding to contemplate the progress in the field of nonlinear dynamical systems (NDS) science based on the work presented in this volume. Dynamical systems approaches have had a significant influence in psychology ever since its early days. Piaget used equilibrium as one of its central tenets in his description of the dynamics of child development (e.g., Piaget, 1967; see also Chapter 8, this volume); Lewin (1947) similarly analyzed the dynamical processes of information exchange in groups in terms of tendency toward equilibrium (see also Chapter 14), and gestalt psychology emphasized the unified whole in perception over its constituent perceptual elements (Wertheimer, 1925, see also Chapter 6). The chapters presented here attest to the responsiveness of psychology to the latest developments in NDS, such as chaos theory, catastrophe theory, fractal geometry, and agent-based modeling, and they illustrate the extent to which these approaches have made inroads in most of the subdisciplines in psychology, such as cognitive, developmental, clinical, and organizational psychology. In each of these areas, NDS provides novel perspectives to long-standing questions to which traditional paradigms failed to offer satisfying answers; NDS inspires scholars to ask various questions about observed phenomena and offers new, more flexible modeling strategies. To appreciate the most recent theoretical developments in the field of NDS in psychology, it is instructive to review some of the earlier work that occurred some two decades ago in the wake of chaos theory (e.g., Prigogine & Stengers, 1984), catastrophe theory (Thom, 1975), and complex adaptive systems theory (Stewart, 1989; Waldrop, 1992). In this chapter, I briefly reflect on some of these early developments as a context of the discussion of some of the common threads that run through this book and how they illustrate the growth that the field of NDS has experienced. The second part of this chapter discusses more broadly current trends in the field of NDS and some potentially interesting growing points.

Psychology as a Sleeping Beauty

Chaos and complexity theory energized dynamical scholarship (e.g., Waldrop, 1992), including research using related approaches such as catastrophe theory and agent-based modeling. It is probably correct to say that in some of psychology's subdisciplines, our understanding of particular phenomena have been shaped by the work that NDS scholars have done, such as in the area of the early development of cognition and action in children (Thelen & Smith, 1994), marital interaction (Gottman, Murray, Swanson, Tyson, & Swanson, 2002), stage transitions in intellectual development in childhood (van der Maas & Molenaar, 1992) and industrial/organizational psychology and organizational theory (Guastello, 1981; Guastello, Dooley, & Goldstein, 1995). This work demonstrates the fundamentally nonlinear nature of some specifically circumscribed phenomena, such as the physical growth processes enabling children learning how to walk, and the qualitative transitions in children's frames of reference when they move from one stage of cognitive development to another. Because of this fundamental nonlinearity, models were required to capture this aspect. In the case of Piaget's (e.g., 1967) theories, the formal description of these models (i.e., stage transitions as catastrophic) is a relatively recent development, although the original theory is an essentially dynamical theory.

In an article titled "The Kiss of Chaos and the Sleeping Beauty of Psychology," Freeman (1995) evaluates the potential of NDS approaches to enhance our understanding of how the brain works. He argued that prevailing doctrines in neuropsychology have predisposed scientists toward a deterministic view of brain functions, disregarding empirical signs that a more holistic conceptualization may better capture these functions. Freeman observed: "The theory of chaos in the very near future will greatly change the way in which the brain function is conceived by psychologists" (p. 19). Similar claims were made in other areas of psychology at the time (see, e.g., Combs, 1995; Peat, 1995; Perna & Masterpasqua, 1997; West & Deering, 1995 and many others). There is a continued tendency among NDS scholars to reflect on their work in terms of a possible major paradigm shift in psychology and other social sciences (e.g., Allen & Varga, 2007; Dore & Rosser, 2007; Fleener & Merritt, 2007).

Freeman's (1995) discussion illustrates in a nutshell the ways in which NDS can broaden our perspective on research and theory building in psychology, while also clearly showing what the limitations were of the NDS perspective at the time. It is therefore worth our while to dwell a little longer on his arguments. They serve as an illustration of how much has happened in nonlinear dynamics, and, for that matter, in psychology during the past 15 years. Freeman identified the neuron doctrine, the doctrine of forward action, and the reflex doctrine as foundational concepts underlying "most contemporary research on the nervous system" (p. 21). The *neuron doctrine* considers neurons as the primary unit of analysis in brain research and reduces behavior to the triggering and action potential generated by individual neurons. More complex behaviors, such as intentional behavior, however, yield neuronal behavior that has so much variability that the available data are difficult to interpret. Consequently, researchers tend to resort to summary descriptions of central tendency, which in turn allows for the observed phenomena to be incorporated into a stimulus–response framework, ignoring both the unpredictability of the behavior of individual cells and the systemic patterns of neurons acting in conjunction. Taking a holistic rather than reductionist perspective on behavioral phenomena, as NDS does, inspires one to question the neuron doctrine and examine patterns of interaction.

The second doctrine, the *doctrine of forward action*, posits that neural activity can be understood exclusively in terms of a unidirectional passage of signals, without consideration of the recursive actions of neurons that would make them interactive elements. A recursive rather than linear understanding of causality inspires one to question the doctrine of forward action and examine feedback patterns. Third, the *reflex doctrine* conceptualizes behavior as a chain of conditioned responses, rather than as an adaptive self-organizing neural structure. An emphasis on the adaptive rather than mechanical aspects of organism–environment interactions inspires one to question the reflex doctrine and study more complex adaptive responses of the organism.

Freeman's discussion illustrates how NDS produces a shift in research priorities. Part of the excitement that radiates from the work in nonlinear dynamics has to do with its exploratory nature and with the sense of breaking truly new ground in psychology and offering the field alternative approaches and conceptualizations and new modeling techniques and analytical strategies. The chapters in this volume offer an excellent opportunity to take stock of how well we have progressed with these endeavors. Much of the work in NDS that was published 10 to 15 years ago, like Freeman's (1995), describes the application of NDS to psychology in very general terms, and provides examples (some of the most vivid ones can be found in Abraham, Abraham & Shaw, 1990), of how those strategies might be applied to psychological processes. Although significant as a first step, this work does not nail down any of the modeling features in a definitive way. A lot has changed since then. The scope of the work reported here may seem modest in comparison to the earlier efforts, but it arguably offers a more substantial contribution to the field, because it provides much more definitive statements about what the proposed relationships are between the various phenomena we observe and try to understand. A significant body of empirical work has been accumulated over the past decade and a half that is explicitly based on dynamical modeling principles. The chapters in this book illustrate how evidence can be collected and analyzed in support of some of the main tenets of NDS theory, such as self-organized criticality, multistability, hysteresis, and discontinuous change. In this chapter, I discuss the significance of this work to the field of psychology and offer some personal observations about recent developments in NDS and the challenges ahead.

The Roles of NDS in Psychology

Why should the psychological community take an interest in what NDS has to offer? Of the many roles that NDS plays in psychology, the work presented in this book best illustrates that NDS (a) clarifies the use of dynamical concepts in psychological research and theory, (b) provides a rich and well-defined lexicon of change concepts, (c) offers a new perspective on old questions in the field, (d) offers an opportunity to revisit and refine old dynamical systems models based on recent developments in nonlinear dynamics, (e) identifies prototypical examples of dynamical and systemic processes, (f) describes the inherently dynamical and systemic nature of many psychological phenomena, (g) facilitates input to the field from other disciplines about systemic behavior, (h) reconciles seemingly controversial issues and integrates disparate areas of knowledge into a broader conceptual framework, and (i) targets specific areas of weakness in traditional linear models.

Clarifies the Use of Dynamical Concepts

It has been argued that for the dialogue within the NDS community to be productive, it needs to attain clarity in its terminology, not so much to use all terms in the same way but to at least know whether we mean the same thing by them (Goldstein, 1995). If we describe a system as chaotic, does that necessarily imply sensitive dependence on initial conditions? Does being "at the edge of chaos" mean being at the edge of a state in which such sensitivity may arise? Nonlinear dynamical terms such as *chaos* and *complexity* are as commonly used outside of the NDS scholarly community as they are within it, often without any reference, explicit or implicit, to their mathematical underpinnings. Within the NDS community, there has been some reflection about whether the use of NDS terms such as *chaos*, *complexity* and *attractor* requires definitions grounded in mathematics. Can we call something a *saddle point bit* when we mean "being at the crossroads" without referring to the mathematical expression? Can we use such terminology outside of these strict mathematical constraints for added flexibility and analytical convenience in the interpretation of observed systemic behavior (Abraham, 1995)? While the verdict may still be out about the productiveness of referring to key NDS concepts without the full understanding of its mathematical referents, the work reported in this book errs on the side of caution. In Chapter 1, and indeed throughout the book, a mathematical grounding is provided for the NDS concepts that are being used, both as deterministic functions informing psychological theory and as modeling strategies used to capture dynamical and systemic processes through stochastic or simulation methods. The availability of these definitions facilitates the adoption of NDS perspectives in the field at large.

Provides a Rich and Well-Defined Lexicon of Change Concepts

Mainstream psychology typically offers an undifferentiated concept of change as gradual and linear (i.e., "first-order change;" Koopmans, 1998). NDS offers a mathematical formulation of a number of distinct change scenarios, which have wide applicability in the field, such as, for example, the transition from a limit cycle attractor state into chaos, described by the logistic map (May, 1976, see also Chapter 1, this volume), synchronization through coupled logistic maps (Chapter 12), hysteresis (Chapters 4, 7, 10, 12), periodic attractors (Chapter 12), nonlinearity and bifurcation scenarios in time series measurements (Chapter 3), nonlinear change in probability estimates (Chapters 3, 4, 12, 15), and emergent order (Chapters 2, 7, 9, 11, 13, 14, 16).

Catastrophe theory is one of the best examples of how mathematical models can enrich our understanding of the nature of change. One of its great merits is that there are clear empirical referents to strictly mathematical concepts, such as hysteresis, bimodality, divergence, and inaccessible regions, and the literature provides compelling examples such as the bimodality in the distribution of outcomes in science learning (Stamovlasis, 2006), hysteresis in perception of speech (Hollis, Kloos, & Van Orden; Chapter 7, this volume), or apparent motion (Ploeger, van der Maas & Hartelman, 2002; Tschacher & Junghan, Chapter 10, this volume). Statistical models based on catastrophe theory in many instances claim superiority to traditional regression analyses in the analysis of nonlinear data, with goodness-of-fit statistics indicating a sometimes spectacularly good fit to the data with some studies reporting R^2 higher than .90 (e.g., Guastello, 1982; Lange & Houran, 2000), indicating an ability to detect complex processes of transformation that may go unnoticed when more traditional models are used. The stochastic use of catastrophe model fitting procedures to analyze variability in data traditionally attributed to measurement error is a potentially major enrichment to the field because it provides us with a means of testing for different scenarios of discontinuity and deviations from our distributional assumptions. A more extensive debate about the implications of findings such as the aforementioned for linear modeling, as well as a detailed assessment of the conditions under which they can be replicated would, in my opinion, greatly benefit the field of psychology.

New Perspective on Old Questions

In a clear example of how NDS can offer a new perspective on questions that have preoccupied the field for a long time, Gregson (Chapter 4) discusses the limitations of the Stimulus-Response function in psychophysics from an NDS perspective. He argues for a broader conceptualization in which the response includes a broad array of actions and experiences that may or may not be measurable. In addition to being too narrowly defined, the traditional S-R function is also incomplete for three reasons. First, the model is static because it ignores the time factor. Incorporating time in the model allows for the study of intermediary neural transmission processes, for example, through measuring delay effects (hysteresis). Second, the traditional S-R function does not specify the conditions under which the relationship breaks down. One needs to fit a nonlinear probability function to do so. Third, the traditional function is one-dimensional in that it does not tell us anything about complex sensory input – the gamma function (see Figs. 4.3. and 4.4, and Eq. 4.3) does that. Gregson's discussion illustrates how modern insights into discontinuity can offer a new perspective on old problems and enables one to model multistability and turbulence into perceptual input–output relationships.

Renaud, Chartier, and Albert (Chapter 6) offer a new perspective on perceptual constancy, also an old problem in psychology. Perceptual constancy enables us to decide that an object can remain stationary while we move in relation to it. Establishment of perceptual constancy by an observer involves the computation of the covariance of the position of the body of an observer relative to the object being observed. Renaud et al. argue that this is a self-organizing process, and they propose a dynamical model that couples the agent and the environment as two interdependent dynamical systems. They propose that the agent limits its visual search space intentionally when extracting invariance from the perceptual space, and they demonstrate the link between the two systems empirically: the link between the spatial position of an object in relation to other objects and the motor processes that constitute an active visual search for the object and its boundary conditions. By invoking NDS, this work demonstrates the adaptive character of perceptual constancy and offers an alternative to traditional information processing accounts.

Revisits Older Dynamical Models

Van Geert (Chapter 8) revisits Piaget's (1967) and Vygotsky's (1978) models of child development as examples of early dynamical models that searched for the underlying mechanisms of developmental change. Piaget's stagewise transitions in the child's intellectual frame of reference and Vygotsky's zone of proximal development at the level of discourse between the teacher and the learner are both examples of discontinuous transitions that occur when adaptive systems acknowledge the need to reorganize on the basis of environmental input. Intellectual development in childhood is an example of how small changes at the local level (e.g., perception of an object and the inability to account for the perceived information within a given frame of reference) can lead to a reorganization of the entire frame of reference (accommodation). We would now call this an emergent process, and it illustrates how organisms seek to create order and replicability in the exchanges with their surroundings (see also Hollis et al., Chapter 7). Contemporary notions of development make a distinction between short-term development (emergence of behavioral patterns) and long-term development (teaching, learning, and maturation), and describe the dynamical interrelation between the two. Classical developmental theories, such as Piaget's and Vygotsky's thus get incorporated into a larger theoretical framework that had not yet been developed at the time.

In Chapter 3, Minelli reviews the use of differential equation systems to predict cell-membrane electric activity and fits a sigmoid probability function to describe membrane potential, both of which have been part and parcel of the study of electrocortical activity from the 1950s onward. However, NDS has enabled us to build bifurcation dynamics and other contemporary notions of discontinuity into those models, thus offering a much richer conceptualization of neural processes.

Dooley (Chapter 14) returns to the work of Taylor (1911), who almost a century ago recognized businesses as social entities but who provided a conceptualization of organizational behavior which, by contemporary NDS standards, seems mechanical because it assumes that such behavior is fully predictable. Contemporary notions of emergence and self-organization allow one to understand the generative mechanisms of systemic behavior in terms of the behavior of lower-level units, making it possible to incorporate unpredictability into the models. The intuitive appeal of these concepts in organizational learning and development is readily apparent in the wide adoption of nonlinear and dynamical concepts in the popular business literature, where talk of *complex organizations* and *leadership emergence* is widespread. This further reinforces the need for a conceptual grounding of NDS concepts to facilitate their discussion in nonscholarly circles. Chapter 13 discusses the modeling features of these phenomena in greater depth.

Prototypical Examples of Dynamical Processes

Both within and outside of the field of nonlinear dynamics, scholarship benefits from the availability of prototypical examples of phenomena particularly suitable for NDS treatment that can serve as reference points in the field. A well-known example is Zeeman's (1976) use of catastrophe theory to explain the dynamics of fight-or-flight reactions in animals. In Chapter 2, Sulis uses collective intelligence as an example of an area of study that is ideally suited to illustrate the value of a systems conceptualization. It is conceptualized as a directly observable phenomenon that can be modeled in terms of ants performing a certain task and in terms of the conditions that need to be met for them to be able to do so. Sulis brings a wide range of modeling features to bear, such as self-organization, phase transitions, and broken symmetry, ultimately to argue that collective intelligence is a prototypical example of emergence. With small numbers of ants present, ant behavior is unfocused and unproductive, but once the size of a colony reaches a critical quantity, a collective pattern snaps into place in which collective ant behavior becomes predictable and relatively insensitive to intervening environmental input.

The study of the processes through which leadership emerges from egalitarian team interactions (Guastello, Chapter 13) is also a prototypical systemic phenomenon in that a qualitative transition takes place at the systemic level that can be understood in terms of the behavior of lower-level units and that is discontinuous in the sense that team situations with and without leadership are qualitatively different. Although there are many examples within the emergence literature of how agent-based, bottom-up processes are used in the explanation of change on the systemic level, Guastello rightly acknowledges the importance of contribution of processes in the opposite direction, that is top-down (supervenience), in which the behavior of individual lower-level units is delineated by systemic boundary conditions (see also Koopmans, 1998, 2001). The phenomenon of leaders emerging from leaderless teams was reported more than half a century ago, but the process was poorly understood. NDS provides us with the means to revisit the issue, both theoretically (emergence) and in terms of investigating the process empirically by quantifying and modeling processes of discontinuous change (catastrophe models). The finding that group size affects the dynamics of leaderless teams mirrors Sulis's findings about the relationship between the size of ant colonies and the behavior of individual agents within the colony. The study of coordination and group learning, as described in Chapters 13, 14, and 15, illustrates how the notion of collective intelligence can be meaningfully applied to the behavior of humans, and it identifies a potentially interesting link between the work on organizational learning and the literature on human intelligence.

Inherently Dynamical Psychological Phenomena

The inherently dynamical character of social processes was recognized by William James and has traditionally been part of social psychology from its beginning. Vallacher and Novak argue in Chapter 12, however, that the emphasis in social psychology has traditionally been on higher-order behavioral and mental phenomena, such as traits, schemata, roles, and norms, rather than the turbulent flow of lower-level elements, such as thoughts, feelings, utterances, and movements, which constitute the ongoing stream of thought and behavior through time. NDS provides a means to bridge the gap between these two levels of description. Traditional models tend to be outcomes oriented and deemphasize the intrinsic dynamics from which those outcomes emanate. The notion of dynamic self-organization from the bottom up is consistent with contemporary notions in complexity theory (e.g., Holland, 1995). The authors describe the synchronization of behaviors in social situations as an example of complex adaptive behavior and as one of the central mechanisms on which social systems are based. The authors use coupled logistic maps to model the dynamical process in simulation studies, which, in turn, can lay the groundwork for empirical studies in this area.

In their assessment of the origins of psychopathological development, Lunkenheimer and Dishion in Chapter 9 focus on the relationship systems (family, peers) on which developing children typically rely most critically, and they discuss how interactions at the microlevel have a shaping influence on the interactive process of the relationship system as a whole. It is of both theoretical and practical interest to study the origins of maladaptive interactive behavior and its systemic ramifications because it may enable us to understand the relationship of psychopathological development in terms of its relational context. The empirical focus in their chapter is on deviant peer interaction and coercive family interaction, but the authors stress the practical need to study adaptive as well as maladaptive interactions, particularly in terms of their developmental effects on individuals, children, and adolescents. In a preliminary study, the authors found that addressing maladaptive dynamics therapeutically within family settings improves the relationships within the family system. The behavior of individual family members is thus understood in terms of the interactional system of which they are part, and maladaptiveness is reframed as a phenomenon at the level of the family system, rather than the individual.

In Chapter 10, Tschacher and Junghan argue that disease is an inherently systemic phenomenon and illustrate this point by linking the clinical symptoms of schizophrenia to perceptual organization. Their research, which compares normal subjects and schizophrenia patients, indicates a relatively circumscribed dysfunction of the internal capacity to organize stimulus materials in schizophrenia patients (i.e., an impairment in the gestalt pattern formation). It appears that positive symptoms of the disorder are associated with excessive perceptual organization, whereas negative symptoms are associated with decreased perceptual organization, suggesting multistability in the interaction of schizophrenia patients with the environment.

The inherently dynamical and systemic nature of brain functions and organic pathology, discussed in Chapter 3 by Minelli, can be seen, in the comparison of the dynamics of neural networks in a resting state in healthy subjects when compared with their highly nonlinear patterns during epileptic seizures and in the dynamics of degenerative encephalopathies such as Alzheimer's and Parkinson's diseases. Minelli also discusses the increased brain complexity associated with the development of intelligence and the analysis of the patterns of connection between regions of the brain when certain types of tasks are performed by experts and by novices. Minelli's chapter makes it clear that the description of patterns of interaction between different regions of the brain to explain such phenomena is hard to accomplish without support of an NDS framework.

Organizational learning is another example of an inherently systemic phenomenon, further discussed in Chapter 15 by Allen, who uses complexity theory to understand the role of evolutionary processes in organizational learning. Allen contemplates what underlying mechanisms organizations need to be successful. As many other NDS scientists in organizational theory do, he argues that a bottom-up process is a crucial element of that success. That is, through the creation of a diversity of ideas generated at the microlevel practices, schemata, and routines employed, a rich pool of adaptive responses and behavior exists that can be either retained or rejected as initiatives or behavioral precedents for the organization. The acquisition of strategies and effective behaviors at an organizational level through fluctuation at the microsystemic level illustrates emergence. In a simulation study, Allen compares strictly Darwinian learning (i.e., firms are launched with random strategies with the unsuccessful ones going under) to several alternative conceptualizations, each of which allows some organizations to benefit from the learning of others. The simulation reveals that strictly Darwinian learning is too costly because too much investment goes into the creation of firms that are ultimately not successful, and therefore other principles of self-organization need to be invoked to ensure long-term viability.

Input From Other Disciplines About Systemic Behavior

NDS scholarship often cuts across the boundaries of traditional disciplines and can be applied as fruitfully in biology, physics, chemistry, art, economics, sociology, economics, and education. Within each of these disciplines, the phenomena being studied may be different, but the NDS vocabulary used is the same (see Chapter 1), and in this way, it facilitates interdisciplinary communication and the cross-fertilization of insights insofar as they concern systemic and adaptive behavior. Like any other discipline, psychology is a beneficiary of such input. In this volume, Van Orden et al., for instance, draw a parallel with physics and biology when they frame their question on the origins of order in cognition. Allen's chapter illustrates the utility of the adaptive principles from theoretical biology for organizational learning, postulating a common systemic basis. Sulis's chapter on collective intelligence illustrates the potential of this cross-fertilization from the vantage point of theoretical biology, a perspective that invites a contemplation of the intelligence as a property of interacting organisms rather than individual ability, the way it is more typically defined when it comes to humans (e.g., Gardner, 1985; Jensen, 1972; Sternberg, 1985, 2007). The collectivity of human intelligence is surely of interest as well, for instance, when one considers such adaptive challenges as the prevention of war and terrorism, poverty, disease, ecological disruption, and global warming, challenges which by far outstrip the intellectual capability of any individual. Dooley argues in this book that studying the coordination of activity between organizations that is required to respond effectively to adaptive challenges of that scale and magnitude is one of the areas where organizational psychology has the greatest potential to contribute effectively to the field, provided it takes an NDS perspective.

Allen describes a probability function to characterize the distribution of the tendencies toward conservation and toward diversity. He argues that through noise, diversity is created at the microscopic level. In that sense, organizational learning is an analogous process to evolution in the Darwinian sense. Allen's analysis of the behavior of the North Atlantic fisheries in Canada serves as an example of the role of diversity in organizational learning. A model that relies on cost-effectiveness alone would result in the depletion of stock; there needs to be diversity in knowledge and strategies for the profession to remain viable, that is, a need for strategies that rely on cost-effectiveness as well as long-term predictions about the effect of one's activities on future availability.

Reconciles Controversial Issues by Integrating Disparate Areas of Knowledge

In Chapter 11, Pincus utilizes NDS as meta-theory to search for coherence in the field of psychotherapy. He takes note of no fewer than 400 psychological theories that guide the work of psychotherapists and argues that almost any therapeutic process, regardless of its theoretical basis, can be seen as an interpersonal process that has self-organizing features, involving a patterned flow of information exchange between the therapist and the client system. Pincus also finds common systemic features within these widely disparate approaches to psychotherapy, such as conflict and rigidity in the client's functioning. Pincus illustrates the implicit dynamical concepts in the various theories of psychotherapy, such as, for instance, Horney's (1970) description of three primary strategies used by individuals in interpersonal relations: moving toward, moving away, and moving against. Pincus's discussion illustrates the broad applicability of the notion of self-organization. There is a trade-off, however, between the breadth of application of such concepts, and their informative value (Allen, 2006), and the recognition that something is self-organizing does not by itself tell one very much. However, such recognition does carry implications about how empirical research can be conducted. Pincus analyzes turn-taking patterns in interpersonal exchanges through orbital decomposition and describes the viability of research that connects interactive behavior to physiological indicators. These are processes that are relevant to many if not most psychotherapeutic situations and may give us a better understanding of the mechanisms that make psychotherapy effective over and above the particularities of the approach taken.

Dooley (Chapter 14) similarly sees a unifying function for NDS in organizational science, because it finds common ground with many traditional organizational science models and reconciles seemingly opposing viewpoints. The normal accident theory assumes all of the elements of system have the same goals, whereas the garbage can theory assumes the opposite. A complexity lens conceptualizes the degree to which goals are shared as a variable that differs across agents within a system and over time within individual agents and thus would treat each theory as an articulation of extremes on the same continuum. NDS offers a fresh perspective on other controversies in the field of organizational theory as well, partly because it can accommodate seemingly contradictory conceptions of organizations, such as the mechanical and organic conceptions. Both require feedback loops between the behavior of individual agents and the larger system that defines their collective action, and, conversely, the delineation of this individual behavior in their interaction with other members of the same system. A complexity science lens focuses attention on the microactions of all members and how these might yield networks that appear more or less mechanistic or organic, as well as how these traits evolve and change over time because of evolutionary, teleological, dialectic, and life-stage forces.

Targets Areas of Weakness in Traditional Linear Models

In Chapter 7, Hollis et al. discuss the contribution of NDS to the study of cognitive processes in light of the failure of the traditional information processing metaphors emanating from cognitive science to account for such basic functions as listening and recognizing objects. The authors view these functions as a process of order creation and organizing experiences. Traditional models think of order as replicability. NDS instead conceptualizes order as an emergent phenomenon, a notion that mirrors Nicolis and Prigogine's (1989) description of the dissipation of heat. Both the interest in *origins* and the identification of *order* as a psychological construct exemplify the NDS approach because they express an interest in the underlying dynamics of cognitive processes. Hollis et al. argue that traditional information processing approaches wrongly assume that cognition is well organized and predictable. These shortcomings were recognized at the time these models were developed, but NDS offers a new perspective by reconceptualizing the notion of order.

Dooley argues in this book that in organizational theory, NDS has the greatest potential in those areas in which traditional linear models appear to be weakest, that is, their continued attachment to a leadership model that explains successful leadership in terms of the personality and persistence of the leader in face of adversity, and so on, rather than focusing on the larger parts of the organizational constellation. A second area of weakness of linear models is the lack of a good conceptualization of the psychology of large-scale, coordinated adaptive responses such as those to Hurricane Katrina, and, finally, planning for possible major catastrophes, such as September 11 and the possible rising of sea levels. Emergency responses, Dooley argues, are characterized by loosely coupled networks interacting in highly uncertain environments, and they are therefore very suitable for NDS treatment.

Aks remarks in Chapter 5 on the robustness of the linear model and the broad applicability of the central limit theorem. However, there are inherent skew and irregularity in response-time and eye-tracking data, and rather than relying on data-transformations to normalize the data, there is a need to address such irregularities as the empirical phenomena that they are and to develop analytical frameworks to analyze them, such as the shape, drift, and diffusion parameters discussed in Chapter 5. The relationship between eye movement and stimulus structure appears to be complex, indicative of a $1/f$ power law. The author proposes a self-organizing process in the behavior of neural networks to account for this trend. Aks's chapter illustrates the role that NDS plays, providing modeling alternatives in situations in which making linear and normality assumptions may result in a concealment of the nature of the relationship between observed phenomena and their underlying neural mechanisms.

Van Geert (Chapter 8) notes a continued reliance among developmental researchers to interpret cross-sectional data longitudinally and to aggregate results across individuals. He stresses the need instead to understand behavior at a given point in time in terms of the behavior displayed at an earlier point in time. This longitudinal understanding of behavior stands in contrast to the long-standing tendency in established research paradigms to look at behavior as "frozen in time."

Context, Evolution, and Growing Points

In the section that follows, I offer some context to the most recent developments in the field of NDS and identify some possible growing points for future work. I make a distinction between two overlapping theories: chaos theory and complex adaptive systems theory.

Chaos Theory Then and Now

In psychology and its neighboring disciplines, systems thinking up to the early 1980s was still largely dominated by the point of view that systems had a proclivity toward being stable and that systemic turbulence is a temporary concomitant to a transition from one state of homeostasis to another (Lewin, 1947). Insights from cybernetics were significant at the time in that they allowed us to understand the behavior of systems in terms of the behavior of its constituent components, as well as vice versa. However, cybernetic theory did not specify the processes or mechanics resulting in novel processes and behaviors, nor did it inspire us to consider systemic turbulence as a more permanent kind of feature to many systems. Chaos theory offers a perspective that recognizes that behavior is not necessarily predictable and that allows systems to operate under a wide range of states of (dis)equilibrium (Goldstein, 1990).

Part of the appeal of NDS approaches is that they provide a set of mathematically derived metaphors to describe complex processes (Peat, 1995; Hollis et al., this volume), in which basic results in other sciences, such as thermodynamics, serve as early examples of dynamical behavior. Although the mathematical definition of chaos dates back to the late 19th century and to the work of the French mathematician Henri Poincaré (Guastello, 1995; Stewart, 1989), it was particularly Prigogine's work (Prigogine, 1997; Prigogine & Stengers, 1984) that stimulated research and theory building in this area by suggesting that chaos theory had a much wider range of application in science than was previously believed. He and his colleagues presented the transition from chaos to order as an important qualification of the second law of thermodynamics (Hollis et al., Chapter 7) and implied that the theory might offer a different perspective on widely cherished theoretical notions in other fields of knowledge as well. There is something deeply intriguing about the notion that unpredictability can be mathematically modeled as sensitive dependence on initial conditions or that chaos acts as a mediator between determinism and randomness (Prigogine, 1997). Much of the perceived potential of chaos theory to produce a paradigm shift may have been inspired by the fundamental nature of its challenge to traditional scholarship as well as the almost metaphysical nature of the following questions: What does randomness mean? What are the limits of predictability? What are the origins and determinants of the order around us, and what are the origins of novelty? How do things come into being? These questions transcend the confine of specific scientific disciplines, and there is reason for excitement when science makes an attempt to reach out to them. The quotes that follow capture some of the excitement:

> Chaos theory is not simply a set of novel procedures that can be imported into the existing establishment of scientific psychology; it in fact represents a fundamental revolution in viewpoint. (Combs, 1995, p. 130)

> Chaos theory has struck such a deep chord in so many different disciplines that it is difficult to account for its attraction in terms of technological advances alone. One reason may be that chaos theory has taken us away from the algebraic and numerical abstraction into the geometry of pattern and form. But another even more compelling reason may be that chaos has an archetypical power of its own. (Peat, 1995, p. 371)

There were early warnings about overestimating the potential of the theory (Richardson, 1991), and doubts were raised because of the seemingly insurmountable challenges posed by deterministic models to our ability to measure psychological phenomena. There are also questions about how common chaos is as a phenomenon. McSharry (2005) identified three fundamental problems with the empirical study of chaotic phenomena in social science contexts. First, it appears that we are able to demonstrate chaos mathematically only in contrived situations (such as the pendulum experiment, see Fig. 1.1K, Chapter 1). Second, many scholars have argued that the use of deterministic models in social science is inherently problematic because our measurements are too imprecise and our data sets tend to be noisy (e.g., Vallacher & Novak, Chapter 12; Tschacher & Junghan, this volume). A related challenge is to distinguish random and nonrandom errors associated with chaos and other forms of instability in the system (Hollis et al., Chapter 7; McSharry, 2005), which is one of our main points of contention with linear scholarship. Third, using a single model – chaos – to explain systemic behavior requires us to assume that the underlying dynamical processes are stationary, and nonlinear scholars would, of course, be the first ones to question that assumption. McSharry (2005) observed that "the attractiveness of finding chaos in real-world systems has the potential to cloud the better judgment of many researchers" (p. 381). Similarly, Kaplan and Glass (1995) found the likelihood of successfully attributing systemic behavior to chaotic patterns so small, that they compared it with the probability of obtaining a Shakespeare play by putting a sufficiently large number of monkeys behind typewriters for a long enough period of time.

It is important to note that none of these arguments negate the theoretical relevance of chaos nor its value in informing empirical work; the discrepancy between these models in their mathematical expressions and the imperfect conditions of measurement is to be expected (Bak, 1996) and not unique to chaos (Freeman, 2000). Freeman clarified this relationship between theory and measurement in a simulation study in which the injection of random error into a system displaying chaos results in a stabilization of the attractor regime. He concluded from his findings that "chaotic attractors, like straight lines and perfect spheres, do not exist in nature, but are mathematical fictions to help in system design" (p. 365). The best our measurements can do is approximate these functions to show their plausibility in the real world. The detection of deterministic chaos, then, may, at least in psychology and the life sciences, carry as little promise as the detection of deterministic straight lines.

The work presented in this book also reflects on the question where we should take things with chaos theory. In a discussion of the erratic nature of mental disorders, Tschacher and Junghan admit that chaos theory has offered insights, but they question whether it has done anything more definitive. Deterministic chaos is difficult if not impossible to determine in real data and therefore may not be the best way to build a theoretical or methodological framework in the investigation of nonlinear phenomena in psychology. The authors recommend that chaos be subsumed as a special case among the many dynamical regimes that can potentially be investigated stochastically, as, for example, Guastello does. Vallacher and Novak acknowledge that chaos has been demonstrated in many biological and physical phenomena and add that although human behavior is admittedly unpredictable, it does not necessarily reflect deterministic chaos. Guastello and Liebovitch discuss some of the methods that have been developed to circumvent these issues, such as the use of surrogate data sets (see also McSharry, 2005), and many others have offered modeling strategies (e.g., Minelli, Chapter 3;

see also Gregson, 2005; Heathcote and Elliott, 2005) that concern themselves explicitly with the analysis of noisy data when fitting dynamical models with or without chaotic attractors.

The Rise of Complex Adaptive Systems Theory

The theory of complex adaptive systems (CAS) describes the adaptive behavior of living systems as self-organizing, and it focuses on how order emerges from within those systems. The degree and intensity with which exchanges take place within a given system signifies whether systems are close to or far from equilibrium. Complexity theory describes systems as often being in a state far from equilibrium, open to change and capable of restructuring into higher levels of complexity (for instance, through differentiation of subsystems) without necessarily being turbulent, and without necessarily returning to stability. Traditional systemic models such as those described, for example, by Lewin (1947) and Bateson (1935/1972) assumed that systems were stable in principle but could be turbulent when in a stage of transformation. Proponents of CAS question that assumption and argue instead that adaptiveness often presupposes that systems are in a state of adaptive instability, characterized interchangeably as "far-from-equilibrium" (e.g., Goldstein, 1990) and "at the edge of chaos" (e.g., Waldrop, 1992), a state in which the variability in interactive behaviors increases the likelihood of adaptive responses at the systemic level. CAS is often associated with the work of Stewart (1989), Waldrop (1992), and Holland (1995, 1998), each of whom, in different ways, demonstrates how CAS can be used as an overarching framework to study the behavior of living organisms and to incorporate a broad variety of theoretical perspectives from biology, molecular genetics, physics, and chemistry into a single framework that deals in a very broad sense of self-organizing and adaptive behavior. Psychological processes quite naturally have their place within this framework.

CAS also questions the systemic determination of the behavior of individuals that can be found, for instance, in Parsons and Bales (1955); but focuses instead on the larger systemic outcomes of local interactions among agents (e.g., Elliott & Kiel, 2004). Understanding the origins of novelty is one of the central problems in the study of adaptive behavior and discontinuous change and is typically defined in terms of how the interaction of lower-level components within a system result in the emergence of order in the exchange of energy and information at a higher systemic level. Several of the chapters describe instances of this process, such as the emergence of order in the collective intelligence (Sulis, Chapter 2), cognition (Hollis et al., Chapter 7; van Geert, Chapter 8), interpersonal exchanges (Lunkenheimer & Dishion, Chapter 9; Pincus, Chapter 11; Guastello, Chapter 13), and organizational learning (Dooley, Chapter 14; Allen, Chapter 15).

The interest in emergence in terms of the behavior of lower-level components also justifies the need for agent-based modeling. Frantz and Carley (Chapter 16) identify the need for psychologists to strengthen their simulation capability given the wide availability of inexpensive software and the fact that simulation can serve as an intermediate step between theory and observation of more complex systemic processes. Agent-based modeling enables researchers to program the distribution and transfer of information within social networks and to model the behavior of individual agents within the context of this information exchange. Agent-based modeling can analyze emergent social phenomena (e.g., the emergence of hierarchy) and evolutionary dynamics (e.g., patterns of change) as being dependent on the behavior and characteristics of individual agents, such as the rate at which they learn and interact with other units. The authors argue that the use of simulation techniques to model dynamical processes has implications for psychology because it becomes possible to model the connections between the behavior of social networks and the motivations, perceptions, and cognitions of individual agents within those networks.

Goldstein (2002) questioned the ability of NDS – attractor and bifurcation dynamics in particular – to describe emergence adequately because by reducing novelty to a chance occurrence, it lacks specificity about inherent systemic features that predispose toward transformation. Therefore a need exists to develop formalisms capable of describing such inherent features, as well as the shift toward a radically novel organization that they are capable of producing. An example of such formalisms is Holland's (1998) proposal of a recursive process that includes novelty operators and combinatorial mixing processes such that redundant elements in the reiteration are negated. Through elimination of redundancies, the system creates a "space" that enables the introduction of novel components. Models that seek to identify the internal determinants of change in this way are of interest in psychology for both theoretical (describing mechanisms underlying novel occurrences) and practical reasons (the identification of factors that predispose a system toward qualitative transformation). However, for these principles to have empirical relevance, measurement strategies need to be articulated to address specific shortcomings of NDS, as well as the ability of alternative models to address those shortcomings. Furthermore, a comparison of the new formalisms with more traditional systemic notions such as attractors and bifurcations may be instructive both on the conceptual level and in terms of the two sets of models to account for our observations in research.

Future Challenges

It would benefit the field to have a candid assessment of the value of detecting chaos. How important is it to us to establish sensitive dependence on initial conditions in our measurements? To what extent are we inhibited by the limitations in our modeling capability? If we succeed in detecting chaos (e.g., Guastello, Chapter 13), what are the replicable features of that success? Perhaps the most intriguing claim to come from NDS theory – and perhaps its most significant challenge to linear models, is its ability to distinguish random from nonrandom errors (i.e., white noise from pink noise) when looking at model deviations. This challenge is interesting because it goes to the heart of what makes traditional linear modeling attractive: the simplicity of the notion that parameters of central tendency and variability are sufficient to characterize distributions and that whatever variability in our observations we cannot attribute to the model must be due to error (see also Chapter 5). The notion of unpredictability obscures this scenario, but we know little about how far that challenge reaches into our linearly derived knowledge base in psychology. The measurement strategies discussed in this book, as well as in other places (e.g., Gregson & Guastello, 2005) offer some pointers as to where this work is heading and give a clear sense of the extent to which NDS can improve on linear models in terms of accurately describing the data.

Given the complexity of NDS models, there is great potential for the wider adoption of simulation studies in the theory-building stage, and this book reports several (Vallacher & Novak, Chapter 12; Allen, Chapter 15; Frantz & Carley, Chapter 16). The use of simulation may help us to learn more about the possibilities and limitations associated with the use of deterministic models to analyze psychological data and provide an assessment of the plausibility of the models and hypotheses of interest, which may facilitate and further inform empirical work.

Psychology at the Edge of Chaos?

There continues to be a need in the field for alternatives to a reductionist version of psychology that isolates phenomena from their systemic context, reduces behaviors to measurements at a single point in time and assumes stationarity. Much of the work in NDS is a continuation of a dynamical tradition that has existed in psychology since its early days, and will most likely continue to be a significant force in the field for some time to come. Is psychology at the edge of chaos? That depends on how the edge of chaos is defined. Waldrop (1992) described the edge of chaos as an intermediary state between order and chaos and suggests that the state characterizes most if not all complex adaptive systems:

> Right in-between the two extremes [order and chaos], ... at a kind of abstract transition called "the edge of chaos," you also find *complexity:* a class of behaviors in which the components of the system never quite lock into place, yet never quite dissolve into turbulence either. These are the systems that are both stable enough to store information, yet evanescent enough to transmit it. These are the systems that can be organized to perform complex computations, to react to the world, to be spontaneous, adaptive and alive. (Waldrop, 1992, p. 293)

Insofar as psychology can be seen as a system of knowledge, of interacting individuals transmitting information pertaining to that knowledge system, and insofar as it can be seen as an open system interacting with the environment to test the explanatory adequacy of its propositions, its characterization as being at the edge of chaos seems evident. The impact of NDS on the field as described in this book is one of the many ways to illustrate the aptness of this metaphor.

References

Abraham, F. D. (1995). A postscript on language, modeling and metaphor. In F. D. Abraham & A. R. Gilgen (Eds.), *Chaos theory in psychology* (pp. 311–342).Westport, CT: Praeger.

Abraham F. D., Abraham, R. H., & Shaw, C. D. (1990). *A visual introduction to dynamical systems theory for psychology*. Santa Cruz, CA: Aerial Press.

Allen, P. M., (2006, March). *Complexity: The challenge of a co-evolving epistemology and onthology.* Keynote address at the Second International Nonlinear Science Conference, Heraklion, Greece.

Allen, P. M., & Varga, L. (2007). Complexity: The co-evolution of epistemology, axiology and ontology. *Nonlinear Dynamics, Psychology, and Life Sciences, 11*, 19–50.

Bak, P. (1996). *How nature works: The science of self-organized criticality.* Oxford: Oxford University Press.

Bateson, G. (1935/1972). Culture contact and schismogenesis. In G. Bateson, *Steps toward an ecology of mind: A revolutionary approach to man's understanding of himself* (pp. 61–71). New York: Ballantine. [Reprinted from *Man, XXXV*, Article 199.]

Combs, A. (1995). Psychology, chaos, and the process nature of unconsciousness. In F. D. Abraham & A. R. Gilgen (Eds.), *Chaos theory in psychology* (pp. 129–137). Westport, CT: Praeger.

Dore, M. H. I., & Rosser Jr., B. J. (2007). Do nonlinear dynamics in economics amount to a Kuhnian paradigm shift? *Nonlinear Dynamics, Psychology, and Life Sciences, 11*, 119–147.

Elliott, E., & Kiel, L. D. (2004). Agent-based modeling in the social and behavioral sciences. *Nonlinear Dynamics, Psychology, and Life Sciences, 8*, 121–130.

Fleener, M. J., & Merritt, M. L. (2007). Paradigms lost? *Nonlinear Dynamics, Psychology, and Life Sciences, 11*, 1–18.

Freeman, W. J. (1995). The kiss of chaos and the sleeping beauty of psychology. In F. D. Abraham & A. R. Gilgen (Eds.), *Chaos theory in psychology* (pp. 19–20). Westport, CT: Praeger.

Freeman, W. J. (2000). *Neurodynamics: An exploration in mesoscopic brain dynamics.* New York: Springer Publishing Company.

Gardner, H. (1985). *The mind's new science: A history of the cognitive revolution.* New York: Basic Books.

Goldstein, J. (1990). A nonequilibrium nonlinear approach to nonlinear change. In D. Anderson, G. Richardson, & J. Sterman (Eds.), *System dynamics' 90* (pp. 425–439). Cambridge, MA: MIT Press.

Goldstein, J. (1995). The Tower of Babel in nonlinear dynamics: Toward the clarification of terms. In R. Robertson & A. Combs (Eds.), *Chaos theory in psychology and life sciences* (pp. 39–47). Mahwah, NJ: Erlbaum.

Goldstein, J. (2002). The singular nature of emergent levels: Suggestions for a theory of emergence. *Nonlinear Dynamics, Psychology and Life Sciences, 6*, 293–309.

Gottman, J. M., Murray, J. D., Swanson, C. C., Tyson, R., & Swanson, K. R. (2002). *The mathematics of marriage: Dynamical models.* Cambridge, MA: MIT Press.

Gregson, R. A. M. (2005). Identifying ill-behaved nonlinear processes without metrics: Use of symbolic dynamics. *Nonlinear Dynamics, Psychology and Life Sciences, 9*, 479–504.

Gregson, R. A. M., & Guastello, S. J. (2005). Introduction to nonlinear methodology, Part I: Challenges we face and those that we offer, *Nonlinear Dynamics, Psychology and Life Sciences, 9*, 371–374.

Guastello, S. J. (1981). Catastrophe modeling of equity in organizations. *Behavioral Science, 26*, 63–74.

Guastello, S. J. (1982). Color matching and shift work: An industrial application of the cusp-difference equation. *Behavioral Science, 27*, 131–139.

Guastello, S. J. (1995). *Chaos, catastrophe and human affairs: Applications of nonlinear dynamics to work, organizations and social evolution.* Mahwah, NJ: Erlbaum.

Guastello, S. J., Dooley, K. J., & Goldstein, J. A. (1995). Chaos, organizational theory and organizational development. In F. D. Abraham & A. R. Gilgen (Eds.) *Chaos theory in psychology* (pp. 267–278). Westport, CT: Praeger.

Heathcote, A., & Elliott, D. (2005). Nonlinear dynamical analysis of noisy time series. *Nonlinear Dynamics in Psychology and Life Sciences, 9*, 399–434.

Holland, J. H. (1995). *Hidden order: How adaptation builds complexity.* New York: Basic Books.

Holland, J. H. (1998). *Emergence: From chaos to order.* Reading, MA: Addison-Wesley.

Horney, K. (1970). *Neurosis and human growth.* New York: Norton.

Jensen, A. R. (1972). *Genetics and education.* New York: Harper & Row.

Kaplan, D., & Glass, L. (1995). *Understanding nonlinear dynamics.* New York: Springer Publishing Company.

Koopmans, M. (1998). Chaos and the problem of change in family systems. *Nonlinear Dynamics, Psychology, and Life Sciences, 2*, 133–148.

Koopmans, M. (2001). From double bind to n-bind: Toward a new theory of schizophrenia and family interaction. *Nonlinear Dynamics, Psychology, and Life Sciences, 5*, 289–323.

Lange, R., & Houran, J. (2000). Modeling Maher's attribution theory of delusions as a cusp catastrophe. *Nonlinear Dynamics, Psychology, and Life Sciences, 4*, 235–254.

Lewin, K. (1947). Frontiers in group dynamics. *Human Relations, 1*, 5–41.

May, R. M. (1976). Simple mathematical models with very complicated dynamics. *Nature, 261*, 459–467.

McSharry, P. (2005). The danger of wishing for chaos. *Nonlinear Dynamics, Psychology, and Life Sciences, 9*, 375–397.

Nicolis, G., & Prigogine, I. (1989). *Exploring complexity: An introduction.* New York: Freeman.

Parsons, T., & Bales, R. F. (1955). *Family socialization and interaction process.* Glencoe, IL: Free Press.

Peat, F. D. (1995). Chaos: The geometrization of thought. In R. Robertson & A. Combs (Eds.), *Chaos theory in psychology and the life sciences* (pp. 359–372). Mahwah, NJ: Erlbaum.

Perna, P. A., & Masterpasqua, F. (1997). The history, meaning and implications of chaos and complexity. In F. Masterpasqua & P. A. Perna (Eds.), *The psychological meaning of chaos* (pp. 1–19). Washington, DC: American Psychological Association.

Piaget, J. (1967). *Six psychological studies.* New York: Random House.

Ploeger A., Van Der Maas, H. L. J., & Hartelman, P. A. I. (2002). Stochastic catastrophe analysis of switches in the perception of apparent motion. *Psychonomic Bulletin and Review, 9,* 26–42.

Prigogine, I., (1997). *The end of certainty: Time, chaos and the new laws of nature.* New York: Free Press.

Prigogine, I., & Stengers, I. (1984). *Order out of chaos: Man's new dialogue with nature.* New York: Bantam Books.

Richardson, G. P. (1991). Caveats about chaos: Informal remarks on embracing the new nonlinear dynamics, intended to stimulate discussion. In M. Michaels (Ed.), *Proceedings of the First Annual Chaos Network Conference* (pp. 1–2). Urbana, IL: People Technologies.

Stamovlasis, D. (2006). The nonlinear dynamic hypothesis in science education problem solving: A catastrophe theory approach. *Nonlinear Dynamics, Psychology, and Life Sciences, 10,* 37–70.

Sternberg, R. J. (1985). *Beyond IQ: A triarchic theory of human intelligence.* New York: Cambridge University Press.

Sternberg, R. J. (2007). Who are the bright children? The cultural context of being bright and acting intelligent. *Educational Researcher, 36,* 148–155.

Stewart, I. N. (1989). *Does God play dice? The mathematics of chaos.* Oxford: Blackwell.

Taylor, W. W. (1911). *The principles of scientific management.* New York: Harper.

Thelen, E., & Smith, L. B. (1994). *A dynamic systems approach to the development of cognition and action.* Cambridge, MA: MIT Press.

Thom, R. (1975). *Structural stability and morphogenesis.* New York: Benjamin-Addison-Wesley.

Van der Maas, H. L. J., & Molenaar, P. C. (1992). Stagewise cognitive development: An application of catastrophe theory. *Psychological Review, 99,* 395–417.

Vygotsky, L. S. (1978). *Mind in society: The development of higher psychological processes.* Cambridge, MA: Harvard University Press.

Waldrop, M. M. (1992). *Complexity: The emerging science at the edge of order and chaos.* New York: Simon & Schuster.

Wertheimer, M. (1925). *Drei Abhandlungen zur Gestalttheorie.* Erlangen: Philosophische Akademie.

West, B. J., & Deering, B. (1995). *The lure of modern science: Fractal thinking.* Singapore: World Scientific.

Zeeman, E. C. (1976). Catastrophe theory. *Scientific American, 234,* 65–83.

Index